ELECTIONS AND
PARTY MANAGEMENT

ELECTIONS AND PARTY MANAGEMENT

POLITICS IN THE TIME OF DISRAELI AND GLADSTONE

by

H. J. HANHAM

Dean of the School of Humanities and Social Science
Massachusetts Institute of Technology

THE HARVESTER PRESS · SUSSEX
ARCHON BOOKS

This edition first published in England in 1978 by
THE HARVESTER PRESS LIMITED
Publisher: John Spiers
2 Stanford Terrace, Hassocks, Sussex

and in the United States of America
as an Archon Book, an imprint of
THE SHOE STRING PRESS, INC., Hamden Connecticut 06514

First published 1959 by Longmans, Green
and Company, Limited

British Library Cataloguing in Publication Data
Hanham, Harold John
  Elections and party management. – 2nd ed.
  1. Political parties – Great Britain – History – 20th century
  I. Title
  329.9'41   JN1120
  ISBN 0–85527–074–8
  ISBN 0–85527–663–0 Pbk

Library of Congress Cataloging in Publication Data
Hanham, H. J.
  Elections and party management.
  Reprint with new introd. of the 1959 ed.
  published by Longmans, Green, London.
  Bibliography: p.
  Includes index.
  1. Elections – Great Britain – History.
  2. Great Britain – Politics and government –
  1837–1901. I. Title.
  JN955.H3 1978   329'.023'41081   78–17593
  ISBN 0–208–01550–7

Printed in Great Britain by
REDWOOD BURN LIMITED
Trowbridge & Esher

CONTENTS

Appendices

PREFACE

THIS is not a book about the House of Commons, or cabinets or statesmen, or the various interests and organisations that sought to influence them. It deals solely with the problems of the ordinary party politician and the growth of party organisation in the country after the 1867 Reform Act. It is, therefore, a study in party history rather than a survey of the 'structure of politics' or a conventional political history. Nor is it intended to stand alone. Another volume will deal with the politicians themselves and the 'pressure groups' with which they were associated.

The subject matter has been divided into three sections. The first deals with the different types of constituencies, their political habits, and the growth of party organisation within them. Its theme is the contrast between the old political world of the counties and small towns, which looked back to the years before 1832, and the new world of the big industrial towns with their masses of working-class electors and their penchant for Birmingham Radicalism. The second section deals with elections and electioneering. Here the principal themes are the end of the confusion of parties which had persisted since the fall of Peel, the emergence of a two-party system, and the development of new electioneering techniques. Subsidiary themes are the rather surprising survival of electoral corruption and the slowness with which working-class politicians grasped their new opportunities. In a bigger book there would also have been room for a discussion of the complicated rôle played by pressure groups like the United Kingdom Alliance. The third and final section deals with the party headquarters in London, their modest efforts to move with the times, and the problems of party finance.

In the seven years that have elapsed since I first started to collect material for this book I have been helped by far more people than there is space to mention here. I must, however, thank Dr G. S. R. Kitson Clark, who gave me invaluable guidance when I was beginning my researches in Cambridge, and Professor W. J. M. Mackenzie and Mr Peter Campbell, who read and commented on my final draft. With them I remember Professor Willis Airey, who first encouraged me to take up historical research. I also owe an immense debt to my wife, who not only interrupted her own research to help me gather material, but also typed out a large proportion of the manuscript.

A large general work of this kind would not be possible without the help of the owners and custodians of private collections of manuscripts. I am, therefore, most grateful for access to their collections: to Captain C. K. Adam, the Marquess of Bath, Viscount Chilston, the Earl of Cranbrook, the Duke of Devonshire, and the Trustees of the Chatsworth Settlement, Viscount Hampden, Lord Hylton, the Earl of Iddesleigh, the Marquess of Salisbury, the Earl of Scarbrough, the Hon. David Smith, the National Trust, the National Union of Conservative and Unionist Associations, the North of England Conservative Agents' Association, and the Manchester Liberal Federation. I should also like to express my thanks to the many libraries and record offices that have assisted me, either by making available their facilities or by courteous answers to troublesome letters.

For guidance on the intricacies of Welsh politics and for permission to quote passages from an unpublished study of South Wales politics I am particularly grateful to Dr I. Gwynedd Jones of Swansea.

H. J. HANHAM

MANCHESTER,
March 1958

INTRODUCTION TO THE SECOND EDITION

TWENTY years after the Reform Act of 1832, which set Britain on the road to American-style electoral democracy, Charles Dod published a 'Political Gazetter' intended to show how the new system was working.[1] What must have struck contemporary readers of the book was not how much things had changed, but how much had remained the same. Here are a few examples. Chatham, which became a parliamentary borough for the first time in 1832, had easily slipped into the pattern of other dockyard towns which returned members of parliament.

> A committee of the House reported, March 8, 1853, that 'a large number of the electors are employed in the dockyard and other public departments', that they are 'under the influence of the government for the time being', and that 'there is no instance of a candidate being elected for this borough who has not had the support of the government'.[2]

Chester, long a preserve of the Grosvenor family, continued to be under their influence, although money was now said to offer a significant source of competition.

> The Marquis of Westminister retains the greater part of the influence which he formerly enjoyed here; with trifling exceptions some member or other of his family has sat since the Restoration. Candidates with good pecuniary resources are said to have great weight in Chester.[3]

Cricklade, once one of the most notoriously corrupt boroughs in the country, had passed through many phases, but its politics still belonged to the eighteenth century.

> Formerly possessed by the second Earl of Carnarvon; next by Mr. Joseph Pitt, a banker at Cirencester; and next by Mr. Robert Gordon of Kemble Park, which last gentleman now divides the influence with Lord Clarendon, Lord Radnor, Mr. Goddard, and Mr. Neeld[4].

The statesmen of the time had grown up in the world of such

[1] Charles R. Dod, *Electoral Facts from 1832 to 1853, Impartially Stated, Constituting a Complete Political Gazetteer*, ed. by H. J. Hanham, Brighton 1972.
[2] *Ibid.*, 58.   [3] *Ibid.*, 61.   [4] *Ibid.*, 76.

boroughs. Lord Palmerston represented one of them, Tiverton, for thirty years; William Ewart Gladstone, who first entered the House of Commons as one of the Duke of Newcastle's members for Newark immediately after the passage of the 1832 Reform Act, continued down into old age to lament the slow disappearance of nomination boroughs; while the third Earl Grey, son of the Lord Grey whose ministry had carried the Reform Act of 1832, was one of those who most vehemently defended the existence of little boroughs, with small populations, on the ground that they supplied the House of Commons with 'men of enlightened views and independent character, but unfitted for encountering the storms of popular election'.[1]

Such men believed that the House of Commons was the only legitimate forum of the nation, where great issues could be expounded and resolved by men specially capable of coming to enlightened conclusions because of their long political training. Statesmen did not, while in office, make major public speeches to party audiences until Gladstone's path-breaking speeches to vast audiences in South Lancashire in 1865 and 1868. And for many years thereafter they were careful, whether in or out of office, to avoid the charge that they were 'stumping the country' for purposes of mere party advantage.

In short, as has been pointed out by William Nisbet Chambers, the style of British politics down to 1867 was about a generation behind that of American politics. In America the so-called second party system (1828-60) had already been in existence for many years before the British party system began to catch up.

> The salient characteristic of the second party system was the mobilization of mass participation in elections and in politics generally. In a time when Great Britain, even after the widely-touted Reform Bill of 1832, could boast an electorate of only about 650,000 out of a population of some 16 million, presidential elections in the United States were drawing turnouts of 1,153,350 in 1828, and 2,409,474 in 1840, even though total population amounted to only about 12 million in 1830 and 17 million in 1840. A venerable piece of doggerel expresses the American enthusiasm for politics in the nineteenth century—
>
> > They marches in parades and they gets up hurrahs
> > And they tramps through the mud for the good old cause.

[1]Quoted in H. J. Hanham, *The Nineteenth Century Constitution*, Cambridge 1969, 144.

This sense of popular engagement came to maturity in the second party system. In an era when men often lived far from one another and even town dwellers were often starved for entertainment and excitement, the party battle took on the form of a game and a major source of entertainment. . . . Thousands *did* march, flaunt transparencies of party hereos, cheer at mass rallies in town squares or rural groves, and go to the polls to vote.

The outburst of popular participation was probably due in part to the ethos of Jacksonian, equalitarian democracy, but other factors were important too. Among these was the fact of nationwide party competition in an era of improved means of transportation and mass communication, including the emergence of a popular, partisan press. Voting turnout jumped from 26.9 per cent of white adult males in the multi-factional presidential election of 1824, in which six states still chose electors by legislature, to 57.6 and 57.8 per cent in 1828 and 1832, in the era of the restoration of parties. The election of 1840 brought voting participation to an unprecedented 80.2 per cent of white adult males. . . . The result was the democratization of parties and the party system, in popular participation and in the sources and kinds of leaders and cadres who came to the fore in both the Democratic and Whig parties.[1]

British politics began to catch up with American politics only after the Reform Act of 1867. Politics for more than twenty years after the 1867 Reform Act became the central preoccupation of the nation. The party system was remodelled to encourage popular participation on an unprecedented scale. The number of votes cast in general elections rose rapidly, each party gaining over a million votes for the first time in the general election of 1874. Political oratory became popular oratory, not just speeches to a small audience in the House of Commons. Disraeli and Gladstone became popular heroes featured on hundreds of thousands of plaques, horse brasses, salt cellars, and tiles. They also became villians, and the object of anonymous scurrilous verse like these four stanzas about Gladstone, printed on a plain sheet of paper and circulated in the north of England:

> Gone from the sweets of office,
> Gone from the head of affairs,
> Gone in the head they tell us,
> Gone, and no one cares.

[1]William Nisbet Chambers and Walter Dean Burnham, eds. *The American Party Systems: Stages of Political Development*, New York 1967, 11-12.

Gone, not to join the angels,
Gone to reflect on the past,
Gone into opposition,
Gladstone's gone at last.

Gone, let us trust for ever,
Gone whither none can tell,
Gone, let us hope to heaven:
There are demons enough in hell.

Says Satan, 'The place is as full as can be
But I'd like to make room if I can.'
So he let Ananias and Judas go free,
And he took in the G. O. M. [1]

The eighteen years that followed the Reform Act of 1867 were particularly important in British history, because they were the years in which the nation accustomed itself to the notion of democracy. The 1867 Act had enfranchised a large proportion of the householders in the boroughs, but had left most of those in the counties unenfranchised. It had created a considerable number of new parliamentary constituencies without abolishing any significant number of old ones, with the result that the size of electoral districts was grossly uneven. It had created mass working-class constituencies in the cities, but it had provided no simple and cheap way of electioneering in them, so that most of the biggest constituencies could only be contested by rich men or by those who had the support of such men. And it had done nothing to check bribery and treating, which reached massive levels in the general election of 1880, well after the introduction of the secret ballot in 1872. Such a system was so clearly provisional that further change was inevitable, and it came in a series of Acts passed between 1883 and 1885. These equalized the borough and county franchises, adopted single-member electoral districts of roughly equal size as the norm, limited the amounts candidates might spend on elections, and introduced new and more stringent prohibitions against corrupt practices.

As Walter Bagehot pointed out in 1872, the mere fact of passing the Reform Act of 1867 did not change very much. 'The people

---

[1] From a fly-sheet in the possession of the author. The G. O. M. [Grand Old Man] was W. E. Gladstone.

enfranchised under it', he commented, 'do not yet know their own power . . .'[1] Its effects, he predicted, would be felt only in the future, when those brought up under the old system had ceased to play an active role in politics, and political leadership was in new hands. And the most notable changes which took place in the years immediately after 1867 were indeed those which flowed from a change in generations. With the death of Lord Palmerston in 1865 and the defeat of Lord Russell's government in the following year the last of the party leaders who had been active before 1820 passed from the forefront of political life. Those responsible for the disestablishment of the Irish Church in 1869, the Irish Land Act of 1870, the Education Act of 1870 and the reforms of the civil service, the army, and the courts of law which took place between 1870 and 1873 were seasoned politicians, but their careers had been made since the Reform Act of 1832. However, such men were not yet accustomed to think in terms of a largely working class electorate. Gladstone and Disraeli had grown up before 1832, and had reached maturity in the context of the quasi-aristocratic politics of the 1840s. Gladstone had first served as a cabinet minister in 1843, Disraeli in 1852. Those who served in their cabinets had for the most part entered political life in the 1840s or 1850s.

Like their predecessors after the earlier Reform Act of 1832, the political leaders of the generation of 1867 were forced to take an active interest in electoral management. For the new electorate created in 1867 had to be managed and led, elections had to be fought, party enthusiasm directed into suitable channels. It is not true, as is still commonly believed, that Robert Lowe, after the passage of the 1867 Reform Act, proclaimed, 'Now we must educate our masters'.[2] But political education was after 1867 a practical necessity. Millions of new voters had to be absorbed into the political system, assimilated into the existing party structure and encouraged to vote. A new generation of provincial political leaders, akin to the party bosses of America, was required to make the system work. And such men speedily emerged. The first and best known of them was Joseph Chamberlain in Birmingham. But by the 1880s most large towns, at least in England and

---

[1]Walter Bagehot, *The English Constitution*, World's Classics edn., London 1949, 260.
[2]For what he actually said see A. Patchett Martin, *Life and Letters of the Right Honourable Robert Lowe, Viscount Sherbrooke*, London 1893, II, 323.

Ireland, had well-established local leaders, who formed the backbone of the first nationwide organizations of party workers, the National Union of Conservative Associations (1867), the National Liberal Federation (1877), and the Irish National League (1882).

Some of the provincial political leaders were also leaders of industry, like the Pullars of Perth, the Kitsons of Leeds, and the Crossleys of Halifax, or leaders of commerce, like the Forwoods of Liverpool.[1] By establishing a close connection between economic leadership and political leadership, such men helped reinforce the central position of politics in British life. But everywhere the normal pattern was for the 'natural' leaders of the community to take their place as political leaders: Liberal and Conservative committees alike were largely composed in rural areas of: the gentry, the clergy, the estate agents, the bankers, the larger farmers, the manufacturers of agricultural implements, and the nonconformist ministers; in the towns of: lawyers, brewers, bankers, manufacturers, merchants, leading shopkeepers, Church of England and nonconformist ministers, and town councillors, plus a sprinkling of dentists, trade union leaders, master craftsmen, and school teachers.

In many parts of the country the political associations to which such men belonged almost imperceptibly became social organizations as well. Some wealthy central city clubs built clubhouses, either in the palatial style of the Manchester Reform Club (1868) or the more modest style of the gentleman's clubs of watering places and county towns, to reinforce the social ties between members. Others were reluctant to tie up their resources in brick and stone and preferred the more spartan traditions of the little clubs that were established in modest houses and were often offshoots of nonconformist chapels. But almost everywhere politics came to occupy a central position in community life. Workingmen's clubs, co-operative societies, friendly societies, and other charitable organizations were often identified with one party or the other.[2] The Conservative bank in a provincial town often glowered at a Liberal bank across the street. Conservative

---

[1]The Pullars were dyers who later became important dry cleaners, the Kitsons were engineers, the Crossleys carpet manufacturers, and the Forwoods merchants and shipowners.

[2]H. J. Hanham, 'Politics and Community Life in Victorian and Edwardian Britain', *Folk Life*, IV (1966), 5-14.

lawyers, active in working for their party, did not expect much business from Liberal clients: nor did Liberal lawyers expect much Conservative business. It was not that Liberal and Conservative did not mix. They often belonged to the same church, attended the same balls, engaged in the same sports, and had attended the same school. Their children were also likely to marry across party boundaries. But in the 1870s and 1880s everybody talked about politics, and worked hard at making the new politics a success, so that politics seemed to matter more than ever before. And when the great crises of the 1880s came—the death of Gordon and Gladstone's conversion to Home Rule for Ireland—politics quite often disrupted social life. Old friends would not speak and crossed the road to avoid one another. Dinner parties were disturbed by political wrangles. And nerves were so taut that it is not surprising that in the years that followed a reaction sets in. In the 1890s politics lost its undisputed primacy in the national consciousness, much as it had already done in America. Attention shifted to the suburban home, with its growing creature comforts, and to the revelations of social investigators who had begun to make it clear that great political issues like the extension of the franchise or Home Rule for Ireland had little bearing on the problem of how to diminish the worst evils of poverty and overcrowding. The trade unions began to assume a more central role in public life. Organized games began to replace politics as spectator sports. The newspapers gradually ceased to report political speeches in full. Society, in short, began to forget its intense love affair with party politics.

In the meantime, however, a whole generation of new politicians had grown up who were attuned to the post 1867 political order. In 1874 the first two working men were returned to parliament. In 1886 a working-class M.P. for the first time became a minister of the Crown, when Henry Broadhurst became Under-Secretary at the Home Office. Trade unions, workingmen's clubs, and friendly societies were added to the list of the social organizations (headed by Eton) which provided a training for a political career.

By 1905, when the *Sheffield and District Who's Who* was published with the avowed purpose of 'giving an outline of the careers of the public men in the city and neighbourhood', the careers of working-class politicians were at last beginning to be regarded as significant enough to merit public attention, though their more aristocratic contemporaries still received disproportionate attention in the newspapers. The typical Sheffield politician was still in 1905 a professional man like Alderman Robert Styring, about whom it was reported:

> The 'Whip' of the Liberal Party in the Sheffield City Council is, professionally, a successful lawyer, partner in the firm of Webster and Styring, solicitors. Sprang from the sturdy middle class, which has for so long been the backbone of the country. He has been in public life for 20 years, entering the Council for St. Peter's ward as a Liberal in 1886, after an initial defeat in the early part of that year. He was successively re-elected for that ward until 1899, when he was appointed an alderman. Has for many years been prominently connected with the Cemetery Road Congregational Church and Sunday School, and in 1889-90 filled the office of Chairman of the Sheffield Congregational Association. Since 1881 he has been hon. sec. of the Sheffield Athenaeum Club, and in 1896 a presentation was made to him by the members to mark their appreciation of his services during 15 years. As a member of the City Council it fell to Alderman Styring's lot to organise the Sheffield Electric Supply Department on the acquisition of the electric light by the Corporation in 1898, and he was Chairman of the Electric Light Committee down to November, 1904. To him mainly is due also the initiation of the Surplus Lands Committee, and the intitiation of the Angel Street and other building schemes of the Corporation, some of which have been the subject of keen controversy. Was actively concerned in the arrangements under which the Corporation purchased the tramways and converted them to the electric system. Took a prominent part in the purchase and subsequent management of the water undertaking. Has been a member of the committee since the date of purchase. It was at his suggestion that the Corporation sought to obtain, and after a protracted Parliamentary struggle succeeded in establishing, Sheffield's claim to a large share of the Derwent Valley water. Since the formation of the Derwent Valley Water Board, has been one of Sheffield's three representatives on that body. Was for some time a member of the University College, and is now on the Court of Governors of the University of Sheffield. For many years has been one of the Corporation representative members of the Technical Department of the University. Is a member of the Education Committee, and a Governor of King Edward VII School at Sheffield.[1]

[1]*Sheffield and District Who's Who,* Sheffield 1905, p. 31.

On the Conservative side such professional men were commonly supplemented by publicans like Councillor Alfred Taylor:

> Native of Sheffield, born in 1849: educated at Trinity Church Schools, Wicker. Served apprenticeship to edge tool and sheep shear trade, and though has now left that business, has maintained close association with his old trade, and remained member of his trade union. Has been a licence holder for 35 years, and is now landlord of the Corner Pin Hotel, and is much respected, not only in the 'trade' but in Sheffield generally. Has occupied position of President of Sheffield, Rotherham, and District Licensed Victuallers' Association; Vice-president Licensed Victuallers' National Defence League (No. 2 branch); trustee of Licensed Victuallers' Institution at Dore, Freemason and member of several Friendly Societies. Has always been prominently identified with Conservative Party in Sheffield, particularly in Brightside Division. Took leading part in elections in Brightside Old Ward when S. Q. L. candidates were 'hammered out'. First elected to City Council in 1894 for old Brightside Ward, afterwards St. Philip's Ward, and was afterwards allocated to Neepsend for which he now sits. Is a member of Health, Tramways, and General Purposes and Parks Committees. Takes great interest in provision of municipal music in the Parks in summer and in the courts and alleys in winter. Cemeteries and public burial grounds also take up a good deal of his time.[1]

But the politics of the post 1867 period was best represented by trade unionists like Councillor A. J. Bailey:

> Councillor Alfred J. Bailey is one of the soundest and least aggressive members of the Labour group in the City Council. Born July 15th, 1868, at Scredington, Lincolnshire, the son of an agricultural labourer. His education was received at a village National School, three miles from Scredington, and then at a new village Board School, the head of which was a schoolmistress. Mr. Bailey, who is a member of the Church of England, commenced work as a ploughboy at thirteen years of age, and stuck to farm work until he was 21. Then he came to Sheffield, and obtained employment as a drayman. On several occasions he lost situations, and found himself out of employment for long periods, owing to his advocacy of trade union principles. Worked at Treeton Colliery as a surfaceman, and was there affected by the miners' lockout of 1893. As a workman he assisted in organising the surfacemen, and in 1896 was appointed

[1]*Ibid.*, p. 38.

official organiser for the National Amalgamated Union of Labour, the membership of which has since increased by over 3,000. Was elected a member of the Sheffield Board of Guardians in April, 1902, and was re-elected in 1904, on both occasions without a contest. He had the unique experience of having to fight for his seat on the City Council twice in the same year. He was elected at a by-election in June, 1904 for Darnall Ward, the vacancy having been caused by the death of the late Councillor Castle. In November he had again to seek re-election, and was again opposed. The majority of 271 in June rose to 533 in November.[1]

Elections and Party Management, which first appeared in 1959, was designed to illustrate the political context in which such men grew up, partly in the world of post-1832 politics, where they were largely outsiders, partly in the world of post-1867 politics, where they gradually became insiders. The book was planned as part of a large and still unfinished study of politics, parliament, and people in mid-Victorian Britain. There were to be two volumes: the first was to examine the electoral system and the relations between the party leaders at Westminister and their followers in in the country, the second, which has still to be written, is to be devoted to politicians in parliament and the country. What was published was, therefore, only the first volume of two.

The findings of *Elections and Party Management* in many ways closely paralleled those of Norman Gash's *Politics in the Age of Peel* which had appeared six years before. But the emphasis was rather different. My interests at the time were chiefly contemporary, and I was, therefore, as much concerned with the continuities between the mass politics of the 1880s and the mass politics of the 1950s, as I was with survival of the political world that had begun to die in 1832. Some of the records I consulted were still held by local party offices, where party agents often had a lively sense of the connections between the world of the 1867 Reform Bill and their own world. There were even, in many places, survivors of the old politics. A man who had known Disraeli (who died in 1881) was still active in one constitutency, a 'Primrose Bud' of the 1880s is another.

I now regret that the book did not include more comparative material dealing with other countries. But at the time there was

[1] *Ibid.*, p. 45.

very little in print that would have helped me to find a way through the sources. I badly needed Seymour Martin Lipset's *Political Man* which was not published until 1960 and Lee Benson's *The Concept of Jacksonian Democracy: New York as a Test Case*, which was not published until 1961. There was not even very much available in print on Scandinavia, though a number of distinguished scholars had been at work for some time. Solid collections of essays on many countries were not to appear until the middle or late sixties.[1] But my main concern at the time was with Britain, not America or Scandinavia. When I began work in 1951 there was no up-to-date study of the Reform Acts of 1832, 1867-8, or 1883-5. Nor was there a single substantial study of a nineteenth century general election or of a nineteenth-century political party. Books that now seem indispensible were a long time in coming: John Vincent's *The Formation of the Liberal Party* (1966), Michael Brock's *The Great Reform Act* (1973), F. B. Smith's *The Making of the Second Reform Bill* (1966), Maurice Cowling's *1867: Disraeli, Gladstone and Reform* (1967), Trevor Lloyd's *The General Election of 1880* (1968), and many others.

The defects of *Elections and Party Management* arose largely from the relative isolation in which it was produced. The critics were for the most part very generous. But I have long thought that I should not have accepted the suggestion of the original publisher to remove the full introduction I had written and that I should not have been quite so optimistic as to believe that I could summarize in list form a very complicated subject in the way I attempted in Appendix III. That Appendix, which consisted of a list of 'Seats Controlled by Patrons', should have been more tentative and have distinguished more clearly between different types of control. I thought at the time that it was something of a tour de force to know as much as I then did about so many constituencies: now I realize that my knowledge was very patchy. The overall picture is probably about right, but here and there I was misled by my sources. Midhurst, for instance, was not as much in his pocket as Lord Egmont for his own purposes liked to make out.

[1] Erik Allardt and Yrjö Littunen, *Cleavages, Ideologies and Party Systems*, Helsinki 1964. Seymour M. Lipset and Stein Rokkan, *Party Systems and Voter Alignments: Cross National Perspectives*, New York 1967, Stein Rokkan and others, *Citizens, Elections, Parties: Approaches to the Comparative Study of the Process of Development*, Oslo 1970, Erik Allardt and Stein Rokkan, eds., *Mass Politics: Studies in Political Sociology*, New York 1970.

The concept of influence and control—or of deference as David Cresap Moore has it[1]—is fraught with difficulties. Party loyalty is one form of it: voting to please a neighbour or a landlord another. In both cases there is to some degree reciprocal relationship involved. Voters hope to get something out of parties or neighbours or landlords when they vote in such a way as to please them. They may be influenced in so voting by pride or ideology or family sentiment or fear, or a mixture of these and other feelings. What one is talking about, therefore, whether writing about the nineteenth century or the twentieth, is the springs of human conduct. To these we have but uncertain guides. Like my old teacher and friend, George Kitson Clark, I prefer to stop short of making definite pronouncements about such matters, because the more I have learnt the less sure I am that information in such fields can be convincingly related to a sound structure of theory.

In *Elections and Party Management* I tried to concentrate attention on those aspects of patronage and control where information of a practical sort was available: in textbooks on the law of elections, records of the trial of election petitions. the archives of railway companies, and in country newspapers, for instance. I tried to cleave as closely as possible to such sources, and particularly to rely heavily upon newspapers, because they occupied a central place in the politics of the 1860s and 1870s and they, therefore, reflected the blend of influences that shaped political life. The idealism of the Gladstonian Liberal Party, for instance, is closely linked in the newspapers to a pragmatic, old-fashioned approach to politics. Such a linkage is nicely illustrated by this extract from the sometimes ultra-Liberal *Western Times* referring to Ashburton in Devon:

> The house of Matheson and Jardine is one of the most extensive of the great mercantile establishments of England, and Mr. Robert Jardine, the present candidate, is a member of that firm. It is highly desirable that the commerce of this country should be duly represented in the House of Commons, and no candidate comes before a constituency with a better right to aspire to the honour of the representation than a first class merchant. Looking at human nature, we may add that there are no benefits which a constituency may honestly expect to obtain from connection with a representative like

[1]David Cresap Moore, *The Politics of Deference: A Study of the Mid-Nineteenth-Century English Political System*, Hassocks 1976.

those which flow from such a connection. They are benefits conferred without corruption, and may therefore be received with all honour. The merchants whose establishments equal the courts of petty princes, have the opportunity of advancing the fortunes of enterprising young men, and the recipients of their favours know at the same time that the obligation is mutual, that the fortunes of the house depend on the fidelity of the service rendered and the patronage thus bestowed exacts a return which exalts and benefits both parties alike.

Mr. Robert Jardine is not only a member of this great commercial house, but he happens to be the largest land-owner in the parish of Ashburton, and takes a local interest in everything connected with the borough.[1]

This was politics in the old style with a vengeance, but it was not unenlightened politics, because it combined deference with a very practical attempt to alleviate the conditions of the people. It wasn't, therefore, so very different in intent from the new politics, which Joseph Chamberlain outlined in a speech at Birmingham in 1885:

I believe, and I rejoice to believe, that the reduction of the franchise will bring into prominence social questions which have been too long neglected, that it will force upon the consideration of thinking men of all parties the condition of our poor—aye, and the contrast which, unfortunately, exists between the great luxury and wealth which some enjoy, and the misery and poverty which prevails among large portions of the population. I do not believe that any Liberal policy, mine or any other, will ever take away the security which which property rightly enjoys; that it will ever destroy the certainty that industry and thrift will meet with their due reward; but I do think that something may be done to enlarge the obligation and responsibility of the whole community towards its poorer and less fortunate members. In that great work, if I am permitted to take any part, I hope I may have, I am confident I shall have, your support and sympathy.[2]

---

[1]*Western Times* (16th June 1865), quoted in H. J. Hanham, 'Ashburton as a Parliamentary Borough, 1640-1886', *Transactions of the Devonshire Association*, XCVIII, pp. 249-250.
[2]Leopold Wagner, ed., *Modern Political Orations*, London 1896, p. 282.

INTRODUCTION TO THE FIRST EDITION

THAT juxtaposition of old and new which gave the period between the Reform Acts of 1867 and 1884 its peculiar character,
was occasioned by two factors: the Reform Act of 1867 itself and
the long period of economic prosperity which lasted almost unbroken from about 1850 to 1879. The one deprived the Radicals
of their most significant grievance against the existing social
order, at the price of admitting them to a much greater share in
the government of the country; the other confirmed both the
popular belief in the inexorable march of progress and the
economic supremacy of the aristocracy and the middle classes.

The 1867 Reform Act almost doubled the old electorate of
close on a million, and gave the county vote to nearly all landowners, tenant farmers and middle-class householders, and to the
better class of village tradesmen, and the borough vote to almost
all settled householders. It withheld the franchise from working-
class householders in the counties, and from all who in county
or borough shared dwelling-houses or occupied them for short
periods or as a condition of employment. In the counties the
chief consequence was to give the rural districts much more
weight than the small towns and mining villages. In the boroughs
the effects were more varied. In the smallest boroughs like Dorchester and Hertford the 1867 franchise was little different from
the old one, since the new voters were agricultural labourers and
small tradesmen dependent on the local 'upper crust' for their
livelihood and not sufficiently numerous to form effective political
associations of their own. In many of them the new electorate
was, indeed, only about fifty per cent bigger than the old. The
medium-sized provincial centres like Cambridge and Ipswich
were more affected, since their electorate was doubled or trebled.
But as the new electors were mostly skilled tradesmen and shopkeepers of the poorer sort (bakers, butchers, carpenters and beer-
shop proprietors were particularly numerous among them), who
already played an important part in municipal elections, there
was again nothing like a sweeping change in the political balance
of forces. This took place only in the industrial towns, and in
Scotland, where the electorate grew beyond all recognition.

There were 1,165 electors in Gateshead in 1866, of whom 110 were working men; in 1872 there were 9,191 electors of whom the vast majority were working men: there were 6,630 electors in Newcastle-upon-Tyne in 1866, of whom 1,559 were working men; in 1872 there were 21,407 electors of whom the vast majority were working men: there were 768 electors in Warrington in 1866, of whom 149 were working men; in 1872 there were 4,848 electors[1], again mostly working men.

What the 1867 Reform Act signally failed to do was to carry out a much-needed redistribution of seats. On paper the fact that no fewer than fifty-three seats were redistributed was impressive, especially when coupled with the introduction of the so-called minority clause in thirteen big constituencies.[2] But in practice it did very little to remedy existing inequalities. At one extreme there were still more than seventy boroughs with a population of less than 10,000, although many larger places were not enfranchised, while at the other there were over forty constituencies with a population of more than 200,000. Portarlington, with less than 3,000 people and 140 electors, was as much a parliamentary borough as Liverpool with 500,000 people and 60,000 electors; Tiverton, with a population of 10,000, had two members, like Marylebone with a population of 477,000; and Rutland, with a population of 22,000, had as many members as South-East Lancashire with a population of 403,000. And these discrepancies were growing every year because the population of the smaller constituencies was either stationary or declining, while that of the larger was rapidly increasing. Moreover, the different classes of constituency by no means enjoyed equal representation. The boroughs had 281 members and the counties only 170, although the population of the counties was considerably larger (13,689,000 as against 12,286,000 in 1881): the boroughs and agricultural counties were over-represented in comparison with the industrial counties (notably Lancashire and Yorkshire); and most glaring of all, the south and west of England were over-represented in comparison with the rest of the country. Wiltshire and Dorset

---

[1] The best general account of the Reform Act and its consequences is given in Charles Seymour, *Electoral Reform in England and Wales*, New Haven 1915. There was no Irish equivalent to the English and Scottish Reform Acts, so that the old Irish electorate remained virtually unchanged until 1885, when the number of electors was actually smaller than it had been in 1866.

[2] For details of the distribution of seats and the minority clause see Appendix II.

still had twenty-five members between them, eighteen for the boroughs and seven for the counties, although their population was no more than 450,000; yet the metropolis with three million people had only twenty-four members, and the West Riding with two million had only twenty-two.[1]

The greatest inequality or discrepancy in the system was not traditional at all. The reformers in 1867 deliberately went out of their way to give the boroughs a franchise entirely different from that of the counties, so increasing rather than playing down the traditional difference between them.[2] They came therefore to differ not only in size, in traditions, and in local government, but also in the whole way in which elections were fought. The counties became the strongholds of the old order; the boroughs, or rather the bigger boroughs, became the field for experiment in 'democratic' political organisation. The distinction was not however a rigid one. Neither 'borough' nor 'county' was a precise term, because of variations in size and character within the two categories, and because there existed, in addition to predominantly urban counties like South Essex,[3] a number of hybrid 'agricultural boroughs' which were a cross between county and borough. These were composed of a small town or village together with most of the neighbouring parishes or tithings, and in some cases included the whole of the hundred in which a town was situated. Some of them were quite small in area, but others meandered for miles—Great Marlow extended over some twenty-two square miles, Droitwich over forty-three, and Wallingford over twenty-eight—while the giants among them were really county divisions: Aylesbury with 108 square miles, New Shoreham with 175, Cricklade with 248, and East Retford with 325.[4] Thirty-seven of the most rural had, in fact, a population of less than one person to an acre, and Wareham actually had a lower ratio

[1] The extent of this over-representation was recognised in 1885 when the southern and western counties were deprived of thirty-eight seats. Cornwall lost 6 members, Devon 4, Dorset 6, Wiltshire 9, Hampshire 4, Berkshire 3 and Sussex 6. For comments on the change see *Spectator*, 27 December 1884.

[2] The electorate of the boroughs of England and Wales was increased by about 134% in 1867, that of the counties by only 45%.

[3] The centre of South Essex was West Ham with a population of 129,000 in 1881. Middlesex, West Kent, South-West and South-East Lancashire and parts of the West Riding had a similar character.

[4] These boroughs were classed by statute with the counties for electioneering purposes, and under the 1868 Act candidates in them were permitted to hire cabs to take voters to the poll.

(0·196) than the very rural county of Dorset itself. Such boroughs inevitably produced queer effects on the electoral map. Buckinghamshire, for instance, was cut in two by the vast borough of Aylesbury, which stretched from Aylesbury itself to Missenden and from the outskirts of Thame to the outskirts of Tring, yet it also possessed three other large agricultural boroughs: Buckingham, Wycombe and Marlow. Similarly, in Sussex, the borough of New Shoreham stretched from the Surrey boundary to the sea, and completely surrounded the still extensive but smaller borough of Horsham. As the size of a borough bore no relation to its importance, the boroughs of Wiltshire, Dorset, Hampshire and Sussex present on the map a most extraordinary jumble: insignificant small boroughs like Bridport and Dorchester, whose parliamentary boundaries were the same as those of the municipal borough and included none of the surrounding parishes; sizeable towns like Brighton, Portsmouth and Southampton; and stretches of countryside like Midhurst, Wareham and Petersfield with scarcely a town in them.

Although the 1867 Reform Act, in spite of these deficiencies, was undoubtedly the first decisive event in what has been called the 'transition to democracy', the twenty years that followed it were far from democratic. As G. J. Holyoake told an audience of working men in 1868

> Though Representation is open to us, we cannot understand too soon, that the House of Commons, like the London Tavern—is only open to those who can pay the tariff. . . . All that the sons of labour have gained at present, is the advantage of being consulted. Whoever is member will have to take them into account. This is a great thing gained. But the electoral machinery of England is centuries old; and the people cannot expect to come into possession of it without conditions, nor to master its use all at once.[1]

For the moment the preoccupations of parliament and the electorate were almost entirely middle class, and the Reform Act was less important because it gave some working men the vote than because it had touched off an era of reform.

The Reform Act of 1832 had called the new forces in English life into the parliamentary forum, but it had not decided what role they were to play. Indeed, after satisfying the most pressing

---

[1] G. J. Holyoake, *Working-class Representation*, Birmingham 1868, pp. 8-9.

demands of their supporters, the reformers had deliberately preserved for the old aristocracy much more power and influence
than its experience of government and prestige alone would
have won it. It still remained for the middle classes to seize
effective power if they wanted it. For a few years it seemed that
they would do so, but the burst of legislative enthusiasm associated
with the disciples of Jeremy Bentham soon died away as a result
of aristocratic inertia and the development of the great national
conflicts over the Charter and the Corn Laws. Until the fierce
antagonisms which gave rise to Chartism and the Anti-Corn-Law
League had burned themselves out, or had been subdued by the
long years of mid-Victorian prosperity, free trade was the only
major issue with which parliament felt bound to deal. Indeed,
for twenty years after the end of the 'hungry forties', men were
too busy taking advantage of the good times which had come
to them, and sampling the pleasures of their new-found power
abroad, to care much for their abstract rights. There was, as a
consequence, a general desire among all but convinced reformers
to shelve questions of reform until Lord Palmerston should retire.
Meanwhile, the reformers belonging to the disparate traditions
of Peel, Bentham and Cobden drew closer together and joined
forces with the Oxford reformers, the Radical working men, and
the political dissenters in accepting Gladstone as their leader.

By 1865, with prosperity seemingly assured, only two things
stood in the way of an era of reform designed to benefit the
middle classes: Palmerston, who obstinately refused to retire, and
the question of parliamentary reform, which had been so much
agitated since 1859 that no other major reforms could well be
given precedence over it. Death removed Lord Palmerston in
October 1865, and in 1867, after two years of political confusion,
the essentially Palmerstonian parliament which had refused reform at the hands of Lord Russell and Mr Gladstone accepted
it at those of Lord Derby and Mr Disraeli. In the very next
session Mr Gladstone brought forward a motion for the disestablishment of the Irish Church in very much the same terms
as that which had first been carried by Lord John Russell in 1835.
He was supported by Bright, and in the new Liberal cabinet
formed at the end of 1868 Whigs, Peelites, and Radicals all
found a place. In the course of the 1868 parliament the middle
classes who had enjoyed nominal power since 1832 at last came

into their own. The army, the universities, and indirectly the Civil Service, were opened to them; the first steps were taken in educational and temperance reforms; and the Irish Church was disestablished.

For the seventeen years after 1867 there was scarcely a break in the catalogue of reforms, even during the life of the Conservative parliament of 1874 to 1880. As Gladstone wrote prophetically in his *Chapter of Autobiography* (1868), the 'movement of the public mind has been of a nature entirely transcending former experience', and the public soon became prepared for changes which had seemed out of the question only a few years before. At the same time, a clear division between reformers and anti-reformers began to emerge, which gradually transformed both political parties, and which had the immediate effect of giving the electors a distinct choice of party programmes for the first time since 1847. Even more important, the reformers, by their own example and by their enactment of the Ballot Act, gave encouragement to the forces of nationalism in Ireland, which soon grew out of the party garments that English politicians would have had them wear.

The extraordinary number of reforms with which these years are associated should not, however, be allowed to obscure the essential continuity of political life before and after 1867. Gladstone and his associates belonged in outlook to the age of Peel and Cobden. The objectives they pursued in the seventies and eighties were almost without exception those which John Bright had been proclaiming twenty years before, just as their social attitudes had been shaped by the belief in the divine right of the middle classes to political leadership and by the ultra-individualism of the Manchester school. And the constituencies themselves continued to be dominated by the magnates of land and industry. The reason for this political continuity was undoubtedly the mid-Victorian period of economic prosperity. Its influence was two-fold: it created the atmosphere of optimism and confidence which made possible the great reforms of the late sixties and early seventies, and it sustained and invigorated the old hierarchical society which in the forties had seemed doomed to decay. It revived in particular that attitude of deference with which Bagehot made such play, and which was so alien to the mood of the Chartists and the world of *Sybil*:

a deference which had the effect of prolonging the privileges of the aristocracy and the landed gentry. What Radical writer of the thirties could have written, as Leslie Stephen wrote in 1867, of the aristocracy as an integral and even essential part of society whose privileges no Reform Act would seriously diminish?

> The main influence . . . of the upper classes undoubtedly depends upon what may be called the occult and unacknowledged forces which are not dependent upon any legislative machinery. England is still an aristocratic country; not because the nobility have certain privileges, or possess influence in certain boroughs. A power resting upon such a basis would be very fragile and would go to pieces at the first strain upon the Constitution. The country is aristocratic, because the whole upper and middle, and a great part of the lower, classes have still an instinctive liking for the established order of things; because innumerable social ties bind us together spontaneously, so as to give to the aristocracy a position tolerably corresponding to their political privileges.[1]

Radicals still carped at the petty tyranny of landlords and resented their wealth, but they could not ignore the fact that landlords were the wealthiest men in the country, that they dominated Society with a capital S, and that they sent more members to parliament than any other class.[2] Moreover, the landowners acted as political chiefs in the constituencies, where seats like Nostell Priory, Knowsley Hall, and Chatsworth House were as much party offices as those in Westminster.

Prosperity also affected the towns. In the oldest ones new industries sprang up: bicycle-making at Coventry, cocoa and tobacco processing at Bristol, agricultural machinery works at Bedford and Lincoln, and Colman's mustard works at Norwich. In those whose prosperity had come with the industrial revolution there

[1] Leslie Stephen, 'On the Choice of Representatives by Popular Constituencies', *Essays on Reform*, London 1867, pp. 106-7.

[2] The number of members who came from families with more than 2,000 acres of land (according to John Bateman's *The Great Landowners of Great Britain and Ireland*, 4 edn, London 1883, and 'The New Domesday') was as follows:

	Number of Members	
	1868	*1880*
2,000–5,000 acres	c. 86	85
5,000–10,000 acres	104	86
10,000–20,000 acres	88	62
20,000–50,000 acres	70	49
Over 50,000 acres	59	40
	407	322

was also a change of tempo as new industries, mainly concerned with engineering, moved in alongside textiles. There were also new towns like Birkenhead, Middlesbrough, Crewe, and Swindon.

These developments directly affected the position of the skilled workmen, whose value in an industrial society was only just coming to be recognised, and whose material position had been steadily improving. Their new houses were better than ever before, and although many of them are today slum property, they made possible a new order and cleanliness which was quite alien to the chaos and filth of Engels' Manchester of 1844. Wages had risen, and by 1871 prices had begun to fall without (except for a short time in 1879-80) any serious rise in unemployment. Trade unionism enjoyed a boom, and for a while spread even to the agricultural labourers. Nor was there any lack of incentives. A skilled man could earn as much as five times the income of an agricultural labourer, and enjoyed all the social advantages which society linked with the successful application of the doctrine of self-help. For the time being, at least, there was no serious call for a movement to redress working-class grievances.

But by 1880 the long period of prosperity which had lasted since the fifties was at an end, although few were yet aware of it. The working classes were not greatly affected at first, but the bulwarks of Victorian society, the landlord, the capitalist, and the church, soon found themselves in difficulties. Now at last the Protectionists of the forties were vindicated as free trade put an end to the unexampled prosperity of English agriculture, and increased competition reduced the return from industrial investments. And the break in English political life, in so far as there was one, came not in 1867 but in the years between 1880 and 1886.

The general election of 1874 was the last to take place in the old conditions. By 1880 the Home Rule movement had grown from small and very respectable beginnings to become a real menace to the English supremacy in Ireland. Through the medium of parliamentary obstruction the Home Rulers had also put an end to many of the comforts which had made parliamentary life agreeable to English country gentlemen. Already sorely troubled by the demands which their constituents were making upon their time, these now began to relinquish parliamentary ambitions altogether. Much of the remaining flavour of mid-Victorian politics also disappeared with the death of Disraeli in 1881—as the nostalgic success of the Primrose League was to show—and was never recaptured. The Conservative party which he had done so much to create took on a new rôle only five years after his death, when the Liberal party finally collapsed as a result of its many internal conflicts.

The machinery of politics changed along with the parties. The Corrupt Practices Act of 1883 which limited election expenditure made it easier and cheaper to get into parliament and gave a new importance to party organisation. The voluntary worker in the constituency, organised by a body like the Primrose League, and the party headquarters, with their large financial resources and supply of posters and leaflets, became for the first time the key to electioneering. The old constituencies inherited from the middle ages were swept away in 1884-5, and the gross inequalities in their size and the difference between the borough and the county franchise went with them. The single-member constituency became the rule, even though it meant breaking up the big towns and creating entirely working-class constituencies without middle-class leaders. As the big towns, the metropolis, and the industrial districts for the first time received their fair share of the seats there was also a great influx of members of a new type, and for the first time the number of commercial men and manufacturers in the House of Commons was greater than the number of landowners.

The chapter of political history that opened with the general election of 1885 was, in short, a completely new one. Leaders, parties, constituencies, were all different from those of 1867, and as such can find no place in a book on the age of Disraeli and Gladstone.

Part I

THE CONSTITUENCIES

Chapter One

COUNTY MAGNATES

I

THE county, even where it had been divided in 1832 and redivided in 1867, was more than a geographical unit. With its own head, the Lord-Lieutenant, its own ecclesiastical organisation, its own courts, and its own foxhounds and beagles, it was a self-contained society. And in many counties, as in Trollope's Barsetshire, the parliamentary divisions created in 1832 had corresponded to real social divisions, so that by 1867 they had acquired an independent character of their own, with their own magnates, their own 'county town', and not infrequently their own Quarter Sessions. The effective government of the county was entirely in the hands of the freeholders and gentlemen of fortune, who could alone become county magistrates and attend to the administration of justice and the business of the county at Quarter Sessions. Within the narrow circle of magnates, squires, beneficed clergy, leading manufacturers, bankers, and merchants whom the Lord-Lieutenant appointed to the Commission of the Peace there were, of course, important differences of social status: some were peers or members of parliament, some kept London houses or stables at Newmarket, some had seats in other counties, while others lived with their foxhounds or parishioners in the county. But if Quarter Sessions constituted something of an élite (there were only 183 county magistrates in the whole of Lincolnshire in 1876),[1] the society of those who mattered was more extensive, reaching from the Lord-Lieutenant at the top to the larger farmers at the bottom. In most counties there was a well-marked hierarchy, such as that which Lord Willoughby de Broke described so agreeably in writing of his Warwickshire youth in *The Passing Years*:[2]

[1] *The Post Office Directory of Lincolnshire*, London 1876, records that among the 183 magistrates were 55 clergymen, 6 peers, 7 sons of peers, 7 baronets and 8 M.P.s. These latter totals include the following in more than one category: a clerical baronet, two sons of peers in holy orders, 3 baronet M.P.s and one M.P. who was a peer's son.
[2] Lord Willoughby de Broke, *The Passing Years*, London 1924, pp. 57-8.

The Lord-Lieutenant,
The Master of the Foxhounds,
The Agricultural Landlords,
The Bishop,
The Chairman of Quarter Sessions,
The Colonel of the Yeomanry,
The Member of Parliament,
The Dean,
The Archdeacons,
The Justices of the Peace,
The lesser Clergy,
The larger Farmers.

It would not be difficult to construct a similar table of precedence for Barsetshire, where the foxhounds and the yeomanry were not perhaps so important as in the eyes of a famous M.F.H.

One thing on which the lists for almost every county would agree would be the status of the county member. In the sixties and seventies he was still a great man, and to be a knight of the shire carried with it a social prestige almost greater than that of cabinet rank. As late as 1868 Edward Fellowes, the Member for Huntingdonshire and later Lord de Ramsey, was able to ride to the hustings at the head of his tenantry, 150 of them, all on horseback, who formed a semicircle round the hustings and waited quietly while he was returned unopposed.[1] In that year only thirteen of the county members were strangers to the counties they represented, and country newspapers were hot against candidates who did not come up to conventional standards: only men of extensive property or local family connections would do. There was a particularly strong prejudice against the nouveaux riches, and most county gentlemen agreed in principle with the Lincolnshire Whig who

> ... hoped they should always have men of good family to represent them—men of good stock. Some might make large fortunes in Australia or New Zealand, and, returning home, wish to become Members of Parliament, but they were not the men to satisfy or represent the agricultural interests of this county.[2]

Even Lord Eustace Cecil was not quite approved in Essex because Lord Salisbury had so little property in the county.[3] Judge

[1] *Stamford Mercury*, 27 November 1868.   [2] *Ibid.*, 24 July 1868.
[3] *Colchester Mercury*, 20 June 1868. Letter from 'A Tenant Farmer'.

then the indignation of the old school when a self-made Wisbech merchant was returned for Cambridgeshire in 1865, in the dissenting and fen smallholders' interest. This 'disgraceful event' was redeemed by his defeat in 1868, but the Tory *Cambridge Chronicle* could regard his candidature only as an unmitigated calamity:

> He is a man who never should have been selected for the important position he fills. . . . He has absolutely no qualification for the position. He is neither innately nor by birth a gentleman. He is perfectly uneducated. The result is we have a county member who is a parliamentary cypher, and a country gentleman (save the mark) whose conversation is on a par with that of his groom. Money, is his only recommendation.[1]

The typical county member was a solid country gentleman, or the son of one of the lesser peers like Lord Lyttelton or Lord Howe. He was not a politician in the ordinary sense of the word, rarely spoke in the House, and spent a great deal of the session in the country. Indeed, most counties positively preferred to elect well-known sportsmen like M. F. Bissett of the Devon and Somerset Staghounds or county administrators like Edward Hicks, vice-chairman of Cambridgeshire Quarter Sessions, whom they knew and understood, rather than statesmen whose preoccupations were alien to them. In one respect, however, the counties were surprisingly unprejudiced. They made no objection to choosing merchants or manufacturers who had set up as country gentlemen if their behaviour warranted it. The Miles family of Bristol, for instance, who were at once merchants and bankers and country gentlemen, were nearly all acknowledged to be excellent country gentlemen once Disraeli's friend Sir William Miles, member for East Somerset 1834-65, had become a spokesman for the Protectionists in the forties.[2]

Henry Chaplin, popularly known as 'The Squire', personified both the strength and the weakness of the tradition of these

---

[1] *Cambridge Chronicle*, 3 October 1868.
[2] Six members of the family entered parliament within a period of sixty years: Philip John Miles, merchant and councillor, M.P. for Westbury 1820-6, Corfe Castle 1829-32, and Bristol 1835-7, his four sons Sir William Miles, banker and Chairman of Clifton Guardians, M.P. for Chippenham 1818-20, New Romney 1830-2, and East Somerset 1834-65, P. W. S. Miles, president of Bristol Chamber of Commerce, and M.P. for Bristol 1837-52, J. W. Miles, banker and councillor and M.P. for Bristol 1868, and C. W. Miles, M.P. for Malmesbury 1882-5, and his grandson Sir Philip Miles, sheriff of Bristol and M.P. for East Somerset 1878-85.

honourable but often obtuse country gentlemen. He was generous, genial, and, within his limits, intelligent. He lived up to his ideals, and behaved as one with a rent-roll of £20,000 a year should— that is to say, he overspent it. He won the Derby of 1867 with 'Hermit', who stood at 1,000 to 15 before the race, and he was master of the Blankney Hounds. He was member for Mid-Lincolnshire, where he was almost universally popular, and he consistently defended the interests of agriculture, even when this led him to embrace the new Protectionism. In parliament he habitually used the ponderous style known as the 'grand manner', which consorted well with his massive figure. Moreover, because he believed in himself, he persistently refused office after he had been Chancellor of the Duchy of Lancaster in 1885, because it was not accompanied by a place in the cabinet, and only gave way in 1889 when he was offered the post of first President of the new Board of Agriculture, which he could not well refuse.

II

The political character of a county was decided almost entirely by its landlords, the recognised leaders of social, administrative and judicial life. The freeholders were still the largest single body of voters (about 400,000 out of 800,000 in England), and pos- sessed an undoubted veto when they cared to use it, but in England this veto was in abeyance because large landlord, tenant-farmer and freeholder tended to share the same outlook and to vote together.[1] There was in England no social or religious barrier between landlord and tenant, between large landowner and small, such as there was in Wales and Scotland, so that tenants, however well-to-do, consciously looked to their landlords for political guid-ance, and almost invariably accepted it when offered. It was, indeed, so much a part of the custom of the countryside that scarcely anybody bothered to dispute it. Even where the land-lord made no attempt to conduct a canvass and ostentatiously allowed his tenants to 'go as they please', the tenants did their best to find out what their landlord really thought. As one

[1] 'Landlords and tenants voted together because they were bound by the same sympathies and interests, and where those interests differed on any important question the tenant would be found, as in Scotland, ready to take an independent course.' Sir Michael Hicks Beach, 3 *Hansard* CCVII, 766 (1871).

witness before the Hartington Committee of 1869-70 said, 'If they were told that their landlord did not care how they went politically, the majority of them would endeavour to find out what would best please him in order that they should so vote.'[1] Landlord and tenant alike regarded this unsolicited obedience to the unwritten law of the countryside as if it were a law of nature. 'I believe it is an evil of having property', a Radical landowner told the Hartington Committee, 'that a man considers that he not only owns this property himself, but that he owns the souls of his tenants, and I confess to a certain extent that personally I have that feeling, I should be even afraid I should be very indignant if my tenant voted against my wishes.'[2]

The ballot made little difference in England because it was accompanied by no change in the relations of landlord and tenant, and in any case everybody in the countryside knew pretty well how everybody else voted. The impetus the ballot and the extended franchise gave to political associations was ample compensation for the loss of the old poll-books which recorded how each elector voted. A Liberal or Conservative Association, or a Habitation of the Primrose League with the squire or parson as president and the estate agent as organiser and collector of subscriptions was, indeed, not very different from the old, more informal arrangements. Moreover, until 1883 when election expenses were limited, it was usual for the polling day to be an occasion for popular celebrations, all the voters in a village driving to the poll in carriages provided by the candidate or squire with stops for refreshment at the squire's expense at each stage of the journey.

Villagers and tenant farmers generally voted along with their landlord not only because it was the accepted custom of the countryside, but also because in everyday life the ordinary tenant was consciously dependent on the goodwill of his landlord. Sir Frederick Pollock's monograph on *The Land Laws*, first published in 1883, sums up this relationship very aptly.

Farm holdings are always or almost always taken by the tenant direct from the freeholder, and there is generally something of a personal relation between them (even where the landlord is a college or other corporate body) beyond the mere receipt and payment of rent. The farmer is legally bound to pay the full amount of

[1] H.C. 352, p. 198 (1868-9). VIII, 198.   [2] *Ibid.*, p. 251.

his agreed rent, without regard to the goodness or badness of the season; but in bad years it is the constant practice for the landlord to remit such a percentage of the rent as to leave the tenant answerable only for so much as the farm seems fairly capable of paying under the circumstances. . . . The landlord in return expects a certain amount of deference and compliance in various matters from his tenant. Not only does the farmer meet him half-way on questions of shooting rights, and allow free passage to the hunt, but his political support of the landlord is not unfrequently reckoned on with as much confidence as the performance of the covenants and conditions of the tenancy itself. In the case of holdings from year to year it may be not unfairly said that being of the landlord's political party is often a tacit condition of the tenancy.[1]

The political concord of landlord and tenant was more than a recognition of quasi-legal obligations. It amounted to a mutual recognition that an agricultural estate was a social institution, with its own code of behaviour and its own loyalties. The landlord did more than collect the rents and make reductions in bad times; he was the head of a community towards which he had recognised duties and obligations, and with which he shared a community of interest. His obligations to his estate were extensive. He was responsible for the repair and reconstruction of farmhouses, and for their progressive rebuilding to meet modern sanitary requirements. He was expected to provide cottages at uneconomic rents or at no rent at all for labourers who worked on the farms or round the big house, and to keep them in constant repair.[2] He was invariably the largest single contributor for the maintenance of old schools, and usually for the provision of new ones, and he was expected to contribute handsomely to the extension of hospitals and the building and equipping of reading rooms and halls. He provided the necessary land, and sometimes the materials, for the construction of churches and chapels, while the great work of nineteenth-century church restoration was largely financed out of his pockets. Charities, too, of all sorts, diocesan and other funds, and agricultural and industrial shows, always looked to

[1] F. Pollock, *The Land Laws*, 2 edn, London 1887, pp. 152-3.
[2] As late as 1912 rents ranged between 1s. and 3s. a week in most English counties and between 9d. and 2s. in Wales: *The Land: The Report of the Land Enquiry Committee*, London 1913, I, 118-19. The tied cottage let with the farm and sub-let by the farmer to the labourer for little or no rent was largely confined to England south of the Trent. *Ibid.*, I, 136-7. For the burden to the landlord see the 11th Duke of Bedford, *A Great Agricultural Estate*, London 1897, p. 83, and A. H. D. Acland, *Memoirs and Letters of the Right Honourable Sir Thomas Dyke Acland*, priv. printed, London 1902, p. 316.

him for help. The lesser tenants, the household staff, and estate workers also required occasional financial assistance, orders for hospitals, help in finding openings off the estate for themselves and their children, and sometimes help towards the cost of educating a clever child.

The political influence of a great magnate was always relatively much greater than that of his lesser neighbours, partly because he lived in greater state, but mostly because his financial resources made the lot of his tenants much happier. The great magnate was better able to withstand a fall in prices or an adverse season than the smaller man, and could help deserving tenants to tide over bad times more easily. He had, in general, more capital, expended it more systematically, and could use both labour and materials more economically because he was able to maintain continuity of management. Men like the seventh Duke of Devonshire, the third Marquess of Salisbury, and successive Dukes of Bedford, who administered their estates as gigantic trusts for the benefit of landlord, tenant, and labourer alike, were able to build up an enviable sense of community. The best of these larger landowners put from twenty per cent (often much more) of their gross rental into developing the estate. Sir Thomas Dyke Acland, for instance, spent at least £200,000 (twenty-five per cent of his gross income) over the years 1871 to 1898 on an estate of a little less than 40,000 acres.[1] The Duke of Bedford's accounts for his Bedfordshire and Buckinghamshire estates over the years 1876 to 1895 give a similar picture:[2] out of a total income of £870,036 (£687,658 from rents, £96,695 from woods, and £85,683 from other sources) only £104,672, or 12·03 per cent, went to the landlord.

The smaller owner could not as a rule hope to live on the scale which had become customary with the landed classes, and at the same time provide the same services on his estate as his bigger neighbours, unless he possessed some additional source of income other than land. In the words of Sir Arthur Acland, 'A clear income in cash of £2,000 a year may be preferable from the purely money point of view—to "take your money where you like"—to an estate of a gross £5,000 a year rental with the usual country house and its amenities to keep up, with tithes, mortgages, family burdens, and the demands of the upkeep of the

[1] *The Land*, I, xlvi-xlvii.   [2] Bedford, *A Great Agricultural Estate*, pp. 226-7.

estate.'[1] Indeed, once the agricultural depression had drained
away their reserves the majority of owners of rural estates of less
than 5,000 acres could not afford to live on their estates unless
they had other sources of income.

Landlord influence was defended by contemporaries on two
main grounds. Most Conservative landlords regarded it as an
unavoidable reflection of the fundamental inequalities of society,
and as a humanising influence. The *Standard*, for instance, answered
a Radical attack in these terms:

> The man who has two or three hundred families living on his
> estate, depending on him more or less for their comfort, deriving
> from him benefits not to be repaid in the shape of rent, and not
> measurable by any commercial term, would be worse than careless
> of one very material part of his duty if he did not use the influence
> of his position . . . for the advancement of the cause which he believed
> to be right.
>
> It is monstrous to argue as though this influence were necessarily
> an evil one, or that it is always harshly used. It is as legitimate a
> kind of influence as any other which a man is free to use—as the
> influence of mind over mind, or of the stronger will over the weaker.
> The mere possession of land cannot make the difference between a
> legitimate and an illegitimate influence.[2]

By contrast, many farmers and Whigs, in particular those active
in agricultural societies where landlord and tenant met on equal
terms, believed that the association of landlord and tenant was
a consequence of their common interests, and that it was desirable that the landlord, who knew his tenants' difficulties, and
who alone had the means to enable him to play a major part in
politics, should represent the estate in the great outside world.
Mr Gladstone went even further and maintained that only by
combining their forces could those who lived on an estate make
their voices heard. 'The influence attaching to [great estates]',
he wrote late in life, 'grows in a larger proportion than mere
extent, and establishes a natural leadership, based upon free
assent, which is of especial value at a period when the majority
are, in theory, invested with a supremacy of political power which,

[1] *The Land*, I, xlvii. There is a 'model budget' for a £5,000 a year squire in Bateman's *Great Landowners*, pp. xxiv-xxv, which shows how a nominal income of £5,000
might easily in practice produce £1,132.

[2] *Standard*, 15 September 1868.

nevertheless, through the necessities of our human nature, is always in danger of slipping through their fingers.'[1]

The objection to these, and all other contemporary defences of landlord influence, was that even on the best-managed estates the 'free association' of landlord and tenant was based on coercion. In many cases it was a very indirect form of psychological coercion, in the shape of an inherited feudal attitude towards landlords, but it was coercion none the less. As James Howard pointed out, there was something wrong with a relationship which ensured that the farmers as a class should be so 'pauperised in spirit' that in spite of the ballot there were 'cases in which the dignity of the tenants would be consulted, and themselves saved from unnecessary trouble, if the proprietor simply had a cumulative vote in proportion to the number of the farmers upon his estate.'[2] He might well have quoted the case of Sir Watkin Wynn's Mostyn estate, where the agent did very little canvassing, wrote no election letters, and received no political instructions from Sir Watkin, but the tenants still voted as he expected them to, even though many of them were Liberals and Sir Watkin was a Tory. As the agent put it, 'I have found on both the large estates that I have been engaged upon scarcely any necessity for pressure upon the tenants; both the landlords stood highly in the opinion of their tenants, and as a rule the tenants were always desirous of studying the landlord's wishes and views.'[3]

There was, of course, a certain amount of direct coercion, particularly on small estates. Usually it took the form of homilies like the one sent by Lord Willoughby de Eresby's agent to his Carnarvonshire tenants in 1868:

> I feel it necessary to explain that Lord Willoughby d'Eresby is a Conservative, and gives all his support to Mr. Pennant; therefore he does not consider it right that you should allow yourself to be led by others to vote against the interest of the estate upon which you live and the wishes of his Lordship.[4]

But sometimes agents went further and threatened tenants with penalties. As the Hartington Committee put it, 'The agent frequently holds language which the landlord would shrink from

---

[1] Sir Philip Magnus, *Gladstone: A Biography*, London 1954, p. 433.
[2] James Howard, 'Landowning as a Business: A Reply', *Nineteenth Century*, XI, 556 (1882).
[3] H.C. 352, p. 327 (1868-9). VIII, 327.
[4] 3 *Hansard* CXCVII, 1311.

using, but which the latter does not think it necessary to disown.'[1]

The dangers of coercion were greatest when a landlord changed his politics. Relatively few did so, and it was by no means uncommon for those estates which had been in the same family for many generations to have political loyalties going back for centuries: in Cumberland, for instance, the major estates had been established in the sixteenth century and had been rivals ever since.[2] But changes did occur, and on such occasions it was necessary for a landowner and his agent to use a good deal of firmness if the estate was to be kept united. Usually landlords were considerate, gave their tenants time to think about the change, and encouraged them to abstain from voting if they felt a strain on their conscience at first. Indeed, the fifteenth Earl of Derby was so discreet when he changed sides in 1879 that many of his tenants were still unconverted by 1886 when he changed back again. But even discreet changes could involve an unpleasant amount of coercion. A typical case occurred in 1904 when landlord influence had long ceased to be seriously defended. The Guest family of Wimborne, Dorset, whose head was Lady Wimborne, after being for many years Conservative, reverted in that year to their former Liberalism. Lady Wimborne began to canvass for the Liberals instead of for the Primrose League and instructed the agent for the estate, a Mr Meaby, to make sure that the tenants had actually voted by checking off their names at the polling booth. When this was mentioned in the course of the trial of an election petition in 1910, Mr Justice Lawrance, an old Tory county member, pointed out that while 'it would be a poor thing for this country if those possessing wealth, position, and so forth, should not exercise some influence upon those . . . subject to their influence',[3] it was monstrous to expect tenants to change their politics at the whim of the landlord.

I do not think for a moment that anybody who saw poor Mr. Meaby, who had been 40 years in the employment of the Wimborne

[1] H.C. 115, p. 5 (1870). VI, 135.

[2] 'The Baronies of Burgh and Gilsland, to this day, have great weight in deciding who shall represent Cumberland. One is as notorious a Yellow [Lowther] stronghold as the other is a Blue [Howard] one. Carlisle, situate as it is between Burgh and Gilsland baronies, was the scene of a strife between the Howards and Lowthers for political influence that lasted from the Restoration to 1802.' R. S. Ferguson, *Cumberland and Westmorland M.P.s.*, Carlisle 1871, p. 284.

[3] H.C. 158, p. 2 (1910). LXXIII, 454.

family and who, during that time, I should think, looking at his benevolent countenance, had been a member of the Primrose League, whose duty it had been possibly to take a penny book and to see whether the Primrose Leaguers had given their votes properly, for years, and who was suddenly called upon to turn round like a weather cock from north to south in a moment and say, 'Now you go and do the same for the Liberals as you did for the Conservatives,' —I say, I do not think anybody who saw Mr. Meaby would conceive for a moment that he could intimidate anybody or anything personally; but, as the representative of those who sent him, even Mr. Meaby might be an influence for evil.[1]

The curious thing is that English landlords rarely went a stage further and evicted tenants for political reasons. The ideal of the English landlord, even where there was nothing in the way of tenant right, was a happy estate, and tenants were evicted only in exceptional circumstances and for non-payment of rent. The Duke of Bedford, for instance, discovered in 1897 that there had never been an eviction of any sort on the Thorney estate since the fens had been drained.[2] This was one of the reasons why the ballot made little difference to English elections, whereas it made a great deal of difference in Ireland and Wales. Even that staunch Cumberland Radical, Sir Wilfrid Lawson, who had listened to tales of how tenants were coerced for years before the ballot, and made much of them, admitted in after years that most of the old stories of landlord coercion were so much humbug. The man who said he preferred to vote one way but was compelled to vote the other was simply taking out a sort of insurance policy to enable him to preserve the goodwill of both sides.[3]

Conditions were not nearly so good in the 'Celtic fringe', where political evictions were by no means uncommon. In Scotland the tenant-right movement received a great impetus from the eviction of two well-known farmers, Scott of Timpandean in Roxburghshire and George Hope of Fenton Barns in East Lothian, the best-known scientific farmer in Scotland, solely because of

---

[1] H.C. 158, p. 6 (1910). LXXIII, 288.

[2] Bedford, *A Great Agricultural Estate*, p. 50 n. It should be added that although landlords rarely evicted farm tenants, neither they nor the farmers on their estates felt the same scruples about evicting agricultural labourers. In Norfolk and Suffolk after 1872 the farmers even banded together in an effort to put down the labourers' unions by evicting all the 'trouble makers' they could lay their hands on: cp. George Edwards, *From Crow-Scaring to Westminster: An Autobiography*, London 1922, *passim*.

[3] *Sir Wilfrid Lawson: A Memoir*, ed. G. W. E. Russell, London 1909, pp. 96-7.

their politics.[1] In Wales numerous political evictions in Carmarthenshire and Cardiganshire in 1859, 1865, and 1868, amounting to as many as seventy cases in 1868, touched off the conflict
between landlord and tenant which was one of the outstanding
features of Welsh politics for the next thirty years.[2] In Ireland
evictions had, of course, long been common, and continued to
be a regular feature of the war between nationalists and priests
on the one hand and landlords on the other.

III

The landlord-tenant alliance dominated county politics, but
it was by no means the only factor of importance. About 54 per
cent of England and Wales (and rather more of Scotland) was
in the hands of owners of over 1,000 acres, and almost 80 per
cent was in estates of over 100 acres, so that the amount of land
occupied by smallholders was not great.[3] But there were about
a quarter of a million smallholders as well as the independent
merchants, manufacturers, cottagers and tradesmen of the small
towns and villages. They had little influence in counties such as
Dorset, where seventy-two per cent of the land was in estates of
over 1,000 acres, but in East Anglia and parts of the Midlands
they formed a far from negligible independent or Radical interest.
In these regions there was a long tradition of religious dissent going
back to the seventeenth century, lately reinforced by the rise of
Primitive Methodism and the opening of new pits and factories
in some of the smaller towns.

[1] For Scott's case see H.C. 352, pp. 305f. (1868-9). VIII 305f.: for Hope's see
George Hope of Fenton Barns, by his daughter, Edinburgh 1881.
[2] Cp. David Williams, *A History of Modern Wales*, London 1950, p. 262, and T. E.
Ellis, *Speeches and Addresses*, Wrexham 1912, pp. 253f.
[3] The figures for England and Wales were

	Owners	Acreage	Acreages as % of total acreage
Peers and Squires with over 1,000 acres	4,217	18,545,949	53·7
Landowners with 100 to 1,000 acres	33,997	8,926,899	25·9
Smallholders with 1 to 100 acres	217,049	3,931,806	11·4
Cottages with less than 1 acre	703,289	151,148	·4
Public bodies	14,459	1,443,548	4·2
Waste	—	1,524,624	4·4
	973,011	34,523,974	100

Source: Bateman, *Great Landowners*, 4 edn, p. 515.

Many Liberals hoped in 1868 that the new £12 occupation franchise would shift the balance of power in favour of the independent interest. But their expectations proved illusory, and it is fairly clear that the landlords had at no time any serious cause for alarm. The owners of the larger estates enjoyed quite as much influence over tradesmen living in neighbouring villages, who were more or less dependent upon the farmers living on the estate for their livelihood, as they had over those living within its boundaries. In villages where there was no large estate the influence of parson and large farmer (both Tory) produced very much the same result. A report on Buckinghamshire made to Disraeli in June 1868 suggests that the Conservatives at least were aware of this.

> The new voters are a body subject to influence much the same as the small freeholders. In the Towns they are chiefly Shopkeepers, Butchers and Publicans, and in the Villages Small Farmers, Wheelwrights, Publicans, & Blacksmiths. Whether the preponderating influence is Conservative or Liberal the majority of the New Voters will follow that influence.[1]

But Brand, the Liberal Whip, sent a long letter of lament to his chief after the election which suggests that he for one had no idea of what was to come.

> In the Home and Midland Counties, where there is no considerable Town Element, we have been, generally speaking, routed. The New Voters in the small Country Villages are wholly dependent on the Clergyman and leading farmers: both these classes have been most active against us, and they have coerced the small traders in the villages—i.e. the Blacksmith, the Wheelwright, the Carpenter, the Mason, the Grocer, the Tailor etc. etc.
>
> In Cambridgeshire I found these voters wholly with us in heart, and they promised for the most part to vote accordingly, but when the pressure came at the last, and they were put upon their trial, their courage gave way. The same result has occurred in all the English Agricultural Counties except where special circumstances favoured our men.[2]

The political effectiveness of the independent interest was weakened on the one hand by its dispersion among the small market towns and the traditionally nonconformist districts, and

---

[1] Wm. Powell to Disraeli, 6 June 1868. Disraeli Papers.
[2] Add. MS. 44,194, ff.108-9.

on the other by its lack of leaders and self-confidence. Take the case of the two neighbouring divisions of West Suffolk and Cambridgeshire. In West Suffolk the great majority of the big landowners were Conservatives, who easily prevailed over the Whig minority, headed by the Bunburys and the Duke of Grafton, to carry both seats. Nearly all the important market towns were either solidly Liberal or evenly divided between the two parties, and there was a district of dissenting freeholders round Lakenheath, Mildenhall and Stowmarket, but the independent interest lacked any sort of cohesion and was therefore powerless.

The district round Mildenhall forms part of a great crescent which stretches from Holbeach Marsh and Spalding in Lincolnshire round the seventeenth-century borders of the fens into Suffolk and Norfolk, which was dominated by its dissenting smallholders. In Cambridgeshire the crescent cut the county in two: the uplands south and east of Cambridge, and the Duke of Bedford's estates to the west, were under the thumbs of their landlords, while the fen country, except for Ely and March, was in the hands of the independent interest, whose headquarters were at Wisbech. As a consequence Cambridgeshire returned one Liberal to represent the fens and two Conservatives to represent the uplands from 1857 to 1885. The independent interest might well have obtained a second seat, had it not been for its lack of organisation. Richard Young, who was M.P. from 1865 to 1868, was too much influenced by personal animosity towards the country gentlemen who refused to regard him as an equal to become a successful leader. Henry Brand, who succeeded him as member in 1868, was prevented from assuming the rôle by his election as Speaker in 1872, and the Whig squires were unsympathetic to the aspirations of the dissenters. The Liberalism of the villages therefore remained more or less surreptitious until 1885.[1]

---

[1] Even Whittlesey, a village of some 4,500 people, and a Liberal stronghold in terms of votes cast, was shamefaced about its Liberalism because it lacked an influential head. Thus Henry Brand wrote to Hugh Childers, nephew of a local landowner, asking him to visit the place to give the local Liberals his countenance: 'Your presence at the poll on Tuesday (early) will be of great value, for the upper crust of Whittlesey town is against us, and they rather sit upon the small voters; your presence will counteract their knavish tricks.' Spencer Childers, *Life and Correspondence of the Right Hon. Hugh C. E. Childers 1827-1896*, London 1901, I, 156.

Chapter Two

COUNTY POLITICS

I

BECAUSE estates voted as a unit, county electioneering was a simple business. Once the register had been checked for errors and duplicate entries and a list of non-resident voters had been drawn up, little remained to be done. First, the county agent had to discover how each big estate would vote. This he usually did by visiting tenants on the estate whom he knew personally and who habitually supplied him with information. Thus Disraeli's agent in Buckinghamshire reported to him well in advance of the by-election which was caused by his elevation to the peerage in 1876.

> We shall undoubtedly win our County Election . . . I yesterday made a point of seeing one of the leading tenants on the Ashridge estate, & he told me, nearly to a man, the Brownlow tenantry, & retainers would go for Fremantle [the Conservative], and as your Lordship well knows, that many a time has that division of the County won the election—I also saw a leading tenant on the Mentmore estate [of Baron Meyer de Rothschild], & he told me they are all to do as they like, and that many would not vote at all, as they did not like the Liberal party. Mr. Treadwell, who you know, & who is one of the Tenants on the newly purchased Winchendon Estate of Baron Ferdinand [Rothschild], told me they could do as they liked—& they should probably vote as they had hitherto done —I think the Brill, Ashendon & Wotton division, will be sound as heretofore—The Claydons & part of Buck[ingha]m will be against us—as Sir Harry [Verney] smarts so, at losing his seat for Buck[m].[1]

At this stage it was essential to persuade any landlord who might be friendly, but whose political allegiance was not clear to his tenants, to make his views known. Thus Henry Brand, the Chief Liberal Whip, wrote to Gladstone during the 1861 Flint-shire by-election asking him to give his support to the Whig cause now that he was a member of a Whig cabinet, and no longer a quasi-Conservative.

---

[1] J. K. Fowler to Lord Beaconsfield, 10 September 1876. Disraeli Papers.

Thanks for your letter about Flintshire, and for your announcement that your agent will vote for Lord Richard Grosvenor. Let me
ask you to go a step further, and to tell him to let it be known to
your tenants that your wishes are with Lord Richard.

And as a postscript:

It is important that you should move your Agent to let your
wishes be known.[1]

Such an appeal from London was not usual, however. Most
landowners acted on their own initiative or were prodded by
their friends and relatives to let their wishes be known. Thus in
1868 old Lord Overstone, the Whig banker, informed the prospective Whig candidate for North Northamptonshire that he
could not support him because of his views on the disestablishment of the Irish Church. Whereupon the candidate, the Hon.
Fitzpatrick Vernon, promptly gave up what had become a hopeless canvass, and published Overstone's letter as a sort of justi-
fication.[2] The Duchess of Sutherland (who was Countess of
Cromartie in her own right) made a similar announcement in
1880 lest it be thought that she had embraced her husband's
Whig politics. She wrote to Lord Beaconsfield, 'I am anxious
to tell you that I have, (as I once told you I would) let my
tenantry know that I expect them to give their votes according
to the principles always held by my house.'[3]

After attending to these essential preliminaries the principal
agent in a county division could leave most of the work of preparing for polling day to the local committees in each polling
district. The only tasks to be dealt with centrally were the allocation of cabs and other conveyances and the distribution of
circulars to non-resident voters. These latter had usually to be
sent details of trains and eating places and to be met at the
nearest railway station.

There could be no general canvass because it was still thought
to be an impertinence to canvass a man's tenants without his
permission, and such permission was not readily given. In any

---

[1] H. B. W. Brand to Gladstone, 20 May 1861. Add. MS. 44,393, ff.41-2.

[2] The Wellingborough correspondent of the *Stamford Mercury* then remarked, 'Of
course it will tie up his own tenants; but it will be a bitter draught which the independent freeholders and the newly enfranchised twelve-pounders will not readily
swallow.' *Stamford Mercury*, 2 October 1868.

[3] Duchess of Sutherland to Beaconsfield, 'Thursday' [1880]. Disraeli Papers.

case, a general canvass was unnecessary because the politics of an estate depended on its landlord. When the Liberals of Mid-Cheshire came to canvass the country districts of the division in 1868 they could discover only two estates whose proprietors professed to allow their tenants any freedom of choice. But even in these two cases the freedom was illusory: on one the tenants refused to pledge their votes without the written permission of their landlord, which he not unnaturally refused to give, while the other was owned by the Liberal candidate's father, Lord de Tabley.[1]

Even local party committees had little to do. Most squires and agents rather liked to do such canvassing as seemed necessary, with the help of their relations and the local clergy. Indeed, we are told that in North Norfolk in 1868 'the parson of the parish, naturally enough, thinking the Church was in danger, and the squire, naturally enough, thinking that he was the great man, were acting in each particular parish as a sort of committee'.[2] One not untypical squire treated the election as a great family event, providing breakfasts and dinners, and conveyances to the poll for his tenants at his own expense. And although this was before the ballot, this expenditure was regarded by the election judge as perfectly legitimate and in no sense an inducement to vote for one party rather than another.[3]

II

The general control of each party in a county division was in the hands of a steering committee composed of the largest landowners and most active politicians, assisted by a prominent solicitor such as the clerk of the peace, the county coroner, or the clerk to one of the more active benches of magistrates. In addition, there were subordinate committees in each polling

[1] H.C. 352, p. 251 (1868-9). VIII, 251. Compare this with the experience of one of the candidates for County Galway in 1872: 'I personally canvassed every town, and I rode through the various estates in the county, and there was scarcely an estate in the county where I did not get the same answer; and I found almost universally the answer—"Sir, we like you very much; but we must vote with our landlords, and if our landlords vote for you, we will vote for you." ' *3 Hansard* CCXII, 1785.

[2] H.C. 352, p. 514 (1868-9). VIII, 514. Evidence of Mr Justice Blackburn.

[3] 'I think he thought he was safe enough without the necessity of his giving this entertainment. His intention was to keep up and promote his own influence; I draw the conclusion that the intention of those feasts was to promote the influence of the squire at some future election, at some future time, not to influence the votes to be given at the then pending election. . . .' H.C. 120-4, p. 278 (1868-9). XLVIII, 280.

district composed of local squires, clergymen and large farmers, under the direction of a member of the central committee as chairman, and also assisted by a local solicitor. These district committees enjoyed a great deal of independence in the larger counties, and it is quite in character that four of the eight district committees in South-West Lancashire in 1868 took little notice of the central committee in Liverpool, even though Mr Gladstone was their candidate. Leigh district, we are told, was 'entirely under the management of Mr. Kirkpatrick who for several years has devoted much attention to the subject and who has required very little attention from the centre'. Ormskirk district was 'under the entire control of Mr. Musgrove and Mr. Hill who have declined any assistance whatever and have strongly deprecated any interference'. Warrington district was managed by George Crosfield, a member of a leading local family, who paid all the expenses himself and employed his own solicitor as agent, while at Wigan there were two committees, independent not only of Liverpool but of one another.[1]

Sometimes the central committee in a division was also the executive committee of a formally-constituted party association, but this was by no means always the case. In 1874 there were Conservative associations in only forty-four of the eighty-two English county divisions. There was, moreover, considerable opposition to the promotion of associations. When the Central Committee of the Conservative party tried to reorganise the counties after the defeat of 1880 it encountered much resistance. The Dorset Conservatives, for instance, positively refused to form an association until dragooned into doing so. The county had been shared between the two parties since 1857, the Conservatives taking two seats and the Liberals one, and the Conservative members could not see what good an association would do them, while they could see that it would cost them a lot of money and that it might make contested elections more likely.[2] Earlier a proposal to set up an association in Cambridgeshire had met with a rather different type of hostility. Both the squires and farmers in the county proper and the townsmen of Cambridge opposed the suggestion when it was first mooted by Lord Hardwicke in 1868, because they feared that they would be called upon to pay

---

[1] Add. MS. 44,416, ff.240-1.
[2] Edward Stanhope to Lord Salisbury, 12 May 1881. Salisbury Papers.

for an association over which they would have no control. The inaugural meeting had to be abandoned because so few people attended, and to make a second meeting a success Hardwicke had to give an undertaking that he would not use the proposed association as a means of financing his family's election ventures, and that the town should have a voice in its conduct.

When once associations had been formed, however, their officers made the most of them. Thus when the thoroughly unrepresentative Cambridgeshire Conservative Association met to choose a candidate in 1874, it was told by its agent, Major Barlow:

> They had a Central Conservative Association and District Associations. The Central Association was formed of the chairmen and vice-chairmen of the district associations as delegates to this central association. By these means the feeling of all the electors of the various districts was ascertained, and that feeling was represented by these delegates at a public meeting of the central association, so that they were aware of the general feeling throughout the county as to who should be the representative for the county.[1]

Yet at this very time there was an independent Conservative candidate in the field (Hunter Rodwell) with the support of the farmers round Newmarket, whose candidature was certain to be successful in spite of the Association.

In divisions dominated by one great magnate or group of magnates, the fiction that a party association or committee represented the electors was utterly transparent, and even important squires had to be content to leave the management of their party to its hereditary leaders. Thus in North Devon, where Earl Fortescue and the Earl of Portsmouth were the recognised Whig leaders, Sir Thomas Acland, M.P. (who owned 35,000 acres in Devon and Somerset), regarded it as perfectly natural that they should lead the party. He wrote in 1885, when it was necessary to find candidates for the new divisions of the county:

> It is very difficult *for me* to stir a finger between the Houses of Fortescue and Portsmouth. Redvers Buller, son of my predecessor, ought not to be lost sight of—he stands well with farmers generally. I think he is Vice-Chairman of the Liberal Association, which is little more than 'nominis umbra'. The Whig Peers have always settled these things.[2]

[1] *Cambridge Chronicle*, 26 September 1874.
[2] Acland, *Sir Thomas Dyke Acland*, pp. 345-6. Acland's attitude of self-abnegation is partly to be explained by the fact that his family had hitherto always been Tory.

This subservience preserved the old custom by which the greatest magnates nominated one of the members in counties where they possessed the preponderant influence. In return for this compliance with his wishes, the magnate paid most of the registration and election expenses and gave his support to a second candidate, who was usually chosen from among the local country gentlemen. He also relinquished the nomination when his family lacked suitable candidates, retaining only an indirect veto in the form of his ability to withhold contributions towards the election expenses and to prevent his tenants from voting for any candidate of whom he disapproved. Sixteen English county seats and a variable number of Welsh, Scottish and Irish seats were in the gift of patrons after 1867, and in addition there were a number of other seats over which great magnates had a more precarious hold.[1]

There had been comparatively little redistribution of power in the counties for fifty years so that the seats which magnates controlled were, for the most part, those which Oldfield had listed in 1816.[2] The attitude of the electors in such counties had also remained virtually unchanged, and it was thought to be part of the natural order of things that the Duke of Bedford should return his heir for Bedfordshire, the Duke of Manchester his for Huntingdonshire, the Duke of Northumberland his for North Northumberland, and the Duke of Rutland his for North Leicestershire. In Gloucestershire, where the Conservative Duke of Beaufort's interest had decayed since 1832, an active Liberal wrote of his part in a by-election in 1867: 'I frequently stated that, had the Marquis of Worcester [the Duke's eldest son] been in the field, I should not have voted against him, as I think it desirable that our future hereditary legislators should have an opportunity of learning their duties in the Lower House.'[3] Some of the greatest magnates were willing to go to extraordinary lengths to keep up their traditional prestige, even in counties where their political opponents had gained a permanent majority. The Liberal committee for South Devon thought that there was nothing odd about a request that they should not start a subscription to help with the cost of Lord Amberley's contest in 1868, on the ground

---

[1] For details, see Appendix III.

[2] Where a county had been divided in 1832 or 1868 the patron's influence had, of course, been transferred to one of the new divisions.

[3] *Manchester Guardian*, 11 November 1868.

that 'the Bedford family would not like a public subscription to be made for anyone of their name', although it meant asking the Duke for £4,000.[1]

A few counties were almost entirely in the hands of great magnates. Westmorland, once monopolised by the Earl of Lonsdale, had since 1854 been shared between him and the Marquess of Headfort (heir of William Thompson, M.P., of Underley Hall); Huntingdonshire had since 1837 been shared between the Duke of Manchester and the Fellowes family; Rutland was habitually shared among four families, the Finches, the Heathcotes, the Noels, and their Lowther connections, and two of the three seats for Cambridgeshire were controlled until 1874 by the Earl of Hardwicke and the Duke of Rutland.[2] A sixth county, Cheshire, although not a family preserve in the same sense, was also dominated by a small group of Tory families: the Egertons, the Leghs, and the Tollemaches, all of them more or less distantly related.[3]

The tendency of Welsh, Scottish and Irish county politics was so strongly anti-landlord, even in 1868, that the great landowners found it extremely difficult to maintain their traditional interests. In 1868 about twenty seats were in the hands of patrons, but by 1880 the number was less than ten, and by 1885 only three remained firm in their allegiance, all of them in Ulster. The only Welsh county completely dominated by great magnates was the half-English county of Monmouth, whose representation had been shared since 1841 between the Duke of Beaufort and Lord Tredegar. In Wales proper, only Sir Watkin Williams-Wynn, who kept his seat for Denbighshire until 1885, and also controlled Montgomeryshire until 1880, exercised a similar influence. He was, as readers of Borrow's *Wild Wales* will remember, more of a national institution than a Tory magnate, and his influence even survived his death by a few months. When he died early in

---

[1] Bertrand and Patricia Russell eds, *The Amberley Papers: The Letters and Diaries of Lord and Lady Amberley*, London 1937, II, 160.

[2] The Duke of Rutland's interest had never been absolutely secure, and on the death of Lord George Manners in 1874 it was tacitly abandoned. The Duke talked of putting up his nephew in 1879 but nothing came of the project. The 4th and 5th Earls of Hardwicke were unpopular with the Cambridgeshire country gentlemen, but the family interest survived intact until the death of the Hon. Eliot Yorke in 1878, when the 5th Earl was forced to abandon it for lack of money. He became bankrupt in 1881.

[3] Three Egertons, two Leghs, and a Tollemache were elected in 1868, two Egertons, an Egerton Leigh, a Legh, and a Tollemache in 1874, two Egertons, a Legh and a Tollemache in 1880. A second Tollemache was elected in 1881.

1885 the Denbighshire Liberals let it be known that they would not offer any opposition to the return of the new Sir Watkin, but that they would oppose any other Conservative candidate.[1] The young Sir Watkin was reluctant, but he eventually came forward and sat for the county until the dissolution, when he was defeated in the new Eastern Division of Denbighshire and the 182-year tenure of the Wynns was ended. The other Welsh interests were very shadowy compared with this: C. R. M. Talbot, who represented Glamorganshire from 1830 to 1890, had an unrivalled personal influence in the county and could doubtless have chosen a successor if he had wished to retire; the Duke of Westminster, Lord Mostyn, and Lord Hanmer controlled Flintshire between them; Earl Cawdor virtually controlled one seat for Carmarthenshire, and Lord Ormathwaite could usually carry Radnorshire.

In Scotland long-drawn-out contests between rival families continued to be a prominent feature of county politics, but family monopolies were few and growing fewer. The Duke of Buccleuch had lost his preponderance in the border counties by 1868, Bute-shire had ceased to acknowledge the rule of the Marquess of Bute and was saved for the Conservatives only by the Duke of Hamilton's control of Arran, and after 1873 the Dundases gradually lost their influence in Orkney and Shetland. As a result, only two 'pocket counties' survived intact to 1885. The Duke of Argyll continued to dominate the county of Argyll in spite of the growth of a formidable Conservative opposition headed by Malcolm of Poltalloch, and the Duke of Sutherland remained master of Sutherland. The latter was, indeed, an almost impregnable interest, since the Duke owned 1,176,343 of the county's 1,299,253 acres (and with them £68,602 of the estimated gross rental of £71,494), and there were only 325 electors.

Ireland shook off its patrons equally decisively. Many of them had with difficulty restored their interests during the fifties after the irruptions which O'Connell had made in them, and they were powerless to resist the Home Rule movement. Twelve or thirteen seats were more or less securely held by great landowning families in 1868, but only five of them were in the same hands by 1880. Patronage was not destroyed, however, for the Ulster reaction against Home Rule in 1885 had the effect of guaranteeing

[1] Rowland Winn to Lord Salisbury, 11 May 1885. Salisbury Papers.

a number of seats (notably Mid Antrim, West Down, and North Tyrone) to their old patrons.

III

The English counties were the chief strongholds of the Conservative party, which regularly won in them more than twice as many seats as its opponents, and actually won five times as many in 1874.[1] However, the individual county constituencies were not so overwhelmingly Conservative as the election results as a whole seem to suggest. Small majorities were by no means unusual, and in Kent and Essex, where there was a large urban element in the county divisions, very small majorities were the rule: thus in 1880 the Conservative majorities in the three Essex divisions were 192, 402, and 625 in a total electorate (for the three) of 241,000. The Liberals were not so much weak as on the defensive, and, because they acted defensively, not as ardent in the fight as their opponents.

It is difficult to overstress the contribution of Whig landowners to the Liberal cause in the counties even as late as the eighties. There were few agricultural counties in which they could not sometimes win one seat and occasionally two, while in the industrial counties they provided candidates and leaders. The typical Whig was not a small country squire but a county magnate enjoying considerable influence. The three largest estates in Bedfordshire were Whig, the Whig Lords Fitzhardinge and Ducie were two of the three largest landowners in Gloucestershire, and five of the estates over 5,000 acres in Durham (total 92,569 acres) were Whig.

On the other hand, although it was often said that all small resident squires were Tories,[2] this was not quite true. Apart from

---

[1] The figures for the English counties (excluding Monmouthshire) were:

	Whigs and Radicals	Conservatives
1868	46	124
1874	27	143
1880	54	116

The Conservative majority had been increased by some twenty-five members in 1867 when thirteen of the existing county divisions were subdivided. In 1865 the Whigs and Radicals had gained 51 and the Conservatives 94 seats.

[2] 'I think the valuable service of small *resident owners*, say squires of 2,000 per annum (all Tories) is apt to be underrated.' Sir Thomas Dyke Acland, quoted in A. H. D. Acland, *Sir Thomas Dyke Acland*, p. 353.

well-known Whigs like Kingscote of Kingscote (3,900 acres), there was a small number of lesser men, as witness the case of Cambridgeshire (Table I).

Table I. Estates in Cambridgeshire, *1868*

Acreage	Liberals	Conservatives	Neutral	Total	Liberal Acreage	Total Acreage
Over 10,000	1	1		2	18,800	37,778
5,000–10,000	1	3		4	7,402	25,864
3,000–5,000	1	4		5	3,157	16,532
2,000–3,000	3	13		16	6,851	37,406
1,000–2,000	8	30	1	39	10,956	50,368
	14	51	1	66	47,166	167,948[1]

Because there were relatively few Whig landowners, and many of them owned big estates, their individual attitudes mattered far more to the Liberal party than those of individual Conservative magnates mattered to the Conservative party. The Conservatives managed quite well without the active support of the Duke of Northumberland in 1868,[2] but the indifference of the Whig Duke of Sutherland almost certainly cost the Liberals a seat in Staffordshire and another in Shropshire.[3] The Duke had already shown that he did not think it worth his while to preserve a troublesome and expensive interest merely to please his friends, for in 1865 he had refused to allow his brother to stand for Shropshire. In 1868 he reiterated his refusal and also refused to contribute to the election expenses of another Shropshire Liberal, thereby depriving the local Liberals of their hereditary leader and of their main source of revenue. He had all the political influence he wanted in Sutherlandshire, for which he could always return one member of his family.

This indifference to their political responsibilities was by no means uncommon among Whig magnates with a distaste for

---

[1] The total acreage for the county was 524,481.

[2] The Duke wrote to Lord Hylton, 4 November 1868 (Hylton Papers): 'I don't feel interested in the elections. If the present government obtain a majority, it will be only an incentive to the Whigs to plunge further into revolution, and between Lord Derby and Disraeli they have let the mob in upon us, and will of course give way whenever they find themselves hard pressed. I would rather see the Whigs in power, and trust to their quarrelling with the Radicals than to the resolution of the present government.'

[3] For the Duke of Sutherland's attitude see Lord Ronald Gower, *My Reminiscences*, new edn, London 1895, pp. 142ff.

Gladstonian Liberalism, and a number of them even encouraged their tenants to vote against Liberal candidates in 1868 and 1874 in order to teach the Liberal party a lesson. Thus the Earl of Yarborough, whose 57,000 acres in Lincolnshire were the main-stay of the Liberal cause in the northern half of the county, refused to move a finger to help the first Gladstone government. When the Whig member for North Lincolnshire (Sir Montague Cholmeley) died in January 1874 he was succeeded by a Con-servative without a contest, and the Liberal *Stamford Mercury* commented:

> Formerly the house of Brocklesby, owing to its political consistency and advocacy of civil and religious liberty, commanded the allegi-ance of a large majority in the division, and one seat at least was safe for the Liberals. The present head of the house, though he inherits the amiable disposition of his forefathers, is less given to public life, and the consequence seems to be that other Whig families have followed his example. Thus the Liberal party is left without an influential head, and much to the mortification of the thinking and independent men in the constituency they are fated to see their political opponents win an easy victory.[1]

Fortunately for his party, Lord Yarborough died in 1875, and during the minority of the new Earl (who came of age in 1880) the estate fell into the hands of strong opponents of the Beacons-field government. The Yarborough interest was accordingly re-vived, and Brocklesby again became the Liberal headquarters in the division. And during the 1880 election, which led to the recovery of the seat lost in 1874, a Liberal meeting at Caistor opened on this significant note:

> THE CHAIRMAN, in the course of his speech, said he had been a Liberal ever since he took an interest in politics, and he had always supported and backed up the Yarborough interest, which had been Liberal for four generations past. He had heard very gratifying accounts of the canvass on behalf of Mr. Laycock, and the present Lord Yarborough himself had assured him that if he had the power to vote he should have supported the Liberal candidate.[2]

Lord Yarborough's neutrality in 1874 and his son's activity in 1880 was typical of a very general change in attitude among the

[1] *Stamford Mercury*, 30 January 1874.
[2] *Stamford Mercury*, 16 April 1880. Lord Yarborough later became a Conservative and held office as Captain of the Gentlemen-at-Arms, 1890-2.

Whig magnates during the life of the Disraeli government. The change was all the more marked by the release of a number of important Whig magnates from parliamentary and official duties for work in the counties.[1] One consequence was a revitalising of the Liberal cause in Northamptonshire, where Lord Spencer became chairman of quarter sessions as well as Lord-Lieutenant, and the return of Lord Spencer's brother 'Bobby' Spencer (afterwards the sixth earl) as member for North Northamptonshire from 1880. In Northamptonshire Lord Spencer was assisted by one of the greatest of Whig magnates, Lord Fitzwilliam, who had recovered his zeal for the Liberal cause in the course of the campaign against Disraeli's foreign policy, and had thrown himself into election work in the West Riding, where he was Lord-Lieutenant, and in Huntingdonshire, as well as in North-amptonshire. But the price of the support of the Fitzwilliam interest was bluntly put before the incoming ministry in a letter to Lord Granville written immediately after the general election.

I have had unusual opportunities of testing the pulse of the voters generally in Yorkshire, Northamptonshire and Huntingdonshire, both rural and urban and I unhesitatingly declare, that, speaking generally, there is no radical feeling in the nation. I believe it is mainly thro my instrumentality that six liberal members have found seats in this parliament. My own political opinions are well known, and I have every reason to believe, that it was confidence in the moderation of my views, which brought about this success—you will therefore understand that I must take a deep interest in the formation of a cabinet which I and mine will have largely contributed to place in power.[2] If the cabinet about to be formed is composed of men who command the respect of the nation, and the approbation of the moderate portion of the liberal party then we have good ground for hoping for wise legislation and an enduring success. . . .You will doubtless have great pressure put upon you to introduce into the government men holding extreme opinions; if that pressure is yielded to, it will speedily bring about the dismemberment of the liberal party.[3]

[1] There had been no fewer than six English Lord-Lieutenants in the first Gladstone ministry, as well as Lord Lansdowne, a great landowner in many counties: Lords Ailesbury (Wiltshire), Carlingford (Essex), Cork (Somerset), Ripon (North Riding), Spencer (Northamptonshire) and Sydney (Kent).

[2] Lord Fitzwilliam had a brother and two sons in the 1880 House of Commons.

[3] Fitzwilliam to Granville, 18 April 1880. P.R.O. 30/22A.

The prophecy was fulfilled: by 1885 Lord Fitzwilliam and Lord Yarborough had had enough, and in 1886 their support was given to the Liberal Unionists or the Conservatives.

IV

The Radicals were potentially much stronger in the counties than the Whigs, because they had the support of the dissenters, and because they had an untapped source of power in the agricultural labourers. But because there was no class in England comparable with the Radical farmers of Scotland, they had no chance of winning any substantial number of seats before 1885. Radicalism came, therefore, to be regarded as an essentially urban product, and suffered from being too closely identified in the rural mind with urban land reformers more interested in dealing a blow at political enemies and spreading the orthodox doctrine of freedom of contract than in the problems of the agricultural community. Mill and Bright, for instance, outraged agricultural opinion in 1866 by attacking the government's proposal to compensate farmers for cattle compulsorily slaughtered during the rinderpest epidemic, and made it plain that they objected in principle to any restriction on the importation of diseased beasts.[1]

Because the Radicals lacked any substantial body of allies among the farmers they were free to take advantage of the strike of the agricultural labourers in 1873-4. Joseph Arch became a Radical hero and was taken up by the National Liberal Federation. The 'ignorant' farmer who put down the labourers became for many Radicals almost worse than the tyrannical landlord of Radical legend, while the wiser Radical leaders used the opportunity to drive a wedge between orthodox Conservatives who disapproved of the farmers' actions and the Tory farmers.[2] Even in 1874 influential Conservative opinion was seriously alarmed, and the *Cambridge Chronicle* hastened to urge Conservatives not

---

[1] *3 Hansard*, CLXXXI, 472-92.
[2] Sir George Trevelyan in bringing forward his usual Bill to extend the County franchise in 1875 pointed out the need which the labourers had of representatives of their own and pointed to two by-elections in the previous year, in one of which (Cambridgeshire) the farmers had insisted on having an anti-labourer candidate and not an orthodox Conservative, and in the other (West Suffolk) where they had forced a Conservative candidate rumoured to be sympathetic to the labourers to withdraw. G. O. Trevelyan, *Speeches on the County Franchise*, Manchester 1877, p. 28.

to allow themselves to become identified with the farmer's campaign against the labourers.

> We echo the sentiment that has been expressed that it would be a dire misfortune if the Conservative Party were identified with the victory of the tenant-farmers in the late unfortunate conflict in this part of England. Our Radical opponents have only been too ready to make capital out of their falsely-assumed position of 'the labourers' friends'. They have represented the labourer as the down-trodden serf; they have villified [sic] and heaped abuse upon the farmer—especially 'the Tory farmer'—and they have helped to pull the strings to set the agitation in motion. The Conservatives are the farmers' and the labourers' true friends, and it would indeed be a pity if it went forth to the world that the Conservatives were returning to Parliament a member who had fought the battle of the farmers against those labourers whose condition their most distinguished leaders are desirous to improve. What has been denounced, and properly so, has been the interested but foolish, if not wicked, action of Mr. Arch and his brother delegates, stirring up strife and discord throughout the country, setting class against class, and raising bitter feelings where before there was contentment and peace. It is against these professional firebrands that just anger has been felt and expressed.[1]

The Radicals at last discovered some allies among the farmers in 1879 when James Howard of Bedford, a manufacturer of agricultural implements, founded the Farmers' Alliance. Its principal objective was a change in the land laws that would allow more flexibility in times of depression and more protection for the tenant farmer, and it attracted the support of many farmers alarmed by the bad times. At the general election of 1880 Howard himself was returned for Bedfordshire and the other leading member of the Farmers' Alliance, Thomas Duckham, for Herefordshire, thanks to the exertions of the farmers. And many farmers in other counties also voted Liberal.[2] But although Howard became a popular figure in the House of Commons, the Alliance never again did so well as in 1880, and made a poor showing

---

[1] *Cambridge Chronicle*, 3 October 1874. It is worth noting that Henry Burgess, vicar of Whittlesey, a violent Tory in ordinary politics, supported the Labourers' Union (*The Times*, 15 April 1874), and that the Cambridgeshire gentry were by no means all sympathetic with the farmers' attitude towards their labourers.

[2] The *Mark Lane Express* claimed that the Farmers' Alliance had won the Liberals sixty seats, but this is obvious nonsense. However, there was a marked swing to the Liberals in Durham as well as in Bedfordshire and Huntingdonshire, and also in parts of many other counties.

at by-elections after 1881. Neither Howard nor Duckham found safe seats in 1885, and by 1886 they had disappeared from the House.

The position of the Farmers' Alliance was in any case an anomalous one. To win elections it had to secure the support of both Whigs and erstwhile Tory tenant farmers—in short, to be moderate—and Howard's address in 1880 was a studiously reasonable document appealing to them.

> I would strenuously oppose any rude attempts to break up the ancestral estates of the kingdom; at the same time I advocate a modification of the law of entail, with a view to prevent the settlement of land upon unborn persons. I desire to see every landowner in the possession of freedom—freedom from those obligations and burdens imposed upon him by his ancestors, which so often prevent him from doing his duty by the land. I advocate the institution of a simple and efficient registration to facilitate the transfer of land from seller to buyer; the abolition of the law of distress; the giving to tenants a concurrent and indefeasible right to ground game; the repeal of the malt tax; the reform of local taxation, and a fair apportionment of local rates between landlord and tenant.[1]

But such moderation, although it attracted the support of Mr Gladstone, who made a bid for the farmers' vote at Midlothian and followed it up by abolishing the malt tax in 1880 and amending the game laws in 1881, tended to defeat its own ends by repelling the urban Radicals. In 1879 and 1880, before the election, this did not matter, because both the Birmingham Radicals and the Irish Land League were pleased to find allies among the farmers at such a time.[2] But by 1881 both of them were beginning to have doubts. Chamberlain was not himself much interested in agricultural questions, but his *alter ego*, Jesse Collings, was the leading parliamentary spokesman of the agricultural labourers. And Collings had got little support for his own policies from the Farmers' Alliance. As his biographer puts it, 'Mr. Collings had not found the farmers, as a class, eager to espouse proposals which he regarded as in the best interests of their workers, although he has always gladly admitted that there have been and are many most worthy exceptions to this general

---

[1] *Agricultural Gazette*, 12 April 1880.

[2] The support of the Land Leaguers caused the Farmers' Alliance a good deal of embarrassment, particularly as F. H. O'Donnell claimed that he and not Howard was its founder. Cp. F. H. O'Donnell, *A History of the Irish Parliamentary Party*, London 1910, I, 347-64, and *Agricultural Gazette*, 19 April 1880.

statement'. Collings was at first friendly towards the Farmers' Alliance, but he soon cooled towards it when he found it reluctant to take up his own reforms. The farmer, he pointed out in September 1881, 'cannot yet see that his natural ally is the people, and not the landlord.... In the reforms advocated by the Farmers' Alliance no notice is taken of the agricultural labourers.'[1] As a consequence, he dissociated himself from the Alliance, and let it be understood that it must be regarded as unsatisfactory by any Radical reformer.

By the following year it was clear that the farmers as well as the Birmingham Radicals had made their choice. As Sir Thomas Dyke Acland told Gladstone, 'Their politics may be summed up in three words, keep down Rates, Rent, and Labour'. As a consequence the *Radical Programme* devoted a chapter to the agricultural labourer, but left the farmers to fight their own battles.

V

The roots of the Conservative strength in the counties lay in the kinship of outlook and interests between landlord, farmer, and villager at the level of half-formed ideas and instinctive reactions. It was an alliance of the hunting-field and the cattle-market rather than of the political meeting, or even the agricultural society. And the Conservatives came, therefore, to be more than a party of squires and parsons. They were as near as possible to being the party of the 'agricultural interest', the party of those who cultivated the land.

After 1866 the agricultural interest had a permanent mouthpiece, the Central Chamber of Agriculture. This was basically a federation of the more active farmers' clubs, agricultural societies, and Chambers of Agriculture, so organised that its committees could 'take charge of measures in the Houses of Parliament, and before the Government, calculated to benefit agriculture' and 'oppose or modify any movement detrimental to that important interest'.[2] Liberals usually occupied the chair in alternate years,

---

[1] Jesse Collings and J. L. Green, *Life of the Right Hon. Jesse Collings*, London 1920, pp. 126-7.

[2] A. H. H. Matthews, *Fifty Years of Agricultural Politics*, London 1915, p. 394. The Central Chamber itself met infrequently and delegated its work to a council and a number of committees, of which the most important were the standing committees on cattle diseases and local taxation. The Local Taxation Committee was a remarkably well-organised pressure group in its own right, whose secretary, Major P. G. Craigie, became first Director of Statistics at the Board of Agriculture in 1889.

but their function was mainly ornamental and, in James Howard's words, the Chamber was not only 'strongly political, but its Tory bias has become proverbial'.[1]

In spite of the existence of the Central Chamber of Agriculture, there was nothing like an agriculturalists' cabinet, and in the country at large the defence of the agricultural interest was left to individual Conservative M.P.s who took up particular questions. Thus Albert Pell spoke for the Poor Law Guardians, and Clare Sewell Read for the farmers, while Sir Walter Barttelot pleaded for the repeal of the malt tax, Sir Henry Selwin-Ibbetson for the legislative repression of rural intemperance, and Sir Massey Lopes for the readjustment of local taxation.[2] It did not matter that some of the issues raised were little more than shibboleths. The malt tax, for instance, was one of the targets of rural Conservatism for nearly half a century, and the agriculturalists were aggravated rather than relieved when the interfering Gladstone repealed it in 1880.[3] Farmers had enjoyed looking back nostalgically to a dim romantic past when malt-houses stood on every farm, crops were better, and the agricultural labourer was not encouraged to injure his health by drinking brewers' beer. In East Anglia the reformers even kept a tame agricultural labourer on view, who attributed his health and vigour to brewing his own beer, and was made much of by Select Committees and other curious persons.

The two most important agricultural issues in the years before 1879, when the depression edged everything else into the background, and rents were reduced on a vast scale, were the prevention of cattle diseases, and the evolution of a system of county government which would be in some sense representative of the ratepayers and yet would not have to impose new financial burdens in the shape of rates. Both questions concerned all sections of the agricultural interest, and on both the principal spokesmen were Conservatives.

The rinderpest epidemic of 1865-7 was the first major agricultural catastrophe, apart from bad harvests, since the repeal

---

[1] *Agricultural Gazette*, 19 April 1880.

[2] It should perhaps be added that these spokesmen were not always popular, even with their own party, and that Pell and Read were often at loggerheads with their constituents. There is a life of Pell, *The Reminiscences of Albert Pell, sometime M.P. for South Leicestershire*, ed. Thomas Mackay, London 1908.

[3] The malt tax attracted a Select Committee in 1868 whose proceedings make entertaining reading: H.C. 420 (1867-8). IX, 235.

of the Corn Laws. In 1865-6 alone there were 27,815 cases in
various parts of the country caused by the importation of infected
foreign cattle—a vast number by twentieth-century standards,
when less than 100 cases would be regarded as a major calamity.[1]
This epidemic was followed in the years 1881-3 by an epidemic
of foot-and-mouth disease of which 18,732 cases were reported
in 1883 alone. The first epidemic forced the government to
legislate, the second to strengthen the new legislation.

It was by no means easy to devise a remedy for the situation
when one was first called for in 1865. In the days before refrigera-
tion it was necessary to import large numbers of live cattle, and
until the establishment of the Foreign Cattle Market at Dept-
ford in 1872 it was very difficult to prevent their dispersion
throughout the country. Farmers were not yet educated in the
belief that compulsory slaughter of diseased animals was justified, and were ignorant of the ways in which infection was
spread; butchers and importers objected to any interference with
their business; free-traders were not convinced that there need
be any restriction of imports, and regarded any tampering with
freedom of importation as a threat to the people's food supplies
and an insidious plot to raise food prices. However, at the end
of 1866, the newly-formed Central Chamber of Agriculture decided on a programme: the limitation of imports to specially
licensed ports with quarantine and slaughterhouse facilities, at
which all fat stock should be slaughtered and all store stock
should be quarantined; the slaughtering with compensation of all
infected beasts; and a tightening up of the regulations governing the transit of animals. But no mention was made of penalties
for the exposure of infected beasts where they might pass on the
disease to others.

By the time these proposals were formulated the government had
accepted in principle both the restriction of imports and restrictions
on the movement of even healthy cattle, at the behest of the Royal
Agricultural Society backed by the agricultural members.[2] These
latter had come back to Westminster when Parliament reassembled in 1866, furious at the ineptitude of a government which
had done little or nothing to stem the epidemic. Led by George

---

[1] cp. Matthews, *Fifty Years of Agricultural Politics*, p. 10.

[2] cp. J. A. Scott Watson, *The History of the Royal Agricultural Society of England
1839-1939*, London [1939], pp. 109-12.

Ward Hunt, who at Northamptonshire Quarter Sessions had taken the lead in trying to restrict the movement of cattle in the county only to find his efforts thwarted by Northampton Borough, which had continued to import diseased animals, they fell on Sir George Grey, the Home Secretary, and badgered him until he agreed to bring in a bill. When Grey brought it in he roused the ire of the agriculturalists still further by going out of his way to conciliate the doctrinaire free-traders.[1] But Ward Hunt was not to be put off: he introduced an alternative bill of his own giving the government greater powers and making adequate provision for compensation for compulsory slaughter, and insisted that his bill and the government's should go forward together. When his own bill was defeated, he virtually took charge of the government bill in committee, carried vital amendments to it, and so humiliated the government that *The Times* contemplated its resignation. It is hardly surprising that in the new Derby-Disraeli government formed later in the year he became Financial Secretary to the Treasury and that in 1868 he succeeded Disraeli as Chancellor of the Exchequer.

The Contagious Diseases (Animals) Act of 1866 gave the agriculturalists just the stick they needed with which to beat a government, since it invested the Privy Council with considerable discretionary powers. Thereafter, each government, Liberal or Conservative, was subjected to a running attack from Tory agriculturalists on the use it made of these powers, and in 1876 Clare Sewell Read even resigned his post as secretary of the Local Government Board under Disraeli in protest against the slackness of the Privy Council Office in applying the Act and its amendments.[2]

In 1883, the foot-and-mouth epidemic called for new legislation, and the agriculturalists on both sides banded together behind Henry Chaplin, who had taken upon himself Ward Hunt's rôle, to carry a motion against the government demanding that a bill should be brought in. The Privy Council staff was by this time more favourable towards the agriculturalists' point of view, and in 1884 the government brought forward a bill which

---

[1] *3 Hansard* CLXXXI, 355-83. The Webbs (*English Local Government: The Story of the King's Highway*, London 1913, pp. 221-2) noted a similar case in which the House of Commons took over from the government the regulation of Turnpike Trusts, whose abolition was eventually forced on the government by the House.

[2] Matthews, *Fifty Years of Agricultural Politics*, pp. 20-2.

proposed to give it additional powers to deal with cattle diseases. But in the eyes of agriculturalists the new bill was inadequate and the House of Lords, where it was first introduced, ignoring government protests, added a number of clauses designed to increase its efficacy. The government tried to defeat the Lords' amendments in the Commons, but failed in spite of its large nominal majority, and the measure which finally emerged incorporated nearly all the agriculturalists' proposals.

The other great question which agitated the agricultural interest was that of local taxation. The Poor Rate had long been so high that agricultural property bore much more than its fair share of the burden of direct taxation. And during the fifties and sixties there was a steady increase in the volume of complaint, as new burdens were imposed on the rates at the behest of parliament. The problem was most acute in counties which had adopted the Highways Act of 1862, but it was also serious (by nineteenth-century standards) in any county where the central government had insisted that the magistrates build new prisons, lunatic asylums, or militia barracks. Two possible reforms were advocated: one called for a reform of county government, and the other for Treasury grants to local authorities.

The demand for a reform of county government was never effective, because the scheme which the Tory reformers adopted, and which the Central Chamber of Agriculture approved, was not a very convincing one. It was proposed to set up County Financial Boards composed of equal numbers of magistrates and Poor Law Guardians (i.e. farmers) to take over the duties of the County Finance Committees as rating authorities. In this way it was hoped both to conciliate the farmers, who were restive about the magistrates' monopoly of effective power in the counties, and to establish a body sufficiently strong to be able to resist the demands of the central government for increased expenditure. But although the scheme secured the support of the farmers in many counties,[1] it had not made much headway before it was overshadowed by the success of the campaign to

---

[1] The *Colchester Mercury* remarked of a meeting of the East Suffolk Chamber of Agriculture in 1868: 'In that, as in this county, the management of the county finances by the magistrates is not looked upon with any degree of suspicion, but it is thought that the ratepayers would have greater powers of resistance to extravagant schemes which Government inspectors and departments required should be carried out.' *Colchester Mercury*, 6 June 1868.

secure relief for the ratepayers both by extending the area of assessment for rates and by means of grants from the Consolidated Fund.

This latter campaign had been opened in 1868, after a good deal of skirmishing, with a circular from the Central Chamber of Agriculture urging its members to take up the question with candidates at the general election. In the following year a Local Taxation Committee was appointed by the Central Chamber to assist friendly M.P.s, and by 1870 the reformers were ready to do battle with the government. In that year the government introduced a bill extending the incidence of rating, but had to withdraw it because of the opposition it encountered, and the lack of parliamentary time. Goschen, as President of the Poor Law Board, also made the tactical mistake of entering into a discussion of the incidence of taxation in town and country, basing his remarks on a statistical analysis by Robert Giffen which purported to show that the agriculturalists had no real grievance. This enabled the Central Chamber of Agriculture to publish a reasoned statement of their case by Dudley Baxter, the Conservative statistician, who demonstrated that the burdens on realty were double those on personalty.[1] Quarter Sessions, meeting shortly afterwards, were urged by agriculturalists to protest against the government's refusal to meet their case, and there was a general hardening of agricultural opinion against it. During the session of 1871 ministers managed to evade the agriculturalists' attack, but in 1872 Sir Massey Lopes carried against them (by 259 votes to 159) the following resolution, which became the agriculturalists' battle-cry until the general election.

> That it is expedient to remedy the injustice of imposing taxation for National objects on one description of property only, and therefore that no legislation with reference to Local Taxation will be satisfactory which does not provide, either in whole or in part, for the relief of occupiers and owners in counties and boroughs from charges imposed on ratepayers for the administration of justice, police, and lunatics, the expenditure for such purposes being almost entirely independent of local control.[2]

One of Disraeli's first acts on taking office in 1874 was to receive a deputation from the Central Chamber of Agriculture

[1] R. Dudley Baxter, *Local Government and Taxation, and Mr. Goschen's Report*, London 1874. This work was originally published as a series of letters.
[2] Matthews, *Fifty Years of Agricultural Politics*, p. 89.

and to express his agreement with their views on local taxation. Sir Massey Lopes took office as Civil Lord of the Admiralty (he was succeeded as Chairman of the Local Taxation Committee by Albert Pell, another Conservative agriculturalist), and had the satisfaction of seeing all his proposals put into force. Sir Stafford Northcote's first budget relieved ratepayers of the cost of prisons altogether,[1] and provided increased grants for police and pauper lunatics, a saving to the ratepayers of £2,000,000 a year, and during the next three years much was done to tidy up local finance. The Central Chamber of Agriculture dropped the subject for the moment, and it was not raised again until 1882. The Tories had shown themselves to be the friends of agriculture, and the agriculturalists were grateful, although (as Mr Gladstone did not fail to point out at Midlothian),[2] other parts of the government's legislative programme showed it rather as the friend of the landlords than as the friend of the farmers.

[1] The prisons were transferred to the Prison Commissioners acting for the Home Office in 1876.
[2] *Political Speeches in Scotland, March and April 1880*, Edinburgh 1880; Eighth Midlothian Speech.

Chapter Three

THE SMALL TOWNS

I

THE old world of quiet medieval market towns like Calne, Eye, and Bridgnorth, or Coleraine and Armagh, although deprived of much of its representation by 1867, continued until 1885 to return more than half the borough members and more than one-fifth of the House of Commons.[1] By 1867 there was a good deal of doubt among politicians as to the wisdom of retaining the very smallest, and the schedules of the Reform Act were not drawn up without a great deal of careful consideration, but in the end they were allowed to remain because they gave the landed interest an opportunity to secure additional representation. None the less, many Conservatives were convinced that Disraeli had made a mistake, because the small boroughs returned more Liberals than Conservatives.[2]

The little boroughs varied a great deal in character. Some were respectable places like Kendal or Christchurch (which included Bournemouth) and possessed a 'middle class' of merchants, manufacturers, bankers, solicitors to county families, nonconformist ministers, estate agents, and retired army and navy officers who acted as their political leaders. There were venal boroughs like Truro among them, but all of them had a certain tone, and usually a fair degree of independence. But the remainder, except for the few cathedral cities, lacked local leaders,

[1] For the purposes of this chapter I class as 'small towns the 113 boroughs with a population of less than 16,000 in 1871, and eight others—Aylesbury, Cricklade, Retford, Shoreham, Stroud and Wenlock (agricultural boroughs with a small town as their centre), the joint borough of Penryn and Falmouth, and the growing town of Windsor. Sixteen thousand is chosen as the dividing line because it avoids classing as small towns places like Bedford, Hereford, and Winchester, which had a well-developed way of life of their own and a well-defined local 'upper class' to control their politics.

[2] The small English boroughs were divided as follows:

	1868		1874		1880	
	Lib.	Cons.	Lib.	Cons.	Lib.	Cons.
Under 10,000	25	29	20	34	27	27
10,000–20,000	43	21	37	23	46	14

more important than an occasional small manufacturer, and the shopkeepers, medical practitioners, and country attorneys, whose clients were sometimes country gentlemen but more often local farmers and tradesmen. As a consequence, few of them possessed any political organisation worthy of the name, and even those few relied on rich candidates or the neighbouring gentry to pay the incidental expenses.[1] They were therefore almost completely dependent for leadership on outsiders, whether local landowners or rich men anxious for a seat in parliament.

The happiest of the small boroughs were those on the borders of a great estate, or within its boundaries, and totally dependent on it. They enjoyed neither political excitement nor political responsibility, but they were usually spared the demoralisation which resulted from corrupt electioneering. Disraeli rather over-coloured the picture of such a borough in the draft of a novel that was never completed, but the essential truth is there:

> Now this noble lord was so fortunate as to have an interest in a borough which his opponents always denounced as a nomination borough, though in truth he had no property whatever in it and could not command a single vote. But he and his wife, being wise and good people, were very civil and courteous to the inhabitants of this borough, which reached almost to their park gates; gave them every year a ball or two, went to theirs, asked them to shooting-parties, subscribed to their charities, presided over their meetings, religious and horticultural, supplied all the wants of the great house from the borough instead of from co-operative stores—and so the lord and lady were what is called 'adored', and the borough always asked leave to return their sons or nephews to Parliament.[2]

This account may be compared with that given by a hostile observer of Stamford in 1868.

> For years past it has been a Pocket Borough belonging to the Marquis of Exeter, who lives close to the Town, and owns a great portion of it. There are no manufactures in the place except a small Firm who make Agricultural Implements, and the Tradespeople depend upon the surrounding Gentry for their custom, so there is

---

[1] In 1874, there were no Conservative associations, even of the variety which never met and had no members, in the seven Cornish boroughs, in eight of the nine Wiltshire boroughs, or in five of the six Dorset boroughs: *Conservative Agents and Associations in the Counties and Boroughs of England and Wales*, London 1874, *passim*.

[2] W. F. Monypenny and G. E. Buckle, *The Life of Benjamin Disraeli, Earl of Beaconsfield*, London 1910-24, V, 535-6.

no independence in the place. . . . Everything in the shape of Liberal organization has completely died out. We had an interview with Mr. Paradise, the Editor of the 'Stamford Mercury' and he assured us, 'that so far as he knew, he was the only liberal of any influence in the Town, and he didn't think there was sufficient energy to form an organization.' This we found to be quite correct, for though a great number felt the degradation of being represented by a nominee, not a single man could we find, who would assist us in starting an organisation to free themselves.[1]

Not all borough patrons were simply landowners. Manufacturers had long sat for small boroughs where their mills or factories were the main source of income and employment. Tiverton, for instance, returned John Heathcoat from 1832 to 1859, with Lord Palmerston as his colleague after 1835, for the obvious reason that in his machine-woven-lace mills he employed 1,200 hands by 1836 and about 2,000 by 1860.[2] Indeed, once its initial coolness had been overcome, the borough was bound irrevocably to him and his family, and in 1868 his grandson and heir, Sir John Heathcoat-Amory, resumed the family representation of the borough which he held unbroken to 1885, when the borough at last lost both its members. In much the same way Cricklade, a vast agricultural borough, whose natural centre, after the opening of the Great Western Railway, was Swindon, came to be represented from 1865 to 1885 by the head of the G.W.R., Sir Daniel Gooch, a Conservative. As his colleague he sometimes had a fellow Conservative, Ambrose Lethbridge Goddard, a Swindon landowner whose family had sat for the county or for Cricklade since the early eighteenth century, and sometimes a Liberal opponent. Gooch made no secret of his claims on the borough and held his seat simply because no one wished to oust so powerful a friend of Swindon. In 1868 he wrote to Disraeli:

Personally I have no wish to be in Parliament. My work as Chairman of this Company is as much as I ought to have on my hands but I feel the Railway Company should have as one of the Members for Cricklade one who will give his attention to their Interest. The 1200 votes of our own men, chiefly liberals—would always

[1] Reform League Report: Stamford. This is the first of many valuable reports in the George Howell Collection at the Bishopsgate Institute cited in this book. For their history see p. 335 below. For Stamford see also J. M. Lee, 'Stamford and the Cecils 1700-1885', Oxford B.Litt. thesis, 1955.
[2] Wm. Felkin, *A History of the Machine-Wrought Hosiery and Lace Manufactures*, Cambridge 1867, p. 263.

command one seat in the liberal Interest, and I believe the Liberals would be content to have only one seat if I was the Conservative to hold the other, in the Railway Interest. . . .[1]

In the eighteenth century it had been customary to recognise a distinction between various types of influence, and in particular between predominant influences and proprietorship in boroughs. 'We must . . . caution our readers', wrote Oldfield in the *History of the Boroughs* of 1792, 'not to confound the influence which prevails in counties, and popular cities and towns, with that which dictates in limited corporations and burgage tenures, which are all private property, and what are termed rotten boroughs, with only ten or twelve houses in each. The influence of the first description is only derived from extensive property, eminent personal qualities, or from good neighbourhood and hospitality. The latter is of the authoritative kind, and is maintained by corruption, persecution, and tyranny, and is carried to market as a saleable commodity, with as little secrecy and caution as an estate is carried to the hammer at a public auction.'[2] This distinction survived into the post-Reform period as a distinction between 'family boroughs' (like Petersfield, where the Jolliffe interest was weak, or Hertford, where Lord Salisbury's interest was strong),[3] where the maintenance of a family interest depended entirely on the personal qualities of the family candidate and of the standing of the family at the time of the election; and proprietary or 'close' boroughs, where the patron could return whomsoever he wished. Thus, when George Glyn, the Liberal Chief Whip, told Gladstone in 1870 that apart from Wilton, which was doubtful, he knew of only three 'close boroughs' on the Liberal side (Calne, Richmond, and Malton), he was not taking any account of the 'family boroughs' on the Liberal side, of which

[1] Sir D. Gooch to Disraeli, 23 October 1868, Disraeli Papers. Also quoted in P. M. Williams, 'Public Opinion and the Railway Rates Question in 1886', *English Historical Review*, LXVII, p. 53, n.7 (1952).

[2] [T. H. B. Oldfield], *An Entire and Complete History, Political and Personal, of the Boroughs of Great Britain*, London 1792, II, 213.

[3] At Petersfield the Jolliffe family's influence had been precarious since the 1820s; in the eighties there were further complications when the Liberal member, William Nicholson, a London distiller who had bought Basing Park in the locality and represented the borough from 1866 to 1874 and from 1880 to 1885, turned Conservative, and fought both the Jolliffes (also Conservative) and a Liberal. For this see Sir Charles Petrie, *The Carlton Club*, London 1955, pp. 121-3. For the Jolliffe family history see Lord Hylton, *The Jolliffes of Staffordshire*, priv. printed, London 1892. For Hertford see A. J. Balfour, *Chapters of Autobiography*, London 1930, pp. 86-7.

there were at least twenty-three.[1] This distinction was supported by stories (usually apocryphal) of landlord tyranny in proprietary boroughs of a type which would have been highly injudicious in a family borough. Lord Sandwich, for instance, was reported to have prevented the Liberals of Huntingdon from building up an effective opposition by striking at them when they began to gain ground at municipal elections in 1866 or 1867. Every tenant who had voted Liberal was turned out, or threatened with eviction, and every such voter who was employed by Conservatives in the town was dismissed, whereupon the Liberal opposition collapsed. Those who had voted for the Liberals were then taken back into favour, and the borough again gave such an appearance of near-unanimity that the Reform League's agents reported bitterly: 'The representation belongs as much to the Earl of Sandwich, as if the seat was given to Hinchingbrooke House instead of Huntingdon, if he sent a negro we couldn't prevent his return.'[2]

The truth is, however, that this distinction had long been an unreal one and that by 1872 it had become quite outdated. Indeed, the press virtually admitted as much by using the terms 'family borough', 'close borough', and 'nomination borough' as if they were indistinguishable.[3] Except in entirely rural boroughs like Midhurst or Woodstock (the population of the 'town' of Midhurst was only 1,615, that of Woodstock only 1,133) the hold of proprietors had so loosened that if the electors could find themselves a rich leader they could easily break away. And

[1] Glyn to Gladstone, 6 December 1870. Add. MS. 44,348, f.63.

[2] Whitehaven (population 19,000) was thought to be in much the same position. It was contested only four times between its enfranchisement in 1832 and 1885 but on each occasion Lord Lonsdale's nominee was elected, although Glyn wrote in 1868 of having hopes of 'beating Lord Lonsdale at Whitehaven' (Add. MS. 44,347, f.168). The town was governed by twenty-one trustees, of whom six and the chairman were nominated by 'the Castle', which also possessed, thanks to the number of houses and other property owned by the Lonsdales, a safe enough majority in the electorate. There is a Reform League report on the borough as well as a number of newspaper articles. See also J. E. Williams, 'Paternalism in Local Government in the Nineteenth Century', *Public Administration*, XXXIII, 440-3 (1955).

[3] The *St James's Gazette*, 6 September 1881, published an article on 'Family Boroughs', but mentioned only what were usually referred to as 'close boroughs': Eye and Woodstock on the Conservative side, Calne, High Wycombe, Marlborough, Richmond and Ripon on the Liberal. A careful anonymous writer in the *Fortnightly Review* in 1885 (n.s. XXXVII, 53) wrote about the Whig control over Ripon, Calne, Tavistock, and Bodmin as if it were like that in the old-fashioned close boroughs, but avoided committing himself to any precise label, apparently because he felt that the time for precise labels, whether 'close borough', 'family borough' or 'nomination borough', had gone by.

after the ballot no patron could count on the unswerving loyalty of a borough unless his reputation for 'good neighbourhood and hospitality' was really a good one.

But although the day of close boroughs and absolute proprietorship in boroughs passed away with the coming of the ballot, few nomination boroughs took advantage of their opportunities. Stamford was captured by a persistent carpet-bagger in 1880, but the case was exceptional, and most patrons easily held their own. Indeed, in 1874 Arthur Balfour replaced Baron Dimsdale at Hertford, and Sir Henry Holland succeeded Lord Egmont at Midhurst without even a contest. Popular sitting members were, if anything, more sure of their seats, as a result of the ballot, since they were no longer made to pay for the sins of the patron. At Bodmin the Hon. Frederick Leveson-Gower, Lord Robartes's Whig nominee since 1859, even enjoyed the support of many of the leading Conservatives when all suggestion of coercion had been abandoned.[1]

Because proprietary influence had become so amorphous it is not always easy to decide whether a patron any longer controlled a borough. However, by following a few simple rules it is possible to draw up a list of nomination boroughs. Where a patron normally succeeded in maintaining a traditional interest by returning the candidates of his choice, he may be regarded as the patron of the borough, and the borough may be classified as a nomination borough. Where, however, there was a regular opposition which sometimes succeeded in defeating the potential patron, as at Petersfield or Leominster, there can be no question of patronage, and the borough must simply be looked upon as one in which the character of electioneering was shaped by the existence of a powerful interest controlled by one family. Such boroughs were not in any real sense nomination boroughs and must therefore be excluded. A list prepared on this basis, but also including six larger boroughs where patrons also played a large part in elections, yields the following results (doubtful attributions included in the totals are noted in brackets):

[1] Bodmin was a typical example of the boroughs which responded to 'good neighbourhood and hospitality'. Leveson-Gower wrote of it: 'Through the intervention of Mr. Hayter, the Whip, Mr. Robartes, the member for the Eastern Division of Cornwall, offered to get me returned for Bodmin. He had considerable property in that borough, and was besides much esteemed there, which enabled him to secure at least one of the two seats for any one he recommended.' E. F. Leveson-Gower, *Bygone Years*, London 1905, p. 243.

Nomination Boroughs 1868[1]

England	39	(4)
Wales	1	(1)
Scotland	1	(1)
Ireland	5	(1)
Total	46	(7)

It is interesting to compare these figures with those for England and Wales in the forties given by Professor Gash in *Politics in the Age of Peel.*[2]

Nomination and Family Boroughs 1847 (England and Wales only).

	Boroughs	Members
Nomination Boroughs	42	59
Doubtful Nomination Boroughs	10	14
Family Boroughs	11	11
	63	84

The reduction in the number of boroughs would appear much less marked if Professor Gash's second and third categories were discounted to make allowance for boroughs where patronage was almost but not quite at an end, and probably amounts in reality to not more than about ten boroughs, of which four were disfranchised in 1867.[3] But the decline in the number of seats was much greater, amounting to over forty. Of these, eighteen were abolished by the Reform Act,[4] and the rest were either freed by the extension of the franchise or more gradually as a result of the course of local politics.

It is difficult to trace in any detail the decline in borough patronage between the forties and the seventies except in a few obvious cases, because there are scarcely any local histories dealing with the subject. The obvious causes of change were the 1867 Reform Act which so extended the electorate at Cheltenham, Christchurch, Kidderminster, King's Lynn, Morpeth, and

[1] For a list of these boroughs see Appendix III. Patrons never controlled more than one seat in a two-member borough after 1867. Hence the number of members returned by patrons was the same as the number of boroughs.

[2] Norman Gash, *Politics in the Age of Peel*, London 1953, pp. 438-9, and 193-201.

[3] Arundel, Ashburton, Reigate and Thetford.

[4] Chippenham, Dorchester, Hertford, Huntingdon, Lichfield, Ludlow, Malton, Marlborough, Marlow, Richmond, Ripon, Stamford and Tavistock lost a member each, and the four boroughs totally disfranchised lost five members in all.

Westbury that the erstwhile patron's tenants or supporters were swamped, and the bankruptcies or near-bankruptcies which destroyed the Duke of Buckingham's power at Aylesbury and Buckingham and the Duke of Newcastle's at Newark.[1] But it is impossible to follow the gradual decline of patronage in such places as Derby, where the Duke of Devonshire seems to have decided at the end of the forties to make no effort to keep up his interest. Thus in 1846 he wrote to his nominee, Frederick Leveson-Gower: 'I am so very happy that you are pleased [to become member], and your letter has gratified me very much. It is quite true that you are the only person to whom I should consent to prolong that sort of interest with Derby.'[2]

II

Nomination boroughs were not completely without excitement: there was sometimes a change of patron and sometimes a change in the patron's politics. The oddest change of patron occurred at Malmesbury. Before 1832 the Corporation returned the members at the direction of Joseph Pitt, a Conservative, but the 1832 Reform Act extended the borough boundaries to include so many of the Whig Earl of Suffolk's tenantry, that they swamped the town voters, and gave him the patronage. The 1867 Reform Act swung the balance of power back to the town and to the still unreformed Corporation.[3] The Corporation possessed no paving, lighting or other local government powers, and was basically a friendly society for the administration of justice and the corporation estates. It was presided over by a High Steward and Deputy High Steward, whose principal duties were to hold feasts, to attend the borough petty sessional court to 'assist' the often illiterate magistrates, and to assist the Corporation in the choice

[1] The Rothschild family soon acquired so much property in Aylesbury that they nominated one member after 1865 in place of the Duke.

[2] Leveson-Gower, *Bygone Years*, p. 237.

[3] Hence this account, which is derived from the *Report of the Commissioners appointed to Inquire into Municipal Corporations not Subject to the Municipal Corporations Acts* [C. 2490] and [C. 2490-1] H.C. (1880). XXXI, 1. The *New Domesday* records that the Corporation owned 650 acres of land worth £1,652 a year, but it in fact owned nearly 800 acres worth considerably more, from which it derived its influence. This land was divided among 316 persons: 280 commoners were entitled to something over an acre each or 8s. a year in lieu of the land; 24 assistant burgesses, who were the oldest commoners, were entitled to 24 acres each; and they in turn elected 12 capital burgesses, who were entitled to 141 acres each.

of its parliamentary candidates, who were always Conservatives. The High Steward from 1856 was Colonel C. W. Miles, a member of the notable Bristol family, who for some years shared his influence with the Reverend Charles Pitt, his Deputy, and the heir to the old Pitt interest. This latter interest was purchased or rented about 1866 by Walter Powell, a young Welshman who went to Malmesbury in the first place for the hunting, and who became Conservative candidate in 1868, after he had succeeded in registering all 150 members of the Corporation with even the slightest claim to a vote under the new Act. He lived at Eastcourt House, the Pitt family seat, and with the help of Miles acted as *de facto* head of the Corporation until he was carried out to sea by a balloon and presumed drowned in December 1881, when Miles succeeded him as M.P.

A curiously old-fashioned change of patron occurred at Launceston, where the Werrington Park estate of some 4,000 acres dominated the borough.[1] For many years it was owned by the Duke of Northumberland, who returned the members both before and after 1832. The Duke sold the property in the early sixties, and in 1865 A. H. Campbell, who had bought it, had himself returned for the borough. Campbell died in 1867, and in 1871-2 the Werrington estate was sold to J. H. Deakin, a Lancashire merchant and Colonel of Volunteers, who wanted it for one of his six sons, who was about to come of age. One of the recommendations of the estate is said to have been that it assured the holder of a 'large voice' in elections, and Colonel Deakin, like the two previous owners, continued to employ the same agent as the Duke of Northumberland had done, both for estate and election purposes. In 1874 Deakin decided to offer himself as a candidate in the Conservative interest, and although he told his tenants they might vote as they pleased, he doubtless counted on their 175 votes, a considerable proportion of the nominal electorate of 795, and was returned quite easily. However, he was ultimately unseated on petition on the novel ground that shortly before the election he had allowed his tenants to kill rabbits on the estate, where previously they had been closely preserved, as a result of pressure at election meetings, and that this was a corrupt inducement to vote for him. The case created

[1] For Launceston generally see H.C. 250 (1874). LIII, 421f., from which the following account is largely derived.

something of a stir, but did nothing to alter the balance of power in the constituency. Colonel Deakin returned his eldest son in his stead, and when the son retired three years later at the instance of the Whips, he was able to return the Solicitor-General, Sir Hardinge Giffard, in his place. Giffard, on becoming Lord Chancellor, was able to bring in Sir Richard Webster (the newly-appointed Attorney-General) as the borough's last member in 1885.

A change of patron which also involved a change in the politics of the constituency occurred at Bridgnorth, since the Restoration a family borough of the Whitmores.[1] From 1832 to 1852 the borough was represented by T. C. Whitmore and from 1852 to 1870 by his brother Henry, who was a Lord of the Treasury in 1858-9 and 1866-8. But the family hold on the borough was weakening by the sixties, and after his brother's death early in 1865 Henry Whitmore's seat was precarious. In July 1865 he retained it only after petitioning against the return of Acton the historian, and in 1868 his majority was fifty-one. By then his nephew had sold the Apley estate[2] and abandoned the family interest in the borough, and in 1870 Henry Whitmore retired from parliament, giving as his reason to Disraeli the disappointment he felt at not having been made Chief Whip in 1868.[3] Whether this was or was not Henry Whitmore's real reason for leaving Parliament—Bridgnorth's reputation for purity in late years had been somewhat tarnished—its effect was to transfer the patronage of the borough to the new owner of the Apley estate, William Orme Foster, a Stourbridge ironmaster who had been Liberal member for South Staffordshire for many years but was defeated there in 1868.[4] Foster returned his son, William Henry Foster, at the 1870 by-election, and even in the black days of 1874 the latter had a record majority. More remarkable, in the course of the 1874 parliament W. H. Foster turned Tory, and was still easily able to hold the seat in 1880.

Droitwich changed in rather the same way as Bridgnorth. Before 1832 the borough had been controlled by the Whig Lord

[1] Sir Lewis Namier, *The Structure of Politics at the Accession of George III*, 2 edn, London 1957, pp. 242f.

[2] *Burke's Landed Gentry*, 5 edn, 1871, II, 1505.

[3] Henry Whitmore to Disraeli, 7 December 1869. Disraeli Papers.

[4] The Fosters were by no means strangers to the borough as James Foster, W. O. Foster's uncle, had managed to capture one of the seats for the duration of the short Reform parliament of 1831-2.

Foley, whose predecessors had ousted the nearest landowner, Sir John Pakington, as early as 1690.[1] The 1832 Reform Act redressed the balance and the Pakington family seat, Westwood Park, was securely placed within the borough boundaries. In 1835 the Whigs were defeated, and in 1837 a Pakington was again returned for the borough, and held the seat without a contest until 1868. This was the Sir John Pakington, afterwards Lord Hampton, who sat in Lord Derby's cabinets and was often compared with Sir Roger de Coverley, and who, through his mother, was the direct heir of that Sir John Pakington who had been ousted in 1690. By 1868, however, great changes had taken place in the borough, and the Pakington interest had been greatly weakened. The district had gained a new prosperity through the rapid expansion of the salt works which John Corbett had purchased in 1852, and the salt-workers had become an important part of the population. In 1868, most of them became eligible for the vote, and the number of electors grew from 400 to 1,500. Corbett, who had in the meanwhile acquired great wealth and considerable celebrity, put up rather half-heartedly against Pakington as Liberal candidate, but the salt-workers were not pressed to support him and he failed.[2] By 1874, however, Corbett was in earnest. The general swing to the Conservatives had no counterpart in Droitwich, and Sir John Pakington was badly beaten, and so lost both his chance of a place in the cabinet, and his control of the borough.[3]

III

Seats in the gift of a patron were usually occupied by members of his family, if only for the obvious reason that they were too scarce to be spared for outsiders. When there was no obvious family candidate it was natural to offer the seat to the party Whips, although some patrons preferred to keep the patronage

[1] T. H. B. Oldfield, *The Representative History of Great Britain and Ireland*, London 1816, V, 258.
[2] For Corbett see *D.N.B.*, 2 Suppl. He was persuaded to stand in 1868, much against his will, by pressure from party headquarters: Add. MS. 44,347, f.168.
[3] The voting was:

	1868		*1874*
Pakington	790	Corbett	787
Corbett	603	Pakington	401
Majority	187	Majority	386

entirely to themselves. Lord Exeter would brook no outside interference at Stamford in 1868, and Lord Wenlock in the same year
was extremely indignant with Glyn, the Liberal Whip, because
he believed that there was a plan afoot to bring in an outsider
to contest the second seat in what he considered (rather oddly)
his borough of Wenlock.[1] Similarly, in 1856 Lord Derby declined
to use his influence with Lord Egmont at Midhurst on the ground
that Lord Egmont was 'rather touchy on such matters'.[2] However, the seventh Earl of Egmont, who was member for the
borough, offered the seat to Hart Dyke, the Conservative Chief
Whip, in 1874, even before his uncle the sixth Earl was dead.
By Dyke it was offered to Ward Hunt, the First Lord of the
Admiralty, in accordance with Disraeli's wishes, in order that he
might offer it to Admiral Hornby.[3] The latter eventually refused
it, and it was then given to Sir Henry Holland, afterwards Lord
Knutsford, then a civil servant in the Colonial Office.

A nominee member naturally experienced considerable embarrassment when there was a change in the political views of his
patron. Lord Alfred Hervey, a Liberal, felt bound to give up his
seat at Bury St. Edmunds in 1868, because of the confusion of
family politics—'The change . . . in my family politics since my
poor Brother's death, and the strong language publicly used by
my Brother Arthur and my nephew Augustus (M.P. for West
Suffolk) in opposition to the Liberal party and policy, made my
position at Bury so disagreeable, that I was compelled to abandon my intention of standing for it again.'[4]

The politics of Lord Ailesbury's family were equally confused.
The third Marquess (a Palmerstonian and a Whig) sat uninter-
ruptedly for the borough of Marlborough from 1832 until he succeeded to the title in 1878, and was succeeded in the borough by
his brother Lord Charles Bruce, also a Liberal. However, in 1880,
during the first contest since 1857, Lord Charles was opposed
unsuccessfully by Lord Ailesbury's son Lord Henry, an ardent
Conservative. At Marlborough the quarrel was at least kept
within the family. At Shaftesbury, which was generally considered

---

[1] Lord Wenlock apparently thought that one seat was in his gift and the other in
Lord Forester's, although there seems to be little other evidence to show that this was
so. Add. MS. 44,347, f.190.

[2] Derby to Sir Wm. Jolliffe, 17 January 1856. Hylton Papers.

[3] Gorst to Disraeli, 7 May 1874. Disraeli Papers.

[4] Lord Alfred Hervey to Gladstone, 27 December 1868. Add. MS. 44,417, f.263.

a close borough of the Marquess of Westminster, it was not. The sitting member in 1868, George Glyn, complained in the course of the general election: 'I wish the people in these parts had a little more spirit—politics are dead here, if I had time I should almost like a contest to stir them up . . .'.[1] And on the death of the second Marquess in 1869 his wish for opposition was realised. The Wiltshire estates went, not to the Whig third Marquess (and first Duke) of Westminster, but to the Dowager Marchioness, a Tory. As a result, when Glyn became Lord Wolverton in 1873, he was succeeded by a Conservative. But the new Lord Wolverton was not a man to be trifled with in electoral matters, and, after leasing a nearby estate, he set about building up an opposition. The Marchioness protested vehemently and tried to get Disraeli, then Lord Beaconsfield, to take action against him, on the somewhat tendentious ground that as a peer Lord Wolverton should not interfere in elections for the House of Commons,[2] but to no avail: in 1880 Lord Wolverton's brother was returned by a majority of thirty-four.

IV

Apart from incidents such as these, nomination boroughs enjoyed a peaceful enough existence, for which they were to be envied. The other small boroughs, too small to stand on their own, became a prey to conflicting interests, and in the end, as often as not, sought consolation in the beer and money-bags of the contending parties. Where there was a patron small majorities mattered little—at Droitwich there was a majority of one in 1835, yet the borough was not contested again until 1868—but where there was no patron it was only too easy to buy a majority or to create an interest which must be placated. The result was a series of fierce localised conflicts, reflecting the shifting of influence in the town and with only an indirect bearing on national politics. Poole actually achieved the distinction of being won from the Liberals by the Conservatives in 1868, of being regained by the Liberals in the Conservative reaction of 1874, and of being won again by the Conservatives in 1880, all for local reasons.

[1] Add. MS. 44,347. f.184.
[2] Lady Westminster to Lord Beaconsfield, 29 March 1880. Disraeli Papers. Disraeli was not very sympathetic and commented after the election, 'Alington ought to have kept Dorchester right, and Lady W. Shaftesbury.' Buckle, *Disraeli*, VI, 521.

The simplest of situations in these masterless boroughs was a battle between rival landowners. The classical struggle was that at Wareham between the families of Erle Drax of Charborough and Calcraft of Rempstone, which lasted for almost fifty years.[1] Before 1832 the Calcraft family had achieved supremacy in the borough by purchasing the property of its rivals, the Pitts and the Draxes, a transaction which earned Oldfield's hearty disapproval. 'The inhabitants', he wrote, 'like so many Russian peasants, have quietly submitted to the transfer, being incapable of breaking the fetters with which a long *prescription* has shackled them!'[2] The extension of the borough boundaries in 1832 restored the Drax interest to much of its former importance, and the heads of the two houses of Drax and Calcraft both offered themselves for the borough. For the first three elections the Calcraft interest (Liberal) prevailed, but in 1841 the Draxes (Conservative) carried the day and remained firmly in the saddle until, in 1857, John Hales Calcraft was again returned, by three votes. He sat until 1859, when he was again defeated, but in 1865 he was able to return his eldest son, another John Hales, who also won the seat in 1868, but died shortly after the declaration of the poll. His brother succeeded to the family interest, but was beaten at the ensuing by-election and never stood again. Mr John Samuel Wanley Sawbridge-Erle-Drax sat on until 1880 when, in his eightieth year and after thirty-three years in the House, he was beaten by an 'outsider', Montague Guest.[3]

Grantham was another town of this sort, but the contest there was complicated by there being two seats. The principal interests in the neighbourhood were those of Earl Brownlow (Conservative), who lived just outside the borough at Belton House, and the Earl of Dysart (Whig), who lived ten miles outside the town at Buckminster Park. The two families of Cust and Tollemache

[1] Gash, *Politics in the Age of Peel*, pp. 71-2.

[2] Oldfield, *Representative History*, III, 420.

[3] Sir William Fraser has the following curious account of Erle Drax. 'One of the Curiosities of the House, very rarely seen, was Erle Drax, for many years Member for a Dorsetshire Borough. He appeared about one evening in the Session: in some Sessions not at all. His appearance was that of a villainous Don Quixote; or Lismahago. At a General Election, on the day previous to the nomination, he put out the following address to his Constituents: "Electors of Wareham! I understand that some evil-disposed person has been circulating a report that I wish my tenants, and other persons dependent upon me, to vote according to their conscience. This is a dastardly lie; calculated to injure me. I have no wish of the sort. I wish, and I intend, that these persons shall vote for me." ' *Disraeli and His Day*, London 1891, p. 263.

(formerly Manners) frequently provided candidates from their own ranks, but the Whig family of Cholmeley of Easton Hall, and the Tory families of Welby of Denton Manor and Thorold of Syston had a traditional interest in the representation, dating back, in the latter case, to the Restoration. It was conventional to regard one seat as in the gift of Lord Dysart, but in fact it was only secure when the second seat was relinquished to the Custs, and neither side was content with one seat except during the period 1857-65. The result was a long-drawn-out struggle whose character was established as early as 1826. Indeed, when Sir Montague Cholmeley put forward his son in 1868, along with Lord Dysart's brother, who had been his colleague from 1826 to 1831, he felt that the battle was exactly the same one he had fought when he first stood for the borough in 1826.[1] A characteristic speech (which was rounded off by the expression of a wish that the young ladies of Grantham would stop working altar-cloths for High-Church clergymen and turn to making flannel petticoats for the poor) set the tone:

> My friends of Grantham, you well know that I have always had a friendly feeling towards you. In this town, some two-and-forty years ago, I made my first essay—a triumphant essay—into political life as your representative . . . I and my friend Mr. Tollemache beat the Custs then, and I hope and believe Mr. Tollemache and my son will beat the Custs now. (Cheers). It depends entirely upon yourselves. . . It is for you to decide whether this borough is again to fall into the apathy which it did, when, for a long series of years, it was arranged before hand who were to be your representatives, and when really the voice of the public had no say in the matter. If you allow the two Liberal candidates, or even one of them to be beaten you will return into the old net, but if you exert yourselves you may depend upon it you will not be beaten.[2]

After this it seems something of an anti-climax to find that the two Liberals were returned unopposed, despite the fact that the Conservatives had won both seats in 1865, and that it was not until 1874 that a Cust came forward—and then successfully.

Buckingham was a third borough of the same type. The Liberals

[1] Frederick James Tollemache, 5th son of William, Lord Huntingtower, sat for Grantham 1826-31, 1837-52, 1857-65, 1868-74. Sir Montague Cholmeley sat for Grantham 1826-31, and for North Lincolnshire 1846-52, 1857-74.

[2] *Stamford Mercury*, 30 October 1868. The *Mercury*, 2 October 1868, had already made the same point about the Custs: 'This is another attempt to make Grantham a nomination borough.'

were represented by Sir Harry Verney, who sat for the borough
from 1832 to 1841, from 1857 to 1874, and from 1880 to 1885,[1]
and the Conservatives, first by the nominees of the Duke of
Buckingham and after 1859 by John Gellibrand Hubbard, later
Lord Addington, a Russia merchant and governor of the Bank
of England, who sat for the borough from 1859 to 1868. Verney
lived at Claydon House and Hubbard at Addington Manor, both
outside the borough but conveniently near to it. In 1868 Verney
and Hubbard, hitherto colleagues, were forced to fight for the
one seat preserved by the Reform Act, which Verney won. In
1874 Verney was ousted by Hubbard's eldest son, Egerton
Hubbard, but in 1880 he regained the seat. This was not the end
of the struggle, for the new Buckingham Division formed in 1885
rather increased than diminished the influence of the two families.
Sir Harry Verney's son won it in 1885, lost it in 1886 to Egerton
Hubbard, and regained it in 1889 (when Egerton Hubbard
succeeded to the peerage), in contest with Evelyn Hubbard, the
late member's brother. In 1891 Verney was expelled from the
house,[2] but Evelyn Hubbard again failed to gain the seat, which
in 1906 was restored to the Verney family, who held it from 1906
to 1918.

At Westbury the struggle was between local millowners on
each side, with county families playing an important part.[3]
Prosperous enough today, Westbury was hard hit in the early
nineteenth century by the decline in the West-Country wool
trade, and had become a scene of desolation. The population
declined by 11·3 per cent between 1831 and 1861, grass grew
in the market place, houses were everywhere unlet, their windows
broken and their roofs falling in, while the hand-loom weavers
went on trying to earn a miserable pittance: those familiar with
Shepton Mallet today will know something of the atmosphere.
The opening of two large mills brought renewed life to the town,
and provided almost the only work in the place. The larger

[1] He was M.P. for Bedford 1847-52.

[2] After the conviction of an accomplice he pleaded guilty at the Central Criminal
Court to conspiring to procure a young girl aged 20 for immoral purposes, and was
sentenced to 12 months' imprisonment: *The Times*, 7 May 1891. He was expelled
12 May 1891.

[3] For the 1868 and 1880 contests the sources are the decisions of the judges at the
trial of election petitions: H.C. 120, p. 191 (1868-69). XLVIII, 191, and H.C. 337-
Sess. 2, p. 87 (1880). LVII, 155; the MS. reports of the trials in the Record Office
of the House of Lords; and a Reform League report.

mill, owned by a Liberal, employed about 200 voters out of an electorate of only 1,000 in 1868, and the smaller, owned by a Conservative, somewhat fewer. Between the two millowners there existed a keen and intensely personal hatred, fanned by political rivalry. Abraham Laverton, the Liberal, had parliamentary ambitions, and in 1868 resolved to try his luck as Liberal candidate, since Sir Massey Lopes, whose family had controlled the borough since 1812, had moved to a county seat and the extension of the franchise had virtually destroyed his interest. The Conservative candidate was John Lewis Phipps of Leighton House, a local landowner of some importance, whose family aspired to the patronage of the borough, and monopolised the Conservative representation between 1868 and 1885. Since the borough included a great deal of agricultural land the county influence was important, but everything else paled before the bitterness of the fight between Laverton and his rival, Harrop. The latter cast all discretion to the winds once he knew that Laverton was in the field; Phipps was brought to interview his workmen and the handful of avowed Liberals, most of them outworkers, were given the option of voting for Phipps or losing their jobs. They were frankly told 'No man can serve two masters'. Those who demurred were dismissed, and eventually found themselves employment with Laverton. The inevitable petition unseated Phipps, who had won by 492 votes to 465, but his brother, Charles Paul Phipps, who lived within the borough at Chalcot, retained the seat for the Conservatives at the by-election. Laverton had his revenge in 1874, when he won by 540 to 518, but he lost the seat to another Phipps, the late member's eldest son, in 1880.

In other boroughs there was a straight fight between land and industry, usually accompanied by a good deal of corruption. At Frome a large mill was pitted against all the local landowners except the Earl of Cork, the Lord-Lieutenant. At Maldon E. H. Bentall was returned in 1868 because he employed so many of the electors in his agricultural implement works at Heybridge within the borough, and the election was enlivened by the threat of his opponent, who was supported by the neighbouring gentry, to start a rival works.[1] At Stroud a similar struggle took place between a number of Conservative landowners and local residents, headed by J. E. Dorington of Lypiatt Park, and the Liberal

[1] *Law Times*, 12 September 1868.

woollen manufacturers of Stroud and their ally S. S. Dickinson, son-in-law of a former member, and father of the first Lord Dickinson. But it was inextricably confused by the development of corruption on a large scale under the guidance of local solicitors, and by a family squabble. The Stanton family, the leading Stroud woollen manufacturers, became divided politically. Walter John Stanton was elected one of the Liberal members in February 1874 but was unseated on petition along with his colleague. In May 1874 he was succeeded as member by his nephew Alfred, who was returned as a Liberal with Dorington as his (Conservative) colleague. However Dorington's election was voided in its turn, and at the second by-election H. R. Brand, the Liberal candidate, was opposed by Alfred Stanton's Conservative brother James. This sudden turn of events led the two Liberal Stantons to placard the borough with a very curious proclamation,[1] and their influence was brought to bear against James Stanton. Brand won by a small majority, but, like his predecessor, he was unseated on petition. Another Liberal woollen manufacturer, S. S. Marling of Stanley Park, who had formerly been a county member, was then called in to contest the seat and not only won it but held it until the general election of 1880. Then Alfred Stanton gave up his seat to his uncle Walter, and Marling relinquished his to Brand, and these two continued to represent the borough until it was extinguished in 1885.

V

Where there were no major interests such as these to give an underlying stability to local politics, the local party leaders were

[1] *To the Electors of the Borough of Stroud.*
Gentlemen,
    We have been much surprised and grieved to find that a member of our family, Mr. James Stanton, has been persuaded by the Conservative party to come forward as a candidate in opposition to Mr. Brand.
    Much as we feel the painful position in which we are placed by this unfortunate occurrence, we are bound to state that we cordially support Mr. Brand, and earnestly appeal to you to use your best endeavours to secure his return to Parliament, and thereby advance the interests of the Liberal cause, with which our name has been so long associated in this borough. . . .
Your obedient servants,
Alfred J. Stanton.
Walter J. Stanton.
Stroud, July, 17th 1874.
[The original is in the Painswick House Collection, Election Addresses Series E, vol. V, f.20a., Gloucester Public Library.]

driven either to make a compact with their opponents to share the representation, or to allow their borough to become the prey to faction. And since the age of compacts was over, because no borough with a population of less than 10,000 had a second member after 1868, faction was in the ascendant.[1] As the *Law Times*'s election expert pointed out:

> In small towns and small constituencies *party* spirit runs high. The fight at the election is nominally between the candidates, but really between the local magnates, the desire of Mr. X. in High-Street being more that *he* shall beat Mr. Y. in East-Street, than for the Constitutional or the Radical cause in the abstract. Thus almost every man in a small town ranges himself on one side or the other habitually: but there is a residuum of indifferent men, or venal men, who care nothing for either party, who stand apart, and who turn the scale when parties are pretty evenly balanced.[2]

There were two quite distinct types of venal small boroughs. There were those which wanted a member who would stay a long time, foster local industries, care for the poor, and subsidise all the local associations and bazaars, and there were those which preferred a well-lubricated and inconclusive tug-of-war between rival candidates which would bring money into the town at election times.

Bridport was a typical example of those boroughs which wanted a milch-cow for their representative. From 1841 until 1875 it was represented by T. A. Mitchell, a London merchant and ship-owner of Scottish parentage, who was a Liberal in politics. His claims on the borough were freely recognised by the Reform League. 'He has been a most generous supporter of all local charities and undertakings, and this constitutes his great power over the working population. . . . He is really more respected for his personal qualities and local influence than for any decided political activity, as he has seldom, if ever, spoken upon any question brought before the House.'[3] Moreover, he enjoyed the support of the principal banker, the Independent minister, four

---

[1] In 1868 compacts still existed at Aylesbury, Bury St. Edmunds, Pontefract, East Retford, Warwick, Wenlock and Weymouth. Of these only three, those at Pontefract, Retford and Weymouth, had been made by the local party managers for their own convenience: the rest were no more than a reflection of the predominance of a local magnate who controlled one seat. The only compact to survive until 1880 was that at Wenlock.

[2] *Law Times*, 18 July 1868.

[3] Reform League Report: Bridport.

important twine millers and merchants, and the three leading working-class Radicals. Mitchell retained the seat without a contest in either 1868 or 1874, and on his death in 1875 was succeeded by another carpet-bagger from London, Pandeli Ralli, of Ralli Brothers, the Greek merchant bankers.

In choosing Ralli, the Liberal managers seem to have borne in mind the Reform League's advice that if it ever became necessary to replace Mitchell a candidate should be sent down 'whose position and influence would enable him *to benefit the trade of the town*', but the choice was a bad one. Ralli, whose later election record was dismal, was neither personally attractive to working-class electors nor sufficiently lavish with his money when there was no election in progress to win him favour in Bridport.[1] Moreover, he was unable to prevent the alienation of the working-class electors from the middle-class Liberal leaders which had threatened to become serious since 1868, and which Mitchell's long experience had enabled him to delay.[2]

Between 1875 and 1880 the indifference of the working-class electors both to Liberalism and to Ralli was played on by the Conservatives, and in 1879-80 the latter were able to provide themselves with what they thought was an ideal candidate. Either this candidate, C. N. Warton, or his agent, managed to turn the Liberal majority of 431 in 1875 into a Conservative majority of 9. The highly original device by which this feat was accomplished has been described in such different terms by different raconteurs

---

[1] *3 Hansard* CCLXVIII, 1593 gives a very inadequate report of a speech by Peter Rylands attributing Ralli's defeat entirely to his failure to foster local industries or to put money into the pockets of his constituents in other ways. A month after his defeat at Bridport in April 1880, Ralli fought Wallingford and was lucky to keep his seat on petition in view of corrupt practices which took place: H.C. 10, p. 23 (1881). LXXIV, 263. He later unsuccessfully contested the Wells division in 1885, Gateshead in 1892 and 1893, Newcastle-upon-Tyne in 1892, and Gloucester in 1900.

[2] The Reform Leaguers had already pointed out in 1868 how serious this division in the Liberal ranks was: 'The Liberal party predominate, and consist of the principal professional, private and mercantile residents, but in all previous elections they have exercised an all powerful influence over the working men of the town; who being their tenants and in their employ, have been almost compelled to vote for the candidate favoured by their employers. But now that the twine trade and, indeed, almost all commerce is in a very depressed state, and numbers of men have been discharged from various factories—so that they feel themselves somewhat independent—it is feared that some of them may vote for the Tory candidate from a mere spirit of opposition. . . .

'The feeling among the working men varies greatly, but it may be described as somewhat *indifferent* to the final issue of the contest, and many would probably vote for the candidate who would spend the most money, without reference to politics, of which the large majority appear completely ignorant.'

that the details are uncertain, but the main outline is clear enough. Not long before the election Warton's friend and agent, one Patch, went down to the borough and was taken ill and given up for dead. On his supposed death-bed the sick man dictated a will to a local Conservative solicitor leaving generous benefactions to the town and to certain individuals. The solicitor could not keep the news secret and it spread like wildfire among the electors. Meanwhile the invalid speedily recovered and immediately became a local notability, and was asked if he knew any suitable Conservative to contest Bridport. Patch promptly recommended his friend Mr Warton to the Conservatives of the borough as a man with £30,000 a year, and property in Southwark besides, and won the seat for him largely by recounting all the ways in which this money could be spent in Bridport. Warton, indeed, nearly spoiled his chances by professing a belief in purity of election, but this *gaffe* was hastily covered up by his supporters. It was only after the election that the local Conservatives discovered that Warton was a comparatively poor man with no intention of spending any money at all in Bridport, and it is said that their rage was so great that he never set foot in Bridport again before, at the end of the 1880 parliament, he accepted an appointment in Australia.[1]

Apocryphal as part of this story may be, it is not far removed from that of Harwich during this period. Harwich had long been notorious for its venality, and was only rescued from certain decay by the opening of a branch railway from Manningtree, and the starting of a line of packets to Rotterdam and Antwerp for which the Great Eastern Railway built docks, quays, and railway yards and the Great Eastern Hotel. In this way the Great Eastern became the largest employer of labour and the most powerful influence in the town. The electors of Harwich naturally looked upon the Company as a milch-cow and determined, irrespective of politics, to do as much as they could to persuade it to spend money in the town. From 1859 to 1885 they had a guarantee for their prosperity in the person of a director or leading shareholder of the Company (always a Conservative) sitting as their

[1] He was appointed Attorney-General for Western Australia. The account given above is set out with greater circumstantial detail in *Vanity Fair*, 10 May 1884. J. W. Lowther (*A Speaker's Commentaries*, London 1925, I, 174) says that it was Warton who took to his bed, and that the rumour of his benefactions was sufficient to have him returned, as it were, *ægrotat*.

representative at Westminster. The member from 1859 to 1880 was Captain Henry Jervis-White-Jervis, the son of an Irish baronet and an officer of the Engineers, who had been introduced to the borough by his father-in-law J. C. Cobbold, who was a large landowner there and at Ipswich, which he represented in parliament. In 1859 Jervis's return was a matter of money and influence rather than a result of his railway connections, but in 1862 he was appointed to the board of directors of the Great Eastern, which was an amalgamation of two local railways, the Eastern Union and the Eastern Counties, and in 1863 he became deputy-chairman of the company.[1] As such he was in a position to profit politically from the company's expansion in Harwich, which received a great impulse in 1863 when the company decided to purchase its own steamboats. Jervis's position on the board was, nevertheless, a difficult one. He was one of the two representatives of the shareholders of the old Eastern Union Railway, who claimed that they had been unfairly treated by the Great Eastern, and in a sense, therefore, the leader of the opposition on the board—'one of the Eastern Union importations' as the *Railway Times* remarked.[2] He was at the same time a Conservative, and inclined to use his influence on behalf of the Harwich Conservatives, whereas the most active members of the board, Bidder and Shaw, were Liberals who objected to his doing so.

The general election of 1865 provoked a major crisis in the company over this latter question. Shortly before the election the board of directors decided to end its arrangement with a local firm, which acted as the company's agent in Harwich, and to appoint its own continental traffic manager. Bidder and Shaw, who dominated the Harwich sub-committee, decided that the transfer must take place before the election: this probably because Jervis was doing unexpectedly well in Harwich, in spite of a decision of the board not to use its influence in the elections.[3] Accordingly, they ordered the secretary and the new continental traffic manager to Harwich a week before the election, where they

---

[1] For details of the G.E.R. and Harwich elections I have relied on the MS. minutes of the Great Eastern Railway in the Record Office of the British Transport Commission, on *Bradshaw's Railway Manual*, the *Railway Times*, *Herepath's Railway Journal*, the Reform League's report on Harwich, and the evidence given at the trial of two Harwich election petitions H.C. 233 (1866). X, 431 and H.C. 227-Sess. 2 (1880). LVIII, 65.

[2] *Railway Times*, 5 August 1865.

[3] Minute of 6 July 1865.

arrived at one o'clock in the morning with fifty or sixty porters from Liverpool Street Station. Jervis met them on their arrival and hotly ordered them back to London on the ground that the chairman of the company knew nothing of their mission and that the porters had merely been brought down as a political dodge. The band from London accordingly retreated and the continental traffic manager reported to the board that they had done so because Jervis threatened a breach of the peace.[1] Jervis followed up this victory by stopping some building work which had been begun on orders from London, and the position remained unchanged until the election, when he was returned with a handsome majority.

The Great Eastern directors censured Jervis for his action and removed him from the deputy chairmanship, but the battle did not end there: Jervis launched a counter attack, accusing the board of going beyond its legal authority in raising money and of maladministration, and brought to his aid his Eastern Union allies. In most circumstances the attack would have been parried at the company's general meeting by the chairman and deputy chairman using proxy votes entrusted to them by absentees, but for some reason (probably the change in the deputy chairmanship) the proxies were all found to be invalid, so that a motion for an enquiry was carried against the board. The majority was not quite large enough to comply with the rules governing the appointment of committees of enquiry, but the company was in a weak financial position, and the board could hardly prevent an enquiry being held without rousing grave suspicions. As a consequence a committee of investigation was appointed, and in a very short time unearthed evidence of technical irregularities, and of illegalities such as the payment of dividends out of loan-capital, which were sufficient to lead an excited shareholders' meeting to pass a resolution calling for the resignation of all the directors. Jervis and his solitary supporter on the board refused to budge, but all the other directors withdrew and a new board was chosen, from which Jervis retired in rotation in 1867.

The reaction of the electors of Harwich was characteristic. The Conservatives, who were greatly attached to Jervis because he spent a lot of money in the borough, were delighted with the victory of their champion. The indifferent felt that Jervis had

[1] Minute of 19 July 1865: *Railway Times*, 19 August 1865.

proved beyond all doubt his ability to champion their interest, and realised that he would be quite as influential as a leading shareholder as in a minority on the board. The Liberals saw in the change in the composition of the board an opportunity for themselves. They accordingly asked the new chairman, Charles Henry Turner, to become their candidate, sure that he would bring with him some pickings for them. Turner went so far as to pay the registration expenses and to visit the borough several times, but when he discovered the quality of the local Liberals he prudently withdrew. No doubt he shared the astonishment of the Reform League's agents who visited the borough shortly afterwards and reported, 'We cannot say that the new voters are Liberals, as venality, bribery and self interest seem to preponderate over politics.' They recommended in their simplicity that 'some of the least venal' should be invited to a course of lectures on the 'points of departure between Liberal and Conservative policy'.

When Jervis finally retired in 1880 so black was the reputation of the borough that the new Conservative candidate, Sir Henry Tyler, had as little as possible to do with the leading Conservatives and contested it solely on the strength of his own claims.[1] These were strong enough. For some years he had combined the offices of Chief Inspector of Railways at the Board of Trade (from which he had recently retired) and Chairman of the Grand Trunk Railway of Canada, and he had lately been appointed to the board of the Great Eastern on the strength of his unrivalled knowledge of railways. In spite of the Liberal reaction he was easily returned.[2] The Liberals rashly petitioned against his return on the ground that he had been guilty, through his agents, of corrupt practices, but the petition came to nothing: Tyler had behaved with the utmost circumspection because he was sure of winning. The petition had the result, however, of showing that the Liberals had themselves been guilty of bribery on a moderate scale and that little or nothing had been done to check it.[3] The Great Eastern connection, even without lavish expenditure, seems to have been sufficient even in 1880 to counteract the more direct appeal of gold.

Few candidates had the moral courage to make their appeal

[1] H.C. 227-Sess. 2, p. 4 (1880). LVIII, 68.
[2] In 1885 he became M.P. for Great Yarmouth where one seat had been under railway influence until 1866-8 when the borough was disfranchised for corruption.
[3] H.C. 227-Sess. 2, pp. 8-9 (1880). LVIII, 72-3.

to the self-interest of the electors an open and avowed one, but there is one amusing exception: John Orrell Lever, who was returned for Galway town (not strictly a small borough) in 1880 as a Liberal-Conservative-Home Ruler. He had represented the borough between 1859 and 1865, when he was defeated, but for the next fifteen years he was kept out of politics by the need to retrieve his commercial fortunes. In 1880, however, he was back again as a candidate, and placarded the town with the following extraordinary poster:[1]

Vote for Lever.— Who was prevented from building extensive mills for the manufacture of flax and cotton by his non-election at his last contest.

Vote for Lever.— Who was ruined by the machinations of opposing interests in 1866, in his endeavours to benefit GALWAY.

Vote for Lever.— Who vanquished his opponents, and is once more in possession of a princely fortune.

Vote for Lever.— Who has no personal interests to serve.

Vote for Lever.— Who, from his extensive experience, influential connections and capital, is now in a better position than he ever was to secure the prosperity of GALWAY.

Most venal boroughs did not care to have a permanent or semi-permanent member because a hotly-fought election brought money into the town. There was, indeed, an almost irresistible tendency towards drawn battles or battles decided by the slenderest majorities, because only these encouraged lavish spending. It was almost as if there was a 'law of diminishing majorities' which, when one side became weak, compensated the weaker side with recruits from among its opponents. There was rarely anything quite as remarkable as the migration of the agents and party manager of each side to the opposite camp which occurred at Horsham in 1847.[2] But in small boroughs where everybody knew everybody else, the transfer of one influential individual set up a chain reaction which might be important enough to carry the borough for the other party.

Some boroughs were, of course, much worse than others. In

---

[1] Quoted in W. Saunders, *The New Parliament, 1880*, London 1880, pp. 249-50.

[2] William Albery, *A Parliamentary History of the Ancient Borough of Horsham*, London 1927, pp. 331-9.

places like Frome and Horsham there was very little deliberate fostering of corruption except on the part of the very lowest class of electors, but to outsiders these boroughs looked black enough, and there are plenty of election reports which read like Thomas Hughes's description of the 1868 election in Frome.

> We had a desperate hard battle and my people staunch as they were had almost given up hope on the night between nomination and the poll when all the publics were ringing with the carousings of the blues. However I stuck to my guns, wouldn't have a single room at any public, and pulled off the victory by the skin of my teeth against such drunkenness violent and open intimidation and secret bribery as I hope never to see again. . . .
>
> I am a convert to the ballot not of course as a principle but as a method worth trying to stop the awful wickedness of our small borough elections.[1]

But such boroughs compare very favourably with the fifteen or twenty towns like Bridgwater, or the majority of small Irish boroughs, which deliberately inveigled rich men to the town in order to lighten their purses. Beverley and Bridgwater in England and Cashel and Sligo in Ireland were the Eatanswills of the sixties, and paid the penalty of their notoriety with disfranchisement. The rest continued little disturbed by election judges or Royal Commissions. In the West, Barnstaple and Taunton were little better than Bridgwater. A month before the 1868 election a Taunton newspaper devoted a leading article to the orgy of bribery which it anticipated when the fight became hot, remarking: 'Those who remember the past will know well enough what will follow, should a really hot fight take place. . . . It seems almost foolish to anticipate a day when electors generally shall throw off the trammels of wretched customs and vile indulgence . . .'[2] The same paper recalled that in 1865 a prospective candidate had found during a preliminary canvass that of the 900 electors of Taunton, between 260 and 270 were resolved to vote for no one unless they were paid. In Ireland there were several small boroughs like Athlone and Mallow, which had been declining since the Famine, and almost literally lived on electioneering. Take the case of Athlone as T. P. O'Connor knew it in the early sixties, and as it remained for another twenty years.

---

[1] Thomas Hughes to Lord de Grey, 20 November 1868. Ripon Papers, Add. MS. 43,519 (uncatalogued).
[2] *Western Weekly Advertiser*, 3 October 1868.

With many of the people the periodic bribe entered into the whole economy of their poor, shrivelled, squalid, weary lives. Men continued to live in houses that had better have lived in lodgings, because the house gave a vote. The very whisper of a dissolution sent a visible thrill through the town, and the prospect of common gain swallowed up amid the people all other passions, religious and political, and united ordinarily discordant forces in amity and brotherhood. There was, as there is, a tolerably strong minority of Protestants in the town; between the Protestant and the Catholic there was irreconcilable difference of political as well as of religious feeling; and, indeed, there was rarely any social intercourse between people of the two creeds. But at election time the Catholic and the Protestant forgot their rivalries, remembered the interests only of their town, and fought strenuously and side by side in loving union for the man who gave the highest bribe. There was a highly respected Protestant tradesman in the town when I was a boy who had a large repute for political wisdom, and was generally esteemed; and I remember hearing a well-known saying of his quoted, which put the philosophy of Irish electioneering in these times in a compendious form. 'I am a Protestant', Ned — used to say, 'and my father was a Protestant, and his father before him; but the man I want to see returned for Athlone is the man that leaves the money in the town.'[1]

In such places corruption often permeated all classes, and the new electors of 1867 had long been accustomed to the habits of the £10 householders before they came to share in the material advantages of the franchise.[2] When the Reform League sent its agents to stir up the working men of Guildford to 'assert their rights' and the dignity of labour, they met with a good natured but negative response. J. B. Leno, a working-class poet, reported in some disgust that, election or no election, regular meetings were held at Tory public houses where punch costing ten shillings a bowl was dispensed to as many as cared to attend. But the vice was not all on one side—

[1] T. P. O'Connor, *The Parnell Movement*, London 1886, pp. 134-5.
[2] It would, however, be churlish not to recognise that these small boroughs, however corrupt, had their good points. Some few could be in part reclaimed; almost all were willing to devote themselves more or less unselfishly to the cause of a really popular candidate when that rare commodity came among them; and the Irish constituencies showed at times a quite heroic attachment to Home Rule which nothing in their previous history had foreshadowed. William O'Brien's victory at Mallow in 1880 was contrary to all the town's past traditions, and the electors of Athlone must have felt positively saintly when they returned Justin Huntly McCarthy unopposed in 1884.

not one, but nearly all with whom we have come in contact, estimate the value of the vote by what it will fetch in the market; and openly proclaim their intention of making what they can of it. On two successive occasions, we have heard men openly proclaim (with the approval of all present, saving myself) that their votes would go to the highest bidder—that candidates for Election were guided by no principle, and hence no discredit attached itself to those who Traded on their desire for personal advancement, and Party supremacy.[1]

A more cynical reporter suggested that the only way to break up a compact between the two parties at Weymouth, which was maintained by general corruption, was to introduce a thorough-going Liberal who 'must not profess very advanced principles' but should form a dock company to attract some of the shipping lines from Plymouth.[2]

The electors of such towns were perfectly open about their attitude to politics. The local party leaders asked the party head-quarters for lists of rich men and selected the richest of them as their candidate if he were not otherwise unsuitable. In a few places there were also bands of electors, sometimes headed by local solicitors, who offered their support to the highest bidder *en masse*.[3] The arrival of a new and reputedly rich candidate was almost invariably the cause of genuine popular rejoicing much more noteworthy than the occasional riots which were reported in the press. Sir Henry Hawkins ('Hanging Hawkins') recalls in his *Reminiscences* the astonishment he felt when he went down to investigate the possibility of standing for Barnstaple in 1865 and was greeted by a cheering crowd.[4] If he had been wise, since he was an advocate of purity, he would have caught the next train back to London. As it was, the word soon got round that nothing was to be had from him: immediately backs were turned and the cheering died away, and it was no surprise to him or anyone else when he was bottom of the poll. A more realistic candidate was Sir Richard Glass, the pioneer manufacturer of submarine cables, who stood for Bewdley in 1868. When he first

[1] Reform League Report: Guildford.　　　[2] Ibid. Weymouth and Melcombe Regis.
[3] There are cases recorded at Brecon, Ipswich and Macclesfield. The worst case was at Brecon in 1868 where one attorney received £500 and four others received £100 each. Mr Baron Martin, possibly bearing in mind similar cases recorded by Oldfield, commented that it 'looked very much like buying a small borough, and paying a man for the interest which he had probably made with a number of electors'. H.C. 352, p. 434 (1868-9). VIII, 434.
[4] *The Reminiscences of Sir Henry Hawkins, Baron Brampton*, ed. Richard Harris, London 1904, Ch. XXVII.

came to the town it was after dark and he was a complete stranger, yet for miles along the road little knots of people turned out to cheer him.[1] In this case the party managers were not mistaken in their man, as Sir Richard had announced that he was prepared to lay out £4,000 for the benefit of the 1,000 electors, and his agents opened twenty public houses to all comers. In this he was perhaps rather old-fashioned, for it made it impossible to preserve the seat on petition, and the money was wasted.

Fortunately, the type of candidate who set out on his own initiative to besiege a borough with a bad reputation and to buy up an interest was extremely rare. The agents of Sir Henry Edwards did this at Beverley, but the only other English case of note occurred at Windsor. Both members for Windsor were unseated in 1866 and long afterwards there was a corrupt element in the town fostered by corrupt practices at municipal elections which gave political life in the borough a bad name.[2] In 1866 Robert Richardson-Gardner went to Windsor in order to create an interest, with only his money and the fact that he was Colonel of the North-East London Rifle Volunteers to recommend him. He determined to indulge in no corrupt practices but to sail as near the wind as possible. He spent money lavishly on clubs, charities and entertainments, and he began to buy up cottage property and to erect model dwellings whose inhabitants he sometimes provided with coals and other gifts. One condition he did make, that he would have only Conservative tenants, and those who voted against him in 1868 were ejected from their homes as soon as the danger of a petition had passed—conduct which Lord Bramwell called 'most disgraceful and most mischievous'.[3] By 1874 he had 306 tenants, 220 of whom were voters, and the rest mainly dependants on his charity, who held the balance between the parties. Richardson-Gardner held the seat until 1890, when he retired, but he never quite lived down a shady reputation, and he never got the baronetcy he hoped for.[4]

---

[1] For Glass's candidature see H.C. 120, p. 6 (1868-9). XLVIII, 6, and H.C. 9 (1868-9). XLVIII, 525.

[2] The evidence on Windsor is contained in the report of the trial of an election petition in 1874: H.C. 373 (1874). LIII, 469f, and in the minutes of evidence taken before the Hartington Committee: H.C. 352 (1868-9). VIII, 1f.

[3] H.C. 152, p. 6 (1874). LIII, 554.

[4] He asked Lord Salisbury for a baronetcy in 1885, and added significantly: 'I may remark that Windsor has cost me a small fortune and that I have never received *the slightest help or favour* from the Party during the whole 19 years.' R. Richardson-Gardner to Salisbury, 31 August 1885. Salisbury Papers.

Chapter Four

THE PROVINCIAL BACKWATERS

I

BETWEEN the really big towns with an active political life of their own and the very small boroughs where political activities were artificially fostered from outside, stood a middle group of about seventy-five boroughs.[1] About half of them were old provincial centres like Hereford, Cambridge, Lincoln, and Shrewsbury, only partly absorbed into the world of modern industry and party politics, where old family connections lingered on and where bribery was customary and even reputable. Local men like the Gurdon Rebows at Colchester, the Clives at Hereford, and the Cobbolds at Ipswich were the candidates of their preference, but carpet-baggers were much more common, and much better able to satisfy the local appetite for gold. The remainder of this group of boroughs were Scottish and Welsh districts which were pure but where politics were localised in the contributory boroughs, and modern towns like Cheltenham, Gateshead, Ashton, and Stalybridge, whose adolescence was uncommonly prolonged.

Most of these boroughs owed such character as they possessed to their employers of labour. Indeed, because they were quite small and the influence of the larger employers was so direct and extensive, they illustrate one of the main features of late Victorian politics, the association of political emancipation with dependence on the great employers. In all the bigger towns both the leaders of the movement for political emancipation and its opponents were themselves employers. The industrialist-politician who took an active part in promoting the welfare of his neighbourhood enjoyed a twofold influence: on the one hand he was a political leader who attracted the support of the independent electors, the small shopkeepers, the self-employed tradesmen, and the independent working men, and on the other he exercised a

[1] This group included all the boroughs with between 16,000 and 50,000 people in 1871, with the exceptions mentioned on p. 39.

direct influence over his own employees, and, through his political associates, over the employees of other firms as well. Indeed, since most of the medium-sized boroughs were quite small, the influence of the proprietor was akin to that of a landlord in a country village.[1]

Because most firms were small the really large mill or works which still retained its family character exercised an enormous political influence. Its proprietor was automatically one of the leading men in the town, and his brothers and sons along with him, while the near-unanimous vote of his employees was sufficient to tip the scales in an election. Take the case of Preston, which was much larger than most of the towns with which this chapter is concerned. In 1883 there were eighty mills in the town, divided as follows:[2]

Number of Hands	*Number of Mills*
Under 100	4
100-300	36
300-500	16
500-1,000	15
1,000-2,000	6
2,000-3,000	2
Over 3,000	1

The smaller mills were pretty evenly divided between the two parties, so that the political allegiance of the town depended on the independent electors and on the one great firm employing over 3,000 hands, Messrs Horrocks. The independent electors favoured the Conservatives for local reasons, but not by a sufficiently large majority to make the latter sure of both seats, or even of one, without the Horrocks vote as well.[3] As a result, the active intervention of the proprietor of the firm in political life was enough to decide elections, just as it had been when John Horrocks became member for the borough in 1802. Thus the decision of Edward Hermon, the sole proprietor of Horrocks's, to come forward as Conservative candidate in 1868, after he had

---

[1] The average mill in the cotton industry employed only 177 operatives in 1870, most of them women, the average woollen mill only 70 operatives, while the average unit in the metal industries of Birmingham, Sheffield and the Black Country employed about 20 operatives. J. H. Clapham, *An Economic History of Modern Britain: Free Trade and Steel 1850-1886*, Cambridge 1932, p. 117.

[2] A. Hewitson, *History of Preston*, Preston 1883, pp. 185-6.

[3] For Preston politics see also pp. 301-2 below.

been invited to stand by both sides, had the effect of guaranteeing the Conservatives his seat and virtually the second seat as
well as long as he chose to stand.[1] Even in 1880 there was so
little chance of beating him that the Liberals left him unopposed,
and concentrated on the seat held by his colleague, Sir John
Holker, a carpet-bagging lawyer.

> As to Mr. Hermon, [says Hewitson, the Preston historian] his local
> commercial status and generosity of disposition rendered his political
> position impregnable. He was the principal partner in the greatest
> cotton manufacturing establishment in the town; was not only a
> large employer of labour, but a liberal patron of all the leading
> institutions; was a warm friend of educational, social, and religious
> movements, especially those associated with the Church of England;
> and his seat was deemed, by all parties, perfectly safe.[2]

More usually an influence of this sort was a family, not an
individual, one. At Carlisle it was that of the Ferguson family,
who were the leading Carlisle Liberals and the leading cotton
manufacturers, and provided the city with two members, Joseph
Ferguson from 1852 to 1857 and Robert Ferguson from 1874 to
1886.[3] One branch of the family owned the old firm of Peter
Dixon and Sons, the other what was known in Carlisle as the
Holme Head firm, but the family owed their influence quite as
much to the fact that they were civic leaders as to their direct
political influence, which was, indeed, restricted, as the Holme
Head works employed only 130 electors in 1868.[4] A Ferguson was
always the leader of the Liberal party, and there was usually at
least one Ferguson on the city council. Joseph Ferguson was
mayor of Carlisle for many years before he became its M.P.,
and his son Robert was first chairman of the Carlisle school
board before he too became an M.P. R. S. Ferguson, the Cumberland historian, writing of his family in 1871, says of them:

> From 1812, downwards to the present, the heads of the firm of
> Peter Dixon and Sons, and of the Holme Head firm, have been
> conspicuous and influential leaders in every local election contest,

---

[1] Lord Edward Howard, his opponent, wrote of him: 'Hermon is the worst opponent
we could have had—very rich—probably led by clergy.' Add. MS. 44,347, f.181.
See also *Preston Guardian*, 12 August 1868.
[2] Hewitson, *History of Preston*, p. 147.
[3] In between there was another 'cotton member', Edmund Potter of Manchester
and Hadfield, M.P. for Carlisle 1861-74.
[4] H.C. 352, p. 540 (1868-9). VIII, 540.

not only for Carlisle, but also for Cumberland. Both firms joined the Orange and Purple against Mr. Curwen, but since then have been strong on the Blue [i.e. Liberal] side. The number of weavers employed by these great firms accounts for the fact that the Caldewgate quarter of Carlisle, mainly inhabited by the weavers, has been always a place of great importance in elections.[1]

Ferguson also records that the Liberal cause had been greatly assisted in recent years by the formation of new works which also possessed a marked political individuality.

> Other important industries have also sprung up in Carlisle, employing large numbers of workmen, and generally strengthening the Blue interest, such as the marble works of Messrs. Nelson, the hatteries of Messrs. Carrick, and the biscuit factories of Messrs. Carr and Slater. . . .
> So long as banking at Carlisle was in the hands of private individuals, and not carried on by joint-stock companies, the influence that the banking interest could bring to bear was generally exerted on the Conservative side. . . . The influence of Messrs. Head's bank has always been exerted on the Conservative side, and has been much augumented by Mr. Head's personal character and large charities.[2]

In Lancashire and North Cheshire, where industry was also old-established, there was an unusually large number of families like the Fergusons. Macclesfield was dominated by the Brocklehursts, who were silk manufacturers, bankers, solicitors, town councillors, and hereditary leaders of the local Liberal party. From 1832 until 1881, when the borough was disfranchised for corruption, they claimed one of the seats, and from 1885 until 1918 they were the obvious Liberal candidates for the Macclesfield division of Cheshire.[3] Between 1832 and 1914 three members of the family were M.P.s, five were mayors, one was created a peer, and another a baronet. Ashton-under-Lyne was dominated by the aggressive Puritan figure of Hugh Mason, a cotton spinner who lived in great style at Groby Hall, and who had very little of the patience which won his more celebrated neighbours, the Ashtons of Hyde, an enviable reputation as

---

[1] Ferguson, *Cumberland and Westmorland M.P.s*, p. 307.

[2] *Ibid.*, pp. 307-9.

[3] There is a brief history of the family: Mary Crozier, *An Old Silk Family, 1745-1945*, Aberdeen 1947.

employers.[1] Mason's hatreds were so universal—they included alcohol, gambling, horse-racing, landlords, the theatre, tobacco, Tories, trade unions, and the Church of England—that he in time stirred up such an opposition against himself that Ashton became a Tory constituency. But until he died in 1886 the Liberal party was absolutely in his pocket, and he felt no compunction in offering the seat to his friends.[2] At Blackburn there were two leading Tory families, the Feildens, who had been important people in the district since the sixteenth century, and the Hornbys, who were eighteenth-century arrivals.[3] The Feildens provided social standing, the Hornbys vigour and leadership: together they were almost unbeatable. The founder of the Feilden interest in the borough was William Feilden, who had been driven into industry because he was a younger son, sat for Blackburn from 1832 to 1847, and was made a baronet by Peel. He was followed during the next thirty years by three other members of the family who sat for Blackburn 1853-7, 1865-9, and 1869-75. The founder of the Hornby interest was William Henry Hornby, who acted as chairman of the Conservative party at the first election in 1832, when he was only twenty-seven. He was leader of the party for almost fifty years, M.P. from 1857 to 1869, Charter Mayor in 1851, and chief promoter of railways in the district. His third son, William Henry the younger, succeeded him as leader of the Conservative party and became first chairman of the Blackburn school board, leader of the town council, Jubilee Mayor, freeman of the borough, M.P. for Blackburn from 1886 to 1910, and the last of Blackburn's great local figures. Two other Hornbys also represented Blackburn 1841-52 and 1869-74.

The influence of those enterprising men who founded great

[1] Mason had succeeded to the influence both of his father, and of his father-in-law, Abel Buckley, a leading Anti-Corn-Law Leaguer and Mayor of Ashton. For his character see W. H. Mills ed., *The Manchester Reform Club 1871-1921*, privately printed, Manchester 1922, p. 11.

[2] In 1879 he offered the seat to George Melly in the following terms: 'Dear Melly, Will you be able to sit for this borough? I know you voted on the Lawson [Permissive] Bill, and would vote for Scottish Disestablishment. We have a majority. Very sincerely, Hugh Mason.' George Melly, *Recollections of Sixty Years (1833-1893)*, privately printed, Coventry 1893, p. 36. Melly refused, whereupon Mason decided to stand himself. He became M.P. for Ashton in 1880 and held the seat until 1885.

[3] There is no good account of them. The account given here is based on a letter from W. H. Hornby to Akers Douglas, 5 October 1891, in the Salisbury Papers, G. C. Miller, *Blackburn: The Evolution of a Cotton Town*, Blackburn 1951, and Burke's *Peerage* and *Landed Gentry*. The Feildens of Blackburn are to be distinguished from the Fieldens of Todmorden, also M.P.s.

industries in small towns and built new towns around them differed from that exerted by manufacturers in old-established towns because there were scarcely any rival influences at work. Thus for one generation, and sometimes for more than one, the founders of new industries became virtually assured of a seat in parliament as soon as their new town was enfranchised. Sir Josiah John Guest, the proprietor of the Dowlais ironworks, became first member for Merthyr Tydvil in 1832, John Laird the shipbuilder became first member for Birkenhead in 1861, H. W. F. Bölckow of Bölckow and Vaughan, ironmasters, became first member for Middlesbrough in 1868, Ralph Ward-Jackson, the founder of West Hartlepool, became first member for the Hartlepools in 1868, and Charles Mark Palmer of the Jarrow shipyards became first member for Jarrow in 1885. The appeal of such men was almost irresistible: 'It is the general opinion of the Working and Middle Class Leaders', the Reform League's agents reported from Birkenhead, 'that there is no hope for Liberalism in this Borough until the death of Mr. Laird or the introduction of the Ballot.' It was an appeal quite sufficient to make the ballot merely an opportunity for a swing away from party allegiance towards the local magnate, and Laird actually increased his majority by 1,230 with the ballot. And it was often all the stronger that it was expressed in local terms. Ward-Jackson, whose interests in West Hartlepool had already passed to the North-Eastern Railway before the 1868 election, none the less firmly rooted his claims in his local services.

> You well know that I appear before you as one long and thoroughly acquainted with this populous and enterprising district. . . Many of the best years of my life have been spent among you; and I can, without egotism, say that the promoting of the commercial and social interests of the Hartlepools has ever engaged and will continue to receive my unceasing and devoted attention. . . .
>
> It is well known that I have been long advocating works in the Bay of Hartlepool, for Enlarged Protection and an increased Depth of Water into the two Harbours. The Electors may rely on my determined and continuous efforts towards the obtaining of that great and necessary Improvement of the Port.[1]

[1] Address to the Electors of the Hartlepools, 1868. *South Durham Herald*, 27 June 1868.

II

The great majority of employers of labour were Liberals, and so were the majority of the small shopkeepers, so that the medium-sized boroughs usually returned Liberal members.[1] But because so much depended on one or two great employers, these boroughs often reflected the fluctuations in their opinion of the Liberal party. This usually meant no more than that one Liberal member who had offended some of his erstwhile supporters was replaced by another, sometimes after a fight, as when R. N. Philips defeated Frederick Peel at Bury in 1865 and Henry Campbell defeated John Ramsay at Stirling in 1868.[2] But in 1874 there were a number of much more complicated upheavals, because many prominent Radicals were disgusted with their party and withdrew their support from the Liberal candidates in their constituency (although without transferring it to the Conservatives). As a consequence, the Conservatives, who had been gaining ground steadily since 1870, met no effective opposition and won twenty-three seats which had been Liberal in 1868 in the medium-sized boroughs alone. In 1880, however, the alienated Liberals returned to their former allegiance, and in most towns there were record Liberal majorities, but not before the Conservatives had made themselves a great deal more effective as opponents than they had ever been before.

The effect of the fickleness of a few leading Liberals is demonstrated in remarkable fashion by the course of events in Lincoln. The two members for Lincoln in the 1865 parliament were Charles Seely, an influential Radical who had sat for the borough at intervals since 1847 and whose seat was perfectly safe, and Edward Heneage, afterwards Lord Heneage, a local landowner

---

[1] A considerable number of the 54 English boroughs with two members but a population of less than 50,000 returned one Whig and one Radical or one Whig and one Conservative, so that it is not easy to generalise about the character of their Liberalism. In 1884 'A Candid Conservative', writing in the *Fortnightly Review*, XXXVII, 48, of the coming redistribution, spoke of the Tory expectation of 'the vigorous resistance of the Whigs, whose political importance has for years been mainly due to that system of two-membered constituencies which has enabled a small faction, holding in most country towns the balance between Conservatives and Radicals, to make terms with either party, and so secure for itself a moiety of the representation'.

[2] Spender, his biographer, records that he first descended on the constituency at a by-election and 'with a shrewd Glasgow lawyer, Mr. Gordon Smith, as his agent, he immediately and without invitation or organisation issued his address . . .' J. A. Spender, *Life of the Right Hon. Sir Henry Campbell-Bannerman*, London 1923, I, 26.

who became Chancellor of the Duchy of Lancaster under Gladstone in 1886 and then a Liberal Unionist.[1] Together they represented the traditional compromise in the medium-sized boroughs between Whigs and Radicals which generally enabled the Liberals to secure both seats. The temper of the town was, however, Radical rather than otherwise, as there was no middle-class to speak of to interpose between the few manufacturers of agricultural implements and machinery, and their workmen who had swamped the old voters.[2] Moreover the heads of Clayton and Shuttleworth, the steam engine manufacturers, were 'great Radicals'. There was, therefore, a good deal of dissatisfaction with Heneage when on the Tuesday before the nomination (which was to be held on the following Monday) he declared his opposition to the ballot and to the repeal of the ratepaying clauses of the Reform Act. On the Wednesday and Thursday the leading Radicals met and determined to support a second Radical candidate instead of Heneage. A meeting of working men (their employees) was called on Friday and adopted the proposal that John Hinde Palmer, who had thrice contested the borough in the past as a Radical, should be invited to stand again. On the Saturday a subscription was opened to finance Palmer's candidature, to which the Conservatives gladly contributed, and two large meetings were held in the Buttermarket. By that evening it was clear that with the largest employers behind the movement as well as the working-class Radicals, nine-tenths of the Liberal electors would favour Palmer.

The following morning (Sunday) a deputation called on Heneage and told him what had occurred, and also that the Conservatives were hoping to bring forward a candidate of their own. Heneage hurried into Lincoln but found his position hopeless. Rather than fight an expensive and useless contest he agreed to withdraw and to announce this withdrawal on the next morning, the day of the nomination. His announcement, made at 8 a.m., immediately put a stop to the Conservatives' plan to run a man of their own, and by 11 a.m. Hinde Palmer had been chosen member for Lincoln without opposition, although

---

[1] His family had a traditional interest at Grimsby, which he represented from 1880 to 1892, and from 1893 to 1895. The details which follow are derived from the 1868 Lincolnshire Poll Book, the *Stamford Mercury*, and the *Lincoln Gazette* for 20 November 1868.

[2] The Reform Act roughly trebled the electorate.

he himself did not know it until much later in the day. Meanwhile, Heneage had placarded the walls of Lincoln with a farewell address.

To the Electors of Lincoln

Having ascertained that a large majority of the Liberals of Lincoln have broken their faith with me at the Eleventh Hour, and pledged themselves to support another Candidate, in a manner so unprecedented and dishonourable, that it seems difficult to realize the fact, and not being inclined to fight a Contest for their amusement, or to put the city into a state of unnecessary disturbance and excitement, I have decided to withdraw my *Claims*.

I again became a Candidate for the representation of your City at the urgent request of the Electors, although another Constituency sought my services, *a course of conduct on my part in marked contrast* to that of my *False Friends*. To my *true* friends I render my best thanks for favours past and present, and regret that I shall no more be able to look upon them as my Constituents.

E. Heneage.[1]

By 1874 the position had again entirely changed. The manufacturers of Lincoln were so disgusted with the Gladstone administration that they encouraged their workmen to vote as they pleased.[2] As a consequence, even Seely's vote was 'greatly reduced by his loss of the foundry influence',[3] while Hinde Palmer's position was hopelessly undermined. The working men gave their votes instead to Edward Chaplin, whose brother Henry was a great favourite at Lincoln because of his magnificent stable. 'Nothing', we are told, 'could have withstood the popularity of Mr. Henry Chaplin.'[4] That he was a Conservative hardly counted. However, in 1880 the position was again what it had been in 1868 and Hinde Palmer was easily returned with Seely. Moreover, when Hinde Palmer died in 1884, he was succeeded by the leading local manufacturer, Joseph Ruston of the great engineering firm of Ruston, Procter and Co. with the full support of the 'foundry influence'.[5]

---

[1] *Lincoln Gazette*, 20 November 1868.
[2] *Stamford Mercury*, 9 April 1880.
[3] *Ibid.*, 6 February 1874.
[4] *Stamford Mercury*, 6 February 1874.
[5] The election results were: 1868 Seely and Palmer unopposed; 1874 Chaplin 2,107, Seely 1,907, Palmer 1,748; 1880 Seely 3,401, Palmer 3,128 Chaplin 2,190; 1884 Ruston 3,234, Hall (C) 2,263.

III

The influence of employers over their own workmen was of such an all-pervading nature that there was rarely any question of bringing direct pressure to bear on them to force them to vote for their masters. The workman would normally vote for his employer because he knew him, because he respected him (or at least regarded him as a symbol of authority), because it was universally expected of him, because the livelihood of so many men depended on the employer that his interests seemed akin to theirs, and not infrequently because employer and employee shared the same political views. Indeed, with some leading manufacturers it was a matter of principle that their workmen should have no pressure brought to bear upon them, yet the result was almost invariably the same. Thus, when a Royal Commission at Norwich in 1869 was investigating the return of J. J. Colman, the Radical mustard manufacturer, in the previous year, and called his manager (an active Liberal) to give evidence, it elicited the following information:

Q. You are the manager of Mr. Colman's works, are you not?
A. Part of the works the pepper and starch.
Q. He has a very large number of men in his employment, has he not?
A. Oh yes; I should think perhaps 800 to 1,000 men.
Q. Did you canvass those men?
A. Not one of them.
Q. Do you mean that you did not ask a single one?
A. I don't believe I asked one single man for his vote; we make it a point not to do so.
Q. How many out of the thousand are voters?
A. That I do not know; I never went through it, and I cannot tell.
Q. You can surely give me some idea of the proportion?
A. I should think there are 400 or 500 voters.
Q. Not more?
A. I should think it was not more; it may be.
Q. Do you know of any influence having been used to induce those men to vote?
A. Never.
Q. Directly or indirectly?
A. Neither one way or the other. I don't believe there is another firm in the city where there is so little influence exercised.

Q. Did some of your men vote for Stracey?
A. Oh, yes, several.
Q. How many out of the 500 voters?
A. I don't know, I am sure; I don't think there was many.[1]

Not infrequently the underlying economic claims of a great manufacturer on his workmen, on the shopkeepers and tradesmen who supplied those workmen, and indirectly on subcontractors and their workmen, were brought out into the open. It was unusual for a manufacturer who became a parliamentary candidate himself to base his campaign on his personal claims, but these claims figured equally prominently with political ones in the minds of his supporters, and sometimes outweighed the political ones altogether. Such was the case in the campaign conducted on behalf of Richard Fothergill, a local iron-master, during the Merthyr Tydvil election of 1868, which has been vividly described by Dr I. G. Jones in a recent and as yet unpublished paper:

> . . . Fothergill unlike any of his fellow-ironmasters, was established as a large employer of labour, in both Aberdare and Merthyr [the two principal parts of the constituency]. In the former valley he was the predominant industrialist, his ironworks and mines extending from Hirwaun to Aberdare and Abernant, stopping short only at Mountain Ash, where the power of Bruce and the sea coal proprietors was predominant. As the owner of the Plymouth Works in Merthyr, which were at this time in as flourishing a condition as the state of trade would allow, he ranked next to Dowlais and Cyfartha in the industrial hierarchy. Potentially, his power in that area was even greater since he owned, and might possibly rehabilitate, the old Penydarven Works. The ever-recurring theme of his supporters was merely a logical extension into a statement of this industrial power in social and political terms. He employed over 4,000 in Aberdare alone: all told more than 20,000 people depended upon him. His Wages Bill was about £1200 weekly:—as it were, a weekly injection of specie without which the society of the valleys would collapse. In political terms the conclusion was clear and not to be argued with: to reject such a pivotal and seminal power would be to commit social suicide. This was an argument which few working men in his employ could possibly fail to appreciate. As one who signed himself 'working-man Elector' wrote, 'it would be a hazardous thing to oppose Mr. Fothergill, for if he took it into his head he could stop all his works

---

[1] [C. 14] p. 354. H.C. (1870). XXXI, 390.

and thereby ruin both the Towns of Merthyr and Aberdare.'[1]
Fothergill as the provider of bread and butter to twenty thousand
souls, the industrial arbiter of Aberdare, at whose bidding whole
works and collieries opened or closed, the man who paid £10,000
per year in rates—this was the figure presented to the electors,
Fothergill as the great and benevolent capitalist.

Unlike the employers of labour, most ground landlords possessed very little direct political influence because their land was
held on long leases. In the past even long leases had had curious
clauses to them, such as that which bound the tenants of the
Duke of Newcastle's Nottingham estate (of which Mr Gladstone
was a trustee) to hold no religious services other than those
of the Church of England,[2] but by the sixties these clauses
were being gradually abandoned. A few optimists thought that
they could continue with old ways. For example, one of Montagu
Corry's correspondents told him in 1874 of an ardent Conservative in East Derbyshire who had 'upwards of forty cottage and
other tenants' dependent upon him, and who intended to make
political conditions before granting new leases: 'The tenant of
his collieries wishes to rent land of him, for the purpose of building 300 cottages; should Mr. Strelley accede to this proposal, it
will be conditional on the cottages being let to men of his own
political views.'[3] Lord Londonderry appears to have insisted on
similar conditions at Seaham Harbour, but there can have been
few such cases. Much more typical was the impotence of Lord
Derby, the principal ground landlord of Bury, in Lancashire.
The Derby family was popular in the town, and had provided
most of its amenities including the public buildings and the
market. The rectory, worth £2,240 a year, was in Lord Derby's
gift, and the garrison was something of a Conservative influence.
But most of the millowners were active Liberals and supported
R. N. Philips, brother of the first M.P. for Manchester, who sat
for the town from 1857 to 1859 and from 1859 to 1885, with
results which Lord Derby himself described to Sir William Jolliffe
in 1858:

> The Dissenting interest is very strong in the Town; and most of
> the manufacturers are Radically inclined—so that although 2/3 of

[1] *Aberdare Times*, 21 September 1867.
[2] A. Tilney Basset, *The Life of the Rt. Hon. John Edward Ellis, M.P.*, London 1914,
pp. 28-9.
[3] O. J. Bourne to Corry, 31 March 1874. Disraeli Papers.

the Town belong to me in Fee, and most of the remaining 1/3 to the Rectory as Glebe Land, yet as they are built upon and leased for very long terms, we have never lately been able to return a Conservative.[1]

In a few towns landlord influence was a major factor in elections because the landlord occupied a quite exceptional position. Chester, where the Duke of Westminster possessed sufficient influence to return one member until the borough was disfranchised for corruption in 1881, was the most notable. It had so much the atmosphere of a small town dependent on the neighbouring magnate that when in 1868 the Conservatives found themselves much in the lead they instructed their remaining voters to split their votes between Henry Cecil Raikes, their candidate, and Earl Grosvenor, rather than plumping for Raikes, lest Grosvenor be defeated with incalculable results to the town.[2] Four other towns were in a somewhat similar position: Gateshead, Huddersfield, and Scarborough, which returned Whigs, and Wigan, which not infrequently returned a relative of the Conservative Earl of Crawford and Balcarres.[3] At Gateshead the main influence was that of Sir William Hutt, who had inherited much of the Bowes estate from his wife. Huddersfield was largely owned by the Ramsden family, who gave their support to E. A. Leatham, and Scarborough was dominated by the Johnstone family, one of whom represented the borough from 1832 to 1837 and from 1841 to 1881.

Occasionally the influence of a great landlord appeared in much less direct forms, with curious results. Thus the Marquess of Westminster exercised a great deal of personal influence in the city of Westminster, for which his nephew, Captain Grosvenor, was returned in 1865, and when he stood again in 1868, Gladstone sent the chairman of his committee a letter commending him to the electors in the following terms:

---

[1] Earl of Derby to Sir William Jolliffe, 9 April 1858. Hylton Papers.

[2] H. St J. Raikes. *The Life and Letters of Henry Cecil Raikes*, London 1898, p. 70. There was probably also some fear of a petition on the part of Raikes's supporters whose hands were not clean. In 1880 the Liberals spent £6,191 and the Conservatives £3,843; of which £2,857 of the Liberal money and £718 of the Conservative was corrupt expenditure. *Ibid.*, pp. 153-4.

[3] A member of the Lindsay family sat for Wigan 1820-31, 1845-57, 1859-66, and 1874-80. After 1885 the family represented one of the county divisions instead; the twenty-seventh Earl sat for the Chorley division, 1895-1913, and the twenty-eighth Earl for the Lonsdale division, 1924-40.

Captain Grosvenor, who was first recommended to us by the connection of his family with the city, and by the cordial and deserved respect in which they are held, has shewn himself to be an able and faithful representative, whom his constituents might well have chosen from his personal merits and ability alone.[1]

Captain Grosvenor himself struck the same note at the declaration of the poll.

Three years ago they had taken him in trust as a member of a Liberal and a respected family. He was thankful to think that his success was now in some degree connected with faithful service in the past.[2]

IV

Although there was often no need for employers to bring direct pressure to bear on their workmen, the right of the master to influence the vote of his servant was frankly accepted, although the extent to which he might carry his influence was a matter of dispute. Some masters made no attempt whatever to influence the votes of their men, either from choice, or because they saw so little of them—as was the case in parts of the mining industry and in most of the building trades—or because the trade union spirit was very strong in the particular works or mill. Others took a very strong line because they felt that unless they did so the men would be corrupted by evil influences. The majority simply expected some deference to their wishes because they thought it natural that working men should look to their 'betters' for guidance. In any case the actual form which employer influence took depended not on the masters but on the managers, foremen and overlookers who were usually, although by no means invariably, of the same political complexion as their employers. These, like the staff of the firm's offices, were chosen not only for their managerial skill but also for their general sympathy with their employer's point of view.

Even the best type of employer, who regarded his employment as a trust, often applied the most curious tests of fitness, the effect of which was not very different from that of open political discrimination. Thus we read of I. and R. Morley, the hosiery

---

[1] Gladstone to Dr Brewer, 21 July 1868, from a circular in the Bishopsgate Institute.
[2] *Standard*, 19 November 1868.

manufacturers, whose head was Samuel Morley, the nonconformist philanthropist:

> In taking young men into his house, the chief inquiries made were, whether they were men of sterling moral character as well as of business qualifications. There was no question raised as to whether they made profession of Christianity—the only question ever put was to ascertain whether they were Protestant, as Mr. Morley would not, for the sake of the others, allow a Roman Catholic to come amongst them lest he should—as in duty bound—seek to propagate the tenets of his Church.[1]

Local politicians usually assumed for practical purposes that the larger mills in a town were close preserves of the master, and thought it was no more odd to negotiate with him than with a landlord in the country about the votes of those dependent on him. It was usual to ensure the success of political meetings by persuading one's friends to close their works or mills in order that their men might be 'enabled' to attend. At Birmingham, for instance, it was the closing of the works by Liberal masters so that their men might take part in a counter-demonstration against a Conservative meeting which led to the notorious Aston riots of 1885.[2] Some manufacturers organised political processions of their workmen, and even armed them with sticks and stones with which to demolish Conservative windows.[3] Others marched their men to the poll after giving them breakfast, in a manner more reminiscent of Ireland than of England.[4]

Because most men worked until late in the evening it was assumed that they must be canvassed at work. Few masters when left to themselves bothered to undertake a formal canvass in addition to making the customary informal enquiries about how their men would vote, and to seeing that suitable posters were put up in the mills, but quite a large proportion of them asked their foremen and overlookers to try to win over the waverers.[5] In some towns the election committees sent each

[1] Edwin Hodder, *The Life of Samuel Morley*, 2 edn., London 1887, pp. 199-200.
[2] J. L. Garvin, *The Life of Joseph Chamberlain*, London 1932, I, 477.
[3] For such a case at Gravesend see H.C. 352, pp. 162f. (1868-9). VIII, 162f.
[4] For a case of this type, again at Gravesend, see H.C. 337-Sess. 2, pp. 47-8 (1880). LVII, 115-16.
[5] One witness before the Hartington Committee said in 1869 of Stalybridge: 'The overlookers and managers of the different mills have gone round to the men under them and canvassed them, and told them how they must vote; told them they must vote in the way that they wished them to do'—and this on both sides. H.C. 352, p. 89 (1868-9). VIII, 89.

employer a list of electors over whom he might have influence and asked him to make a return showing how they would vote.[1] The Blackburn Conservative committee in 1868 rashly went a stage beyond this and issued a special circular asking every manager, overlooker, and tradesman, and any other person having influence, to use their exertions to return the Conservative candidates.[2] Unfortunately for the committee, there was something like a reign of terror in several mills after this, the responsibility more of foremen and ordinary workmen than of the masters, and the circular was held to be proof that the foremen were acting as agents of the Conservative members, who were accordingly unseated. Such cases enable one to understand why the Conservative working men of Ashton were so apprehensive in the same year, although the great majority of Liberal masters had made it clear that they would not dismiss workmen who voted against their wishes.[3] Nor is it altogether surprising that there was a certain amount of cynicism in Stalybridge at the efforts of the mayor, a prominent Liberal, to be 'non-political' during his term of office, when his partner was all the time an active Liberal and his mill was placarded with Liberal posters.[4]

So widely recognised was the right of an employer to influence his workmen's vote, that before the Ballot Act the employees of local authorities were often regarded as if they were employed by a Liberal or Conservative master. In some towns it was even believed that corporation officials chose their workmen on political grounds. At Ashton the Conservatives were sure that all the men employed on public works after the Cotton Famine were forced to vote Liberal if they did not wish to be dismissed before their mates when the scale of the works was reduced, but they were probably quite wrong in thinking so.[5] On the other hand the Carlisle corporation seems on the face of things to have encouraged the appointment of Liberals to posts in its gift. In 1868 when there were thirty-five Liberals and only five Conservatives on the council and the city treasurer, the city surveyor,

---

[1] *Ibid.*, p. 106.
[2] *3 Hansard* CXCIV, 1483.
[3] The Ashton Conservatives attributed their fears to reports that there had been, or were to be, wholesale dismissals at Hibbert and Platt's works in Oldham. It afterwards transpired that these fears were groundless, and John Bright reported that at least 400 of Hibbert and Platt's men had voted Conservative, although the head of the firm, John Platt, was one of the Liberal candidates. H.C. 352, p. 107 (1868-9). VIII, 107.
[4] *Ibid.*, p. 158.   [5] *Ibid.*, pp. 101f.

and the rate collector were Liberals, twenty-three or twenty-four of the municipal scavengers voted Liberal and only five Conservative. Similarly, at the municipal gasworks eight men voted for the single Conservative candidate, whereas twenty-one voted for both Liberals and three others plumped for one of the Liberal candidates.[1]

Every responsible politician knew that intimidation was as reprehensible in the towns as it was in the counties. But the distinction between influence and intimidation was difficult to draw, and there can be no doubt that in England at least cases of open intimidation were far from rare. Moreover, they were magnified in the minds of many of the voters themselves until they looked for intimidation everywhere. 'Many a workman imagines intimidation that was never intended', said the Home Secretary in 1869, 'but his fear is none the less real to himself.'[2] Very few workmen were prepared to speak of employer influence in the neutral tones of a witness from Carlisle before the Hartington Committee. 'I find it in this way', he said, 'that wherever the master's opinions are pretty well known, the men generally go with him.'[3] A much more typical reaction was that of the Conservative agent from Ashton, who was very conscious that the majority of the local millowners were Liberals. 'I will not call it intimidation, but from the position of the masters, and from the nature of the voting by the persons residing on their premises or working in their mills, there is some kind of influence which you can only account for on the principle of undue influence. . . .'[4]

Three undoubted cases of intimidation will demonstrate how far some employers or their managers were inclined (albeit in exceptional circumstances) to carry their influence.[5] The first is from Ashton in 1868. After the 'Murphy riots' of 1867-8 had shown

[1] H.C. 352, p. 540. (1868-9). VIII, 540.
[2] 3 *Hansard* CXCIV, 652.
[3] H.C. 352, p. 539 (1868-9). VIII, 539.
[4] *Ibid.*, p. 101.
[5] I leave aside isolated cases of intimidation of an unsystematic nature which are impossible to deal with in general terms. They included threats of eviction from work and home, and miscellaneous threats like that in the following extract from a letter sent to an elector in Burton-on-Trent. 'However, if you persist in your intention of voting for Popery, you must excuse my stating that I intend to remove my money from your property, and place it where it can assist Conservatism and Protestantism, and therefore request that within fourteen days you will pay to me about 8*l*. 16*s*., being the amount of interest due; and also, as it will be needful to offer the property for sale by auction, whether you have any choice as to the auctioneer.' (*Law Times*, 31 October 1868.)

that the Liberals were by no means supreme, a number of Liberal millowners apparently made up their minds to put down all opposition, simply by dismissing men who were politically unreliable. The Conservatives set up a special fund to lend assistance to the alleged victims in Ashton and in Stalybridge, of whom thirty-eight received relief.[1] The most flagrant intimidation took place in the mills of one Oldham Whittaker, who discharged some forty of his eight hundred men for their vote and made no secret of the fact.[2] He also adopted the near-universal custom of the town and ostentatiously withdrew his custom from his Tory ironmonger.[3] Moreover, no sooner were his actions denounced to the Hartington Committee than a notice appeared in one of his mills which read as follows:[4]

Election of Members of the Local Board.

As the masters in these mills pay all the rates of tenants living in their cottages, it is expected that they will vote for the persons nominated by Mr. Whittaker; the other workpeople are requested to do the same.

By order; Hurst Mills,
April 12th, 1869.

The interest of the other two cases of intimidation lies in the fact that the employer involved was a limited company—the London and North-Western Railway—and not an individual employer. Railway companies as such had no political interests, and most boards of directors were ready to pass resolutions asserting their neutrality, and even to order the erection of posters assuring their employees that they might vote as they pleased.[5] In practice, however, few railway companies could avoid some involvement in local politics, both because they were the largest ratepayers in the country, and because their workmen tended to look to them for guidance. Moreover, as the cases of Harwich and Cricklade have already indicated, a railway town tended to seek railway directors as its members, if only as a form of safeguard

---

[1] H.C. 352, p. 99 (1868-9). VIII, 99.

[2] *Ibid.*, pp. 102-7. Whittaker was the only employer of any importance in Hurst, a suburb of Ashton. His private chapel and family memorials are still the most prominent feature of St John's Church there.

[3] *Ibid.*, pp. 109-110.

[4] *Ibid.*, p. 107.

[5] The North Eastern Railway issued a notice to this effect in 1868, but in Carlisle, at least, it was ignored; *ibid.*, p. 368. The Great Eastern decided to do the same but changed its mind later: MS. Minutes of 7 and 20 August 1868.

against a possible removal of railway yards or workshops to another town. The railway vote was even sufficiently important, after the ordinary railwayman had been enfranchised in 1867, to engage the attention of George Grenfell Glyn, the Liberal Chief Whip, whose father was a leading figure in the railway world.[1] He made it his deliberate policy to approach unfriendly boards of directors, in order to secure formal resolutions of neutrality, and did his best, although unavailingly, to oust Sir Daniel Gooch from Cricklade.[2]

The boards of directors of the railway companies had very little corporate political influence, because they rarely interfered with the management of their lines, and because the directors did not all belong to the same party. The directors of the bigger companies did not even enjoy the influence that they might have obtained had they taken an active interest in appointments to the railway staff: most of them were afraid that they would be inundated with applications if they did so, and Sir Henry Tyler, of the Great Eastern, once commented: 'Of course directors have applications from men to recommend them for employment, and they might send in their names to the officers, but any director who asks, as a favour, to have any man employed is a fool. . . .'[3] The directors of the smaller companies were in a rather different position, since they had much greater knowledge of their lines, but few of them were clearly identified with the actual management except in unusual circumstances, such as those which prevailed in Carlisle, where the old Lancaster and Carlisle line had been absorbed by the London and North-Western Railway,

[1] George Carr Glyn was chairman of the London and North-Western Railway, and afterwards of the Railway Clearing House. His son, George Grenfell Glyn, who succeeded him as 2nd Lord Wolverton in 1873, also held the latter post. The railwaymen's votes were not used only by the directors. In 1880 the railwaymen's trade union took an interest in elections and there was considerable pressure on candidates for constituencies where there was a big railway vote to support a bill giving railwaymen compensation for accidents: cp. *Railway Times*, 3 April 1880.

[2] George Howell, the secretary of the Reform League, was deputed by Glyn to act in the matter. He reported to him on 30 September 1868 (Howell Letter Book, Bishopsgate Institute):

I have been to Swindon and intend setting things all right with the railway men there. But it is most desirable that a minute should be passed by the Directors similar to that passed by the Bristol and Exeter. If this be done not only can you secure one seat but two by a majority that would astonish you. Some say 700.

If you can get this minute passed do so at once and I will call a meeting of the Railway men at which meeting the decision of the Directors shall be made known.

Even the refusal of the Board to pass such a resolution will do great good.

[3] H.C. 227-Sess. 2, p. 114 (1880). LVIII, 178.

and the railway officials regarded the local directors as their chief safeguard against the encroachments of Crewe. The railways owed their peculiar political flavour not to their directors but to their administrative staffs. The managers, engineers and foremen who controlled the actual operation of the lines, unless specifically requested not to do so, thought it their duty to direct the railway vote in such a way as seemed to them best for the company, just as so many other employers of labour were in the habit of doing.

By the sixties the biggest railway in the country, the London and North-Western, whose main lines ran from Euston to Birmingham, Liverpool, and Manchester, was usually classed as Conservative in politics. It possessed in common with the Great Western a tradition of strong chairmen who exercised an almost despotic sway over the general policy of the line, and Sir Richard Moon, who was chairman from 1861 to 1891, was essentially a Conservative. He issued no directives to his subordinates on political issues, unless he did so informally, but he ostentatiously ignored the implications of the regular canvasses by Conservative candidates conducted with the approval of local officials, while Liberal requests in 1868 that he should ask the board to issue a declaration of the company's political neutrality were met as if they were an attempt to interfere with the administration of the line. He simply announced, after consulting the board, that no such declaration was necessary, and declined to do anything more.[1]

What happened at the Carlisle workshops of the company in 1868 may be taken as a characteristic result of Moon's attitude.[2] The Lancaster and Carlisle railway which terminated at Carlisle had formerly been an independent line, with its own workshops and board of directors. The growth of Crewe and the standardisation of equipment over the whole of the company's lines threatened to render the Carlisle workshops superfluous, so that it was natural for the local management to enlist themselves as supporters of an influential local director, William Nicholson Hodgson, who had been a director of the old independent company, and who was M.P. for Carlisle at intervals between 1847 and 1868, when he was defeated in the city but

[1] H.C. 352, p. 368 (1868-9). VIII, 368. There is nothing in the minutes of the board of directors for this period to indicate that the question was in fact raised at a board meeting.
[2] The evidence for what follows is in H.C. 352, pp. 367-72 and 535-47 (1868-9). VIII, 367-72, 535-47.

was elected for East Cumberland. Hodgson, a Conservative, was a member of an old Carlisle family, had been mayor in 1834, and took a considerable interest in the railway, so much so that his recommendations for employment were apparently more than usually acceptable to the company's officials. Curiously enough, the leading Liberal candidate after 1859, Sir Wilfrid Lawson, was a director of the Maryport and Carlisle Railway, whose employees voted solidly Liberal.

At the general election of 1865 the political alignments of the two railways were already established, and we owe our knowledge of what happened in 1868 to the fact that Hodgson's margin over Lawson in 1865 was that of the L.N.W.R. vote— 'the railway screw' the Liberals called it. The Reform Act increased the L.N.W.R. vote from 30 to 154 and naturally the Liberals were alarmed. As it happened the railway officials also had grounds for anxiety, although for a different reason. They had caught wind of a proposal to reduce the Carlisle establishment, and canvassed for Hodgson in 1868 with great energy, presumably in an effort to win a friend on the board. A number of men who had been hitherto known as Liberals were 'talked over', and great pressure was put on the rest. To cap it all, the superintendent determined to secure the presence of Hodgson, who had deliberately avoided attending the workshops lest he be accused of intimidating the railwaymen. In the end he agreed to come, although much against his better judgement. The officials seized this chance, called for a show of hands and cheers when they had the dissidents in the superintendent's office, and secured the reluctant adherence of most of the waverers.

It is doubtful whether Hodgson himself was aware of the effects of his canvass, but the Liberal railwaymen drew the obvious conclusion. As one of them put it:

> I believe Mr. Hodgson, as a gentleman, canvassed them fairly; he sought to do the best he could for himself and for his party, and I do not know that in any case he used any undue influence apart from the consideration of his being present at all in the works; that in my opinion, and in the opinion of many others, was sufficient of itself; ... I do not say that there was anything unfair in Mr. Hodgson endeavouring to secure votes for himself; but you see the influence he carried with him in visiting the works as a director.'[1]

[1] H.C. 352, p. 543 (1868-9). VIII, 543.

Possibly the superintendent's zeal was not all self-interested—he was so keen for Hodgson's victory that he held back until after the election the official notification of the impending reduction of staff when it finally came from Crewe. But it was effective: of the 154 men who voted, 136 voted for Hodgson, 3 for Hodgson and a Liberal, and only 15 for both the Liberals.[1]

Immediately after the election the reductions were undertaken. All those who had voted Liberal in the department selected for reduction, five in all, were discharged, along with seventeen others. The Liberals protested furiously, and brought the case before the Hartington Committee, and before the annual meeting of the railway shareholders,[2] although rather pointlessly, since Hodgson had been defeated and had moved to the county. The whole episode ended on a curious note, with the L.N.W.R. superintendent organising a counter-protest of Liberal and Conservative workmen, who were ordered to testify that they had been subjected to no undue pressure.[3]

At Crewe, the setting for our other example of railway politics, the railway workshops drifted into politics after the town had become a borough in 1877 because of their position as the main avenue of employment.[4] After the first municipal elections the Chief Mechanical Engineer at Crewe, F. W. Webb, discovered that there were no railway officials on the council. He was, reasonably enough, put out by the apparent slight to the source of the town's existence and prosperity, and thought that the company should have some means of watching over its interests. At the elections held in the following year, the Liberals, who had a substantial majority on the council, met his objections by running three 'Independent Railway Company' candidates, who were all elected. In the course of the elections, however, Webb issued a statement which contained the ominous remark that 'if the people of Crewe do not study the Company's interest, I shall not be responsible for what the directors will do in reference to

---

[1] The voting in 1865 had been: plumpers for Hodgson 27, splits between Hodgson and a Liberal 2. *Ibid.*, p. 368.

[2] In reply to Sir Wilfrid Lawson, Moon, as Chairman of the L.N.W.R., 'said that the matter might be dropped; the board had never noticed such matters. He hoped that Sir Wilfrid Lawson and other members of Parliament would attend to interests of the company in the House.' *Herepath's Railway Journal*, 27 February 1869.

[3] H.C. 352, p. 544 (1868-9). VIII, 544.

[4] For a fuller account of Crewe politics see W. H. Chaloner, *Social and Economic Development of Crewe 1780-1923*, Manchester 1950, Ch. VI.

putting on the rates.'[1] In 1880 he went a stage further, and after much prompting from the Conservatives, formed a committee of works foremen to promote the return of the company's officials as Independents, allied, of course, with the Conservatives. The result was that by 1885 there was an 'Independent' majority on the council which held control until 1891. By then, Webb's position had been rendered untenable by the consistent victimisation of all those who declined to accept the management's policy. The directors at last intervened, shortly before Moon's final retirement, and the whole policy of intervention was abandoned along with any claims to control the votes of the railwaymen.

[1] Chaloner, *Social and Economic Development of Crewe*, Manchester, p. 146. 'Putting on the rates' appears to imply dismissing men whose maintenance would have to be paid for out of the rates while they were unemployed: cp. 'to put on the parish'.

Chapter Five

THE BIG TOWNS IN 1868

I

THE agricultural counties and small market towns belonged to a different world from that of the larger provincial and industrial centres. In the countryside of Cranford and Barchester and Eatanswill, custom and traditional allegiances counted for everything, and even the village Radicals, the Felix Holts, belonged to an essentially rural pattern. In the industrial districts each big town had its own character, shaped by its particular industry and its industrial magnates, to which it persistently clung, but the atmosphere was one of bustle and of change. The successful capitalist who was visibly building a new society, the young man bent on making a career for himself, were as much the symbols of urban England as the tradition of log cabin to White House was of rural America. Moreover, while most of rural England remained loyal to the Church of England, much of industrial England was committed either to indifference, or to dissent, and with it to an attack on privilege in Church and state. Thus, although some Conservatives looked to the big towns for support, there is no doubt that their whole pattern of life inclined the latter to a militant Liberalism or to Radicalism. The *Radical Programme* of 1885 had good reason to proclaim that its message was that of the towns.

> The great towns as they now are, constitute the source and centre of English political opinion. It is from them that Liberal legislation receives its initiative; it is the steady pressure exercised by them that guarantees the political progress of the country.[1]

The Conservatives were gravely handicapped in the towns by their association in the public mind with aristocratic exclusiveness, with the privileges of the Church of England, and with hostility to industry and free trade. And before 1867 there was little they could do to disarm popular prejudice except in Liverpool,

[1] *Radical Programme*, London 1885, p. 5.

Birkenhead, Preston and Belfast, where there was a strong Conservative tradition, and in some of the older towns like Nottingham and Norwich, which were more or less open to the highest bidder. There is even a certain amount of truth in the gibe that the Conservatives won borough elections only by bribery.

> The expedient adopted by the Conservative party was simply this: the counties were left to take care of themselves, and the boroughs were fought by bribery. Enormous sums were spent in corrupting the electorate, and a candidate who was not prepared to 'make a good splash' had no chance whatever.[1]

Nor was the position much better after 1867. The only changes of any importance were the growth of Conservative support in the South-East Lancashire boroughs, and the emergence of a Conservative majority in the Cities of London and Westminster and in Greenwich.[2]

Before 1867 politics meant to the ordinary elector in most of the big towns very much what they did to his counterpart in the smaller ones: the opportunity to vote for one of several candidates, who either offered themselves to the electors uninvited, or were put up by the local party managers. In either case the candidate's chances of success depended on the amount of money that he was prepared to spend and on the weakness of his opponents, rather than on the support of a popular association. Sometimes the local party managers called themselves a committee or an association, and on the Liberal side there was often both a Whig and a Radical committee, but, whatever their name, all these committees and associations were in fact self-perpetuating oligarchies of subscribers to a registration fund, who managed the constituency with the aid of a registration agent.

---

[1] H. E. Gorst, *The Earl of Beaconsfield*, London 1900, p. 125. The importance of Harold Gorst's remarks, more of which are quoted in subsequent chapters, are that they reflect the (rather jaundiced) views of his father, Sir John Gorst, for many years election manager to the Conservative party. While he was writing his book, Harold Gorst was private secretary to his father at the Education Department of the Privy Council and an occasional writer in the press.

[2] The figures for towns with a population in 1871 of more than 50,000 (in the whole of the United Kingdom) were as follows:

	Liberal seats	Conservative seats	Home Rule seats	Total seats
1865	78	22	—	100
1868	89	25	—	114
1874	68	44	2	114
1880	87	24	3	114

Once a year the members addressed their constituents and occasionally there would be meetings of Liberal electors. But the only opportunity for the poorer elector or the non-elector to discuss political questions was afforded by organisations which did not exist primarily for party purposes: friendly societies, chapels, sectarian organisations like the Liberation Society, temperance societies, and public-house clubs of trade unionists, Radicals or Tories.

After 1867 the whole shape of electioneering and of party organisation in the big towns began to change. Men came to think of a party, not in terms of individual candidates and party committees, but in terms of a core of party members of all classes in every constituency, united in pursuit of common aims, acting as canvassers in the wards, and meeting together regularly to discuss current political questions, to elect their officers, and to choose parliamentary candidates. This change took place in three main stages. The first, which lasted from 1867 to 1876, was primarily a transitional stage: the old self-perpetuating committees still survived, but they were supplemented by party clubs and working-men's associations and took a new interest in municipal elections. During this period, too, the provincial press, which had been freed of tax in 1855, obtained a new influence and authority. The second stage overlapped the first and lasted from 1870 to 1879. During this time John Gorst did his best to establish Conservative associations all over the country, while on the Liberal side there was a resurgence of anti-party, or sectarian, pressure groups on the model of the Anti-Corn-Law League. The third stage, which began about 1876, was characterised by the formation of effective 'popular' associations of electors, the triumph of party feeling over sectarianism, and the emergence of the National Liberal Federation. During this period, which lasted until 1886, first the Liberals and then the Conservatives developed the forms of party organisation which became general in the late eighties and which have, after some modification, lasted ever since.

II

Almost everywhere the 1868 election was fought on an *ad hoc* basis by an organisation specially formed or adapted for the purpose by the old party leaders. But there was, particularly among the Liberals, a new readiness to conciliate the working classes, and to make concessions to working-class organisations on questions of organisation and in the choice of candidates. The extent of these concessions naturally determined the form of the party machinery for the election. In Birmingham, where a new Liberal Association had been formed in 1866, the existing machinery was already adequate, but a more vigorous leadership was called for to make it effective. In Manchester, where the Whig and Radical sections of the party had united in 1867, under the name of the United Liberal Party, to return one Whig and one Radical M.P., an agreement was made with the local working-class organisations to adopt as a third candidate a nominee of the working men, Ernest Jones.[1] In Leeds there was a three-way bargain between the old official Liberals, the Radical Association, and the working-class organisations, to adopt the sitting Whig member (Edward Baines), and an advanced Radical (Alderman R. H. Carter) acceptable to the working men. Other towns followed the example of little Whitby (one member), where, although W. H. Gladstone enjoyed the support of all sections of the party, there were two separate committees, one middle-class and the other working-class.[2]

In towns with strong Radical traditions shrewd leadership often enabled the old party leaders to conciliate the new electors with only formal concessions. At Stockport the Liberal leaders accepted the advice of one of their members, J. B. Smith, that they should go out of their way to encourage the new electors to attend party meetings.

> We are entering upon a political phase as it appears to me wh. will require some prudence & tact to guide. 5 or 6000 voters who have never before exercised the franchise have suddenly obtained it & taking it for granted that the majority have liberal tendencies they are likely to be somewhat jealous of any assumed control over their actions & opinions. The old reform voters are only 6 or 700 represented by the Reform Assn. Nothing would suit the Tory tactics better than any false move which would enable them to raise the cry of reform room dictation: allow me therefore to suggest that you be careful to avoid this rock . . . and suggest whether it would not be better to invite the co-operation of the newly enfranchised liberals, to hear their opinions & wishes before you decide on what Candidates the Liberals should invite to represent them. By this course you might secure united action as no one could justly complain & an immense amount of trouble & agitation in the election

---

[1] See pp. 310-11, below.   [2] Reform League Report: Whitby.

would be saved by thus uniting voters of all classes in one common object.[1]

Very few Liberal committees followed the example of Bristol and Blackburn and encouraged the Reform League to send its agents from London to help them.

The dangers of ignoring the working men altogether were strikingly demonstrated at Dewsbury. The management of the Liberal party there was in the hands of a committee which had been formed before the borough was enfranchised in 1867 to fight county elections.[2] Its members were advanced Radicals, but in choosing a candidate they made the fatal blunder of not consulting the working-class organisations or the Whigs. Their choice fell on Handel Cossham, a well-known Bristol Radical who had Bright's support, and would in most circumstances have been welcomed by the working men. But the Trades Council had already been working quietly for six months on behalf of Ernest Jones, the former Chartist, and Cossham's adoption, without any pretence at consultation on the part of the Liberal leaders, decided them to bring his name forward publicly. Great meetings were held on Jones's behalf, a canvass was entered upon, and every preparation (apparently in part Tory financed) was made for a hot contest. In September 1868, however, Jones decided to accept an invitation to stand for Manchester, and in his farewell address and in subsequent statements suggested that his followers should support Cossham.[3] By then it was too late to end the split, and the working men soon found themselves another candidate in Serjeant Simon, a leading Jewish barrister,[4] who secured the

---

[1] J. B. Smith to Alderman Barr, 16 July 1868. J. B. Smith's Papers, Manchester Central Library, MS. 923.2/S. 341, f.93.

[2] The account which follows is taken from the columns of the *Manchester City News*, *Manchester Guardian*, *Leeds Mercury*, and *Dewsbury Reporter*.

[3] *Manchester City News*, 12 September 1868.

[4] For his legal career see *D.N.B.* He represented Dewsbury from 1868 to 1888. His opponents at first accused him of being a Tory in disguise, but he countered the accusation with a letter from the secretary of the Liberal Registration Association which admitted his *bona fides* (*Leeds Mercury*, 31 August 1868). However, he certainly had so much Conservative support in 1874 that a Conservative candidate refused to fight because the voters were already committed (W. W. Bean, *Parliamentary Representation of the Six Northern Counties of England*, Hull 1890, p. 803). Simon's position could never, of course, be an orthodox nonconformist one like Cossham's, and he took a peculiarly independent line on questions of foreign policy: in December 1879, for instance, he attacked Gladstone for his attitude towards the Jews, particularly in Germany and Eastern Europe, whom Gladstone, along with other Liberals, had denounced as favouring Turkish supremacy in the Balkans. He even warned him that the Jews might be driven to secede from the Liberal party 'to which three-fourths

support of George Potter and managed to win the seat by a comfortable majority.

III

In many ways the most interesting experiments of the 1868 election were not those made by the ordinary party managers, but those of unorthodox politicians who hoped that the new constituencies would be more friendly to novel electioneering devices than the old.[1] The best-known experiment had already been inaugurated by John Stuart Mill in 1865 in the hope of securing greater independence of members and a reduction in the cost of electioneering. When he stood for Westminster he declined to canvass or to spend money, and refused to hide his heterodox views, but was none the less returned.[2] At the same election Mill's blind disciple, Henry Fawcett, carried out a similar experiment at Brighton and was elected without the aid of paid agents or canvassers, and without holding any meetings in public-houses.[3] Both stood on the same terms in 1868, but although Fawcett was re-elected, Mill lost his seat. Their attitude was also shared in part by W. E. Forster, who resolutely advocated the view that no man should be allowed to stand between the candidate (or member) and the electors as a whole, and that party managers who tried to do so were dangerous. In 1868 his supporters at Bradford persuaded him to coalesce with Edward Miall, but he did so only with the greatest reluctance. 'I should have had probably no committee at all, certainly only a few gentlemen, and I should have thrown myself generally on the constituency . . .', he told an election court in 1869.[4]

The second experiment involved what is now called a primary

of them belong' (*The Times*, 22 December 1879). In both 1874 and 1880 Simon's old enemies, the Liberal Association, unsuccessfully put up a candidate against him, but he was by then sure of popular support. In 1879 the association was reorganised on the Birmingham plan, but Simon still refused to recognise it, spoke against it in much the same terms as Forster had used at Bradford (*The Times*, 6 October 1879), and demonstrated its ineffectiveness in 1880 by defeating both its candidate and a Conservative. It is significant that in 1880 Simon's Liberal opponent was adopted on the vote of only 156 electors (*Dewsbury Reporter*, 28 February 1880).

[1] Proportional representation was much discussed at this time, not only by J. S. Mill and his disciples, but also by the working-class politicians of the Reform League; but its advocates' only real success was in the adoption of the cumulative vote for school board elections in 1870. The minority clause in the 1867 Reform Act was generally denounced by the advocates of P.R. as a bogus device.

[2] J. S. Mill, *Autobiography*, World's Classics edn, pp. 239-40.

[3] Leslie Stephen, *Life of Henry Fawcett*, 3 edn, London 1886, p. 242.

[4] H.C. 28, p. 194 (1868-9). XLVIII, 896.

election, but which was known at the time as a 'trial ballot', for the selection of Liberal candidates. This seemed on the face of things to solve most of the problems of candidate selection without calling for a complicated local organisation, since it gave all Liberals a share in the choice of candidates. But the trial ballot was soon shown to be of little practical value both on account of its expense and because of the indiscipline and corruption in the Liberal ranks, and by 1870 it had been thoroughly discredited. It is difficult to be sure how many trial ballots were actually held or when the idea of holding them became popular. As far back as the 1830s there was talk of trial ballots, and an unofficial poll was taken in Bolton as a result of the unpopularity of one of the members, Peter Ainsworth, but the idea does not seem to have been applied to a big constituency before 1867. Between 1867 and 1870 there were, however, five important trial ballots at Maryport, Stafford, Sunderland, Manchester and Bristol.

The most successful trial ballot took place in Manchester immediately after the 1868 election. At the general election two of the three Liberal candidates, Sir Thomas Bazley and Jacob Bright, had been returned, but the third, Ernest Jones, had been defeated by a Conservative. The Liberals immediately petitioned against the return of the latter (Hugh Birley), on the ground that his firm held a number of government contracts, and fully expected to unseat him. To make sure that there should be no division in the Liberal ranks at the by-election which would then take place, the Liberal Committee resolved to hold a trial ballot. At this the candidates were Ernest Jones and T. Milner Gibson, a former member for the borough who had been President of the Board of Trade under Palmerston and Russell. All electors who had voted for the Liberal candidates at the general election, and other avowed Liberals, were eligible to vote, and most of the former were sent an identification card by post, which they exchanged for a voting paper at the polling booth.[1] Polling took place in forty-one booths and extended over two days, at a cost to the party of something over £400. 11,475 of the 18,000 persons entitled to vote (62 per cent) actually voted, giving Ernest Jones a large majority. The result was unexpected, but the party managers were so pleased with the smooth functioning of the arrangements for the ballot that they despatched the chairman of the

[1] H.C. 352, pp. 521-30 (1868-9). VIII, 521-30.

committee responsible to give evidence on behalf of the 'Manchester system' to the Hartington committee, which was investigating different systems of conducting elections by ballot. This appearance must, however, have been their only consolation, as their hopes were dashed soon afterwards: Ernest Jones died, and the Select Committee appointed to consider Birley's case decided that he was not disqualified from sitting.

The weakness of the trial ballot as a means of settling disputes between Liberal candidates was clearly demonstrated at Sunderland, a town which had a long history of wrangling between 'Whigs' and Radicals going back to 1832. The immediate background of the trial ballot was a three-cornered contest at the general election of 1865 between Henry Fenwick and John Candlish, Liberals, and James Hartley, Conservative, in which Fenwick and Hartley were successful, and a by-election in February 1866 when Candlish defeated Fenwick, who had sought re-election on taking office as a Lord of the Admiralty. Candlish, a local shipowner, was certain to be re-elected at the general election, but the fate of the third seat was in doubt between two new Liberal candidates, Edward Gourley, another shipowner who had been twice mayor, and T. C. Thompson, a landowner and colliery proprietor. Both were Radicals, and both had the support of a cross-section of the party. Indeed, Thompson, although the candidate of the old 'Whig' connection, was supported by the secretary of the Reform League and other working-class Radicals. Attempts were made to secure a compromise, and eventually the two candidates agreed to put their claims before the Liberal electors at a trial ballot, towards the cost of which each side put down £75. According to the report made by the Reform League's agents all went well until halfway through the day of the poll, when Thompson's supporters discovered, or claimed to have discovered, a number of forged 'test papers', and forthwith repudiated the poll. Their figures gave Gourley 3,271 votes and Thompson only 419.[1] Oddly enough, however, the local newspapers suggest that both sides took fright at the last moment at the thought that the ballot might be rigged, and withdrew with mutual recriminations before the poll could be held.[2] The Reform League sent men down to the borough on two

[1] At the general election Gourley polled 4,901 votes and Thompson 3,596.
[2] *Sunderland Times*, 4, 7 and 11 July 1868.

occasions, but they were unable to reconcile the two opponents. At the general election no Conservative stood, and Gourley won the second seat by a substantial majority, and retained it until 1900.

The Bristol trial ballot, which finally discredited such tests of opinion, took place as the result of the death of the Hon. Francis Berkeley, the celebrated advocate of the ballot, in March 1870.[1] There were three Liberal contenders for his seat, but the real opposition lay between George Odger, supported by the working-class Radicals, and Elisha Smith Robinson, a local councillor, the chosen of the manufacturers and merchants. The trial ballot passed off without much excitement and was won by Robinson; the other candidates withdrew, and he was returned at the by-election. The Conservatives then brought a petition against Robinson's return on the novel ground that the trial ballot had not been pure. They were able to show that one of Robinson's committee, a hide and skin broker, had employed a Tory publican to corrupt voters, and that the man had secured a considerable number of votes. The trial judge remitted the case to the Court of Common Pleas for a ruling on the point of law involved—whether the two elections, the trial ballot and the by-election, were inextricably connected—but the question was hardly in doubt, and Robinson was unseated. Thereafter, except for occasional calls for a trial ballot by eccentrics like Dr Pankhurst at Manchester in 1883,[2] the whole idea was allowed to lapse as impracticable.

IV

Although the 1868 election led to only temporary changes in the management of elections, other changes of the time were more permanent: the foundation of political clubs and Conservative working-men's associations, the rise of the provincial press, and the growth of a new interest in municipal elections.

Before 1867 there were very few clubs, social or political, for ordinary business men, country politicians, or working men. The great London clubs, Brooks's, the Carlton, the Conservative, and the Reform, had no room for City men or for party workers from the provinces who might come up to London on political business.[3] There were no political clubs in the City of London,

---

[1] H.C. 309 (1870). LVI, 179.   [2] *Manchester Examiner and Times*, 29 September 1883.
[3] cp. Earl of Malmesbury, *Memoirs of an Ex-Minister*, one vol. edn, London 1885, p. 579.

and scarcely any party organisation beyond an office and secretary on each side. Neither party made any attempt to provide social facilities for the increasing numbers of business men who required some *pied-à-terre* in the City more comfortable than their office, now that they lived in Kent or Surrey. The position was no better in the provinces. Few of the provincial clubs which had been founded in the thirties and forties on the model of the Carlton and Reform had survived, and those few, like the Eldon Club at Norwich, were too exclusive to be of any political value. Whatever the rules might say, membership was in practice restricted to the leading professional men of the town and those country gentlemen who preferred to spend a few hours in a club on market days rather than in a public-house. Their political influence was often much less than that of the old-fashioned dining clubs which had been in existence since Pitt Clubs flourished at the end of the Napoleonic War, or even longer—clubs like the True Blue Club at Gloucester and John Shaw's Club in Manchester.[1]

In London a new era opened in 1868. Since the foundation of the Conservative Club in 1840, only one major metropolitan political club had been formed, the still-aristocratic Junior Carlton in 1864.[2] Now there was a rush of new building. The City Carlton was formed in 1868, the St Stephen's (a Conservative club near the House of Commons) in 1870, the City Liberal in 1874, the Devonshire (Liberal) in 1875, the Beaconsfield in 1879, the National Liberal in 1882, the Constitutional in 1883, and the City Conservative and the City Constitutional in 1884. Both the National Liberal and the Constitutional were avowedly designed

---

[1] It is difficult to know how many of these old clubs still existed, as most of them were not affiliated to the party offices, and so do not appear in the official lists. For instance, there is only one Pitt Club in the Conservative list for 1874, that at Holbeck near Leeds, although there were undoubtedly more, including the London Pitt Club which still meets as a dining club. John Shaw's Club in Manchester has been in continuous existence as a dining club since 1738, and its history by F. S. Stancliffe (*John Shaw's 1738-1938*, Manchester 1938) is a good example of the use to which the records of these old clubs might be put.

[2] Because so many country gentlemen were Conservatives there was a much greater pressure on the accommodation of the Conservative clubs. Thus, John Bateman gives the following list of the club membership of the great landowners (over 3,000 acres) in 1879. (*Great Landowners*, p. 497.)

Conservative			Liberal		
Carlton	.	. 642	Brooks's	.	. 216
Junior Carlton	.	. 112	Reform	.	. 103
Conservative	.	. 65	Devonshire	.	. 29
St Stephen's	.	. 37			

to provide facilities for provincial politicians, and their example was followed by the last clubs founded during the period, the Primrose (1886), the Junior Constitutional (1887), and the Junior Conservative (1889). Throughout the seventies and eighties the Carlton and Reform also made special efforts to extend their membership to certain classes of provincial politicians who had hitherto found it difficult to enter. The Reform, for instance, altered its rules in 1877 to allow the selection by the committee of two prominent Liberals each year, a provision which was used to admit a number of distinguished provincial and Scottish newspaper editors and poor M.P.s like Thomas Burt.[1] In addition to these there were a number of new clubs, of which the Eighty Club and the Cobden Club were the most important, which were political dining clubs or associations rather than clubs in the ordinary sense, and possessed no club-house. The number of members of the political clubs with club-houses is given in Table II.

Table II. London Political Clubs in 1868 and 1885[2]

Conservative Clubs

1868			1885		
Carlton	. . .	800	Carlton	. . .	1,600
plus peers and M.P.s			Conservative	. .	1,200
Conservative	. .	1,500	Junior Carlton	. .	2,100
Junior Carlton	. .	2,100	City Carlton	. .	1,000
			St Stephen's	. .	1,500
			Beaconsfield	. .	900
			City Conservative	.	1,500
			Constitutional	. .	4,054
			City Constitutional	.	1,500

Liberal Clubs

1868			1885		
Brooks's	. . .	575	Brooks's	. . .	600
Reform	. . .	1,400	Reform	. . .	1,400
			City Liberal	. .	1,150
			Devonshire .	. .	1,500
			National Liberal .	.	4,500

[1] L. Fagan, *The Reform Club*, London 1887, p. 112.

[2] These figures, which are approximate only, are mainly from *Whitaker's Almanack*. In 1904 the maximum permissible membership of the political clubs in London was as follows (those clubs marked with an asterisk are now extinct): *Conservative:* Carlton 1,800, Junior Carlton 2,100, *City Carlton 1,000, *Conservative 1,300, *Junior Conservative 5,500, Constitutional 6,500, *Junior Constitutional 5,500, St Stephen's 1,500, *Primrose (no club-house) 5,000. *Liberal:* Brooks's 650, Reform 1,400, Devonshire 1,200, *City Liberal 900, National Liberal 6,000, Eighty (no club-house) 700. W. J. Fisher, 'Liberal Clubs and the Liberal Party', *Monthly Review*, December 1904, pp. 128-9.

Provincial clubs began to be established in some numbers after 1865, usually without any prompting from London. The Manchester Reform Club, possibly the most influential of all the provincial political clubs, elected its first members in January 1867.[1] The Liverpool Reform Club was opened in 1879, the Manchester Conservative Club in 1876, the Liverpool Conservative Club in 1883, the Scottish Conservative Club at Edinburgh in 1877, and the Glasgow Conservative Club in 1880. A Cobden Club was formed in Leeds in 1865, but it failed three years later, and it was not until 1881 that the Leeds Liberal Club opened its doors, and 1882 when the Leeds and County Conservative Club was established.[2]

The Liberals usually gave their opponents credit for greater acumen in the formation of middle-class clubs, particularly after the secession of the Liberal Unionists in 1886, but consoled themselves (especially if they were teetotallers) with the thought that such clubs were often of no political value. An article in the *Monthly Review* in December 1904, which attempted one of the very few serious discussions of the subject, simply repeated what Liberals had been saying at local party gatherings ever since the seventies, when it remarked that

> no one can have familiarised himself with the working of the average local political club without being struck by its ineffectiveness. What should be a centre of political activity is too frequently a lounge—better than the public-house certainly, but filling no higher place in men's lives—where the drink is probably better, even if it is not cheaper, and cards, billiards, and smoking concerts are the chief attractions.[3]

What the Liberals usually failed to realise was that the numerical inferiority of the Conservatives in most of the big towns before

---

[1] Mills, *Manchester Reform Club*, p. 18.
[2] Their initial membership was as follows:

	Leeds Liberal Club	Leeds and County Conservative Club
Life Members	92	102
Town Members	745	724
Country Members	126	488
	963	1,314

The Liberal Club lost members from 1882, when it had 1,045 members, to 1888; there was then a revival and in 1893 there were 1,502 members, the peak from which the membership declined to 711 members in 1910. The figures are from the reports of the two clubs in the Leeds Central Library.
[3] *Monthly Review*, December 1904, p. 136.

1886 was so marked that they needed a social centre, such as the Liberals could safely dispense with, in which leading Conservatives could meet and feel that they were on friendly ground.[1] It did not even matter that these clubs were primarily social centres, so long as they were centres, and in places like Birmingham and Bradford the Conservative organisations which were gradually developed in the late seventies and early eighties could never have been built up so successfully without them. Moreover, on both sides the clubs were useful meeting places for town councillors and other local politicians, and provided facilities for holding receptions to distinguished guests as well as for holding meetings which were likely to be dwarfed and made uncomfortable by large halls.[2]

Both parties also attempted after 1867 to provide social-cum-political centres for working men in the wards of the larger towns. Where the club movement was strong an attempt was made to set up a club in every ward to act as the party headquarters for the ward, just as the middle-class club was the party headquarters for the town as a whole.[3] The result can still be seen at Bury in Lancashire, where there is a central Conservative club with a three-guinea subscription which acts as an adjunct to the party headquarters nearby, and ward clubs in nearly all the wards with a subscription of between 7s. 6d. and ten shillings. The model for the ward clubs was the public-house, in which trade unions and friendly societies met (with the bar as the chief attraction), but there were also temperance clubs, and Archibald Salvidge, himself a brewery manager, insisted that for local reasons all the Liverpool Conservative clubs should be dry.[4] The great thing, as Captain Middleton explained to a correspondent in 1887, was to keep the facilities as plain and homely as possible.

---

[1] The position was, of course, very different after 1886. For a typical comment on the importance of Conservative Clubs in the earlier years see a speech by Robert Heath, M.P. for Stoke in 1874, quoted by R. T. McKenzie, *British Political Parties*, London 1955, p. 161.

[2] The Manchester Reform Club, for instance, had a special 'corporation table' for councillors and aldermen to dine at, and was much used for political meetings. Mills, *Manchester Reform Club*, pp. 80-1.

[3] The chronology of club-building is an obscure subject, but the following dates for the Bolton Conservative clubs seem fairly typical. Central Conservative Club (£10,000) 1870, Little Lever C.C. 1878, Westhoughton C.C. 1879, West Ward C.C. 1881, Derby Ward C.C. 1882, Halliwell C.C. 1884, Ainsworth C.C. 1886, Moses Gate C.C. 1886, Tonge Moor C.C. 1887. J. Clegg, *Annals of Bolton*, Bolton 1888.

[4] Stanley Salvidge, *Salvidge of Liverpool*, London 1934, p. 16.

Always begin as inexpensively as possible—for a Club, hire a suitable house & get a few friends to guarantee the rent for say 3 years—if funds are not forthcoming furnish as simply as possible on the hire system i.e. paying so much per month—have your subscriptions, Ordinary Members 4/-, Hony Members 10/-, Vice Presidents 20/-, per annum. If possible avoid building & avoid elaborate furniture—the latter simply drives working men out of the place. Clean, bright, rooms, with the means of playing drafts & bagatelle is the chief want . . . all our successes begin in this way—our failures begin in elaborate Club Houses and furniture more suited to a London Club than a working man's home.[1]

In Lancashire it was not uncommon for the party associations to give grants to clubs, and even the Manchester Liberal Association, which believed that the wards should finance their own ventures, began in 1880 to make grants towards the cost of furnishing and maintaining clubs, the latter ostensibly in return for the use of a room as an office at elections.[2] In Salford the Conservative organisation was based entirely on clubs, the ward associations being identical with the ward clubs.[3]

The orthodox party clubs were supplemented by a new type of political club, whose importance was barely recognised at the time and has not been much noticed since. This was the political debating society or local House of Commons, sometimes with a formal constitution and sometimes of that informal sort which Trollope poked fun at when writing in *Ralph the Heir* of Ontario Moggs, the hero of the 'Cheshire Cheese' and the Percycross Young Men's Association. The younger members were zealous for any cause they took up, practised if not elegant speakers with some knowledge of political problems, and usually only too anxious to work for any candidate who sought their aid. The first formally-constituted local House of Commons was formed at Liverpool in 1860, and the movement soon spread to the other big towns. By 1883, when an article on the movement appeared in the *Nineteenth Century*, over 100 towns had local Houses, and

[1] Middleton to Lord St Oswald, 8 March 1887. Chilston Papers. In 1894 Middleton formed the Association of Conservative Clubs to strengthen the club movement.

[2] In May 1880 £20 was given to the Beswick club to cover part of the cost of furniture, and in September of the same year the debts of the St John's Club were paid off. The usual annual grant was £5. From the MS. Minutes of the Manchester Liberal Association.

[3] This is still the case in some constituencies. The Glossop Conservative Club, for instance, is also the Glossop Conservative Association.

there was a total membership of over 35,000.[1] Each House possessed its government and opposition. Twenty-six of the fifty-nine Houses about which there was information had Conservative majorities in 1882, and thirty-three had Liberal majorities. Many of the Houses were by no means composed exclusively of young and uneducated men, and we are told that 'Clergymen, justices of the peace, well-known political figures, persons of local influence, the richer local tradesmen, grave city merchants, are among the prominent amateur legislators . . .'[2] They also very soon became a school for budding politicians who had been debarred by poverty or family tradition from going to one of the older universities. The first of these really to make his name was Sir Edward Clarke, Solicitor-General from 1886 to 1892, whose career at the bar had also been forwarded by a friendly solicitor whom he had met at the Crosby Hall Debating Society. And among other distinguished local parliamentarians were Andrew Bonar Law, who joined the Glasgow parliament in 1879, Rufus Isaacs, later Marquess of Reading, who became a member of the Hampstead parliament in 1892, and William Joynson-Hicks who was a member of local parliaments at Highbury and Bromley in the eighties.[3]

V

In Lancashire and Yorkshire the club movement on the Conservative side became merged with a much older movement, that of the Operative Conservative Societies. These had developed originally in sympathy with Oastler's democratic Toryism in the thirties and forties,[4] and the Wigan Operative Conservative Society actually claimed an unbroken existence since the forties.

---

[1] B. Jerrold, 'On the Manufacture of Public Opinion', *Nineteenth Century*, XIII, 1080. (1883). The membership figures were as follows: Bethnal Green 120, Bradford 800, Brighton 530, Bristol 780, Bury 440, Cardiff 640, Cheetham 410, Derby 500, Dumfries 248, Dundee 350, Eastbourne 220, Edinburgh 680, Glasgow 1,000, Hackney 1,000, Hull 680, Kirkcaldy 265, Lambeth 1,200, Leeds 794, Leicester 400, Liverpool 618, Manchester 1,312, Newcastle-on-Tyne 1,050, Newport 582, Norwich 658, Nottingham 560, Oldham 700, Plymouth 700, Rochdale 300, Scarborough 400, Sheffield 652, Shrewsbury 320, Southwark 300, Stockport 837, Sunderland 651, Swansea 550, Sydenham 6-700, Tottenham 250, Worcester 400.

[2] *Ibid.*, p. 1,086.

[3] D. Walker-Smith and E. Clarke, *The Life of Sir Edward Clarke*, London 1939, p. 44; The Marquess of Reading, *Rufus Isaacs, First Marquess of Reading*, London 1942, I, 55-6 and 69-70; Robert Blake, *The Unknown Prime Minister*, London 1955, pp. 29-30; and H. A. Taylor, *Jix, Viscount Brentford*, London 1933, pp. 19-23.

[4] cp. W. Paul, *History of the Origin and Progress of Operative Conservative Societies*, 2 edn, Leeds 1838; C. Driver, *Tory Radical: The Life of Richard Oastler*, New York 1946.

Such continuity was rare, however, and when the movement was revived in 1867 most of the old associations had disappeared, and there was no opposition to a change of name to that of Conservative Working Men's Associations. But there were occasionally echoes of the old Operative Conservative Societies, as when the Rawtenstall Conservative Industrial Co-operative Society was founded in 1872.

The revival of 1867 was primarily due to a group of young Conservatives in London who were in the habit of assisting the party managers. They formed an association (later known as the National Union) to assist in the promotion of Conservative Working Men's Associations, and Leonard Sedgwick, the first secretary of the National Union, and a number of volunteers spent most of 1868 travelling the country in order to explain how Conservative Working Men's Associations could best be formed. The Union also sponsored a series of pamphlets entitled *Conservative Legislation for the Working Classes*, of which the most influential was on legislation for mines and factories. The new associations were not confined to Lancashire and Yorkshire, where they had become firmly established quite early in the reform crisis of 1866-7, but they were strongest there. Indeed, the new movement was almost a failure in London and the South-West, where it suffered a series of setbacks.[1] However, by 1874 there were at least 150 Conservative Working Men's Associations distributed over 57 boroughs and five counties. A few associations boasted 2,000 members, and the Birmingham Association had as many as 3,000 members by 1868, but the effective membership of most of them was of the order of 100-500.[2] There are so few records of the early life of Conservative Working Men's Associations outside Lancashire that there is no means of knowing whether they developed according to any pattern, but this seems unlikely. Those about which there is information varied enormously among themselves. Some followed the example of the Wigan Operative

[1] The Reform League was so strong in London that it was even for a time able to prevent the Conservatives from holding public meetings in support of the movement, and an inaugural demonstration was deliberately broken up.

[2] Membership figures are hard to come by, even in the official publications and MS. records of the National Union, and most newspaper reports are untrustworthy. The figures given above are 'intelligent guesses', based on a wide reading of newspaper reports. In Lancashire during 1867 and 1868 meetings organised by the local Conservative Working Men's Associations were quite often attended by nearly a thousand working men, and even Ashton-under-Lyne could muster between 600 and 700: *Stockport Advertiser*, 26 April 1867.

Conservative Society and met in public-houses on three or four nights a week. Others met in schools or church halls until they could find a club house.[1] Yet others grew round a club established by the local party leaders. This diversity seems to have been caused by a very general lack of money and by differences in the standard of generosity of middle-class patrons.

The one association directly fostered by the central party managers may perhaps be taken as typical of the better-endowed associations which found it difficult to win supporters in spite of their financial advantages. The London and Westminster Working Men's Constitutional Association was got up partly by the local party leaders in Westminster, headed by W. H. Smith, and partly by a few politically-minded artisans. W. H. Smith, as candidate for the City of Westminster, thought it 'necessary to furnish the Conservative working men of London with an organisation which could bring together all persons sympathising with them without being so heavy a tax upon them as to render it impossible for them to bear the cost of doing it wholly themselves'.[2] The association held meetings in public-houses in different wards of the city and endeavoured to build up an informal membership based as much on good fellowship as on politics, although the officers also sought to establish ward committees and canvassing teams. The fifteen members of the Executive Committee and the officers met weekly in the office of the Westminster Registration Association to co-ordinate their activities and to receive guidance from the party agent. Appropriately enough, their leader, the secretary of the Association, was employed as a smith to keep in order the metal window sashes of the Houses of Parliament.

The objects of the London and Westminster Association were high-flown, 'to unite the friends of constitutional principle in resisting any attempt to subvert the Protestant faith or the Constitution of the Country; to protect the prerogative of the Crown; and to defend the rights and privileges of the People'.[3]

[1] An impecunious Conservative Working Men's Club at Knaresborough met from 1869 to 1881 once a month in the Charity School. Each member was entitled to a pint of beer but no more: [C.2777] p. 9. H.C. (1881). XLII, 9. At Ashton-under-Lyne the Conservative Working Men's Association met in the Church Institute, and was called the Ashton-under-Lyne Working Men's Church and Conservative Association.

[2] Disputed Elections (H.C.): Evidence given at trials; Westminster 1869. MS. in Record Office, House of Lords, p. 11.

[3] *Ibid.* p. 54. This may be compared with Oastler's slogan: 'The Altar, the Throne and the Cottage'.

Membership was open to any working man who paid a shilling, but few of the 'members' actually paid up, and a nominal membership which increased from 300 or 400 in June 1867 to 1,600 to 1,800 in 1868 (when 'branches' were formed in Mile End, Mayfair, Long Acre, Pimlico and Lambeth) and settled down to about 1,000 by February 1869, included less than 150 paid-up members. Between April 1867 and May 1868 149 working men paid their shilling, but in the following nine months only forty-six, and the total income from this source was only £10 11s. 0d. over the whole period. The expenses were met by W. H. Smith as president (£60), his solicitor (£30), his agent (£5), and a number of M.P.s who lived in the constituency. The only meetings which were held were somewhat disreputable ones in public-houses where drinks were not infrequently provided gratis. Nor were all the members respectable, and in 1868 many of them became engaged in corrupt practices which very nearly cost W. H. Smith his seat.[1]

The emphasis placed on Conservative Working Men's Associations by the party leaders gradually changed after 1868. In 1867, when most of them were first projected, they had been adopted as the obvious solution to the problem of securing the new working-class vote. Disraeli was even then not very happy about the idea, and was only with difficulty persuaded to give his support to the infant National Union (known at first as the Conservative Union) which had grown out of a conference of local Conservative leaders and a few Conservative working men held in London in April 1867.[2] Later, in a well-known speech at Glasgow in 1873, he came out strongly against associations limited strictly to working men. 'I have never been myself at all favourable to a system which would lead Conservatives who are working men to form societies merely confined to their class.'[3] In the intervening years his followers had been converted to much the same point of view. The National Union had become a federation

---

[1] H.C. 120, p. 198 (1868-9). XLVIII, 198.

[2] At the beginning of November 1867 Disraeli stopped the issue of circulars calling for support for the 'National Union of Conservative and Constitutional Working Men's Associations', but his reasons for doing so were only indirectly connected with his views on working men's associations. He feared that the government might be compromised by incautious agitators. There is a long correspondence on the subject in the Disraeli Papers.

[3] Quoted in M. Ostrogorski, *Democracy and the Organization of Political Parties*, trans. F. Clarke, London 1902, I, 256. Disraeli later modified his views when his followers came to act too literally on his advice.

of all Conservative Associations and not simply of Working Men's Associations, and the emphasis in the constituencies had gradually shifted from the new working-men's associations and clubs to the ordinary party associations fostered by Gorst. Some of these new party associations from the first attempted to gain the best of both worlds by calling themselves Conservative Working Men's Associations, among them those of Huddersfield and Nottingham. But in most cases there was a tendency to induce active working men to join the committee of the Conservative Association proper, and simply to provide club facilities or something very like club facilities for the ordinary working man anxious to enjoy a pint of beer after work. Thus, by 1874 the Conservative Working Men's Associations had reached their peak except in Liverpool, and thereafter they tended to become simply local Conservative Clubs for working men.

VI

The growth of the provincial press after 1855 gave a tremendous boost to local politics because it enabled the provinces for the first time to receive up-to-date political news almost as soon as London, and because it increased the self-confidence of local politicians. It was a very different press from that of the thirties and forties: cheaper, more self-conscious, more courted by the politicians. In the smaller towns there were still parallels to the heroic struggle between the *Eatanswill Gazette* and the *Eatanswill Independent*, but in the larger towns the end of the newspaper tax had prepared the way for a new journalism quite as important as that of the *Daily Telegraph* in London. After an initial burst of newspaper-making in the late fifties, the number of provincial dailies continued to grow year by year, and by 1868 fourteen of the largest English provincial towns possessed daily newspapers. There were as yet none in East Anglia or the Potteries, and the south coast was quite bare from Dover to Exmouth, where the three Exeter dailies circulated, but in the early seventies these gaps were filled, and by 1885 forty-seven English towns, including nearly all the larger parliamentary boroughs, had daily papers of their own.[1] Similarly, in Wales the one daily at Cardiff in 1868 had by 1885 been joined by two others at Cardiff, two at Swansea,

[1] These figures are taken from the *Newspaper Press Directory*.

and two at Newport. In Scotland and Ireland, which had been well served even before 1855, the change was relatively much less important, although new dailies were established in Aberdeen, Paisley and Waterford.

The provincial daily press aimed, not to displace *The Times*, which remained indispensable reading for the well-informed, but to occupy in the provinces a place equivalent to that of the *Daily News*, the *Daily Telegraph* and the *Standard*, which were building up what were for those days enormous circulations in London and the Home Counties.[1] They could not hope to build up similar circulations: the *Daily Telegraph* with a circulation of 191,000 in 1871, 242,000 in 1877 and 250,000 in 1880, or the *Standard* with a circulation of about 200,000 by 1880, were giants.[2] But the more modest figures of *The Times*, 60,000 in 1879 sinking to 40,000 in 1890, were a possible target. The *Yorkshire Post* moved from a circulation of 11,222 in 1869 to 15,863 in 1870, 28,465 in 1875, 40,167 in 1880 and 46,637 in 1885. The *Manchester Guardian* reached 30,000 copies by 1880, the *Birmingham Post* 27,000, the *Liverpool Daily Post* about 20,000. The figures for the Scottish papers were similar; *The Scotsman* sold about 30,000 copies in 1870, and by the end of the eighties the *Glasgow Herald* was selling about 42,000 copies. The importance of the major provincial papers was emphasised by their extensive circulation outside their home market. Even in 1858 the *Manchester Guardian* was selling 60 per cent of its copies outside Manchester, and some went as far afield as Newcastle, Leeds, Hull, Carlisle, Whitehaven, and Liverpool.[3] By the early seventies the *Guardian* was more firmly established in Manchester proper, but much of the Manchester district, from Crewe to Cumberland, had fallen into the hands of the *Examiner and Times*, which appears to have had a comparatively small circulation in Manchester itself except among active Liberals and nonconformists.[4] The *Guardian* made energetic

---

[1] The most accessible account of 'the new journalism' of the unstamped newspapers is in *The History of the Times—The Tradition Established 1841-1884*, London 1939, Ch. XIV.

[2] These figures and those which follow are from A. P. Wadsworth, *Newspaper Circulations, 1800-1954*, reprinted from the *Transactions of the Manchester Statistical Society* for 1954-5.

[3] *Ibid.*, p. 21.

[4] The *Examiner and Times* was eventually bought by the Liberal Unionists whose investigations (recorded in the Devonshire papers at Chatsworth) prompt the above remarks. Its standing in nonconformist circles is reflected in the editor's decision not to review *Robert Elsmere* because to do so would cause offence to its public: E. R. Russell, *That Reminds Me—*, London 1899, p. 68.

efforts to recapture this market, and by 1873 was also challenging the *Leeds Mercury*, another pushing paper, in East Lancashire and Yorkshire.[1]

The larger provincial papers soon attracted to their staffs young men for whom the shaping of a newspaper became their life's work and who depended for their success on sheer good writing and good journalism. Most of them were men who had known great poverty in youth, and had worked their way to the top by way of obscure provincial weeklies.[2] Some of them soon won national recognition such as even the most eminent of the older editor-proprietors, like the two Edward Baineses, had only gained through membership of the House of Commons.[3] Such men as Edward Russell (Lord Russell of Liverpool), editor of the *Liverpool Daily Post* 1869-1919, Wemyss Reid, editor of the *Leeds Mercury* 1870-87, Henry Dunckley, editor of the *Manchester Examiner and Times* 1855-89, and, most distinguished of them all, C. P. Scott, editor of the *Manchester Guardian* 1872-1929, had no need to enter the House of Commons to know that they were a power in the land.[4]

It was this generation of editors who exploited the electric telegraph to enable the provincial papers to overcome their worst disadvantage, distance from the capital. After 1874, when the *Leeds Mercury* was almost the only provincial newspaper to carry next morning the news of Gladstone's sudden dissolution of Parliament and a copy of his election address, London offices became almost obligatory.[5] The possession of up-to-date news considerably strengthened the position of editors and leader writers because it killed the old custom of provincial journalism that an editor should not put pen to paper without first seeing *The Times*. The bigger provincial papers became independent in comment as well as in management, and were able to maintain their new-found independence with the utmost ease until Harmsworth's 'new journalism' developed in the nineties.

[1] *Memoirs of Sir Wemyss Reid 1842-1885*, ed. S. J. Reid, London 1905, pp. 200–1.

[2] cp. H. W. Lucy, *Sixty Years in the Wilderness*, London 1909, *passim*.

[3] The Baineses were editor-proprietors of the *Leeds Mercury* and M.P.s for Leeds.

[4] Both Russell and Scott were in fact Liberal members for a time, but this was an unimportant episode in their careers.

[5] The *Leeds Mercury* had recently established a joint office with the *Glasgow Herald* which enabled them to employ a night editor to relay such news: *Memoirs of Sir Wemyss Reid*, p. 208. This book also gives an interesting account of the making of the new provincial journalism, pp. 163f.

The provincial papers had had a strong Liberal bias for many years before the newspaper tax was repealed, and this was strengthened by the growth of the dailies, and of the new week-lies and bi-weeklies which were started in great numbers in the fifties, sixties and seventies. In 1885 forty-five of the provincial dailies were Liberal and only twenty-nine were Conservative,[1] while most of the twenty-five 'Independent' dailies were also generally sympathetic to the Liberals. In Wales and Scotland the disparity was even greater: there were four Liberal dailies and only two Conservative in Wales, and ten Liberal dailies and three Conservative in Scotland. Add to this the weekly and bi-weekly press which brought the number of newspapers in England and Wales to over 2,000, divided into 590 Liberal papers, 379 Conservative papers and 1,200 neutrals (most of them 'enemies in disguise' of the Conservatives),[2] and one has a picture of the overwhelming numerical superiority of the Liberal press.

The disparity in numbers was generally reflected in the content and circulation of Liberal and Conservative papers. Scottish Conservatives generally took *The Scotsman* in preference to Conservative papers, and the Conservative *Manchester Courier* was unable to compete on equal terms with the Liberal *Guardian* and *Examiner*. The Conservative leaders were, rightly or wrongly, more concerned with the London press and with provincial papers in the south than with those in the industrial districts and the north, and the best of the provincial Conservative journalists were drawn away to the *Standard* or *Globe* or *Morning Post* or to the West-country papers rather than encouraged to remain in the provinces and develop the press there. Thus, while there was no shortage of old-fashioned editor-proprietors like Sir Thomas Sowler of the *Manchester Courier*, there was no Conservative Wemyss Reid or C. P. Scott. On the other hand, many of the minor Conservative papers made successful bids to lighten their reading matter and to give better reports of local affairs. Thus the *Cambridge Chronicle*, although short of revenue from advertisements, was a more readable paper than the *Cambridge Independent Press*, and the *Bolton Chronicle* than the *Bolton Journal*.

Many Conservatives were alarmed at this state of affairs and made efforts to start local papers. As one of them put it,

---

[1] *Newspaper Press Directory*, 1885.   [2] *National Review*, V, 635. (1885).

The influence of the metropolitan press, although it is still much larger throughout the country than is generally assumed, does not extend to the lower classes of electors in the provinces. They must be got at, if they are to be reached at all, by local newspapers, in the general contents of which they take an interest. They cannot be reached by pamphlets, and, as a general rule, are not to be approached through public meetings. They take no side in politics, or, if they accept the impeachment that they are partizans, would call themselves Radicals.[1]

But the Conservative party had an uphill task because there was no central fund out of which to finance newspapers, and there was a lack of technically competent people to run them. Indeed, after the experience of many failures, the Conservative Central Office did its best to discourage new projects unless they had very powerful backing. Even the proprietors of existing papers were given a stereotyped reply when they applied for help in improving their papers, such as that which Captain Middleton sent to Lord Dartmouth (who wanted help for the Midland Press Ltd of Wolverhampton) in 1887.

There is no fund from which I could obtain a loan or a gift. The number of applications we have are so numerous and the amount required so heavy that we find the only chance of successfully coping with the requirements of each district is to induce gentlemen residing in the immediate neighbourhood concerned to interest themselves in the local press or other matter requiring assistance. I would suggest that the best plan to adopt would be—

1st To endeavour to get local gentlemen to take shares.

2nd To endeavour to get existing shareholders to increase their number of shares

3rd To mortgage the plant & goodwill of the papers

4th To obtain a loan from a bank upon the personal guarantee of any gentleman or gentlemen who may be interested in the success of the paper. . . . If I can assist by inducing any residents to interest themselves & a list is sent to me I shall be only too happy to do anything in my power.[2]

[1] *National Review*, V, 635 (1885). There is an interesting account of the influence of a local Conservative paper in Southwark in Sir Edward Clarke, *The Story of My Life*, London 1918, pp. 150-1.
[2] Middleton to Dartmouth, 16 February 1887. Chilston Papers.

Chapter Six

THE EARLY SEVENTIES

I

THE overwhelming success of the Liberals at the 1868 general election encouraged them to rest content with their existing organisation. The old Liberal committees continued with the work they had done before 1867, arranging occasional meetings, financing the registration of electors, and looking for new candidates. But almost everywhere the temporary arrangements made with working-class committees for the purposes of the general election were allowed to lapse, and the course of events soon led to the re-emergence of the old division between Whig and Radical.

The Conservatives, on the other hand, were moved by their failures in 1868 to improve their organisation, especially in Lancashire, where they had secured an unexpected amount of popular support. Their efforts were not particularly enthusiastic until it became plain that the Liberal government was failing, but encouragement from headquarters ensured that they did not relax their efforts. The Conservatives were too far behind in numbers and organisation to wish to do more for the moment than to set up a basic organisation in every town of importance. And Gorst, who became party agent in 1870, made this his principal objective between his taking office and the general election of 1874. In the words of his son:

> The first step to be taken was the organization of local committees in the towns and county divisions. In order to carry out this object it was necessary to pay a personal visit to every constituency throughout the country. Arrangements were made to meet the most influential local Conservatives at each place, and to persuade them to form a committee for the purpose of propagating Conservative principles and arranging about a local candidate. These committees, when once they had been established, rapidly grew into Conservative associations. Intelligent working-men were easily persuaded to join them, and they are now known everywhere by the common appellation 'Conservative Working-Men's Associations'. In the counties these

associations always remained aristocratic in character, and chiefly consisted of country gentlemen and the superior class of farmers; but in the manufacturing districts of counties like Yorkshire and Lancashire, and in large towns such as Birmingham and Sheffield, they spread at the most astonishing speed among the masses of the electorate.[1]

Once they were established the local committees quickly asserted their independence, and the pace of development within the constituency therefore depended entirely on them.[2] Moreover, Gorst was not entirely successful in achieving his objective, and in 1874 the Conservative organisation in the forty-nine boroughs with a population of more than 50,000 varied enormously: two still had no Conservative organisation at all, three possessed a solicitor-agent but no committee, three were controlled by Conservative clubs, eight were controlled by registration associations, and thirty-three possessed a self-styled Conservative association.[3] The thirty-three, however, included both Birmingham and Bradford, where the Conservative association was coextensive with the middle-class Conservative club.[4]

The model adopted by most associations which wished to extend their membership to include working men was that of the small number of popular associations which were already in existence by 1867. The Coventry association as it was in 1867 may be taken as typical of them. Coventry in the sixties was an unusually Conservative place because the Cobden Treaty of 1860 (with France) had ruined the silk-ribbon industry and the excessive amount of unemployment was associated with free trade and the Liberal party.[5] The Conservative organisation was divided

[1] H. E. Gorst, *Earl of Beaconsfield*, pp. 126-7.

[2] Harold Gorst's remarks about the National Union are an interesting commentary on this local independence: 'An attempt was made to affiliate these local associations to a central organization by the establishment of the "National Union", an idea which emanated principally from Mr. Cecil Raikes. But the local Conservative committees were jealous of outside control, and would not surrender their independence; the National Union has consequently become more than anything else a centre for distributing pamphlets, cartoons, and other electioneering literature.' *Ibid.*, pp. 126-7.

[3] The position in the 34 boroughs with between 30,000 and 50,000 people was much worse: 9 were in the hands of solicitors, 1 in those of a club, and 5 in those of registration associations, while two had a 'Chairman of the Party' but no party association. These figures are taken from the official party list.

[4] T. Wright, *Life of Colonel Fred Burnaby*, London 1908, pp. 147-8, and *The Times*, 16 November 1885.

[5] 'The Working Class used to be Liberal, but a large number of the most ignorant are filled with the notion that the French Commercial Treaty has ruined the Trade of Coventry, and as a Liberal Government passed that Treaty, they say Liberalism is responsible for the effect.' Reform League Report: Coventry.

into two parts.[1] The Conservative Registration Association managed elections by means of ward managers originally 'elected' when the Association was first formed in 1863, who together formed the committee of the Association and who took charge of the work of the canvass in the wards. They were given general guidance by the election agent, a solicitor who took charge of the technical work of the election, but the Association relied largely on working-class volunteers to canvass the wards. The Conservative Working Men's Association to which they belonged was quite distinct from the Registration Association, although there was an overlapping membership. It had its own club rooms and a part-time paid secretary, who had formerly been a weaver, and was supported by subscriptions from gentlemen who desired 'to provide a room and papers for working men, to come and sit and read; nothing more'.[2] The Reform League's agent reported that there were at least 500 voters in this association (as compared with an estimated 700 in his own) and regarded it as a serious political challenge.

There was also a more complex model, not dissimilar to the later Liberal associations, which was adopted as the basis of the new Leeds Conservative Association in the seventies.[3] The basis of the organisation was not the ward, but the polling district, because the wards were too large to be managed undivided except on polling day. The chairman of each polling district, and the chairman and secretary of each of the wards (who had been appointed by the founders of the association in the first place), plus such subscribers of a guinea or more to the funds of the association as were elected to it (or chose to belong to it), formed an executive committee in which was vested control of the party as a whole. Its membership in 1885 was as follows:

Chairmen of 32 polling districts . .	32
Chairmen of 16 wards . . .	16
Secretaries of 16 wards . . .	16
Total Representatives	64

[1] cp. H.C. 275, pp. 111-17 (1868-9). XLIX, 433-9.

[2] The secretary of the association was also a traveller in spirits, possibly his chief recommendation for the post.

[3] *The Times*, 16 November 1885.

Subscribers of one guinea and upwards
elected at the annual meeting   54

Total Executive Committee   118

This was only the façade, of course. *The Times* correspondent noted that in 1885 the association was in the hands of the fifty-four subscribers of one guinea, and it is clear from the local newspapers that the executive committee was dominated by a group of subscribers who were also chairmen of wards and polling districts.

II

While the Conservatives were slowly putting their house in order, the Liberal party had begun to disintegrate as its non-conformist wing reacted against the measures of the Gladstone government. The 1867 Reform Act had effected something of a revolution in the political status of the urban nonconformists. Since the religious census of 1851 nonconformists and Wesleyans combined had been assured of something like numerical equality with the practising members of the Church of England.[1] Now, as the largest, most active, and most high-principled section of the Liberal party, they seemed to be in a position to claim the redress of their grievances: Cross Street and Carr's Lane Chapels seemed at last to be within measurable distance of claiming equality with Chatsworth as seats of Liberal orthodoxy. But although the nonconformist position was potentially an extraordinarily strong one, because so many nonconformists now possessed the vote, the nonconformists were in no position to take advantage of it. The effective strength of nonconformity was

---

[1] The figures for England and Wales for those attending the most popular service were:

Church of England	3,773,474
Protestant Nonconformists (including Methodists)	3,153,490
Roman Catholics	305,393
Other groups	28,685

The figures for the principal dissenting bodies were: Wesleyan Original Connexion, 907,313, Independents 793,142, Baptists 587,978, Primitive Methodists 266,555, Calvinistic Methodists 180,725, Wesleyan New Connexion 61,319, Presbyterians 60,131, Wesleyan Association 56,430, Wesleyan Reformers 53,494, Bible Christians 38,612, Unitarians 37,156, Society of Friends 18,172.

concentrated in the inadequately represented bigger towns, particularly those of the Midlands and Yorkshire. The Wesleyans and Baptists were ill-organised and short of leaders. And there was a lack of any generally accepted notion of what political action was appropriate to nonconformists *quá* nonconformists. One influential group of nonconformists headed by Samuel Morley, M.P. for Bristol and proprietor of the *Daily News*, was committed to wholehearted support for Mr Gladstone, and felt that nonconformists stood to gain more from loyal support for the Liberal party than from direct action. Indeed, Samuel Morley resigned from the Liberation Society in 1868 because he felt that purely sectarian issues should not be allowed to take precedence over the other major issues of the day.[1] A second group was interested in social reform rather than religious controversy, and acted as a brake on the militant nonconformists, but felt unable to identify itself wholly with a Liberal party for which social reform was not a primary interest. Its most prominent members were Quakers like William Fowler, M.P. for Cambridge, who sided with the militants against the Contagious Diseases Acts, and the Education Act, but with the government on most other issues. Finally, there were the militants who believed in direct action and were indifferent whether their activities harmed the Liberal party so long as they achieved their ends.

In 1868 the Irish Church issue had served to unite all but the most militant nonconformists behind Gladstone. But the temporary nature of the arrangements made for the election, except in a few places like Birmingham and Bradford, meant that the degree of nonconformist participation in local Liberal associations was as yet undecided. Therefore the orthodox channels through which to express nonconformist grievances and aspirations were still those independent nonconformist, or mainly nonconformist, organisations like the Liberation Society and the United Kingdom Alliance, which were designed to emulate the Anti-Corn-Law League.[2] There was a fairly general expectation that much of their work

[1] Hodder, *Samuel Morley*, pp. 276f.
[2] There are as yet no adequate histories of these organisations. The Liberation Society is best studied through its pamphlets, its official journal, the *Liberator*, and the *Life of Edward Miall* by Arthur Miall, London 1884; the United Kingdom Alliance through its annual reports, Henry Carter, *The English Temperance Movement: A Study in Objectives*, London 1933, and M. H. C. Hayler, *The Vision of a Century 1853-1953: The United Kingdom Alliance in Historical Retrospect*, privately printed, London 1953. For their income see Appendix IV.

might now be taken over by the Liberal party, but that was all.

The illusion that the Liberal party would become the mouth-piece of the nonconformists was soon shattered. The Education Bill of 1870 and the Licensing Bill of 1871 antagonised all but the loyalists who followed Samuel Morley. Militants like the veteran Edward Miall and the youthful Joseph Chamberlain spurred on their associates to undertake a bitter and far-reaching agitation, and the Liberation Society, the United Kingdom Alliance, and the newly-formed National Education League became in their different ways the acknowledged spokesmen of the political dissenters.[1] The initiative passed in the big towns from the Liberal associations to the local branches or committees of these nonconformist organisations, and to the independent Radical associations they fostered. The only exceptions occurred in those towns where the advanced Radicals already controlled the only Liberal association.

III

The curious thing about the nonconformist campaign from 1870 to 1874 was that its effects were so limited. It made a great splash in the press, it disturbed the constituencies and led to a number of independent Radicals opposing orthodox Liberals at elections, but it made comparatively little impression on the ordinary Liberal voter, unless he were already thinking of voting Conservative or abstaining, in which case it confirmed him in his intention. There were four main reasons for this. The first was that the great nonconformist organisations were much more like modern pressure groups or the Lord's Day Observance Society than they were like the Anti-Corn-Law League. They appealed not to the pockets and stomachs of their supporters but to their idealism, and were intended to influence parliament and the leaders of public opinion rather than the man in the street. Their income was sufficient to enable them to publish a considerable number of pamphlets and other literature and to employ a staff of lobbyists in London and of missionaries in the provinces. This gave an impression of great activity and influence. But the fact

[1] For the National Education League see its *Monthly Paper*, Francis Adams, *History of the Elementary School Contest in England*, London 1882, and the biographies of Joseph Chamberlain, W. E. Forster, H. W. Crosskey, and R. W. Dale.

that the best-organised of them, the United Kingdom Alliance, had a staff of about thirty, an income of nearly £13,000 a year, and a weekly newspaper, the *Alliance News*, with a circulation of about 25,000 copies, gave it influence rather than power. Its activities were too often directed into unproductive channels, such as the annual campaign in favour of Sir Wilfrid Lawson's Permissive Bill, with its carefully organised approaches to M.P.s and its interminable petitions, or the equally unproductive meetings of the faithful. Even the National Education League, with more limited resources but better leaders, followed the same method, so that its organisation remained simply a loose network of some 430 committees of local notables, whose task it was to make a noise when requested to do so by headquarters.

The second reason was more fundamental. The ordinary nonconformist, and particularly the ordinary Wesleyan, had no wish to be an agitator except perhaps for better living conditions. Where there was not an overwhelmingly strong Radical tradition or an outstanding group of Radical leaders there was, therefore, little chance of the militant nonconformists winning over the majority of their co-religionists to agitation. Even at the height of the Education Act controversy this indifference to purely sectarian agitation was so marked that the Education League on several occasions suffered what Garvin described as a 'pitiable fiasco at the polls' at by-elections.[1] The intransigence of the United Kingdom Alliance, which refused to support any measure of temperance reform unless accompanied by local option, thereby defeating the 1871 Licensing Bill, which the government was not strong enough to carry without its support, did a great deal to discredit independent agitation. Many moderate Liberals and nonconformists agreed with Stanley Jevons, who called the Alliance 'the worst existing obstacle to temperance reform', and attacked it because, 'It absorbs and expends the resources of the temperance army on a hopeless siege, and by proclaiming no quarter, it drives the enemy into fierce opposition to a man'.[2] This feeling was so widespread that the nonconformist militants made substantial progress only in places like Sheffield where they could associate themselves with an existing Radical faction.

---

[1] Garvin, *Joseph Chamberlain*, I, 134.

[2] W. S. Jevons, *Methods of Social Reform and Other Papers*, London 1883, p. 247.

In places like Bradford where they worked hardest they suffered disastrous defeats.

Thirdly, there was the fact that so much depended on a few outstanding men in each locality. Because they were active people, influential as employers and civic leaders, their defection was a serious matter for the Liberal party, and they were able to conduct an energetic campaign for their beliefs. But they were too few to carry on long without help. The most active nonconformist leaders like H. J. Wilson of Sheffield[1] were stretched to the limit of their capacity in organising the local branches of the Liberation Society, the Education League, and the Alliance, campaigning against the Contagious Diseases Acts up and down the country, and doing their best to build up Radical associations. For the moment their nuisance value was enormous, but it was clear before 1874 that they must come to terms with more moderate Liberals if they were to exert any permanent influence. There was, therefore, nothing really surprising in the *détente* in the relations between Radical nonconformists like H. J. Wilson and the orthodox Whigs and Liberals they had been attacking, when it finally came after 1874.

Finally, there was the timing of the general election of 1874. Given adequate preparation the Education Leaguers might easily have brought about considerable changes in the organisation and representation of the Liberal party, by making them a condition of their support. As it was they were given no time for manœuvre, so that no bargains could be struck. The militant nonconformists were caught unawares in the middle (or rather towards the end) of a campaign against the Liberal government, and except in those constituencies where they had candidates of their own in the field they were at a loss how to act. Some followed the line laid down by R. W. Dale in the *Congregationalist* and remained hostile to the government. Others simply drew in their horns and decided to take no part in the campaign, except where there were good local reasons for doing so. This was the policy advocated by the *Liberator*, the official journal of the Liberation Society, which lamented 'the impossibility of completing arrangements which, had time permitted, would have enabled us to enter on the contest with deliberation and confidence'.

[1] Mosa Anderson, *Henry Joseph Wilson, Fighter for Freedom 1833-1914*, London, 1953.

What, then, is our duty . . . ? Not to wage war upon the Government, but to make the advancement of our objects, rather than the safety of the Government, our chief concern. If we can serve the Liberal party while serving our cause, so much the better for that party; but we are not called upon—as, under some circumstances, we might be—to make sacrifices on its behalf. A Liberal party and a Liberal Government are valuable only in proportion as they adopt Liberal principles and pass Liberal measures.[1]

After they had recovered from the first shock of defeat the nonconformist Radicals began to see the extent of their folly. They had foreseen defeat, but a defeat of the government, not of the Liberal party or of so many nonconformist candidates. There was, therefore, a very strong feeling that the policy of independence had failed and that Radicals must throw in their lot frankly with the Liberal party and endeavour to reform it from within. It was on this feeling that Chamberlain drew when he set up the National Liberal Federation in 1877 and merged the National Education League into it.

But the Birmingham Radicals were not the only ones to change their policy. The United Kingdom Alliance and the Liberation Society went through a similar process of realignment which led them to become officially recognised auxiliaries of the Liberal party by 1891. The Alliance actually changed before the Education League. The debates on the 1871 and 1872 Licensing Bills had so confirmed Conservative suspicions of the Alliance that by 1874 it was extremely difficult to be both a good Conservative and a member of the Alliance. The two Conservative members for Manchester in 1874, Hugh Birley and W. R. Callender, were Alliance men, but their position was exceptional.[2] Liberals alone seemed likely to take up local option, although Hartington and Chamberlain both opposed it, and the Alliance trimmed its sails accordingly. The annual report of the executive for 1874 frankly (and verbosely) accepted the view that the proper course for the Alliance to follow was now one of infiltration into the Liberal party.

Is it possible that in any successful reconstruction of the Liberal programme, the claim to popular control of the traffic in drink can

---

[1] *Liberator*, 2 February 1874.

[2] In 1859 twenty-one Conservatives and fifty-seven Liberals supported the Permissive Bill (Dawson Burns, *Temperance History*, London [1890], I, 426). By 1880 only one Conservative, Hugh Birley, supported it as against 145 Liberals (Carter, *English Temperance Movement*, p. 200).

be ignored? . . . In the future Liberal party it will be the fault of the Alliance Liberals themselves if they are hampered with any of the old difficulties. Let them take care that those who have now preferred their trade interest to their party associations be not trusted again, and that any reconstructed party shall at least be pure and free from association with a trade which brutalises the people, and dims the intelligence of those to whom Liberal politicians profess to appeal.[1]

The process had begun which led to the adoption of the Alliance's policy by the Liberal party in the Newcastle programme some seventeen years later.

The Liberation Society soon followed this lead, and at the 1877 triennial conference of the Society Charles Miall, the founder's son, advised his fellow-Liberationists that the time had gone by for dealing with disestablishment from 'an exclusively religious, or Non-conformist point of view'.[2] He urged them to think of themselves rather as a ginger-group working within the Liberal associations than as an independent society.

The time has surely come when support should be absolutely withheld from Parliamentary candidates, who, under whatever guise they present themselves, openly avow an intention to vote against our principles. Such men can hardly, under existing circumstances, claim to be regarded as Liberals. In all large constituencies the friends of religious equality have a valid right to object to nondescript, or unreliable, men being foisted upon them. *Their* cause will never be advanced by professional wirepullers, or political adventurers, against whom they need always to be on their guard. Hence it follows that the real battle will be fought not so much in the polling-booth as in the *committee-room*. . . . It may also be urged that every great popular constituency, where Dissenters, and working men who are like-minded, greatly preponderate, ought to be, and might be, with rare exceptions, represented at the next general election, by members who, in addition to other qualifications, loyally adhere to the policy of disestablishment. Further, it may be reasonably claimed that one candidate in all two-member boroughs, where Nonconformists are an influential section of the Liberal party, should be perfectly sound on this question. . . . It might also be urged that a severer test may fairly be applied in the case of new candidates than to those who have already served a constituency.[3]

[1] *Twenty-Second Report of the Executive Committee of the United Kingdom Alliance,* Manchester 1874, pp. 6-7.
[2] C. S. Miall, *The Disestablishment Question in Relation to the Liberal Party and Electoral Action,* London 1877, p.1.
[3] *Ibid.,* pp. 6-7.

The consequences of this policy were seen on the eve of the general election of 1880. The Liberal party was recognised as the only possible ally, and, except in a few exceptional cases, an amnesty was granted to all Liberal candidates shortly before the election. In so far as the Society intervened in the election at all, it did so discreetly by enjoining unity on all Liberals and by erecting posters in 200 towns, 'of a kind calculated to promote the success of the Liberal as well as of the Liberationist cause'.[1] This moderation won the Liberationists a considerable advance in the public estimation. Many moderate Liberal candidates, not hitherto committed, expressed sympathy with the principle of disestablishment, and the Society showed a new appreciation of political realities by not pressing them further. The result was that, along with the sixty-three Liberationists in the new House (sixteen of them members of the Society's executive committee), there were a large number of sympathisers, bringing the total number of those generally in favour of some measure of disestablishment to almost half the Liberal strength. Moreover, the Society won a significant tribute from Gladstone. In a speech at Marylebone he pointed out the danger of faction weakening the Liberal cause at the elections, and went out of his way to salute the nonconformists:

There is a noble example, however, to the contrary in the largest section of the Liberal party—the Nonconformists. If there is any section of the Liberal party which is entitled to urge and to force its own peculiar opinions, irrespective of times and circumstances, that section is the Nonconformists. What is the peculiar opinion? Their special and distinctive opinion relates to Disestablishment. They have in their own minds and consciences, not merely a political idea, but a religious conviction on that question. And yet what is their conduct? What an example, what a model, are they placing before us! They are putting their own views into the shade in order that they may not interfere with the success of the cause in which they believe their particular idea is included and absorbed.[2]

[1] *Liberator*, 1 May 1880.   [2] *Liberator*, 1 April 1880.

Chapter Seven

THE RISE OF THE CAUCUS

I

THE most pressing problem of the Liberal party after 1874 was the need to reconstruct the urban Liberal associations. In towns like Manchester, Leeds, and Sheffield, where the Liberals had suffered particularly galling defeats at the general election, this reconstruction was carried out within a year or eighteen months of the election: elsewhere it was delayed until 1876 or 1877, or until the formation of the National Liberal Federation in June 1877 had given a new impetus to association-building.

The first reformed Liberal associations were not copied from any particular model. Sometimes the local Liberal leaders had Birmingham connections and drew on the experience of the highly successful Birmingham association, but more often they merely improved the rules of their own association or borrowed those of a neighbouring one. The aim was not to put into practice any theory of representation, but to provide a framework within which all sections of the party could work together, and within which nearly all the local leaders, Whig, moderate, or Radical, could be found a place. This unity was not in practice easy to achieve. The essential condition of success for any association had become an unrestricted membership, with working-class Radicals at least nominally on an equal footing with prosperous Whigs. And the presence of a strong Radical element meant that constant pressure was brought to bear on the leaders of the association to follow the programme enunciated by Joseph Chamberlain and his fellow Radicals in Birmingham and to break altogether with the Whigs.

This was particularly the case in Leeds, of which there is an interesting account by Wemyss Reid. The new association had scarcely been formed before it was called upon to select a candidate for a by-election, so that the underlying conflicts within the association were immediately brought into the open. Two distinct groups of Liberals had coalesced to form the association:

the old-fashioned nonconformist Liberals and Whigs, headed by the Baines family, three of whom had represented the borough since 1832, and the advanced nonconformists of the Education League, with their Radical allies from the old Radical association, headed by John Barran, a former mayor who was made president of the united Liberal association. Each of these groups had a candidate for the vacancy: Sir Edward Baines, who had lost his seat in 1874, was put forward by the old Liberals, and John Barran, who eventually secured the candidature, was put forward by the Radicals.

It was the first meeting of that description I had ever attended, but it was typical of many that I have attended since then. As I expected, it was proposed by those who had long been recognised as the leaders of the Liberal party in Leeds that Sir Edward Baines should be the candidate. Forthwith a most violent opposition was offered to the proposal by men who had never before been heard of in Leeds politics, and some of whom had only been resident in the town for a few months. I remember that the most violent of these gentlemen was a schoolmaster from Birmingham, who denounced Sir Edward Baines for the assistance he had given in the passing of that iniquitous measure, the Education Act. Another gentleman denounced him with equal violence because he was the proprietor of the *Leeds Mercury*, a journal which had dared to speak disrespectfully of the truest and most honest Liberal of the day, Mr. Joseph Chamberlain. . . . On all sides I heard extreme opinions expressed by men whose faces and names were quite unfamiliar to me, and I found to my dismay that the more extreme the opinions, the warmer was their reception by these representative Liberals. They would hardly listen to their old leaders, who had grown grey in fighting the battles of Liberalism. They treated with contumely any words of soberness or moderation. They applauded even speakers who were palpably selfish and insincere. As I listened to that debate, my eyes were opened, and I realised the fact that a great revolution had been suddenly and silently wrought, and that the control of the Liberal party had, in a great measure, passed out of the hands of its old leaders into those of the men who managed the new 'machine'.[1]

The prospect of meeting and mastering men whose outlook was so different from their own was often too much for the older leaders of local Liberalism, who soon dropped out of politics

[1] *Memoirs of Sir Wemyss Reid*, p. 221-2. The reports and balance sheets of the Leeds Liberal Association are preserved in the Leeds Central Library.

altogether. But too much should not be made of this change. The older leaders were literally older—usually over seventy— and were in any case on the verge of retirement. Most of them belonged to the political generation of the Anti-Corn-Law League whose leaders had nearly all left parliament by 1874. A new generation had grown up (John Barran was twenty-one years younger than Sir Edward Baines) which was hostile to the Man- chester school on many points, and was strong for local option and usually for disestablishment. Even in Manchester, where the National Education League and Birmingham Radicalism had few friends, there was a complete revolution in outlook as one political generation gave place to another between 1870 and 1880. By 1882 the Manchester Liberal Association was com- mitted to supporting the programmes of the United Kingdom Alliance and the Liberation Society, and to nearly all the doc- trines enunciated by Chamberlain in the *Radical Programme* of 1885, while Thomas Gair Ashton, the treasurer, whose father was president of the Association, was a strong Home Ruler, and many of the other officers believed in the enfranchisement of women.

This did not mean that there was any change in the rôle of the local Liberal leaders or in their social composition: there was just the inevitable transfer of power from one generation to another. Manchester was still dominated by cotton magnates,[1] as Birmingham was by the leaders of the metal trades. Moreover, there was still a strong feeling that the leaders of local industry should be brought into the Liberal associations and encouraged to take office. In Sheffield, where the steel magnates had never been closely associated with the old Liberal leaders, A. J. Mundella had great difficulty at first with men like Sir Frederick Mappin, the cutler. ('The separation of classes in Sheffield is wider than in any other place I ever knew', he wrote in November 1875, 'and there will naturally be reluctance on the part of such men to break through the traditions of their order.'[2]) But he was not unduly troubled by this, as he could see that the association would unite the more troublesome elements of the party, and

[1] In 1884 eight of the nine officers of the Liberal Association were engaged in the cotton industry, but after 1885 new men, headed by C. P. Scott of the *Manchester Guardian* and Sir Henry Roscoe of Owens College, became prominent.
[2] W. H. G. Armytage, *A. J. Mundella, 1825-1897. The Liberal Background to the Labour Movement*, London 1951, p. 160.

that men like Mappin, who became an M.P. in 1880, would come in in the end. 'The swells will come in hereafter when we have made it a success. No Association can influence or bind them. This is not the case with the working men and the lower middle class, they are loyal to their party and their friends. Let us only *get enough* of them and we shall soon have our share of the upper crust, and if not, we must do without them.'[1]

Because these pre-1877 Liberal associations were formed as a result of essentially local compromises, there were considerable differences between them in the sort of leadership they developed once their initial difficulties had been overcome. In Sheffield there was a genuine compromise between the moderate leaders, the Leader family, and the Radicals, headed by H. J. Wilson, which enabled A. J. Mundella as member to arbitrate between them and preserve the original balance of the association. In Manchester the management of the association became vested in about ten moderate Radicals, most of whose families had played an active part in the Anti-Corn-Law League. As the General Purposes Committee of the association, they arranged an approved list of candidates for the offices and places on the Executive and other committees, and nominated them *en bloc*.[2] In Leeds almost all the founders of the association were too old or too busy to take an active part in its work, and in 1877 a trio of newcomers took charge: Wemyss Reid, James Kitson (later Lord Airedale) and John S. Mathers (whom Reid described as 'the best organiser and wire-puller I ever met in the course of my life'): a newspaper editor, an ironmaster, and a building society manager.[3]

Of course, there was always an opposition. But it could be successful in diverting the managers of the association from their chosen path only if it embraced a popular cause. Thus in 1880 the still-turbulent Leeds 'opposition' managed to get Herbert Gladstone chosen as Liberal candidate in place of his father,

---

[1] Armytage, *A. J. Mundella*, p. 160.
[2] In 1882 the General Purposes Committee proposed and carried the names of 24 persons to serve as co-opted members of the Executive Committee and 93 persons to serve as members of the General Council: the General Purposes, Finance, and Registration Committees were re-elected without change. The only elections held at the annual meeting were for the 6 places on the Executive Committee and the 7 on the General Council which the General Purposes Committee had not bothered to fill. The MS. Minutes of the Association give full details of the election.
[3] *Memoirs of Sir Wemyss Reid*, pp. 278-9.

who had elected to sit for Midlothian, because the officers of the association were rash enough to propose the contemned Sir Edward Baines for the seat.[1] But most managers were not so rash as to offer their opposition such a challenge. At Manchester it even proved possible to build up such a stock of confidence that when the managers of the Liberal association decided not to contest a by-election in 1883 they were able to prevent an unofficial Liberal candidate from winning more than a very small number of votes.

The success of the Manchester Liberal managers was a consequence of the complicated system of consultation developed since 1874, which showed to best advantage in 1879, when it became necessary to replace one of the sitting members, Sir Thomas Bazley, who had decided to retire at the general election. The leaders first approached Mr Gladstone, who would have been a universally popular candidate. When he refused they called a special general meeting to suggest suitable candidates. Ten names were selected from among those mentioned, and were referred to the Executive Committee for consideration.[2] The Executive narrowed these down to two, Alderman Abel Heywood and John Slagg, and referred their claims to a selection committee, which preferred Slagg. After a hot debate this choice was confirmed by the Executive Committee by 59 votes to 20, and referred again to a general meeting, which accepted the recommendation by an overwhelming majority.

This elaborate system of consultation engendered such confidence that when Hugh Birley, the minority Conservative member, died in 1883 and Dr Pankhurst announced himself as an independent Liberal candidate for the vacancy, the vast majority of the Liberal electors was prepared to abide by the decision of their leaders as to how they should act. Dr Pankhurst had been at loggerheads with the association for some years, and was unlikely to stand down in favour of any other candidate; the registers were in an unsatisfactory state; and there was no

---

[1] *Ibid.*, pp. 289-90; also Sir Charles Mallet, *Herbert Gladstone: A Memoir*, London 1932, pp. 76f.

[2] Eight of these were local men (Henry Dunckley of the *Manchester Examiner*, Alderman Abel Heywood, a veteran Radical who had contested the borough in 1859 and 1865 and was now old and infirm, Dr Pankhurst, R. N. Philips, M.P. for Bury, Herbert Philips, Oliver Heywood, John Slagg, and Sir Joseph Heron, the town clerk); two were outsiders (Lord Hartington and T. Milner Gibson, a former member and minister). There are full reports in the MS. Minutes of the Association.

money for a contest, so that the Liberal leaders thought it better not to put forward a candidate at all and to make it a test of loyalty to the Association that good Liberals should abstain from voting. Pankhurst and his friends were furious and challenged the decision of the officers, but to no avail. A long series of meetings of the association went against them, and the ordinary members remained loyal. So loyal, indeed, that even with the help of a letter of approval from Parnell, Pankhurst secured only 6,216 votes, although Slagg in 1880 had secured nearly 25,000, and there were at least 20,000 Liberals on the register.[1]

The basic unit of organisation in these reorganised associations was the municipal ward or polling district. Each of them was permitted to conduct its own business and to send representatives or delegates to a General Committee or General Council, which was charged with the oversight of the association's work and with the ultimate choice of parliamentary candidates. In addition to the General Committee there was an Executive Committee which attended to the day-to-day management of the association's business, either directly or by means of sub-committees. This Executive Committee was usually chosen partly by the General Committee, and partly by co-optation. A good idea of how the system worked can be gained from a glance at the composition of the committees of the Leeds and Manchester Liberal Associations in 1883.

Leeds Liberal Association

Executive Committee

The Officers (elected at the annual meeting) . .	7
One Representative of Each Ward (*appointed* by the Ward Committee)	16
Twenty Other Members (elected at the annual meeting)	20
Total	43

All members of the Executive Committee to be subscribers to the funds of the Association.

[1] There is a good account of the contest in the *Manchester Guardian*, 29 September 1883 and succeeding days. Money was a vital factor in the situation: the 1880 election had cost the Liberals £10,468, as compared with £3,933 in 1874, and it was estimated that a contest would cost £8,000 and be unsuccessful in returning a Liberal member. But the Liberals were no doubt also influenced by the fact that the leaders of the association were divided on the Home Rule issue.

General Committee—The Six Hundred

The Executive Committee (if not chosen by the wards) . *up to*	43
Not less than Twenty Representatives of Each Ward (*elected* at public ward meetings—minimum 320) . *up to*	480
Thirty Members added by the Executive Committee .	30

Total up to 553

Manchester Liberal Association

Executive Committee

The Officers (elected at the annual meeting) . . *about*	7
Representatives of Each Ward (*elected* at public Ward meetings)	103
Thirty Co-opted Members	30

Total about 140

General Council

The Executive Committee (if not chosen by the Wards) . *up to*	140
Representatives of Each Ward (*elected* at public ward meetings) . . . . *up to*	618
One Hundred Co-opted Members	100
Forty Members added by the Executive Committee .	40

Total up to 898[1]

By no means all the members of the committees of the Leeds and Manchester associations were subscribers to their association's funds. The Leeds Executive Committee complained in 1884 that fewer than 250 of the 480 ward representatives on the General Committee were subscribers, although it hastened to add that it did not wish a 'money subscription' to be a condition of membership.[2] The Manchester Executive Committee made a similar calculation and found that only 553 persons subscribed to the association's funds, many of them not office-holders, although there were 750 members of the General

---

[1] The actual attendance seems to have been usually in the neighbourhood of 150, although on one occasion in 1882 750 were present, and 476 attended a selection meeting in 1879.

[2] Annual report for 1883, p. 8.

Council.[1] Both associations derived most of their income from the middle classes, but the pattern of contributions was different. The Manchester association was managed by wealthy men who made little attempt to economise or to avoid a deficit. They and a number of equally wealthy friends contributed £400 to £800 a year in lump sums of £50, £100, or even £200, when they felt that it was their turn to give, and on one occasion in 1884 the Ashton family added a 'loan' of £500. The sums contributed by smaller subscribers were sufficient to meet only the routine office expenses. Two appeals for funds were launched in the early eighties, in one of which it was asserted that 'We should prefer a large number of small subscribers to a few large ones', but the amount collected was quite inadequate for the Association's purposes, since it was already £900 in debt.[2]

The Leeds association was managed by relatively poor men who paid more attention to costs, and it was therefore able for a time to live on small subscriptions. From 1877 to 1885 the largest regular subscribers were John Barran, M.P., who gave £25, and Sir Andrew Fairbairn, who gave £10, and two-thirds of all subscriptions were contributed by those who gave a guinea or less. Working-class subscribers were comparatively unimportant, since they could not afford to give much,[3] but in such a broadly-based association they were naturally much more important than in Manchester. Unfortunately for the Liberal party, the dominance of the small subscriber was short-lived. As the association extended its activities it became less able to finance them from small subscriptions. By 1883 it had already overreached itself in financing the School Board elections, and an enquiry into the activities of the Headingley guardians. The resulting debt of over £400 could not be met from subscriptions and had to be bequeathed to posterity. With the division of the

---

[1] Minutes of the Executive Committee, 11 November 1884.

[2] The first appeal in 1880 attracted 141 subscriptions in response to 900 circulars; but they were worth only £197. 3. 0; the second appeal to 'upwards of 200 gentlemen' attracted only 50 subscribers.

[3] The subscribers in 1881 may be divided roughly as follows:

	£	s.	d.
171 Middle-class subscriptions (£1 to £25) .	278	2	0
114 Intermediate subscriptions (6s. to 11s. 6d.) .	58	13	0
396 Working-class subscriptions (1s. to 5s.) .	59	9	0
681	396	4	0

borough in 1885 even routine expenses were very greatly increased and appeals had to be made for big subscriptions. Thereafter, until the First World War, the association (renamed the Leeds Liberal Federation) was chiefly financed by about twenty large subscribers, whose defection ultimately completed the destruction of the Liberal party in Leeds.[1]

II

Before 1877 the new Liberal associations had neither a distinctive outlook nor a common model. They had been created to meet specific local needs without much thought for the future, and had borrowed ideas from any association of which they had heard: Newcastle and Manchester had looked back to the traditional Lancashire associations, Bradford and Leeds had come under Birmingham influence, while Sheffield had simply borrowed at random. With the formation of the National Liberal Federation in 1877 all this was changed. The Birmingham Radicals supplied the associations with both an ideology and an organisational model which thereafter became almost obligatory.

The ideology was described by Frank Schnadhorst, secretary of both the Birmingham Liberal Association and the National Liberal Federation, in a letter to *The Times* in 1878:

> Our constitution represents an honest attempt to put the management of the party (by means of a thoroughly representative committee) where we think it should rest—in the hands of the people themselves.
>
> We object to self-elected leaders, however respectable; we object, especially, to manipulation by legal agents; we object to constituencies being made the instruments of personal ambition or the victims of crotchet mongers.
>
> We are anxious to promote the unity and strength of the Liberal party. We think without organization this is impossible.[2]

In the previous year a description of the organisation of the association had been circulated at the inaugural conference of the National Liberal Federation:

[1] The report of the Federation for 1905 drew attention to the fact that three quarters of its income was derived from twenty subscribers. The accounts for 1908 (*Liberal Year Book*, Leeds 1909, pp. 47-51) show that the twenty-two people subscribing over £10 gave a total of £861. 5. 0 out of a total subscription income of £1,128. 12. 0.

[2] *The Times*, 23 August 1878.

The Birmingham Liberal Association consists of all Liberals who are elected to serve on any of its committees, or who signify their adherence to its objects and organisation. The *objects* of the Association are the return of Liberal members to Parliament and to local governing bodies, and the general promotion of Liberal principles. Its *organisation* is entirely representative in character. The central body, having charge of the whole direction of its affairs, is termed the 'Committee of Six Hundred', and is composed of members freely chosen at public meetings of Liberals, held annually in each municipal ward of the borough. The constituency of the 'General Committee' is, therefore, the whole Liberal party publicly called together in the various districts of the borough. Every Liberal who chooses can attend in his own ward, and take part in the election of ward representatives.

The General Committee discusses political subjects, selects School Board and Parliamentary candidates, and decides the general policy of the Association. It is an established rule, that if any person consent to be nominated as a candidate of the Association, in case he is not selected he must submit to the decision of the Committee.

Each ward elects a certain number of members to constitute an Executive Committee. The Executive Committee, which is thus also a directly representative body, calls a meeting of the General Committee upon all important occasions, takes its opinion, and carries out its decisions.

In each ward a Ward Committee, appointed at a public meeting, watches over its special Liberal interests; the Chairman and Secretary of each Ward Committee being, by virtue of their offices, members of the General Committee and of the Executive Committee. Candidates at municipal elections are selected for each ward by the Ward Committee.

The principles upon which the Association is based are, therefore, the following:—

(1) The whole body of Liberals in the borough is recognised as the constituency of the Association, and every Liberal has a vote in the election of its committees.

(2) Political responsibility, and the ultimate power of control, belong to the largest representative body, and the policy of the Association is loyally guided by its decision.

(3) The decision of the majority, in the selection of candidates and other matters of practical business, is regarded as binding upon those who consent to be nominated, as well as upon the general body of members.

(4) A broad and generous meaning is given to Liberalism, and no subject of public or political importance is excluded from its deliberations.

The width of the base on which the Association rests prevents the divisions so often caused by sectional interests; and its representative character is so thoroughly sustained that combined action is rendered not only possible, but vigorous, determined, and enthusiastic.[1]

In practice there were a number of important variations from the Birmingham model, even among associations formed after 1877. Many Liberal associations declined to do away with subscriptions as a test of membership. Indeed, at the inaugural conference of the National Liberal Federation the secretary of the Halifax association said that 'he believed the bulk of the associations throughout the country, as at present constituted, were of a similar opinion',[2] and threatened that his association would not join the Federation unless the member associations were free to adopt their own tests of membership. In order to avoid a row, Chamberlain thereupon made a vague statement to the effect that variations from the norm would be overlooked. More serious was the fact that an increasing number of associations found that they had not got sufficient members to enable them to differentiate between their General Committee and a general meeting of the members of the association. As a consequence, the two were often amalgamated, either in name or in fact, and the General Committee became the annual general meeting of the association.[3] Even some of the bigger associations found that they had committed most of the wards to electing more ward officers, ward committee men, and ward representatives to the Executive or General Committees than there were active Liberals in the wards. As early as 1877 the Leeds and

---

[1] *Proceedings Attending the Formation of the National Federation of Liberal Associations*, Birmingham 1877, pp. 5-6. There is a more extensive account in H. W. Crosskey, *The Liberal Association—The '600'—of Birmingham* and in J. Chamberlain, *A New Political Organisation*, both published separately by the Federation in 1877, the first being a reprint from *Macmillan's Magazine*, Vol. XXXV, and the second a reprint from the *Fortnightly Review*, Vol. XXII.

[2] *Proceedings*, p. 29.

[3] Thus, although the Manchester Liberal Federation to this day retains its General Council, the latter is now no more than a general meeting. Section 6 of the Constitution approved on 22 March 1947 reads: 'The General Council shall consist of all members of the Liberal Party in the Manchester Divisions who have subscribed to the funds of the Federation during the preceding twelve months, either directly or through a Division Association or other recognised unit of the Party.'

Bradford associations found themselves in this embarrassing situation, and at Leeds the Executive Committee was driven to issue placards imploring the Liberals in the wards to attend ward meetings. But to no avail. The annual report for 1885 admitted that 'Even now the principle of simple election is far from being perfect, for at many of the public meetings called for the purpose of electing representatives they are not always well attended, and in some instances there are actually fewer present than the number of representatives to be elected.' The ward meetings became less and less active, even in Birmingham, and more and more was expected of, or left to, the Executive Committee.

After the split with the Liberal Unionists in 1886 it was often not even worth while to pretend that the associations were representative of anything but themselves, and an article in the *Westminster Review* in 1887 catalogued an extraordinary list of deficiencies.

The associations have not been representative owing to the principal ward meetings having proved unworkable in practice. Many associations have become more or less close bodies, representative of a few, and out of touch with the bulk of the Liberal party. It has been so common as to be almost a rule, in ordinary times, for small ward meetings to elect more members to the association than there have been persons present at the meetings. Selected lists of names have been put to the meeting, and carried as a matter of the commonest routine. Then, again, there has been a tendency to let the work drift. There exist only vague and superficial relations between the associations and the electors; the central body takes little or no trouble to ascertain the opinions of the masses; the whole policy is of a general and indefinite character; and the association in effect represents, in the true sense of the term, too frequently no-one at all but the members themselves. When the time of an election comes, there is a most praiseworthy activity, and the party managers endeavour with most laudable zeal to accomplish in a few days what ought to have been, and might have been, the gradual work of as many years. It is common enough in such constituencies—and they may be counted by the hundred—to hear complaints of the apathy of the Liberal party; and it is not too much to assert that this apathy is mainly the reflection, outside the association, of the indifference, routine, and inactivity which prevail within it.

The cardinal faults of the present system of local organization are:

The non-representative character of the associations;

The faulty system of election;

The dangerous practice of issuing mere machine-made opinion;

The indifference of the bulk of the Association to the political condition of the rank and file of the party;

The lack of any methodized system of political education;

And the want of any organized method of apportioning work and responsibility among individuals.[1]

III

The National Liberal Federation was founded by the Birmingham Radicals in 1877 in the hope that it would become a second Political Union, such as Attwood had built up in 1829, and give them unquestioned leadership of Radical opinion in the country.[2] That other instrument of Birmingham imperialism, the National Education League, was wound up, and its members were urged to devote themselves to keeping the Liberal associations in line with Federation policy laid down in Birmingham. Chamberlain and his associates (chief among them William Harris and Frank Schnadhorst) had chosen their time well. The Eastern crisis had given rise to Gladstone's pamphlet on *The Bulgarian Horrors and the Question of the East* in September 1876, to widespread indignation among Liberals of all shades of opinion, and to the belief that the time had come for the party to put its house in order before the next general election. And by the beginning of 1877 the bigger Liberal associations were already sufficiently strong and self-conscious to feel the need for some channel through which to express their views, particularly where they differed from those of Lord Hartington. On the other hand, although they were not indisposed to join a federation of which Mr Gladstone approved, they were not yet sufficiently sure of themselves to wish to campaign against the supremacy of Birmingham.[3]

The Federation was described by its founders in their circular as follows:

[1] *Westminster Review*, CXXVIII, 395 (1887).

[2] The standard account of the foundation of the Federation is that of F. H. Herrick, 'The Origins of the National Liberal Federation', *Journal of Modern History*, XVII, 116-29 (1945).

[3] The first officers of the Federation were Joseph Chamberlain, president, William Harris, chairman of the General Committee, Jesse Collings, honorary secretary, J. S. Wright, treasurer, and Frank Schnadhorst, secretary. All of them came from Birmingham. Jesse Collings succeeded Chamberlain as president in 1880, and was followed in 1881 by Henry Fell Pease, and in 1883 by James Kitson.

It is proposed that all Liberal Associations, established on a similar popular basis, should enter into a Federal Union.

While local circumstances will, of course, cause variations in points of detail, yet a popular basis is essential in order that a Liberal Association may obtain the hearty co-operation of its members, and occupy its just position in the Liberal party.

No interference with the local independence of the Federated Associations is proposed or contemplated. Each one of the Associations will arrange the detail of its own organisation and administer its own affairs; but from time to time, and on all occasions of emergency, the representatives of all the Associations in union will be convened to consider the course of action which may be recommended to their respective organisations. No formal political programme will be submitted for general acceptance.

The Federation is designed to assist the formation of Liberal Associations, on a popular representative basis, throughout the country; to bring such organisations into union, so that by this means the opinions of Liberals, on measures to be supported or resisted, may be readily and authoritatively ascertained; and to aid in concentrating upon the promotion of reforms found to be generally desired the whole force, strength, and resources of the Liberal party.

The essential feature of the proposed Federation is the principle which must henceforth govern the action of Liberals as a political party—namely, the direct participation of all members of the party in the direction of its policy, and in the selection of those particular measures of reform and of progress to which priority shall be given. This object can be secured only by the organisation of the party upon a representative basis: that is, by popularly elected committees of local associations, and by the union of such local associations, by means of their freely chosen representatives, in a general federation.[1]

In practice no attempt was made to restrict the membership of the Federation, as had been intended, because only suitable or more or less suitable associations showed a desire to join.[2] The number at first was forty-six, but fairly soon nearly all the larger associations came in (see Table III), even including several from the metropolitan boroughs, although their position was an anomalous one.

The attitude of the London elector towards politics was quite

---

[1] *Proceedings Attending the Formation of the National Federation of Liberal Associations*, p. 7.
[2] Brighton, Edinburgh, Cheltenham, Lincoln, Weymouth, and Woodstock, which were represented at the inaugural conference, stayed out of the Federation until after 1885, and Derby, which was also represented at the inaugural meeting, did not join until 1883.

different from that of his provincial counterpart, and there were
no popular Liberal associations in the metropolis when the

Table III. Associations affiliated to the National Liberal
Federation: English and Welsh Boroughs[1]

Population in 1871	Joined 1877 after Inaugural Conference	Total affiliated in 1884	Boroughs not affiliated in 1884
Under 7,000 . . .	3	6	25
7,000 to 10,000 . . .	1	6	20
10,000 to 20,000 . . .	5	14	24
20,000 to 30,000 . . .	3	7	13
30,000 to 50,000 . . .	12	18	16
50,000 to 100,000 . .	9	17	6
100,000 to 200,000 . .	9	12	1
Over 200,000 . . .	5	8	5

Federation was formed. J. F. B. Firth, later member for Chelsea,
told the inaugural conference that 'Even if they divided it into
districts, a Liberal Association in London would not carry with it
what Liberal Associations with a smaller population did elsewhere.
Political life in London was almost non-existent, except under
special circumstances, as at Chelsea, where they had an association
connected with the working classes, and another with the middle
classes.'[2] A special London and Counties Liberal Union was
eventually formed in 1881 to cope with the problem, but Chelsea,
Finsbury, Lambeth, the Tower Hamlets, Westminster and the
City did not appear in the Federation list of Associations until
after 1885. However, their omission was not very disturbing to
the Federation, since its marked provincial bias was one of its
greatest political assets. Even in 1886, when the Federation's
headquarters were moved from Birmingham to London, the provincial Liberals were insistent on this point. Spence Watson points
out in his official history that the move was only undertaken
'with the distinct understanding that the provincial character of
the Federation was not to be diminished, and no step should be
taken which, in any sense, would separate the Executive of the

[1] In addition, Aberdeen, Dundee, Glasgow and Kilmarnock were affiliated by 1884
and also about ten English county divisions.
[2] *Proceedings*, p. 38. A correspondent writing to the *Spectator*, 15 March 1884, alleged
that there was no Liberal organisation in Middlesex except for one agent who was
responsible for 30,000 electors.

Federation from the active and vigorous political life of the provinces from which it had received its chief strength and inspiration'.[1]

Scotland was, if anything, even less closely associated with the
Federation than the metropolitan boroughs, although (unlike
Ireland) it was within the Federation's orbit. Four Scottish
Liberal associations joined the Federation as individual members,
but the remainder resisted affiliation to what was essentially an
English organisation. Instead, they joined the purely Scottish
federations created by the party Whips.[2] A National Liberal
Federation of Scotland was eventually formed in April 1886, but
survived for only eight months, after which it was swallowed up
by the Scottish Liberal Association.

The Federation did not itself undertake a systematic propaganda
campaign in all parts of the country, and its resources were small.
Its income (and consequently its expenditure) remained well
below that of the great nonconformist propaganda agencies and
did not even approach that of its predecessor, the National
Education League. Whereas the National Education League had
had an income of £3,741 in 1876, when it was near its end, the
National Liberal Federation obtained only about £1,500 a year
in the early eighties. It was thus comparable with the Conservative National Union with about £1,000 a year, not with the
Liberation Society with an income of up to £10,000 a year or
the United Kingdom Alliance with up to £13,000. Indeed, the
two latter outran the normal resources of the two party headquarters.

IV

The foundation of the National Liberal Federation touched off
one of the classical debates of nineteenth-century politics—a pro-
tracted discussion as to the merits and demerits of political
organisations in general and of the Birmingham caucus in particular—which was not brought to a close until the publication of
Ostrogorski's reflections on the relationship between party organisations and democracy in 1902. The questions at issue were clear
enough. Were party machines in every town to be allowed to dictate
to the mass of Liberal electors the way in which they should vote?

[1] R. S. Watson, *The National Liberal Federation*, London 1907, p. 60.
[2] See p. 159 below.

Was a nation-wide federation of these machines to determine current political orthodoxy? And was the party outside parliament to become almost as important as the party within it? But they became so cluttered up with American parallels (concisely discussed by Mr Henry Pelling in a recent book[1]), and with controversies about particular constituencies and policies, that they were never argued to any sort of conclusion. Indeed, the whole controversy has now little more than antiquarian interest because it had so little direct effect on events.[2]

The views of both sides were equally extravagant. The Birmingham Liberals with transparent mendacity claimed that not only the local associations but also the National Liberal Federation were truly democratic. Joseph Chamberlain at Ashton in December 1882 said that 'the federation is thoroughly representative of the party, and not of any clique within it, in every constituency in the kingdom, and it is a central body in its operation representative of the committees of all the different districts sending delegates in proportion to their population, and by constant communication and conference the opinions of the whole are ascertained and brought together for simultaneous action'.[3] The opponents of the Federation and of the new associations denounced it as a monstrous conspiracy. McCullough Torrens, for instance, writes of it in his autobiography as follows:

> Under the name of organising for the purpose of registration, active committees were formed, widening slowly into societies of the idler and more fanatical members of the community, and assuming the pretentious names of Liberal Associations: all of them adapted and directed from a central seat of usurpation.
>
> Mechanical ingenuity was applied to reduce the free spirit of party to unquestioning uniformity. . . . The rules of each separate club were stereotyped impressions of those ordained at the central office of the Caucus, and furnished to those who would accept them in the various constituencies throughout the kingdom as dictates to thought and fetters to local action. . . . Where existing members could not be made amenable to the factious or fantastic tests dictated from headquarters, new candidates more compliant were introduced

---

[1] Henry Pelling, *America and the British Left: From Bright to Bevan*, London 1956, Ch. III.

[2] There is a brief bibliography in Ostrogorski, *Democracy and the Organization of Political Parties*, I, 201 n.2.

[3] *Manchester Guardian*, 20 December 1882.

to unsuspecting notice in the local press, and by degrees at gatherings yclept meetings of the Liberal Association, where the old and influential party leaders seldom if ever appeared, and were never expected to appear.[1]

The truth lies, of course, somewhere between the two extremes, as most of the party leaders realised at the time. Disraeli, although he did his best to blacken the character of the Federation, did not hide his own opinion that it was one of the major causes of the Liberal victory in 1880. Gladstone, although he saw the danger of unrepresentative associations capturing a constituency, saw little wrong with the objects of the Federation or with the new associations. W. P. Adam, the Liberal Chief Whip, approved of the Federation and did his best to help the new-style Liberal associations, because he thought that they would help to end Liberal dissension in the big towns.[2] Even Lord Hartington, who could not approve of the Federation as such, objected more because it tended to upset the balance between Whig and Radical in the party than from any abstract dislike of party organisation.[3]

Moreover, middle-class fears that moderate Liberals would be shut out of parliament by violently Radical caucuses, although not extravagant, were not as yet justified. When attacked by one of the small minority of unrepresentative associations, moderates like W. E. Forster at Bradford,[4] W. J. Fitzwilliam at Peterborough, E. A. Leatham at Huddersfield, and Sergeant Simon at Dewsbury,

[1] W. T. McC. Torrens, *Twenty Years in Parliament*, London 1893, pp. 356-8.

[2] Adam wrote to Hartington in December 1878 advising him to give his countenance to the Federation: 'The organization is not applicable to small boroughs or to counties but it operates well I think in large towns & tends to prevent that division of the Liberal party at elections which is the bane of the party. . . . I do not think the fact of the organization being unpopular in many constituencies need prevent your giving it a helping hand to develop itself among constituencies where its working is really beneficial.' Devonshire Papers, 340.783, ff.1-2.

[3] B. Holland, *The Life of Spencer Compton, Eighth Duke of Devonshire*, London 1911, I, 245.

[4] For Forster's case see T. Wemyss Reid, *Life of the Right Honourable William Edward Forster*, new edn, London 1895, pp. 246f. Bradford's troubles had little to do with the Federation. At by-elections in 1867 and 1869, and at the general election of 1868, the Liberal party had been hopelessly divided between Whig and Radical. In 1870 the fact that Forster, the author of the Education Act, and Edward Miall, its chief opponent in the House of Commons, were both members for Bradford also split the Radicals. Forster was forced to coalesce with the Whigs at the 1874 general election, but easily defeated the Miallites, who thereupon retaliated by forming a Liberal association on the Birmingham model. However, after long controversy, during which the National Liberal Federation had to disown some of its protégé's views (*The Times*, 20 August 1878), agreement was reached between the two factions, each of which returned a member in 1880.

were all able to keep their seats without undue difficulty. And really independent Liberals like Leonard Courtney (who sat for Liskeard and then for the Bodmin Division) could always find a seat for a rural or a Scottish constituency. The caucus opened the way to the practice of modern electorates, which vote more or less automatically for the candidate of the party association, and against independents of any sort. But because of the divisions within the Liberal party, and the great shortage of candidates after the redistribution of 1885, this was not a problem of the immediate future.

Chamberlain himself did his best to underline the unreality of the controversy in a letter to *The Times*, immediately after the 1880 general election.

The Caucus

Sir,—A few days after the dissolution of Parliament it was said by a writer in the Press that the elections would 'test the efficiency of the new democratic machinery of which Birmingham is the capital'.

It may interest your readers to learn the result of the experiment. Popular representative organizations on the Birmingham model, sometimes called 'The Caucus' by those who do not know what a caucus really is, and have not taken the trouble to acquaint themselves with the details of the Birmingham system, exist in 67 of the Parliamentary boroughs in which contests have just taken place. In 60 of these Liberal seats were gained or retained. In seven only the Liberals were defeated, but in three at least of these cases a petition will be presented against the return on the ground of bribery.

This remarkable success is a proof that the new organization has succeeded in uniting all sections of the party, and it is a conclusive answer to the fears which some timid Liberals entertained that the system would be manipulated in the interest of particular crotchets. It has, on the contrary, deepened and extended the interest felt in the contest; it has fastened a sense of personal responsibility on the electors; and it has secured the active support, for the most part voluntary and unpaid, of thousands and tens of thousands of voters, who have been willing to work hard for the candidates in whose selection they have for the first time had an influential voice.

Among other results must be noticed the fact that the gentlemen who have commended themselves to these popular and somewhat democratic committees have been, on the whole, more decided in their Liberalism than was usually the case of the nominees of the small cliques of local politicians whom the new organization has superseded. A long purse has not been an all-sufficient passport, and the candidates who are 'so thundering eminent for being never heard on', have been passed over again and again in favour of others who have won their spurs in political conflict, and have given proof of steadfastness to their principles and of ability in maintaining them.

The restricted franchise in the counties and the large area of these constituencies have hitherto prevented any considerable extension of the plan outside the boroughs. One of these difficulties will now shortly be removed; the other may be overcome; and I expect that at no distant date the electors will universally demand a preliminary voice in the selection of candidates.

Meanwhile, in ten county constituencies in which the caucus has, in spite of all obstacles, been already established, and where contests have taken place, the Liberals have won seats in all; and it may be affirmed that in most of these cases there would have been no contest but for the energy and determination of the new element imported into the councils of the party.

Altogether, for good or for evil, the organization has now taken firm root in this country, and politicians will do well to give it in future a less prejudiced attention.

I am, Sir, yours obediently,

J. CHAMBERLAIN.

Birmingham, April 10.[1]

This letter, although it claimed too much for the National Liberal Federation, at least by inference, had sufficient truth in it to impress even Chamberlain's opponents.[2] And it is significant that Disraeli told the Queen a few days later that 'the Conservatives had been too confident, and that they had not had that same organisation or worked as hard as the Liberals had. That the Liberals had worked on that American system called caucus, originated by the great Radical, Mr. Chamberlain.'[3] It was the

---

[1] *The Times*, 13 April 1880.

[2] The letter claims too much in four ways: it takes no account of the national swing to the Liberals, which accounted for Liberal gains in a clear majority of the boroughs where they occurred; it gives no credit to Liberal organisations outside the Federation which were responsible for striking gains in seven boroughs; it ignores the inconvenient fact that at Chester and Gloucester the caucus was neither more nor less than an instrument of corruption; and it does not mention the fact that many of the boroughs in which the Liberals made gains were two-member boroughs which still returned a Conservative. Of the 67 boroughs Chamberlain mentions 46 were Liberal in 1868, 11 Conservative and 10 divided. In 1874 the numbers were 32 Liberal, 14 Conservative, and 21 divided. In 1880 they were 49 Liberal, 8 Conservative, and 10 divided.

[3] Buckle, *Disraeli*, VI, 535.

Conservatives who made much of the new organisation (without copying it minutely) after 1880. Very soon, indeed, the Conservatives had built up Associations in most parts of the country quite as representative and popular as those on the Liberal side, although usually less pretentious, and after 1885 there was little to choose between the local organisations of the two parties. A recent Conservative party publication even reads strangely like an echo of the manifesto issued by the Birmingham Liberals in 1877 which has already been quoted.

An association consists of all men and women resident in, or connected with the constituency, who declare their support of the objects of the association and subscribe annually to its funds. . . .

The chief business to be transacted at the Annual General Meeting is to receive, discuss and adopt the report and accounts of the Association for the past year, and to elect officers. Discussion on the report and accounts affords opportunity for constructive criticism or suggestions. . . .

The management of the affairs of an association between general meetings should be in the hands of an Executive Council. This is the governing body, and all sections of the organisation must accept its decisions. It should consist of all the officers of the association and representatives of each ward or polling district branch. . . .

The finance and general purposes committee forms an inner executive and has responsibility for most of the essential routine work of the association between meetings of the executive council. Its membership should consist of a small number of suitable persons able and willing to devote their time and energy to the work. . . .

Whenever it is necessary to select a parliamentary candidate the executive council of the association should appoint a selection committee. . . . When one or more persons are selected the committee makes its report to the Executive Council, and finally there is a general meeting of the association to adopt as prospective candidate the person eventually chosen.[1]

V

The accession to office of the Liberal government of 1880, in which its president was a cabinet minister, radically changed the position of the National Liberal Federation. Hitherto it had been primarily concerned with questions of organisation and with the

[1] *The Party Organisation*, Conservative and Unionist Central Office, Organisation Series No. 1, 1958 edition, pp. 24-5.

defeat of the Disraeli government. Now it became a semi-official organisation committed to the support of a particular government and its measures, and concerned with all the constituencies, not simply with the big towns. The change was not an easy one for the Birmingham Radicals to adapt themselves to, but by 1885 the officials of the Federation, at least, had adapted themselves, and the main outlines of the modern party machine had been established. Its work has been described vividly by Ostrogorski.

As soon as the Ministry met with resistance or with a display of hostile feeling in either House, the managers of the central Caucus let loose the Associations, urged them to hold meetings, to send monster petitions to Parliament, to vote resolutions of protest or indignation, to remonstrate with their members or even to give them direct orders. 'We ask you', ran the Birmingham circulars sometimes, 'to put yourselves at once in communication with your representatives in the House of Commons, strongly urging them to be in their places on . . . next and to vote for. . . .' As the legislative measures in regard to which this intervention was demanded seemed in themselves worthy of support to a large section of opinion, the Associations had no difficulty in complying with the proposals which came from Birmingham; without exactly wishing to honour or obey the Committee of the Federation, they co-operated in a common cause. The mode of action recommended to them provoked all the fewer scruples because the Associations were chiefly composed of militant politicians, and then it invested them with a power, with an authority, the exercise of which is always welcome. . . .

By force of habit the co-operation of the local Associations with Birmingham became, so to speak, automatic; those who were jealous of their independence asserted it by paraphrasing the resolutions sent from Birmingham, but they voted them all the same, convened public meetings, inveighed against the members who were not loyal to Mr. Gladstone, etc. A mere telegram from the bigwigs of the Caucus was enough to set the Associations in motion throughout the country, and the lion growled, screamed, roared, with pleasure or with anger, as occasion required.[1]

The fact that the headquarters of the Federation were in Birmingham was if anything a help to the government, since it enabled pressure to be brought to bear on dissentient Liberal members such as could not be exerted by a Liberal prime minister. Members were as yet too familiar with the easy-going habits

[1] Ostrogorski, *Democracy and the Organization of Political Parties*, I, 209-10.

of the sixties to accept very readily the dictates of their own party leaders, and were reluctant even to accept modest restrictions on the freedom of the House to talk at will on any subject, such as those brought about by the adoption of the closure (subject to generous safeguards) in 1882. Moreover, there was as yet no party election platform, no mandate, which would justify the use of this pressure by ministers. The latter simply conferred among themselves and then introduced their measure to an expectant House, irrespective of its bearing on Liberal principles or on pledges given by individual members.

The disadvantage of having the party headquarters in Birmingham was that there was no way of softening or toning down the injunctions issued by the Federation. The Federation was so much a Radical organisation that it automatically acted as if the Liberal party were not an alliance of men of different views but a unitary party committed to a Radical programme. This attempt to force the party into one groove was widely resented by those who conceived of the party in different terms. Not that the attempt was successful, as the history of the Liberal party after 1885 shows. However, in so far as the Federation's appeals were primarily directed to Liberals in the big towns, as they usually were, it was difficult to resist them because the opinion of Birmingham in such cases was almost invariably also the opinion of Manchester or Glasgow. Opinion had changed so much in these towns since the sixties that they allied themselves rather with Gladstone and Chamberlain than with Hartington and the moderates, although by no means all of them accepted Chamberlain's leadership. The real opposition to Chamberlain's views came from London, the counties and the small towns, which were stronger in M.P.s and peers than in organisation and were virtually unrepresented in the National Liberal Federation.

None the less, an opposition did develop within the Federation, which gradually became more important, although it was still not strong enough to seize the reins of power in 1886 when Chamberlain himself went over to the enemy, and left the Federation to Birmingham's erstwhile allies. This opposition had always existed, and was not, as Ostrogorski believed, simply a matter of local pique.[1] Chamberlain himself had recognised that it was likely

---

[1] *Ibid.*, I, 290-1.

to develop, and that efforts would be made to prevent Birmingham from doing as it liked. 'I think it is a great mistake to ask Manchester and Leeds to join Birmingham in starting the Federation . . .', he wrote to Jesse Collings. 'If these two associations are joined with us they will seriously hamper our action and they will claim equal representation on all the committees of the Federation . . .'[1] The officers of the Leeds, Sheffield, and Newcastle associations eventually joined in issuing the invitation to local associations to attend the inaugural meeting. But they had no doubt that they were being made use of for the purposes of Birmingham, and several of them lent their names only because they felt that by so doing they might be able to prevent Birmingham excesses. Spence Watson of Newcastle afterwards explained that he had doubts about signing the circular, and that he had agreed to do so only because he was attracted by the idea of a 'working federation': 'At first he had some fear, when this thing was mentioned to him, lest it should be allowed in any way to interfere with the independence of their local associations. That fear had been very much dissipated.'[2] Robert Leader of Sheffield was even less enthusiastic, and remained for many years an opponent of the Federation.[3] Suspicion of Birmingham was even voiced at the inaugural conference of the National Liberal Federation, where delegates from Halifax, Manchester and Leicester expressed serious misgivings and declined to commit their associations to join the Federation until they had referred the question back to their committees.

These misgivings did not trouble the Birmingham leaders unduly because they were convinced that they could 'manage' the Federation easily enough, as events proved that they could. However, they took the precaution of providing themselves with a core of faithful supporters who could always be relied on to outvote any dissentients at meetings: five local associations in Birmingham, three in Wednesbury, two in Wolverhampton, and eight more in other towns and villages near Birmingham (a total of eighteen associations) which nearly always followed the lead given them by the officers of the Federation. In practice, however, the real defenders of Birmingham in case of a conflict on

[1] Garvin, *Chamberlain*, I, 259.
[2] *Proceedings Attending the Formation of the National Federation of Liberal Associations*, p. 28.
[3] Armytage, *Mundella*, p. 179.

questions of policy were men like H. J. Wilson of Sheffield, who had been a stalwart of the Education League and who could be relied upon always to take the most extreme view of a question. Such men could split their local associations and prevent them from revolting against Birmingham policies, and also assist the Birmingham men directly in their capacity as delegates to the annual meetings of the Federation and the occasional meetings of its General Committee.

The main centre of opposition to the Federation was in Lancashire. The Federation had friends in Tory Liverpool among the younger Liberals of the Junior Liberal Association, and also in a few local magnates like Hugh Mason of Ashton,[1] but very few in Manchester. In the Manchester district and the cotton districts of North Lancashire the lecturing and publishing work, which was performed in the Midlands by the National Liberal Federation, was attended to by the National Reform Union. The climate of Lancashire opinion was also different from that of the Midlands: the Education League had never fully established itself, partly no doubt because denominationalism was so strong; and Chamberlain still ranked as a pushing fellow who had in Lancashire contributed very little towards the Liberal reorganisation after 1874 and nothing towards the Liberal victories of 1880. Moreover, the Manchester Liberal Association, which was generally recognised as the leader of Lancashire opinion, represented the rival tradition of the Anti-Corn-Law League.

Before 1880 the Manchester Liberals had very little to do with the National Liberal Federation.[2] R. N. Philips, member for Bury, held office in both the Manchester association and the Federation, but he had a large estate in Warwickshire, and his Vice-Presidency of the Federation was little more than a recognition of this dual personal connection. The only Manchester Liberal who regularly attended Federation meetings was J. F. Alexander, the paid agent of the Liberation Society in Manchester, who was closer to the Birmingham Liberals than his colleagues, and A. G. Symonds, the secretary of the National

[1] The October 1881 annual conference was held in Liverpool, and the 1882 conference in Ashton-under-Lyne.

[2] The relations between the two were first drawn to my attention by Dr Philip Whitaker, and were later followed up in the minute books of the Manchester Liberal Association and in the press.

Reform Union, who often had business to transact with Schnad-horst.[1] After 1880, when the Federation began to issue its circulars urging support for the government, Manchester became increasingly uneasy at the way in which the Federation was taking on itself the task of deciding which measures were particularly worthy of support. The Manchester Liberals were finally provoked to action by a circular issued by the officers of the Federation on Saturday, 11 February 1882, which called upon Liberal Associations to rally behind the government scheme for changing the procedure of the House of Commons as a counter to Irish obstruction. This circular was printed by all Liberal papers on the following Monday and was commended by the *Manchester Examiner and Times*, which generally reflected the views of the leading Manchester Liberals. The Manchester Liberals objected not to the contents of this circular—they resolved at the usual meeting of the General Purposes Committee next day to take steps to call a meeting to support the government—but to the fact that it had been prepared by the officers of the Federation without any pretence of prior consultation with the General Committee of the Federation. The Executive Committee of the Manchester Liberal Association accordingly resolved at its next meeting on 2 March:

> That this Committee recommend that the General Committee of the National Liberal Federation should appoint a Consulting Committee consisting, in addition to the Officers, of Representatives of seven of the most influential Federated Associations to whom the draft of all Circulars on important matters should be submitted before they are issued.

The Secretary was instructed to take this resolution to the next meeting of the General Committee of the Federation to be held four days later in Birmingham, but it met with no support from the other associations. Powell Williams and Schnadhorst who had issued the circular simply explained that they had received 'such information from the highest authorities in the House of Commons as led them to believe that its immediate issue, without calling a meeting of the Committee or consulting anyone—

[1] The Manchester Liberals who did attend Federation meetings reported back formally to their committee, but there seems to have been little discussion of their report. See, for example, the minutes of the General Purposes Committee, 19 February 1880.

thus risking delay—was urgently demanded'.[1] Hardly a comforting reply, since the Committee no doubt assumed that the 'highest authorities' were Mr Joseph Chamberlain and his friends, but one with which they had perforce to be satisfied.

The Manchester Liberals still felt strongly on the subject when the next meeting of the General Committee of the Federation was announced, and after a good deal of discussion the General Purposes Committee of the Liberal Association unanimously resolved:

> That the Executive Committee be recommended to consider the desirability of this Association withdrawing from the National Liberal Federation on account of the issue of circulars on National policy without the knowledge and approval of any of the Federated Associations.[2]

A week later the Executive Committee set up a committee almost identical with the General Purposes Committee to confer with the Federation, the two opponents of the motion not putting their views to the test of a vote. The officers of the Federation managed to postpone a meeting with the new committee for seven months, until the annual meeting of the Federation on 19 December at Ashton-under-Lyne, during which time the Manchester press held its peace. And when the meeting at last took place on 19 December, neither Schnadhorst nor the Federation's treasurer attended, and the Birmingham delegates simply asked the Manchester officers to prepare a draft amendment to the constitution incorporating their views.[3] However, in the evening the Manchester Committee had its revenge when the Federation's meeting at Ashton was addressed by Chamberlain: the only prominent Lancashire Liberals present were William Summers, M.P. for Stalybridge, Benjamin Green, the paid secretary of the Manchester Liberal Association, Alexander of the Liberation Society, and J. W. Southern, a comparatively young Manchester Liberal.

---

[1] Minutes of Executive Committee, Manchester Liberal Association, 14 March 1882.

[2] Minutes of General Purposes Committee, 2 May 1882.

[3] The Manchester Committee reaffirmed their original resolution when the Birmingham delegates had left, resolving that 'This Committee is unanimously of opinion that no declaration with reference to public policy or party action should be published by the General Committee or the Officers of the Federation, and that suggestions should be issued as information or advice to the local Associations'. Minutes of the Executive Committee, 9 January 1883.

The platform was thus almost entirely confined to delegates from Birmingham and the Midlands.[1]

Chamberlain chose this occasion to make the characteristic defence of the Federation which has already been quoted,[2] and which was little more than a deliberate insult to the Manchester Liberals. Next morning the Radical *Manchester Examiner* came out with a full-scale attack on the Federation, which was followed next day by a similar one in the more moderate *Manchester Guardian*. The *Guardian* very sensibly confined its case to Chamberlain's statement that the National Liberal Federation was truly representative of the member associations, and in doing so stated the viewpoint of all the leading Manchester Liberals.

> Now representative in any real sense the Association most surely is not. At annual meetings . . . it may be possible to get together a good number of representatives from different constituencies. . . . But its annual meetings are the least important part of the work of the National Liberal Federation, and the ordinary meetings of its General Committee are both far less representative and undertake a far more exalted function. They profess at critical moments to give the cue to the political action of the constituencies all over the kingdom, and, being in fact made up in an overwhelming proportion of representatives from the immediate neighbourhood of Birmingham, they affect to 'focus' opinion and to pull the strings for the whole country. An organization of this kind which aspires to guide the policy of the Liberal party and to shape the policy of Ministries would, if it were efficient for the purpose, be in fact a sort of second and larger Parliament, meeting in order to control or supersede the first. Being, as it is, in the highest degree inefficient and wholly incapable of any such function, its chief effect is to supply a ready means of misrepresentation to the opposite party, and to give to the spontaneous movements of popular opinion among the constituencies an appearance, belying the reality, of mechanical subservience to a moving power. This result, we admit, is the consequence, not necessarily of the existence of such an organisation, but of its mistaken activity. There is plenty of good work for the Federation to do in acting as a consultative body for leading Liberals, and aiding the party to become more thoroughly organised, especially in the smaller boroughs and country districts. But when it assumes an executive function we venture to say that it entirely oversteps its proper use, and against this aberration, encouraged, or indeed

[1] *Manchester Guardian* and *Manchester Examiner and Times*, 20 December 1882.
[2] See p. 141.

originated, as it may be by MR. CHAMBERLAIN, Liberals who have the welfare of their party at heart will do well to protest.[1]

The Manchester Liberals must by now have despaired of any compromise with Birmingham, and can hardly have been surprised when at the meeting of the General Committee of the Federation the officers denounced Manchester's proposed amendment to the constitution, with the result that it was almost unanimously rejected.[2] Some of the Manchester Liberals now toyed with the idea of forming a rival federation of Liberal associations, but most of them were content to wash their hands of Birmingham. The idea of a 'Moderate Liberal Union' which would show 'both a readiness to accept compromise and an abandonment of all effort to force on premature measures by violent language and fanatical agitation',[3] continued to be discussed during the next twelve months. And the draft constitution which Ostrogorski saw was provided with revealing marginal comments: 'Liberal party used to be the party of freedom; now Liberals are becoming a party of coercion', 'The chief character toleration—even Chamberlain admissible if he were not so violent and domineering', 'No horse to be ridden to death', 'Temperament the bond of union'. But the scheme was always a shadowy one and was never taken up by any Liberal association as such, and when it was referred to the 'great Whig chiefs in London' (probably Lord Hartington and Lord Derby) cold water was poured on it for fear it should break up the party.

When the split between Birmingham and the other associations finally came over Home Rule in 1886 the Manchester Liberals took little part in the manœuvres which led to Chamberlain's expulsion. There was not even a contest between Birmingham and other provincial towns, although the president for the year, James Kitson of Leeds, was anxious to reduce the power of Birmingham. Everything turned on the attitude of men like Alfred Illingworth of Bradford and H. J. Wilson of Sheffield, who had been Birmingham's friends in the local associations. It was these men, through their spokesman, John Edward Ellis, who carried the hastily summoned conference at the Westminster Palace Hotel against the Liberal Unionists, not Birmingham's old

[1] *Manchester Guardian*, 21 December 1882.
[2] Minutes of the General Purposes Committee, 8 May 1883.
[3] Ostrogorski, *Democracy and the Organization of Political Parties*, I, 248.

opponents from Manchester and Sheffield.[1] Many of the old opponents of Birmingham, indeed, supported Lord Hartington and opposed Home Rule, and had more to gain from staying away from such a meeting than from attending it, since if Radical could be persuaded to defeat Radical the militant caucus would be at an end.

[1] The day before the meeting (on 5 May 1886) Ellis, Illingworth, Wilson and E. R. Russell met and decided to support Home Rule. Until the actual meeting there appears to have been a good deal of confusion among the provincial Liberals. The best account is J. E. Ellis's given in Bassett, *Life of John Edward Ellis*, pp. 74-8.

Chapter Eight

SCOTLAND, WALES AND IRELAND[1]

I

AT the beginning of the nineteenth century the Scots and Irish were as ill-represented in parliament as the population of the industrial districts of England. The Scottish constituencies were little better than a string of pocket or rotten boroughs and counties in the hands of the party managers, while the Irish constituencies were entirely in the hands of the Protestant minority and elections were managed by the English Chief Secretary.[2] As a consequence, the reforms of the 1830s, which in England had the effect of transferring political initiative to the provinces—to the Manchester school and eventually to the Birmingham caucus —had the effect in Scotland and Ireland of restoring the representation to the nation at large. The Scots reacted to the change by giving their wholehearted support to the Whigs and the Radicals who had come to be regarded as the champions of the national interest. The Irish, whose nationalism was more ardent and who, unlike the Scots, regarded themselves as a temporarily conquered people, were also sympathetic to the Whigs, but the characteristic expression of Irish nationalism (hampered as it still was by English endeavours to repress it) was a series of national movements which attempted from the days of O'Connell to those of Sinn Fein to restore the Irish parliament and solve the Irish land problem. Only Welsh nationalism was unaffected by the reforms, and that because it was essentially a development of the forties.

In Scotland there were no decisive political changes between the 1832 Reform Act and the break up of the Liberal party in 1886. By 1868 the Liberals, as the party of national patriotism,

[1] This chapter is not a comprehensive account of the political life of the 'Celtic fringe', but an attempt to fill conspicuous gaps in the general discussion of the various types of constituency which precedes it.
[2] For the Scottish and Irish constituencies see Oldfield, *Representative History*, vol. VI, and E. and A. G. Porritt, *The Unreformed House of Commons*, Cambridge 1903, vol. II. Sir Charles E. Adam's *View of the Political State of Scotland in the Last Century*, Edinburgh 1887, also gives an interesting account of the Scottish constituencies.

could count on carrying all but six or seven of the sixty Scottish seats, although their hold on the counties was not altogether secure and there was a Conservative reaction in them in 1874.[1] Such political issues as arose were usually thrashed out, not between the two parties but within the Liberal party, with the result that Scottish politics had a unique air of permanence.

This stability was only possible because Scotland, unlike Wales and Ireland, was either not conscious of the dominion of England or welcomed the English association.[2] The Scots and English regarded themselves as cultural partners rather than as ruler and ruled, and both were content that Scottish problems like those which grew out of the Disruption of the Scottish Church, and the need to reform the Scottish law of landlord and tenant, should be thrashed out in Scotland. Scotland was prospering, Clydeside was not yet a problem,[3] and all except the crofters were aware of the material advantages of the English connection, so that for the moment government from London, and even the hateful name 'North Britain', were not associated with material disadvantages. Moreover, there was no ostentatious challenge to national feeling like the Anglican church in Wales and Ireland, or the English administration in Dublin: the symbols of Scottish national culture, the education system, the legal system, and the church, remained intact.

The closeness of the English connection and the predominance of the English Liberal party caused Scottish politics to develop along the same lines as those of England. Scottish electors asked

---

[1] The figures for all Scottish Constituencies are:

	Liberals	Conservatives
1868	54	6
1874	41	19
1880	54	6
1885	62	10

[2] cp. Sir Reginald Coupland, *Welsh and Scottish Nationalism: A Study*, London 1954, Ch. VI.

[3] The position of Clydeside at this time was akin to that of Tyneside or Belfast: standing somewhat apart from other provincial centres but closely linked with them. The textile and iron industries were prosperous and threw up political leaders, most of them Liberal, who allied themselves with newspaper editors, Church and Free Church ministers, and solicitors to form a political upper crust similar to that found in Manchester, with which it had close commercial and family connections. Clydeside failed, however, to produce a leader recognised as such outside Glasgow, and as it boasted only nine of the sixty Scottish members (although Dunbartonshire, Lanarkshire and Renfrewshire with their burghs contained almost a third of the population of Scotland) it remained something of a backwater until the 1885 redistribution gave it more members.

their candidates questions about Scottish problems, such as the position of the church, the game laws, the law of hypothec, and the need for a Scottish Secretary of State, and Scottish Radicalism was largely the product of Scottish, not of English, nonconformity. But Scottish elections were ultimately decided by issues which affected the whole of the Liberal party in the three kingdoms, or which were purely local, not by those of a Scottish character. Gladstone's Midlothian speeches were delivered to Scots in Scotland and contained frequent references to Scottish issues, but their theme was not just a Scottish one, and their effects were felt, and intended to be felt, with equal force in England and Scotland alike. Indeed, unless Gladstone is to be regarded as a Scot, which he was by descent, although he was almost wholly English in education and outlook, the leaders of the Scottish parties, with the exception of Duncan McLaren, were all English. Gladstone ·was flanked by Hartington and Bright and Chamberlain, not by Lyon Playfair, W. P. Adam or Henry Campbell-Bannerman, who were eminent Scots but not eminent Scottish party leaders. Even Duncan McLaren, the leader of the Scottish Radicals and the strongest personality among the Scottish M.P.ş, was content to follow the advice of his close friend and brother-in-law, John Bright, on general questions, and to regard himself as 'the member for Scotland' rather than as the leader of a Scottish Radical party.[1] Moreover, when McLaren retired from parliament to make way for his son in 1881, Joseph Chamberlain took his place as the leader of Scottish dissent, and conducted a fierce campaign for Scottish disestablishment.[2]

This dependence on English leadership was reflected in the attitude of the party managers, who treated Scotland as if it were an extension of England. The Lord Advocate and the Scottish Lord of the Treasury acted in no more exalted capacity than that of assistants to the Chief Whip at elections. And although they were deputed to attend to disputes about candidates where local knowledge was essential, and to suggest the names of possible Scottish candidates, the Chief Whip kept the actual allocation

[1] cp. J. B. Mackie, *Life and Work of Duncan McLaren*, 2 vols, Edinburgh 1888.
[2] There was more than the overwhelming social and economic predominance of England to account for this dearth of leaders. The quality of the Scottish M.P.s was deplorably low (as it still is) because the ablest Scots did not go into politics. As a consequence, there was not a single Scottish M.P. (apart from Englishmen who sat for Scottish constituencies) in the cabinet between 1835 and 1885. Scottish interests were represented, if at all, by peers.

of seats in his own hands. This was the more natural in that the Scottish Liberals had difficulty in finding candidates at home, and that Scotland was coming to be regarded as a refuge for prominent Liberals who found it difficult to keep a seat in England. Henry Austin Bruce, the Home Secretary, was put up for Renfrewshire in 1869, Gladstone for Midlothian in 1880, S. D. Waddy for Edinburgh in 1882, and by 1885-6 the tradition was so well established that Goschen, Childers and Mitchell Henry put up for Scottish seats along with a number of other Englishmen, including H. H. Asquith and Edward Russell of Liverpool. They were soon joined by other prominent Englishmen, including Augustine Birrell, Lord Wolmer, and John Morley.

The Scottish Conservatives were as dependent on English leadership as the Scottish Liberals, and had, in addition, to rely on the Whips to find English seats for them until 1886. The nominal leader of the Lowland Conservatives, the Duke of Buccleuch, was old and discredited, and the nominal leader of the Highland Conservatives, the Duke of Richmond, Lennox and Gordon, was both an Englishman and incapable of leading anybody. The Scottish Conservative M.P.s with moderately safe seats (six in all) were respectable lairds but nothing more.[1] The others were too transitory to count, and ranked rather with the optimistic advocates, solicitors, younger sons, and Glasgow merchants and ironmasters who contested the Scottish burghs. Almost all the able Scottish Conservatives had either to be brought in for an English constituency or to take refuge in England after losing one of the precarious Scottish seats. Men like Sir John Hay, Sir James Fergusson and the Balfour brothers all sat for English boroughs. But even these men were by no means leaders in Scotland. Indeed, in so far as the Scottish Conservatives had an effective political leader, it was Lord Salisbury, who had no wish to meddle in Scottish affairs, but had a special position in Scotland as brother-in-law of the Earl of Galloway, uncle of the Balfours, and friend of Campbell of Blythswood.

During the seventies the control of the party headquarters in London was strengthened by the formation of branches of the

[1] The six in 1868 were a representative band: Charles Dalrymple of Newhailes, brother of Sir James Fergusson of Kilkerran; the Hon. James Grant, later 9th Earl of Seafield; Lord Elcho, afterwards 10th Earl of Wemyss; Donald Cameron of Lochiel; Sir G. Graham Montgomery of Stanhope; and Lord Garlies, afterwards 10th Earl of Galloway.

party organisations in Edinburgh. The more efficient of these was that created for the Liberals by W. P. Adam in 1876 and formally inaugurated in January 1877, which lasted until the First World War. This consisted of two parts, the East and North of Scotland Liberal Association in Edinburgh with a secretary who acted as the agent of the party for the whole of Scotland, and a West and South-West of Scotland Liberal Association with offices in Glasgow. These two parts were federated in 1881 to form the Scottish Liberal Association, which became the Scottish counterpart of the Liberal Central Association (i.e. the party offices). In December 1886 it also absorbed the nascent National Liberal Federation for Scotland, and came to be officially described as the 'Scottish Liberal Association, being a Federation of the Liberal Associations in Scotland'.[1] John James Reid, advocate, the first secretary of the East and North of Scotland association, was a close associate of W. P. Adam, and acted under Adam, Rosebery and Craig Sellar as general manager of the Midlothian campaign in 1880. He also made a tour of all the Scottish constituencies before the election, and, encouraged by Adam, interfered with the local committees to an extent which would hardly have been tolerated in England. No doubt the fact that he had a private fund at his disposal made up for his excessive zeal.[2]

The Conservative organisation, like the Liberal, was theoretically divided into two parts, one for the East and one for the West, but in practice it was controlled by a single committee of lawyers (there were others on it but the lawyers did the work). This committee had very little success, in spite of the prompting of successive Scottish committees at the Central Office in London, until in 1883 Reginald MacLeod, Sir Stafford Northcote's son-in-law, was appointed Central Office agent in Edinburgh, but thereafter it began to make an impression. It raised over £5,000 for fighting the 1885 election—almost entirely from the peers and lairds—as well as the £1,000 a year or thereabouts which was necessary to keep the office in Edinburgh and the National Union for Scotland in working order, and it started an unsuccessful

---

[1] *Liberal Year Book*, London 1887, pp. 140-1.

[2] Adam seems to have supplied Reid with considerable sums of money in addition to those raised in Scotland, both for general purposes and in order to build up a secret reserve. There is an obscure correspondence on the subject in the Adam Papers and an account of the secret fund, which amounted to £1,588. 12. 0 in November 1880. For Adam's relations with the Scottish constituencies see *The Scotsman*, 16 and 17 March 1880.

newspaper, the *Scottish People*, to run in association with the heavily subsidised (£8,000-£10,000 a year) *Glasgow Evening News*. In addition it was able to employ a number of lecturers. Its efficiency is a little difficult to judge, as MacLeod was distrusted by his colleagues in London, who were perturbed by what they deemed his Highland irresponsibility, but it is clear from letters in the Salisbury papers that by 1886 it had built up the morale of Scottish Conservatism sufficiently to enable it to take full advant-age of the split in the Liberal party.

Although Scotland was usually treated as if it were part of England, there were two important differences between the con-stituencies in the two countries. The first was the overwhelmingly Liberal character of the Scottish burghs (between 1832 and 1885 the Conservatives never held more than three of the twenty-three, or after 1867 twenty-six, burgh seats, and they won none at the general elections of 1857, 1859, 1865, 1868, and 188·), and to a lesser extent of the Scottish counties. If the Scottish counties had not been small enough for the Conservative can-didates to be known personally to a large proportion of the farmers, it is conceivable that no Conservatives would have been returned in 1868 and 1880. The few Conservative strong-holds, the counties of Bute, Dunbarton, Inverness, and Wigtown, were either the creation of a few local landowners or the con-sequence of a Conservative tradition going back to the eighteenth century. Bute, for instance, was Conservative almost entirely because of the twelfth Duke of Hamilton's hold on the islanders of Arran, and was lost soon after he died in 1895.[1]

Until Disraeli became party leader the Conservatives were in-clined to accept this state of affairs as inevitable. Even in 1868 they contested only twenty-one of the fifty-six Scottish constitu-encies. Sir Graham Montgomery, the Scottish Whip, when asked for his views on the party's prospects, was frankly pessimistic. He thought that something might be done with the counties by taking up Scottish measures—as was done in 1874, when private

[1] Graham Murray (Lord Dunedin) was able to scrape home in 1900 as a result of the Boer War, but the seat was lost at a by-election in 1905 when Graham Murray was appointed Lord Justice-General. Middleton had written to McDonnell in October 1899 to warn him of the impending loss: 'I fear the Bute seat cannot be considered a safe one. Graham Murray has alienated some of his followers there by his foolish habit of not answering letters and since the death of the late Duke of Hamilton we cannot reckon on the solid 450 Arran votes he used to take to the poll on our behalf.' Salisbury Papers.

patronage in the Church of Scotland was ended by the Conservative government, to the fury of the Scottish dissenters, who wanted the establishment to remain as imperfect as possible. But he held out no hope for the boroughs: 'their case is nigh hopeless. One or two, however, might be contested.' Indeed, the reasons he gave for the Liberalism of Scotland were so all-embracing as to suggest that the Conservatives had no hope at all.

Before the passing of the Reform Bill of 1832 Scotland had no real representation. The county members were elected by small bodies of Freeholders. A man with an estate of £5000 a year unless he happened to be a Freeholder had no vote. The Borough members were elected by the self elected Town Councils. This state of things has never been forgotten by the people & they are continually being reminded of it, consequently they can't tolerate the supremacy of a Party that opposed the Reform Bill of /32 & tried to keep them out of the power in the constituencies which they now possess.

Then I think the Presbyterian form of church government is democratic in its tendencies, though I admit it is not so in the north of Ireland. In Scotland the Presbyterian dissenters are a very numerous & powerful body. Their enmity to the Established church is bitter and undying. They look upon conservatives as greater friends to and stronger supporters of the Established Church than the liberals & hence their support of the latter at the elections.

One other thing that tells against conservative opinion spreading amongst us is that most of the newspapers are on the liberal side & so are the best conducted & clearest written papers and too many conservatives I am sorry to say take the leading whig paper the 'Scotsman' in preference to their own leading Journal.

Some soreness certainly rankles in the breasts of the Tenantry as to our preservation of game at present, but as liberals are quite as great transgressors in this matter as any of us, I don't see that much stress can be laid upon that alleged ground of our unpopularity. The loss of Aberdeenshire [in 1866] was generally attributed to that feeling amongst the farmers, but I have it on the best authority that Sir James Elphinstone's mismanagement was the real cause and I believe that seat will be regained either by Mr Leslie or one of the Aberdeen family.[1]

Disraeli was not satisfied with defeatism of this sort, and determined to enliven the Conservative organisation as much as he could. After the 1868 election (and again after the 1874

[1] G. Graham Montgomery to Disraeli, 21 January 1867. Disraeli Papers.

election) a committee was appointed to go into the matter, and Gorst and Keith-Falconer from the Central Office spent much of their time in Scotland.[1] The result was a gradual increase in the number of constituencies contested (21 in 1868, 37 in 1874, and 42 in 1880), and a general improvement of Conservative morale. This was specially noticeable in 1874, when the rank and file of tenant farmers in the Lowlands were dissatisfied with the Liberal government and ready for a change, and the Conservatives made big gains in the Lowland counties. But organisation was not enough to give the Conservatives any permanent advantage, and the tenant farmers returned to their old allegiance with a rush in 1879-80, largely as a result of the series of bad harvests.[2]

The second characteristic of the Scottish constituencies that requires notice is the oligarchical character of Scottish Liberalism. It has often been said that the Scottish education system and presbyterianism were essentially democratic, at least in their tendencies. But in terms of the nineteenth century with its hierarchical social structure and its enormous differences of income, this is true in only a limited sense. The Scottish system of education made it possible for a few exceptionally gifted ploughboys to live in palaces, and for an appreciable number to occupy manses, bank parlours, and captains' cabins, and to become members of clubs in India, but it did little for the ordinary farmhand. Presbyterianism made it possible for the laity to play a considerable part in church government, but too often this merely set the seal of ecclesiastical approval on secular success. In the Church of Scotland the leading men in the parish were, in the small towns, respectable shopkeepers and professional men, in the countryside the lairds and leading farmers (whose long leases and big farms made them more independent than in England), and in the big towns the leading manufacturers or merchants. And among the Free Churchmen and United Presbyterians the position differed only in degree.

The same contrast existed in Scottish Liberalism. The best type of Scottish Liberal, personified by James Bryce, was an

[1] For the committee on Scottish organisation after 1874 see Basil L. Crapster, 'Scotland and the Conservative Party in 1876', *Journal of Modern History*, XXIX, 355-60 (1957).

[2] The Conservatives won 6 county seats in 1868, 15 in 1874, and 6 in 1880. There should have been a seventh in 1880, but Sir A. H. Gordon (East Aberdeenshire), who had been elected in 1875 as a Conservative, changed his allegiance on the Eastern question (*3 Hansard* CCXLIII, 793-8) and was returned unopposed as a Liberal.

intelligent idealist. 'I find', wrote Taylor Innes of the history of Scotland, 'in every age a passion for the ideal, and a sense of the obligation of men who deal with public affairs to build upon nothing less than principles of right.' 'I am a Liberal because I am a Scotchman.'[1] And there were other admirable features of Scottish Liberalism, such as the independence and sense of public duty characteristic of the provost and bailies of Scottish burghs, and the purity of Scottish elections. But along with these good qualities, the effects of which were wholly admirable, went other Scottish characteristics with political results which were not always so desirable: caution, undue respect for age and experience, and a weakness for long pedigrees. Caution bred apathy, reluctance to change, unwillingness to go outside established families for parliamentary candidates, and distrust of working-class politicians. Respect for age and experience led Liberal associations into choosing retired soldiers, sailors, Indian civil servants, merchants and manufacturers as candidates, rather than men of dash and ability. The great majority of the members for the big towns were over fifty, and it was looked upon as something of a revolution when in 1874 Charles Cameron of the *North British Daily Mail* was returned for Glasgow at the age of 33. Fondness for long pedigrees meant (particularly in the counties) the choice of the scions of old local families whose influence alone would have been insufficient to secure them the seat.

These characteristics did not diminish the genuine Radicalism of the constituencies or of the members, and it is significant that the majority of the Scottish Liberal members preferred W. E. Forster to Lord Hartington as their leader in 1875.[2] But they did give the Scottish constituencies a somewhat old-fashioned air. The typical burgh Liberal association was popular enough in tone. Almost all the leading men in the burgh belonged to it, and there were often extended arguments about policy which were sometimes carried to the length of a temporary secession. But it was dominated by a small coterie of leading men, and its

---

[1] *Why I am a Liberal*, ed. Andrew Reid, London, n.d., p. 64.

[2] Those whose preferences were recorded in the Adam Papers were: for Hartington (8)—Henry Campbell-Bannerman, Edward Ellice, Edward Jenkins, A. F. Kinnaird, Samuel Laing, Duncan McLaren, D. R. Macgregor, John Pender: for Forster (14)— George Anderson, Sir Windham Anstruther, Charles Cameron, Sir Henry Davie, J. J. Grieve, J. F. Harrison, William Holms, Peter McLagan, William Mure, Ernest Noel, Lyon Playfair, John Ramsay, Robert Reid, James Yeaman.

Member of Parliament was almost always sufficiently wealthy or important to be able to hold himself aloof from the ordinary factional arguments. Scottish burghs were, indeed, very prone to be 'member-ridden', because they selected as the candidates great manufacturers like Stewart Clark, the Paisley thread manufacturer, or entrepreneurs like Sir Thomas Sutherland of the P. and O. steamship company, or landlords like Edward Ellice the younger. In much the same way the typical county Liberal association, although less member-ridden (unless the member were a man like Robert Jardine or Alexander Matheson of the great firm of Jardine, Matheson and Co.), was dominated by a small group of lairds, big farmers or cattle breeders, and professional men. Robert Farquharson's principal supporters in West Aberdeenshire were two lairds, two cattle breeders, a retired banker, the Provost of Huntly, the editor of the *Huntly Express*, and a family of 'farmers and gentlemen'.[1] Significantly, he had secured the Liberal nomination largely because his leading tenants went along to the adoption meeting to support him.[2]

By the standards of most English counties, with their committees of landowners, such associations were almost popular in character. But they were no less exclusive: the small laird, the big farmer, the banker, the newspaper editor were just as much the leaders of society in a small Scottish county as the great landowners were in an English one. And where there were leading landowning families on the Liberal side, it was quite as usual for them to monopolise the representation and to dominate the Liberal association as it was in England. The two Liberal families of Sinclair of Ulbster and Traill of Rattar shared the representation of Caithness between 1832 and 1885, and although their monopoly was broken by Dr G. B. Clark, a crofter candidate, in 1885, the present Viscount Thurso (who belongs to the fifth generation of Sinclairs to have contested the county) was returned for Caithness and Sutherland from 1922 to 1945. A number of counties were habitually contested by the partisans of two rival houses of different politics. In Wigtownshire the Conservative Earl of Galloway fought the Liberal Earl of Stair. The representation of Roxburgh was shared by two families

---

[1] Robert Farquharson, *In and Out of Parliament: Reminiscences of a Varied Life*, London 1911, pp. 184-7.
[2] *Ibid.*, p. 179.

for an even longer period. The two rival houses of Douglas (afterwards Montagu-Douglas-Scott) and Elliot, whose chiefs were the Conservative Duke of Buccleuch and the Liberal Earl of Minto, had fought each other since the seventeenth century, and were not to be allied until in 1886 the Elliots became Liberal Unionists.[1] The partisans of each side imputed every political virtue to their champions and every political vice to their opponents, and there is something delightfully naïve about the adulation heaped upon the Elliots in 1880 by that staunch opponent of landlordism, *The Scotsman*.

> With Roxburghshire the last of the Buccleuch counties is wrested from the Buccleuch grasp. The men of Tweed and Teviotdale have once more restored the county to its rightful position. Many Roxburghshire people—many Liberals throughout Scotland—have a vivid recollection of fights long ago, when Elliots fought with Scotts, when Minto warred with Branxholm, for the representation of the county. More than once Minto had to succumb, because all the electoral arts, which have been used wherever the Duke of Buccleuch has sway, were used to keep the independent electors from asserting themselves. This time these arts have proved of no avail. Public indignation has swept them away, as they have been swept away in Dumfriesshire, in Selkirkshire, and in Mid-Lothian. The Duke is now free to devote himself exclusively to the nomination of the Peers he thinks fit to represent Scotland. He will probably not meet in that task with the same firm front that has been presented to him in the constituencies; but that is comparatively a small matter. It is of more importance that the men of Roxburghshire should have chosen the Hon. Arthur Elliot for their representative in Parliament—that Minto should have once more successfully led the battle for independence and Liberal principles.[2]

Scotland is a small country closely knit by kinship, the universities, the bar, the churches and the press, and it is scarcely surprising that the family atmosphere of individual Liberal associations also characterised Scottish Liberalism in general. Candidates moved freely from constituency to constituency (particularly where they had family connections or land in more than one place) if they were not successful the first time; usually

[1] The latest member of the two families to represent the county was Lord William [Montagu-Douglas-] Scott, M.P. for Roxburgh and Selkirk 1935-50.
[2] *The Scotsman*, 10 April 1880. Elliot subsequently became a Liberal Unionist, editor of the *Edinburgh Review*, and the biographer of Goschen.

from the county to the local burghs or vice versa, but often much further. T. R. Buchanan, who started his career in East Lothian in 1880, moved to Edinburgh in 1881, to East Aberdeenshire in 1892, and to East Perthshire in 1903, and Sir John Pender, who contested Totnes in 1865, Linlithgowshire in 1868, Stirling in 1886, and the Govan division of Lanarkshire in 1889, and was returned for Wick 1872-85 and 1892-6, were the most travelled members, but a considerable number had contested three constituencies. Except in the far north the leading members of the various local associations also got to know one another well, as they mixed freely with the committees of neighbouring constituencies at shows, markets and meetings, and with the leading Scottish Liberals during visits to Edinburgh. The University electors, and particularly the doctors, helped to encourage this fraternisation, since they took a great interest in the personalities involved in university elections and not infrequently held meetings at which they tried to measure them against such heroic academic figures as Lyon Playfair, who had been a professor in Manchester, London and Edinburgh, secretary of the Science and Art Department and an F.R.S. before becoming M.P. for the universities of Edinburgh and St Andrews in 1868 and Postmaster-General in 1873.

There is an agreeable informality about the correspondence of Scottish Liberals of the period as a result of these close personal links. J. J. Reid's reports to W. P. Adam in 1879, for instance, have the ring of intimate personal knowledge. Thus he writes of Kirkcudbrightshire, where John Lawson Kennedy of Knocknalling hoped to succeed the sitting member at the dissolution:

> The objections to Knocknalling are insuperable unless I have utterly mistaken the constity. & I know it so well I do not think I have. He *is* unsound on Rabbits & he *is* (or at least *was*) unsound on the Trinity. He would not command 50 votes. I am glad we are rid of Caird for he also was weak, very weak. The suggestion of young Carrick Moore (ætat 30) of Corswall is not a bad one; young Munches I am pretty sure won't go. He has not the money & Munches will never give it him. The local paper named these two.
>   If Kennedy will submit to a reference to Lord Hartington or to you it would be all right. They have named a comm: of 10 to look out for a candidate. Walter McCulloch, J. Gordon Brown, McNeillie

of Castlehill, Starke, McCall of Caitloch, Dr. Lewis, Neilson of Queenshill & others.[1]

Again, he writes a week later of Inverness-shire, a Conservative county, for which Adam had suggested a Mr Lyall or Lyell [? Leonard Lyell of Kinnordy, Forfarshire, afterwards M.P. for Orkney]:

> For this Mr Lyall would do very well, we have *no local man whatever*, & the next best thing is a laird & a Scotchman. The pity is that Forfarshire is not further North. I hope he wears a Kilt, if he is up Glenisla way he very likely does. Perhaps I might have a chance of seeing him next week in London when I come. The expense will be not inconsiderable but the seat may be won.

The most impressive feature of Scottish Liberalism was that it was able to adjust itself, in spite of its oligarchical character, to most of the new demands which were made upon it. It was as unsuccessful in keeping the allegiance of the labour movement as was the English Liberal party,[2] but it was able to reconcile the demands of churchmen and disestablishmentarians and it was able to deal with the problem of the crofters. The principal reason for this success was that the large Liberal majorities in most constituencies made it possible to do without a close-knit organisation on the Birmingham model, with the consequence that political issues could be fought out by the old method of appealing to the electors. Twelve constituencies were fought by superfluous Liberals in 1868, seven in 1874 and twenty-two in 1885; only in 1880 was there anything like a respite, when only two constituencies were fought by extra Liberals.

The primary issues in the great majority of cases were ecclesiastical, as might be expected since the Disruption of the Scottish church had taken place comparatively recently. J. J. Reid in

---

[1] J. J. Reid to W. P. Adam, 10 July 1879. Adam Papers. The Caird mentioned was Sir James Caird, M.P. for Dartmouth 1857-9 and for Stirling 1859-65, the famous agriculturalist whose seat, Cassencary near Creetown, was in the county (where he owned over 2,000 acres). 'Munches' is a reference to Wellwood Herries Maxwell of Munches, M.P. for Kirkcudbrightshire 1868-74. Kennedy ultimately withdrew his candidature (*The Scotsman*, 16 March 1880) and the seat went to John Heron Maxwell-Heron of Kirroughtree.

[2] The seventies and eighties were not an important period for Scottish working-class politics, because the influence of Gladstone was so strong. cp. Thomas Johnston, *The History of the Working Classes in Scotland*, 3 edn, Glasgow [1939], pp. 261-3. For a trades council during this period see K. D. Buckley, *Trades Unionism in Aberdeen 1878 to 1900*, Aberdeen 1955.

1879, for instance, reported one such dispute in East Aberdeenshire, where there was talk of endorsing the candidature of Sir Alexander Gordon, who had originally been elected as a Conservative and who was a churchman: Reid was afraid that if the Liberals adopted Gordon 'the dissenters may start a man of their own'.[1] As in England, there were also difficulties with temperance men, and Reid was much alarmed lest they should split the Liberal vote in Edinburgh, where there had been a contest between rival Liberals in 1874.

A meeting anent the Representation is called for Saturday. The P.B.s [Permissive Billers] & such like are signing a requisition to Trayner who is moving heaven & earth—Several members of the Committee have spoken to me, & I have said their best policy is to take their sitting members *both* of them.[2]

However, in the end both Liberal sitting members were re-adopted.[3]

The most interesting case is that of the crofters, whose interests were almost entirely neglected before 1885. Indeed, many of the evictors were themselves Scottish members. The crofters had suffered from the great rise in the value of agricultural land and sporting properties which had taken place during the first half of the nineteenth century, because it had encouraged Highland landlords to let their properties for grazing or for shooting, and to reduce as far as possible the amount of land held by the crofters at low rents.[4] The result was a series of clearances, most of which had taken place long before 1868, which drove a large number

[1] Reid to Adam, 17 July 1879. Adam Papers.

[2] *Ibid.*

[3] Mr W. H. Marwick of the University of Edinburgh has kindly informed me that John Trayner, who was appointed a Lord of Session by the Gladstone government in 1885, had been active in connection with the Scottish Permissive Bill Association and that he took part in a meeting with Sir Wilfrid Lawson early in November 1879. Both Duncan McLaren and James Cowan, the sitting members, supported the Permissive Bill, but Cowan was thought to be insufficiently active in support of it and of other Radical measures, and Trayner was anxious to replace him. At the meeting of the Liberal executive committee on 14 March 1880 Trayner was nominated as an alternative candidate to Cowan, but his claims were rejected by 16 votes to 9 (*The Scotsman*, 15 March 1880). Trayner's supporters then appealed to the 'Aggregate Liberal Committee', where several trade unionists supported his claims, but he was again rejected by 146 votes to 43. (*Edinburgh Courant*, 15 March 1880.) On each occasion there were a number of abstentions.

[4] There are many accounts of the crofters' problems. The most accessible are J. S. Blackie, *The Scottish Highlanders and the Land Laws*, London 1885; and D. W. Crowley, 'The "Crofters' Party", 1885-1892', *Scottish Historical Review*, XXXV, 110-26 (1956).

of crofters off the land altogether, and restricted most of the remainder to poor soil and extremely small uneconomic holdings. Before 1885 very few of them had the vote, with the result that the typical Highland Radical was a grazier—the crofter's enemy —like William McCombie of Tillyfour, M.P. for West Aberdeenshire 1868-76, and that the wrongs of the crofters were largely ignored. The onset of the agricultural depression, however, forced their grievances on the attention of the public, for it made it impossible for the ordinary crofter to pay the high rent that was still asked of him (since the market value of the land remained the same because it was in demand for deer runs). The result was a new series of attempted evictions which culminated in the spirited resistance of some of the Skye crofters in April 1882 at the 'Battle of the Braes', and the beginning of a new approach to the crofters' problems. In 1881 the Irish Land Leaguers led by Davitt took up the question in Glasgow, in 1882 the Highland Land League was formed to advocate a peasant proprietary in the Highlands, and in the same year Dr Charles Cameron, M.P. for Glasgow and proprietor of the *North British Daily Mail*, took up the crofters' cause in parliament and in his paper. The government, and especially Chamberlain, appreciated the need to do something to relieve the crofters, but their hands were tied by Irish obstruction, and nothing had come of their good intentions by the general election in 1885. As a consequence, Radical 'crofter candidates' were run in six constituencies (Sutherland, Ross, Caithness, Argyll, Wick and Inverness), three by the Highland Land League and three by local Radicals, all but one of whom were successful in ousting the more orthodox Liberal candidate. The 1886 Liberal government took the hint and passed the first of a series of Liberal Crofters' Acts, and by the next general election the 'crofter candidates' had with one exception become orthodox Liberals. 'Crofter candidates' of Henry Georgeite or socialist views continued to contest Highland constituencies for the next forty years, usually under the auspices of the Highland Land League, but with little success except in the Western Isles. Until the Second World War the crofter constituencies remained predominantly Liberal.

II

The feeling that there were significant political differences between Wales and England was still quite new in 1868, since
modern Wales is a product of the industrial revolution and of
the evangelical revival of the early nineteenth century.[1] The one
created a new urban Wales alongside the old Wales of the hills,
the other cut off the mass of the people from the old ruling
classes. For politics, religion was more important than industry,
because the religion of the chapels created the social climate of
the new Wales. On the one hand, standing apart, were the clergy,
the gentry, the large farmers, and the narrow circle of Anglican
and public-house working men—less than a quarter of the total
population—on the other was the mass of the people. Between
the two lay an immense gulf. The gentry looked to England,
spoke English, belonged to the Church of England, and, apart
from a few Whig houses, were Tory. From the people they were
separated by social custom and religion, and even the relations
of landlord and tenant had become almost entirely commercial.
The lower clergy, although usually conscientious and Welsh-
speaking, were cut off from most of the laity; from the lower
classes by difference of language, outlook and creed, and from
the gentry by birth, since they were largely drawn from the class
of small farmers. Dissent, on the other hand, was a popular
Welsh movement. It emphasised Welshness, and the need to re-
vive the national language and culture. It erected between the
ordinary people and their natural leaders the dual barriers of
language and belief, and provided a new leadership in the ministers and deacons, who supplied the want of a native middle class.
These leaders (like so many of the priests in Ireland) were of
humble origin and won their leadership the hard way, by showing that they possessed more intelligence, more eloquence,
more spirit, than their congregations. But unlike the Irish clergy,
few of them received a regular stipend and few of them were tied
for long periods to one chapel: they enjoyed a large measure of

---

[1] The best accounts of Welsh politics are contained in Coupland, *Welsh and Scottish
Nationalism*; T. Evans, *The Background of Modern Welsh Politics, 1789-1846*, Cardiff
1936; David Williams, *A History of Modern Wales*, London 1950, and *The Rebecca Riots*,
Cardiff 1955; Henry Richard, *Letters on the Social and Political Condition of the Principality
of Wales*, London 1866 (also published as *Letters and Essays on Wales*, London 1884);
and in R. T. Jenkins, 'The Development of Nationalism in Wales', *Sociological Review*,
XXVII, 163-82 (1935).

independence, and they owed this independence to the greatest test of all, the willingness of the congregations to pay for their services. Nor were they tempted to move away to England. The Welsh language freed them from dependence on English culture, but it also cut them off from migration except to the Welsh chapels in the great cities—a mere handful.

The early preachers were too busy to attend to politics, which, in any case, they despised. But by the forties the Baptists and Congregationalists were beginning to raise political questions and to associate themselves with militant dissent in England. They felt most strongly the need for a system of primary education outside the church, but they were also very conscious of the church's privileges and hostile to the establishment. By the fifties the growing strength of the Oxford movement in the church and the report of the commissioners on Welsh education had also wakened the Methodists to their affinity to the old dissenting bodies. Moreover, an influential dissenting press had sprung up, which used the Welsh language and agitated nonconformist grievances, and which in 1859 was reinforced by the most influential of all Welsh-language newspapers, Thomas Gee's *Baner ac Amserau Cymru*.[1] Gee had a vivid style and immense determination, and as a Methodist minister as well as a publisher himself typified the change which was taking place in Welsh Methodism.

To demand the ending of such grievances of dissent as church rates, the church monopoly of burial grounds, tithes, the church control of education, and the establishment itself, involved both a political and a social challenge, since the gentry, who were churchmen, controlled the Welsh representation. For tactical reasons the dissenters denounced Toryism as their enemy, but in practice they were quite as concerned to overthrow the Whigs as the Tories. The fact that in 1859 and 1865 there was nominally a small Liberal majority in the Welsh seats was irrelevant to them, because on ecclesiastical questions both parties voted together. Indeed, the Whigs were often stiffer opponents than the Tories, and were in no sense Radicals: one-third of the Liberal members in 1862 called themselves 'Liberal-Conservatives', seven

[1] Gee was a Denbigh publisher. The *Baner ac Amserau Cymru* incorporated Gee's own paper *Y Faner* (1857), and *Yr Amserau*, a fortnightly published in Liverpool and edited by William Rees, an active politician, which had exercised an extraordinary influence in its day in drawing the attention of dissenters and Methodists to their political disabilities.

were Lord-Lieutenants, two were sons of peers, one was the brother of a peer, and three were baronets. The advocacy of dissenters' grievances, therefore, involved not only a political campaign, but an attack on the privileged position of church and gentry, and the capture of the Welsh representation by the dissenting majority. This imparted a bitterness to Welsh politics, a sense of social grievance, which had no real counterpart in England. Moreover, since the gentry were well aware of the challenge to their position they were tempted to counter-attack with the consequence that the eviction of tenants for their politics, hitherto almost unknown, became a commonplace in certain Welsh counties. The result was not only the creation of a myth which magnified their number beyond all recognition but a general deterioration in the relations between the dissenting majority and the church minority.

There was no possibility of the dissenters gaining a working majority in any of the Welsh constituencies before 1867. Most of the Welsh constituencies were counties with a very restricted franchise, and all but three of the boroughs were predominantly rural and subject to landlord influence. An active friend of the dissenters, Dillwyn, represented the Swansea district, but Merthyr Tydvil, the largest borough in Wales in point of population, had a very small electorate (1,387 electors in 1866, although the population was over 85,000), which included only 126 working men, and returned a nominee of the Guest family, while Cardiff was under the influence of the Marquess of Bute. Even after 1867 traditional influences were very powerful, but the Reform Act did put the dissenters in a majority in almost all constituencies. In the larger boroughs it was an overwhelming majority —Merthyr's electorate grew from 1,387 to 14,577—but in the counties it was still by no means a large one, and unless the dissenters were unusually well organised they had to side with Whig country gentlemen against Tory country gentlemen rather than work for their own candidates. There was, therefore, no question of sweeping nonconformist gains until after 1885.

The first open assault by the dissenters occurred in Merioneth in 1859, but was defeated, and resulted in the inauguration of political evictions on a scale which soon gave the election a legendary significance. As there seemed no immediate prospect of winning a seat, the experiment was not tried again in 1865:

instead, a new emphasis was placed on organisation, and a serious attempt was made to build up a nonconformist electoral organisation. The initiative in this reorganisation was taken, not by the Welsh themselves, but by the Liberation Society, an English organisation in which two émigré Welshmen, Henry Richard and Carvell Williams, were leading figures.[1] These two, with the Society's founder, Edward Miall, held a conference at Swansea in September 1862 to discuss the question, and enlisted the aid of a number of rich English nonconformists, of whom the most generous was Samuel Morley. Thereafter every effort was made to encourage the chapels to take a greater interest in political questions, and particularly in disestablishment. Meetings were held all over Wales by Liberationists, committees were formed to promote political action, and two Registration Associations were formed to attend to the routine work of electoral organisation in north and south Wales.[2] These efforts were not by any means equally successful in all parts of Wales, but in a few constituencies the essential framework was established, while in the others much was done to complete the political education of the dissenters. By 1867 it was only a question of where the new organisation was to try its strength.

In the end two constituencies selected themselves: Merthyr Tydvil and Denbighshire, and in them the battle was accordingly fought. Merthyr was the industrial centre of South Wales, an enormous straggling constituency running from valley to valley where the pits and ironworks lay, and taking in Aberdare, Mountain Ash, Merthyr and Dowlais. It was also one of the main centres of Welsh nonconformity with eighty-one congregations and sixty ministers.[3] The sitting member was Henry Austin Bruce, a local man who had been stipendiary magistrate for Merthyr and Aberdare from 1847 to 1852, when he entered the House of Commons as successor to Sir John Guest. He was himself a coal owner, but he derived most of his considerable influence from his association with the Guest family, for whom he acted as one of the trustees of the great Dowlais ironworks after

[1] There is an account of their activities in C. S. Miall, *Henry Richard, M.P.*, London 1889, and in the *D.N.B.* article on Richard.

[2] The north Wales meetings were often held at Liverpool rather than in Wales itself, and a special 'Conference of Welsh Reformers' met there shortly before the 1868 elections. *Liverpool Weekly Courier*, 6 June 1868.

[3] I owe these figures to Dr I. G. Jones. The *Nonconformist*, 2 December 1868, gives various accounts of the election from the dissenting point of view.

1855. Although never a popular figure, Bruce had made a name for himself in the House of Commons as Under-Secretary at the Home Office, 1862-4, and Vice-President of the Committee of Council on Education, 1864-6, and was almost certain of a place in the next Liberal cabinet (he became Home Secretary). In normal times he would have been sure of keeping his seat, although the fact that he was a churchman, and an opponent of the ballot and of trade unionism, made him an unsympathetic candidate for such a constituency. But the times were not normal: the Reform Act not only trebled the electorate; it gave Merthyr a second member, and the two candidates who came forward to claim it were both exceptionally strong.

The first and stronger claimant was Henry Richard, by this time the most respected and influential of Welsh dissenters. Richard had made his reputation in England as minister of the Marlborough chapel in the Old Kent Road, 1835-50, as an advocate of international arbitration and secretary of the Peace Society since 1848, and as a leading member of the Liberation Society. But he had retained an active interest in Welsh dissent, and had provided it with a reasoned statement of the dissenters' grievances in his *Letters on the Social and Political Condition of the Principality of Wales*, first published in the *Morning Star* in 1866. The second candidate was Richard Fothergill, also a dissenter, who was one of the largest employers of labour in the borough and enjoyed the support of a number of influential ministers. His claims were those of a great industrialist rather than those of a militant dissenter, but he was none the less an exceptionally strong candidate, as has already been pointed out,[1] and a threat to Bruce rather than to Richard.

The form which the contest was going to take was decided during the winter of 1867-8 when Bruce gradually lost touch with the electors in the valleys, and particularly with the Chartist element among them. By the beginning of 1868 his strength was no greater than that of Fothergill in spite of his long start, and the more Radical dissenters were growing restive. Thomas Gee's *Baner ac Amserau Cymru* pointed out in February that he was unsympathetic to the causes dear to the heart of all dissenters, and that as Vice-President of the Committee of Council on Education he had generally favoured church schools. By August, when

[1] See above, p. 78.

Gee began to attack Bruce in earnest, the whole climate had changed and Bruce was in grave danger; by September Gee's avowed preference for Fothergill had tipped the scales decidedly against him; by October it was merely a question of how big Fothergill's majority would be. The *Baner* was the decisive influence because it brought men to look on the election solely from a nonconformist point of view. Gee attacked Bruce on the ground that henceforth mere sympathy for the nonconformists was not to be enough: dissenters needed as their representatives fellow dissenters who could be trusted to go along with them the whole way to disestablishment. In particular, he called for a firm stand on the education question, on which Bruce took a strongly Anglican line, and pointed out, rather unfairly, that Bruce had failed to subscribe to the movement for a Welsh university, that he had appointed two English-speaking churchmen to inspect Welsh schools, and that he had shown in office a strong partiality for church schools in dealing with disputes at Gellifer and Lingen. Finally, Bruce was opposed to the ballot, the symbol of Welsh independence. Although most English dissenters, including Jacob Bright, George Hadfield, and Samuel Morley, and even Henry Richard, preferred Bruce to Fothergill, once the issue of the election was stated in these terms the chapels were bound to give their support to the latter and Bruce was doomed. Richard himself wrote to Gee: 'Bruce certainly deserved all he got in the *Baner*. I certainly agree with you that we ought to take high ground and not submit to be snubbed by these so-called liberal churchmen.' Bruce was accordingly driven out, to take refuge in Renfrewshire, and Fothergill and Richard were returned for Merthyr.[1]

The issue in the other symbolic contest, in Denbighshire, was the same, but it was complicated by the fact that it involved, as well as straightforward religious issues, the relations of landlord and tenant. Denbighshire was not only the home of Thomas Gee, whose influence was decisive in the campaign; it was the headquarters, as it were, of territorialism in Wales. A member of the Wynn family had represented it continuously since the eighteenth century, and the Wynns were the greatest landowners in all Wales with some 150,000 acres, 29,000 of them in Denbighshire. Sir Watkin Williams-Wynn, who had sat for the constituency since

---

[1] Richard (L) 11,683, Fothergill (L) 7,439, Bruce (L) 5,776.

1841 as a Conservative, had since 1852 been content to share the representation with a Whig landowner, Robert Myddleton-Biddulph of Chirk Castle, who was Lord-Lieutenant and brother of Queen Victoria's Keeper of the Privy Purse, and in this way the dissenters were shut out of the representation. Sir Watkin was too strong to dislodge (he kept his seat until his death in 1885), so that it was clear from the first that the dissenters would have to attack Biddulph if they wanted a seat, however much they might protest that they were equally indifferent to both members. Gee was lucky enough to secure as his candidate George Osborne Morgan, the son of a vicar of Conway, who had had a brilliant university career before taking up journalism and the bar. Osborne Morgan was a passionate believer in the new non-conformist Wales, although himself a churchman, but he was first and foremost a champion of the Welsh farmers against their landlords. In Denbighshire the issue of the election thus came to depend more on the tenants' reaction to his campaign for tenant right than on religious issues such as those raised in Merthyr. There was nothing new in the questions raised, but the fact that tenancies were much less secure in Wales than in England and that rents had been gradually increasing imparted to the whole question an almost Irish immediacy, and gave Osborne Morgan a seat by a narrow majority.[1] Moreover, the landlord-tenant issue was underlined after the elections by political evictions in Carmarthenshire and Cardiganshire from which stemmed the agricultural Radicalism of 'Young Wales' in the eighties. However, in Denbighshire itself there was a curious quiet after the elections and Sir Watkin and Osborne Morgan were returned together unopposed until 1885.

After the 1868 elections Henry Richard and Osborne Morgan joined forces to draw public attention to the evictions in Wales, to promote a burials bill, and to work for disestablishment. But Welsh questions were almost immediately overshadowed by the agitation against the 1870 Education Act and the other unpopular measures of the Gladstone government. Henry Richard himself was the most able of the government's critics in the education debates, and threw himself into the activities of the National Education League. In 1874, when Edward Miall gave up his

[1] Sir W. W.-Wynn (C) 3,355, G. O. Morgan (L) 2,720, R. Myddleton-Biddulph (L) 2,413.

seat because of failing health, he also became the leader of the English Liberationists. He was thus drawn away from Wales into English politics just as Welsh political dissent was ready for a further advance, and in need of a strong leader. As a consequence, the particularism which was always a marked feature of Welsh nonconformity shaped events between 1870 and 1880: North Wales turned to tenant right and local causes, while South Wales tended to split up into its component parts and to become absorbed in local disputes.

Wales was rescued from this particularism by an Englishman, Stuart Rendel, and by the Midlothian campaign, which gave Welsh dissenters in common with those in England a new sense of purpose. Rendel was one of the partners in the great Elswick works started by Lord Armstrong, the Newcastle engineer and inventor of the Armstrong gun, and by Rendel's father. He was an advanced Radical, but he had no acquaintance with Wales before he became candidate for Montgomeryshire in 1878, and was a churchman—hardly the popular conception of a Welsh leader. What he did in Wales was almost entirely done by personal charm, lavish expenditure—he hired a special train to carry his voters to the poll—and great natural abilities. He first captured the Welsh imagination in 1880 by winning Montgomeryshire, one of the oldest and most firmly established Conservative strongholds in Wales, which had been held by a Wynn without a break since 1799. He then set himself to supply from the House of Commons the leadership which Henry Richard had failed to provide. Here his election address was an extraordinary asset, since it had been inspired by A. C. Humphreys-Owen, one of the best informed Welshmen of his day, and incorporated all the points with which 'Tom' Ellis became associated ten years later: disestablishment, tenant right, the establishment of a truly Welsh education system headed by a Welsh university, and the end of tithes. Here, too, Henry Austin Bruce, now Lord Aberdare, was a great help to him, because it was the Aberdare Committee's report on intermediate (i.e. secondary) and higher education in Wales that mapped out a solution to the most difficult of Welsh problems.

But the secret of Rendel's leadership lay in his determination to form a Welsh national party within the Liberal party and to endow it with practicable objectives which would appeal to the English Radicals in the House of Commons. He differed from Henry Richard in wanting a Welsh party distinct from the nonconformist wing of the Liberal party, and in sympathising with those who wished to form a Welsh Land League on the Irish model: but he also differed from the latter in believing that agrarian agitation for its own sake would alienate the English Radicals on whom the Welsh reformers depended for support in Parliament. His own programme for a Welsh party was Radical enough, but it was also eminently practical: disestablishment for Wales alone, the creation of a new educational system along the lines suggested by the Aberdare committee, and a system of tenant right for Wales. By restricting his objectives to purely Welsh ones Rendel reduced English opposition to the minimum, and created a Welsh party in the House of Commons. As he wrote many years later:

> Some striking demonstration of the growing Nationality of Wales was then needed. Skilful manœuvring and small doles for undenominational education could not create or constitute a party. The true policy appeared to be to declare a grievance and to claim a remedy on a scale worthy of a distinct Nationality, and for my part I believed that it was almost essential to reject for the time the undoubted claims of Welsh land and to concentrate upon Welsh disestablishment.
>
> Of course, I had no hope of even proximate success in any measure itself. It would be success enough to bring Wales, whole and united, into a definite position in relation to England. Welsh disestablishment meant a clear and effective issue with all Anglicising influences in Wales, and a practical declaration of the case for Welsh Nationalisation outside Wales.[1]

At one jump Wales became a force in the House of Commons, and the careers of T. E. Ellis and Lloyd George became possible.[2]

The old particularism and attachment to the landed families remained strong, particularly in Brecknockshire, Denbighshire, Montgomeryshire and Radnorshire, but in 1885 Wales returned only four Conservatives, while there were thirty Welsh Liberals or 'Lib-Labs'. Moreover, the first county council elections gave

---

[1] *The Personal Papers of Lord Rendel*, ed. F. E. Hamer, London 1931, p. 306.

[2] There is a useful account of Welsh politics and their bearing on the career of Lloyd George in W. Watkin Davies, *Lloyd George 1863-1914*, London 1939. For Ellis see T. I. Ellis, *Thomas Edward Ellis*, 2 vols, Liverpool 1948 (in Welsh).

the nonconformists control over local government as well as over the parliamentary representation. The result was that by 1889 the political representation of the country (Table IV) at last reflected the results of the religious census of 1851.

Table IV. Religion and Politics in Wales[1]

	Number of persons at the most numerously attended service on Census Sunday 1851.		Results of the first County Council Elections January 1889.				Parliamentary Representation January 1889.		
	Church	Nonconformists	C.	L.	L.U.	Ind.	C.	L.	L.U.
Anglesey	2,374	16,604	6	34	1	1	–	1	–
Brecknock	6,234	19,375	21	20	3	1	–	1	–
Cardigan	10,517	34,571	9	38	–	1	–	1	–
Carmarthen	8,685	31,918	8	40	2	1	–	3	–
Carnarvon	7,328	41,781	15	33	–	–	1	2	–
Denbigh	9,138	29,153	14	33	1	–	1	1	1
Flint	4,931	13,046	14	25	–	3	–	2	–
Glamorgan	11,997	81,141	15	45	4	2	–	9	1
Merioneth	2,360	20,168	9	33	–	–	–	1	–
Monmouth	16,026	48,201	16	29	–	3	2	2	–
Montgomery	8,370	22,441	17	22	2	1	–	2	–
Pembroke	8,989	21,839	15	31	1	1	–	1	1
Radnor	4,259	3,958	10	12	1	1	1	–	–
	101,208	384,196	169	395	15	15	5	26	3

III

In spite of the Fenian movement which threatened armed rebellion in parts of the south and west, Ireland in 1868 still appeared to most English observers to share the political assumptions of England itself. Chichester Fortescue, Liberal Chief Secretary for Ireland under Russell and Gladstone, wrote to the latter at the beginning of the election campaign:

Our prospects in Ireland are very good. The old spirit of so-called 'Independent Opposition', playing into the hands of rebels on one side and of the Tories (who encourage it) on the other, has almost died out in the light of the Church question, and your Irish policy,—

[1] The figures are taken from Henry Richard's *Letters on the Social and Political Condition of the Principality of Wales*, p. 77; the *Daily News*, 29 and 31 January 1889, and the *Constitutional Year Book for 1895*.

so that the R. Catholic body, with small exceptions, is unanimous in supporting the Liberal party here, and yourself.[1]

Yet by 1874, even before the rise of Parnell, this superficial resemblance to England had disappeared, and Fortescue himself was struggling to avoid defeat in County Louth and clinging pathetically to the once-despised support of the Conservatives:

> I believe I am beaten. Home Rule, with Fenianism behind it, has probably carried both seats for this county. Fenianism revenges itself on me and 'coercion Fortescue' & 'Amnesty' are the popular cries. I have been almost abandoned by the R.C. priests. Many are violently against me—& those who are friendly are intimidated, & do nothing. On the other hand, I have a large amount of Protestant Conservative support.[2]

The Liberals were routed everywhere except in Ulster, and the old fight between the two English parties was at an end.

The general election of 1868 was not only the last to be fought between Liberals and Conservatives; it was also the last to be fought in the peculiar conditions of Irish politics before the ballot. Parliamentarianism was discredited in the eyes of the mass of the people, and the voters were for the most part content that landlord or priest or briber should decide their politics. The great majority of the seats were allocated without any reference to the people at all, as fifty-four of the sixty-four county seats and eleven of the thirty-nine borough seats were uncontested. But even where there was a contest the voters were rarely left to decide for themselves. In the towns (even in Dublin) money and mobs were the masters, with the consequence that petitions were presented in eleven of the twenty boroughs contested.[3] In the countryside— the rural outskirts of the boroughs and the counties—the landlords or their agents escorted their tenants in batches to the polls. Where the landlords were Conservatives the priests put up such resistance as they could, sometimes (as at Drogheda) organising mobs to 'rescue' voters, sometimes (as at Sligo) threatening those who voted Conservative with spiritual penalties. Bishop Gillooly of Sligo, for instance, declared before the election that 'Catholic

---

[1] Add. MS. 44,121, ff.66-7.
[2] Add. MS. 44,123, ff.81-2.
[3] Belfast, Carrickfergus, Cashel, Drogheda, Dublin, Galway, Limerick, Londonderry, Sligo, Wexford, and Youghal. Cashel and Sligo were disfranchised after the elections.

voters who voted for Major Knox should make reparation before
they could be reconciled to God', and after the election he and
his priests sent those who had voted for Knox out of their churches
to hear mass in the church porch.[1] On the other hand, where
the landowners were Whigs whose candidate favoured the disestablishment of the Irish Church, the priests gave them every
assistance in bringing their tenants to the poll. They seem to
have been particularly active at Limerick, where the two Liberal
candidates were opposed by a Conservative and a self-styled
Fenian (Richard Pigott of the *Irishman*, afterwards notorious as
the forger of letters from Parnell) whose supporters seem to have
coalesced.[2]

Because it was a tradition of Irish politics to employ mobs to
'protect' the candidates on each side, few contested elections were
fought without violence, and the army was parcelled out for election duty to prevent serious disturbances. Not that it was very
successful in carrying out this distasteful duty. On many occasions the soldiers themselves became the target of the rioters,
because tradition decreed that the way to prevent disturbances
was for the soldiers to marshal each landlord's voters on his estate
and march them to the poll in a body, and the object of the
popular party was therefore to liberate the escorted voters. The
army had no illusions about what it was doing. Major-General
McMurdo who commanded the Dublin Infantry Brigade in 1868
told the Hartington Committee, 'It is very well understood by
the officers of the army that the majority of those voters go under
the escort very much against their own inclination, in order to
vote according to the wishes of the landlords'.[3] When asked
whether the soldiers regarded the voters as free men or prisoners
he replied, 'Practically as prisoners; in receiving charge of a
number of men, with orders to take them to a polling station,
the officers are bound, according to their ideas of military usage,
to take care of those men, that they do not escape and that
others do not injure them'.[4] Indeed, the officers were given orders
that they were not to allow voters to escape, since it was generally thought that the wretched men were anxious to do so. It is
hardly surprising that the Hartington Committee, looking back

[1] [C. 48] p. viii. H.C. (1870). XXXII, 628.
[2] H.C. 352, pp. 206-16 (1868-9). VIII, 206-16.
[3] H.C. 352, p. 289 (1868-9). VIII, 289.   [4] *Ibid.*

on this election in the following year, was less than content with
what it found.

> In Ireland . . . the influence of the landlord is often opposed by
> that of the Roman Catholic clergy. Organized mobs also appear to
> be an almost generally recognized part of the system of conducting
> an Irish election. The object of their employment is either to
> intimidate an unwilling voter, or one who is supposed to be under
> coercion, so as to force him to vote on the side of the popular party,
> or to prevent, by physical force, the voters of the opposite side from
> reaching the poll. To so great an extent is this system carried, that
> the employment of troops in aid of the police, is the ordinary rule at
> an Irish election. The military force in the country is distributed
> before a general election with a view to that event, and not only are
> the troops employed to preserve order at the polling-places, but
> escorts are frequently given on the requisition of candidates or
> their agents, for the purpose of protecting voters coming from a
> distance. It is alleged that in some cases the voters go under the
> charge of these escorts against their will, and consider themselves
> under coercion. Notwithstanding these precautions, scenes of
> violence, including loss of life, are not unfrequent.[1]

The party divisions of English politics had meaning only in
Ulster where, as in Liverpool and other parts of Lancashire, there
was a strongly Protestant working class with Conservative sympathies which made Belfast a Conservative stronghold. However,
as Belfast had only two members and only two of the other nine
Ulster boroughs (Londonderry and Newry) had a population of
more than 10,000, the real interest of Ulster politics was centred
in the counties. In them there was a strong minority Presbyterian
and tenant-farmer movement whose traditions were those of the
old Tenant Right League,[2] and whose natural affiliations were
with the Liberal party. Before the ballot the tenant righters had
little success at elections, and at the general election of 1868 their
cause was so depressed that none of the Ulster counties was contested and seventeen of the eighteen county members were Conservatives. But with the ballot the tenant righters emerged as a
strong Liberal force in Ulster county elections, although they
chose an independent Conservative, J. W. Ellison-Macartney, to

---

[1] H.C. 115, pp. 5-6 (1870). VI, 135-6.

[2] For the League and for subsequent Irish movements see T. P. O'Connor, *The
Parnell Movement*. Its objectives, the three F's (fixity of tenure, fair rents and free sale),
were essentially those of the English Radical land reformers.

be their candidate for Tyrone in 1874.[1] The result (see Table V) was that in the two general elections of 1874 and 1880 the Liberals were able at long last to meet the Conservatives on something like even terms and were able to gain a number of seats by posing as the party of the villager and small farmer.[2] As if to emphasise this character the Liberal candidates were rarely land-owners: the eight Liberal county members returned in 1880 were respectively a merchant and farmer, a Presbyterian mini-ster, a Congregationalist manufacturer from Kidderminster, a merchant from Belfast, a solicitor, a Dublin brewer, and two barristers. But although the Liberals seemed likely to do even better at any future general election fought under similar condi-tions, they were not given the opportunity, because by 1885 Parnell had given a new turn to the Home Rule movement. The Conservatives became once more the party of Ulster Protestant-ism and the Union, with the result that the Liberal candidates (unless they were Liberal Unionists) were consistently rejected.

Table V. Ulster Members

	Liberal	Liberal Unionist	Conservative	Home Rule
1868	5	—	24	—
1874	7	—	20	2
1880	9	—	18	2
1885	—	—	16	17
1886	—	2	15	16
1892	—	3	16	14

The transformation which took place in southern Irish politics between 1868 and 1874 had two main sources: the Home Rule movement and the ballot. The Home Rule movement intro-duced a purely Irish party into Irish politics, while the ballot destroyed the political power of the landowners who were the principal supporters of the two English parties. For ten years after the formation of the Home Government Association in 1870 the direction which the new party would take and the attitude of the priesthood to it remained uncertain. But when Parnell had

[1] For this election see Lawrence J. McCaffrey, 'Home Rule and the General Election of 1874 in Ireland', *Irish Historical Studies*, IX, 190-212 (1954).

[2] The Liberal county seats increased in number from 1 in 1868 to 3 in 1874 and 8 in 1880.

become leader of the Irish parliamentary party in 1880 the direction was clear at last, and the history of Irish politics ceases to be the history of the English political parties in Ireland.

The Home Government Association founded by Isaac Butt in 1870, which touched off the Home Rule movement, was not itself a popular body. It was an association of prosperous professional men, merchants and landowners; some of them, like Butt himself, Conservatives. But it won the sympathy of many of the farmers and old repealers, with the result that it won no fewer than seven by-elections in 1871 and 1872. Most of the lower clergy also supported it, and one of the successful Home Rule candidates, Captain Nolan, was unseated in Galway because the priesthood (in this case from the Archbishop downwards) had used spiritual intimidation on his behalf. But there was still a wing of the Roman Catholic hierarchy which was firmly Liberal, and at the Kerry by-election the Catholic bishop unsuccessfully supported a Catholic landowner, James Dease, who was the nominee of the Earl of Kenmare, against the Protestant candidate of the Home Rulers. Moreover, the growing disillusionment with the Gladstone government's Irish policy after 1871 encouraged many Liberal Catholic M.P.s to look with sympathy on the idea of establishing a federal system in the United Kingdom which would not change the position of the churches or the tenure of the land but would give Ireland a parliament of its own for local purposes. When Butt called a Home Rule conference in November 1873 no fewer than twenty-five M.P.s attended, with the result that the new movement received a sudden access of respectability.

The general election of 1874 was fought in an atmosphere of general confusion because, although it was clear that the Home Rulers would gain a large number of seats, the lack of a central organisation (the Home Rule Conference had constituted a Home Rule League but had not had time to provide it with an organisation or funds) meant that the initiative needed to return Home Rule candidates had to be local. In the case of the twenty-seven Liberal M.P.s who had formally joined the Home Rule League and the five Home Rulers who had been returned at by-elections there was no difficulty. But in the cases of the other thirty-one Home Rule candidates there was room for wide differences of approach, and many were no more than nominal Home Rulers.

The majority of them were landowners belonging to the old political families, who were allowed to obtain seats because there was no alternative. Nor were all the Home Rulers Liberals: Butt himself, Lord Robert Montagu, George Morris and Colonel King-Harman were all Conservatives.

In spite of the confusion of the 1874 election there was a clear-cut result: the Liberal party was effectively destroyed as an Irish party: fifty-five Home Rulers were returned for the three southern provinces, but only five Liberals. The Conservative minority, whose candidates had contested a record number of constituencies, thus became all at once the only effective representative of the English ascendancy. The rejection of Chichester Fortescue in Louth was the most important symbol of this new alignment of parties, although there were also important contests in Limerick and Westmeath. Fortescue as Chief Secretary for Ireland at the time of the disestablishment of the Irish Church and the Land Act was the leading Irish exponent of Gladstone's Irish policy. But he was vulnerable as a Protestant and as a landowner and was, therefore, easy to discredit when Gladstone's Irish policy had itself been discredited by the fiasco of the Irish University Bill. Moreover, the Home Rulers had two strong candidates to put up against Fortescue and his colleague Mathew O'Reilly Dease: A. M. Sullivan, proprietor of the Home Rule organ, the *Nation*, and Philip Callan, who also stood for Dundalk. The Catholic Archbishop of Armagh favoured Fortescue, but the majority of the clergy were strong Home Rulers and went with the popular cause. As a consequence the two Home Rulers won a remarkable victory and Fortescue was driven to ask for a peerage.[1]

For a time during the seventies, after it had become clear that parliament would not tolerate a federal solution of the Irish problem, it looked as though the destruction of the Liberal party was more a matter of form than of substance, and that the Home Rule League would simply become another not very Radical pressure group on English lines. The nominal Home Rulers soon tired of their new rôle and hankered after their old position in the Liberal party. T. P. O'Connor did not exaggerate when he wrote in *The Parnell Movement*: 'The accession of a Liberal

[1] The result was: Sullivan (H.R.) 1,250, Callan (H.R.) 1,202, Fortescue (L) 608, Dease (L) 265.

ministry would have immediately completed the disaster which the defeat of Butt's proposals had begun. At least half the party would at once have become applicants for office, and probably a considerable number would have realised their wishes. The remainder, coalescing with the Liberal party, would gradually have sunk deeper and deeper into a position of obedience to the Liberal whips. . . .'[1]

The Home Rule movement was saved by the rise of Parnell. While not yet leader of the party, he was able in 1879-80 to link the parliamentary movement started by Butt with the Land League, which had been fostered by Davitt and had the support of Archbishop Croke of Cashel and most of the lower clergy, and of the ordinary peasantry. He was able to divert part of the enthusiasm roused by the Land League agitation into parliamentary channels so that when the Land League was dissolved in 1881 the parliamentary party headed by himself became its natural successor.[2] All this did not happen in a day, and the general election of 1880, although much less corrupt than past elections, was fought in quite as much confusion as that of 1874. But there was a difference in that the lead was now taken by Parnell and the nationalists and not by Shaw (Butt's successor) and the moderates, and that the struggle of Home Ruler against Liberal took a new form. In six constituencies there were symbolic contests between nominal Home Rulers and nationalists in which the latter were the more successful, although the narrow franchise placed them at a considerable disadvantage. But the election had come before either Parnell or Shaw was ready for it, with the result that it was impossible to prophesy the result or even to analyse it precisely after the event. The *Irish Times*, for instance, divided the Home Rule members into four categories:[3]

The Left: Parnell and his supporters.	. .	17
The Right: Shaw and his supporters.	. .	24
The Centre (mostly to become Parnellites).	.	18
Old Repealer: P. J. Smyth	. . . .	1

And even Parnell's leading supporters were in doubt as to who would be elected party leader. In the end, because many of the

---

[1] O'Connor, *The Parnell Movement*, p. 240.
[2] For Parnell's rise see R. Barry O'Brien, *The Life of Charles Stewart Parnell 1846-1891*, 2 vols, New York 1898, and N. D. Palmer, *The Irish Land League Crisis*, New Haven 1940.
[3] *Irish Times*, 19 April 1880.

Home Rule members were absent on the day the leader was chosen, Parnell was elected by twenty-three votes to seventeen, and the career of Parnell's Irish parliamentary party which Dr Cruise O'Brien has so ably recorded, was launched.[1] For although Shaw and his leading associates seceded to the Liberals a year later, it required only one more general election and the organisation of the Irish National League to give Parnell absolute mastery over the Irish representation and for Shaw and his colleagues to be driven to look for seats in England or Scotland.

[1] C. Cruise O'Brien, *Parnell and his Party 1880-90*, Oxford 1957.

Part II

ELECTIONS AND ELECTIONEERING

Chapter Nine

ELECTIONS (1)

I

It is idle to expect that a study of Victorian elections will confirm either the myth that in the good old days of the nineteenth century men gave their votes for principle rather than for party or self-interest, whereas in the twentieth century men give their votes chiefly from habit, or the more recent myth that Victorian elections were festivals of beer and bribery. It is equally idle to expect of such a study the statistical sophistication which 'psephologists' have displayed in analysing British elections since 1945. The reason is an elementary one: nineteenth-century elections bore only a superficial resemblance to their twentieth-century counterparts, with the result that comparisons become not so much odious as meaningless. It was not merely that the franchise was different in counties and boroughs and in Great Britain and Ireland, or that the election registers were inefficiently put together, or that the election results were carelessly recorded; nor that there were complications like the minority clause and the tendency for superfluous candidates to come forward. It was primarily that general elections were not general. Only about half the seats were contested by both parties, and even when both parties were in the field with the same number of candidates, local or regional or 'national' issues tended to be as important as those which agitated the whole of the three kingdoms. There was not even any agreement on election colours; blue was a Liberal colour in Cheshire and Westmorland, and a Tory colour in Lancashire; purple and orange were Conservative colours in Surrey and Kent, and Liberal colours in Wiltshire, and there were numerous other variations.[1]

There is, however, a narrow basis for comparison, and for a more or less scientific analysis, in the minority of constituencies

[1] There is a long correspondence on the subject in *Notes and Queries*, 4th Series, vols. II and III. Even today, of course, election colours do not all follow the same pattern, but there is very little of the diversity of the 1870s.

which were contested at every election by sufficient candidates to enable us to say that the contest was a party contest as well as a local one. And a study of these constituencies does seem to show that where both parties were sufficiently strong to keep up a contest over a number of elections, the electors behaved very much as their grandchildren and great-grandchildren have been behaving in the middle of the twentieth century. But it must be emphasised that these constituencies were exceptional; they included none of the Scottish burghs, none of the Irish counties or larger boroughs, and only one quite exceptional London constituency, Westminster. Their value lies in the tendencies they point to, not in their representative character.

The constituencies chosen for this sample are those which were chosen by John Biddulph Martin, the banker-statistician, for a similar purpose in 1874.[1]

They belong to five categories:

I 14 small English and Welsh boroughs.
II 14 large English boroughs.
III 12 English and Welsh counties.
IV 7 Scottish counties.
V 5 small Irish boroughs.

———

52

———

The number of electors in each of the five groups was as follows:

				Total Electorate		
				1868	*1874*	*1880*
I	.	.	.	12,667	13,172	13,897
II	.	.	.	178,933	203,442	231,909
III	.	.	-.	124,889	130,184	159,421
IV	.	.	.	21,479	26,484	25,895
V	.	.	.	3,006	3,411	4,072
All constituencies	.			340,974	376,693	435,194[2]

[1] J. B. Martin, 'The Elections of 1868 and 1874', *Journal of the Statistical Society*, XXXVII, 193-201 (1874).

[2] It will be observed that the rate of increase differed from group to group, partly with population shifts, partly with improvements or changes in the system of registration.

The proportion of electors who actually voted (Table VI) differed in these constituencies more with the type of constituency
and the zeal of the party workers than with the state of the registers, as was often the case in less hotly-fought constituencies.
Indeed, some of the big towns managed to poll over 90 per cent
in 1880, an extraordinary proportion for this type of constituency, and there was a continuous tendency to improve the
registers so that the poll should not be an artificial one.

Table VI. Percentage Poll, 1868-80

	1868	1874	1880
I	86·78	89·07	90·57
II	76·86	79·42	82·51
III	74·36	79·44	79·26
IV	78·80	72·31	87·89
V	89·79	90·56	92·24
All constituencies.	76·55	79·37	81·99[1]

In the sample constituencies as a whole there was a swing to the
Conservatives of five per cent in 1874 and a similar swing back
to the Liberals in 1880, so that the position of the two parties
was almost identical in 1868 and 1880 (Table VII). On the other
hand, the swing was by no means uniform: the small boroughs

Table VII. Percentage of the Poll won by each Party, 1868-80

	1868		1874		1880	
	Lib.	Cons.	Lib.	Cons.	Lib.	Cons.
I	50·28	49·72	45·26	54·74	48·91	51·09
II	53·49	46·51	50·03	49·97	55·14	44·86
III	49·50	50·50	43·11	56·89	48·39	51·61
IV	55·34	44·66	48·93	51·07	55·43	44·57
V	52·24	47·76	49·53	50·47	47·10	52·90
All constituencies	52·04	47·96	47·37	52·63	52·46	47·54

[1] A different selection of 169 English and Welsh constituencies which were fought
by both parties in 1874 and 1880 gives a 76·10 per cent turn-out in 1874 and a 79·80
per cent turn-out in 1880. cp. Alfred Frisby, 'Voters *not* Votes: The Relative Strength
of Political Parties as shown by the last two General Elections,' *Contemporary Review*,
XXXVIII, 635-46 (1880).

both in England and Ireland were much more Conservative in 1880 than they had been in 1868, and the English counties slightly more so: the Scottish counties after an exceptionally big swing against the Liberals in 1874 returned to their 1868 allegiance: the big English boroughs after a comparatively small swing of three per cent in 1874 reacted so violently against the Conservatives in 1880 that the Conservative proportion of the poll fell below the 1868 level.

These figures have their counterparts in those showing the increase in the electorate and in the party strengths between 1868 and 1880 (Table VIII). After the Conservative reaction of 1874 had worn off the parties returned in 1880 to almost the same relative positions as they had occupied in 1868, although the distribution of their strength among the various classes of constituency was now different. The Liberals had gained ground in the big towns by almost ten per cent, but this increase was nullified by a Conservative increase in the small Irish boroughs and the English counties.

Table VIII. Increased Electorate and Votes, 1868-80,
Expressed as a Percentage

	Electors	Voters	Liberals	Conservatives
I	9·71	14·49	11·38	17·64
II	29·61	39·14	43·42	34·21
III	27·65	36·06	33·01	39·05
IV	20·56	34·47	34·70	34·18
V	35·46	39·16	25·46	54·15
All constituencies	27·63	36·70	37·81	35·50

The variation in the party strengths between each election is in itself an interesting phenomenon. In 1874 (Table IX) two things happened. First, the Liberals failed to win their share of the new voters in all types of constituency, and actually lost votes in the small towns and the English counties. Unfortunately, it is impossible to find out to what extent this setback was caused by abstentions or by changes of party allegiance between elections. The only type of constituency in which the Liberals continued to make a good showing—although there too they suffered a setback—was in the big towns. There the Conservatives possibly owed their better position to winning the votes of those who had abstained in 1868 or who voted for the first time, rather than to the conversion of former Liberals. Secondly, the Conservatives increased their vote by about one-quarter in all types of constituency except the small towns, and emerged from the elections a very much stronger party than they had been in 1868.

Table IX. Increased Vote, 1868-74, as a Percentage[1]

			All voters	Liberals	Conservatives
I	.	.	.	6·72	−3·93	17·49
II	.	.	.	17·49	9·88	26·25
III	.	.	.	11·36	−3·01	25·45
IV	.	.	.	13·15	0·04	29·40
V	.	.	.	14·45	8·51	20·95
All constituencies			14·54	4·26	25·70

In 1880 (Table X) the rôles of the two parties were reversed. The Conservatives still obtained nearly eight per cent more votes than they had won in 1874, and did particularly well in the counties and Irish boroughs. But the Liberals easily carried the day with an enormously enlarged poll which increased their strength by almost a third. The deciding factors on this occasion were the popular excitement and the improved Liberal organisation, particularly in marginal constituencies, where there was in

Table X. Increased Vote, 1874-80, as a Percentage[2]

			All voters	Liberals	Conservatives
I	.	.	.	7·28	15·93	0·12
II	.	.	.	18·42	30·53	6·30
III	.	.	.	22·18	37·15	10·85
IV	.	.	.	18·84	34·64	3·70
V	.	.	.	21·59	15·62	27·45
All constituencies			19·34	32·17	7·80

[1] The corresponding increase in the *electorate* was: I 3·99 per cent, II 13·70 per cent, III 4·24 per cent, IV 23·30 per cent, V 13·47 per cent, All constituencies 10·48 per cent.

[2] The increase in the electorate was I 5·50 per cent, II 13·99 per cent, III 22·46 per cent, IV −2·22 per cent, V 19·38 per cent, All constituencies 15·53 per cent.

many cases an increase of as much as ten per cent in the proportion of the electorate which voted (as against about three per cent in the rest of the country). In addition there was a great increase in the size of certain constituencies where the Liberals had worked hard between 1877 and 1880 to secure favourable registers. This was particularly the case in London, where there was a quite extraordinary increase. Whereas in the sample constituencies the increase in the number of voters was 19·34 per cent, in almost all the metropolitan boroughs it was over fifty per cent.

This pattern of nation-wide swings is familiar enough to the twentieth century, but in studying the nineteenth an additional factor must be taken into account: local influence. Its importance may be gauged in three ways: by the extent to which both parties gained seats, by the number of uncontested elections, and by the 'personal' vote received by individual candidates in multi-member constituencies. At every election the party which lost

Table XI. Election Results[1]

| | | Liberal Gains | | |
	England	Wales	Scotland	Total
1868 . .	41	6	4	51
1874 . .	25	1	2	28
1880 . .	100	8	12	120

| | | Conservative Gains | | |
	England	Wales	Scotland	Total
1868 . .	44	1	2	47
1874 . .	76	5	11	92
1880 . .	18	–	–	18

| | | Balance Sheet | |
	Liberal gain	Conservative gain	Net gain
1868 . .	51	47	L. 4
1874 . .	28	92	C. 64
1880 . .	120	18	L. 102

[1] The changes at later elections were

	Liberal gains	Conservative gains	Total changes
1886 .	14	156	170
1892 .	100	17	117
1895 .	14	112	126
1900 .	42	30	72
1906 .	246	4	250

A. L. Lowell, *The Government of England*, New York 1908, II, 107n.

the election gained some seats because local factors were sufficiently important in some constituencies to counteract the effects
of the national swing of opinion. In other words, both parties
gained and lost seats, even when no third party intervened, and
the result of the election as a whole was obtained by subtracting
the losses from the gains in the manner shown in Table XI.

During the fifties it had been customary to leave hopeless or
near-hopeless seats altogether uncontested: the Conservatives
could not find candidates in the boroughs and the Liberals could
not find candidates in the counties. The consequence was that
in 1859 no fewer than 374 seats were uncontested. After 1867
more seats were worth contesting, and the party managers were
more anxious that they should be contested, with the result that
the number of uncontested seats fell rapidly until 1880, when
it reached the level which came to be regarded as the norm
until 1922—about 110 seats.

1868	.	.	210
1874	.	.	187
1880	.	.	110

The chief change was in Ireland, where the Home Rulers destroyed the quietude of the fifties and early sixties in dramatic
fashion.

1868	.	.	65 seats uncontested
1874	.	.	20 seats uncontested
1880	.	.	17 seats uncontested[1]

The number of seats which were uncontested was, however,
only one factor in the situation. There were in addition a number
of seats which were contested only by rival candidates of the same
party, and others in two-member constituencies which were virtually uncontested because the weaker party put up only one
candidate.[2] Moreover, the emergence of Home Rule soon put
an end to contests between Liberals and Conservatives in Ireland (except in the smallest boroughs and in Ulster), as one party
or the other usually withdrew and left its erstwhile opponents
to fight the Home Rulers. The result, as Table XII shows, was

[1] Ten of these seats were held by Home Rulers.

[2] The strategy of this was often disputed, as a candidate ran the risk of losing because
his supporters gave their second vote to his opponents. On the other hand, there was
always a chance in the counties and in boroughs where the majority party was
divided, that a single candidate might attract 'protest votes'.

that about half the 650-odd seats were either absolutely uncontested or virtually uncontested in 1868 and 1874, and about two-
fifths of them in 1880.

Table XII. Seats not Contested by a Liberal

	1868	1874	1880
Conservatives unopposed	90	127	56
Conservative *v.* Conservative	2	3	–
Home Rulers unopposed	–	1	10
Home Rule *v.* Home Rule	–	–	11
Conservative *v.* Home Rule	–	11	33
One Liberal in two- or three-member constituency	24	36	46
	116	178	156

Seats not Contested by a Conservative

	1868	1874	1880
Liberals unopposed	120	59	44
Liberal *v.* Liberal	40	15	11
Home Rule unopposed	–	1	10
Home Rule *v.* Home Rule	–	–	11
Liberal *v.* Home Rule	–	30	8
One Conservative in two- or three-member constituency	53	45	48
	213	150	132

Seats not Contested by both major parties

	1868	1874	1880
No Liberal	116	178	156
No Conservative	213	150	132
	329	328	288
Less Home Rulers included twice in above table	–	1	21
Total	329	327	267

The importance of local factors is most clearly indicated by the different vote received by two candidates running as colleagues for a two-member constituency. In a good many cases the result was a division of the representation between the parties, either with or without a contest, depending on the circumstances of the constituency (61 seats were shared in this way in 1868, 62 in 1874 and 50 in 1880[1]). It is not easy to arrive at any general estimate of the extent of the 'personal' vote which led to such a state of affairs, but it was rarely less than three per cent and was often nearer ten per cent, rising in some cases to as much as fifty per cent. The most closely fought two-member constituency I have been able to discover was Bolton in 1880, when there was a 95·56 poll, an extraordinary record. The result was

J. K. Cross (L)	6,965
J. P. Thomasson (L) . . .	6,673
T. L. Rushton (C) . . .	6,539
Hon. F. C. Bridgeman (C) . .	6,415

The straight party vote on each side was 6,594 (49·45 per cent) for the Liberals and 6,262 (46·96 per cent) for the Conservatives, and only 480 persons (3·60 per cent of those who voted) failed to give a straight party vote. Bolton had long been a well-disciplined constituency, and it is interesting to note that even in 1874 the number of electors who failed to give a straight party vote was only 553 (4·8 per cent of the voters), but that this small number of dissidents was sufficient to divide the representation between the parties. The two successful candidates were popular local men for whom 292 of the 553 voted irrespective of party, with the following result:

John Hick (C)	5,987
J. K. Cross (L)	5,782
William Gray (C)	5,650
James Knowles (L) . . .	5,440

[1] In addition to these seats nine constituencies were held by a Liberal or nominal Home Ruler and a Home Ruler in 1874, and two in 1880. Of the constituencies divided between the two parties, eleven in 1868, twelve in 1874, and eleven in 1880 were ones in which the minority clause was in operation.

It is useful to compare these results with those for a loosely organised county division, where there were only three candidates. In the East Riding of Yorkshire a single Liberal unsuccessfully fought two Conservatives, Christopher Sykes and W. H. Harrison-Broadley, in 1868 and 1880: in 1868 793 of the 2,603 Liberal voters split with one of the Conservatives, and 330 of the Conservative voters were plumpers; in 1880 801 of the 3,707 Liberal voters split with a Conservative and 265 of the Conservative voters were plumpers. Similar results also occurred in loosely organised boroughs like Greenwich, where in 1874 Gladstone obtained 718 votes more than his Liberal running mate, and his Conservative fellow-member obtained 632 votes more than the second Conservative candidate.

II

When Disraeli died in 1881 the party election manifesto was still a personal appeal from the party leader, not a statement of future policy prepared and endorsed by the leading men in the party. Parties had 'principles' (although they were never very sure what they were), but the party policy at an election was never clearly defined: the electors were expected to draw their own conclusions from the confused and often contradictory statements made by individual candidates. These statements were of course shaped by the speeches of the party leaders, the particular interests of the individual candidate, and the activities of the numerous organisations which existed to influence public opinion, from the Political Economy Club to the Birmingham caucus. Thus in 1868 there was a consensus of opinion among Liberals that (*a*) Gladstone should be the next Liberal Prime Minister, (*b*) the Irish Church should be disestablished and disendowed, and (*c*) there should be a reduction in public expenditure, because these were the views stated or implied in Gladstone's election address and in those parts of his speeches which were generally taken up by Liberal candidates in the country. But in addition to this, there was also a feeling that (*d*) a national system of education should be introduced, (*e*) the army should be reformed, (*f*) the universities should be opened to dissenters, and (*g*) something should be done about liquor licensing, all issues on which Gladstone made only very general pronouncements.

This equation of party policy with the consensus of party opinion meant that the party leaders were left relatively uncommitted to any particular scheme of reform. It also meant that it did not much matter who the nominal party leader was: in 1880 when Liberal opinion was largely shaped by Gladstone and Chamberlain, nobody could be sure in advance whether Gladstone, Granville, or Hartington would be the next Liberal Prime Minister, yet very few Liberals bothered about the problem. Similarly, provided a leading Liberal did not set himself against the consensus of party opinion at an election, there was no reason why his past opposition to the party leaders on a particular issue should disqualify him for office after the election. Robert Lowe and the Adullamites who had opposed Russell's Reform Bill in 1866 returned quite naturally to the party fold in 1868: indeed, Lowe's election address went far beyond those of the other leading Liberals in sketching out the reforms he contemplated.[1] By contrast, however, Goschen in 1880 so set himself against the consensus of Liberal opinion that the county and borough franchises should be assimilated, that he automatically excluded himself from cabinet office.[2]

The tone of an election campaign owed almost everything to the leading personalities on each side. Occasionally, as was the case in the Liberal party in 1880, the party leader was not the popular leader, but the peculiar character of the three elections of 1868, 1874 and 1880 depended very largely on the contrasting appeals of Gladstone and Disraeli. Both parties built their campaigns round the two pugilists in much the same way as the Conservatives magnified the appeal of Sir Winston Churchill in 1945. Other personalities, like Lord Derby, or Lord Hartington, or Joseph Chamberlain, made an individual appeal to sections of the electorate, but there was little or no attempt to exploit

[1] He told a group of London University graduates who had asked him to become their first member: 'I have ever striven, to the best of my ability, to reform our law by bringing it within the principles of enlightened jurisprudence, to abolish all distinctions and disabilities founded on religious belief, to keep our practice in strict conformity with the principles of political economy, to substitute merit for patronage as a means of entering and rising in the public service, to promote the education of all classes, to enforce economy in the public expenditure, and to restrict the interference of the State within narrow and definite limits so as to leave the utmost scope consistent with order and good government to private enterprise and discretion': *Manchester Examiner and Times*, 12 February 1868.

[2] Morley, *Gladstone*, II, 625. There is an interesting analysis of the state of Liberal opinion in 1880 in a short pamphlet, possibly by W. T. Stead, *The Approaching General Election: A Political Catechism*, London 1880.

the cabinet or shadow cabinet as a team. When Disraeli spoke of the 1868 cabinet as 'a range of exhausted volcanoes' each of which had erupted in turn, he conveyed a just impression of the individualism of most governments.

An election was usually fought around one issue, and it was the duty of the party leader to decide what this issue should be and to provide his followers with a 'cry'. Gladstone, for instance, put forward the disestablishment of the Irish Church in 1868, the abolition of the income tax in 1874, the Turkish atrocities in 1880, and Home Rule for Ireland in 1886. Thereafter the public, the press, and the candidates, could be relied on to strike out for themselves along lines which Lord Palmerston's successful appeals to the country had made familiar. To a generation which read parliamentary debates verbatim, and derived a good many of its political attitudes from *Punch*, the music hall, and the prize-ring, the personal rivalry of Gladstone and Disraeli underlined everything they said. But the lasting novelty of the period was the new campaign methods which Gladstone developed after 1868.

Gladstone was the first major statesman to stump the country.[1] He experimented first in South-West Lancashire in 1868, and then carried the new technique to its logical conclusion in the two great Midlothian campaigns of 1879 and 1880. At Midlothian Gladstone, no longer official party leader, felt himself free to set out a fairly comprehensive programme for a future Liberal government, but the essence of his campaigns was that they resembled those of an American presidential candidate rather than those of a modern British party leader. Gladstone, like American presidential candidates, tried to give a lead to the country as a whole, but he made no attempt to fetter the liberty of candidates to adjust their own election addresses to the needs of their locality. The party candidates had been chosen by the constituency associations for local reasons, and it was not for the party leader to interfere with their freedom of choice, by making too precise a statement of his intentions. In 1868, two years before the 1870 Education Act, Gladstone's address contained only the following ambiguous comments on the Education question, and

[1] How new was the idea is shown by Robert Lowe's reaction to a speech at Liverpool in 1866 in favour of the government's Reform Bill. This he denounced as 'a sort of Ministerial agitation' which might have developed into 'an influence of terrorism'. A. P. Martin, *Life and Letters of the Right Honourable Robert Lowe, Viscount Sherbrooke*, London 1893, II, 279.

candidates were free to commit themselves to whatever educational reform they themselves favoured.

No question is at the present day more complicated by differences of opinion than that of primary education. But all are agreed both upon its vital importance and upon its pressing urgency. In the year 1839, Earl Russell . . . placed upon official record the desire of Her Majesty that the rights of conscience should be respected, and that the youth of the country should be religiously brought up. Further measures are certainly required to establish and secure the first of these great principles; and they need not in my opinion involve the slightest disparagement to the second. I think that the declaration of Earl Russell still marks the proper basis of national policy in Education for the three Kingdoms. But it has become increasingly desirable that the State should stand clearly apart from responsibility for the teaching of particular and conflicting creeds in schools aided by grants from any national fund.[1]

Gladstone deliberately refrained from narrowing the gap between himself and his supporters. He viewed the Liberal party as a federal party and interference with the independence of his followers seemed out of place. Equally, he expected them not to interfere with him, and he particularly deprecated the Conservative practice of discussing a major bill at a party meeting before it was introduced in the Commons. When Derby revealed the first draft of the 1867 Reform Bill to his followers, Gladstone commented:

after an experience of thirty-four years, it is a practice entirely novel for a Minister of the Crown to gather to his house those Members of Parliament who he thinks agree with him, and state to them, days in advance of the House of Commons, the particulars of a great measure which it is his intention to submit to Parliament.[2]

Gladstone's views on such questions were derived from the excessive regard for the independence of Ministers and of their supporters which distinguished the Peelites. This led him on the one hand to withdraw into his shell when his followers were dissatisfied with him, rather than attempting to win them over by gentle persuasion and gossip in the Tea Room of the House of Commons; as when in 1867 he complained that he could 'hardly

[1] W. E. Gladstone, *Speeches in South-West Lancashire, October 1868*, Liverpool 1868, p. iv.
[2] *3 Hansard* CLXXXVI, 27.

speak a word . . . with any confidence that some man will not rise on the Liberal side to protest against it', and as a consequence took a resolution to await a 'spontaneous action from within the bosom of the party' in his favour, and meanwhile 'to avoid all acts of leadership which can be dispensed with'.[1] On the other hand, it prevented him from forcing a more comprehensive programme on the party when his leadership was temporarily unquestioned, as in 1868 after he had carried the Irish Church campaign into the country. It is arguable that the 1868 ministry would have been much more successful in its later years if Gladstone had given a stronger lead on the education question, liquor licensing, and the Irish land question. At least the Liberal rank and file would have been forewarned and much subsequent conflict could have been avoided.

Gladstone's technique when stumping the country was simple. He directed a series of speeches at the whole country, but gave them within a comparatively narrow compass of towns so that they acquired a unity of sense and purpose which they might otherwise have lacked. Each series was concerned with one great theme, but it was accompanied by a minor or secondary theme to set it off, and each speech was designed to cast new light on each of these themes so that the speeches as a whole read together as if they were a course of lectures. The two themes were almost invariably the same: first the iniquity, injustice and depravity of some institution and of his opponents' policy in supporting that institution, and secondly, the financial extravagance of his opponents and their inability to appreciate the principles of good government (economy, and the interests of the community rather than those of a class). The subject of his denunciation was in turn the Irish Church, the Turks and their allies the Beaconsfield government, and the union with Ireland. The note was, therefore, always one of high moral indignation and of fervent appeal to the better feelings of his audience, conveyed in the ringing tones which meant so much to his followers, and it varied little from that of his first election address as party leader in 1868. Of the Irish Church he said:

> In the removal of this Establishment I see the discharge of a debt of civil justice, the disappearance of a national, almost a world-wide reproach, a condition indispensable to the success of every effort to

[1] *Later Correspondence of Lord John Russell*, ed. G. P. Gooch, London 1925, II, 362-3.

secure the peace and contentment of that country; finally, relief to a devoted clergy from a false position, cramped and beset by hopeless prejudice, and the opening of a freer career to the sacred ministry.[1]

Gladstone's technique had more than the charm of novelty for his followers: it was by its nature almost the only appeal which could reach the great mass of nonconformist electors, who became after 1868 his most numerous and effective supporters. However much they came at times to feel that he had gone wrong or been misled, they could never forget after 1868 that he was the one man in political life who seemed to be moved by principle. They alone appreciated to the full his sacerdotal turn of phrase, and he did them only justice when he recorded in 1868: 'Our three *corps d'armée*, I may almost say, have been Scotch presbyterians, English and Welsh nonconformists, and Irish Roman Catholics.'[2] The great majority of Congregationalists, Baptists and Unitarians would, indeed, have wholeheartedly endorsed the letter which Henry Allon of the *British Quarterly* addressed to Gladstone when forwarding a resolution in favour of the disestablishment of the Irish Church.

> You do not need to be assured of the great esteem and hearty sympathy of Nonconformists . . . if now—or by and bye—any public expression of their feeling could in any way strengthen your hands . . . they would eagerly throughout the country give such a demonstration of their feeling as no public man for the last generation could have elicited.
>
> It may interest you to know that in the public prayers which in nonconforming Churches are offered for the nation and its rulers and statesmen—the Divine Blessing has been very generally implored upon you and your proposal—of course in general yet unmistakeable terms. Since the agitation on the Slavery question such a thing I imagine has scarcely occurred. It springs from a conviction of the deeply religious character of the question. . . .[3]

This is not to say that all nonconformists straightway became ardent Gladstonians, or that all Liberals were pleased with Gladstone's campaign methods. There were many Liberals who

---

[1] Gladstone, *Speeches in South-West Lancashire*, p. v.
[2] Morley, *Gladstone*, II, 259.
[3] Add. MS., 44,095, f.311. Compare this with F. T. Palgrave's remark, 'When I say the Lord's Prayer I use the Revised Version and say "Deliver us from the Evil One" and I mean Mr. Gladstone.' *Listener*, 4 July 1957.

agreed with every one of Gladstone's proposals, and endorsed the views expressed in his speeches, yet could not bring themselves to trust him very far. A leading article in the *Pall Mall Gazette* sensibly pointed out as early as 1868 that Gladstone was imperfectly in sympathy with his party because his traditions were neither Whig nor Radical, but Tory, and that it was very difficult to be one of his followers because his proneness to allow ideas, his own or those of others, to grasp him, made his actions almost unpredictable.[1] It also expressed the view, commonly held by London Liberals, that the Irish Church was not 'a question in itself of such paramount magnitude and urgency as to be entitled to throw all others into the shade', and prophesied that difficulties would arise for the Liberals when the Irish Church had been disestablished and other questions had to be dealt with. Similarly, critics in 1880 felt that Gladstone's preoccupation with the Eastern question had blinded him to the needs of the moment at home and in Ireland, and after 1880 they saw in the travail of his ministry the natural consequence of his earlier folly. Indeed, Gladstone's restlessness was such that he filled friend and foe alike with apprehension, particularly when, as in his apologia for his change of opinion on the Irish Church question, the *Chapter of Autobiography*, he elevated his notion that it was the duty of statesmen to move with the times to the dignity of a system.

Gladstone's hustings oratory faced Disraeli with a clear choice: he must either follow his rival's example at the risk of alienating his followers and being outmatched by him, or he must find an alternative way of presenting the Conservative case, more in line with tradition. The former course was in fact hardly open to him because he was too old and infirm for a strenuous campaign, and there was nobody to deputise for him: Lord Randolph Churchill was the first Conservative to set up as a hustings orator in Gladstone's style. There was in any case the strong political objection to stumping the country, that Gladstone's vigour foreshadowed the end of the Palmerstonian Liberal party and promised the Conservatives a monopoly of Conservatism if they could only show that they were a Conservative party and not just an alliance of country squires and adventurers. All Disraeli need do was to wait, and in the meantime to do as little as

---

[1] *Pall Mall Gazette*, 3 November 1868. At this time the *P.M.G.* was a Conservative paper.

possible to antagonise the middle-class Palmerstonians who were gradually changing their political allegiance. Simple opposition to Gladstonian Liberalism, combined with a clear exposition of a Conservative policy such as he gave in his Crystal Palace speech of 1872, would enable him to assemble a national Conservative party. Buckle is quite beside the point when he remarks of the 1868 election that 'so absolutely incapable was [Disraeli] of demagogic arts that he neglected, almost to a culpable degree, to endeavour to utilise his great legislative achievement'—the Reform Bill.[1] Disraeli could not afford to stump the country, because to do so would have been a remarkable innovation. As it was, his election address with its undertones of appeal to religious feeling on behalf of the Church of Ireland, was bitterly denounced by Goschen, a very moderate Liberal: 'The Prime Minister has not scrupled to turn his sceptre of office into an incendiary torch. The cry has been raised of "Protestantism in danger", and religion is invoked against the cause of justice.'[2] The same sort of objection was raised even against Disraeli's manifesto to the electors of Bath at a by-election in 1873. W. H. Smith, a Palmerstonian Conservative, regarded the very issue of such a manifesto as worse than shocking, while its wording, although moderate enough by twentieth-century standards, was thought to be quite outrageous, even by the *Annual Register*. Disraeli wrote:

> For nearly five years the present Ministers have harassed every trade, worried every profession, and assailed or menaced every class, institution, and species of property in the country. Occasionally they have varied this state of civil war by perpetrating some job which outraged public opinion, or by stumbling into mistakes which have always been discreditable, and sometimes ruinous. All this they call a policy, and seem quite proud of it; but the country has, I think, made up its mind to close this career of plundering and blundering.'[3]

The truth is, that the orthodox weapons were quite adequate for any party leader with a Conservative message. The occasional speech at a gathering of political supporters, or at a great banquet, or on becoming Lord Rector of a Scottish University,

[1] Buckle, *Disraeli*, V, 87.
[2] A. R. D. Elliot, *The Life of George Joachim Goschen*, London 1911, I, 97.
[3] Sir Herbert Maxwell, *The Life and Times of the Right Honourable William Henry Smith, M.P.*, Edinburgh 1893, I, 244. Smith commented on the Bath letter: 'Disraeli has ruined himself, and rendered reconstruction of parties—a new choice of leaders—almost inevitable.'

coupled with the annual address to one's constituents and a few major public appearances in the provinces, were quite sufficient, supported by the turn of events in parliament, to catch the ear of the country. There was no question of speeches not being reported: with a very few exceptions they were reported verbatim even in papers hostile to the speaker: and they were read. That in itself was enough for a 'conservative' party, provided that the party leader was careful to attach to himself any 'splinter groups' within the party, as Disraeli was usually able to do, and provided that the Liberals sufficiently antagonised the most active rank-and-file Conservatives, the clergy and the publicans, to make them zealous supporters before election day. In such circumstances the election address to the leader's constituents (framed on the model of the Tamworth manifesto) was quite sufficient to set the tone of the actual election campaign, and nothing more rigorous was required.

Chapter Ten

ELECTIONS (2)

I

THE three elections of 1868, 1874 and 1880 took place in quite different circumstances. The 1868 election was more a matter of establishing or consolidating the position of the parties in the new constituencies created by the Reform Act than a choice between alternative governments, since everybody knew in advance that the Liberals were going to win, and that the Conservative minority government was only a temporary expedient. The 1874 and 1880 elections, on the other hand, were straight fights between two great parties, each of them with a reasonable expectation of holding office, decided by the public reaction first to a strong Liberal government and then to a strong Conservative one. As such, they became the first 'modern' elections in British history. With them the party struggle became a clear-cut appeal to the electors to establish one party or the other in power, and the era of ministries made by the House of Commons came virtually to an end.

The 1868 election was essentially a sequel to the events of 1867. During 1867 a Conservative government in a minority of about seventy in the House of Commons had carried a Reform Act. Similar Acts were required for Scotland and Ireland, and there were various other technical measures relating to the conduct of elections to carry in the session of 1868. But with the main Reform Act out of the way it was only a matter of time before the Liberals reunited to turn out their opponents, and before the old parliament elected in 1865 was dissolved and a new one elected from the new constituencies. In consequence, the government's position was perceptibly weaker when Disraeli succeeded Derby soon after parliament had reassembled in February 1868, and new issues occupied the minds of members.

The foremost of these new issues was the state of Ireland, where the Fenian movement had been at its strongest in the previous

year. Statesmen turned to it from their absorption in the problems
of parliamentary reform with something like a consciousness of
neglect, and the redress of Irish grievances, frequently mooted
since the suspension of Habeas Corpus early in 1866, suddenly
became a matter of urgency. Bright and Gladstone were united
on the need for reform, and it was clear that they would raise the
question as soon as parliament met, if only to embarrass the
government. The obvious target for Liberal attack was the Irish
Church, whose disestablishment had been called for by Lord
John Russell as early as 1835, and whose constitution was scarcely
capable of wholehearted defence by the government, since
several members of the cabinet were known to favour reform.
And the cabinet itself was so well aware of the fact that it tried
hard to find an acceptable policy of its own which would stop
short of disestablishment. The first two cabinets held by the
Disraeli administration (2 and 3 March 1868)[1] were devoted
to Ireland, but nothing like a consistent Irish policy emerged.
An old scheme of Lord Mayo's for granting a Charter to an
Irish Roman Catholic university was revived, although the
insistence of the cabinet that there should be a lay majority on
its governing body effectively dispelled any chance that the Irish
hierarchy might be prevailed upon to accept it. It was also
decided to set up yet another Royal Commission on land questions,
and pending its report to bring in a land bill to deal with points
on which both parties were agreed, a colourless measure which
was greeted with almost universal contempt. The Church
question was relegated 'to the decision of the new Parliament',[2]
but in the inevitable debate on Irish grievances Lord Mayo,
as Chief Secretary for Ireland, managed to cover this awkward
gap with hints of something like concurrent endowment of all
churches in Ireland.

The government's manifest weakness played into Gladstone's
hands. He came to the House with a coherent programme which
had been drawn up in conjunction with his leading colleagues:
disestablishment and disendowment of the Irish Church, subject
to the preservation of vested interests, together with the withdrawal of the Maynooth grant and Regium Donum. Bright, who
would have preferred a land bill, and some of the Whigs were

---

[1] *Letters of Queen Victoria*, second series, ed. G. E. Buckle, London 1926, I, 509.
[2] *Ibid.*, p. 511.

not altogether happy about the new policy, but they were prepared in the circumstances to accept it. Gladstone's preliminary
statement was speedily followed by the introduction of three
resolutions (23 March 1868) designed to secure a vote on the
principle of disestablishment and disendowment, and also pray-
ing the Queen to place at the disposal of parliament her interests
in the Irish Church. A government amendment was rejected by
a majority of 60, and on 30 April the first resolution was carried
by a majority of 65.

Disraeli held the trump card, however, and without consulting
the cabinet,[1] determined to play it: he secured from the Queen
her approval for a dissolution of parliament if the opposition
should carry a vote of no confidence. He then (3 May) announced
to the House his intention of retaining office until the reform
programme was completed, offering as a sop full facilities for the
passage of Gladstone's resolutions towards their inevitable ship-
wreck in the Lords, and a dissolution in the autumn, once the
hurriedly-prepared new registers were ready. The ground was
well chosen, for although Gladstone and the opposition had won
the initiative, not one of the opposition leaders dared bring in
a no-confidence motion. Gladstone fulminated against penal dis-
solutions,[2] and the iniquity of a government clinging abjectly to
office, but he went no further even when taunted to do so by
Disraeli. The demoralisation of the reform debates was still to
be felt among the Liberal rank and file. It required more than
two divisions to restore faith in the Liberal leadership, and to
steel members to face two general elections within a year on different franchises.[3] There were, indeed, those who thought that
the Liberal party would do better out of office for the time being,
since a party on the attack is always more effective at a general

---

[1] The cabinet was kept in ignorance of Disraeli's intentions, apparently because he
felt that it might not support him. Hardy, Stanley, Malmesbury, Richmond, and
Cairns seem all to have favoured resignation: Journal of Lord Cranbrook, 3 May
1868. Cranbrook Papers.

[2] *3 Hansard* CXCI, 1710.

[3] Lord Granville consulted Erskine May on the question and found him distinctly
pessimistic: 'I asked him what was the temper of the House. He said pleased at the
consolidation of the majority, and having struck a blow at the Irish Church with
impunity to themselves, but utterly unreliable for any purpose which may be met by
a dissolution. We should as likely find ourselves in a minority of 70.' (Add. MS.
44,145, ff.165-6). The Speaker was just as pessimistic: 'If a vote of want of confidence
in the Government had been proposed, a considerable number of the majority would
not have voted.' J. E. Denison, *Notes from my Journal*, privately printed, London 1899,
p. 225.

election, and there would be no disputes about the composition of the cabinet or about its policies.[1]

During the hiatus between the defeat of the government on Gladstone's resolutions and the elections in November, both parties did their best to conciliate their supporters and to win new friends, but apart from Gladstone's speeches in South-West Lancashire in October very little unusual happened. The only two sections of the community which appear to have changed their political allegiance were the Wesleyans and the Roman Catholics. The alignment of active dissenters on one side of the conflict, and of active churchmen on the other, gravely embarrassed the Wesleyans. Traditionally the allies of the Conservatives, they were aware that their association with the Conservative party had become very tenuous during the previous decade, and that they were drifting into an alliance with the Liberal nonconformists. The Wesleyan Conference resolved to remain neutral on the Irish Church issue, but it was an unfriendly neutrality, and Conservatives found little comfort in the words of the incoming president:

> We are *not* the allies, much less the partisans of a State Church. Neither are we Dissenters, in the proper, strictly historic, and Anglican use of that polemic term. And it is only in the maintenance of this midway position we are able, we think, to maintain our independence.[2]

Many Wesleyan ministers and lay preachers remained Conservatives, and there were two Wesleyan Conservative candidates, but the majority of Wesleyans gave their support to the Liberals. Some did so after long argument and fortified by the thought that one vote would not commit them permanently to the Liberal party.[3] But many of them welcomed the opportunity for the break with the Church and the Conservative party towards which they had long been drifting. As one Wesleyan minister put it: 'Uneducated men feel more than they think, and the mass of our Church . . . is composed of uneducated men, who naturally are opposed to a religious body whose members appear to scorn and dislike them because they belong to another communion.'[4]

---

[1] *Leeds Mercury*, 5 May 1868.

[2] *Primitive Methodist*, 27 August 1868.

[3] George Melly spent most of polling day at Stoke attempting to persuade a few leading Wesleyans that they might properly vote for a Unitarian: Melly, *Recollections of Sixty Years*, p. 26.

[4] *Standard*, 11 November 1868.

The assault on the Irish Church made it even more difficult for Roman Catholics to vote Conservative or remain neutral. Both Archbishop Manning and Cardinal Cullen had been flirting with the Conservatives while the project for an Irish Roman Catholic university was under consideration,[1] but they and their followers returned emphatically to the Liberal camp as soon as Gladstone took up the case against the Irish Church. Conservative Catholics were left to manage as best they could, with the result that many of them, including Disraeli's friend Sir Robert Gerard, determined to be neutral.[2] The last Conservative stronghold was the *Tablet*, which supported the government assiduously until it was purchased for Manning in November and the editorial chair transferred to Mgr Herbert Vaughan.[3] Until November the *Tablet* urged that Catholics should support the Conservatives, since they were pledged to pass a landlord and tenant bill for Ireland and to grant a charter to an Irish Catholic university, and because they might repeal the Ecclesiastical Titles Act: reform of the Irish Church might wait until the next session. In April an editorial even ventured to attack the Irish bishops for supporting disestablishment, on the ground that the union of Church and State had been declared sacred by the Pope, and that such matters were under the direct jurisdiction of the Holy See. 'We can't adopt the creed of the English Dissenters, and become a Cromwellian, an Independent, a Voluntaryist, and a seculariser of Church property, merely for the sake of applauding a party move of MR. GLADSTONE's.'[4] Vaughan, however, completely changed the paper's line and strongly advocated the 'disestablishment and disendowment in Ireland of the most hostile and powerful organization which has ever enslaved the mind of man since the date when Arianism passed away'.[5]

Disraeli tried to counterbalance these losses by mobilising the Anglican clergy on his behalf, a task made easier by the feeling which had been whipped up against Gladstone in the Oxford

[1] Buckle, *Disraeli*, V, 5-10.

[2] The chief effect in the House of Commons was that most of the Conservative members for Irish constituencies who were Catholics or unenthusiastic supporters of the Irish Church abstained or voted against their party on Gladstone's resolutions. Of the nine Conservatives who supported Gladstone, six sat for Irish constituencies.

[3] E. S. Purcell, *Life of Cardinal Manning, Archbishop of Westminster*, 2 edn, London 1896, II, 387-91.

[4] *Tablet*, 4 April 1868.

[5] *Ibid.*, 7 November 1868.

election of 1865. He endeavoured, in particular, to trade on the anti-Catholic prejudices of the evangelical clergy, and the widespread fear of ritualism. He told the Queen in March before Gladstone's resolutions had been discussed:

> He thinks that Mr. Gladstone has mistaken the spirit of the times, and the temper of the country. The abhorrence of Popery, the dread of Ritualism, and the hatred of the Irish, have long been smouldering in the mind of the nation. They will seize, Mr. Disraeli thinks, the opportunity long sighed for and now offered, to vent their accumulated passion. . . .
>
> In the Boroughs there will be revived, with terrible earnestness, the no Popery cry: in the counties, the clergy and gentry will rally round the sacred and time honoured principle of Church and State.[1]

Disraeli seems to have thought that a few Evangelical appointments to deaneries or canonries, and a number of monster meetings organised by specially appointed committees, would set off a train of Protestant enthusiasm, but in this he was mistaken. Lord Shaftesbury and other prominent Conservative churchmen persuaded the Church Institution, the Ulster Protestant Defence Association, the Central Protestant Defence Association, the United Protestant Defence Committee, and the National Union, to join together to form a 'Central Board' for the defence of the Irish Church. And this Board held a meeting in St James's Hall on 6 May at which the four Archbishops were present (the United Protestant Defence Committee held a similar meeting in Dublin). But its main work was the preparation and despatch of circulars and the winning over of individual churchmen and Wesleyans to its cause, scarcely the best way of rousing popular enthusiasm. The task of rousing Protestant feeling in the constituencies therefore fell by default to ultra-Protestant bodies such as the National Protestant Union, which was generously financed by the Duke of Portland. But even this body was not very successful. It sent deputations all over the country and published numerous pamphlets in the hope of winning over erstwhile Liberals like the Duke of Portland himself, but found it difficult to convince them that Disraeli and his colleagues were vigorous anti-Papists, or that the Union's efforts would not be better directed towards

---

[1] *Letters of Queen Victoria*, 2 series, I, 517-18.

resisting the growth of Romanism in the Church of England.[1]

Except in Lancashire, where there was a strong feeling against the Irish (see Chapter XIV), only a few candidates tried to pursue a distinctively Protestant line. The effect was usually mildly ludicrous. Sir Henry Edwards at Beverley, who had a Roman Catholic opponent, distinguished himself by making one of the 'discoveries' of the election, that Gladstone was a Roman Catholic in disguise, but few candidates took advantage of it. Sir Henry told his hearers in November that he had no objection on principle to genuine Roman Catholics, but Gladstone he regarded as by no means genuine.

> But gentlemen, I hate these perverts—I don't want to have in this country a Roman Catholic Prime Minister. I don't say that Mr. Gladstone is a Roman Catholic, but he looks deuced like it. The experience I have had in the House of Commons has not gone for nothing. I have there had an opportunity to study men, and the principles of men. Gentlemen, I tell you plainly and frankly that I believe Mr. Gladstone is a thorough Roman Catholic, and of the worst description, because he is a Jesuit.[2]

Although the anticipated anti-Popery movement did not develop, except in Lancashire, Disraeli was right in expecting support from the evangelical clergy. They were active almost everywhere, and Henry Allon's report on events in his parish was typical of many made at the time to both Gladstone and Disraeli.

> Everywhere the Evangelical clergy have moved heaven and earth to excite fears about the church. In my own parish the vicar has had meetings of his clergy at his house since July—& the most perfect & strenuous organization has been brought into operation.[3]

On the other hand, many of the High Church clergy and the laity were indifferent, while those High Churchmen and Liberal

---

[1] Nugent, the secretary of the Union, was none the less convinced that much might have been done if there had been more time. 'There can be no doubt', he wrote to Disraeli on 25 August, 'that there are many earnest zealous Protestant Liberals in general politics, who would cordially support our cause, and vote for Protestant Conservative Candidates, if they felt assured that it was the determination of the Government to support Protestantism throughout the Empire at all hazards—and to resist firmly but decisively the aggressions of the Roman Church. . . .' The Union was active in all the Lancashire constituencies and in 48 others in 1868, and supplied most of the Protestant pamphlets and leaflets used in the Lancashire elections by the Conservative candidates.

[2] *Manchester Guardian*, 7 November 1868. I have omitted the various interpellations of cheers and hisses.

[3] Add. MS. 44,095, ff.317-18.

Churchmen who had supported Gladstone at Oxford continued to support him. Indeed, neither High Churchmen nor 'Liberals' had much sympathy with the ultra-Evangelical Church of Ireland, and most of them had doubts about the value of the establishment even in England. The Duke of Buckingham found that the High Church clergy in his district would not even sign a petition expressing sympathy and support for the Irish Church in its tribulations.[1] As for the laity, Lord Stanley, the leading opponent of the Irish Church in the cabinet, told Disraeli in September that two-thirds of the Conservatives had no hope of saving the endowments of the Irish Church, and that they therefore favoured compromise and reform.[2] This was clearly an exaggeration, but there is no doubt that few of the laity felt comfortable about defending an institution in such obvious need of reform, and that they only did so because they feared that Irish disestablishment might be followed by English disestablishment.

The results of the election were, by and large, the expected ones. The Liberals increased their lead in Wales, Scotland and Ireland and in the bigger towns: the Conservatives gained ground in their strongholds in the English counties, and won a great deal of additional support in Lancashire. After the general election of 1865 the two parties had been divided roughly as follows.[3]

	Conservatives	Liberals	Liberal majority
England . . .	221	247	26
Wales & Monmouth .	14	18	4
Scotland . . .	10	43	33
Ireland . . .	49	56	7
	294	364	70

After the 1868 election the Liberals increased their majority by about forty. Almost all of this increase took place outside England: the Liberal majority in the Celtic fringe grew from forty-seven in 1865 to no less than eighty-four in 1868.

Individual members of both parties lost their seats in the mêlée,

---

[1] Duke of Buckingham to Disraeli, 18 April 1868. Disraeli Papers.

[2] Stanley to Disraeli, 24 September 1868. Disraeli Papers.

[3] These tables are derived from an analysis of the election results made specially for the purpose, but like the numerous contemporary estimates, the totals are only tentative, because of the difficulty of classifying several Liberal-Conservatives.

	Conservatives	Liberals	Liberal majority
England . . .	217	243	26
Wales & Monmouth .	10	23	13
Scotland . . .	7	53	46
Ireland . . .	40	65	25
	274	384	110

and the Liberals lost a number of important political leaders. Gladstone and two former Liberal cabinet ministers, Lord Hartington and Milner Gibson, were defeated in Lancashire, and H. A. Bruce, a member of the incoming cabinet, was defeated at Merthyr Tydvil. Gladstone was able to take refuge in Greenwich, where a seat had been kept open for him by the Whips, but Hartington and Bruce had to wait for vacancies (in the Radnor boroughs and Renfrewshire respectively), and Milner Gibson was unable to find another seat. Among other prominent Liberals or quasi-Liberals who were defeated was J. A. Roebuck at Sheffield. On the Conservative side the most important casualties were the law officers, the Attorney-General (Sir John Karslake), the Solicitor-General (Sir Richard Baggallay), and the Lord-Advocate (Edward Strathearn Gordon). More important than these individual defeats was the emergence of a new national movement in Wales, and of a strong local movement in Lancashire (which are dealt with elsewhere), and the victories of Lord George Hamilton and W. H. Smith in Middlesex and Westminster, which pointed the way to further victories in 1874, and removed from the House two idiosyncratic personalities, Henry Labouchere and John Stuart Mill.

As soon as the elections were over the Disraeli government established an important precedent by resigning without meeting parliament. There was a good deal of adverse comment in the Liberal press on this move at first, but a little reflection soon convinced the public that the move was a wise one since there was no purpose to be served by delay. Mr Gladstone was accordingly requested to become Prime Minister and took office.

II

The new government was an unusually talented team, but it soon got into difficulties with its supporters, and was forced to rely on the Opposition to carry its Education Bill through the House more or less intact. The left wing of the Liberal party became increasingly restive as a consequence, and tended in the constituencies to support the advocates of particular nostrums against the official government candidates. At the same time the scope of the government's measures was regarded by many moderates as being too wide, with the result that there was a gradual but steady loss of enthusiasm on the part of the Liberals and a corresponding gain on the part of the Conservatives. And, unfortunately for the government, there was a very large number of by-elections during the life of this parliament—135—so that this dissatisfaction showed itself in by-election results.[1]

These by-elections cost the government both prestige and seats, and showed in a remarkable way the dangers by which any Liberal government was beset in the period before the institution of an effective party organisation in the constituencies. There was not perhaps anything quite as remarkable as the defeat of the Liberal candidate at Stoke in 1875 by Dr Kenealy standing as the defender of the Tichborne claimant.[2] But time and again Liberals found that their supporters, and even influential local leaders, seemed to have deserted their party before a by-election occurred. This was particularly the case with the constituencies in which Josephine Butler and the opponents of the Contagious Diseases Acts interested themselves.[3] They had scarcely any

---

[1] At first, largely as a result of election petitions, the Liberals gained a few seats, but thereafter they lost them regularly: thus, 1869 gain 2 loss 4, 1870 gain 4 loss 5, 1871 loss 6, 1872 loss 7, 1873 loss 7, 1874 loss 1. (Figures from the *Constitutional Year Book*.) There were 152 vacancies in the Commons during this parliament, made up as follows: deaths 54, succession to the peerage 18, creation of peers 11, members unseated on petition 30, member unseated by resolution of the House 1, acceptance of office 15, 'resignations' 23 (*The Times*, 6 February 1874).

[2] In 1874 the Liberal vote had been split between three candidates but there was a clear Liberal majority of about 3,000. In 1875 when George Melly retired to attend to his business the voting was Kenealy 6,110; Walton (L) 4,168; Davenport (C) 3,901.

[3] The C.D. Acts provided for the compulsory inspection and, if necessary, the compulsory medical treatment of prostitutes in towns with naval and military barracks. Introduced in 1864 they were ultimately repealed in 1886 as the result of a long parliamentary campaign conducted by James Stansfeld. For an account of the campaign see Josephine E. Butler, *Personal Reminiscences of a Great Crusade*, London 1898, and J. L. and Barbara Hammond, *James Stansfeld, A Victorian Champion of Sex Equality*, London 1932.

organisation and could send only a handful of workers (plus strong-arm men to protect them) to fight any one election, but until 1872 they were a serious threat to the Liberal majority in any small or medium-sized borough. Their most successful campaign was that against Sir Henry Storks, the general who acted as Cardwell's chief assistant at the War Office. At the end of 1869 or early in 1870 it was decided to bring him into the House of Commons in the specially-revived office of Surveyor-General of the Ordnance, and the Whips were asked to find him a seat. Storks had been a colonial governor noted for his rigid enforcement of the Contagious Diseases Acts and was regarded by the repealers as a particular enemy. They therefore decided to oppose his election in order to show the government their strength.

Storks was not a strong candidate because he lacked popular appeal and had no local connections worth speaking of, so that he could be put up only for a small borough. He chose first to stand for Newark at the beginning of 1870, but the agitation got up against him was so strong that he soon withdrew, and in October 1870 he stood for Colchester, where one of the sitting members had died. By now the repealers, who were mostly Liberals, were determined to accept no compromise. In May the government had answered their arguments during the first debate in parliament on the Contagious Diseases Acts by proposing a commission of enquiry, but the setting up of the commission had been tactlessly delayed until November. The Colchester by-election came therefore to be regarded as an opportunity to teach the government a decisive lesson. The town was a military one and the Contagious Diseases Acts were in force there, so that Storks's candidature afforded just such an opportunity as the repealers had hoped for. Josephine Butler herself, and many other supporters of repeal, descended on the constituency and got up a formidable agitation in spite of a great deal of violence on the part of their opponents. Not content with simple opposition, they put up a candidate of their own to split the Liberal vote, and were lucky enough to obtain for the purpose Dr Baxter Langley, a well-known Radical who had made way for Gladstone at Greenwich in 1868 and who contested Greenwich along with him in 1874. Glyn as Liberal Whip did his best to persuade Langley to withdraw, and he eventually did so after he had been formally nominated, but by then it was too late. Storks obtained only 841 votes, whereas the former member had secured 1,467 in 1868, and as the Conservatives retained all their 1868 votes and won a few new ones, the Conservative candidate was returned by a large majority.[1] For a time it seemed as though Storks might altogether fail to find a seat, although he clung to the view that he could win Newark if allowed to contest it and urged Glyn to give Bristowe, the new member, a government appointment. Glyn was very sceptical of this, however, and wrote to Cardwell:

> I am not satisfied that Storks could win Newark *till* the question of the C. Diseases is at rest—nor do I think Carmarthenshire would be safe—you see the determination with which these people act—and I fear the Welsh dissenters would not be sound—*both* candidates at Newport have had to pledge themselves for Repeal.[2]

Eventually in 1871 a suitable vacancy was created when Rear-Admiral Lord John Hay, a Naval Lord of the Admiralty, retired from Ripon, a pocket borough controlled by a member of the cabinet, Lord De Grey, and Storks was safely returned.

The loss of by-elections and waning enthusiasm for the government sapped the energies of its supporters in the House of Commons, and by 1872 it was only a question of time before there was a major defeat in the House. Gladstone apparently rather hoped for such a defeat because it would, in all probability, have led to another minority Conservative government, and a breathing space which would give the Liberal leaders time to re-deploy their forces. But by 1873, when the defeat finally came on the Irish University Bill, Disraeli had decided that the day of minority Conservative governments was over. He refused to take office, and insisted that the government should be allowed to stumble on to face the electors at the polls, the logical conclusion of his own resignation in 1868. There is no way of knowing exactly what would have happened had the Conservatives taken office in 1873 and dissolved immediately, but it is clear that the Conservatives would have been very lucky to obtain a working majority. The lesson of 1867-8 was that Liberal disunion soon ceased in opposition once the old bones of contention were disposed of. If their principles were at stake Liberals were willing

---

[1] *The Times*, 4 November 1870.
[2] Glyn to Cardwell, 17 November 1870. P.R.O. 48, 5/25, f.118.

to fight Liberals, even if it meant the loss of seats to the Conservatives, but once they had made their protest the dissidents
were surprisingly willing to return to the party fold and to help
to restore the party vote to its 1868 level: no fewer than ten of
the seats which the Conservatives had won at by-elections between 1868 and 1874 were re-captured by the Liberals in 1874
because the force of the reaction against the government was
spent. The acceptance of office by the Conservatives would have
been widely regarded as sufficient punishment for past errors,
and the party would have been given a chance to close its ranks.
In the circumstances, a Conservative dissolution in 1873 would
almost certainly have resulted either in a small Conservative
majority of about ten seats, or in an equally small Liberal majority.
By waiting and allowing the Liberal divisions to become deeper
the Conservative position was immensely strengthened.

The general election, when it did come in 1874, differed from
that of 1868 in that it was utterly unexpected. Gladstone's address
to the electors of Greenwich was issued on 24 January without
the slightest warning, and took everybody by surprise by announcing an immediate election (in February) to test public feeling
on the abolition of the income tax. A by-election at Greenwich
had been expected (at least by the well-informed) as a consequence of Gladstone's decision to assume the office of Chancellor of the Exchequer in addition to that of First Lord of the
Treasury. It was also expected that he would fail to secure re-
election, since the other Greenwich seat had been captured by
the Conservatives at a by-election in 1873. But this was not
thought to be an adequate reason for dissolving parliament in
the middle of winter shortly before it was due to meet, and
without any warning to the government's supporters. The
sudden dissolution was followed by a quiet campaign and, of
course, a brief one. Few speeches were made by the party leaders
because few were needed: the government's case lay in its record,
the opposition's in its hostility to an administration which had
'harassed every trade, worried every profession, and assailed or
menaced every class, institution and species of property', and in
the need for a period of quiet. Gladstone's offer to abolish the
income tax was very little noticed by either side. The only people
active in the constituencies were the Conservatives, who were
stronger in the boroughs than at any time since 1841, the Radical

pressure groups, and (in Ireland) the Home Rulers: the more orthodox Liberals were quiescent.

The Conservatives benefited chiefly from four things: the unprecedented zeal and success of the borough Conservative associations, the unexpected vigour of the landed magnates in the counties, the improved central organisation of the party, and the activity of the Conservative publicans who became, for the first time, active politicians rather than the recipients of disguised bribes in the form of payments for the use of their premises as 'committee rooms'. The Liberals, on the other hand, suffered for the foolishness of their government in alienating its supporters in the Liberal associations, on whom it relied to prevent the popular reaction against its reforms from getting out of hand. The most energetic party workers of 1868 were either indifferent or had gone over to the anti-government pressure groups, the National Education League, the United Kingdom Alliance and the Home Rule League, and to make matters worse there was scarcely any central direction of the election campaign. Not only was the timing of the election a surprise to the Liberal party, it came also at a time when Arthur Peel, the newly-appointed Chief Whip, was ill and unable to undertake the vital work of weeding out surplus Liberal candidates.

This election has often been described by Liberal historians in terms of a 'torrent of gin and beer' (Gladstone's description of it immediately after the election), and Sir Robert Ensor even goes so far as to construct a general theory of late nineteenth-century politics on the basis of the activities of the licensed victuallers.[1] His thesis falls into two parts. First, that 'from midsummer 1871 till the dissolution of 1874 nearly every public-house in the United Kingdom was an active committee-room for the conservative party. The consequences of this upon actual voting, well attested by contemporary evidence, probably outweighed all the other factors in the government's unpopularity.' Secondly, that until 1871 the liquor industry, like most of the other 'permanent interests', had been Liberal, and that the Conservatives had consequently been starved of workers and money. But that from 1871 onwards the Conservatives made good this lack:

> Money, workers, and support of every kind flowed to it inexhaustibly from the liquor trade. The more the liberals came to rely on the

[1] R. C. K. Ensor, *England 1870-1914*, Oxford 1936, pp. 21-2.

chapels, the more the public-houses rallied to their opponents. When political 'machines' developed in the eighties, the need for a permanent large income at the head-quarters of each party was vastly increased. But for money derived from brewers and distillers, it is very doubtful if the conservatives could have met it. . . . Nor was money all. Few people are so well placed to influence voters as publicans; and there practically ceased to be any liberal publicans.

The view that the publicans were largely responsible for the government's defeat in the constituencies is derived from some hasty words of Gladstone's after the election, from a number of Liberal newspapers (and in particular the *Daily News*),[1] and from the pronouncements of the United Kingdom Alliance. It comforted Gladstone to attribute the Liberal defeat to the licensed victuallers because he always liked to think of elections as a battle between the children of darkness and the children of light, and had no doubt that the licensed victuallers belonged to the category of 'publicans and sinners'. Moreover, he had some reason for feeling strongly on the subject, since the licensed victuallers' organisations were strong in his own constituency, Greenwich, and because since 1873 the other member for Greenwich had been T. W. Boord, a Conservative distiller. But those in Gladstone's immediate family circle, and later even Gladstone himself, rightly attributed the Liberal defeat to much more general causes.[2] The Liberal newspapers, too, soon changed their tone, and began to accept the more cautious interpretation of papers like the *Methodist Recorder*, which was sure that there had been a Conservative reaction but doubted whether it could be attributed to any particular cause. Moreover, it is clear from a study of the licensed victuallers' own press (chiefly the *Licensed Victuallers' Guardian* and the *Morning Advertiser*) that there was nothing like a systematic attack on the government. Until 1873 there was not even an effective national organisation for sending circulars to M.P.s, and even after an elaborate conference in Birmingham in January 1873 to discuss the 1872 Licensing Bill, very little was done to concert the activities of local associations of licensed victuallers.

---

[1] The views of the *Daily News* were pretty accurately reflected in the *Annual Register* which is, therefore, an untrustworthy source.

[2] *The Diary of Lady Frederick Cavendish*, ed. John Bailey, London 1927, II, 168. For another balanced view see *A Journal of Events During the Gladstone Ministry, 1868-1874*, by John, Earl of Kimberley, ed. Ethel Drus (Camden 3 Series xc), London 1958, pp. 43-4.

As soon as the election was announced the Licensed Victuallers' Protection Society called for a two-fold campaign in favour of proved friends on the one hand and against the advocates of local option on the other, but it did not call for an attack on the government. On the advice of the Licensed Victuallers' National Defence League local organisations of licensed victuallers also confronted candidates with a questionnaire on licensing issues. But care was taken not to adopt a party line, and the Ramsgate and St Lawrence Licensed Victuallers' Association was solemnly rebuked by the editor of the *Licensed Victuallers' Guardian* for supporting the Conservatives when there was a friendly Liberal (Sir Henry Tufton) in the field.

> We much regret that the Ramsgate and St. Lawrence Association should have decided on throwing Sir Henry Tufton overboard on political grounds alone. The honourable Baronet has ever taken a lively interest in the welfare and charities of the Trade, and has furthermore withstood all overtures from the Permissive party. On these grounds we think it would have been more prudent to have allowed the Trade vote to take its natural course. Much as we have contributed to the overthrow of a ministry which has acted unwisely in its legislation on the Licensing question, we must not visit the sins of the Government upon those Liberals who are disposed to deal justly towards us. The Licensing Act of 1872 was as much the work of the Conservatives as of the Liberal party, and organised hostility towards friendly Liberals will do us no good in the long run.[1]

This cautious attitude was reflected in many of the constituencies where the Liberal candidates were either friendly towards the licensed victuallers or hostile to local option. In Westminster, for instance, the candidates of both parties were hostile to the 1872 Licensing Act. And there were many others in which the complexity of local politics was such that the licensed victuallers' influence was negligible. Thus in Leicester, where the local licensed victuallers' association decided to support one of the Liberal members, P. A. Taylor, against his colleague William McArthur,[2] there was no significant difference between the number of votes received by them. In such constituencies few, if any, Liberal publicans changed their allegiance. Indeed, there was no reason why they should, any more than Liberal brewers like the Basses, the Buxtons, and the Whitbreads, or old friends of

[1] *Licensed Victuallers' Guardian*, 14 February 1874.   [2] *Ibid.*

the licensed victuallers like Edward Knatchbull-Hugessen. The licensed victuallers took a decisive line against the Liberals only where there was already a Conservative majority among them (as at Ramsgate), or where temperance Liberals were strong. In the latter case (and particularly in the constituencies where one or more of the 150 or so supporters of local option were standing) there really was a rush to the Conservatives, although it was mainly confined to those publicans who had been only nominal Liberals in 1868. It was not so much the Gladstone government as the temperance movement and the gradual identification of the Liberal party with the United Kingdom Alliance which finally drove the publicans into the Conservative camp.

Nor is the hypothesis of a grand movement by the publicans necessary to explain the Liberal defeat in 1874. The issues before the electors were so clear and the swing against the government was so strong, that no amount of free beer was likely to have a decisive effect on the result.

The second part of Ensor's thesis must be entirely rejected. The main support of the Conservative party was and remained the landed interest, although after 1874 it was also supported by a large proportion of the middle classes. And the landed interest was still sufficiently prosperous even in 1895 to supply the great majority of the Conservative party funds. It is simply not true that the Conservative party was short of money before 1871 or that after 1871 it was financed by the liquor interest. As yet we have no complete list of the contributors to the party funds, but the figures given in Chapter XVIII and other lists of contributors to the party funds in England and Scotland which the present writer has seen, suggest that at least until 1892 the Conservatives obtained nearly all their money from the traditional sources.

The most important and permanent result of the 1874 election had nothing to do with the liquor interest at all. This was the marked swing to the Conservatives in middle-class constituencies. There had already been an indication of the way in which the tide was flowing in 1868 when W. H. Smith in Westminster and Lord George Hamilton in Middlesex had won unexpected victories in erstwhile Liberal strongholds. W. H. Smith summed up the change in his own person: his father had been a Wesleyan and a Liberal, and he had himself only gradually broken with the family creeds to become a churchman and Conservative. In the early sixties he was in some demand as a Liberal candidate, but did not finally agree to stand for a constituency until 1865. He then stood for Westminster as a Palmerstonian Liberal against the Radical John Stuart Mill, appealing to the 'more moderate or Conservative portion of the constituency', whom he offered an 'opportunity of marking their disapproval of the extreme political doctrines' of the other candidates.[1] As a successful commercial man, with something like national celebrity because of his successful development of his firm's business as wholesale news-agents, and as a man of monumental common sense, he seemed to be a typical Palmerstonian Englishman. Moreover, although he was still nominally a Liberal, his reasons for supporting Palmerston were entirely Conservative ('I feel that the country owes a debt of gratitude to him for having preserved peace, and for the resistance he has offered to reckless innovation in our domestic institutions'), and suggested that he would find it impossible to remain in the Liberal party when Palmerston had gone. Even in 1865 he was toying with the idea of a Liberal-Conservative party composed of the Palmerstonian elements in both parties. By 1868, with Gladstone leader of the Liberal party, he found himself firmly if reluctantly established in the Conservative camp as official Conservative candidate for Westminster.

By 1874 the same change had taken place in individual commercial men all over middle-class London: the City itself, suburban Surrey, Kent and Essex all changed their allegiance, while Middlesex and Westminster each returned two Conservatives by substantial majorities. By 1880 the Liberals had lost control of suburbia altogether.

The change in Middlesex, where the electorate had become a predominantly suburban one as a result of the new railways to the City, was particularly significant. The constituency was overwhelmingly Liberal in the fifties, and even in 1867 Henry Labouchere was returned unopposed because no Conservative could be found to contest such a hopeless seat. But some years before 1867 the character of the constituency had begun to change as more middle-class houses were built, almost all of which were enfranchised by the 1867 Reform Act, and in 1868 the two parties were fairly evenly balanced. Lord George Hamilton had quite

[1] Maxwell, *W. H. Smith*, I, 123.

a substantial majority, but this was more the result of open warfare between the two Liberal candidates than of the political
views of the constituency.[1] The voting was:

Hamilton (C)	7,850
Enfield (L)	6,507
Labouchere (L)	6,397

By 1874 most of the remaining Palmerstonians had gone over to
the Conservatives, who also won over the new voters, with the
result that the Liberal poll fell by approximately a thousand votes,
while the Conservative poll increased by 2,500.

Hamilton (C)	10,343
Coope (C)	9,867
Enfield (L)	5,623
Lehmann (L)	5,192

The electorate grew by about 6,000 between the elections of
1874 and 1880, but even this change did not greatly help the
Liberals, and the result of the 1880 election was:

Hamilton (C)	12,904
Coope (C)	12,328
Gladstone (L)	8,876

A similar and equally decisive change took place in the other
parts of suburbia, as a result of which all twenty-one divisions of
Middlesex, Kent and Surrey returned Conservatives from 1885
to 1892.

III

The Disraeli government was much more fortunate than its
predecessor in by-elections. It lost fifteen seats between 1874 and

[1] Labouchere denounced both Lord Enfield, the other Liberal, and Lord George
Hamilton in the most violent terms and plunged the Liberals into internecine warfare
which even the Committee of the Reform Club failed to end. cp. A. L. Thorold, *The
Life of Henry Labouchere*, London 1913, pp. 78-84, and Lord George Hamilton, *Parliamentary Reminiscences and Reflections 1868 to 1885*, London 1916, pp. 1-9. The figures for
the poll given below are taken from a letter by Dudley Baxter to the *Standard*, 27
November 1868: those given in the two biographies differ wildly.

1880, but it gained ten,[1] and until 1878 it probably more than held its own in the country because the ministry's foreign policy won a measure of approval from a section of the Liberals and from the metropolitan Liberal press, headed by *The Times*. On the other hand, there is no real reason to suppose, as has often been assumed, that a dissolution at the time of the Congress of Berlin would have secured the ministry another term of office with a safe majority. The boroughs were still very largely Liberal, and the Conservatives had already begun to suffer heavy losses at municipal elections, losses which became more numerous in 1879; the Home Rulers were stronger than they had been in 1874; and the chances of Conservatives again profiting by Liberal dissensions to slip into parliament were remote. The Conservatives would probably have kept a majority, but it would have been either a majority of three or four or a majority over the Liberals, but not over Liberals and Home Rulers combined. The situation would, in short, have been very much the same as it would have been if Disraeli had taken office in 1873 and afterwards dissolved, except that in 1878 the Conservatives would have attained their position because of their own strength, whereas in 1873-4 they would have done so because of their opponents' weakness.

Whatever the might-have-beens, Disraeli did not dissolve, and by 1879 the government was faced with serious difficulties, the extent of which it completely failed to gauge Of these, the campaign which Gladstone carried on against its Eastern policy was, if not the least important, at least of only subsidiary importance. It made a great impression on the nonconformists and on the working classes, and by reviving the loyalties of 1868 made it possible to reunite the party but, like the Birmingham caucus, it failed to give that jolt to public opinion which was necessary to overthrow the government. This was provided by the unexpected deepening of the agricultural and industrial depression,

---

[1] The results of by-elections were:

			Gains	Losses
1874	.	.	3	—
1875	.	.	1	4
1876	.	.	1	4
1877	.	.	1	2
1878	.	.	3	3
1879	.	.	—	2
1880	.	.	1	—
			10	15

which the government tried to pass off as a temporary phase and
consistently underestimated as a source of disquiet. In England
bad harvests and the agricultural depression inaugurated a not
very extensive but none the less significant Liberal reaction in
the counties, and the beginnings of a flight of the farmers from
the Conservatives, who seemed to be doing so little to ease their
burdens, to the newly formed Farmers' Alliance. In Ireland
they led to a famine whose dimensions threatened to rival those
of the 'great famine', and to support for the Land League,
founded, like the Farmers' Alliance, in 1879. After this the Conservatives lost all chance of gaining any ground outside Ulster, and
even in Ulster began to lose seats to the Liberals. In Scotland the
depression also led to a sudden resurgence of anti-landlord feeling
which cost the Conservatives all their gains of 1874.

The industrial depression gave a similar shock to industry,
which led to widespread unemployment on a scale unknown for
many years. The trade unions were hard hit and some disintegrated under the strain. Those that remained had a glut of work-
less men to care for. From an average figure of one or two per
cent unemployed in 1871-4, the unemployment rate rose to 6·8
per cent in 1878 and 11·4 per cent in 1879 before falling again
in 1880 and 1881.[1] During the elections the Liberals unashamedly
exploited the hard times. Election posters and cartoons blamed
the Conservatives for them. In Manchester a leaflet was circulated
which simply contained the statement seen on p. 230.[2]

This was a most unpromising background for an appeal to
the country, but the government made the position worse by
delaying the election from 1879 (when it would normally have
been held) until 1880. Until the middle of 1879 the Liberals
had no marked advantage, although their morale was good, but
by July they had begun to gain ground. W. P. Adam, the Chief
Whip, was ready for an election at any time after that, and was
able to weed out a record number of superfluous Liberal candidates, while the 'new model' Liberal associations attained their
maximum efficiency about November, when Gladstone opened his

[1] The figures for the decade are: 1870 3·9 per cent, 1871 1·6 per cent, 1872 0·9
per cent, 1873 1·2 per cent, 1874 1·7 per cent, 1875 2·4 per cent, 1876 3·7 per cent,
1877 4·7 per cent, 1878 6·8 per cent, 1879 11·4 per cent, 1880 5·5 per cent, 1881 3·5
per cent. W. T. Layton and G. Crowther, *An Introduction to the Study of Prices*, 3 edn,
London 1938, p. 274.

[2] A copy of this leaflet is now preserved in Manchester Central Library.

FACTS ARE STUBBORN THINGS
SALFORD WORKHOUSE

When Gladstone took office there were	901 Inmates	3375	Receiving Out-Door Relief.	
When he retired there were	851 ,,	1922	,,	,,
DECREASE	50 do.	1453	do.	do.
When Lord Beaconsfield took office	851 ,,	1922	,,	,,
And on 1st of January, 1880	1718 ,,	4760	,,	,,
INCREASE	867 do.	2838	do.	do.

So much for TORY RULE, with its Bad Trade, Heavy Rates & Taxes.
IF YOU HAVE NOT HAD ENOUGH OF THESE, VOTE FOR THE TORIES.

first Midlothian campaign. The Conservatives, on the other hand, were allowed to bask in a false security, and to let their organisation get slack. Few of them had expected to win such a decisive victory as that of 1874, and even fewer understood its implications, so that there was a tendency to regard it almost as an Act of God, a favour towards His chosen people, which had opened the way to decades of Conservative rule. Sir Stafford Northcote as leader of the Commons did little or nothing to prepare his supporters with arguments for the constituencies, and did even less to rouse their spirits, while James Lowther, the Chief Secretary, managed to convey a completely false picture of the state of affairs in Ireland. Even worse, the party machine had been allowed to decay since 1876. As a result, when Disraeli finally chose to dissolve in March 1880, after two by-elections had unexpectedly favoured the government, the Conservatives were completely unprepared and his dissolution had the same effect on his party as Gladstone's equally badly-timed dissolution of 1874.

The election of 1880, like those of 1868 and 1874, was fought on issues already before the public, and the speeches made after the dissolution probably had little effect except in swelling the number of electors who actually voted. Disraeli's address, like Gladstone's in 1874, utterly failed to make an impression on the public mind because there had been no preparation for it. Oracular warnings about the dangers of Irish separatism meant as little to the public as conditional promises to repeal the income tax had done in 1874. Gladstone and Chamberlain had already captured public attention with their declarations on foreign and social policy and continued to hold it from the opening of the first Midlothian campaign (24 November to 8 December 1879) until the poll was held in April. Indeed, Disraeli's election address was completely forgotten during the second Midlothian campaign (16 March to 5 April 1880), during which Gladstone gave such an unrivalled exhibition of oratorical virtuosity that it held the attention of the entire country. Gladstone was right when he wrote to Rosebery after the elections were over:

> As to Midlothian the moral effect, before and after, has I think surpassed all our hopes. The feeling until it was over . . . was so fastened on it, that it was almost like one of the occasions of old when the issue of battle was referred to single combat.[1]

The result was a sweeping Liberal victory more complete even than that of 1868. Nearly all the Liberal losses of 1874 were regained, and most of the marginal seats held by the Conservatives in 1868 were also captured by the Liberals.[2] Moreover, the Liberals made significant advances in their own strongholds, Wales and Scotland: Wales returned only two Conservatives as against twenty-eight Liberals, and Scotland only seven Conservatives as against fifty Liberals. Only in Ireland was there cause for Liberal anxiety: there the 'Whig' Home Rulers, who were supporters in general of the Liberal party, suffered a setback at the hands of the much more independent Parnellites, so that in Ireland the election results were:

Conservatives	26
Liberals	16
Moderate or Whig Home Rulers .	37 } 61
Parnellites	24 }
	103[3]

[1] Morley, *Gladstone*, II, 614.

[2] 49 Conservative and 49 Liberal seats had been won with majorities of less than 10 per cent in 1874, and 45 of the 49 Conservative seats changed hands in 1880. In addition 20 of the 48 Conservative seats held by majorities of less than 10 per cent in 1868 were also captured. (11 others had been won by the Liberals in 1874.)

[3] The Liberals and Conservatives each gained 5 seats and the Home Rulers gained 10 from the Conservatives. The moderate Home Rulers soon tended to merge with the Parnellites, leaving a core of about 20 'Whigs' who lost their seats in 1885.

The only comfort which the Conservatives could derive was that they could not very well do much worse, since in England they were reduced to the level of 1857, their lowest since 1832.

In the old parliament there had been:

Conservatives	351
Liberals	250
Home Rulers	51
	652
Conservative majority . . .	50

In the new parliament the position was reversed:

Liberals	353
Conservatives	238
Home Rulers	61
	652
Liberal majority	54

Chapter Eleven

ELECTION MANAGERS AND REGISTRATION AGENTS

I

ALTHOUGH political associations and party committees were becoming increasingly important after 1867, most of the work of political organisation in the constituencies continued until long after 1885 to be done by those who were paid for their services. These were the (usually part-time) registration agents and their counterparts, the election agents. In some of the big towns and in a few counties there were already by 1868 professional party organisers who combined the functions of secretary of a Conservative or Liberal association, registration agent, and election agent; but this was unusual. The majority of the party associations preferred to divide the work between a number of solicitors or professional election agents, who were competent to deal with the problems of electoral and registration law but were ill-fitted to encourage voluntary effort by individual electors.

The key figure in all election work was the registration agent. He was expected to advise the local party leaders on all problems of local organisation, to make himself generally available at elections (often under the orders of an outsider), to act as a general correspondent for the party headquarters, to seek out and register his political friends, and to disqualify as many of his political enemies as could be shown to possess no valid qualifications for the vote. In addition, the inefficiency of the registration machinery thrust on him the further duty of supervising the whole business of registration.[1]

Long before 1867 the inefficiency of the Overseers and revision courts alike had forced the party agents to take upon themselves the main work of registration, and by 1880 they were extraordinarily good at it. In the big towns where there were full-time agents, even the preliminary register had come to be prepared by them, and the party associations employed men to

---

[1] For the registration system see Appendix II.

visit each house to note any changes in the tenancy. The Liberal registration agent for Liverpool, for instance, presided over an elaborate machinery which he described to his fellow agents in 1883 in these terms:

> Our method of procedure is, a month or so before the Register is published, to make a house to house survey of the whole city, to make out street registers of all persons on our side of politics who are not on the present list and ought to be on the new list, and correct errors in the present Register by giving to the Overseers information obtained in our survey, so that such errors shall not reappear. As a rule, they receive such information, check it, and if correct, insert the names. On an average we send 14,000 to 15,000 names of persons entitled to be placed on the list, and the later our survey is made so much the better, for we can then send information to correct the Register almost up to the time it is in the printer's hands.
>
> Our city is divided into four townships and one parish, and persons who have removed from one township to the other are enrolled for the new township on producing from the old one a note stating in effect that all rates have been paid. In this way a great amount of useful work is done, and certainly more than three-fourths of our friends are placed upon the Register without any trouble or loss of time to them. After publication it has been our practice to make the usual claims for persons omitted, and also objections, and from time to time it has been my duty to object to from between 4,000 to 5,000 voters.[1]

As soon as the preliminary register had been published, both parties examined it carefully and issued claims and objections. The agents of the two sides then met and compared their lists of names, and agreed to allow certain claims and objections (often a large number) and to confine the attention of the revision court to cases which raised questions of principle. In this way a great deal of time was saved: as one agent put it, 'We often save very many hours of trouble by comparing the information received from the persons objected to, and satisfying each other that an objection is useless, and getting it withdrawn.'[2] This habit of co-operation also had the salutary effect of discouraging the creation of faggot votes, with the result that they became more and more uncommon, except in Peebles and Selkirk and Midlothian.

Three types of case were actually heard in the registration

[1] *Liberal Secretaries' and Agents' Association. Report of its Formation, Rules, and Conferences*, Liverpool 1883, p. 28.
[2] H.C. 360, p. 54 (1870). VI, 262.

courts, at which the parties were usually represented by a local solicitor if the registration agents were not themselves qualified solicitors. First, there were those cases that raised legal points, such as the definition of 'occupation' in the 1867 Act and whether the word 'female' in the 1869 Municipal Franchise Act included married women (it did not). Secondly, there were those which arose from changes whose implications the agents did not understand, such as the creation of a lodger franchise in 1867. Thus in 1868 there were large numbers of objections to lodger claims, designed to exclude from the franchise qualified lodgers who could not or would not attend the revision courts to give evidence. However, when once the agents realised how apathetic the lodgers were and how few of them actually possessed a twelve months' residence qualification, the number of such objections decreased markedly. Finally, there were the purely political cases—still quite common. A good example occurred in Manchester between 1880 and 1885. Between 1874 and 1880 the Conservatives had neglected the registers, with the result that the Liberals had made very considerable gains, to which they were only doubtfully entitled, and easily won two of the three seats at the general election. After the election the Conservatives raised a fund to enable them to purify the registers, and by confining themselves to cases about which there could be little dispute they reduced the Liberal strength by 2,772 voters at the October 1880 registration. The Liberals were naturally very much upset and decided to counterattack, with the result that in October 1881, 2,033 Liberals, 2,133 Conservatives, and 2,876 neutrals were struck off the registers, and the electorate of the two principal working-class wards was reduced by 5,489. The battle continued every year until the final revision in the old constituency in October 1884, when the electorate was 8,945 smaller than in 1880.[1] It is scarcely to be wondered that the Liberals refused to fight a by-election in 1883 when the Conservative minority member died, or that they fared badly at the 1885 general election.

II

The task of the election agent was quite distinct from that of the registration agent. Elections were isolated events, only indirectly

---

[1] These figures are from the MS. minutes of the Manchester Liberal Association.

connected with the work done in the registration courts and
by the party associations, and were organised on a different basis.
The election agent was essentially a man who organised a team
of up to several thousand paid workers, so that they got through
the essential work of canvassing and making arrangements for
taking electors to the polling booths with the minimum of friction, with the maximum of noise and publicity, and with as few
breaches of the law as seemed to him desirable. In the counties
and most of the big towns this task was performed by the registration agent on behalf of the local party leaders, and the candidates had little part in the management of the campaign. Indeed,
in many counties the whole of the election organisation, from
the solicitor-principal-agent at the top to the solicitors' clerks
and their hired roughs at the bottom, was almost entirely hereditary, and even the local magnates had little control over it. In
the remainder of the constituencies conditions varied. In the corrupt ones there was a ready-made hereditary organisation which
sold itself to the candidates, who usually called in their own
solicitors or an outside agent to keep the bill within reasonable
proportions. In the apathetic ones there was scarcely any organisation at all, except for municipal purposes, and the candidate
was forced to import an election manager, who then set about
hiring local solicitors and other notables to work for him. In the
remainder there was a skeleton organisation provided by the local
solicitor-registration-agent and his associates, but extra help had
usually to be imported at elections. In all of them there was
ample opportunity for any energetic solicitor or solicitor's
clerk to find employment as a ward or district or sub-district
agent.

The rewards were always adequate. A chief agent expected
£50 to £100 in a small borough, £150 to £250 in a medium-
sized or large borough, and £500 if his duties were particularly
onerous. District agents received between £15 and £50 each,
plus any surpluses they managed to accumulate and were not
asked to account for, any professional fee charged for particular
services, and, if they were lucky, a retaining fee between elections.
At Oxford the Liberal agents received a total of £577 in 1868,
£525 at the general election of 1874, £210 at a by-election
in 1874, £420 at the general election of 1880, and £420 at
another by-election in 1880, while the Conservative agents

received £367 in 1868 and £210 at the general election of 1880.[1]

The local solicitor who became chief agent at an election usually belonged to a firm which specialised in political business, and the office of agent not infrequently descended from father to son.[2] Such men knew little law, but had picked up a good deal of knowledge of human nature at the local counterpart of Dotheboys Hall, and knew that they could always bring in experts on electoral law to keep them out of trouble. The outside 'experts' who were in such demand at elections were a mixed bag. The best type was a solicitor of some standing either in a big provincial town or in London. Samuel Leech was mayor, under-Sheriff, and agent for Michael Bass, M.P., at Derby, and Liberal agent for South Derbyshire, and specialised in getting up cases for election courts and in fighting by-elections.[3] Horace Philbrick was a partner in the City firm of Philbrick and Corpe and had a number of important clients, but maintained an interest in elections inherited from his father, the leader of the Colchester Liberals, and encouraged by the firm in Halifax with which he had served a year of his articles: he acted as sub-agent at Colchester in 1865 and 1868, at Halifax in 1874 and at Chester in 1880, and as chief agent at Colchester in 1870, and also did occasional work in local revision courts.[4] Lower in the social scale, but still enjoying an established position, there were professional election agents with offices in London. One of the best-known of them was James Acland, an advanced Radical who had been a lecturer for the Anti-Corn-Law League and who later became a member of the Council of the Reform League, of whom George Howell has left an engaging account.

He was broadminded in his views, an able platform speaker and well versed in all the chicanery of election plots and devices. He was agent for Sir Robert Clifton when he first stood for Nottingham, and he told me what difficulties he had in coaching Sir Robert in politics. But he was equal to any emergency. At the first meeting he placed a man in the back part of the room, and when the candidate halted, stammered, and got into a muddle, the man cried out 'Damn

[1] [C.2856-I] pp. 4-8. H.C. (1881). XLIV, 4-8.
[2] T. H. Winder, *A Life's Adventure*, privately printed, London 1921, contains an account of one such family.
[3] H.C. 225, pp. 1-10 (1875). VIII, 457-66.
[4] [C. 2824-I] pp. 727-8. H.C. (1881). XL, 759-60 and P.R.O. 48, 5/25, ff.107-10. Philbrick's brother was Recorder of Colchester from 1870 until his appointment as a County Court judge in 1895.

politics, Sir Robert, tell us who is to win the Derby.' Sir Robert was at home, he could chaff and talk about horses; he became popular, and went in by over 1,400 majority, over the Earl of Lincoln, both then standing as Liberals. Acland's motto was to win the election— never mind the expense: a defeat, he would say, is the most expensive of all contests.

Mr. Acland dabbled in all sorts of election work. He did a good deal in connection with the Corporation of the City of London and could have told a tale as to who prepared some of the elaborate defences which were issued from time to time. The 'Vindication' was, I think, wholly compiled by him.[1] He was an adept at Election addresses. He knew how to say nothing and to say it well. None of his candidates could be convicted of breaking election pledges after their election. His difficulty was with the heckling, when a candidate would sometimes say more than Acland thought prudent, but the 'address' was after all *the* test; an extempore answer could be explained away.

In the pursuit of his profession he was not always on one side; I found him out on one occasion nicely. He was Tory agent for Worcester: one of his lieutenants was agent for Droitwich, but Acland pulled the strings. I made speeches against him in both constituencies, but Acland's men won. . . . He was free and generous to a fault. He could never save money, however much he earned. . . . He was a willing helper without fee or reward when the person wanting help was too poor to pay. But as regards the rich candidate, who had his own game to play, he felt justified in spoiling the Egyptians. But he never sold his Candidate; never relaxed his efforts to get him returned. The system was corrupt; that was not his fault. He advocated a better system. Parliament refused it. The candidates liked the system; why should he complain. He lived to see the change: hustings abolished, open voting driven away with the ballot carried and the Corrupt Practices Acts amended and strengthened.[2]

James Acland had managed to climb the very steep ladder which led from the uncertain and often disreputable life of a political lecturer to the eminence of a fashionable election agent. But he was unusual. Most clerks or working men with a taste for politics and without any trade-union connections could aspire

[1] This was the well-known defence of the city corporation; *A Statistical Vindication of the City of London; or, Fallacies Exploded and Figures Explained* by Benjamin Scott, F.R.A.S., London 1867.

[2] The manuscript of this pen portrait is with others in the George Howell collection in the Bishopsgate Institute. For Acland see also Norman McCord, *The Anti-Corn Law League*, London 1958, pp. 56f. Acland had been a Methodist minister and journalist in early life and was well advanced in years by 1868.

to no more than the rôle of temporary political lecturer. Political lecturers had been in great demand since the time of the Anti-Corn-Law League, and could earn thirty shillings a week and their expenses in fighting elections or in canvassing. Some were employed by the party headquarters, which also tried to keep an accurate list of suitable men in order to recommend them to constituencies. The best of them were honest politicians with a message, but there was an unusually high proportion of black sheep among them who drank too much or lived by extorting money from too-innocent M.P.s for services never performed.[1] William Gregson and Joseph Howes are typical of the better type, possibly because their work kept them away from the flesh-pots of the metropolis.[2] Gregson was brought up as a weaver at Ribchester and moved in 1835 to Low Moor near Clitheroe, where he became a member of a temperance organisation and a leading temperance advocate. He was soon employed as a professional temperance missionary, and held appointments at Blackburn, Brighton, Bolton, Hull and York, before, in 1856, becoming an agent of the British Temperance League. In his new capacity he was encouraged to take an active part in politics and worked for a number of Liberal candidates. He also became a town councillor and leader of the Liberal group on the council in Blackburn. Howes started work in a Nottingham boot factory at the age of thirteen and became an active politician while still in his teens. He joined all the Radical organisations in Nottingham, including the Republican Club, and kept up his Radical activities when he moved to Leeds in 1875. There he soon became chairman of the Labour Representation League and a successful hustings orator, and attracted sufficient attention to be appointed a paid lecturer for the National Reform Union, a post he held for the next twenty-five years while campaigning in the north of England.

III

Although solicitors continued for many years to form the most numerous class of political organisers, a new class of full-time

---

[1] cp. *Nineteenth Century*, XIII, 1083 (1883). The correspondence of the party leaders is full of references to these miserable people.
[2] Both have *Lives*: J. G. Shaw, *Life of William Gregson, Temperance Advocate*, Blackburn 1891, and Joseph Howes, *Twenty-Five Years' Fight with the Tories*, privately printed, Leeds 1907.

agents had come into existence by 1885. Full-time registration agents had been appointed occasionally between 1832 and 1868, and the Liverpool Constitutional Association appears to have had one continuously from 1848, but such appointments were rare. The party agent first emerged as a professional man in the north of England, and particularly in Lancashire, where there was a stronger belief in permanent organisation than elsewhere, and where, thanks to the Anti-Corn-Law League and its successors, which possessed offices and a full-time staff from 1841 to 1870, solicitors had never had a monopoly of registration work. After 1868 the Conservatives were readier than the Liberals to employ full-time agents and in 1874 only Clitheroe, of all the Lancashire boroughs, was managed by solicitor-agents on the Conservative side. Some of the agents were men with other occupations, like James Hampson of Ashton-under-Lyne, who was an auctioneer and 'general agent' as well as Conservative agent, but these occupations were usually not such as to demand a great expenditure of time.

It is not easy to arrive at an estimate of the number of full time registration agents at work by 1885. In 1874 there were fifty-four constituencies in England with Conservative agents who were not solicitors: of these, eight were in the metropolitan area, twenty-eight in Lancashire and twelve in Yorkshire. There was, however, a certain amount of doubling up—for instance, J. C. Shaw, the Central Office 'travelling agent' at Sheffield, acted as registration agent for the borough of Sheffield and, jointly with solicitors, for the Southern Division of the West Riding and for East Derbyshire—so that the actual number of agents who were not solicitors was less, namely fifty-two. Of these, about thirty appear to have been primarily election or registration agents.[1] On the Liberal side the number was appreciably lower in 1874, but it had increased by 1880. As, however, there are no records of the names of the Liberal agents, it is difficult to form any conclusions about them.

The first sign that the new 'lay' agents had been appointed in sufficient numbers to be considered at least an incipient profession was the foundation in 1872 of the North of England Conservative Agents' Association, which has continued in existence

---

[1] These figures are derived from a comparison of the *Law List* with the official party return of agents.

ever since. Its founders were all Lancastrians, and its first secretary
was W. F. Gayter, for many years secretary of the South-East
Lancashire Conservative Registration Association, whose headquarters were in Manchester. The early minute books have been
lost, but by 1886, the date of the first of the surviving minutes,
the association was in a flourishing state with forty-eight members
from all over the north of England who met four times a year,
each time in a different constituency, to discuss professional
matters and to consume a substantial meal.[1] These meetings took
the members as far afield as Southport, Bradford, Nottingham,
Liverpool and Sheffield, but the home of the association continued to be the Manchester district. The attendance after 1886
ranged from twelve to nearly forty members, and the business
discussed ranged from registration and election law and the latest
cases decided in the courts, to arrangements for co-operation between constituencies and the functions of an agents' association.
There was no National Society of Conservative Agents until 1891.

The Liberal agents were slower to organise themselves and were
in general rather worse paid and less regarded than their Conservative counterparts. Moreover, although there were more full-
time agents who were not solicitors in Lancashire and Yorkshire
than in the Midlands, Schnadhorst and the National Liberal
Federation claimed a general jurisdiction over them which was
not recognised by the agents themselves. A Liberal Secretaries'
and Agents' Association was founded in London in 1882 by
some twenty-six agents who met at the Westminster Palace Hotel
under the auspices of the National Liberal Federation. But the
new association was dominated by northerners (the officers were
Green of Manchester, Finnie of Leeds, Cooper of South Derbyshire and Croxden Powell of South-West Lancashire) and until
1885 it escaped the supervision of Birmingham. The first regular
meeting was held at Manchester in June 1883, attended by
eighteen agents from Lancashire, three each from Yorkshire and
Staffordshire, and five others from Derby, Coventry, Kendal,
North Leicestershire and Carnarvon.[2] Since the National Liberal

---

1 This part of the business (it is understood) is still an important feature of the
proceedings.
2 *Liberal Secretaries' and Agents' Association. Report of Its Formation, Rules, and Conferences*,
Liverpool 1883. The report does not publish a full list of agents, but of the 26
mentioned in connection with the inaugural conference 7 were from Lancashire and
Cheshire, 2 from Yorkshire and the rest from isolated constituencies over the rest of
the country.

Federation was unrepresented, it is difficult to escape the conclusion that at this time the new association was in all but name
a counterblast to the Conservative agents in the north rather
than a national association.

The immediate difficulty of the agents in their attempt to establish themselves as a profession was their uncertain social status,
which was a direct result of the lack of a general understanding
as to payment. In general, full-time agents were paid either at
the same rates as part-time solicitors, or less. In the larger boroughs
the rate was usually £150 a year—Elihu Finnie, Liberal agent
for Leeds, was paid £140 until 1883 and then £180—but some
agents were paid thirty shillings a week (£78 a year) or even
less. In 1908 Lowell wrote of agents: 'Their salaries, which vary
much, run all the way from forty pounds to four hundred pounds,
with about one hundred and fifty pounds as the average, the
scale of pay having risen somewhat of late years.'[1] In 1900, when
the number of full-time Conservative agents was about the same
as the number of solicitor-agents, the Council of the National
Society of Conservative Agents even felt it necessary to pass a
resolution 'that the salary of full-time agents should be not less
than £150 p.a. in order to ensure them fitting social positions,
without financial anxiety.'[2]

The Conservatives did their best to raise the social status of
their agents by encouraging gentlemen to take an interest in
electioneering. John Gorst, who became principal agent of the
party in 1870, was a university man, an ex-M.P. and the son
of a country gentleman. His assistants were nearly all of the same
or of a higher class: the first secretary of the Central Office,
Major Keith-Falconer, was a former Hussar officer and a peer's
son; his successor, Lieutenant-Colonel Edward Neville, was an
officer of the Scots Guards, son of a Dean of Windsor, grandson
of a peer, and brother of a county member; and he in turn was
succeeded in 1880 by the Hon. FitzRoy Stewart, another peer's
son. Nor was this all. A number of gentlemen were persuaded
to become constituency agents after the celebrated 'Bob' Grimston
had shown what sport an election could be at Westminster in
1868.[3] The first of these was Wollaston F. Pym, who was

---

[1] Lowell, *Government of England*, I, 482-3.
[2] Quoted by E. Halliley in 'A Short History of the National Society of Conservative
and Unionist Agents', supplement to the *Conservative Agents' Journal*, December 1947, p. 6.
[3] F. Gale, *The Life of the Hon. Robert Grimston*, London 1885, Ch. XIII.

appointed principal agent for the county of Middlesex in 1869.[1]
He was a member of a well-to-do Bedfordshire family, his grandfather had represented the county, and his brother became M.P.
for Bedford borough in 1895. And he himself had seen a good
deal of the world in looking for fortune and adventure in the
colonies. Pym endeavoured to interest men of his own type in
the work he had undertaken, and was supported in the quest
by Gorst (whose own agent at Chatham in 1890 was Lieutenant-
General G. W. Forbes). In time they were rewarded for their
zeal, for among Pym's pupils was Captain Middleton, who became Principal Agent of the party early in 1885, and was a
brilliant success.[2]

IV

The primary importance of the new professional agents was
that they enabled associations of voluntary party workers to get
rid of the solicitors if they wished to do so. There were constituencies with big party associations where solicitors continued
to act as secretary and part-time agent because they were
genuinely interested in politics. But where solicitors stood for an
outmoded system of electioneering they could now be displaced
by an efficient professional. This was particularly the case in
London and the South of England, where the old order had to
be driven out by the new. In Kent the 'Kentish gang' was at
work among the Conservatives as early as 1873, and by 1874
had driven out the solicitors at Dover, Maidstone, and Rochester.[3]
By the eighties they had even secured the appointment of a full-
time agent for West Kent, a vast constituency.

However, the employment in some constituencies of professional registration agents who were not solicitors had little immediate effect on the position of the solicitor-agents. Trained

---

[1] Lord George Hamilton, *Parliamentary Reminiscences 1868 to 1885*, pp. 9-10.

[2] Middleton was a navigating lieutenant whose eyesight failed in 1877 after 17 years
in the navy. He was only 31 years old, and drifted into politics, becoming successively
secretary of a club at Blackheath (1882), agent for West Kent (1883), and Principal
Agent of the party (1885-1903).

[3] Sir William Hart Dyke wrote to Disraeli, 23 August 1873 (Disraeli Papers):
'I have a deal of trouble with our Kent Boroughs: they have all been left for years in
the hands of local attorneys, who have only cared for the filthy lucre, & have been
content to lose any seat, so long as the victim they brought forward paid the bill.
Now, a spirit of energy has sprung up at Greenwich & Rochester & other places,
which disturbs the "attorney elements" & will prove most valuable in the end, but
at present I have my hands full, between contending parties.'

registration agents were few in number, there was a prejudice against their employment, and many of them were thought to be incompetent to conduct an election efficiently, because of their lack of legal training. Cox and Grady's celebrated election manual for the use of solicitors was, therefore, largely justified in its prophecy of 1868 that solicitors would find more election work to do and not less as a result of the Reform Bill.

> With the increased constituencies, more than ever is the assistance of the solicitor necessary to success at an election. More depends upon *management* now than formerly. To watch the registration, to keep up the interest of the candidate among the electors, and to determine the order of battle, is a *business*, to be learned only by experience, and requiring a clear head and a firm hand. Only the solicitor, who combines a knowledge of law with the training that forms the legal mind, can master this *business*.[1]

The weakness of the solicitors was that they were identified by their clients with paid canvassing, corrupt practices, high fees, and indifferent service. Candidates felt that solicitors 'gave only secondary thoughts to their political duties; they were far too stationary in their offices, and very expensive'.[2] They were, therefore, an obvious target for reformers who felt that voluntary rather than paid organisation should be the basis of electioneering. The better class of solicitors felt the isolation of their position, and were anxious to promote political associations and to squash corrupt practices. But they were too late. The Birmingham caucus was already in existence, and other election agents were at hand. Even in London, the least organised of the big urban centres, the day of the solicitor-agent and his armies was passing. Parts of London still answered to the description of it given by the *Law Times* in 1868:

> In London, the electors are so numerous that nobody values the franchise. Who cares to be one of fifty thousand? The consequence is, that one half of the constituency never goes to the poll at all. Three-fourths of the entire body are altogether indifferent to politics, and will not trouble themselves to walk across the street to record their votes. It matters not to them whether Mr. A. or Mr. B. is returned; so the election is really left to the candidates who most exert themselves to bring the voters to the poll. It is all an affair of organisation

---

[1] E. W. Cox, and S. G. Grady, *New Law and Practice of Registration and Elections*, 10 edn, London 1868, p. cxlvii.
[2] Hamilton, *Parliamentary Reminiscences 1868 to 1885*, pp. 9-10.

and cost. How are the electors to be induced to vote for you? Canvass is out of the question; they are careless of politics, with the exception of a few noisy cliques. The first step, then, and the only one, is to form committees in every district of persons known in that district, who will persuade the voters to go to the poll, not for the sake of the candidate, but to oblige their neighbour, the committeeman. These committees must hold their meetings at public-houses, and eat and drink, and employ assistants, and many of themselves expect payment for their services. But even to oblige a committee no voter will walk to the poll, though it be but five hundred yards distant. He must be taken to the poll in a cab. Consequently, the candidate is compelled to hire for the day all the cabs he can procure. The mere sending round of the address by the penny post costs 500 *l*. It will thus be seen how it comes that many of the metropolitan elections cost 12,000 *l*, and few fall below 6000 *l*.[1]

But this description was no longer true of all London. John Stuart Mill and Thomas Hughes were unsuccessful in their attempt to secure volunteer canvassers in 1868, but in 1874 Henry Fawcett won a seat at Hackney and established a new system there. He refused to pay for armies of helpers, he refused to use public-houses, and he insisted on the local Liberals bestirring themselves. As a consequence, he and his colleague spent only £914 in 1880 and got over 18,000 votes, whereas in Southwark, a stronghold of the old order, Thorold Rogers and Arthur Cohen spent £8,000 for just over 9,500 votes.

The rise of the caucus and the end of the solicitors' monopoly of election agencies would probably not have been enough alone to lead to a frontal attack on the system of electioneering with which the solicitors were associated. Bruce as Home Secretary in 1869, and many official and party spokesmen since then, had denounced them with little effect.[2] But the revelation of the extent to which corrupt practices had prevailed at the general election of 1880 made essential the drafting of a new Corrupt Practices Act; and it became clear, as soon as the government had decided that the Act must include provision for the restriction of election

---

[1] *Law Times*, 2 May 1868. Those who are inclined to think this picture overdrawn are recommended to read Charles Coburn's reminiscences of elections in the Tower Hamlets in *The Man Who Broke the Bank*, London n.d.

[2] For Bruce's attack on solicitors for encouraging useless contests see *3 Hansard* CXCIV, 650. Lowell (*Government of England*, I, 486 n.) reports an outspoken attack on solicitors by the chairman of the National Union in 1880.

expenditure, that the position of the solicitor-agents must be called in question.

There was therefore no surprise when Sir Henry James announced that the government's objects, in setting a limit on election expenditure, were to check corrupt practices, to encourage men of small means to come forward as candidates, and above all to give a more healthy character to elections by emphasising principles rather than organisation.[1] James was supported by Gorst and Hart Dyke, the acknowledged election experts on the Conservative side, and by the general feeling of the House. Indeed, by the time the bill came up for consideration for the third time (it had been delayed by Irish business) the opposition to the change had almost disappeared except in one corner of the House, and some of the Liberal members wished to limit expenditure to a much smaller sum than James proposed. The Baron de Ferrières, for instance, held that the 1880 election had cost £3,000,000, of which £1,000,000 went to lawyers and their dependants, £1,500,000 to the publicans, and only £500,000 was spent legitimately, and implied that expenses should be limited accordingly.[2]

The opposition that remained came from the leading spokesman of the solicitors in the House, Charles Lewis, member for Londonderry, who had acted as election agent for several members of the House, among them Hart Dyke. He attacked the bill as both impractical and dishonest: impractical because it was not possible to fight elections with volunteers, and dishonest because it suggested that the government had a higher standard of morality than the people. Gladstone's ministers, he pointed out, had paid for their seats in the usual way, while as for bribery, the tradesman who took a bribe or was employed by his party at elections was behaving no worse than peers who accepted Lord-Lieutenancies or Garters—'The fact was that the whole course of public and Party life in this country, illustrated in various

[1] On this last point he said, 'I think that the real object of consideration for the House is whether we could not base the political contests, not upon results produced by organization, or by agents, but rather upon the honest expression of political opinion, and upon the voluntary efforts of men actuated by a desire that their political views should prevail.' *3 Hansard* CCLVII, 266.

[2] Even under the much less generous schedule of 1918 elections generally cost about £1 million, plus the expenses of the Returning Officers (cp. D. E. Butler, *The Electoral System in Britain 1918-1951*, Oxford 1953, pp. 169-70), so that it is manifest that the Baron's speculations were wild ones.

ways, was nothing more nor less than bribery—payment for value received and services rendered to Party.'[1] A curious echo, this, of a passage in Cox and Grady's manual, 'The hypocrisies of the politician in the Legislature, the pretension to purity and the affectation of confidence in the wisdom and virtue of constituencies, which those who court their favour are compelled to put forth in addresses and speeches, would insure certain defeat, if within the doors of the committee room they were permitted to influence action.'[2]

Of the leading politicians who had any knowledge of electioneering 'in the raw', only W. H. Smith sympathised with Charles Lewis, and he confined his sympathy to letters from his yacht. He wrote to Salisbury on 14 August 1883:

> The machinery of an election has had to be provided at somebody's cost hitherto, and much of this is to be prohibited in future. The result will be, I am afraid, that we shall not poll anything approaching our strength.
>
> The Radicals have the Trades Unions the Dissenting Chapels and every society for the Abolition of property and morality working for them.
>
> Our supporters only want to be let alone, to be allowed to enjoy what they have; and they think they are so secure that they will make no sacrifice of time or of pleasure to prepare against attack or to resist it.
>
> So, to stave off the evil day as long as possible I should wish to retain the power of fighting elections by paid agency if necessary as in the past:—but I am afraid I am in a small minority in the Party in the House of Commons—who only think of one thing—lessening the cheque to be drawn on their bankers.[3]

As Smith took no part in the debate James had an easy task in replying to Lewis. He alluded to Lewis's own well-known generosity and suggested that solicitors would willingly accept the new system since only the less reputable ones thought of elections entirely in terms of money. But agents of the old type he denounced with quite unusual vigour and with the manifest approval of most of the House.

> Electioneering agents added strength to neither Party. Let both Parties fight without them. There would be found, in their absence,

---

[1] *3 Hansard* CCLXXIX, 1661.
[2] *New Law and Practice of Registration and Elections*, 10 edn, p. cl.
[3] W. H. Smith to Salisbury, 14 August 1883. Salisbury Papers.

the real strength of each Party, proved according to the true convictions of those who would then labour and fight. The candidates would then depend on the zeal and enthusiasm of those who laboured voluntarily in the interest of the cause which they considered to be right. An election would not then depend upon the clever trickery of an electioneering agent fighting with all his knowledge against those who would be raw and unskilled in the fight. The two Parties ranged on each side on this question were those who were candidates representing the public, and those who represented the interests of the electioneering agents.[1]

The Corrupt and Illegal Practices Act of 1883 proved in practice to be much less unfriendly to solicitors than had at first seemed likely. Their fees were reduced, and they were prohibited from employing paid canvassers or assistants (except in very small numbers), and from using hired carriages, so that the old and profitable type of election conducted with the aid of paid assistants came to an abrupt end. But the new law gave solicitors a special importance as legal advisers, and made it inevitable that party associations which could not afford a full-time registration agent should continue their part-time solicitor-agents in office. Indeed, because so many new constituencies were formed in 1885, there was for a time a great shortage of election agents of all sorts and local solicitors with election experience were in great demand. Only the richer associations with full-time registration agents could afford to do without them, and even these often appointed a solicitor as secretary or honorary secretary in order to keep them straight on legal issues and to represent them before the registration courts.

[1] *3 Hansard* CCLXXIX, 1700.

Chapter Twelve

COUNTING THE COST

BEFORE the Corrupt Practices Act of 1883 there was no legal restriction of election expenditure, and elections were fought by paid party workers. The Corrupt Practices Act of 1857 exerted a certain amount of moral pressure by requiring each candidate to submit an account of his expenses, and this account was subsequently published, but that was all.[1] Some constituencies paid their candidates' expenses, but most of them clung gratefully to the conventional picture of an M.P. as a rich man overflowing with good things.[2] There was, indeed, a considerable financial inducement for constituencies to fight elections, not by way of associations which required local effort and local expenditure, but by way of a temporary arrangement between the candidates and their solicitors, who hired canvassers and other election workers. By the same token, any proposal to limit election expenditure was bound to be both an attack on the system of conducting elections by means of paid workers, and an incentive to voluntary party associations.

The total cost of a general election varied considerably. In 1868 it was about £1,500,000, and in 1880 about £2,000,000, but the 1874 election cost considerably less.[3] These sums were made up in two ways: from the charges made by the Returning

[1] The natural consequence was that the returns were habitually falsified or not submitted at all. The limitations of the 'official' figures may be judged by a remark made by Thomas Hoskins, legal agent to the Liberal party, in 1880. 'I consider that the election expenses are the legal and proper election expenses, and that any illegal and improper payment is not an election expense which ought to be returned to the returning officer.' [C. 2777] p. 11. H.C. (1881). XLII, 11.

[2] There was no pattern in the matter of local payment of expenses. The Manchester Liberals found their candidates' expenses, the Bolton Liberals did not. Even in corrupt Chester, while one Conservative candidate and both Liberal candidates were shamelessly robbed, the other Conservative, Henry Cecil Raikes, had most of his expenses paid by subscription: [C. 2824-I] p. 742. H.C. (1881). XL, 774.

[3] These figures are based on the official returns but include estimates (which err by under-estimating the costs rather than by over-estimating them) for those constituencies for which no return was made. The official figures for elections from 1880 to 1910 are useful for comparative purposes: 1880 £1,736,781; 1885 £1,026,645; 1886 £624,086; 1892 £958,532; 1895 £773,333; 1900 £777,429; 1906 £1,166,858; 1910 (Jan.) £1,295,782; 1910 (Oct.) £978,312: *Constitutional Year Book for 1914*, p. 265.

Officers for conducting the election, and from the candidates' election expenses proper. The total cost of the Returning Officers' expenses was not very great—approximately £92,000 in 1868, or an average of £310 per constituency—but it was not evenly distributed. Counties cost more than boroughs (see Table XIII), and large boroughs more than small ones. In 1874, for instance,

Table XIII. Average Returning Officers' Charges per Candidate at English and Welsh Contested Elections

	1868	1874	1880
Counties .	£166. 15. 1	£296. 13. 4	£201. 8. 2
Boroughs.	£98. 0. 0	£119. 17. 3	£104. 5. 0

the Returning Officer at Richmond charged £12, his colleague at Manchester £1,457, and his colleague in Middlesex £2,373, while in Scotland most of the charges were borne by the rates. Many English reformers were anxious to see the charge transferred to the rates in England, but when the government itself proposed the change in 1871, Sir William Harcourt and other Liberals defeated it (by a majority of 96), because they held that members of parliament should be men of independent means.[1] A series of Private Members' Bills to the same effect were also regularly defeated during the next twenty years.

The cost of fighting a constituency varied with the length of the campaign and with its character. The 1868 election cost most candidates considerably more than that of 1874 because the election campaign lasted for three months, whereas that of 1874 lasted only three weeks. County constituencies, because of their size and the need to employ more paid agents and cabs, cost much more than boroughs, and boroughs differed markedly among themselves. Thus Manchester, which was fought by paid canvassers, cost the Liberals £9,538 in 1880, while Birmingham, where volunteer canvassers were used, cost only £4,468. Similarly, in Chatham in 1880 John Gorst spent £1,300, while Admiral Glyn, his Liberal opponent, spent £3,000. The average cost of counties and boroughs in England, Scotland and Wales (the Irish members rarely bothered to make a return, although it was required by law) is given in Table XIV.

[1] *3 Hansard* CCVIII, 607-20.

Table XIV. Average Election Expenses per Candidate
(excluding Returning Officers' Charges)[1]

	1868	1874	1880
Counties .	. £3,011. 13. 9	£2,893. 7. 4	£3,128. 1. 0
Boroughs.	. £988. 12. 9	£741. 18. 11	£1,212. 9. 4

These figures may be set in perspective by a comparison with the limits of expenditure fixed by the 1883 Corrupt Practices Act. Broadly speaking it halved the amount spent in 1868 and 1880: in the boroughs £350 might be spent if there were fewer than 2,000 electors, and £380 plus an additional £30 for every additional 1,000 electors if there were more than 2,000 electors; in the counties £650 might be spent if there were fewer than 2,000 electors, and £710 plus an additional £60 for every additional 1,000 electors if there were more than 2,000 electors.[2] This meant that in a smallish borough constituency like Durham, with 2,350 electors in 1880, the expenditure was now restricted to £410 on each side, whereas the two Liberal candidates in 1880 had spent £1,609 between them, and the single Conservative £1,038. For Preston, a large borough with 12,100 electors in 1880, the limit was fixed at £710, whereas at a by-election in 1881 the two candidates had spent £2,225 and £1,396 respectively. The limits for the counties were higher than those for the boroughs, but they were by no means generous. The limit for East Cumberland, with 7,798 electors in 1880, was fixed at £1,070, although the single Conservative candidate had spent £5,846 at the general election of 1880 and the two Liberals £2,477:[3] that for South-East Lancashire, with 26,037 electors in 1880, was fixed at £2,210, although the two Conservatives had spent £13,141 at the general election and the two Liberals £12,640.

The variations in cost between county and county depended not so much on the size of the constituency as on the length of the candidates' purses. Thus an impecunious candidate with

---

[1] The 1874 figures included the Returning Officers' expenses, but as certain items were excluded from the returns in that year, the omissions probably counter the additions. These figures are taken from the official returns.

[2] There were special provisions with regard to Ireland. The limit for Irish boroughs with less than 500 electors was fixed at £200; for those with from 500 to 1,000 electors, £250; and for those with from 1,000 to 1,500 electors, £275. Expenditure in Irish counties with less than 2,000 electors was restricted to £500 and in those with more than 2,000 electors to £540 plus £40 for each additional 1,000.

[3] At a by-election in 1881, however, the single Liberal candidate spent £3,907.

strong public backing might be able to do without paid assistance and hired carriages, while a rich man might rely entirely on
paid assistance to carry him through. The contrast was most
remarkable in the case of James Howard and Thomas Duckham,
the two Farmers' Alliance Candidates in 1880. In Bedfordshire
Howard spent £620, including £195 on agents and canvassers, £46
on the hire of carriages, and £335 on printing and advertising. His
Whig colleague, the Marquess of Tavistock, spent £4,502, including £2,245 on agents, clerks, messengers and canvassers, £1,025 on
the hire of carriages, and £380 on advertising; and his Tory
opponent, Colonel William Stuart, £3,102, including £1,706 on
agents and the like, £643 on carriages, and £330 on advertising.
In Herefordshire, Duckham spent only £296, of which £44 was
spent on agents, £3 on carriages, and £128 on advertising. The
Whig candidate, Michael Biddulph, spent £2,587, including
£1,907 on agents and the like, £440 on carriages, and £387 on
advertising. The two Conservatives had a common expense account and spent £2,862 each, including £1,706 on agents, etc.,
£643 on carriages, and £236 on advertising. According to the
official returns the average figures for the counties of England,
Scotland and Wales were:

Agents, Clerks, etc. .	.	.	.	£1,350. 19. 9
Conveyances .	.	.	.	£739. 8. 11
Printing and advertising .		.	.	£625. 13. 8

In the boroughs variations in expenditure corresponded more
closely with the size of the constituency (see Table XV), although
there were, of course, differences between candidates in the same
constituency and between boroughs with different standards of
electoral morality. The principal variations not due to size, apart
from those already mentioned, were between pure and corrupt
boroughs and between those in which the law relating to the use
of cabs was respected and those in which it was not. The 1867
Reform Act prohibited the use of hired carriages or cabs in all
boroughs except the five which were classed with the counties
for election purposes, but as a breach of the law did not necessarily
affect the validity of an election, many agents ignored it.[1] By
1879 evasion had become so widespread that the law was amended
to allow the use of hired carriages in boroughs in the coming

[1] *Law Times*, 3 October 1868.

general election. Even then, not all candidates profited by their opportunity, and out of an average expenditure of £1,212. 9. 4 only £148. 6. 9 was spent on cabs, as against £495. 6. 10 on agents, etc., and £333. 8. 3 on printing and advertising.

Table XV. Average Election Expenses per Candidate, English, Welsh and Scottish Boroughs (official returns)

Population	1868			1880		
	£	s.	d.	£	s.	d.
Under 7,000 . . .	343	13	0	536	2	10
7,000-10,000 . . .	589	7	2	717	2	3
10,000-20,000[1] . . .	572	10	9	802	12	0
20,000-30,000 . . .	766	0	1	1,095	9	2
30,000-50,000 . . .	1,024	17	5	1,294	7	3
50,000-100,000 . . .	1,241	12	7	1,406	8	8
100,000-200,000 . . .	1,607	14	4	1,743	10	8
Over 200,000 . . .	1,886	5	6	2,426	6	11

The cost of electioneering for the successful or rich candidate was swelled in a variety of other ways. The cost of keeping up the register was essentially a local responsibility in all the big towns in the north, but elsewhere it fell upon the candidate. The cost of a divisional registration association in North Devon was estimated by Sir Stafford Northcote in 1867 to be more than £300 p.a., and of an association embracing the whole county to be twice as much, of which about £300 might be raised locally.[2] On the other hand the cost of the association founded by Sir George Elliot in 1868 in North Durham was £700 p.a., all of which he paid himself while he was member.[3] Most county members seem to have paid about £150 p.a., while a few paid about £300 p.a. In the boroughs everything depended on local circumstances. In some places a few magnates paid all the registration expenses or employed their own solicitors as registration agents. In others all the local solicitors were paid a retaining fee of ten guineas by one side or the other and the register was neglected

---

[1] This group of constituencies was one of the most corrupt and the one from which most fictitious returns were received (e.g. the Rochester Conservatives returned their expenses in 1874 as £600 and actually paid £2,000: *The Times*, 15 September 1879); hence the low figure in 1868.

[2] Northcote to S. Kekewich, 28 July 1867. Iddesleigh Papers, 1104/4.

[3] See pp. 260-1 below.

between elections. Shortly before an election an expert would be specially brought down from London at a cost of perhaps £75-£100 to attend the revision court. More usually a firm of solicitors attended to the register at a cost of about £100 p.a. The actual cost depended on registration methods. J. G. Dodson, President of the Local Government Board in Gladstone's 1880 cabinet, paid £200 p.a. towards the cost of registration at Chester until 1879, when the method of printing the registers was changed and the whole process much simplified, with the result that the cost of the annual registration was reduced to £70. On the other hand, his Conservative colleague, Henry Cecil Raikes, always paid a fixed sum of £100 p.a.[1]

In addition to these routine expenses a member or prospective candidate was expected to give handsome subscriptions to all the charities and institutions in his constituency. A few candidates held out against the system, either by refusing all requests for money or by allocating a fixed annual sum to charity which they entrusted to the mayor or some other local dignitary, but the great majority recognised that their constituents had a conventional claim on their purses. The amount of money which a member spent depended more on the length of his purse than on the needs of his constituents. At one extreme there was W. H. Smith, a very wealthy man, whose Westminster constituents lived on his doorstep and expected him to give them dinners as well as donations, and robbed him unmercifully at elections. There were also the Liberal members for Boston, whose principal supporters habitually 'borrowed' £100 from them when they were in need, and occasionally as much as £700 and £1,300.[2] At the other extreme were the sturdy Scottish Calvinists of the more remote constituencies who regarded even canvassing with the strongest disapproval.[3] In between lay the overwhelming majority of constituencies who expected their members to give as much as they could. Henry Brassey, who gave £489 in 1877, £551 in 1878, £573 in 1879 and £315 in the first three months of 1880 to the various institutions of Sandwich (population 15,000), was

---

[1] [C. 2824-I] pp. 708; 742. H.C. (1881). XL, 740; 774.

[2] [C. 2784-I] pp. 609-10. H.C. (1881). XXXVIII, 633-4. The extent to which even nonconformist ministers would go in begging is demonstrated by a letter from a Surrey minister quoted in *3 Hansard* CCLXXX, 581-2.

[3] Farquharson, *In and Out of Parliament*, p. 190. Even in England there were, of course, members who refused on principle to 'spoil' their constituents, but they were few.

thought to be somewhat lavish.[1] At Chester (population 38,000)
Henry Cecil Raikes, by no means a wealthy man, gave £30 p.a.
towards the race-plate, about £30 p.a. in small subscriptions,
and between £20 and £100 p.a. towards the cost of the annual
Conservative outing to such places as Belle Vue Gardens, Rhyl
and Knowsley. His mother also gave a further sum, say £50
p.a.[2] By way of comparison, it is interesting to note that in 1891
Aretas Akers-Douglas, M.P. for the St Augustine's Division of
Kent, was paying £200 p.a. for registration expenses and £350
p.a. in subscriptions, and that he estimated the annual cost of
the Ashford Division at about £400 p.a., including registration
expenses.[3]

In addition to these more or less recurrent subscriptions there
were non-recurrent items, such as the building of a new club or
the endowment of a local museum. A member who had represented a borough for a long time not infrequently presented such
a building to the local party association or to the town as a whole,
to commemorate his service to the town. Only the shrewd minority
built an institute for their own workpeople, or provided a club
which they rented rather than presented to the local party
association.[4]

The standard of subscription-giving was kept up by the richer
members, who gave parks and libraries to their constituencies, and
treated their constituents as if they were tenants of their own
estates. When there was a wedding in the member's family or
one of his sons came of age, banquets were held for the well-
to-do and bedding and coals were distributed to the poor. When
his wife or a distinguished relative died, he endowed a memorial

---

[1] [C. 2796] p. xv. H.C. (1881). XLV, 15.

[2] Mothers were a useful asset in other constituencies. W. J. Ingram, M.P. for Boston,
had a mother who gave his constituents coals to the tune of £100 p.a., and his Conservative opponent Fydell Rowley had one who gave a 'general entertainment' to
the town. [C.2784] p. ix. H.C. (1881). XXXVIII, 9.

[3] Akers-Douglas wrote to S. K. McDonnell, Salisbury's secretary, on 28 November
1891 (Salisbury Papers): 'I think Pomfret [M.P. for the Ashford Division] may have
overestimated the expenses of the Ashford Divn. I should say the Contest would cost
£1500 & subscriptions including Registration at about £400 but cannot see how it
can be cut down lower. My own Election in the adjoining divn. cost in 1885 £1500
& I have to pay yearly £200 for Registration & my subscriptions come to about
£350 & I do not see how it can be done for less. You must recollect that in Kent the
constituencies are large averaging about 14,000 electors . . .'

[4] W. J. Ingram built a club-room for the Boston Liberals at a cost of £2,000 but
constructed it in such a way that it was an extension of a public-house he owned, the
White Hart, and charged the club £40 p.a. for using it. [C. 2784-I] p. 604. H.C.
(1881). XXXVIII, 628.

park, garden, library or chapel. When trade was bad, his alms were distributed to the poor on a large scale. To a man accustomed to be generous to the tenants on his estate there need be no corrupt intention behind such gifts, only a somewhat old-fashioned paternalism. A rather extreme example of this type of man was Captain J. A. Morrison, who won East Nottingham as a Conservative in 1910.[1] He came of a very wealthy family, and had been presented with considerable estates in Berkshire by his uncle, Walter Morrison, Radical M.P. for Plymouth, 1861-74. In the parliament of 1900 he had sat for the Wilton division, but he lost his seat in 1906, and turned his attentions to East Nottingham a little more than a year before the 1910 election. As soon as he was established as candidate he began to distribute his money as lavishly in Nottingham, where there was much unemployment, as he was already doing in Berkshire. In one year he spent £700 on the poor and another £600 in organising a system for administering his charity so that it went only to the deserving. About all this he was quite open. Of his estate he said:

> I think I can quite honestly say I have never refused help to anyone who I believed to be deserving, and I always adopt the same principle there. I send down a letter through my secretary, or if I do not do it myself, to my agent, and he then makes inquiries locally as to whether the people are deserving or not, and if they are reported on as such I have always helped them.[2]

In Nottingham he behaved in exactly the same way.

> I gave explicit instructions, as I always have done, even before I ever came to Nottingham, that politics was to have nothing to do with charity; and we also went so far as to lay down the general rule that if any political allusion was made in any letter asking for charity, that under no circumstances was any to be sent to those people till they thoroughly understood that it was sent for the merits of their case and not for politics.[3]

His attitude to bazaars was perhaps the only unusual thing about him.

> I used to come down and address meetings and open a certain amount of bazaars, and do the customary things which every candidate for parliamentary honours always does . . . At nearly every

---

[1] The date is immaterial. The type was common between 1832 and 1914.
[2] H.C. 170, p. 310 (1911). LXI, 776.
[3] *Ibid.*, p. 306.

bazaar, as far as my memory serves me, I was in the habit of making purchases instead of sending a cheque. Most of those purchases were in the nature of something useful either for old women or for children and a certain number of old men. Those articles I invariably gave back to either the minister or the clergyman, or some responsible person, and asked them to see that they were given away to deserving cases in the district in which they lived. And I think on nearly every occasion (I may have omitted to do it) I said, 'I hope you will see they come from you, and that my name does not appear.'[1]

Curiously enough, when Captain Morrison's opponents petitioned against his return, the case was decided in terms of a judgement given thirty years before in a similar case brought against Sir Edward Bates, old Walter Morrison's colleague at Plymouth. Bates, like Morrison, had treated his constituents lavishly in time of depression, giving them coal and bedding and much else, and his opponents protested that this was nothing more than corrupt treating. However, Mr Justice Lush, in a judgement which was quoted *in extenso* by the judges in the East Nottingham case, rejected the notion on the grounds that such gifts were habitually expected of members.

One argument was used which surprised us: it was, that the Respondent had no property in Plymouth and no other connection with the borough than that of being its representative in Parliament, as if it were a novelty, and *primâ facie* a crime, for a Member to bestow gifts upon the borough which he represents. Is not this what every Member is expected to do, and what a great many Members constantly do? There are modes of benefiting the constituency which may be preferable to distributing clothing, bedding, fuel, and such like comforts, because they are not capable of being misused or misrepresented, but every man is at liberty to bestow his benefactions in the form which he prefers. One builds a library, or endows a hospital or a church, another provides a park or place of recreation, while a third prefers to give to the poor.[2]

It is scarcely necessary to add that Morrison kept his seat for East Nottingham.

The figures for subscriptions may be related to those for election expenses to give a very rough picture of the 'average' expenses of members of parliament, thus:

[1] *Ibid.*, pp. 305-6.   [2] H.C. 337—Sess. 2, p. 65 (1880). LVII, 133.

Counties

Returning Officer's Charges. . . .	£200
Cost of Election	£3,000
Five years' Registration[1] Expenses at £150 p.a.	£750
Five years' Subscriptions at £350 p.a. . .	£1,750
	£5,700

Equivalent to an annual expenditure of £1,140

Boroughs

Returning Officer's Charges. . . .	£105
Cost of Election	£1,210
Five years' Registration Expenses at £100 p.a.	£500
Five years' Subscriptions at £150 p.a. . .	£750
Total	£2,565

Equivalent to an annual expenditure of £513[2]

There still remains the cost of a possible petition. In 1868 no fewer than 111 members were petitioned against,[3] and a total of 51 petitions were actually brought to trial during the 1868 parliament.[4] A petition was nothing short of a financial nightmare for all concerned with it, apart from the solicitors who got up the evidence[5] and counsel who appeared before the judges. When the trial of election petitions was transferred to special election courts in 1868 it was agreed that these should be conducted on ordinary common-law lines and that in all but exceptional cases the costs should 'follow the event', subject to taxation. This meant that although the winning side might claim its costs from its opponents the costs were to be assessed according to a fixed scale

[1] The 1868 parliament lasted 5 years 3 months; the 1874 parliament 6 years 2 months; and the 1880 parliament 5 years 6 months.

[2] Clearly this figure would be much higher for the larger boroughs; perhaps twice as high.

[3] 3 *Hansard* CCVII, 562.

[4] 30 members of the 1868 parliament were unseated on petition, 28 members of the 1874 parliament and 24 members of the 1880 parliament.

[5] This was a highly specialised business in which one or two solicitors were pre-eminent. The best account of the business of petitioning is in the minutes of evidence taken by the Select Committee on Corrupt Practices Prevention and Election Petitions Acts, H.C. 225 (1875). VIII, 437, from which the details which follow are taken.

and not according to the actual expenditure incurred. The consequence was that the most expensive items in either the petitioner's or the respondent's bill of costs were automatically scaled down by the taxing master, with the result that both sides knew in advance that they would lose at least £1,000. Even in 1868, when expenses were lower than they afterwards became, the average taxed costs of ordinary cases in England was £1,061,[1] with the result that the unsuccessful party was in most cases faced with a bill for at least £3,000 (£2,000 for his own expenses, £1,000 for his opponent's), while by 1880 even successful petitioners had become used to the notion of paying out several thousand pounds.[2]

The most expensive items in a petitioner's bill were those for the feeing of counsel. Sir Henry Hawkins, the leading advocate in the election courts, demanded 500 guineas on the brief and a retainer of 100 guineas a day, sometimes for as many as twelve days. Barristers in the second rank agreed among themselves to accept no less than 200 guineas on the brief and 50 guineas a day.[3] What this meant in terms of a big case can be seen from four examples. In the Taunton case in 1869 the successful respondent spent £4,519, of which £2,385 was for counsel; in the first Stroud case in 1874 the successful petitioner spent £2,717, of which £1,117 went to counsel, and the respondent spent £2,397, of which £1,329 went to counsel; in the second Stroud case the successful petitioner's bill was £3,140, of which £1,205 went to counsel; and in the third Stroud case the successful petitioner's bill was £5,155, of which £1,820 went to counsel, and the respondent's bill was £6,624, of which counsel received £2,621. At Taunton only £775 out of £2,385 for counsel was allowed by the taxing master, in the first Stroud case only £355 out of £1,117, in the second Stroud case only £404 out of £1,205, and in the third Stroud case only £971 out of £1,820. Indeed, in all these cases all the costs were scaled down drastically. At Taunton £4,519 was reduced to £2,391, at Stroud in the first case £2,717 was reduced to £1,290, at Stroud in the second case £3,140 was reduced to £1,467, and at Stroud in the third case £5,155 was reduced to just over £3,000. In other words, the *successful* petitioner or

[1] H.C. 395 (1868–9). L, 197.
[2] 3 *Hansard* CCLXVIII, 1430.
[3] H.C. 225, p. 63 (1875). VIII, 519. The leading barrister in the second rank was Serjeant Ballantine, a master of cross-examination.

respondent in these cases was himself required to pay £2,128, £1,427, £1,673 and £2,155 respectively, and the unsuccessful petitioner or respondent had to pay about £9,822, £3,687, £6,889 and £9,624 respectively.

These figures and those for election expenditure generally may be put in perspective by reference to the case of the most lavish candidate of his day, Sir George Elliot, Conservative member for North Durham and afterwards for the Monmouth district. Sir George, the son of a pitman still alive in 1872, had made his way in life by his own exertions after starting as a boy working at the pit face. By 1868, when he first contested North Durham, he was one of the leading colliery proprietors and mining engineers in the country, with collieries in Durham and South Wales and an extensive business as a wire-rope and cable manufacturer in partnership with Sir Richard Glass, and in 1874 he was made a baronet. Between 1868 and 1885 his election expenditure was roughly as follows:[1]

Election expenses in North Durham:

1868	£22,000
1874 (1)	£11,000
1874 (2)	£9,000
1880	£13,000
1881	£9,000
Total	£64,000

Petitions in North Durham (three):

About	£15,000
Contributions to funds of Conservative Association at £700 p.a.	£11,900
Total expenses, 1868-85	£90,900

Although Sir George Elliot had spent £90,900 or about £5,350 a year during these seventeen years, this was not his only expenditure. In 1874 and 1880 he returned his son for Northallerton, where he kept a factory going at a loss to win him votes (it had

---

[1] His expenditure is recorded at length in a memorandum drawn up for Lord Salisbury in 1892, now in the Salisbury Papers, which is confirmed in its main outlines by the official returns. Elliot's colleague paid £2,000 towards their joint expenses in February 1874, and the party fund provided an additional £3,000 in 1881.

cost him £120,000 to buy it), and in 1874 he paid the expenses, returned at £326, of the Conservative candidate for Whitby. After 1886 both father and son were returned for new constituencies, and by 1892 Sir George estimated that his twenty-four years as a politician had cost him £124,000 in election and organisation expenses for the pair of them, quite apart from donations to charities.

Chapter Thirteen

CORRUPTION

I

THE gradual elimination of electoral corruption is one of the characteristic features of late nineteenth-century electioneering, but the process was a slow one, and was by no means completed by the end of the century. In the first decade of the twentieth century party officials still estimated that a score or two dozen constituencies, mostly in the south of England, were corrupt,[1] and there can be few active politicians today who have not heard stories of isolated cases of corruption in the 1920s, quite apart from the flagrant case of overspending which cost Mr Frank Gray his seat for Oxford in 1923.[2] The very nature of the subject, however, makes it an elusive one, and it is never possible to arrive at a precise estimate of the extent of electoral corruption at any period. Even the best index, the number of cases before the election committees or courts, is of limited value, because some of the worst cases of corruption were deliberately kept from them for fear that the constituency might be disfranchised. At Gloucester in 1874, for instance, the agents and leading men on both sides met and agreed not to sponsor a petition,[3] while at Canterbury in 1880 the Conservatives went a stage further, and tried to buy off a petition after they had won both seats, by offering to give up one of them, to pay the cost of getting up the Liberal petition, and to pay £1,000 to the Liberal candidate who was to lose all chance of winning a seat. Unfortunately the latter held out for £2,500, so nothing came of the proposals.[4] Similarly, at Shrewsbury there seems to have been a tacit agreement from about 1870 to 1902 that neither side should bring a petition lest it reveal the extent of corruption at municipal elections.[5] None the less, the trials of election petitions

---

[1] Lowell, *Government of England;* I, 238.
[2] cp. F. Gray, *The Confessions of a Candidate*, London 1925.
[3] [C. 2841] p. 5. H.C. (1881). XLI, 9.
[4] [C. 2775] p. x. H.C. (1881). XXXIX, 10.
[5] [Cd. 1541] *passim.* H.C. (1903). LV, 505f.

and the memoirs of the barristers who took part in them (notably those of Ballantine, Hawkins, and Montagu Williams) together make it clear that undoubted cases of corruption occurred in at least sixty-four English boroughs *at parliamentary elections* between 1865 and 1884. The full number was probably nearer one hundred, while many other boroughs were accustomed to corruption in certain wards at municipal elections. Whatever figure one accepts as accurate it is certain that corrupt practices occurred in between one-third and one-half of the English boroughs on sufficient scale for them to be noticed.[1]

Contemporary politicians were almost unanimous in blaming corruption on the dregs of the community, an element which Bright aptly called the 'residuum'. But it is unfair to blame electoral corruption solely on the lower orders. The residuum was much more extensive than Bright imagined or pretended, amounting to a clear majority in about a score of constituencies, and elsewhere fluctuating in size from election to election with the heat of the contest and the amount of money involved. In the smallest towns the quinquennial hiring of committee rooms and distribution of bribes was an essential element in their economy. In most of the larger towns, on the other hand, corruption took the much less exceptionable form of quasi-legal libations provided by generous candidates for those who enrolled themselves members of their 'committees'. In either case there was nothing but public opinion and fear of a petition to deter those who wished to corrupt the electors, because the local police forces, particularly in the smaller boroughs, were entirely inadequate for the task of patrolling during an election. Bribery could take place in the market place without a finger being lifted to prevent

[1] The English boroughs that can be shown to have possessed a corrupt element between 1865 and 1884 were as follows (those marked with an asterisk were extensively corrupt): Abingdon, *Barnstaple, *Beverley, *Bewdley, Bodmin, *Boston, Bradford, *Bridgwater, Bridgnorth, Bristol, Cambridge, *Canterbury, Cheltenham, *Chester, Coventry, Derby, Devonport, Durham, *Evesham, *Gloucester, Gravesend, Guildford, Harwich, Hastings, Helston, *Hereford, Horsham, Ipswich, Kidderminster, Knaresborough, *Lancaster, Lichfield, Ludlow, *Macclesfield, Maidstone, Maldon, Northallerton, *Norwich, Nottingham, Oxford, Penryn, Poole, *Reigate, Rochester, Rye, St Ives, *Sandwich, *Shrewsbury, Southampton, *Stafford, *Stroud, *Taunton, Tewkesbury, *Totnes, Truro, Wakefield, Wallingford, Walsall, Westbury, Westminster, Wigan, Windsor, Worcester, *Great Yarmouth. Of these boroughs (64 in all) twenty had a population of less than 10,000, fifteen a population of between 10,000 and 20,000, twenty a population of between 20,000 and 50,000, and eight a population of over 50,000. Only eight of them (Bradford, Cheltenham, Devonport, Kidderminster, Macclesfield, Stroud, Wakefield, and Walsall) were creations of the 1832 Reform Act and only one (Gravesend) of the 1867 Act.

it, while riots often occurred simply because there was no one to stop them.[1]

Corruption was confined to a mere residuum only in the big towns where the dregs of the population tended to accumulate. The size of this residuum varied considerably. In Bradford, Leeds, Liverpool, and Manchester it was restricted to one or two of the central wards where the poorer classes lived and where corruption usually took place only at municipal elections. The worst ward in Leeds, Kirkgate Ward, was a small central ward with about 600 voters, who were mostly small shopkeepers and lodging-house keepers living near the markets.[2] In Bradford there was a whole district in the centre of the town inhabited very largely by Irishmen who could be won over by beer, and the Liberal candidates in 1868 catered amply for their taste. The independent Liberal, Henry Ripley, spent £7,212 and hired rooms in 158 public-houses, in 115 of which 'refreshments' were supplied to any who enrolled themselves as 'committee men': his opponents, W. E. Forster and Edward Miall, spent £3,397 and hired rooms in 127 public-houses, in 62 of which refreshments were available.[3] In Liverpool as many as twenty per cent of the electors in St Anne's Ward appear to have been paid in the 1865 municipal elections, when the price of votes rose from 5s. to £1 and even to £5.[4] In Manchester the Liberals were constantly on the look-out for Tory corruption in the central wards and brought several petitions in 1872.[5]

The residuum was larger in towns like Nottingham and Norwich, where bad electoral traditions were firmly established. The

[1] Two extreme cases occurred at Newport, Isle of Wight, and King's Lynn, where there were riots in 1868 which the police did nothing to quell. On investigation it was found that Newport possessed only five elderly policemen, and King's Lynn eighteen (*3 Hansard* CCII, 1355-7). It is significant that the most notable riots in 1880 occurred in towns without an adequate police force: Barrow, Bath, Buckingham, Carlow, Chester, Dorchester, Exmouth, Leamington, Monmouth, Neston, Newton Abbott, Northwich, Portadown, Rotherham, Shaftesbury, and Tullamore (Saunders, *The New Parliament, 1880*, pp. 230-5). The most spectacular riots of the period, in North Durham in 1874, also took place in small towns (H.C. 374, pp. 57-61 (1874). LIII, 175-9). Liverpool, which was well policed, was extraordinarily quiet at elections in spite of the large Irish community (*3 Hansard* CCVII, 804).

[2] H.C. 352, p. 67 (1868-9). VIII, 67.

[3] H.C. 28, p. 192 (1868-9). XLVIII, 894, and H.C. 120, pp. 35-44 (1868-9). XLVIII, 35-44.

[4] H.C. 352, p. 69 (1868-9). VIII, 69.

[5] They also employed a band of six detectives in 1884, at a cost of about £17, to watch the Conservatives during the municipal elections, but the detectives found nothing. Minutes of the Executive Committee of the Manchester Liberal Association, 11 November 1884.

Mayor of Nottingham told the Hartington Committee in 1869
that in his opinion about one-third of the electors required money,
and gave details to show that at least 2,320 persons out of the
14,168 electors could easily be proved to be corrupt.[1] The numbers willing to take money at any time apparently varied with
the amount offered, as small shopkeepers would take ten shillings or a pound, but not half-a-crown. In the municipal elections
in Byron Ward votes cost 3s. 6d. at midday in 1867, 2s. 6d. at
midday in 1868, and in both cases rose to 5s. later in the day.
At Norwich at least 5,000 of the electors were ready to sell their
votes unless carefully watched. As one of the agents remarked,
'there are a lot of people who, if they are looked after by a foreman or person of influence, will vote in a particular way, but
who, if they are left to themselves, will vote for 5s. or 10s.'[2]

In a place like Norwich or Nottingham the corrupt section of
the community, although large, was not a majority, and there
was on both sides a readiness to denounce corruption. A man
of the highest integrity like Jeremiah James Colman at Norwich
and Samuel Morley at Nottingham could stand and be returned
without being in any way mixed up in corrupt practices, while
the fact that corruption was gradually stamped out in Nottingham shows that the pure stood by their principles. But there were
other boroughs, besides the very small ones like Cashel and Sligo
and Totnes, where corruption was an integral part of the political life of the community—ranging from Beverley and Bridgwater with just over 10,000 people to Gloucester and Macclesfield with over 30,000.

Beverley and Bridgwater, which were disfranchised in 1869,
were (along with Cashel and Sligo) the first of the extensively
corrupt boroughs to come before Parliament after the 1867
Reform Act. The cases were quite different. Beverley had been
comparatively pure in the early fifties, but in 1857 Sir Henry
Edwards, a former member for Halifax and a manufacturer there,
became one of its members. Thereafter his agents deliberately
bought up the borough in his interest. The town council and

---

[1] H.C. 352, p. 1 (1868-9). VIII, 1.

[2] [C. 14] p. 12. H.C. (1870), XXXI, 48. The best account of Norwich elections is in
the *Report of the Royal Commission Appointed to inquire into the Existence of Corrupt Practices at
the Last Parliamentary Election for the City of Norwich*, [C. 1442] H.C. (1876). XXVII, 1,
from which the details which follow are derived: there are other reports for 1869, 1870,
1872, 1875 and 1886. There is an account of some of the Norwich politicians in Sir
Robert Bignold, *Five Generations of the Bignold Family 1761-1947*, London 1948.

the pasture commissioners became mere nominees who distributed patronage and charities in such a way as to supplement Sir Henry's own expenditure to the best political advantage, and the only factory in the town, an agricultural implement works, was bought up to give him a direct influence over the workmen. Bribe as they might, Sir Henry's Liberal opponents could do nothing, and their only claim to the attention of posterity is that one of their last candidates was Anthony Trollope.[1] By 1868 they had despaired of success, and petitioned, knowing full well that the borough would almost certainly be disfranchised. At Bridgwater 'the man in the moon' was an old friend. Gold had been freely distributed from time immemorial, and the Liberal agents actually possessed books showing the sums paid out in bribery as far back as 1807. The price of votes had fallen in 1832, and occasionally there was a pure election, but the voters on both sides continued to expect to be paid for their vote and both parties were organised accordingly. A Conservative Working Men's Association was even formed specially to distribute largesse, and one of the Liberal candidates and the brother of another (Kinglake of *Eothen* fame) were directly involved in the distribution of money.[2]

The House of Commons chose to regard these cases as quite exceptional, and several members, among them ministers, expressed the view that bribery was dying out. George Dixon of Birmingham, for instance, said that treating was now the real enemy, 'for while bribery appeared to be diminishing in this country, treating seemed to be on the increase'.[3] Subsequent events suggest that this view was based on very inadequate evidence, and that the members mistook for a change of heart a temporary abandonment of the traditional corrupt practices in some constituencies, while the party managers waited to see the effects of the Reform Act and the Election Petitions Act of 1868. In fact, after this brief exploratory pause the old ways were resumed with a new zest, and by 1880 were flourishing on a larger scale than ever before. The only change effected by the Reform Act was that the price of votes fell because the number willing to sell their votes had grown. As for the ballot, in the words of

[1] cp. L. O. Tingay, 'Trollope and the Beverley Election', *Nineteenth-Century Fiction*, vol. 5, No. 1, June 1950.
[2] They were eventually prosecuted: 3 *Hansard* CXCIX, 767-8.
[3] 3 *Hansard* CXCIV, 666.

the commissioners who investigated a by-election at Sandwich in May 1880:

> It did not appear that the mode of taking votes by ballot had the slightest effect in checking bribery. On the contrary, while it enabled many voters to take bribes on both sides, it did not, as far as we could ascertain, render a single person unwilling to bribe for fear of bribery in vain.[1]

Seven towns particularly attracted attention in 1880: Boston, Canterbury, Chester, Gloucester, Macclesfield, Oxford and Sandwich, and each of them was temporarily disfranchised. On the other hand a number of towns which should have been on the list escaped notice, of which the most important were Ipswich, Shrewsbury and Worcester. In all of these towns except Oxford, and perhaps Sandwich, corruption was general, and the political leaders on both sides were deeply involved. At Gloucester and Macclesfield, where Royal Commissions were able to conduct the most thorough investigations, it was discovered that at least 2,185 and 2,872 persons respectively could be shown to have given or received money—although the total number of suspects was much higher. More remarkable still were the numbers of influential local persons so much involved that they were 'scheduled' by the commissioners:[2] at Boston six magistrates (three of whom were also councillors), an alderman and three other councillors, a Unitarian minister, the secretaries of both party associations, the agents of both parties and a Conservative candidate; at Canterbury four magistrates, an alderman and a councillor; at Chester the mayor, four aldermen, eight councillors (one of them a magistrate) and two other magistrates; at Gloucester three magistrates (one of them an alderman), two other aldermen, fifteen councillors, six Poor Law guardians, an overseer and five solicitors; at Macclesfield four magistrates, three aldermen, thirty-one

---

[1] [C. 2796] p. xv. H.C. (1881). XLV, 15. Serjeant Ballantine made exactly the same point in his memoirs: 'I do not believe that the ballot will ever be effectual to prevent the practice, and, moreover, it introduces an additional moral taint. A voter may make a solemn promise, take advantage of the secrecy to break it, and of course tell lies to prevent the discovery of his treachery.' W. Ballantine, *Some Experiences of a Barrister's Life*, new edn, London 1898, p. 240.

[2] Those who were scheduled for bribery (which was so defined by a resolution of the House as early as 1677 as to include treating), were disqualified for seven years from sitting in the House of Commons, from voting, from holding municipal or judicial office, and from being appointed or acting as a justice of the peace. Those guilty but not indemnified by judges or commissioners might also be proceeded against in the courts.

councillors, both Liberal members and the agents of both parties; at Oxford two magistrates (one of them a councillor), four other councillors and the town clerk; and at Sandwich the candidates and agents on both sides and all their leading supporters. In all, no fewer than twenty-eight magistrates were found guilty of corrupt practices at this one general election and all but two had their names removed from the rolls.[1]

The Macclesfield case was the most unexpected.[2] The borough had been first enfranchised in 1832 and had, therefore, no old-established tradition of corruption. But by the 1840s it had become the custom to give men refreshment tickets after they had voted, a six-shilling ticket for a single vote and a twelve-shilling ticket for both votes. The custom was rather fostered than otherwise by the Brocklehurst family, one of whom was Liberal member continuously from 1832 to 1880, but it declined during the fifties. In 1865, however, with the arrival in the borough of David Chadwick, a Manchester accountant and a Liberal, a new element was introduced, in the form of general and undisguised treating. Public-houses were opened on every side, and the Brocklehurst solicitors (who included a son of John Brocklehurst, M.P.) were involved in corrupt practices of various sorts.[3] In 1868 W. C. Brocklehurst and Chadwick coalesced, and both parties introduced considerable changes in their organisation, which remained virtually unchanged from then until 1880. The Liberals set up a standing committee of seventy or eighty members in each ward, with its own officers who attended to the business of the ward except at elections. These committees were supplemented by a central Liberal Association, nominally open to all Liberals but practically restricted to members of the corporation. However, as it had no funds because the Liberal candidates paid for elections, its influence was limited. The Conservatives also set up ward committees or associations with about 100 or 120 members, but unlike the Liberals they established a strong central organisation. Each Conservative ward organisation sent six persons (three working men and three 'gentlemen') to act as its

---

[1] *3 Hansard* CCLXIV, 360-1.

[2] The evidence for the Macclesfield case is contained in [C. 2853] and [C. 2853-I] H.C. (1881). XLIII, *passim*.

[3] The expenditure on the Liberal side (Chadwick and Brocklehurst not running in harness) was: Brocklehurst: published £336. 9. 2, unpublished £820. 10. 6; Chadwick: published £820. 10. 2½, unpublished £716. 18. 10¼.

representatives on an Executive Committee of thirty-six members, which was in turn guided by an inner committee of seven or eight. This central association had its own funds—subscriptions of between half a guinea and five guineas were collected from about 100 of the 700 members whenever they were needed —and was not dependent, like the Liberal association, on the generosity of its parliamentary candidates.

These new organisations revived the old custom of paying or treating voters. Committeemen were paid ten or fifteen shillings a day during the elections, with sixpence or a shilling for refreshments on canvassing nights, and many other voters were employed as 'day men' at five shillings a day. In addition, each party paid the rates of its poorest supporters in 1868 to protect their vote (£320 was spent on 700 voters), and every effort was made to see that the poorer voters were compensated for the loss of wages on polling day. Money bribery was not common until it was introduced at municipal elections in 1874. The Liberals had monopolised the aldermanic benches for some twenty years and in both 1874 and 1877 the Conservatives tried unsuccessfully to win a majority among the councillors sufficient to displace some of the Liberal aldermen when they came up for re-election. By 1877 the Liberals were seriously alarmed, and decided to resort to open bribery. They secured a warehouse in No. 6 Ward and used it as an office for the distribution of bribes, whereupon the Conservatives erected a tent from which a magistrate and councillor also distributed money. After this experience both parties decided to be well prepared for the coming parliamentary election, and the Liberal steering committee seems actually to have appointed 'money captains' in the wards.

The 1880 election took the form of a struggle between the money bags of the two parties. The Liberals employed 870 canvassers, the Conservatives 950 canvassers and 48 personation agents, and these men, who were each paid five shillings or seven-and-six, constituted the regular forces on each side. The irregular forces were legion. In No. 5 Ward, where 560 of the 817 electors were eventually scheduled for bribery, there were 103 Conservative canvassers and 157 Liberal ones. In addition, the Conservatives had 231 'day men', of whom 101 were later bought off by the Liberals and so were not paid, seven were employed and paid by both sides, and sixteen were Liberal canvassers who had infiltrated into the enemy camp. In this ward the Liberals spent £420. Conditions were as bad in No. 6 Ward, where 400 of the 605 voters did not mean to vote unless paid. In the borough as a whole at least 4,000 people were paid in one way or another, and the Royal Commission which investigated the case had no difficulty in discovering 2,872 persons to schedule for bribery. Just how easy it was to obtain money was shown by fifty men in a copper works who intended for the most part to vote Liberal, and who were determined to make as much out of the election as possible. They delegated two of their number to bargain for their votes, whereupon both parties offered ten shillings for each man and fifty shillings for the two delegates. The Conservatives actually paid £36 and the Liberals £38, which enabled the delegates to buy refreshments for all the fifty and to distribute one pound to each man, reserving to themselves a good round sum.

Gloucester had been a corrupt constituency long before Macclesfield, and its behaviour had been more than once investigated, the last occasion being in 1859. But the 1859 commission had little effect, beyond scheduling a number of electors for bribery. The borough (which had been temporarily disfranchised) had its representation restored to it in 1862, and continued to return two members until 1880 when its representation was reduced to one. In 1865 the disqualification of the two members unseated in 1859 expired and they were again returned. The 1865 and 1868 elections were, however, comparatively pure, whether because the two members (W. P. Price and C. J. Monk) were tired of corruption or for other reasons, but in 1873 the borough again fell into evil ways. Price, who was chairman of the Midland Railway,[1] was appointed a Railway Commissioner in that year and vacated his seat. J. J. Powell, one of the members from 1862 to 1865, visited the city to test his popularity, but found that he had been forestalled by the leader of the local Liberals, Thomas Robinson. Robinson had been found guilty of bribery in 1859, and was to be again found guilty of bribery in 1874 and 1880, but this was no disqualification in the eyes of the electors of Gloucester, and he became not only mayor of Gloucester four times but also M.P. for the borough in 1880 and from 1885 to

[1] Price was also the father and grandfather of M.P.s. His son W. E. Price sat for Tewkesbury from 1865 to 1880 when he was unseated for corruption. His grandson M. Philips Price was M.P. for the Whitehaven division from 1929 to 1931 and has since 1935 sat for one of the divisions of Gloucestershire.

1895. In 1873, however, he was unsuccessful as the first election under the ballot returned a Conservative, W. K. Wait. The return was petitioned against, but the petition failed.

In 1874 Robinson stood down and Monk and Powell became the Liberal candidates. The Conservative candidates were Wait and Sir Trevor Lawrence. Price helped the Liberals on this as on subsequent occasions, but the real strength of the Liberal Registration Association was a group of councillors headed by Robinson which formed itself into a committee for the corruption of the electors. Unfortunately for Robinson and his friends, however, the two candidates refused to reimburse them for their expenditure on the ground that their consent to it had not been obtained, although they did agree to pay for certain quasi-legal expenditure. The expenses therefore fell into three categories:

Paid by the candidates:
Published expenses £1,443. 13. 8
Quasi-legal expenses £1,000. 0. 0

Paid by Robinson and other councillors:
Illegal expenditure £1,604. 18. 6

Total expenditure £4,048. 12. 2

The Conservatives, who spent virtually the same amount, also engaged in wholesale bribery and employed at least 900 men during the election. Both parties paid from five shillings to a sovereign for a vote, and their method of disposing of the money was the only thing which distinguished them. The Liberals professed to have scruples about public-houses and gave out their bribes either in the streets or in private houses; the Conservatives made three public-houses their distribution centres, the *New Pilot* (£714), the *Leopard* (£40), and the *Haulier's Arms* (£80), and the party agents in them afterwards presented their accounts, which were settled by Wait, the sitting member.

The result of the election was a draw, as one Liberal (Monk) and one Conservative (Wait) were returned, and as neither side could afford a petition the leaders met and agreed to let the result stand.[1] The Liberals soon afterwards formed a Liberal

[1] Each side signed an agreement undertaking not to present a petition or to aid anyone else in prosecuting a petition if one should be brought: [C. 2841] p. 5. H.C. (1881). XLI, 9.

association on the Birmingham model, headed by Robinson, and the Liberal Hundred now became the dominant influence on the Liberal side. Significantly, its chief interest, apart from municipal elections, became an attempt to force Monk, the Liberal sitting member, to pay the bills for bribery incurred at the last election. Monk did all he could to keep clear of entanglements, but he could not avoid working with the association because it controlled all the electoral machinery on the Liberal side, and before the general election of 1880 he was driven to accept Robinson as second Liberal candidate. The Conservatives again brought in an outsider, St John Ackers, a Gloucestershire country gentleman, to run with Wait.

The 1880 election was a repetition of 1874, but with corruption on a larger scale. On both sides the machinery was more efficient and the money penetrated further, but the inspiration was still that of the town council. On the Liberal side three councillors provided about £1,500, which was distributed by councillors, magistrates and volunteer party workers in various parts of the city. Canvassers 'brought up' the voters to committee rooms where they handed in a card with a sum of money marked on it by those who brought them to the poll, and this they exchanged for coin before voting. Some received five shillings or two pounds, but most received a sovereign. Much the same amount was distributed on the Conservative side by publicans, magistrates and miscellaneous volunteers, such as a Poor Law Guardian and a railway foreman, most of it in public-houses. The two parties between them spent at least £3,600 on bribery, and 1,916 persons subsequently admitted to having been bribed, while at least 840 more had received money but were not identified. In addition to the 2,756 voters out of 4,904 who were bribed, there were at least 198 bribers and numerous paid canvassers and the like. Almost all the members of the corporation were involved in one way or another, and it was discovered that bribery was the rule rather than the exception at municipal elections. While the Royal Commission was sitting the annual municipal elections took place, and the Liberals were given the opportunity of showing their contempt for outside opinion: the Liberal Hundred deliberately re-adopted self-confessed bribers as its candidates, and after the elections the Liberal majority on the council nominated a leading briber to the aldermanic seat vacated by a Conservative briber, while the place on the council thus vacated was filled by another briber. The Commission, as a consequence, reported:

> The evidence of facts before us combined with the strongly expressed opinions of many of the chief partisans of both political parties in the city has satisfied us that it is impossible to expect a pure election at Gloucester with such a constituency as at present exists.[1]

II

These cases, coming at a time when the increasing cost of elections was causing considerable alarm, administered a very considerable and salutary shock to public opinion. They created, almost for the first time, a climate of opinion favourable to drastic legislation against corrupt practices. Sir Henry James himself attributed his Corrupt Practices Act very largely to them:

> When the summer and autumn of 1880 had closed, when the country knew there had been electoral corruption, which seemed to increase as the constituencies grew in size, when it was found that that corruption had been applied to that portion of the constituencies not long existent—he meant those men who had been lately enfranchised, and whose poverty rendered them an easy object to those who wished to corrupt—there was a general feeling that some steps must be taken by the Legislature to prevent the spread of corruption at elections.[2]

This is not to suggest that previous attempts to curb corrupt practices had not been intended to be effective. The Corrupt Practices Act of 1854 had established both adequate definitions of what constituted corrupt practices, and the procedure by which an election might be voided if these practices could be shown to have come within the cognisance of an avowed or tacitly recognised agent of the sitting member.[3] It was a valuable piece of legislation which in essence has remained unaffected by subsequent Acts. But until 1866 the administration of the law was

---

[1] [C. 2841] p. 15. H.C. (1881). XLI, 19. Strangely enough, although both Robinson and Monk who had won the election were more or less involved in corrupt practices, only Robinson lost his seat. Monk kept his until 1885, when Robinson took his place (the borough having been reduced to one member), and in turn replaced Robinson in 1895.

[2] *3 Hansard* CCLXXIX, 1697.

[3] Seymour, *Electoral Reform*, Chs. VIII and XIII.

lax. The committees of the Commons which tried petitions were notoriously partisan and gave the impression that they had no intention of enforcing the law where it would be embarrassing. About 1866, however, there was a change in the attitude of both politicians and lawyers. The election committees of the House of Commons began to take their duties more seriously, and a greater effort was made by the parties to gather adequate evidence and to secure able counsel.[1] Moreover, constituencies proved to be generally corrupt at the time of the 1865 election were not simply temporarily disfranchised as Gloucester had been in 1859, but under the 1867 Act lost their members altogether. The isolated precedents of Sudbury in 1844 and St Albans in 1862 were applied not only to the insignificant boroughs of Totnes and Reigate, but also to Lancaster with a population of nearly 20,000 and Yarmouth with a population of over 40,000, eight times the size of several existing constituencies. Two years later Beverley, Bridgwater, Cashel and Sligo were also disfranchised. Even more important, in 1868 Disraeli's Election Petitions Act transferred the trial of election petitions to special election courts, presided over by a judge of one of the Common Law Courts, sitting without a jury. Disraeli himself insisted that the change was important not so much because it altered the investigating tribunal as because it moved the venue of the trials from Westminster, where evidence was difficult to come by, to the constituencies themselves.[2] But at least as important was the fact that the courts encouraged the public to believe that breaches of the electoral law were a species of crime, and that they would be investigated as carefully as any other form of crime.

The immediate effect of the Ballot Act of 1872 was to suppress undue influence, not to put down bribery, but it did affect bribery and other forms of electoral corruption in two important ways. The main provision of the Act, the introduction of secret elections, gave a great impetus to reform because it enabled reformers for the first time to argue that bribery did not pay. It could now be pointed out that the briber had no proof that his money was

---

[1] Ballantine, *Experiences*, p. 239; *Law Times*, 7 March 1868.

[2] In speaking of the Act in 1871 Disraeli said '. . . the character of the investigating tribunal in that Act is but of secondary importance. What was so efficient in that Act, and what dealt such a deadly blow against bribery, and what, if persisted in, will terminate bribery altogether, was the provision which insured a local investigation of the matter.' *3 Hansard* CCVII, 848.

not being wasted, although the force of this argument was somewhat weakened by the fact that most of those who accepted
bribes did in fact vote as they had promised. The subsidiary provision of the Act which extended the law relating to parliamentary
elections to municipal elections, and the Corrupt Practices
(Municipal Elections) Act of the same year which provided a
special tribunal to try municipal election petitions, were of
greater immediate significance because they struck at the roots
of electoral corruption. Hitherto it had been impossible to
challenge the seat of a councillor except by obsolete *Quo Warranto*
proceedings, and the only penalty for bribery at municipal
elections had been the Common Law penalty of a forty-shilling
fine. In practice electoral corruption had gone unchecked at
municipal elections as the forty-shilling fine was difficult to obtain,
and the cost of preparing evidence was prohibitive. The Leeds
Liberals spent over £200 in 1865 in getting up a case against a
councillor, but although they succeeded in winning their case the
councillor was quite unconcerned and was in due course re-
elected.[1] The only practical limit on electoral corruption was the
fact that most councillors were comparatively poor men. The 1872
Act did not check corruption in itself, but it enabled the pure
section of a borough such as Leeds, where only one or two wards
were corrupt, to take action against the corrupt minority. The
number of petitions brought under the Act was never very great,
but there was a steady trickle in the first year after 1872 which
enabled the public to see that the Act was not wholly ineffective,
although where there was a tradition of corruption (as at Shrewsbury) it continued into the twentieth century.[2]

The weakness of all the reforms made before 1883 was their
dependence on public opinion to make them effective. No power
was given to officials to bring petitions in the public interest, and
individual electors were deterred from petitioning by its expense
and by its unpopularity. And an appreciable proportion of the
party managers, aristocracy and middle classes who could
have afforded the cost thought that corruption was inevitable,

[1] H.C. 352, p. 61 (1868-9). VIII, 61. Bernal Osborne told the House of Commons
in 1871 that he had known of £1,500 being spent at a municipal election: *3 Hansard*
CCVII, 752.
[2] The number of petitions tried was 4 in 1873, 6 in 1874, 10 in 1875, 2 in 1876,
4 in 1877, and 3 in 1878: H.O. 53. 1-30 (Public Record Office).

and that a law like the Corrupt Practices Prevention Act of 1854 which was in advance of public opinion should not be enforced. Many speakers and writers compared the public attitude with that of earlier generations towards duelling. Where it differed from duelling was in the fact that direct bribery—quite apart from colourable employment—was confined to no one class; squires, clergy, magistrates, lawyers, tradesmen, even judges,[1] were all engaged in it. Serjeant Ballantine declared in his *Experiences*, published in 1882, that he had never found any force of public opinion against bribery. 'I should be glad to know', he wrote, 'whether the gentry in the neighbourhood have ever withdrawn their custom from a tradesman found guilty of accepting bribes, or whether any gentleman has been excluded from society because he has given them.'[2] He went on to relate some of the familiar sights in the election courts: the leading solicitor complacently disclosing a skilfully organised system of bribery, one of the bribed giving his evidence in a jocular way to the evident enjoyment and admiration of a circle of friends. He might have recounted the great triumph of Sir Henry Edwards at York Assizes in 1870, when the case against him was withdrawn: he was complimented by the judge and left the court accompanied by a vast concourse of admiring friends. Events in Beverley forgotten, he returned to Halifax to play his usual part as chairman of the bench of magistrates and Provincial Grand Master of Freemasons.[3] He might, too, have mentioned the curious events at Macclesfield where there was great local discontent that 'two highly respected and intelligent solicitors' should be imprisoned merely for bribery in 1881 and that six magistrates should have been removed from the bench.[4] Indignation meetings were held and pamphlets were published proving the iniquity of the punishments, although not with much effect on the Lord Chancellor or Home Secretary.

---

[1] W. H. Cooke, Q.C., county court judge for Norfolk, who had been standing counsel to the Carlton Club until six months before the 1868 election was scheduled by the Beverley commissioners in 1869 (*3 Hansard* CXCIX, 1364-5), and so was the registrar of Boston county court in 1880. Mr Baron Huddleston narrowly escaped the same fate at Norwich in 1876.

[2] Ballantine, *Experiences*, pp. 239-40.

[3] *Law Times*, 13 August 1870.

[4] J. White, *Borough of Macclesfield: Corrupt Practices (Disfranchisement) Bill, 1882: Speech of Mr. Alderman White, J.P.*, Macclesfield 1882, p. 5. As was to be expected an Association was formed by a number of M.P.s and others to work for the release of those imprisoned for bribery: cp. their advertisement in *The Times*, 21 December 1881.

Nor were the party officials altogether guiltless in the matter. The Liberal Whips, egged on by Gladstone, were much concerned about the moral liability which the possession of a party fund for assisting candidates imposed upon them.[1] They were therefore always on the watch for signs of corruption and anxious to put it down. Disraeli, too, was a strong opponent of corruption.[2] But the party agents on both sides were much less scrupulous, and there were a number of Conservative Whips who were by no means averse to corrupt practices. In 1853 William Beresford, an ex-Whip and Secretary at War, was censured by the House of Commons for corrupt electioneering, while his successor as Whip, Forbes Mackenzie, was unseated for corruption. In 1859 Rose, the party agent, retired under a cloud after a most damaging series of revelations with regard to his part in corruptly compromising election petitions.[3] Spofforth, his successor, came under grave suspicion for his advice in the selection of a candidate of 'the commercial spirit they required' for a contest at Totnes, and again for his advice to the local agents at Beverley in 1868-9 which led them to cover up their tracks by destroying papers and bustling the chief briber out of the country.[4] Gorst, Spofforth's successor, did his best to stamp out bribery, but in 1880 the corrupt elements of the party again got rather out of hand. The party fund was very laxly administered during the general election, and Lord Henry Thynne, one of the Whips, apparently instigated the secretary of the Junior Carlton Club to corrupt practices at a by-election at Oxford immediately afterwards, with the result that the latter was forced to 'disappear' during the sittings of the investigating commission.[5] When Gorst returned to the Central Office later in the year he had again to make war on corruption, and was most reluctant to employ J. C. Shaw, the Sheffield agent, and a protégé of the Chief Whip, Rowland Winn. He told W. H. Smith that he objected to Shaw for a variety of reasons, but for this above all.

---

[1] Henry Brand, an ex-Whip who had become Speaker, noted in his Journal in 1875 when he was forced to announce that his son had been unseated at Stroud: 'Few men have laboured more earnestly than I and with practical effect for a long and active career, to attain greater purity at Elections. Yet it has come to this!' The Journal is among the Hampden Papers.

[2] Malmesbury, *Memoirs of an Ex-Minister*, p. 304.

[3] *3 Hansard*, CLV, 1276-96.

[4] [3776] p. xii. H.C. (1867). XXIX, xii and [C. 15] p. ix. H.C. (1870). XXIX, 9

[5] [C. 2856] pp. 9f. H.C. (1881). XLIV, 9f.

Chiefly he is prone to corrupt practices, which accounts for his being in such request among corrupt constituencies. What Winn's phrases about not appreciating the money spent by Birmingham come to is that I won't fight corruption by corruption. To this I plead guilty: it is our policy to force the government to pass an Act that will stop as much corruption as possible, and if Harry Thynne & his friends will have corrupt practices on our side they must have them locally not fostered & organized from headquarters by Mr. Shaw or anybody else. Armit & the sugar people are an example of how we become the prey of dupes when we seek to influence elections by questionable means.[1]

Even in the House of Commons, proved bribers were subject to no disability or social disadvantage. One of the most notorious corruptors of constituencies, although not of his own, since he confined his supplies of gold to the service of his friends, was Alexander Brogden, a railway contractor and ironmaster.[2] After he had frankly admitted supplying gold at Yarmouth and Bridgwater his position did lead to some comment in the House of Commons, and a Select Committee was set up to consider his and similar cases. But it recommended that no action be taken, as might have been expected since John Bright, long after the Yarmouth episode, had specially recommended Brogden to the electors of Wednesbury. The House of Commons was occasionally attacked by fits of conscience, and there was then talk of the danger of the House being swamped with new-made men with more money than scruples. But although effective speeches were sometimes made on the subject and one lavish spender, Christopher Weguelin, was denounced by name in the House in 1868,[3] members were far more concerned with the uncertainties of the electoral

[1] J. E. Gorst to W. H. Smith, 8 September 1880: Hambleden Papers. For R. H. Armit see Benjamin H. Brown, *The Tariff Reform Movement in Great Britain 1881-1895*, New York 1943, pp. 16f.

[2] Brogden was one of a singular trio of corrupt candidates, the other two being Henry William Schneider and Philip Vanderbyl. Vanderbyl's gold (supplied by Brogden) largely contributed to the disfranchisement first of Yarmouth in 1867 and then of Bridgwater in 1869, while Schneider was almost entirely responsible for the disfranchisement of Lancaster in 1867. Brogden was M.P. for Wednesbury 1868-85, and Vanderbyl for Bridgwater 1866-9 and for Portsmouth 1885-6. All three were keen Liberals. There is an account of Schneider in J. D. Marshall, 'Corrupt Practices at the Lancaster Election of 1865', *Transactions of the Lancashire and Cheshire Antiquarian Society*, LXIII, 117-30 (1952-3).

[3] Weguelin had spent £5,000 in winning 127 votes at Youghal. For a typical speech against new-made men who corrupted constituencies see P. H. Bagenal, *Life of Ralph Bernal Osborne, M.P.*, privately printed, London 1884, p. 323. That such protests were not uncalled for was demonstrated in 1868 when W. H. Smith spent £8,910 at Westminster and George Elliot £15,302 in North Durham.

law which unseated upright men like Samuel Morley and left corrupt constituencies practically undisturbed, than with particular scandals.

The election courts created in 1868 were generally admitted to be an improvement on the old election committees because they removed the trials from the political arena, but they were by no means perfect.[1] The very fact that the judges, unlike the old committees, gave reasons for their decisions meant that they were driven to formulate what was virtually new law to cover the many cases which did not come clearly under the 1854 Act or under one of the few previous decisions of the Court of Common Pleas. Election law in general turns on the need to establish that a person guilty of a corrupt practice was an agent of the successful candidate, and there had been very few cases in the past which bore directly on the question. The judges therefore became entangled in a network of analogies derived from the master-servant and sheriff-undersheriff relationship which were often far from illuminating. In particular they had to grapple with the position of political associations *vis-à-vis* the candidates. Here there was room for real differences of legal opinion and for judgements which seemed to non-legal minds flatly contradictory.[2] Moreover, some of the judges lacked experience of elections and were too ready to give credit to unreliable witnesses. Serjeant Ballantine thought that the application of the rules of procedure prevailing in the ordinary courts, to election cases, made the new courts far less satisfactory judges of fact than the old committees and no more impartial,[3] while Spofforth, the Conservative petition manager, thought the new tribunals quite as easy to hoodwink as the old.[4]

The first election judges in England, Mr Baron Martin, Mr Justice Blackburn and Mr Justice Willes, were very conscious of the danger they ran of giving partisan judgements, and although they did not satisfy everybody, they convinced most of those

[1] Much greater objection could be, and was, taken to the composition of the Royal Commissions which were set up under the Act 15 and 16 Vic. c. 57 of 1852 to investigate cases of general corruption reported by the election committees or judges. However, the Beverley and Bridgwater commissioners were so universally condemned by the legal profession and by M.P.s in 1869 (*Law Times*, 23 and 30 October 1869 and 3 *Hansard* CC, 1797-8) that later commissions were more carefully chosen and those appointed in 1880 included many men later notable, among them A. V. Dicey.

[2] For an example of 'contradictory' judgements see *Law Times*, 13 March 1869.

[3] H.C. 225, p. 133 (1875). VIII, 589.

[4] *Ibid.*, pp. 97-111.

connected with election business of their honesty and independence.[1] Moreover, their experience convinced them that the task
imposed upon the judges was not as difficult as the bench had
at first anticipated.[2] However, all judges were not so discreet.
The Irish judges had always been regarded as more 'political'
than the English, and their decisions would have been watched
more critically than those in England even if the notorious Judge
Keogh had not been on the bench. Keogh regarded his rôle in
election cases as that of a defender of the Protestant ascendancy
rather than that of a judge, and in 1872 he brought a storm down
upon him over the Galway County case. In the course of the
trial he baited the Roman clergy, denounced their tyranny and
praised the landlords; and in his judgement, as well as scheduling
most of the clergy in the county (from the Archbishop of Tuam
and the Bishop of Galway downwards) for 'spiritual intimidation', he launched into a long eulogy of Oliver Cromwell and
a denunciation of witnesses: one was an 'obscene monster', and
of another he said that 'he had never climbed a father's knee or
embraced a mother's neck'.[3] Isaac Butt raised the matter in the
Commons, where there was a long debate,[4] which resulted eventually in the provision that in future two judges should try each case.

This helped to solve the particular problem of Irish cases, but
in England it merely increased the uncertainty of a petition,
since no result could be achieved unless the judges were agreed.
Moreover, it made the position of a judge who held out against
both his colleague and public opinion extremely difficult. This
was demonstrated in 1906, when Mr Justice Grantham, a
'political judge' and an outspoken Conservative, delivered judgements in the Bodmin and Yarmouth cases which appeared to be
inconsistent. His judgement in the Yarmouth case in particular
seemed to most Liberals, and apparently to Grantham's colleague
also, to be flagrantly partisan, and to reflect the views he had

[1] Ballantine had a brush with Mr Justice Willes, but otherwise there was no direct
imputation of motives: Ballantine, *Experiences*, pp. 250-2. The *Law Times*, 23 January
1869, provides an outsider's view of Ballantine's attitude to judges.
[2] Mr Baron Martin and Mr Justice Willes expressed this changed view to the
Hartington Committee in 1869. H.C. 352, pp. 423f. (1868-69). VIII, 423f. For
the original attitude of the judges see C. Fairfield, *Some Account of George William
Wilshere, Baron Bramwell of Hever and His Opinions*, London 1898, p. 39, and H.C. 50
(1867-68). LVI, 491.
[3] *3 Hansard* CCXIII, 805. The official report of the trial was carefully expurgated:
H.C. 268, p. 20 (1872). XLVII, 244.
[4] *3 Hansard* CCXII, 1763f. and *3 Hansard* CCXIII, 760f.

expressed in what was almost a party speech at the reception given to the judges before the trial. The matter was raised in the House of Commons, where Grantham's *obiter dicta* and speech were pretty generally condemned, but the House was restrained from condemning him outright by a recognition of the difficulties of the judges in such cases.[1] Campbell-Bannerman summed up the whole position very fairly by saying that although he was not satisfied with existing arrangements, there seemed to be no alternative to the election courts because it was impossible to go back to the old partisan committees.

III

In spite of the uncertainties of the law, the 1885 election was much purer than any election in preceding years, and after 1885 corruption of the more blatant sort steadily decreased. Petitions were still presented, but few raised serious issues, and even fewer members were unseated.[2] The change has often been attributed (quite mistakenly) to the Ballot Act, or to the Corrupt Practices Act of 1883. Together they certainly made a great deal of difference to the conduct of elections, and the 1883 Act limited drastically the scope allowed to the corrupt agent. But corruption was by no means killed in 1883, and there is a much more prosaic reason for the change in 1885, the disfranchisement of corrupt constituencies. Until 1865 the corrupt constituencies listed on page 263 possessed one hundred and thirteen seats. Four constituencies were totally disfranchised in 1867 and twelve of the remainder lost one seat. Beverley and Bridgwater were disfranchised in 1869, and Macclesfield in 1881. Finally, as part of the general redistribution of 1885, another twenty-five constituencies were totally disfranchised and most of the rest lost their second member. Thus, whereas in 1865 the sixty-four corrupt constituencies possessed one hundred and thirteen seats, by 1885 the thirty-four which remained retained only forty-six seats.[3]

[1] The Yarmouth judgement was published as H.C. 169 (1906), XCV, 1f.

[2] In England 5 petitions were presented in 1885, 2 in 1886-7, 9 in 1892-3, and 4 in 1895; 3 members were unseated in 1885, 1 in 1886, 4 in 1892-3, and 1 in 1895.

[3] Boston, Bradford, Bristol, Cambridge, Canterbury, Cheltenham, Chester, Coventry, Derby, Devonport, Durham, *Gloucester, Gravesend, Hastings, Hereford, *Ipswich, Kidderminster, *Maidstone, *Norwich, Nottingham, Oxford, Penryn, *Rochester, *Shrewsbury, *Southampton, Stafford, Taunton, Wakefield, *Walsall, Westminster, Wigan, Windsor, *Worcester, *Yarmouth (disfranchised 1867, member restored 1885). Those marked with an asterisk were still more or less corrupt after 1885.

About fifteen or twenty of the thirty-four hitherto corrupt constituencies which survived the holocaust of 1885 continued corrupt long afterwards. At Ipswich and Norwich in 1885 there was considerable bribery out of a secret fund, known to the inhabitants of the town for many years, which cost the members their seats, and local tradition suggests that it continued at municipal elections for many years afterwards. The Ipswich case is a good example of how relatively ineffective the 1883 Act was in really corrupt towns. Elections had been voided in 1835, 1838 and 1842, when an extensive system of bribery was revealed, but a petition in 1857, although it disclosed eight cases of bribery by individual electors, did not affect the seat, and no more petitions were brought to trial until 1885. Yet the borough was hardly a whit purer in the meantime. The bribers simply went underground, and offered their services to both parties. A letter from a leading Ipswich Liberal to Lord Hartington in 1879, in perfect good faith, attributed all corrupt practices to the Conservatives.

> There is a practice amongst Conservatives of dividing Boroughs into districts; over these agents are appointed, who by the distribution of very small sums of money buy up the electors by wholesale— the payments being frequently made on the plea that they are compensations for loss of time. It is excessively difficult to discover who finds the money and to trace up the agency to the candidate, hence the immunity from punishment which the perpetrators enjoy.[1]

The difficulty felt most by this worthy Liberal was the expense of taking action against the candidates concerned, so he offered as a solution that £500 might be subscribed to buy up the venal voters! When a petition was finally presented it was against the two Liberal members, who both told the court quite frankly that they thought corrupt practices had occurred on a large scale in 1885, but on whose orders they did not know.[2] It appeared on investigation that the town still bore all the marks of systematic corruption. In one ward the principal agent for the sale of votes was a shoemaker who had thirty or forty voters under his influence whose support he offered first to the Conservatives and then to the Liberals. In addition to examples of private enterprise of this sort, it was found (as at Gloucester) that there was an agency at work distributing bribes, which had no connection with the candidates.

[1] A. Tyler (?) to Lord Hartington, 19 July 1879. Adam Papers.
[2] A report of the trial is given in H.C. 177, pp. 39-53 (1886). LII, 339-53.

Other towns were just as corrupt. At Worcester in 1906 there was still a general belief that as many as 1,000 voters were corruptible, although the price of votes was only half-a-crown, but a Royal Commission was more moderate. It held:

> That there exists in Worcester a class of voters numbering approximately 500, and consisting mainly of the needy and loafing class, but including a considerable number of working men in regular employment, who are prepared to sell their votes for drink or money.
>
> That this state of things has existed since the date of the limit of our Inquiry, viz. 1883.[1]

At Shrewsbury in 1903 a municipal election petition revealed the fact that extensive corrupt practices had occurred for many years past, and certainly since 1870, and that in the 1902 municipal elections, of the 667 voters who polled in the Castle Fields Ward about 400 had been paid, of whom 248 admitted receiving either half-a-crown or three shillings.[2] Corrupt practices on a similar scale also occurred at Rochester and Taunton, and to a lesser extent at Pontefract, Lichfield, Southampton, Maidstone, Great Yarmouth, and Walsall.[3] Even the most stringent legislation had clearly not killed corrupt practices, and it was some years before public opinion finally did so.

[1] [Cd. 3268] p. 5. H.C. (1906). XCV, 481.
[2] [Cd. 1541] pp. 3-5. H.C. (1903). LV, 507-9.
[3] Reports on these constituencies are to be found as follows: Rochester, H.C. 25, pp. 79-85 (1893-4). LXX, 883-9; Pontefract, H.C. 25-I, pp. 3-12 (1893-4). LXX, 915-24; Lichfield, H.C. 63, pp. 15-22 (1896). LXVII, 421-8; Southampton, H.C. 63, pp. 37-44 (1896). LXVII, 443-50; Maidstone, H.C. 92 (1901). LIX, 15-114; Great Yarmouth, H.C. 169 (1906). XCV, 1-254; Walsall, H.C. 25, pp. 61-8 (1893-4). LXX, 865-72; Taunton, Add. MS. 44,253, f.84.

Chapter Fourteen

A LANCASHIRE ELECTION: 1868

I

THERE were (and still are) three Lancashires, of which the capitals were Liverpool, Manchester, and Preston. Liverpool, a great port with an outlying bastion across the Mersey on the Wirral, devoted its energies to the import of raw cotton from America and the export of finished goods from the cotton towns. As it was not a manufacturing town in any sense, it possessed neither manufacturers nor skilled operatives, the main supporters of Liberalism in the cotton towns. Manchester, although the centre of a ring of cotton towns, most of them in Lancashire but a few in Cheshire or Derbyshire, was not itself primarily a manufacturing town even by the 1860s, but rather a great trading centre, directing an industry which extended well into north Lancashire. Preston united two very different functions as the capital both of old Lancashire, which extends from Coniston to Prescot, and of the north Lancashire cotton district which lies between Blackburn and Clitheroe. By 1833, when Lord Derby shut up his Preston town house and stables, these districts had ceased to be dominated by the great landed families, but they continued for the rest of the century to be greatly influenced by them, and particularly by those magnates who had interests in local mineral deposits, harbours, sea-side resorts, and cotton mills.[1]

Social differences begat political differences. Liverpool was a Tory stronghold, standing aloof from the rest of the county.[2] Society centred round the great merchants and shipowners, almost a hereditary caste, most of whom were Conservatives. There was

[1] Such as the Duke of Devonshire who opened up the iron workings north of Barrow and was largely responsible for the building of Barrow itself, Sir Peter Hesketh-Fleetwood who developed Fleetwood, and the Feildens of Blackburn who were both landowners and cotton-manufacturers.

[2] The best accounts of Liverpool politics are in B. D. White, *A History of the Corporation of Liverpool 1835-1914*, Liverpool 1951; W. W. Biggs, *Some Reasons for the Conservatism of Liverpool by Vindex*, Liverpool n.d.; T. Burke, *Catholic History of Liverpool*, Liverpool 1910; E. F. Rathbone, *William Rathbone, A Memoir*, London 1905; and A. B. Forward, 'Democratic Toryism', *Contemporary Review*, XLIII, 294-304 (1883).

an influential Liberal minority headed by the Rathbones and Holts, but they lacked the support which the Conservatives gained from the clergy and professional men, and never quite succeeded in getting to know the boisterous dockyard workers as their opponents did. They laboured, too, under the disadvantage of a past which could not be lived down. Liberalism was ineradicably associated with the anti-slavery movement, which had been largely directed against Liverpool whence half the slave-ships came, while Toryism was associated with the defence of local interests. Liberalism was even more closely (and fatally) associated with the cause of the Irish Roman Catholics, whose presence confused and embittered Liverpool politics to a degree unknown elsewhere. During the 1830s the Liberals had rashly come forward with a scheme for secular education designed to cater for the children of Roman Catholics and had brought out against themselves the formidable Canon McNeile. Church schools were strong in Lancashire and Orangemen were numerous in Liverpool, while the unending stream of pauper Irish able and willing to undersell their English competitors in the unskilled labour market of the docks was intensely unpopular, even hated. The whole town lived in an atmosphere of white-hot religious and racial passion, kept up by the press and the clergy of all denominations.

The Anti-Corn-Law League made little impression on a Liverpool entirely wrapped up in its internal feuds. It was in any case preaching doctrines virtually irrelevant to the town's economy, and alien to its political traditions. 'Liverpool', wrote Bright to Villiers in 1852, 'is a place corrupted by the old *protections*, infested with Orangeism, and afflicted with a large number of old freemen upon its register. Liverpool is too monstrous a thing to affect public opinion except adversely to its own course.'[1] The Liberals occasionally won parliamentary elections, although almost always for local reasons of a temporary nature, but they lost control of the corporation in 1842, and did not regain it until 1892. The majority of the English were unshakeable Conservatives, and the Irish kept them so. A Liverpool pamphleteer put it thus:

> In towns outside Lancashire . . . generally speaking, the proportion of Tories and of Roman Catholics is too small to produce except in a mild form, the friction and antagonism here referred to . . .

[1] G. M. Trevelyan, *Life of John Bright*, London 1913, p. 201.

Here, however, in Liverpool, the position is very different. A church-man here does not stop to ask himself whether the Catholics are as numerous all through England as they are in Liverpool—he sees them in large numbers here—his Protestant instincts and antipathies are fully aroused, and he joins the ranks of the Conservatives.[1]

The Manchester district, unlike Liverpool, was solidly Liberal (with some few exceptions) between 1832 and 1867. Ashton, Bury, Salford and Manchester itself returned none but Liberals, Rochdale returned a Conservative only in the exceptional circumstances of 1857, and Oldham and Stockport returned Liberals without exception after 1852. Only Bolton usually returned one Liberal and one Conservative. Indeed, after the early fifties the old-established but numerically weak Conservative and Chartist movements were hopelessly outnumbered in the middle-class borough constituencies, and made scarcely any pretence of keeping up the unequal struggle. In the cotton towns, although not in Manchester itself, they persisted at municipal elections, but even there they were in a minority. There was, then, some point in Grant Duff's speech to a Lancashire audience in 1868 which held up Manchester Liberalism to the admiration of the country.

> Ever since the Reform Act of 1832, and still more ever since the Anti-Corn Law League agitation, Liberals in other parts of the country had looked to the manufacturing districts of Lancashire as to a political Mecca, and they had repeated, not with jealousy, but with warm sympathy and admiration, our proud county saying, 'What Lancashire thinks to-day, England thinks tomorrow'.[2]

But such a speech could not have been made after 1868, for in 1868 and 1874 Manchester deserted its traditional Liberalism and the leadership of the Liberal party passed to Birmingham.

The rest of Lancashire was more diverse, and the *Manchester Guardian's* description of Mid-Cheshire would have been equally true of it.

> It is composed in a manner which affords a picture on a small scale of that rivalry between rural and urban interests which goes far to form the essence of political warfare in England. Between the vicinity of great towns on the one hand, and the existence of large landed estates on the other, it includes very wide diversities of calling

---

[1] Biggs, *Some Reasons for the Conservatism of Liverpool*, p. 11.
[2] *Manchester Guardian*, 10 August 1868.

in industry and habits of life. Nor is there wanting, as the names of the candidates show, a fair illustration of that conflict between Conservative and Liberal territorial influences which also enters largely into the sustaining motives of political activity in this country.[1]

The leading territorial influences in the county were those of Lord Derby, Lord Ellesmere, Lord Sefton, the Duke of Devonshire, and the group of large landowners in North Lancashire, many of them Roman Catholics.[2] But the influence of the fourteenth Earl of Derby stood out from all the rest. As a Radical observer remarked in 1864, 'Lord Derby holds a position in the Empire hardly second to that of any other subject of the Crown. He is a great lord in Lancashire by right of lineage and property, but neither the splendid annals nor the wide domains of his House would have won for him the position he holds by the higher right of personal genius and character.'[3]

Territorial influence was as strong in the boroughs as in the county divisions. County families nearly always provided Conservative candidates for Preston, Wigan and Burnley, while in Blackburn and Warrington Liberal manufacturers were usually opposed by Conservative manufacturer-landowners like the Hornbys, the Feildens, and Sir Gilbert Greenall, a class of politicians virtually unknown in Manchester. The more hopeless the seat the more likely it was that a borough candidate on the Conservative side would be a member of a county family. Thus Radical Burnley's first three Conservative candidates were Lieutenant-General Sir James Yorke Scarlett, a son of Lord Abinger, William Alexander Lindsay, grandson of the twenty-fourth Earl of Crawford and Balcarres, and Lord Edmund Talbot, third son of the fourteenth Duke of Norfolk and afterwards Lord-Lieutenant of Ireland and Viscount FitzAlan of Derwent, who was put forward as a candidate in the Towneley interest.[4]

---

[1] *Manchester Guardian*, 2 September 1868.

[2] Lancashire had been much less affected by the Reformation than the rest of the country, and had been a stronghold of Toryism and Jacobitism in the eighteenth century. But although most of the country gentlemen (and particularly Catholics like Sir Robert Gerard) were Conservatives, Lord Sefton and the Duke of Devonshire were between them able to support a very considerable Liberal interest composed largely of millowners set up as landed proprietors.

[3] R. A. Arnold, *The History of the Cotton Famine*, London 1864, p. 236.

[4] The Towneleys were an old Roman Catholic family. Lord FitzAlan had married in 1879 Lady Mary Bertie, whose mother was a Towneley. *The Tablet*, 3 April 1880, noted that he was the only Roman Catholic candidate in England in 1880.

The power of the great landlords over their tenants was, however, less than in other parts of the country, and personal qualities counted for more. Thus when Lord Derby (the great Lord Derby's eldest son) left Disraeli's cabinet in 1878 over the Eastern Question and agreed to act with the Liberals, he himself placed little reliance on the possibility of his tenants following him. Disraeli had, in any case, done his best to prevent this by putting Derby's brother in the cabinet in his place, a Machiavellian move which was thought at the time to be in rather bad taste. Thus, when Lord Granville, who was staying at Knowsley in June 1879, approached Derby on the subject in the hope of winning some support for Lord Hartington who was to fight North-East Lancashire at the coming general election, he got little but sympathy, and reported to Hartington:

> He is of opinion that the influence of a landlord in Lancashire, quâ landlord and apart from his personal & political character is exaggerated.
> As regards the Stanley influence it is probably the strongest in the agricultural division which his brother represents.[1] . . .
> In the South Eastern division his property is chiefly in building land, which gives little political influence.
> He has no property in the North Eastern division.
> With regard to the division which Cross represents[2] he does not think it would be becoming for him to campaign actively against a late colleague. He should remain neutral. He does not think his agents would contradict his views.[3]

Early in the following year Hartington himself asked Derby for help in North-East Lancashire, where he was fighting a difficult election. Derby replied:

> I have your note, and will see to the matter you refer to.[4] I will write at once to my steward in East Lancashire. But your friends must remember that the position is delicate. Farmers and others who have not followed recent public events, and who have always voted Conservative under the lead of my family, are puzzled by a change

[1] North Lancashire.

[2] South-West Lancashire.

[3] Devonshire Papers 340.818. The letter has been corrected in pencil by Derby.

[4] Apparently asking for assistance from Derby's agent. There is no record of it at Chatsworth.

of front and I can't press them to go against what they may suppose to be their convictions.

My letter to Sefton ought to make my wishes clear.[1]

II

At the dissolution of the parliament elected in 1865 the Lancashire members were evenly distributed between the parties, although there were variations from district to district.

	Conservative	Liberal	Total
Liverpool and Birkenhead . .	3	—	3
The Manchester boroughs . .	1	11	12
The County divisions . . .	3	2	5
Preston and the other boroughs .	7	1	8
	14	14	28

The 1867 Reform Act had in the meantime given Lancashire eight new seats, all of which were to be contested for the first time. Three of them had been given to the county (which had accordingly been subdivided into North, North-East, South-East, and South-West Lancashire) and one each to Liverpool, Manchester, and Salford and to the new boroughs of Burnley and Stalybridge. This increased the representation of the county as follows:

	1865 Parliament	1868 Parliament
Liverpool and Birkenhead . .	3	4
The Manchester boroughs . .	12	15
The County divisions . . .	5	8
Preston and the other boroughs .	8	9
	28	36

The interest of the 1868 election lay from the first in Mr Gladstone's contest in South-West Lancashire, in Lord Hartington's

[1] This letter made it clear that Derby now supported Gladstone, but that there were personal and family difficulties in the way of vigorous support at the moment. However, as it was printed in most of the leading papers on 14 or 15 March 1880 (e.g. *The Scotsman*, 15 March 1880), and placarded all over Lancashire with the promise of support for Gladstone boldly emphasised, it is hardly surprising that *The Times*, 15 April 1880, contained a report that Derby had intimidated his tenants on behalf of the Liberals. The letter quoted above is from the Devonshire Papers, 340,909.

contest in North Lancashire (and to a lesser extent in the contest in Preston, the North Lancashire capital), and in the elections in the Manchester boroughs. Liverpool, it was clear, would return two Conservatives and one Liberal (under the minority clause), and Birkenhead would return John Laird. 'The great complaint made by all prominent Working Class Liberals', the Reform League's agents reported, 'is the apathy of their class. The Orange element is strong, and we believe the majority are Conservative from conviction.'[1] The contest in the boroughs outside the orbits of Liverpool and Manchester would, it was equally clear, be decided more by local factors than by anything else, and neither party put much faith in any of them except Burnley. In this they were amply justified, since in both Warrington and Wigan there was the greatest confusion on election day. In Warrington a polling clerk failed to record a number of votes because of a crush of voters, while his superiors added up the votes wrongly at the end of the day, and a Conservative victory was announced, although the Liberals had in fact won. In Wigan, where there were two rival Liberal committees, there was even greater confusion as riotous mobs of miners roamed the streets and there also both parties thought they had won. Once again the Liberals actually won the election, but in both towns the Conservatives won the 1874 election and had their revenge.

To those living outside Lancashire the only contest which mattered was Mr Gladstone's in South-West Lancashire. The electors of South-West Lancashire received his first election address as party leader and listened to his first sustained burst of popular electioneering, the prelude as it were to the Midlothian campaign. The constituency was in any case a remarkable one, and included the county voters of Liverpool, Warrington, and Wigan along with the townsmen of Southport, Ormskirk, St Helens, and many smaller places. The total population was about 350,000, and there were about 20,000 electors. Moreover, the division included Lord Derby's seat at Knowsley, from which the Conservative campaign in the county was conducted, and also the Liberal Lord Sefton's seat at Croxteth. Lord Derby's chosen champions were Richard Assheton Cross, afterwards Home Secretary, who had been barrister, chairman of quarter sessions,

---

[1] Reform League Report: Liverpool.

member of parliament, and banker in turn, and Charles Turner, a Liverpool merchant who was one of the sitting members.[1] Lord Sefton's interest was represented by his cousin H. R. Grenfell, M.P. for Stoke since 1862, who agreed to become Gladstone's colleague only after Lord Sefton's brother had refused the nomination.[2]

Gladstone's connection with Lancashire went back to his boyhood in Liverpool, but when he became a candidate for South Lancashire in 1865 he had not fought an election in the county since he had contested Manchester as a Conservative in 1837. The 1865 contest was in any case a *pis aller*. Henry Brand, the Chief Whip, had furthered his candidature not because Gladstone wanted to become member for a popular constituency, but because it was essential that the Chancellor of the Exchequer should have a seat, and there was reason to think that he would be defeated at Oxford. Both of them treated the matter very casually: Brand hardly mentioned it in his letters, and even his notification that the candidature had been arranged was sandwiched in between other news. 'You will probably have heard that you are to be put up for South Lancashire in conjunction with 2 other candidates—Sir J. Shuttleworth and Mr. Thompson have been named as the other two. I hope that you continue to get good reports from Oxford and Chester.'[3] And until two days before the election Gladstone did no campaigning. Then he hastened to Manchester (arriving, as he said, 'unmuzzled') and to Liverpool

---

[1] R. A. Cross (1823-1914) cr. Viscount Cross 1886, M.P. for Preston 1857-62, S. W. Lancashire 1868-85, Newton div. 1885-6, Home Secretary 1874-80, 1885-6, Secretary of State for India 1886-92, Lord Privy Seal 1895-1900. Cross was a very distant relative of the Asshetons of Downham near Clitheroe, and had been at Rugby and Cambridge with Lord Stanley. Charles Turner (1803-75) was a shipowner and railway magnate of great influence. He was M.P. for Liverpool 1852-3, for South Lancashire 1861-8, and for South-West Lancashire 1868-75.

[2] William Rathbone and the other members of the Liberal committee tried hard to obtain a Molyneux or, failing a Molyneux, a Cavendish, and were much relieved when Grenfell agreed to stand. Alfred Billson told George Melly, who was Grenfell's colleague at Stoke, that at the committee meeting which adopted Grenfell 'it was evidently thought to be a most splendid hit—as Trimble observed "all the advantages of a Molyneux *with* brains" '. (Billson to Melly, 23 July 1868. Melly Papers XIII, 3,023.) H. R. Grenfell (1824-1902) was a member of the firm of Morgan, Grenfell and Co., bankers in the City of London, and a Governor of the Bank of England. He was M.P. for Stoke 1862-8, and unsuccessfully contested Chester in 1857, Lymington in 1860, South-West Lancashire in 1868, Truro in 1874 and Barnstaple in 1880. He was also a prospective candidate for St Ives in 1868. His mother was a daughter of the second Earl of Sefton; his son was created Lord St Just in 1935.

[3] Brand to Gladstone, 25 June 1865. Add. MS. 44,193, f.119. Gladstone's son William was standing at Chester with the support of the Marquess of Westminster.

to get in two speeches on the same day. Brand had already made arrangements for him to retire to Bury (where R. N. Philips had offered to give up his seat) if he failed in the county, so that it was felt that there was no need for extraordinary exertions.[1] But in the event Gladstone won his election by a small majority and was returned with two Conservative colleagues.[2]

The victory in South Lancashire in 1865 was an important milestone in the development of Gladstone as a popular statesman, but it was also something of an embarrassment. The old South-Lancashire constituency was so large as to be practically unmanageable, yet it was a marginal constituency requiring constant attention such as no hard-worked minister could give it. The two new divisions of South-East and South-West Lancashire were, if possible, worse. Although not as big as the old division each of the new divisions had roughly the same number of electors, and was quite as unsafe for a Liberal as the old. And for the 1868 elections the registers were so delayed that a decision about candidates had to be arrived at before it was possible to canvass either division. Gladstone accordingly left entirely to Brand the decision whether he should stand again, and which division he should contest if he did stand.

The choice was complicated for Brand by three factors. First, the leaders of Liberalism in South-East and South-West Lancashire formed a closely-knit connection (William Rathbone of Liverpool, in particular, was related to, or on friendly terms with, nearly all the leading men in both Liverpool and Manchester). Secondly, the Liberal leaders in the South-Eastern division headed by George Wilson were also the leaders of one faction of Manchester Liberalism—that associated with the successors of the Anti-Corn-Law League—and had become unpopular on account of their high-handedness. Thirdly, the centre of the South-Western division was Tory Liverpool, and there had been a Conservative majority in that portion of the old division. Eventually, on 29 July, Brand decided to accept the advice of the Liberal leaders in Liverpool that the old registers were not an accurate guide to the political views of the South-West division, and advised Gladstone to stand in his native

---

[1] Add. MS. 44,193, f.126.

[2] Egerton (C) 9,171, Turner (C) 8,806, Gladstone (L) 8,786, Legh (C) 8,476, Thompson (L) 7,703, Heywood (L) 7,653.

district.[1] Next day Brand saw Henry Grenfell and arranged for him to stand as Gladstone's colleague.

> All is serene with regard to S.W. Lancashire.
>
> Grenfell will stand, and I have no doubt will be your colleague.
>
> Lord Sefton cordially concurs, & subscribes £2000, a good test of his goodwill.
>
> The Deputation from S.W. Lancashire satisfied me yesterday that to start you alone exposed you to considerable risk, as they could not rely upon the whole of your votes being plumpers. There is always a disposition among weak voters, & ignorant men, to utilize their second vote.
>
> So I had no hesitation in exerting myself to secure Grenfell.
>
> A second seat in S.W. Lancashire is of more importance then a victory at St. Ives.[2]

The only difficulty now was to break the news to the Manchester Liberals, who were certain to take it amiss if the wrong people got to hear of it first. Brand left this delicate task to Gladstone himself, but he also passed on some good advice on the conduct of the election in general.

> You are a better judge than I am whether Wilson is the proper man to whom such a communication should be addressed. If he is *the* man with whom you have corresponded on the matter, you can hardly pass him over: but Wilson is the impersonation of that League or Society in the Salford Hundred of which your friends in W. Derby are jealous.[3] If you can take another name without offence to Wilson it would, I think, be better. . . .
>
> I presume that after the Rathbone dinner you will be asked to put out an Address—I need not remind you that this should be framed not only for Lancashire, but for the United Kingdom.
>
> The temper of the Public mind is, I think, strongly in your favour; but in many quarters there is apprehension that the Church & the rights of property are not safe in your hand!!!
>
> I speak plainly; and I know that you will forgive me for plain speaking.

[1] Brand saw a deputation consisting of George Melly, M.P. for Stoke, William Rathbone, Alfred Billson, a solicitor who had been Melly's agent at Stoke, who was secretary of the South-West Lancashire Liberal Association, and who later became an M.P., and T. D. Hornby, the Whig leader in Liverpool. Together they went through the registers and decided that they showed a Liberal majority of about 500. Add. MS. 44,194, ff.60-3. An alternative seat was held in readiness at Greenwich in case of failure.

[2] Where Grenfell was already a candidate. Add. MS. 44,194, ff.64-5.

[3] Salford Hundred and West Derby Hundred had been adopted in 1867 as the basis of the two new divisions of South-East and South-West Lancashire.

It seems incredible; but the truth is that your detractors have so persistently stated this that some people, even among our friends, are weak enough to believe it.

I hope that in your Address, & in your speeches in Lancashire you will say something to reassure men on these points. . . .

As to finance; you know I suppose that the Division finds the ways & means, Ld Sefton contributing £2000.[1]

There now only remained the timing of the election address, which was of more than local importance.

As to the time of your Address, I should be disposed to say—*now*.

The note of war is being sounded all over the Country, & your followers are looking to you for watchwords.

In 3 months the General Election will be upon us: but the fight has begun already.

Your Address now will sound the right note for Candidates, & the Press. It will follow naturally, & almost necessarily, it appears to me, upon the invitation to stand. If you put out no more than a declara- that you will stand, I fear that there will be a sense of disappointment in the Country.

Our friends are watching & waiting for something more.

It is for us, who have right and reason on our side to agitate the question of the Irish Church between this & Nov: the sooner it is discussed, & the more it is shewn up the better. It takes some time for a question of this sort to permeate the masses.[2]

The campaign thus set on foot achieved a triumphant vindication in October, when Gladstone opened his round of election speeches. Between the 12th and the 23rd of October he delivered seven major speeches to vast audiences of working men and reporters in the main centres of the division, Warrington, Liverpool, Newton, Leigh, Ormskirk, Southport, and Wigan. Their effect was felt all over the country and their manner clearly foreshadowed the Midlothian campaign, but the vindication was a national, not a local one, for the South-West Lancashire election never went really well for the Liberals, even where the vast meetings were most successful. Liverpool was, in truth, the worst possible place in which to launch a campaign designed to favour

[1] Brand to Gladstone, 1 August 1868. Add. MS. 44,194, ff.66-9. By 21 August £6,545 had been promised and ultimately the total reached £8,215. Melly Papers XIII, 3066.

[2] Brand to Gladstone, 4 August 1868. Add MS. 44,194, ff.74-5.

the Roman Catholic Church at the expense of a Protestant
church, while the agricultural districts showed themselves as
staunchly Conservative in Lancashire as they were proving in
most parts of the country. Even the unspectacular qualities of
the two Conservative candidates were in this case of advantage
to them, since there was nothing for waverers to object to.[1] The
margin between the two parties was not great, but it was decisive,
and Gladstone was forced to take refuge in Greenwich.

Cross (C)	.	.	.	.	7,729
Turner (C)		.	.	.	7,676
Gladstone (L)	.	.	.	.	7,415
Grenfell (L)	.	.	.	.	6,939

Brand was taken completely by surprise.

> I feel full of remorse at having advised you to raise the standard
> in Lancashire. I am utterly confounded at the result, for certainly
> the figures presented to me in the summer were widely different
> from those declared at the Poll. The truth is, Lancashire has gone
> mad, & the contest there has been one of race, Saxon against Celt.
> This is a sad state of things. Be the cause what it may I crave your
> forgiveness for my ill advice.[2]

The Liberal Committee called for an investigation, but the
report that resulted was of little value, and merely recounted
that things had gone wrong everywhere. Its principal interest for
us is that it showed clearly that the farmers in general had gone
against the wishes of their landlords and against Gladstone wherever they were expected to change their vote from the last
election. 'There can be no doubt,' says the report, 'that the
Gerard tenantry voted as the Tories they are. And not as Catholics
and that the refusal of Mr. Moubert the Steward to do more
than vote for you left the Tenants free to vote as they always
have done.' Moreover, although eighteen omnibuses and thirty-
two other conveyances were sent to Ormskirk to bring voters in,
thirty of Lord Sefton's tenants voted Conservative 'and there can

---

[1] It is amusing to note that William Rathbone had written to George Melly at
the beginning of the contest (Melly Papers XIII, 2998) welcoming their candidature:
'I am very glad Turner & Cross are out . . . I was afraid they were only dummies to
conceal some more formidable opponents.'

[2] Brand to Gladstone, 28 November 1868. Add. MS. 44,194, f.107.

be no doubt that many of the Scarisbrick Tenants plumped for you or split between you and one or other Conservative to some extent.'[1]

III

Lord Hartington's campaign in North Lancashire is interesting for the light that it casts on county electioneering. Hartington had first been returned for North Lancashire in 1857 as the representative of the Cavendish estates (12,681 acres) at the age of twenty-four, and until 1868 had been returned unopposed. His colleague, Colonel John Wilson-Patten (afterwards Lord Winmarleigh) had represented the division since 1832, and was a moderate Conservative and a former Peelite with many friends among the Liberals. But the 1868 division was different from its predecessor in that the more or less Liberal Blackburn Hundred had been separated from it to form the new North-East Lancashire division, leaving North Lancashire as a long straggling division stretching from Cumberland some sixty miles south to the outskirts of Wigan. And the new constituency, being mostly agricultural both north and south of the Ribble, was deemed sufficiently promising for the Conservatives to encourage them to put up a second candidate in the person of Frederick Stanley, Lord Derby's second son, who was already member for Preston. Lord Derby himself had represented the old North Lancashire division in his younger days and was burning for a fight—even to the tune of £25,000[2]—and Patten, who was a schoolfellow and lifelong friend of Derby's, could hardly refuse to accept his son as a colleague.

The whole contest had, none the less, a curiously old-fashioned flavour. Patten, who had a strong aversion to making public speeches, was one of the last survivors of the old-fashioned independent country gentlemen. As the leading authority in the House on questions of Private Bill procedure and the friend of Gladstone and Hartington, he did not feel called upon to take an exclusively party line on public questions. Indeed, he found but little to interest him in general politics, although at various times he had

---

[1] Add. MS. 44,414, ff.240-1. Sir Robert Gerard was neutral on this occasion. The Liberals expressed much indignation with the Sefton tenants (60 in all) who voted the wrong way, although it had been made clear to them that they should vote for Mr Gladstone (Melly Papers XIII, 3018).

[2] Sir Herbert Maxwell, *The Life and Letters of George William Frederick, Fourth Earl of Clarendon*, London 1913, II, 347.

accepted office to please Derby. At Derby's express request he had become Chancellor of the Duchy of Lancaster in 1867, in the hope of early release and despite his distrust of Disraeli, but to his great distress Disraeli persuaded him in September 1868 to exchange this pleasant office for the much less desirable post of caretaker Chief Secretary for Ireland with a seat in the cabinet. Patten knew nothing about Ireland, and resisted the offer, but he eventually gave way on condition that he should have as little as possible to do.[1] The arrangement was quite fantastic, since a general election was already being fought on the Irish Church question, and Lord Mayo, the late Chief Secretary, was on his way to India as Viceroy and could be of no possible assistance.

When poor Patten came to address his constituents he was in something of a dilemma, as he had no notion at all of the government's policy on the Irish Church, and a request for instructions from Disraeli produced only an enigmatic response.

> With regard to your constituents, they cannot expect a Cabinet Minister to tell them the course wh. H.M. Government must communicate, in the first instance, to Parlt. All you have to tell them, [is] that the question will receive the most deliberate consideration of H.M. Govt., & that they will be prepared to advise that course wh. they think most conducive to the public interests. As a member of the Cabinet your mouth is necessarily closed on questions of such magnitude wh. must be brought before the consideration of Parlt.[2]

Fortunately for Patten the character of the division was essentially Conservative, and the public was more interested in

---

[1] His memorandum, dated 16 September 1868 and now among the Winmarleigh Papers, reads as follows: 'In consequence of Mr. Disraeli's letter of the 15th. I went immediately to London & had a personal interview with Mr. D. I stated to him that I still felt the greatest difficulty in undertaking the post which he proposed for me. That I should have the whole Irish policy to learn & that I was unaccustomed to take part in debates on public affairs, & that my health was not strong enough for me to undertake any great amount of work—I especially alluded to the Church & Election questions, with which I was not acquainted. He assured me that I should have nothing to do with the Elections, that as to questions of public policy, he would himself be responsible for them, & that in debate I should be called upon only to substantiate, explain, or enlarge upon what had been previously said. He said that I greatly over rated the difficulty & a good deal more of an assuring kind & I told him that under all the circumstances I did not feel myself justified in declining the post & that I would do my best to fill it, but that I hoped he would remember if I should fail in satisfactorily discharging the duties, that I had forewarned him & hoped that he would not be disappointed. He said that he would write to the Irish Government to announce the matter & that I should receive suggestions either from Lord Mayo or from himself as to the best mode of proceeding.'

[2] Disraeli to Patten, 11 October 1868. Winmarleigh Papers.

Hartington's plight than in the Chief Secretary's speeches. Everything was going badly for Hartington, who had never liked the
idea of a contest in the new division. At the beginning of July
he was used as a go-between in persuading Grenfell to stand for
South-West Lancashire, only to find later in the month that
his own position was much worse than Gladstone's and that
neither a second candidate for North Lancashire nor sympathy
were to be had. On 24 July 1868 he wrote to his father from
Lancaster.

> I am sorry to say that things look very black here. The result of
> the canvass here is that we have got 4976 promises & that we know
> of 3561 who will vote for Patten & Stanley. This leaves about 4500
> who have either not promised, or have not been canvassed. Of course
> some of these will vote for me, but the greater part of them will be
> against. In fact even if all my voters could be depended on to plump,
> it would not look well, and if as they certainly will a good many
> split, and divide their votes between me & Patten or me & Stanley
> it will be very much against us. They do not seem to think that we
> can depend on a great many not splitting for Stanley: neither do
> they think that a second candidate would do any good.
>
> I have told them that I would take the returns up to London, &
> consult my friends what shd. be done. They have promised to keep
> it quiet for the present, but I am afraid it will soon get out. I cannot
> see that it will be any use going on; as we are more likely to lose than
> gain in the time between now & the election; but for the sake of
> other elections it may be necessary to hold on for a time. You had
> better write me a line to say what you think about it. I am just off to
> London.[1]

Hartington arrived in London to find Glyn, the Chief Whip,
about to depart for a rest at the seaside, and in an optimistic
mood which induced Hartington to comment sadly: 'Glyn
does not think that the result of the canvass looks so bad as I
think it: but he does not know much about it I am afraid . . .'[2]
Fortunately, Brand took up his case in the intervals of making
arrangements for Gladstone, and there followed a period of consultation between Hartington, Brand, Drake (a former party
agent), and the local leaders. Brand wanted Hartington to press
on, come what might, but Drake persuaded him that a compromise would be better if one could be arranged, and in the

[1] Devonshire Papers 340.354.
[2] Hartington to the Duke of Devonshire, 25 July 1868: Devonshire Papers 340.355.

end it was decided to try to reach some sort of agreement between the parties as to both North Lancashire divisions. This meant in the first place entering into an understanding with the Liberal leaders in North-East Lancashire, where the Liberal candidates were Ughtred James Kay-Shuttleworth (afterwards the first Lord Shuttleworth), then aged only twenty-four, who had been put up by his father, and William Fenton, the popular candidate, whose father had been M.P. for Rochdale in the thirties.[1] Both, at the beginning of August, felt themselves sure of success, but it was thought possible that Kay-Shuttleworth, as the younger man, might be persuaded to retire in favour of Hartington if the Conservatives were willing to withdraw their candidates in the North-East division in return for a clear run in the North division. On this latter point it was decided to sound Lord Derby, either through Patten or through some other agent.[2]

The plan for a compromise came to nothing, although at first there was an optimistic belief that something would turn up, and Brand told Gladstone as late as 8 August, 'The compromise in N. Lancashire is in hand: we must be content with half the representation, taking the Eastern side, & giving up the Western— Hartington may be moved from West to East. It is a complicated operation, but I hope that it may be affected [*sic*] without public discredit.'[3] Brand even undertook to give Shuttleworth an undertaking (in Glyn's name) that he would have the first claim on the party for a vacancy after the general election. But the negotiations came to a sudden end a few days later. Hartington met Sir James Kay-Shuttleworth (on a railway platform!) and put the proposition directly to him, adding that he personally was averse to it. Sir James thereupon declined to withdraw his son and made it clear that, as the candidates had been formally adopted by the local leaders, they could only withdraw if pressed to do so by the leaders of the party in the party interest.[4] Immediately afterwards it was learned that the Conservatives were not prepared to compromise either, and Brand reported to Gladstone:

---

[1] Sir James Kay-Shuttleworth (formerly Dr Kay) was the principal manager of his son's campaign: Frank Smith, *The Life and Work of Sir James Kay-Shuttleworth*, London 1923, p. 336. Sir James, who owned over 3,000 acres in Lancashire, was a celebrated educationalist and sanitary reformer, and had been prominent in relief work during the cotton famine.

[2] Add. MS. 44,194. f.71, and Devonshire Papers, 340.361.

[3] Brand to Gladstone, 8 August 1868. Add. MS. 44,194, ff.84-5.

[4] Hartington to Colonel Bowdon, 11 August 1868. Devonshire Papers 340.365.

We now hear that the Conservatives in the East are in high spirits profiting by the unpopularity of Shuttleworth. In the meantime Shuttleworth declines to retire in favour of Hartington.

Shuttleworth's Com*ee* are dissatisfied with him, & they may press him to withdraw. Other influences may be brought to bear upon him: but if he is obstinate, I fear that we may lose that seat, as well as Hartington's in the west—Hartington & Fenton would make both seats safe in the East.

I shall advise Hartington, in the event of the failure of negotiations, to fight the Western Division even if it be a forlorn hope.

I cannot say whether he will make this sacrifice for the Party, but I shall advise it.

It is possible that he might be shifted to E. Derbyshire, Egerton going to Surrey; but all such changes of front in the face of the Enemy are dangerous.[1]

Three days later Brand passed on the news that the failure was complete.

The attempt to compromise North Lancashire, East & West, has fallen through. I advise Hartington to fight a forlorn hope in the West. It is much to ask, I know, considering the many seats at the command of his father.[2] But I believe that it will be better not only for the Party, but for himself, that he should fight it out. I have told him that if he fails, he will be entitled to the first vacancy which offers; & the General Election is sure to present some casualties by which he may profit.[3]

The certainty of defeat cast an understandable gloom over Hartington's campaigning, which was further deepened by an unpleasant incident. Two of his principal supporters in North Lancashire were men with a past. E. M. Fenwick, the chairman of his committee, and H. W. Schneider, one of his most active committeemen in Barrow, had been unseated for bribery at Lancaster in 1865 and scheduled by the commissioners who reported on the election. Their position was, therefore, a delicate one, and it seems curious that their disqualification from voting and holding office had not been thought sufficient reason to exclude

[1] Brand to Gladstone, 13 August 1868. Add. MS. 44,194, ff.89-90.
[2] One seat for North Derbyshire was the only one absolutely in his gift, but his large properties in England and Ireland would have made a member of his family welcome in perhaps a dozen other constituencies.
[3] Brand to Gladstone, 16 August 1868. Add. MS. 44,194, ff.91-2. Hartington was found a seat for the Radnor district in 1869 at the price (paid in 1874) of a baronetcy for the sitting member.

them from Hartington's committee from the first. However, no notice was taken until the lists of the committees were published, when some agitation was felt by Hartington's more reputable supporters. The opinion of counsel was then taken, and as it proved adverse to the two men (there was even some question as to whether their serving on one of his committees might not disqualify Hartington himself), Hartington had to ask them to retire.[1]

The only support on which Hartington could absolutely rely came from the Cavendish estates themselves. These were mostly, if not all, North of Lancaster, either about Holker Hall, the family seat, or in the Furness peninsula round the family iron workings at Ulverston, Dalton and Barrow. Lancaster itself had a Liberal majority, but only a small one, while Preston was too much concerned with its own affairs to take much notice of what was happening in the country. Preston had a large Irish population, 3,000 of whom belonged to the Irish Liberal Association according to the Reform League's report, but an Irish population which had been half-Tory since the controversy over the so-called 'Papal Aggression' in 1850, and strongly Tory while C. P. Grenfell, a strongly Protestant Liberal, was a member from 1857 to 1865.[2] Gladstone's campaign against the Irish Church temporarily won over these Irish voters, and the Liberals sought to capitalise on this advantage by adopting as one of their candidates Lord Edward Howard, afterwards Lord Howard of Glossop, a prominent Roman Catholic. But they overstepped themselves when they brought out a Wesleyan, J. F. Leese, as his colleague in order to win both the Catholic and the Methodist vote.[3] Lord Edward found his co-religionists restive, while the Methodists were not reconciled to the alliance with Rome by Leese's candidature, and held aloof.[4] The Conservatives had in any case countered the Liberal move with two much more satisfactory candidates, Sir Thomas Fermor-Hesketh of Rufford Hall, who had been a popular member since 1862, and Edward Hermon, the sole

[1] Devonshire Papers, 340.380.

[2] For Preston politics see W. Dobson, *History of the Parliamentary Representation of Preston*, 2 edn, Preston 1868, Hewitson, *History of Preston*, H. A. Taylor, 'Politics in Famine-Stricken Preston' *Transactions of the Historic Society of Lancashire and Cheshire*, CVII, 121-39. (1955), and pp. 69-70 above.

[3] There was also a third Liberal candidate, Edward German, but he retired too early in the campaign to affect the result.

[4] Add. MS. 44,347, ff.179-82.

proprietor of the great firm of Horrocks, both of whom easily won a majority of over 1,000, or over ten per cent.

When North Lancashire finally polled, Hartington did even worse than he had expected in his most pessimistic mood, and the Conservatives obtained a large majority.[1] Hartington had a majority of 829 in Furness and Cartmel (1,527 votes to Stanley's 698), and of fifty in Lancaster (500 votes to Stanley's 450), but only one other polling district, the tiny one of Brindle near Preston, gave him a majority, and that of only five. Next day he wrote to report the event to his father.

> My defeat yesterday was much more complete than I expected. I have not yet seen the actual numbers at the close of the poll, & I expect that the last returns will probably rather diminish the majority. I believe that N. Lonsdale [Furness and Cartmel] will have done about what was expected & that we had about 1,000 majority there. Lancaster was also quite as good as expected. Carn-forth I think worse, Garstang & all the bad districts much worse. I imagine that there has been a great deal of pressure put on lately especially for Patten; but I don't think that I can ever have really had a chance, & the returns must have been very incorrect.[2]

Hartington characteristically left his account of the cause of his defeat to a footnote about the contest in East Sussex where Lord Edward Cavendish was standing.[3]

> I am afraid we must make up our minds to lose Sussex, as I imagine that the strong Protestant feeling has had a good deal to do with my licking.

IV

Cotton gave the Manchester district a common interest, but it was by no means a social unit. Each town was consciously in-dependent of its neighbours and specialised in one branch of cotton manufacturing: some in spinning, some in finishing, some in printing, some in machine making, and a few in weaving. And both the employers' associations and the cotton trade unions were organised on a federal basis. Manchester, as the place where

[1] Stanley (C) 6,832, Patten (C) 6,681, Hartington (L) 5,296.
[2] Hartington to the Duke of Devonshire, 21 November 1868. Devonshire Papers 340.383.
[3] Lord Edward was beaten but his Liberal colleague J. G. Dodson, afterwards Lord Monk Bretton, was successful. There was a good deal of Cavendish property in the division.

cotton was stored and sold, as a shopping and cultural centre, and as the home of the Anti-Corn-Law League whose influence still pervaded the cotton towns, naturally dominated the district. But it was not so dominant that the cotton towns were unable to maintain their independence.

Such unity of attitude and purpose as there was existed below the level of the mill, the warehouse, and the political association in the character of the ordinary South-Lancashire working man. In his every-day life he was both conservative and independent, often owning his own house or buying it through a building society, and a member of a co-operative society; he was even in some parts a 'capitalist' owning a few shares in one of the larger mills. He was also a strong trade unionist (the cotton unions were the best organised unions in the sixties), a patriot, a bit of a jingo, and a Protestant. As a Protestant he was more likely to be a member of the Church of England or an indifferentist than a dissenter, and had probably been educated in the rudiments at a Church school. Above all he was a man who had gone through the cotton famine of the early sixties with singular courage and fortitude. Yet with all these 'respectable' characteristics went a curious volatility. The Lancashire operative was unmistakably the man for whom Blackpool was soon to be built, and he was strangely unlike the Yorkshireman. Indeed, it was this volatility which most impressed visitors from across the Pennines like Sir Alfred Pease:

> I find these Lancashire audiences extraordinarily different to our Yorkshire ones. Superficially they are enthusiastic but very noisy and frivolous; no political question seems to be serious to them, it is just an entertainment at which they enjoy cheering and a noise. They will cheer *anything* you say or any name they have heard which they think is their colour, or cheer and shout about nothing at all. It is just like a lot of excited Arabs burning powder in a Fantasia.[1]

The general election in South-East Lancashire was decided by a combination of two factors: by a revulsion of feeling against the Irish caused by the Fenian movement and by an Orange lecturer named Murphy, which made it extremely difficult, if not impossible, for Liberals to convince the public of the need for concessions to Ireland, and by the alienation of the operatives from

---

[1] Sir A. E. Pease, *Elections and Recollections*, London 1932, pp. 197-8.

the Manchester School, which led to the Conservatives being regarded as the party of the working-classes.

The Fenian movement, although not very well led, was extremely strong among the Manchester Irish in 1867, and had connections, through men like Michael Davitt of Haslingden, with Fenian lodges all over the county. The actual number of Fenians and Fenian sympathisers was probably about 5,000, but rumour magnified their number to as many as 50,000.[1] On 18 September 1867 the Fenians scored a great success. Two Fenians, 'Colonel' Kelly and an associate, had lately been captured by the police, and were being driven down Hyde Road from Belle Vue prison to the New Bailey prison in Salford, when they were rescued by a number of other Fenians who incidentally shot and killed the unarmed sergeant of police who was riding with the prisoners. Popular feeling was immediately roused on both sides, the English against the Fenians, the Irish on behalf of the suspects who had been arrested and charged with the murder of Police-Sergeant Brett. Fenian activity elsewhere, which led to the blowing up of Clerkenwell prison in London, to a number of outrages in Ireland, and to an attempt to capture Chester Castle, provoked fears of a general rising, and the Irish quarters of the Lancashire towns were the objects of great suspicion. The press, and particularly the Radical *Manchester Examiner*, was full of reports of plots and made the most of the twelve dead and 120 injured at Clerkenwell, of ominous despatches from Canada reporting American preparations to invade Ireland, and (in April 1868) of the Australian Fenian who had shot the Duke of Edinburgh in the back while he was on a visit to Sydney and had narrowly missed killing him.

William Murphy, the Orange lecturer, came to Lancashire at the beginning of 1868, a flaming fox sent by the Protestant Evangelical Mission and Electoral Union among the corn of Lancashire. His one object was to whip up popular feeling against Rome and Irish Roman Catholics in general, to show them 'in their true light' as the murderers and assassins of truth as well as of men. Murphy was already a well-known, not to say notorious,

---

[1] This was the number which Sir Robert Gerard passed on to Lord Derby on 1 November 1867, and which Derby passed on to Gathorne Hardy. The letter is now in the Cranbrook Papers.

figure, and one of the greatest showmen of the age.[1] At Wolverhampton in February 1867 he had scored his first major success
when he provoked a riot sufficiently serious to force the magistrates to call in the military to protect property. At Birmingham
in June, he had done even better: the prospect of excitement had
lured between fifty and a hundred thousand people into the
streets and a riot was easily started. One street inhabited chiefly
by Irishmen was sacked, and the army was again used to disperse
the crowds.

Murphy's message was not political in the ordinary sense of
the word, but it had political implications in the circumstances
of 1867-8 which could not be overlooked. His peculiar skill lay
in his methods. He was an unusual master of abuse, even for an
Ulsterman, and delighted his hearers with vigorous denuncia-
tions of Purgatory, Transubstantiation, and the Adoration of
the Virgin. From abuse he went on to harrowing tales of nun-
neries, of the young women imprisoned there against their wills,
and of the babies that were regularly slaughtered in them.
Then came the *chef d'œuvre*: a mock confession box was set up on
the stage and Murphy interrogated one of his assistants from it
to the delight of his audience. Such meetings (limited to men
only) were specially advertised as a sort of obscene treat ('Protestants! Come and Hear the Questions put to the Married
and Unmarried in the Confessional, and Save Your Wives and

[1] The only full account of his doings in 1867-8 is in the Home Office papers at
the Public Record Office: H.O./45.O.S.7991. They include the posters and telegrams
from which quotations are given below. The programme of the Protestant Evangelical
Mission is summed up in the questionnaire for parliamentary candidates it produced
in 1872 (*The Monthly Record of the Protestant Evangelical Mission and Electoral Union*,
March 1872, p. 39).

1. Will you *deliver* and *protect* the Roman Catholics of this Empire from tyranny,
   illegal taxation, and fraud, by the Pope's Agents, acting under the authority of
   Rome's Canon Law?
2. Will you give the protection of British Law to Nuns who may be imprisoned in
   Convents against their wills?
3. Will you aid and encourage the Queen in the observance of her Coronation Oath
   to 'Maintain the Laws of God, the true profession of the Gospel, and the
   Protestant Reformed Religion'—The Constitution of 1688?
4. Will you advocate the reading of the Word of God in all schools and educational
   establishments in the Empire receiving any support from the Government?
5. As Romish priests are the agents of an 'alien, hostile power,' and as they are
   trained to educate British subjects in theft, lewdness, falsehood, perjury, treason,
   and murder, will you vote for the withdrawal of all money grants to said Priests?
6. Will you vote for the Repeal of the *mis*-called RELIEF BILL of 1829, by which
   the nominees of an alien, hostile priesthood are permitted to *legislate for* 'this
   Protestant kingdom,' but who in that capacity are doing their utmost to subvert
   our National Institutions in the interest of the Pope?

Families from Contamination') and an obscene booklet, *The Confessional Unmasked*, and the report of a debate on *The Depravity of the Priesthood and the Immorality of the Confessional* were on sale where the police did not seize and burn them. Everything possible was done to advertise these meetings, from posters and processions to telegrams to the Home Secretary (one from Bacup read HONOURED SIR CANNOT GET PROTECTION FROM THE POPISH SUPER-INTENDENT WILL NOT LET POLICE DO DUTY I HOPE YOU WILL PROTECT ME FROM POPISH MOB LAW) and both the Home Office and local watch committees were reduced almost to despair in their efforts to restrain Murphy's campaigning. There was relief all round when he was set on by Irish miners at Workington on St Patrick's Day 1872 and so injured that he died soon afterwards.[1]

Murphy secured his greatest triumphs in Lancashire, for wherever he went he conjured up a riot. The mere announcement of his arrival was sufficient to throw the Irish into a frenzy, while at Bacup, where they were quietest, Murphy and his followers sought them out, parading the street behind a man bearing a naked sword.[2] The ugliest riots occurred at Ashton and Stalybridge where there had already been anti-Catholic riots during the cotton famine. For several days in May 1868 armed bands controlled the town and on one occasion columns of demonstrators converged from neighbouring towns and attacked the Irish quarter of Ashton where whole streets were demolished, every house being forcibly entered and the furniture thrown, along with the doors and window frames, into a great bonfire in the street.[3] There was for some time a fear lest Irish attacks on Murphy, which were usually well organised, were the work of Fenians, and a detective was imported from Ireland (the Metropolitan police could not spare any of its thirteen detectives) to investigate. But he could discover no connection between the riots and the Fenians: when he mingled with the crowd at Oldham he 'never heard the word Fenian directly or indirectly uttered', although he did hear a good deal about Murphy. At Oldham the cause of the riot was simply the endeavour of some Irishmen to rescue one of their

[1] For the attack see *The Monthly Record of the Protestant Evangelical Mission and Elec-toral Union*, April 1872. There is an account of it from the Irish point of view in T. M. Healy, *Letters and Leaders of My Day*, London [1928], 1, 23-5.

[2] At Rochdale one of Murphy's assistants actually fired a pistol at the police and was sentenced to sixteen months' hard labour. *Sunderland Herald*, 20 March 1868.

[3] *Annual Register*, 1868, pp. 55-8.

compatriots from the police, which so roused the anger of the English that they set upon their old enemies.[1]

The climax of Murphy's campaign came in September with what the *Annual Register* called 'Murphy riots at Manchester'. These were not really riots at all but they attracted a good deal of attention because of their location. Murphy had arrived in Manchester quietly, and had been immediately lodged in Belle Vue prison while sureties for his good behaviour were secured. While in gaol, he hit upon the ingenious plan of announcing himself a candidate for the representation of Manchester, and issued an address to the electors. This had one theme, 'whatever may be your feelings with regard to points of less consequence, I desire to stake the whole contest upon this one question: Are the electors of Manchester prepared to vote for Protestantism, or for the tools of Rome?'[2] Immediately on his release he called an 'election meeting' on an open space in Chorlton Road. Long before the meeting was due to begin a large crowd had collected which was eventually joined by a considerable band of Irishmen bent on mischief and armed with sticks and stones which they used freely. The police found it difficult to make an impression on a crowd of five or six thousand people, but they were able to restore order before Murphy himself arrived. When he had concluded, a vote of confidence was moved and passed, which assured him that he was a fit and proper person to represent the Protestant interest in Parliament, three cheers were given for the Queen, three more for William, Prince of Orange, and three groans for Popery. Thereafter, Murphy took to indoor meetings, many of them for 'fashionable' audiences, and no more was heard of his candidature.[3]

These riots, following so closely on the Fenian outrages and coming at the same time as Gladstone's campaign against the Irish Church, gave public thinking on this issue a direction which was inevitably unfortunate for the Liberal party. The Irish Church question tended, among working men in particular, to be identified with the old struggle between English and Irish, Protestant and Roman Catholic. Moreover, the riots encouraged Conservative controversialists, and particularly clerical controversialists, to go much farther than they would otherwise have done. One vicar described Gladstone as Antichrist, another spoke of him as a

[1] H.O./45, O.S. 7991/48.   [2] *Manchester Guardian*, 5 September 1868.
[3] *Manchester City News*, 19 September 1868.

Roman Catholic in disguise, a third erected Orange placards in his church and Sunday school. The following notice, for instance, appeared in Preston:

THE QUEEN OR THE POPE?

Englishmen, which will you have to reign over you? The Queen or the Pope? Will you permit Gladstone to take away the supremacy of your Sovereign, and hand it over to the Pope? Dr. Manning, the Pope's emissary, says it is evident that the supremacy of the Church perisheth, and the supremacy of the Pope enters. Englishmen, assert your rights, and show that Union is Strength. Vote only for candidates who will pledge themselves to support the Protestant religion, and maintain the Institutions of the country.

Britons never shall be slaves.[1]

Although Murphyism was responsible for the atmosphere in which the election was fought, the decisive election issues in South-East Lancashire were not those connected with it, but questions of capital and labour. The cotton operatives were well organised, comparatively well paid, and very conscious that they had never fully shared the political views of the Liberal merchants and manufacturers who had dominated the old constituencies. The Reform Act had for the first time enabled them to play a part in elections, and circumstances conspired to make it a decisive part.

The old electorate in the cotton towns, although it included a minority of Chartists and Tories, was largely composed of those who had supported the Anti-Corn-Law League, and their descendants. The issues which divided it were issues which had by-and-large divided the Anti-Corn-Law League; for instance, the left wing which followed Bright favoured manhood suffrage, while the right wing which followed Sir Thomas Bazley favoured a narrower franchise such as Russell's 1866 Bill had proposed. In the eyes of Cobden, who had for a time united them for his purpose, the two wings of the League were so different in their political attitudes that there was no possibility of their continuing to work together after the repeal of the Corn Laws.[2] But in

---

[1] *Preston Guardian*, 28 November 1868.

[2] Cobden wrote to a friend in 1857: 'The great capitalist class formed an excellent basis for the Anti-Corn-Law movement, for they had inexhaustible purses, which they opened freely in a contest where not only their pecuniary interests but their pride as "an order" was at stake. But I very much doubt whether such a state of society is favourable to a democratic political movement . . .' John Morley, *The Life of Richard Cobden*, London 1881, II, 199.

the eyes of working men who had given their adherence to Chartism rather than the League, there was little to choose between Bright and Bazley on issues which concerned them. Bright's idealism generally held out more promise for the future, but his opposition to the Ten Hours Movement, and to the Factory Bills which Shaftesbury had introduced, his general distrust of trade unions, and his avowed opposition to labour representation in Parliament, had prevented him from winning over a majority of working men.[1] Bazley's much more positive dislike of trade unions, and his advocacy of employers' associations (he became the leading member of the National Federation of Associated Employers in 1873) necessarily made him an even less desirable political leader.

There was, moreover, a further serious complication which hampered Bright and his followers in their search for working-class votes. This was the continued existence in Newall's Buildings in Manchester of the machinery created by the Anti-Corn-Law League and its more Radical successor-Leagues for manipulating elections. The distrust which Liverpool Liberals felt towards those who controlled this machinery, and particularly for George Wilson, its manager, has already been mentioned. But the distrust felt in some Manchester circles was equally strong. Wilson and his allies, headed by Hugh Mason and Sir Elkanah Armitage, seemed unable to resist the temptation to meddle and intrigue in parliamentary and municipal elections in such a way that they always appeared to be putting forward candidates without prior consultation with their fellow Liberals. In 1857 this had cost them dear, since the feeling that the ghost of the League was endeavouring to dictate the politics of Manchester was an important factor in the defeat of Bright and Milner Gibson in Manchester when Palmerston appealed to the country after his defeat in the House of Commons on the question of British intervention in China. For the *Manchester Guardian* this was, indeed, the chief issue of the campaign,[2] and Cobden (who was deputising for Bright, who was ill) took it very seriously. In a letter to his wife before the elections he wrote: 'There have been many defections, and unless our friends are giving themselves needless

[1] For Bright's views on labour representation see *The Public Letters of the Right Hon. John Bright, M.P.*, ed. H. J. Leech, London 1885, pp. 179-81.

[2] *Manchester Guardian*, 20 March 1857 and *passim*.

alarm, I fear the chances are greatly against us. The cause chiefly assigned is less an alteration of opinion than a feeling of resistance towards the ghost of the League, which still persists in haunting Newall's Buildings, and, as is alleged, dictates to Manchester.'[1]

Wilson and his friends hastened to patch up a truce with their opponents after the 1857 election. They succeeded almost at once with the Palmerstonian Liberals, whose spokesman was Thomas Bazley, and he was adopted as a Newall's Buildings candidate in 1859.[2] But the left-wing Radicals, many of them with Chartist connections, were not so easily pacified, and put up their own candidate, Abel Heywood, in both 1859 and 1865. However, in 1867, they, too, came into the alliance and formed the United Liberal Party, whose first candidate, Jacob Bright, was returned to parliament at a by-election later in the year. Early in 1868 Newall's Buildings extended the coalition still further by making an alliance with the Reform League and other working-class organisations for the purposes of the coming election. Three candidates were thereupon adopted: Bazley to represent the Whigs and Palmerstonian Liberals, Jacob Bright to represent the middle-class reformers who looked to his brother's leadership, and Ernest Jones, the former Chartist, to represent the working-class Radicals and the Irish electors with whom he had lately made a name as counsel for the defence of the Fenians who had shot Police-Sergeant Brett.[3]

The weakness of this arrangement, like all of those which came out of Newall's Buildings, was that it was so obviously contrived. It smacked of dictation, of corrupt manipulation, and of bartering principles for temporary political advantage, and because it was arrived at behind closed doors there was no opportunity to conciliate potential opposition or to arouse popular enthusiasm. The whole thing seemed to be a sort of conjuring trick capable of making men gape but not of winning their

---

[1] Morley, *Cobden*, II, 192. This was not, of course, the only cause. Other Cobdenite candidates were defeated simply by an alliance of Conservatives and Palmerstonian Liberals.

[2] The old struggle was still carried on in Salford, however, and in 1859 Henry Ashworth stood against W. N. Massey, a 'Whig' who had defeated Sir Elkanah Armitage in 1857. This contest still rankled in 1868 and a contest between rival Liberals was only narrowly averted by the adoption of Massey as one of the Liberal candidates for Liverpool.

[3] The final arrangements were reported in the *Manchester City News*, 20 June 1868. There is a file of clippings and miscellaneous material concerning Jones's candidature in the Manchester Central Library. See also J. Saville, *Ernest Jones, Chartist*, London 1952.

sympathies. Thus when a right-wing opposition was got up, there was no corresponding left-wing enthusiasm to counter it. The 1868 election thus got off to a very bad start, and the lost ground was never recovered, since it proved almost impossible for Bazley, Bright, and Jones to find a common platform beyond the conventional Liberal platitudes. There was, indeed, something almost comic about the way in which Bazley talked about Indian cotton, Bright about women's suffrage, and Jones about the conditions of the agricultural labourer, as a substitute for a programme.

The nature of the opposition which had developed from the right made the position of the three allies all the more embarrassing. For Mitchell Henry, who came forward as an 'Independent Liberal' candidate, based his campaign solely on opposition to the unnatural alliance between Ernest Jones and the more orthodox Liberals. 'For his own part he was convinced that if Mr. Ernest Jones maintained the principles for which, in the political field, he had long been celebrated, they were not the principles which belonged to true Liberalism, or which were in favour with this constituency.'[1] He was fortified in his candidature by a requisition containing 11,000 names, by the support of the *Manchester Evening News* (which he himself financed), and by the implied support of the *Manchester Guardian*, which gave his meetings much more attention than those of his opponents. On the other hand, Mitchell Henry himself, although of vaguely Radical leanings and afterwards Isaac Butt's chief lieutenant in the Commons, was not the man to win working-class votes without the support of the 'official' party leaders, and it was tacitly assumed throughout that he would end his campaign at the bottom of the poll.[2] Of trade unions, for instance, he said: 'He had no fear of trade unionists but, on account of the outrages which had been practised, he should like the name to be got rid of, and that they should be called "Friendly Trades Societies".'[3] He made it clear, too, that like Bazley, and to a lesser extent even Bright, he shared the *Manchester Guardian's* view that trade unions were objectionable in principle because they were

established solely and avowedly for the purpose of keeping down the number of workers in each particular branch of labour, and the rate

[1] *Manchester Guardian*, 2 September 1868.
[2] For Henry see *D.N.B.*, 2 supplement. See also an able pamphlet by W. Stokes, *The Representation of Manchester. Who shall be its Third Member?* Manchester 1868.
[3] *Manchester Guardian*, 1 September 1868.

of speed at which the work shall be done, in order that the unionists may obtain the most money for the least work. There is not even a pretence that the public good is served by a selection of superior workmen or any test of capacity. The unionist may or may not be skilled and apt in his work; all that the union knows or cares concerning him is that he pays his subscription regularly and obeys the orders of the Committee as to how little work he shall do in a given number of hours and how much money he shall insist upon as wages.[1]

The Liberal party in the cotton towns round Manchester suffered in much the same way as the Liberal party in Manchester itself from the imputation that it was controlled by wire-pullers. The feeling was strongest in the 'border' towns of Salford, Stockport, Stalybridge, and Ashton, and in Stockport an attempt was made by J. B. Smith, as we have seen,[2] to minimise it. North of Manchester it was weaker, being of practically no importance in Rochdale and Bury, where the Liberal members were personally very acceptable to the electors, and counting as only one factor among many in Oldham and Bolton, where Liberal organisation was extremely weak. In the case of Bolton, in particular, the charges against the wire-pullers had been almost lost sight of because the Liberal party was divided on the temperance issue. The Reform League's agents reported from the town in September 1868: 'The political position in this borough is peculiar. Liberalism is very strong, but the Liberal candidates, Pope and Barnes, being Teetotallers, many of the liberals will be opposed to them on that account. The Magisterial Bench is mostly composed of teetotallers, and in some cases which have been brought before them they exhibited a very intolerant spirit.'[3] The situation was the more unfortunate for the Bolton Liberals in that one of the candidates, Samuel Pope, had been more or less forced upon the party, although the fact that he was honorary secretary of the United Kingdom Alliance made him a dubious asset as a candidate, because he was the only candidate who could be found who was willing to pay his own expenses.

The Conservatives had had so little success in their attempts to woo the old middle-class electors of South-East Lancashire before 1867, that it was not until the 1868 election campaign was

[1] *Manchester Guardian*, 14 October 1868.
[2] Above pp. 94-5.   [3] Reform League Report: Bolton.

well advanced that it became apparent that they were much more successful with the new electors. And by the time the elections were over it was clear that the Conservatives had scored a great victory, and had put an end to the comfortable old struggle between Liberal and Liberal. Instead of one Conservative being returned and eleven Liberals as was the case in 1865, eight Conservatives were returned and seven Liberals. Bury and Rochdale remained firmly Liberal by substantial majorities, but in Oldham the Liberal majority was only six, and the town returned a Conservative at a by-election in 1872 and again at the general election in 1874, while all the rest of the boroughs returned at least one Conservative.[1] The size of the Conservative vote was, if anything, even more impressive than the number of Conservative victories. At Oldham where the Liberals held on to both seats the 1868 poll was:

Hibbert (L)	6,140
Platt (L)	6,122
Cobbett (C)	6,116
Spinks (C)	6,084

whereas the 1865 poll had been:

Hibbert (L)	1,105
Platt (L)	1,076
Cobbett (C)	898
Spinks (C)	845

Conservatism had long been much stronger in the cotton towns around Manchester than in Manchester itself, particularly at municipal elections.[2] The absence of a Conservative 'upper crust'

---

[1] Ashton and Stalybridge each returned one Conservative, Bolton and Salford two, Manchester one Conservative and two Liberals, and Stockport one Conservative and one Liberal.

[2] The close connection between the triumph of the Conservative party in 1868 and its previous success at municipal elections was emphasised by the chairman of the Ashton Conservatives in a letter to the *Manchester Guardian*, 27 November 1868:

The municipal suffrage is . . . household suffrage with a three year's residence. The new Reform Bill is a household suffrage with a one year's residence. Before the Reform Bill, when the four wards in the borough were all contested at the same time, the Conservatives had a majority on the burgess roll. The Reform Bill having given an equal franchise to the parliamentary electors, they have carried out the same principles and returned a Conservative to Parliament.

of millowners and merchants had given it a popular flavour, which was increased by the establishment of Conservative working men's associations. In places, too, there were pockets of the old democratic Toryism of the forties, whose leader had been Oastler. His old lieutenant, Joseph Rayner Stephens, was the centre of one of these pockets, living on at Stalybridge until 1879, editing local newspapers, and (at intervals) corresponding with members of the Cobbett family, likewise democratic Tories of the old school.[1] Even middle-class Toryism was of a much more popular character than middle-class Liberalism. In each town there were a few traditionally Tory families like the Birleys in Manchester, the Heskeths in Bolton, and the Fernleys in Stockport, who formed the 'aristocracy' of the local Conservative party, whose attitude to the working classes was benevolent and paternal, and who almost automatically provided chairmen of the party. But the leading Conservative workers were usually the clergy, professional men and merchants rather than manufacturers, and most of them were Churchmen and philanthropists even before they were Conservatives.[2] In Manchester many of them belonged to John Shaw's Club, which cultivated old-fashioned ideas of Church and Queen, but which somehow preserved the tradition that it was the duty of Conservatives to succour and defend the working classes. Indeed, the benevolent Toryism of the forties was in process of revival twenty years later, as the older anti-incorporation, almost Eldonian, Tories died out, and were replaced by younger, more adaptable men.

The Tory revival was, however, quite as strong in Manchester itself as in the neighbouring towns, and the 'new Toryism' also drew its leaders largely from Manchester. Two of these personify in their different ways the tendencies of this new Toryism. John William Maclure (1835-1901) was son of the Manchester agent of the Guardian Assurance Company, a keen Churchman who handed on to his son the happy knack of making money easily. He entered his father's office young after a wild boyhood, and immediately became involved in the work of the leading Anglican

---

[1] G. J. Holyoake, *Life of Joseph Rayner Stephens*, London 1881, *passim.* John Morgan Cobbett, son of William Cobbett, was first Liberal and then Conservative M.P. for his father's old constituency, Oldham, 1852-65, 1872-7. It was probably the influence of Stephens that led the Ashton and Stalybridge Conservatives to support the ballot.

[2] Not everyone was content with the tacit alliance of the Church and the Conservative party, but even the energy of the Liberal Bishop Fraser was not sufficient to disturb it. cp. J. W. Diggle, *The Lancashire Life of Bishop Fraser*, 6 edn, London 1890.

charitable and missionary societies. He became secretary of the Central Relief Committee and its chief executive officer during the cotton famine, and in this way became known in London and won the friendship of Lord Derby and Lord Sefton (whom he used to meet once a year for a hot-pot supper and a visit to the pantomime). After the famine he was appointed treasurer of the South-Lancashire Conservative Association under W. R. Callender, and from this post he was promoted in 1868 to become chairman of the Manchester Conservative Association. His rubicund countenance and stock of jokes made him a capital platform speaker, but he never took politics seriously enough to become ambitious for office and did not enter parliament until 1886. His interests lay more with the Church of England, in particular with Manchester Cathedral, of which he was churchwarden for seventeen years and of which his brother was Dean from 1890 to 1906, in the building of parish churches, in business, and in his hobbies, of which the best known was his own invention, the Early Rising Association.[1]

William Romaine Callender the younger (1825-76), was a man of very different type. He was a puritan where Maclure was a *bon viveur*, and he came of a Liberal nonconformist family. His father was a cotton manufacturer, an active Liberal and city councillor, and a leader of the Anti-Corn-Law League, but young Callender reacted against the narrowness of his father's Liberalism and before he was of age became associated with the Conservatives. He was troubled by the conditions in which working men lived and became a champion of trade unions and co-operative societies (along with Thomas Hughes), and a strong temperance man under the guidance of his father-in-law Samuel Pope, the honorary secretary of the United Kingdom Alliance. His abomination was what he called 'the degrading doctrines of the so-called "Manchester School"'.

> There are, unfortunately, a large number of persons who look to the laws of so-called political economy and the accumulation of profits, rather than the welfare of the people; they regard an increasing trade and cheap production as the best, if not the only test of our national welfare; and they have uniformly opposed any legislation or combination which might shorten the hours of labour, improve the

[1] *Manchester Courier*, 29 January 1901, gives a good account of his career, for which see also *D.N.B.*, 2 supplement.

condition of the workman, or reduce the possibility of accident to the lowest average.[1]

In addition to his strong grasp of principle Callender was a born organiser and created the Conservative organisation in South-East Lancashire. His death in 1876, two years after he had become member for Manchester and shortly before he was to be made a baronet, was a great loss to the party.[2]

Men like Maclure and Callender concentrated all their energies on winning the support of the working men they liked and understood. And they found in the trade unions themselves a number of able lieutenants. Some of these, like Thomas Birtwistle of the Weavers and James Mawdsley of the Spinners, were members of the cotton unions, technicians skilled in negotiating complicated agreements between workmen and masters. But others were members of skilled trades in Manchester, including S. C. Nicholson and W. H. Wood, respectively president and secretary of the Manchester Trades Council, who were both members of the Typographical Association. They had no sympathy with the Manchester school—how could they when one of its leading advocates could say in 1884, 'The majority of men were subject to the law of supply and demand, and received no more for their services than their ability entitled them to. . . . He knew that pensions had one effect, to discourage thrift and put a premium upon idleness.'[3]

None the less, it came as a surprise to both Liberals and Conservatives to find that the elections went so decisively in favour of the latter. The Conservative campaign had all along been attuned to working-class attitudes but it had been a quiet campaign, as if the candidates knew that they were untried men and that they had little chance to do more than assert their principles and to wait for better days.[4] The candidates in Ashton, Bury,

[1] W. R. Callender, Jun., *Trades Unions Defended*, Manchester 1870, p. 11. Callender also published *Suggestions on Reform*, Manchester 1866, and other pamphlets.
[2] It was partly compensated for by the emergence of W. H. Houldsworth as a political force after 1880. Houldsworth held very much the same views as Callender and was another skilful organiser. For Callender's life see *Manchester Courier*, 24 January 1876 and *Manchester Guardian* 31 January 1876.
[3] *Manchester Examiner and Times*, 12 March 1884, report of speech by George Mason. On this occasion the Manchester Liberal Association passed a resolution disapproving of pensions for public servants.
[4] Spofforth, the Conservative agent, alone seems to have expected victory, and told Taylor the Whip so, as early as May 1868: T. E. Taylor to Disraeli, 1 May 1868. Disraeli Papers.

Rochdale, Salford, Stalybridge and Stockport had never fought an election before; in Manchester itself Hugh Birley had likewise never contested a seat, although Joseph Hoare, his colleague, was a carpet-bagger who had sat for Hull. On the other hand it is easy to see where the strength of the Conservative candidates lay: in the fact that their decided political views made a strong appeal to electors who were anxious to try something new now that the cotton industry had recovered from the famine.

All the unknown Conservatives preached the same parable, which was probably borrowed from W. R. Callender—the importance of the Protestant Church of England to the community and the need for social legislation along the lines already laid down by Lord Shaftesbury and his followers. Nearly all of them pledged themselves unreservedly to support the protection of trade union funds and the legalisation of trade union action,[1] and two of them, T. W. Mellor in Ashton and James Sidebottom in Stalybridge, advocated the adoption of the secret ballot. Even Joseph Hoare, who handled the subject as if it were unfamiliar to him, none the less made the same points as his colleagues.

> The difference between the Conservative and the Liberal creed was as great as that of light and dark. The true liberality of which the Liberals boasted was that it was better to destroy everything than let anything alone; but what was the Conservative creed? To preserve, and, if possible, increase the usefulness of what was good, and to sweep away all that was bad. He should like to know whether the future historian of England would not show 50 years hence, that the Conservatives had cut away what was bad? Was it not the Conservatives who did away with that abominable truck system? . . . Then, who was it that passed that most beneficent act, the Ten Hours' Bill, by which working men and women in the great hives of industry were relieved from the slavery of long hours? It was the Conservatives . . .[2]

But the Conservatives' most effective speakers were Nicholson and Wood, who held a packed meeting of working men in the Free Trade Hall at which only working men were allowed to speak. There they took up what was by now the orthodox

---

[1] The Bolton Conservatives, and Conservative borough members from outside the Manchester district, were not as friendly towards trade unions as the Manchester Conservatives. For instance Edward Hermon, M.P. for Preston, supported Gladstone's Trade Unions Bill, but held that combinations of employers or workmen were harmful: *3 Hansard* CCIV, 2043.

[2] *Manchester Guardian*, 2 November 1868.

Conservative viewpoint, which Nicholson subsequently expressed more concisely in a controversy with a Radical painter in the *Manchester City News*.

Has it for a moment entered the head of our Sir Oracle that most of the 'champions' of his adoration including John Bright . . . are opposed to any legislative interference between the interests of employer and employed, and are advocates of free labour, the doctrine of the notorious Evans? The speeches of John Bright and his followers throughout all the debates upon the Factory and Bleachers' Bills, and other measures of a similar character, having for their aim the improvement of the social status of the working classes, and which were nobly supported by the Conservative party, have been fraught with opposition on that ground. John Bright, however, says he has changed his views with regard to the Factory Bill. . . . But how will he go on with similar enactments which may in future spring up? We all know that he and his party are free traders, and that they believe as much in free trade in labour as in merchandise. It remains, then, to be seen, when the legislation on trade societies is brought forward next season, what party will be the real 'champions' of the rights of labour; and, if I am not very much mistaken in judgment, the bulk of them will be found on the Conservative side of the House, including our worthy senior member.[1]

In Manchester the Conservatives had also the advantage of the reputation of their leading candidate, Hugh Birley. The Birley family's mills figure in *Coningsby*, but the three Birley brothers in Manchester during the sixties, Hugh, Herbert, and Thomas, were partners in Macintosh's, the india-rubber garment manufacturers, and were best known as the leading philanthropists in the city. Hugh devoted his energies mainly to Church extension while Herbert (who had been much influenced by his brother) concentrated on the education of the poor. By 1870 the three brothers were supporting forty schools, in several of which they took classes, as well as helping to provide food and clothes for the poorest children, and in 1875 Bishop Fraser said that they had established at least seven churches costing over £100,000.[2] Hugh felt strongly on the Irish Church issue, although he had never been a politician, and was prevailed upon to stand for Manchester in 1868. Herbert refused to enter politics but became

---

[1] *Manchester City News*, 12 December 1868.
[2] For the Birley family see *Manchester Guardian*, 10 September 1883 and 27 January 1885, *Manchester Courier*, 10 September 1883 and 21 November 1890, and *Manchester City News*, 14 April 1917.

first chairman of both Manchester and Salford School boards in 1870 by the unanimous wish of both parties and held the two offices (except for a short interval between 1885 and 1888 when the more ardent Manchester churchmen chose a clerical chairman) until his death in 1890. Nobody could quarrel seriously with either of the brothers, because they were so sensible, and Jacob Bright in speaking of Hugh after the declaration of the poll in 1868 said that the new member was 'a man of character, and one who in all his private relations will do honour to the town'.

The Manchester result is an interesting one because it shows more clearly than the others how the new electors were divided. The result declared was as follows:

Birley (C)	.	.	.	. 15,486
Bazley (L)	.	.	.	. 14,192
Bright (L)	.	.	.	. 13,514
Hoare (C)	.	.	.	12,684
Jones (L)	.	.	.	10,662
Henry (Indep. L)	.	.	.	5,236[1]

The votes may be distributed between the various parties roughly as follows:

Liberals	.	.	.	. 18,491
Conservatives	.	.	.	13,121
Liberal-Conservatives and Right-				
Wing Liberals	.	.	.	4,722
Indeterminate	.	.	.	763

But the real interest of the votes lay in the way in which they were distributed in various parts of the city (Table XVI). Jones, as was to be expected, did very badly in the middle-class suburbs and the city centre and not very much better in the mixed middle- and working-class districts. But both he and Birley were over 600 votes ahead of the other Liberals and Hoare in Ancoats and Miles Platting, where the Chartists had always been strongest and where there was also a Conservative tradition.[2] The most remarkable

[1] Henry announced his withdrawal at 1 p.m. but too late to affect the result. The official figures given above do not exactly correspond to those in Table XVI because the returns for some of the wards were inaccurate.

[2] W. R. Callender in *Suggestions for Reform*, p. 7, spoke of the Ancoats district as always having been regarded as 'most unfavourable to the Liberal party'.

Table XVI. The Manchester Election, 1868

	Conservative		Liberal		Indep. Liberal
	Birley	Hoare	Bazley	Bright	Jones	Henry
Middle-class districts (St Ann's and St Luke's Wards)	1,523	1,198	1,271	1,193	864	608
City Centre (commercial and mixed residential) (Exchange, St James's, St John's, Oxford, and Collegiate Church Wards)	2,548	2,133	2,514	2,355	1,046	892
Mixed Residential districts. Cheetham, Newton, Ardwick, and Beswick and Bradford Wards)	3,123	2,549	3,003	2,709	1,724	1,239
Working-class districts N. (St Michael's, New Cross, and St Clement's Wards)	4,327	3,646	3,719	3,747	4,477	1,233
Working-class districts S. (St George's, Medlock St and All Saints' Wards).	3,983	3,158	3,685	3,514	2,551	1,264

result was that in Hulme and Chorlton-on-Medlock, the South Manchester working-class districts in which the Birleys did most of their social work; there Jones was 600 votes behind Hoare, 900 below Bright and 1,400 below Birley. Hulme, in other words, had already become the Tory stronghold it was to remain (except for occasional lapses) until 1945, and the home of the Manchester Conservative working man.

An outsider's comments on the election serve to complete the picture. A few days after the polling was over Engels wrote to Marx to report the results in Lancashire.

> What do you say to the elections in the factory districts? Once again the proletariat has discredited itself terribly. Manchester and Salford return three Tories to two Liberals, including moreover the milk-and-water Bazley. Bolton, Preston, Blackburn, etc., practically nothing but Tories. In Ashton it looks as if M. Gibson went to the wall. Ernest Jones nowhere, despite the cheering. Everywhere the proletariat is the tag, rag and bobtail of the official parties, and if any party has gained strength from the new voters, it is the Tories.

The small towns, the half-rotten boroughs, are the salvation of bourgeois liberalism and the roles will be reversed: the Tories will now be in favour of more members for the big towns and the Liberals for unequal representation.

Here the electors have increased from 24,000 to not quite 48,000, while the Tories have increased their voters from 6,000 to 14,000-15,000. The Liberals allowed much to slip by them and Mr. Henry did a lot of damage, but it cannot be denied that the increase of working-class voters has brought the Tories more than their simple percentage increase; it has improved their relative position. On the whole this is to the good. It looks at present as if Gladstone will get a *narrow* majority and so be compelled to keep the ball rolling and reform the Reform Act; with a big majority he would have left it all to Providence as usual.[1]

V

The 1868 election was not the end of the flight from Liberalism in Lancashire. For several years more the Conservatives continued to gain ground at municipal elections—in some cases until as late as 1877—while the 1874 general election was another Conservative triumph. Some seats won in 1868 were lost again, but in a spectacular fight between Hugh Birley and W. R. Callender on the Conservative side and Sir Thomas Bazley and Jacob Bright on the Liberal, the Manchester Conservatives carried both their men and ousted Bright. Moreover, contrary to all expectations, the Conservatives were able to hold all eight county seats won in 1868. North Lancashire and South-West Lancashire, where Hartington and Gladstone had been defeated in 1868, were yielded to the Conservatives unopposed, and in South-East Lancashire there was a Conservative majority of 1,500. The Liberals were in sight of victory only in North-East Lancashire where there was a nominal Liberal majority on the register and where the 1868 dispute about candidates had been settled by putting up Lord Edward Cavendish and Sir James Kay-Shuttleworth, who came within a hundred votes of a seat.

After 1874, however, the pendulum began to swing against the Conservatives. The Conservative majorities, even in 1874, were not large enough to offer any hope of a permanent Conservative supremacy, yet instead of working hard to retain the allegiance of their supporters, many of the Conservatives, particularly in

[1] *Karl Marx and Frederick Engels on Britain*, Moscow 1953, pp. 499-500.

Manchester, were inclined to become complacent and to let the party organisation decay. They were, therefore, quite unable to cope with the bitterness and political confusion which arose from the great labour disputes of the late seventies, and from these the Liberals profited. Indeed, while the Liberal National Reform Union issued thoroughly dishonest circulars and placards blaming the Conservative government for the depression in the cotton industry, on the ground that it had increased government expenditure and had imposed a tariff in India, the Conservatives did nothing.[1] As a consequence, the Lancashire electorate was attracted, almost as much as the electorate in the rest of the country, by the promise of prosperity and good times to come held out from Midlothian. The prospects of the Liberals were in fact so good by the end of 1879 that Lord Hartington emerged again from Wales and put up in his brother's place for North-East Lancashire, where he won the seat from which the Shuttleworths' obstinacy had kept him in 1868. North Lancashire and South-West Lancashire remained Conservative, but both North-East and South-East Lancashire were lost to the Liberals, along with Ashton, Bolton, Clitheroe, Oldham, Salford, Stalybridge and Warrington, and the second seat for Manchester, and the Conservatives had to wait until 1885 to regain their lost ground. Then they won thirty-eight of the fifty-eight seats granted to Lancashire under the Redistribution Act, including eight out of nine in Liverpool and five out of six in Manchester.

[1] There is a selection of Liberal and Conservative circulars and cartoons of the period in the Manchester Central Library.

Chapter Fifteen

WORKING-CLASS RADICALISM

I

THE chief interests of working-class leaders for the twenty years after 1867 were social and not political. They were concerned to win, both for the skilled working men and for their trade unions, a much more prominent position in society, and in particular a legal revolution in their relations with the employers. The task seemed urgent because the year of the Reform Act was also the year of the Royal Commission on Trade Unions which seemed at first to threaten the very existence of trade unionism, and the year before the decision in Hornby v. Close deprived trade unions of all legal protection for their funds because their objects were held not to be such as the law could approve.[1] The storm soon passed, however, and in its wake came both a friendly Conservative government, which gave the unions all the legal protection they asked for and (in a concealed form) the nine-hour day, and a boom in trade unionism. From 1867 to 1876 the union leaders made almost continuous advances, which seemed to be so great that direct political action was unnecessary. In the eloquent words of the Webbs:

> In 1867 the officials of the Unions were regarded as pothouse agitators, 'unscrupulous men, leading a half idle life, fattening on the contributions of their dupes', and maintaining, by violence and murder, a system of terrorism, which was destructive, not only of the industry of the nation, but also of the prosperity and independence of character of the unfortunate working men who were their victims. . . . In 1875 the officials of the great societies found themselves elected to the local School Boards, and even to the House of Commons, pressed by the Government to accept seats on Royal Commissions, and respectfully listened to in the lobby. And these

[1] For trade unionism at this period see S. and B. Webb, *The History of Trade Unionism*, new edn, London 1920, G. D. H. Cole and A. W. Filson, *British Working-Class Movements: Select Documents 1789-1875*, London 1951, and B. C. Roberts, *The Trades Union Congress 1868-1921*, London 1958. For working-class Radicalism see G. D. H. Cole, *British Working-Class Politics 1832-1914*, London 1941.

political results were but the signs of an extraordinary expansion of the Trade Union Movement itself. 'The year just closed,' says the report of the Parliamentary Committee in January 1874, 'has been unparalleled for the rapid growth and development of Trade Unionism. In almost every trade this appears to have been the same; but it is especially remarkable in those branches of industry which have hitherto been but badly organised.'[1]

Even the sudden end of this prosperity in 1878-9 did not convert the unions to political action. This was partly, no doubt, because the trade unionists felt themselves still to be members of a minority movement. In terms of the total labour force of the country the trade unionists were little more than an élite, numbering perhaps a million and a quarter at the peak of the boom in 1874-5 (about 600,000 were regular unionists as distinct from temporary adherents), and not much more than three-quarters of a million in 1878-9.[2] But the real reason for the apathy of trade unions was the firmly rooted belief in *laisser-faire*, which was almost universally held by all classes, and the fact that the political imagination of the electorate was already dominated by the rival claims of Joseph Chamberlain and Gladstone on the one hand, and of Beaconsfieldism on the other. Even the one nationally-recognised working-class political organisation of the day, the Labour Representation League, was dwarfed out of existence by their rivalry. At the same time the growth of the new popular Liberal Associations virtually destroyed such opportunities as working men had hitherto possessed of promoting the candidature of independent working-class Radicals or of striking a bargain with the local Liberal leaders, with the result that there were fewer working-men candidates in 1880 than in 1874: six against eleven.[3]

Such working-class political activity as there was between 1867 and 1880 was restricted not only by the comparative indifference of many trade unionists, but by divisions in the working-class world. Four different sets of people concerned themselves with the welfare of the working classes. First, there was the 'Junta' of

---

[1] S. and B. Webb, *History of Trade Unionism*, pp. 325-6.

[2] There are no precise figures: for some estimates see the Webbs' *History of Trade Unionism*, p. 326, and G. D. H. Cole, *Short History of the British Working-Class Movement 1789-1947*, London 1948, p. 275.

[3] Three of them were successful as against two in 1874. One of them, Henry Broadhurst, was a creature of the caucus, and was later transplanted from Stoke to Birmingham.

trade union officials, who from 1860 to 1870 dominated the trade union movement through the London Trades Council and its successors, headed by Henry Broadhurst, who alike 'believed that a levelling down of all political privileges, and the opening out of educational and social opportunities to all classes of the community, would bring in its train a large measure of economic equality'.[1] Secondly, there were the increasingly influential provincial trade union leaders, whose interests were largely confined to the welfare of their own unions and their own districts, but who had London connections, first through the Junta's rival, the London Working Men's Association, and afterwards through the Trades Union Congress. Thirdly, there were the Radical clubs all over the country, some of them lingering remnants of Chartism, some no more than trade union lodges or friendly societies which met in a congenial public-house, some semi-revolutionary underground organisations with mysterious continental or Irish connections. They were the forcing ground both for the local trades councils which grew up during the sixties and seventies, and, to a lesser degree, for the First International. Finally there were the middle-class patrons of working-class organisations; some philanthropists like Samuel Morley, some deeper politicians like Frederic Harrison and the Positivists.

The Junta was very conscious of the need to bring all four elements in the working-class world together. The national character of the amalgamated unions gave it extensive union connections in the provinces, although it was prevented from making full use of them by the hostility of the leaders of the independent provincial unions, who in 1868 formed a rival organisation, the Trades Union Congress.[2] The Junta also did its best to build up through its offshoot, the Reform League, a permanent alliance of the Radical clubs, rather in the Chartist tradition, and was in time able to hand on these country connections to the Labour Representation League. Above all, the Junta was on friendly terms with all the middle-class Radicals friendly to trade unionism and working-class political organisations. But the influence of the Junta was nearly spent by 1868, and during the next

[1] S. and B. Webb, *History of Trade Unionism*, p. 241.
[2] A. E. Musson, *The Congress of 1868: The Origins and Establishment of the Trades Union Congress*, London 1955.

five years it steadily declined as a national force. The Reform League (with which this chapter is primarily concerned) came to an end after the general election of 1868: Robert Applegarth was driven out of his union in 1871 as a result of a personal vendetta against him,[1] George Odger, the Junta's protégé and orator, abandoned trade unionism for republican politics about the same time, and William Allan of the Amalgamated Engineers died in 1874.

The break-up of the Junta left a vacuum which no one was able to fill. The most prominent individual trade unionists after 1874 were men like Henry Broadhurst and George Shipton, who followed very closely the traditions of the Junta, and who led the Parliamentary Committee of the Trades Union Congress, which had been set up in 1869 to watch over the legislative interests of the trade union movement.[2] But they were rather skilled negotiators than generals. Effective power in the trade union world had passed to the miners and the cotton unions, but they had no desire to lead a national movement, and were only mildly interested in the Trades Union Congress. Their work was confined to certain districts, their trade battles were not national battles, and their interest in politics was an essentially local one. The miners were pioneers of labour representation, and counted among their number the first two working-class M.P.s, Thomas Burt and Alexander Macdonald, and six of the eleven working men elected in 1885. But they had no theory of representation beyond the general belief that it was good that working men should sit in parliament, and they had no particular programme beyond that of orthodox Radicalism. The miners' leaders were sent to parliament primarily because the miners formed a closely-knit community, loyal to its leaders, and constituting a majority of the electors in Morpeth, and, after 1885, in a number of other constituencies. By contrast, the members of the cotton unions were so scattered that there was no question of their returning a member of their own, and so divided politically that political action by the unions was almost impossible. Several of the

---

[1] He resigned voluntarily, but the bitterness of disputes within the union had made his position extremely uncomfortable if not untenable. There are interesting MS. biographical sketches of working-class leaders at this period in the Howell Collection at the Bishopsgate Institute.

[2] S. and B. Webb, *History of Trade Unionism*, p. 362: Roberts, *Trades Union Congress*, pp. 65f.

leading cotton union officials were Tories, including the most able of them, Thomas Birtwistle, and in any case, Lancastrians were primarily Lancastrians, not trade unionists. There was very little pressure for labour representation in the cotton towns until the late eighties, when the old party balance was destroyed by the alliance of Conservatives and Liberal Unionists.

The particularism of the miners and cotton men had always been shared by the local political 'clubs', and it was the failure to mobilise them in favour of a specifically working-class policy which really determined that there should be little in the way of national working-class politics after the decline of the Junta and the Reform League. The Labour Representation League (1870-80) depended almost entirely on the local clubs for opportunities to put forward candidates and to propagate the idea of labour representation, but it was in every way an amateurish body and speedily came to an end.[1] Instead of working-class connections the clubs obtained middle-class connections, which were necessarily local. Occasionally leading working-class spokesmen like Odger or Howell or Potter would go on a mission tour in the provinces and address the clubs, but usually they had to rely on the local middle-class Radical leaders who financed them. Indeed, in many cases the clubs had deliberately been formed by local employers of Radical sentiments for political ends of their own. One of the Reform League's most effective 'branches' was at Braintree in Essex under the auspices of Courtaulds, and one of the first actions taken by John Edward Ellis after assuming the management of a new pit at Hucknall in Nottinghamshire was to form a Radical organisation among his workmen.[2] Such clubs soon became the most effective support of the Radical wing of local Liberal associations, and where the 'Birmingham model' was adopted, were soon quite absorbed in the Liberal machine. In Leeds even the branch of the Labour Representation League seems to have been virtually absorbed in this way.[3] Small wonder that men like Lloyd Jones and George Howell protested that whatever the situation in Birmingham, the usual effect of the

[1] Cole, *British Working-Class Politics*, Chapters V and VI. I have avoided treating the Labour Representation League in detail because its story duplicates so much of that of the Reform League. The papers of both bodies are preserved in the Bishopsgate Institute.

[2] Bassett, *John Edward Ellis*, pp. 22f. Ellis's political influence is all the more interesting in that he had a good deal of labour trouble over wages in the colliery.

[3] Howes, *Twenty-Five Years' Fight with the Tories*, Ch. III.

caucus would be 'traps in which to shut up the working men of the country'.[1]

The current was running so strongly during the seventies in favour of absorption of all working men in the Liberal party that even the First International succumbed, and it was not until 1881 that the Democratic Federation was founded by Hyndman, and the Labour Emancipation League grew out of the East London Radical clubs. Thereafter the socialists formed an important element in working-class politics, although by no means the dominant one, and the way was prepared for the rise of the Labour Party.[2]

The trade unions' middle-class friends headed by Frederic Harrison, E. S. Beesly and A. J. Mundella, reached the height of their influence in 1867-8 with their successful manipulation of the evidence presented to the Royal Commission on Trade Unions. Thereafter, men like Mundella (who was returned to parliament for the first time in 1868) became relatively less influential, not because they were less active but because the status of the trade unions themselves had grown. The sort of victories which could be won by lobbying could be won just as effectively by the lobbyists of the Trades Union Congress as by its middle-class friends. And after 1874 the presence of two working men in the House itself greatly reduced the need for spokesmen there to put a purely working-class point of view. The old friends of the trade unions still kept up a 'family correspondence' with the union leaders, but it made no great claim to political significance.[3] Few of them, in any case, were interested in labour representation or working-class politics except within the context of the Liberal party. They were all or nearly all very orthodox Radical back-benchers of Gladstonian sympathies, and could not envisage a working-class political movement outside the Liberal party. They occupied, in short, the office of honorary

[1] Lloyd Jones in the *Industrial Review*, 31 August 1878, quoted by Pelling, *America and the British Left*, p. 46. Howell wrote an article for the *New Quarterly Magazine* (X, 579-90) in 1878 to point out the danger that the caucus system would in practice put power in the hands of those who paid the expenses of local associations while seeming to give it to working men.

[2] For this period see Henry Pelling, *The Origins of the Labour Party*, London 1954, and Cole, *British Working-Class Politics*, Chapters VII and VIII.

[3] For two interesting accounts of this correspondence see H. W. McCready, 'The British Election of 1874: Frederic Harrison and the Liberal-Labour Dilemma', *Canadian Journal of Economics and Political Science*, XX, 166-75 (1954), and 'British Labour's Lobby 1867-75', *Ibid.*, XXII, 141-60 (1956).

family solicitors to the trade union movement, not that of political leaders.

II

The most important and most interesting working-class political organisation of our period was the Reform League, which had been formed early in 1865 in an attempt to unite working-class Radicals all over the country in pressing for manhood suffrage and the ballot.[1] It had a middle-class president, Edmond Beales, and various middle-class members, but most of its members were working men, and its secretary was George Howell, a leading trade unionist. Moreover, although its headquarters were in London (it had offices off the Strand) its influence was largely derived from its provincial branches, of which there were 430 by mid-1867, and from associated Leagues in Scotland or Ireland, most of which were really independent local 'clubs'. On the other hand its influence was limited by the activity of two rival organisations, the National Reform Union in Manchester, a middle-class body with less Radical objectives and with a considerable working-class membership in parts of Lancashire and Yorkshire, and the London Working Men's Association, a trade union organisation set up as a rival of the London Trades Council.[2]

The League won for itself during 1866 and 1867 an unenviable reputation for extremist views and violence, because it was engaged in the Hyde Park demonstrations during which the railings round the park were torn down and many inflammatory speeches made, particularly by Charles Bradlaugh. But it was in fact quite a moderate organisation. Indeed, its moderation was such that Disraeli's Reform Bill quite took the wind out of its sails, and its leaders scarcely knew what to do next. Even worse for an organisation of its type, the Reform Bill meant the end of subscriptions from middle-class Radicals who had been paying for an agitation for parliamentary reform, not for the formation of a working-class

[1] For its early history see F. E. Gillespie, *Labor and Politics in England 1850-65,* Durham, North Carolina, 1927. The account which follows is based on its MS. records in the Bishopsgate Institute, London.

[2] The L.W.M.A. had only 5 branches and 600 members in London in 1867, whereas the League had about 100 branches in London and a correspondingly large number of members. G. D. H. Cole in his *British Working-Class Politics* rather overemphasises the importance of the L.W.M.A., which for all practical purposes came to an end in July 1868 and was not re-formed until much later.

political movement.[1] For a time, therefore, the League became little more than a weekly debating society where ill-digested ideas on current questions were aired by such members of the London clubs as cared to attend. Indeed, it very nearly broke up when an energetic firebrand named Finlen carried a resolution in support of Fenianism, which had later to be rescinded at the insistence of the officers.

The officers of the League were determined not to allow it to die, and set themselves to work out a new policy going farther than the original objectives. The northern branches, which in common with most of the others had come to have only nominal contact with headquarters, were invited to give their views at a conference held in Manchester in May 1867. But nothing emerged from the conference except the obvious fact that the branches were waiting for a lead from London.[2] This the London Executive Committee set out to provide, on the assumption that the members wished to see the League transformed into a national association of working-class Radicals capable of expressing a distinctively working-class point of view on questions of the day. The first steps were rather prosaic: in July 1867 James Acland was appointed 'election and registration adviser', a sub-committee was set up to select League candidates and to find constituencies for them, and an appeal for money was directed to the League's middle-class sympathisers.

But although Howell undertook a tour of the northern towns to ask for money, very little was actually forthcoming. A timely £250 from Samuel Morley enabled a course of lectures to be held during the winter, in the vain hope of attracting public attention, but there was not enough money to put the Executive's programme into operation. All that could be done for the moment was to endorse a number of candidates already in the field, either for existing seats or for new seats created by the Reform Bill, as 'League candidates'. These were Edmond Beales for the Tower Hamlets, the Hon. E. Lyulph Stanley for Macclesfield, Colonel

[1] The League's income was derived roughly as follows:

	Income from branches	Middle- and working-class subscriptions	Middle-class donations
April 1865-April 1866	£21. 15. 10.	£116. 6. 0.	£476. 17. 4.
April 1866-April 1867	£236. 5. 11.	£633. 17. 11.	£2172. 17. 0½.
April 1867-April 1868	£43. 19. 3.	£273. 6. 2.	£983. 11. 6.

[2] *Manchester Guardian*, 1 June 1867.

L. S. Dickson for Hackney, and Dr Baxter Langley for Greenwich.[1]

By June 1867, however, it was already clear that there were serious divergences of opinion even within the Executive as to what a 'working-class policy' should be, and in particular as to the approach which should be adopted in the coming elections towards Liberal candidates who were not Leaguers. The dominant school, which was led by Howell and supported by Beales, favoured a frank alliance with Gladstonian Liberalism, and their voice was sufficient to carry a resolution (by six votes to five) that the League should pledge itself 'to secure the return . . . of Members of Parliament pledged to Liberal principles'.[2] Howell and Beales both looked to the gradual rapprochement of the middle and working classes by negotiation and arbitration in political and social matters as much as in the field of labour relations. For, as Beales pointed out, the working classes were themselves fast becoming capitalists.[3] And both regarded middle-class participation in working-class movements as necessary for their success. In Howell's words,

> The greater the element of our Middle Classes in these movements the less violent, and more progressive, will be the results. For then there will be no fear of counter-plotting and reaction.[4]

On the other hand they had no sympathy for the Whigs and Howell encouraged the provincial branches to put up men against them.

> We must go in for the best men we can get to come forward, but better have *new* liberals than old Whigs. *I hate the Whigs.* They have ever been our enemies and are now. . . . We must fight the next election tooth and nail and *if the Whig is doubtful* I personally should prefer a Tory. But of course this is a delicate matter and one which requires care in the working out, but we must tell the professing

---

[1] Howell to G. Jackson, 11 May 1868. Both Stanley and Langley later withdrew their candidature.

[2] Executive Minutes, 17 June 1867.

[3] 'The working classes are themselves deeply interested in the preservation of law and order, of the rights of capital and property, of the honour, and power, and wealth of our country. They are, as members of co-operative, building, and other societies, daily becoming themselves capitalists and landowners.' *Speech of Edmond Beales, Esq., M.A., President of the Reform League, at the Meeting at St. Martin's Hall,* London 1865, p. 11.

[4] Howell to Dr Black, 22 February 1868.

Liberals that their programme must be a good and bold one and their pledges must be kept or they will not do for us.[1]

A second group of Leaguers was less happy about a middle-class alliance, and objected to the proposal to support all Liberals other than Whigs. On the other hand they were unwilling to oppose any reasonably good Liberal, and felt that in cases of doubt rival candidatures (even if one of the candidates were a working man or a League nominee) should be submitted to arbitration. This was broadly speaking the viewpoint of George Odger, who agreed to withdraw from his candidature at Chelsea after arbitrators had recommended him to do so, and of the Manchester and Leeds Reform Leaguers, who felt that for the time being at least they must support all the local Liberal candidates because they had been allowed to nominate one of them. But in practice those who held this viewpoint soon relinquished it either for out-and-out republicanism and hostility to all non-republicans, as was the case with Odger, or for complete identification with the National Education League and the Birmingham caucus.

A third group of Leaguers was composed of what might be called the old-fashioned independent Radicals; men who were very conscious of their principles and who were unwilling to concede anything to circumstance. This group, which was much nearer to the middle-class ultra-Radicals in outlook than to the trade union leaders, was headed by Charles Bradlaugh the atheist, and Benjamin Lucraft, a cabinet-maker, and constituted the most important opposition to Beales and Howell.[2] A fourth group, which was composed mainly of Fenians and continental revolutionaries, objected to anything short of revolutionary action, and was the least influential, although it managed to win some support for its policy of land nationalisation. All these differences of opinion were, of course, reflected in the provincial towns, but the resolute Independents were in a majority in only a few, notably Northampton, Dewsbury and Stafford, and among the Northumberland and Durham miners, and the revolutionaries only among the Irish.

The Reform League was not placed in any immediate difficulty by these differences because Howell and his friends were able to capture a large majority of seats on the Executive in the November

---

[1] Howell to G. Jackson, 11 May 1868.
[2] Bradlaugh eventually became M.P. for Northampton in 1880. Lucraft contested Finsbury in 1874 and the Tower Hamlets in 1880, in each case against two other Liberals and a Conservative.

1867 elections and to use the machinery of the League for their own purposes. In any case action of any sort was out of the question until the election was nearer, or until more money was available. And the most formidable opponent of the Liberal alliance, Bradlaugh, was safely out of the way looking for a seat, so that there was no immediate prospect of trouble from that quarter.

III

By the end of 1867 Beales had virtually dropped out of the inner circle which controlled the Executive of the League, as was natural once it had given up the great popular meetings where his oratory counted for so much. As a result the direction of the League's affairs fell very largely into the hands of George Howell, as secretary. There was nothing he could do at first as the League's funds had 'dwindled down to only a pound or two just to keep our bank acc*t* open' by the beginning of November 1867.[1] A few lectures were given in London and the provinces but that was all. Then came the 1868 parliamentary session with Gladstone's attack on the Irish Church and the provision for an election in November. The electoral sub-committee was revived and a member of the Executive was despatched to help Beales in the Tower Hamlets at the League's expense, and the feeling grew that the organisation built up by the League over the previous three years would be of great importance in the elections. The first result was that at Samuel Morley's request six members of the League, led by Howell, went to Bristol to help him in the by-election he was fighting there as official Liberal candidate.[2] Morley was the League's oldest friend among the middle classes and had always been its chief financial support. At Bristol the old constituency was large, badly organised, corrupt, and factious: the Liberals could never agree among themselves, and the temperance men among them were strongly opposed to Morley (a teetotaller) because he would not support the Permissive Bill; and both candidates lost the election: Morley was defeated and his opponent Miles was unseated on petition. But Howell thought that at Bristol, where much had been done to organise the trade unionists, the result of the League's intervention

[1] Howell to G. T. Floyd, 6 November 1867.
[2] For Morley's connection with the League see Hodder, *Samuel Morley*, pp. 268f. Hodder misinterprets certain events but the main outlines are right.

had been important, and that similar work might be done for other approved candidates elsewhere; or in other words that the doctrine of the middle-class alliance could best be worked out in practice in this way.

To extend the League's activities, however, a great deal of money was required and after the Bristol by-election Morley and James Stansfeld, a leading Liberal and a friend of the League, who had become connected with it through the Italian revolutionaries, agreed to find some. They looked for it in the obvious place, in the Liberal party offices, and interviews were accordingly arranged between Howell and W. R. Cremer, representing the League, and Scudamore Stanhope and W. P. Adam representing Glyn the Chief Whip, who was out of town recovering his health.[1] These interviews were duly reported to the Executive of the League on 15 July, and a resolution was passed which authorised Howell and Cremer to enter into full negotiations with power 'to mention special Boroughs and also to speak in general terms'. The basis for negotiations was a list of boroughs represented by Conservatives which James Acland had already drawn up.[2] Howell proposed that if money were found these seats should become the target of the League's attack, together with any others in which the League or Glyn might be particularly interested, and his scheme was accepted. Stansfeld as a potential cabinet minister wished to avoid any formal connection with the League, and Glyn's name had also to be kept in the background for fear of Whig or Ultra-Radical hostility to the compact, so Morley became treasurer of the 'Special Fund' which he distributed to Howell as necessary.

Howell and Cremer seem to have estimated the cost of their operations as £2,000 to £5,000 with the former as the more likely figure, but they were given only £1,000 for the moment. In the first instance this sum was found partly by Morley, partly by Stansfeld, probably because Glyn had none to spare.[3] There was

---

[1] W. R. Cremer was a leading member of the Amalgamated Society of Carpenters and Joiners, and afterwards became M.P. for the Haggerston division and secretary of the Interparliamentary Union: cp. Howard Evans, *Sir Randal Cremer, His Life and Work*, London 1909. Stanhope, afterwards Earl of Chesterfield, was Glyn's secretary.

[2] This list of 92 constituencies was derived from Acland's *Imperial Poll Book*, London 1867.

[3] The only coherent account of these transactions which survives is contained in letters from Howell to Morley and Stansfeld written in December 1868 and January 1869, and the details are somewhat difficult to disentangle, as so much is assumed as common ground between writer and reader.

then a delay until October when a second grant of £1,000 was made available, as it was necessary to make sure that the money advanced by Stansfeld should be repaid, and that the matter should be kept secret. 'Mr. Stansfeld and Mr. Glyn strongly object to their being known in connection with the matter', Howell remarked in a later letter, and added, 'It was [because of] the fear . . . that these matters would be discussed at our General Council that we had some delay in getting additional cash'. But in spite of these complications a little short of £2,000 was paid over to Howell and spent between July and November.

The League's election operations were conducted in two stages. In the first stage the League sent off delegates in pairs to collect information from those boroughs returning Conservatives. Most of the fifteen men who were sent out were members of the Executive of the League, and all were leading working men either in politics or trade unionism. They were given ten shillings a day for expenses, another ten for loss of earnings, and second-class rail fares—quite a liberal allowance—and gave good value in return, as some of the reports already quoted in this book have shown. The delegates' first task was to visit all the leading trade unionists and Reform Leaguers and any other friendly Liberals to obtain information about the state of the borough in general and about working-class politics in particular. They had then to form a branch of the Reform League or a working-men's Liberal Association if none existed, to hold a general meeting to start it off on the right footing, to settle any internal feuds they had discovered, and to send off a report to London before they went on to the next borough on the list. These reports were sent to Glyn, who was enthusiastic about them in his letters to Gladstone.

> The Reports I have had through the working men from many *doubtful* places are most assuring. . . . They are so sound and so sensible and in most places their great object is to unite the sections of the party for you and not to put up their own or very extreme men.[1]

[1] Add. MS. 44,347, f.154. On the other hand Glyn was rather nervous about his connection with the League, and by next day he was writing, 'I have got into indirect relations with that body and find it most useful but dare not talk about it—they go *for you*.' After he had met Howell and Cremer he was even more nervous: 'Nothing can be more striking than the moderation of these men and their loyalty to *your* cause *but* direct communications with them is a very delicate matter. . . .' Add. MS. 44,347, ff.158 and 212-13.

At this stage the League also entered into an agreement with the Liberation Society and the Peace Society to distribute their pamphlets and other propaganda in return for a donation—£50 in both cases—and quite early in the year over 100,000 Liberation Society pamphlets and leaflets had been sent out.[1] They were useful to the League, since its delegates not infrequently asked that suitable parcels of literature from these and other sources should be sent to key men in the constituencies they had visited.

The second stage of the League's operations was a more systematic attempt, on the lines already mapped out at Bristol, to organise the working-class voters of particular towns. Howell had already offered to help Reform League branches in this way and in some cases to help other Radical associations. Thus at the beginning of August he wrote to one enquirer.

> Our desire is to enquire as to whether we can give some little aid to local effort by operating upon the working class vote through their Trades Societies and other Associations.
>
> We think we can, and are willing to do all in our power to assist to return advanced Liberals to the next Parliament.
>
> *Quite understand that we do not intend interfering with local action in any way.*
>
> If we can supplement local effort we will.[2]

Now, the League began to send delegates to boroughs suggested by Glyn, or to those suggested by Howell and approved by Glyn. Every effort was made to avoid committing the particular Liberal candidate: 'in all instances we take independent action, so as not to commit the candidates in any way. They pay us by giving a donation to our Special Fund.'[3] Most candidates seem to have been actively hostile to the League's endeavours, fearing that any acknowledgement of the League's presence might imply endorsement of the League's policy. But Howell was used to handling such people and could usually quieten their fears. Indeed, his

---

[1] There is a correspondence on this subject in the League's papers with Carvell Williams of the Liberation Society and Talbot of the Peace Society.

[2] Howell to W. Burnfitt, 13 August 1868.

[3] Howell to Leigh Ellis of Wigan, 12 October 1868. The rest of this letter is also informative: 'We are taking very important action in reference to Trade Societies but we must deal with each Borough separately and distinctly. We are managing the unions in Blackburn, Bristol, Preston and a great many of the large towns at this moment and will if you desire it send down a man at once to do something in Wigan. At Sheffield our delegates have done what the local agent could not do viz. unite the numerous trades into one committee for electoral purposes.'

approach to candidates or their agents was quite disarming. Thus he wrote to William Rathbone of Liverpool.

> I am desired to write to you suggesting the desirability of prompt action being taken to get the whole of the organised bodies of Liverpool to aid your election.
> We feel certain of being able to do it but we want to act perfectly loyally to you and to do nothing without your (at least tacit) approval.
> If you desire any testimony as to work already done address a letter either to Mr. James Stansfeld or to Mr. Samuel Morley . . .

> You are quite mistaken as to the import of my letter. You are not supposed to *endorse anything, only tell us to serve you.* We know sufficient of you already . . . in no case would you in any way be mixed up with our movement either in Liverpool or here.[1]

Howell himself undertook a number of special missions for Glyn, notably one to Swindon, but the League's attentions were really concentrated on a small number of boroughs: Blackburn, Rye, Sheffield, Stoke, Brighton, Shoreham, Northampton, Stafford, Worcester, Northallerton, Preston, and a few others. In all these places there was a difficulty in persuading the existing Liberal leaders to coalesce with the working men—Glyn told Gladstone that 'the great difficulty is that the old party managers do not realise the altered state of matters and if they do they are extremely slow to coalesce with the new men'.[2]—or else the working-class voters were seriously disorganised or divided. Both the League and Glyn seem to have thought the most important constituency was Sheffield, where A. J. Mundella, an old friend of the League's, was endeavouring to oust J. A. Roebuck, a famous Radical who was hostile both to Gladstone and to trade unions. William Dronfield, the secretary of the Sheffield Trades Council, had urged the League to help Mundella before there was any question of an alliance with Glyn: 'He is just the right man for Sheffield and will be a great accession to the cause of Labour in the House of Commons.'[3] Goldwin Smith, who was helping Glyn, also asked the League for help at Sheffield, and at

---

[1] These letters from Howell to Rathbone are dated 22 and 27 October 1868.
[2] Glyn to Gladstone, 8 October 1868. Add. MS. 44,347, f.190.
[3] Dronfield to Howell, 27 June 1868. For the Sheffield election see M. Higginbotham: 'A. J. Mundella and the Sheffield Election of 1868', *Transactions of the Hunter Archaeological Society*, V, 285-93 (1943).

the end of August Mundella himself repeated the plea, so there was no lack of encouragement, although the League did very little until in September Glyn mentioned Sheffield as particularly in need of attention. Then two men were despatched who remained there for a fortnight.

Glyn who had for the sake of the party to appear to remain neutral, meanwhile tried to bring other pressure to bear in order to persuade the third Liberal candidate, George Hadfield, to give up his coalition with Roebuck.[1]

In a few places the League's delegates were called upon to suppress unwanted candidates who threatened to split the Liberal vote, and men were driven out of Kidderminster and Brighton in this way. But the League had no success with Bradlaugh at Northampton, although they tried hard, and Glyn had to tell Gladstone that nothing could be done about him. 'Bradlaugh will do harm . . . [He] is not amenable to the League or I think I could manage him.'[2] On the other hand, both Howell and Cremer put up as 'forlorn hope' Liberal candidates with Glyn's backing, in agricultural boroughs where a compact was in force which provided for the return of one Liberal or Whig and one Conservative member. But although Howell was able to win a good deal of support from the agricultural labourers in Aylesbury and Cremer was able to build up a working-men's association in Warwick, both of them were too urbanised ever to have any real chance of success. For a time there was some hope that Baron N. M. de Rothschild would throw over the compact at Aylesbury, as Glyn pressed him to do, but he refused, and Howell finished at the bottom of the poll. Glyn was surprised at Howell standing at all, and regretted that he had left it so late, but there was nothing he could do but lament to his chief:

Howell has no chance at Aylesbury *but* I am very much disappointed at the line Rothschild has taken—he has refused today to coalesce or act & in strong terms. I have done all I can. Howell is a true man and has been of great use to me—he has unfortunately chosen the wrong place & went to Aylesbury against my advice—a stranger cannot win there & Rothschild's treatment has done harm & will create a bad feeling. The upper part of our party are so jealous & sensitive just now. I have written to Howell. Morley, Goschen,

1 Add. MS. 44,347, f.238.
2 Glyn to Gladstone, 10 September 1868. Add MS. 44,347, ff.157-8.

Forster & others have all written to me today in his favour. The
League are very angry but they have waited too long. I much regret
now I did not put one or two of them forward earlier, but though
they constantly sent to me & helped me, the men, Howell & Cremer,
who I shd like to see in the House, never expressed any wish to
become candidates![1]

IV

Meanwhile two prominent members of the League, Bradlaugh
and Dickson, had launched independent candidatures in opposition to other Liberals and were expressing views flatly contradictory to those of Howell and the champions of the Liberal alliance.
Of the two, Bradlaugh was by far the more important, because
his secularist views made him a target for nation-wide abuse, and
made it difficult for any orthodox Liberal to support him or even
to negotiate a compromise with him.[2] He was, as it were, the
independent working-class Radical incarnate, and on this ground
rather than any other John Stuart Mill gave him £10 towards
his expenses. His objectives, as listed in his election address,
summed up the views of the left wing of the Reform League,
whether Christian or atheist.

1. A system of compulsory National Education, by which the State
shall secure to each child the opportunity of acquiring, at least, the
rudiments of a sound English education preparatory to the com-
mencement of the mere struggle for bread.
2. A change in our Land Laws, commencing with the abolition of
the laws of primogeniture and entail; diminishing the enormous legal
expenses attending the transfer of land, and giving greater security
to the actual cultivator of the soil for improvements made upon it.
3. A thorough change in our extravagant system of national expenditure; so that our public departments may cease to be refuges for
destitute members of so-called noble families.
4. Such a change in the present system of taxation, that for the
future the greater pressure of imperial taxes may bear upon those
who hold previously accumulated wealth and large tracts of devised
land, and not so much upon those who increase the wealth of the
nation by their daily labour.

[1] Glyn to Gladstone, 13 November 1868; Add. MS. 44,347, ff.107-8. Cremer's
candidature was apparently financed by Glyn: S. Higenbottam, *Our Society's History*,
Manchester 1939, p. 88.
[2] For his candidature at Northampton see H. B. Bonner, *Charles Bradlaugh, A Record
of his Life and Work*, London 1895, Vol. I, Ch. XXVI.

5. An improvement of the enactments relating to capital and labour; so that employer and employed may stand equal before the law; the establishment of Conciliation Courts for the settlement of Trade disputes, and the abolition of the jurisdiction in these matters of the unpaid magistracy.

6. A complete separation of the Church from the State; including in this the removal of the Bishops from the position they at present occupy as Legislators in the House of Lords.

7. A provision by which minorities may be fairly represented in the legislative chambers.

8. The abolition of all disabilities and disqualifications consequent upon the holding or rejection of any particular speculative opinion.

9. A change in the practice of creating new Peerages; limiting the new creations to Life Peerages, and these only to be given as rewards for great national services; Peers habitually absent from Parliament to be deprived of all legislative privileges, and the right of voting by proxy in any case to be abolished.

10. The abolition as a governing class of the old Whig party, which has long since ceased to play any useful part in our public policy.[1]

Bradlaugh went out of his way to challenge the Executive of the League in the columns of his paper, the *National Reformer*, by boldly reporting that, 'Our candidature is announced with the sanction and knowledge of the Reform League.'[2] The Northampton branch alone had supported Bradlaugh when this announcement was made: the London Executive had given no opinion and was far from sympathetic. George Odger was despatched to Northampton two days later to investigate the situation, to help Bradlaugh if he felt justified in doing so, and to say a few words on his behalf in any case. But when he reported back the Executive declined to endorse Bradlaugh's candidature, and instead passed a resolution which called upon him and Lord Henley, the Whig sitting member, to submit their claims to a meeting of the electors—which Henley could not do without alienating his supporters.[3] One of the first results of the agreement with Glyn was that Howell and Cremer visited Northampton in an effort to make Bradlaugh withdraw. In public they spoke in general terms of their wish that Reform League branches should be independent and of the danger of splitting the Liberal ranks, particularly on religious issues:[4] in private they made it

[1] *National Reformer*, 5 July 1868.   [2] *Ibid.*
[3] Executive Minutes 8 and 22 July 1868.   [4] *National Reformer*, 23 August 1868.

clear that they were opposed to Bradlaugh's candidature and that he would get no help from London. Bradlaugh appealed against this decision to the League's General Council, but as the Council did not control the purse-strings the attack was allowed to drop until after the elections, while Bradlaugh himself returned to Northampton.[1]

By the time the elections were over Bradlaugh had found new allies who were disappointed with the election results and began a full-scale attack on the League's Executive.[2] In Howell's words,

> Mr. Bradlaugh thought that we should give *him* pecuniary and other help. This *we* absolutely refused. Because the money was given in trust to us for a *special object* viz to try and win a number of seats from the *Tories*. We had a list given to us containing the names of 92 Boroughs returning no less than 109 Conservative members all of which were open to attack. Not one shilling of the money was given to us to empower any men to fight against Liberals, unless indeed we include Mr. Roebuck under this term. Now I felt, as the man having more control over the fund than any one else, as the Executive officer that I should not be doing my duty if I allowed the money so subscribed to be used in Northampton against Lord Henley.
>
> In addition to this Col. Dickson thought that we could find him money for the contest in Hackney and deputations were sent asking for large sums.
>
> This Mr. Cremer and myself refused. Even Mr. Odger seemed aggrieved that we did not turn our attention to Chelsea. We felt obliged to refuse except sending a speaker to aid now and again when they had returned to town for a day or so.
>
> This has placed us rather in antagonism . . .[3]

Bradlaugh's theme was that Howell and the Executive, by allying themselves with the 'official' Liberals, had betrayed the working classes, and that the mysterious Special Fund was the price the official Liberals had paid for the quiescence of the Reform League. He demanded an account of the way in which the Special Fund had been used (which he got) and made various

[1] *Ibid.*, 13 September 1868.

[2] This was conducted partly in the Council of the League on 25 November 1868 and partly in the Executive on 3 December (when Howell underwent what he called 'five hours badgering') and again on 5 December.

[3] Howell to Morley, 1 December 1868.

accusations against Howell personally.[1] His case was then taken up by Odger, who claimed that the working classes had been betrayed by Howell and Cremer, who had plotted to prevent working men or their middle-class friends from being returned to parliament. In particular, they had connived at the sudden candidature of Joseph Samuda in the Tower Hamlets which had led to the defeat of Beales, and had not done what was right by 'cutting all connection with the miserable Whigs' in the party offices who were supposed to have supported Samuda.[2] As for the arbitration at Chelsea which had led to Odger's own retirement, it was nothing but a sham and the arbitrators were merely the tools used by 'that miserable Tory Sir H. Hoare' for getting rid of the 'working man's candidate', and quite as bad as Howell's and Cremer's sabotaging of Bradlaugh. Odger's attack rather misfired, however, and Cremer was able to launch a counter-attact against him and to obtain a commission of enquiry into his activities at Stafford, where he had been announced as a candidate but had later withdrawn on condition (or so it was alleged) that his expenses should be paid.

This bitter quarrel killed the League, because it was no longer possible for its leading members to work together, and Howell set about winding it up and looking about for a new occupation.[3] When the Labour Representation League and the Parliamentary Committee of the T.U.C. were formed in 1869 some of the threads drawn together by the Reform League were gathered up again. But the problems which had agitated the Reform League were now viewed from a somewhat different point of view. The Labour Representation League avoided middle-class 'entanglements' as much as possible and concentrated on putting up working-class candidates where they seemed to have a chance of success without seriously endangering Liberal seats. The Parliamentary

[1] During the next few years he also tried unsuccessfully to obtain custody of the League's books and was very unpleasant to Howell about them.

[2] Howell was instructed to ask Glyn for an explanation, which he did, but accompanied his formal letter with a friendly note. By the time Glyn had answered, denying any part in the transaction, the League was virtually defunct. Beales himself had seen Glyn when Samuda's unwelcome candidature was announced but Glyn felt that he could do nothing because Beales was so unpopular with the party. See *inter alia* Add. MS. 44,347, ff.212-13.

[3] Thanks to Glyn, Howell was able to set up as an election agent and Beales was appointed a county court judge. Bradlaugh returned to secularist propaganda; Odger became a republican lecturer; and Cremer broke up the Amalgamated Society of Carpenters and Joiners, before becoming a professional pacifist.

Committee of the T.U.C., with Howell as its secretary from 1871 to 1875, took over the work of negotiating with ministers and friendly M.P.s and of trying to secure better conditions for trade unionists. The Liberal alliance was thus perpetuated on both the political and the trade union fronts, while the idea of the independent Radical candidature became increasingly a middle-class one, symbolised by the adoption of Bradlaugh by the Northampton Liberal Association in 1880.

Part III

THE PARTY MACHINERY

Chapter Sixteen

CENTRAL PARTY ORGANISATION

I

THE chief characteristic of party organisation in the nineteenth century was its impotence. Shorn of the patronage of the eighteenth century, and not yet fortified by the financial strength and undeviating party vote of the twentieth, the Whips and party managers found their influence drastically circumscribed. The local party leaders were sovereign authorities within their own domain, free to select virtually any candidate they wished, and, as long as they had a candidate or local magnate willing to pay the registration and election expenses, financially independent. All they needed from party headquarters were good candidates when the local supply ran short, cheap pamphlets, competent lecturers, a certain amount of help with registration, and occasional help with the expenses of a poor candidate. Any other help which they needed could be supplied more cheaply and more efficiently by organisations like the Liberation Society or the National Reform Union. By 1885 Parnell's Irish party had already developed a new form of organisation, dominated by the party leader and his inner executive committee, but it had for the moment almost no influence on the English parties.

The party managers were not entirely powerless, but to get their way they relied more on their prestige than on their ability to withhold contributions from the party fund or any patronage that might come their way. It was difficult for local leaders, conscious of rivalry within their own association that might at any time lead to their own displacement from office, to resist a Chief Whip or Principal Agent backed by the authority of the party leader. Resistance was possible, particularly when it came to the selection of candidates, but local leaders had to be sure of their ground before risking it. On the other hand, the party managers were powerless to overcome local indolence. Thus Edward Stanhope, the head of the Conservative organisation, wrote to Lord Salisbury at the end of 1883:

It is a fact, unfortunately, that in spite of incessant bullying there are still a large number of constituencies, even in England & Wales, without candidates. It is true that this is partly due to the badness of the candidates on our list, but it is more often the result of laziness on the part of the local leaders, or jealousies amongst them, while the bulk of our friends urgently desire a candidate. . . . Bartley's [the Principal Agent's] resources are exhausted, and though we are going to try a new plan of endeavouring to hold in certain parts of the country meetings of representatives from the constituencies within the district—which may or may not answer—there will still remain a good many which we cannot arouse.

Take for instance, Norwich. Not only ought it to be fought, but its being properly organised is of the greatest importance to 2 county constituencies. Yet nothing will induce the chairman to allow anything to be done—and I despair of moving him until it is too late, without some further pressure [from the party leaders personally].[1]

The days when the party managers had Treasury or Admiralty boroughs in their gift were, of course, long gone by. Very occasionally a patron still gave them the nomination for a borough, and rather more frequently they were deputed to find candidates with long purses for small corrupt boroughs,[2] but none of these seats was directly in their gift. Dover was probably the last to return a man whose claim on the constituency was primarily that he held office in the Admiralty, but even Dover gave up the practice after 1859, and by 1873 it was being described as 'a place influenced much by private and corrupt motives, and little by public spirit'.[3] The party managers, instead of bestowing seats, were now constantly pestered by dockyard members seeking favours for their constituents, usually in the form of new contracts and better rates of pay. They were also approached before most elections with a request to use their influence with the Admiralty to make sure that the Home Fleet was in the right place on polling day. Drummond Wolff, for instance, wrote to Montagu Corry in 1880 to make sure that he would have the help of the fleet at Portsmouth: 'It is of the greatest importance that the

---

[1] Stanhope to Salisbury, 29 December 1883. Salisbury Papers.

[2] George Melly, for instance, was told in 1859 that if he would hand £2,000 to the Chief Whip immediately and leave London for Ireland that night he could be Liberal member for an Irish borough within a week. Melly, *Recollections of Sixty Years*, p. 22.

[3] Gorst to Disraeli, 11 September 1873. Disraeli Papers. For Dover in 1859 see Bagenal, *Bernal Osborne*, pp. 159-68, and J. B. Jones, *Annals of Dover*, Dover 1916, p. 400.

Channel Fleet should be here before the election. We have a devil of a tough fight & want all the assistance possible. . . . The only excuse for not doing this is that an old order exists for the Fleet to go to Gibraltar.'[1]

II

The organisation of the Liberal party, both in parliament and in the country, was entrusted to the Chief Whip in the House of Commons.[2] He himself was required to make sure that M.P.s were in their places at the right time, to select potential candidates, to interview local leaders, to arrange the election campaigns of the party chiefs, to recommend suitable men for honours and for office, and to distribute the party funds which stood in his own name in the bank of his choice. Almost everything, therefore, depended upon his personality and on his being long enough in office to learn his job. There were four Liberal Whips between 1867 and 1885, George Grenfell Glyn (1867-73), Arthur Wellesley Peel (1873-4), William Patrick Adam (1874-80), and Lord Richard Grosvenor (1880-5). Glyn and Grosvenor were Gladstone's personal friends, and, like Peel who was one of his protégés, owed their appointment as much to this as to their ability. Adam, best known to posterity as the original of Scud East in *Tom Brown's Schooldays*, and the most efficient of the four, was made Chief Whip after the débâcle of 1874 because of his long experience as Scottish Whip, although this was nominally a step down from his former post as First Commissioner of Works, an office which sometimes (though not in his case) went with a seat in the Cabinet.

The Whip had so much to do that it was difficult for him to perform all his work equally well, and faults of character soon betrayed themselves. None of Gladstone's Whips before 1885 was as successful as Edward Marjoribanks was to become between 1892 and 1894, and it was perhaps for this reason that contemporaries thought him the model Whip. Robert Farquharson, for instance, lists Marjoribanks's personal qualities as those which every Whip should possess: 'He had a good level head well screwed

---

[1] H. Drummond Wolff to M. Corry, 21 March 1880. Disraeli Papers.

[2] The best account of the Liberal organisation in action is in A. F. Thompson, 'Gladstone's Whips and the General Election of 1868', *English Historical Review*, LXIII, 189-200 (1948). For the work of the Chief Whip as Patronage Secretary of the Treasury see my forthcoming article in *The Historical Journal*, 'Political Patronage at the Treasury, 1870-1912'.

on; he was a man of the world, active, but not obtrusively so, pleasant-mannered, well-born, rich, hospitable, never in a hurry, but always ready to stop and have a "crack", and advise, or warn, or help.'[1] George Glyn, Gladstone's close friend and Whip, who was the despair of his colleagues because of his impulsiveness, stood at the other extreme. Indeed, even his close friend Algernon West thought his charming wife alone made up for his defects:

> His was a strange character; and he possessed in almost equal proportions the qualifications which a Whip should have and the disqualifications a Whip should not have. Among the former were his energy, his fidelity, and not only his fidelity but his blind admiration of and devotion to his master, his entire absorption in his work, and his sharpness and ability. On the other hand, his devotion made him blind and obstinate, and he was overbearing to those who even ventured to differ from anything Mr. Gladstone thought right. He was perhaps tactless and apt to be tyrannical, very fidgety, and possessing none of that calm which enables a man to weather the political storm.[2]

The Liberal Whip was always desperately short of assistance. At elections he could rely on the Lord Advocate and Scotch Whip for help in Scotland and on the Chief Secretary and Irish Whip for help in Ireland, but the campaign as a whole was his own responsibility. Between 1865 and 1886 there was not even a party manager or agent to help the Whip, as Schnadhorst and Robert Hudson were able to do after they moved to London from Birmingham in the latter year. The party offices were those of the Liberal Registration Association (at 41, 42 or 43 Parliament Street), which was renamed the Liberal Central Association by W. P. Adam. These offices acted as a reception centre for visitors from the constituencies and as a permanent home for the Whips (who also had their own room in the House of Commons). But it was usually necessary to take additional offices for general election purposes, from which the Whip could conduct negotiations about seats.

The registration work, and much of the routine work of the office, was performed by Thomas Nicolls Roberts, who had been appointed secretary of the Liberal Registration Association in 1861, and who exchanged this title for that of secretary of the

[1] Farquharson, *In and Out of Parliament*, pp. 221-2.
[2] Algernon West, *Recollections, 1832 to 1886*, 2nd edn, London 1899, I, 349-50.

Liberal Central Association in 1877.[1] But Roberts, who drank too much, was a minor official, a sort of registration agent, and by 1868 he ranked below Glyn's private secretary, H. Scudamore Stanhope, in the office hierarchy. In the early seventies his subordination was formally recognised when Stanhope was appointed to act as Honorary Secretary of the Registration Association, and this arrangement was continued by Adam, whose private secretary, Alexander Craig Sellar, became first Honorary Secretary of the Liberal Central Association. Sellar soon became in effect manager of the party offices, because his chief spent much of his time in Scotland, and employed a second private secretary to attend to his work outside the office. But Sellar was as much a bird of passage as Stanhope had been, and there was no question of making him permanent manager of the office.

The party organisation had not always been so much the personal concern of the Chief Whip. Before 1857 the Liberals had relied for assistance with their election arrangements on freelance election agents who also acted as parliamentary agents for election petitions, of whom the best known were Joseph Parkes and James Coppock. When Coppock died rather suddenly in 1857, however, it was decided to follow the example already set by the Conservatives and to appoint a Principal Agent from among the leading parliamentary agents, to attend both to electoral work and to the extensive business in election petitions. The post was given to William Richard Drake, who was then forty years of age, a leading solicitor in the City of London, and one whose interest in Venetian ceramics and marbles made him a well-known figure in the artistic world.[2] Drake was a complete contrast to Coppock; straightforward, wealthy, well-connected, devoid of the usual low cunning of the successful free-lance agent, and by no means a specialist in election work. Indeed, he was such a success as a solicitor to big City merchant houses, and particularly to the leading banks, that even in 1857 it must have been clear that it was only a matter of time before he would have to give up the party agency for his other work. This he eventually did in 1865, but he never completely retired: he remained for many years 'in close and confidential relationship

[1] Roberts had earlier been head of the Anti-Corn-Law League's electoral registration office: McCord, *The Anti-Corn Law League*, pp. 173-4.

[2] *The Times*, 6 December 1890.

with the leaders of the Liberal party, and especially the Parliamentary Whips',[1] was one of the founders of the Devonshire Club in 1875, and was one of Adam's principal assistants in 1880.

Drake described his work as agent to the Bridgwater Bribery Commission in 1869.

> The duties of the parliamentary agent for the Liberal party . . . involved advising the leaders of the party, members of parliament and candidates on matters connected with election law, and communications with candidates seeking seats in Parliament, and with constituencies seeking candidates, and the placing the former in communication with the latter through the local parties. . . . No salary or payment whatever is made to the agent by the party. The only pecuniary remuneration attaching to it arises from the usual professional charges as parliamentary agent in the conduct or defence of petitions placed in the agent's hands.[2]

Drake and the Whip of the day, Henry Brand (1859-67), were together responsible for the formation of the Liberal Registration Association, which became the most stable element in the organisation after 1860. Its purposes were set out in a circular asking for funds.

> Every day's experience shows, that the main reliable source of success in Electioneering is a careful supervision of, and attention to, the Registration. In many of the principal Constituencies care is taken of this most important matter by local Societies, with which (when properly managed) it is not possible to interfere, or to do more than place the association in communication with them. There are, however, a vast number of Constituencies where no organised plan of registration is adopted, and where attention to the Register is either altogether neglected, or is dependent on individual efforts inadequate to the task. To constituencies such as these a *Liberal Registration Association* would afford much valuable assistance.[3]

Drake's retirement was carefully timed so that he would have time to initiate his successor, Joseph Travers Smith, in the secrets of political management during the general election of 1865. Travers Smith was sufficiently involved to prepare himself a full list of constituencies with a record of their peculiarities, but he found the work unprofitable and uncongenial, and threw it up immediately

---

[1] *The Times*, 6 December 1890.
[2] [C. 12] pp. 1163-4. H.C. (1870). XXX, 1,225-6.
[3] Add. MS. 44,193, ff.12-13.

after the election.[1] Brand, rather than find another agent, took over most of the agent's work himself, deputing the legal business to a firm of parliamentary agents, Wyatt, Hoskins and Hooker,[2] and mere matters of routine to the Registration Association.

The most delicate and important part of the Liberal Whip's work was that which arose from rival candidatures. The Whip never found much difficulty in offering both constituencies and candidates long lists of 'opportunities', but this side of his work was always of subordinate importance. Lord Richard Grosvenor in 1885, in a letter to Gladstone from the Highlands, described the work that really mattered:

> Killing duplicate Candidates goes on much faster & better than killing stags, the number of duplicate Candidates has been, why I know not, greatly exaggerated in the papers, and instead of 30 or 40 as reported to you there are 13 in Metropolitan Constituencies, all of which I have in hand, & most of these are sham & disappear by degrees, & in the rest of the country there are 14, only 2 or 3 of which are really serious—notably the Camborne Divn of Cornwall & Lincoln City. I am fostering a Candidate in Kirkcaldy Burghs to keep out Sir J. Campbell.[3]

The Liberal Whips were always haunted by the fear that they would be thought other than impartial in their dealing with constituencies. They were bound to adopt in public the attitude of strict neutrality which Gladstone himself always adopted towards disputes in the constituencies, and to avoid siding with one section of the party. And they rather encouraged Gladstone to send out formal letters like the following, which was sent to one of the Liberals of Banbury in 1868.

> I feel that I have no title to take any part as between gentlemen of the Liberal party who may be competing for the same seat in Parliament; but, as your enquiry relates to matters of fact, I beg to

[1] His methods are, however, of some interest. He told the Bridgwater Bribery Commission that he kept a register of constituencies in which he would 'make a memorandum to this effect, that at a former election the men would not vote for anybody except for a man professing certain opinions; that at such and such a place the dissenting question was strong, or the evangelical question was strong, or that they would not vote for men who were not strong on the question of the ballot; but it was a political question not a question of money.' [C. 12] p. 977. H.C. (1870). XXX, 1039. The Conservative agent kept no register but sent out requests for information to all the constituencies before each election. *Ibid.*, p. 804.

[2] H.C. 225, pp. 59-71 (1875). VIII, 515-27.

[3] Lord R. Grosvenor to Gladstone, 25 September 1885, Add. MS. 44,316, f.40. There is an account of Lord Richard at work in Katherine Parnell, *Charles Stewart Parnell*, London 1914, II, 88-107.

state that Mr. Samuelson voted for the motion made by me in relation to rating, on which hung the issue of that portion of the provisions of the Reform Bill, and that I fully believe in Mr. Samuelson's
loyal adherence to the principles of the Liberal party.[1]

Any letter which went beyond the personal qualifications of the
candidates concerned and their votes in the House was certain to
make the Whips partisans rather than arbiters, and to class them
with the sectional leaders who did give personal endorsements to
particular candidates: Bright, Mill, Chamberlain, Samuel Morley, and Duncan McLaren. Occasionally the Whips went further
and brought pressure to bear on behalf of a particular candidate,
or Gladstone himself was prevailed upon to intervene. Glyn in 1868
did all he could to support A. J. Mundella in the three-cornered
fight at Sheffield where Mundella was fighting that most unorthodox of Liberals, J. A. Roebuck. Similarly, Gladstone lent
his support to Charles Gilpin and Lord Henley at Northampton
in 1868 when they were attacked by Bradlaugh. But such cases
were decidedly exceptional, and were always liable to raise an
outcry in the press. Thus W. P. Adam, who had in 1879-80 done
all he could in a series of interviews up and down the country to
help constituencies to find suitable candidates and to persuade
surplus candidates to retire, was attacked by the Radical nonconformist press for his pains. He was accused of trying to preserve
the seats of 'unsound' Liberals like N. G. Lambert (Buckinghamshire), Alfred Watkin (Grimsby), James Yeaman (Dundee), J. D'A.
Samuda (Tower Hamlets), W. B. Beaumont (South Northumberland) and John Walter (Berkshire) who had supported Disraeli's
foreign policy, although only Beaumont and Walter actually kept
their seats.[2] For the *British Quarterly Review*, then edited by Henry
Allon, the very effort to maintain party unity was something of
a mistake.

As to any central organization, the party lost at least as much as
it gained. Mr. Adams [*sic*] was very zealous, but the wisdom of some
parts of his tactics, and especially of their most distinctive feature,

---

[1] *The Times*, 7 November 1868. There is a correspondence between Gladstone and
the Whips on the question of letters to candidates in 1885 in Add. MS. 44,316, ff.75-7
and 115.

[2] It is interesting to speculate what they would have said in 1868 if they had known
of Glyn's negotiations with the Tory Whip, Taylor, which he reported to Mr Gladstone thus: 'I forgot to tell you that Taylor engages to withdraw Heygate, to negative
Clinton (if he cannot stop him) & to assent to the *withdrawal of Maguire*.' Add. MS.
44,347, f.109.

was extremely questionable. He was bent on maintaining the union of the party, and in order to do this was content to tolerate some so-called Liberals who had distinguished themselves by their steady opposition to the foreign policy of their leader. More than one of this class owes his seat to the resolute discouragement of the central committee to any attempts to disturb them on the part of more enthusiastic Liberals who were not content to be thus misrepresented. We can only hope that those to whom this place of repentance has been opened will show a due appreciation of the forbearance with which they have been treated.[1]

Much the same criticism was brought against the Whips from the extreme Left for the way in which they selected candidates. The fact that they were always short of money was not generally appreciated, whereas the fact that rich men found no shortage of constituencies to contest was notorious. Sir Sydney Waterlow the printer and stationer was offered five or six possible constituencies in 1868 (including Maidstone, Mid-Kent, and Dumfriesshire), and eventually contested Dumfriesshire in 1868, Southwark in 1870, Maidstone in 1874, Gravesend in 1880, and the Medway Division in 1885.[2] *Reynolds's Newspaper*, in particular, made much of the failure to support working-class candidates although it wrongly attributed the blame to the Reform Club rather than to the Whips.

> Let the working classes be assured that the Reform Club, which had deluged the country with electoral candidates destitute of all political principle, but possessed with weighty money-bags, has but one object in view, and that is the recovery of place, power, and patronage. . . . The Reform Club has done more to shut out working men from Parliament than the Tory Carlton. Wherever a working man has presented himself to a working-class constituency, he has been met with the rattle of Whig money-bags in his face. . . .[3]

This criticism was in fact only partially justified, since both Glyn and Adam did their best to help suitable working men. Glyn tried to persuade the Rothschilds to support George Howell at Aylesbury in 1868, and is reported to have subsidised W. R. Cremer's candidature at Warwick, while Adam certainly subsidised Henry Broadhurst's candidature at Stoke in 1880.[4]

[1] *British Quarterly Review*, LXXII, 180 (1880).
[2] He was returned for Dumfriesshire, but was unseated because he was a government contractor. He won Maidstone in 1874 and Gravesend in 1880. For the 1868 offer see H.C. 78, pp. 2f. (1868-9). VII, 260f.
[3] *Reynolds's Newspaper*, 1 November 1868.
[4] For Howell and Cremer see pp. 329-43 above, and for Broadhurst p. 380 below.

The Reform Club, it may be noted in passing, had by this time almost entirely ceased to play a positive part in the affairs of the constituencies. A Political Committee was appointed in 1869, with an impressive list of duties:

1. To promote the political organization of the Liberal party, and to aid the several constituencies in securing suitable candidates for seats.
2. To arbitrate between conflicting Liberal candidates at Parliamentary Elections contesting the same seat or seats, in order to prevent the loss of seats by division in the Liberal ranks.
3. To suggest and carry out such changes in the rules and regulations of the Club as may from time to time be found necessary to secure its useful political action.[1]

But in practice the Club was rarely called upon to take any initiative on its own, and in 1878 W. F. Rae, a member of the Club since 1860 and chairman of the Library Committee, did his best, in an article in the *Nineteenth Century*, to show that the Club had handed over its functions to the Whip's office.

> The Reform has a committee empowered to manage the political affairs of the club; but this body never interferes in the conduct of elections, unless at the special request of the parties concerned, and then only with a view to smooth over differences and to act as a court of conciliation. That committee have no fund at their disposal, so that the insidious manner in which the Reform Club is said by the imaginative correspondents of country newspapers to thwart one candidate or help another is pure fiction. When impecunious candidates and needy but conscientious electors apply to the club for money, they never receive anything more satisfying than good advice.
>
> The only body acting on behalf of the Liberal party as a whole is the Liberal Central Association, established in 1860, and having an office in Parliament Street, Westminster.[2]

III

The main outlines of the Conservative party organisation were established when the party was in opposition in the early fifties.[3]

---

[1] Fagan, *The Reform Club*, p. 112.

[2] W. F. Rae, 'Political Clubs and Party Organisation', *Nineteenth Century*, III, 919-20 (1878).

[3] I have avoided giving a full account of the early history of the Conservative Central Office in this section as the story is extremely complicated, and I hope to be able to tell it elsewhere.

Broadly speaking, the arrangement which was arrived at was similar to that which the Liberals adopted when Brand was Liberal Chief Whip and Drake was Liberal party agent: the Chief Whip in the Commons was given a general oversight over the party organisation both in and out of the House, but the routine work of organisation in the country was entrusted to a Principal Agent who was not in the Commons at all. Initially this division of function was the consequence of the break-up of the party in 1846. F. R. Bonham, Peel's organiser, together with the great majority of the local Conservative agents, had remained loyal to Peel, and had left the Protectionists without even the most elementary organisation. Until the Derby ministry of 1852 the work of reconstructing the party took precedence over the reconstruction of the party organisation, but after the Derby ministry had fallen this, too, was undertaken. Sir William Jolliffe (afterwards Lord Hylton), a leading country gentleman, was made Chief Whip in the hope that he would improve the morale of the party in the House, and Philip Rose, Disraeli's own solicitor, was made Principal Agent and given charge of the party management out-of-doors. Rose was one of the partners in the great firm of Baxter, Rose, Norton and Co., solicitors and parliamentary agents, which provided him with an assistant in the person of his own eventual successor in the agency, Markham Spofforth. Rose, as 'Principal Agent',[1] attended to the work of interviewing candidates and advising constituencies: Spofforth, who was only twenty-eight, set about reconstructing the system of local agents which Peel's secession had destroyed. And there was no substantial change in this arrangement until 1859. Spofforth succeeded Rose in 1859 and was given an assistant of his own, Dudley Baxter, the statistician, and later an additional assistant to act as the secretary of a Conservative Registration Association.[2]

Disraeli himself took a great deal of interest in questions of

[1] The title of 'Principal Agent', although freely used, appears never to have been formally conferred on any agent before Middleton, and it is doubtful whether even he was invested with it. Spofforth said in 1866: 'I do not consider myself the agent of the Conservative party', and when asked whether he had been agent in 1853 said that it was then that he was 'first consulted by the persons who came about seats and that sort of thing'. [3776] p. 979. H.C. (1867). XXIX, 979.

[2] This was set up in 1863 or 1864 to handle the laborious negotiations with county out-voters on the same plan as the Liberal Registration Association. The first secretary, Henry Smith, was also secretary of the Conservative Land Society, and occasionally acted as an election agent for Spofforth. [3776] pp. 1,003-5. H.C. (1867). XXIX, 1,003-5.

organisation, but he preferred to leave the detailed work of supervision to someone else. Until 1870 this deputy was Lord Nevill,
afterwards fifth Earl and first Marquess of Abergavenny, a born
party manager who exercised an enormous influence behind the
scenes because of his disinterestedness and ability. Until 1868,
when he succeeded to the peerage, he worked regularly at the
party offices; thereafter, until Lord Salisbury's retirement in 1902,
he was the confidential adviser of successive party leaders, the
virtual manager of the Carlton and Junior Carlton Clubs (and
founder of the Constitutional), principal trustee of the party
funds, a formidable *grand seigneur* and an expert on patronage.
Abergavenny was also the inspiration of a school of party
managers, known colloquially in the nineties as the 'Kentish
gang', which included Sir William Hart Dyke and Aretas Akers-
Douglas, Chief Whips 1874-80 and 1885-95 respectively, and
Captain R. W. E. Middleton, principal agent 1885-1903.[1]
Abergavenny had no real successor as adviser on electoral matters,
but Disraeli's practice of entrusting someone (either formally or
informally) with an oversight of the party organisation was continued. In 1868 a committee was associated with Abergavenny
and formally given responsibility for the elections; between 1874
and 1880 Sir William Hart Dyke was *de facto* entrusted with their
management as Patronage Secretary; and again in 1880 a special
committee was appointed, which survived until 1884.

The passage of the 1867 Reform Bill was the prelude to a change
in the office of party agent. The arrangement with Baxter, Rose,
and Norton had never been an altogether satisfactory one, and
Spofforth was not thought to be a suitable man to inspire popular
constituencies, although he gave his encouragement to the formation of the National Union in 1867. After a row in June 1868 a
committee was set up to take charge of election arrangements,
which elbowed Spofforth out of what had hitherto been his most
important activities, and at the end of 1869 he finally resigned
because the new arrangements for the trial of election petitions
had destroyed the profitability as well as the power of the agency.
John Gorst, who was appointed to succeed him, was a young

---

[1] T. H. S. Escott, *Club Makers and Club Members*, London 1914, p. 222n, refers to
them more elegantly as 'the Kentish group'. Other Whips were Sir William Jolliffe
1853-9, Colonel T. E. Taylor 1859-68 and 1873-4, the Hon. Gerard Noel 1868-73,
Rowland Winn, 1880-5; and other agents were Philip Rose 1853-9, Markham Spofforth
1859-70, J. E. Gorst 1870-7, 1880-2, W. B. Skene 1877-80, G. C. T. Bartley 1882-4.

barrister who had lost his seat in parliament at the general election, and who agreed to hold the office on a part time basis.[1] He established his headquarters in the offices occupied by the Conservative Registration Association (which had been reorganised in 1867), which were eventually moved in 1875 from 53 Parliament Street to St Stephen's Chambers, where the St Stephen's Club and the Metropolitan Conservative Alliance were also housed. An important consequence of Gorst's appointment was that Major Keith-Falconer, the secretary of the Registration Association, became the first secretary of the Central Conservative Office and took charge of its routine activities. He also took charge of the Central Press Agency when it was bought for the party in 1871 to help foster the Conservative provincial press, and, along with Gorst, acted as joint-secretary of the National Union. As a peer's son and a soldier with a good record in the Crimean War he was in many ways more acceptable personally than Gorst himself, and as a Scot he could deal with Scottish business as no Englishman could. He was, moreover, perfectly loyal to Gorst, and there can be no doubt that the party lost a great deal when he accepted a vacant Commissionership of Inland Revenue in 1874. His successors (it became the custom to appoint two joint-secretaries) were certainly not his equals, since they regarded their office as essentially subordinate to that of the Principal Agent, as Keith-Falconer had never done.

The work done by the Central Office increased slowly but steadily after 1870, although it did not yet attain the dimensions it reached under Middleton after 1885. Even by 1874, however, it was systematically organised along the lines which Gorst set out in a memorandum for Lord Beaconsfield in 1881, and the machine was running so smoothly that Gorst called at the office only for a very short time each day.

Ordinary work of Conservative Central Office

Registration. Enquiries are made as to the residence & qualification of the outvoters of all counties in England & Wales. Forms, instructions, & advice are furnished to both Counties & Boroughs.

---

[1] It is perhaps worth noting that there is nothing in the Whips' correspondence of the period to suggest that Gorst's appointment was to be a new departure in terms of function. Gerard Noel simply wrote to Disraeli: 'As I think it is important that Spofforth's place should be filled up with as little delay as possible I should be very much obliged if you would kindly let me know your opinion about Mr. Gorst as his successor.' Noel to Disraeli, 2 April 1870. Disraeli Papers.

Elections. Local leaders are assisted in finding suitable candidates. Forms, instructions, and election literature is supplied. County outvoters are canvassed.

Organization. Formation of new Associations is promoted and assisted. Model rules &c are supplied. An annual list of clubs & associations is compiled.

Meetings. The continual holding of small local meetings is advised and encouraged. Speakers and hints for speeches are provided. Special meetings (as for example on the Irish question) are from time to time recommended and promoted.

Publications. Pamphlets & leaflets on current political topics are issued: important speeches are reprinted and circulated.

Press. A weekly publication, called the 'Editors' Handysheet', is issued to provide materials for political articles to the Conservative Provincial Press. Political telegrams are sent from the Lobby to several provincial papers.

Parliamentary. All Bills affecting the interests of the party are circulated amongst the local leaders. Petitions are from time to time promoted.

Statistics. Facts respecting elections, Parliamentary & Municipal, are collected & tabulated. An Index of political events during the past 10 years is in course of formation.

Correspondence. Enquiries are answered upon such subjects as Finance, Foreign Affairs, Army & Navy administration, Election statistics & procedure, India, Irish affairs, Licensing, Education, Friendly Societies, &c &c.

Interviews. People of every class call at the office on political business, and every endeavour is made to treat them with courtesy & consideration.

Visits. Constituencies are visited by emissaries from the Central Office of two sorts:—

    (*a*) Experienced agents to advise on the registration & electoral machinery.

    (*b*) Gentlemen to stir up dormant constituencies, & recommend local organization & effort.

Special Work of Conservative Central Office since August 1880

The Hon. FitzRoy Stewart (our new Secy.) has read up the correspondence of the last 6 years respecting each constituency.

He has seen a great number of candidates for Parliament, & has made out a list of candidates with their qualifications.

He has also appended to each constituency the names of suitable candidates, amongst whom a selection could be made in case of a vacancy.

As the candidates for any constituency become definitely fixed, they are of course noted.

A great deal of his time has been taken up by interviews with persons who have schemes for starting every description of newspaper, and who persist in explaining them to somebody who represents the Party.

The National Union which broke out into discord with the Party managers after the general election has been brought into concord.

A new association 'The Constitutional Union' formed by barristers in the Temple, has been induced to act in harmony with the Central Office.

Constituencies have been visited by the agents of the Central Office & reports made upon their electoral prospects. Stewart has commenced visiting those in which the organization is unsatisfactory. Arrangements are being made for several gentlemen of position to assist Stewart in this work.

A committee on County organization has been formed by Hon. E. Stanhope, which has held many meetings & examined a large number of County members: it is to report to the Central Committee.

A Committee on Ireland has held one meeting & holds its second on Feby. 25th. It has been delayed until Col. Taylor's arrival from Ireland.

A Committee is now being formed to consider the Corrupt Practices Bill.

Mr. Dawson, an Oxford B.A., has been employed since January under the supervision of Stanhope in making an Index of Political Events of the last 10 years for reference.[1]

Although it was very busy, the Central Office was not a happy place after the Conservatives had won their victory in 1874. Gorst felt that he had not been properly rewarded for his services, although he was made a Q.C. in 1875, and he resented the fact that his failure to gain a seat at the general election had cost him his chances of office. As a consequence he became embittered and wayward, and refused an Under-Secretaryship when he did get back into parliament in 1875, on the ground that the head of the department was in the Commons.[2] Moreover, he failed to get on

---

[1] Gorst to Beaconsfield, 24 February 1881. Disraeli Papers.

[2] He was apparently offered the secretaryship of the Board of Trade, a department that needed strengthening: W. S. Childe-Pemberton, *Life of Lord Norton*, London 1909, pp. 219f. Gorst afterwards realised that he had made a mistake. 'I am to blame', he wrote to Disraeli, 4 April 1878, 'for not having asked for an interview with you before declining the offer you so kindly made me in 1875. But I then believed that, for a person like myself without social interest the acceptance of such an office meant political extinction: and I turned to the Bar as the only avenue to public life that was open to me.'

with Sir William Hart Dyke, the new Chief Whip, who had fallen into the Liberal habit of managing electioneering matters from the Treasury, and who regarded Gorst as his employee.[1] They quarrelled over questions of patronage (and particularly over Gorst's attempt to secure an official post for his brother Thomas), and they quarrelled over the demarcation of their respective functions, with the result that in 1877 Gorst was replaced after a year of fierce bickering.

Already in 1877 the party machine was running down. Gorst thought it to be in a worse state than it actually was, but there is no doubt that he was right in warning Disraeli in his farewell letter that an election might bring disaster.

> Our organization in 1877 is greatly inferior to what it was in 1874; and the attempt to renovate & improve it has not come a day too soon. But to succeed in the attempt you must put a stop to that which has been the chief cause of all the mischief that has occurred —the system which Sir W. Dyke has been required to follow of managing elections at the Treasury. I always thought this a most unwise policy on the part of the late government, and since we have been in office, experience has justified that opinion. Instead of the management being vested in my office, under Sir W. Dyke's control, I have been consulted intermittently, in certain elections only, and at certain stages only of the elections: money has been spent against my advice and without my knowledge; and I have had a mere fragmentary and imperfect acquaintance with what has been going on. The established principle of non-interference with local leaders has in many instances been neglected; and those leaders have been constantly offended and alienated both in the distribution of patronage and in other matters. . . . Whether our majority will endure beyond the present Parliament I do not pretend to foretell, but I am certain that unless some energetic measures are speedily adopted our organization, whenever the election does take place, will be as inferior to that of our opponents, as it was superior in 1874, and from the operation of very similar causes.[2]

Gorst's forebodings were soon shown to be justified. His successor, W. B. Skene, lacked Gorst's enthusiasm and the knowledge and force of character which in Gorst compensated for his lack of standing in the party, and was content to let the Whips

[1] Dyke wrote to Disraeli, 8 December 1874 (Disraeli Papers): '[Gorst] is I am bound to say, of great use to me with all his crotchets', and again, 'Things are so quiet now that I am much disposed to keep Gorst in hand crotchets & all.'
[2] Gorst to Beaconsfield, 3 March 1877. Disraeli Papers.

rule the party from the Treasury right up to the end of 1879. Then the system disintegrated because Dyke fell ill from overwork. No one felt himself responsible for the party organisation in general or for the preparations for the general election in particular, with the result that all those in any way connected with the party organisation did what they were inclined to do. W. H. Smith, Skene, the assistant Whips (Rowland Winn and Lord Henry Thynne) and Colonel Taylor all had a finger in the pie, while the task of distributing the party election fund was undertaken by Colonel W. P. Talbot, once Lord Derby's secretary and now Serjeant-at-Arms to the House of Lords, who understandably regarded the situation as little short of utter chaos and distributed the money according to no particular principle.[1] After the election the Conservative press and some of the associations howled for vengeance on the organisers of defeat.[2] Skene hastily retired to Oxford and his Scottish estates; Rowland Winn became Chief Whip; Gorst was recalled to take charge of the Central Office; and a special committee was appointed having as its chief members W. H. Smith as chairman, Edward Stanhope as Vice Chairman, and Lord Percy representing the National Union, to consider ways in which the party organisation might be improved.[3]

The new arrangement soon became permanent. The 'Central Committee' took charge of all questions of organisation outside the House of Commons with Gorst as its executive officer, and the Whips were confined to their House of Commons work. It soon appeared, however, that once again a mistake had been made. Sir Stafford Northcote as leader in the Commons gave the Central Committee little encouragement, even when Lord Randolph Churchill began to attack it. Lord Abergavenny disliked committees on principle and wanted the Central Committee's powers to be transferred to the Chief Whip.[4] And there were endless difficulties about personalities even before the Fourth Party had become militant in the House of Commons. Both Smith and Gorst took an unnecessarily extreme view of their powers. Smith

[1] [C. 2856-I] pp. 480-5. H.C. (1881). XLIV, 510-15.
[2] Even the ultra-Tory *Blackwood's Magazine*, CXXVII, 804-10, thought drastic reorganisation essential.
[3] The appointment of the committee was announced at the Bridgewater House meeting: Buckle, *Disraeli*, VI, 576.
[4] He was in the habit of making trenchant remarks such as 'Too many cooks spoil the broth' (Abergavenny to Salisbury, 13 May 1883. Salisbury Papers), and 'As to the Central Committee the sooner it is abolished the better' (Abergavenny to Salisbury, 14 April 1884).

regarded himself as general director of the party organisation, the committee as a rubber stamp for his decisions, and Gorst as his employee. Gorst respected Smith and at times even liked him, but he objected to interference from any source, and had little or no respect for the committee. The result was a tension which soon destroyed the usefulness of the new arrangements.

Nor did the almost simultaneous retirement of both Smith and Gorst in 1882 mend matters. Edward Stanhope, Smith's successor, was able to effect many salutary changes at the Central Office but his appointment made the Committee's relations with the Fourth Party much worse because Lord Randolph Churchill disliked him. Bartley, Gorst's successor, although he too was a hard worker, also had serious defects. He looked upon the agency as a stepping stone to high office, and a means of participating in discussions on policy held by the party leaders—an honour to which no other agent was ever so presumptuous as to aspire. He campaigned strongly behind the scenes against the decision of the Lords to hold up the 1884 Franchise Bill until the government should table its scheme for redistribution, and even issued circulars to the press setting out his views and denouncing those of his chiefs. Finally, in November 1884, he resigned, and destroyed whatever reputation he still enjoyed with Lord Salisbury by submitting his letter of resignation to the press, and by writing an article denouncing the party leadership for the Radical *Fortnightly Review*.[1] He never held any office again, although he sat for North Islington from 1885 to 1906, and eventually brought his political career to a suitable climax by declaiming against the number of Lord Salisbury's relations in the government.[2]

Worse than all this, however, Gorst joined Lord Randolph Churchill in active opposition to the party leaders. Hitherto the members of the Fourth Party had merely been *frondeurs*; now they became a serious threat both to the party leadership and to the existing system of party management.[3] The genius and popular appeal of the quartet—reduced after 1882 to a trio—derived from Lord Randolph Churchill, but the direction which their

[1] G. C. T. Bartley, 'Conservative Organisation', *Fortnightly Review*, n.s. XXXVII, 611. See also *The Times*, 19 March 1885.

[2] Blanche E. C. Dugdale, *Arthur James Balfour, First Earl of Balfour*, London 1939, I, 238-9.

[3] The standard accounts of the Fourth Party are contained in H. E. Gorst, *The Fourth Party*, London 1906, W. S. Churchill, *Lord Randolph Churchill*, new edn, London 1951, and A. J. Balfour, *Chapters of Autobiography*, London 1930.

efforts took in their attempt to overturn the party leadership in 1883 and 1884 was a natural consequence of Gorst's close association with the mechanics of the party organisation until 1882. Lord Salisbury, who was better informed of the true state of the party (thanks to Arthur Balfour) than Northcote was, warned the latter early in the 1883 session that 'We have to contend, I fear, against considerable bitterness on Gorst's part, arising out of the differences of last year',[1] although as a matter of fact, Gorst was much less hostile to Northcote than Churchill was. Gorst attempted to discredit such reports, but his efforts were more damaging to him than the reports themselves. Thus he wrote to Northcote two days after Salisbury had done so, to protest against 'the calumnies which had been circulated by your supporters in the lobbies of the House of Commons', over a debate on the Transvaal, and claimed Northcote's protection against their 'malevolent mis-statements'.

> The continued persecutions to which I have been subjected in the Conservative ranks since 1874, and against which I have vainly looked for some support from the leaders to whom I have always been so loyal, are not in my judgment calculated to consolidate a party, nor to advance the common object which we all profess (though I fear many very hypocritically) to have in view.[2]

But Gorst had gone too far with Lord Randolph not to go the whole way. By the end of April he was committed to support Lord Randolph's bid for the party leadership, and had turned his mind to the way in which the party machinery might be captured from Sir Stafford Northcote. The weakest link in the official armour was the National Union, which had already threatened in 1880 to break away from the passive rôle allotted to it by the party managers, and Gorst and Lord Randolph now decided to capture it. The National Union had been founded by a group of young Conservatives headed by Henry Cecil Raikes in 1867, and had secured the support of Spofforth, Nevill and the Whips because it promised to be of assistance in organising the newly enfranchised working men.[3] Raikes and his friends had intended the Union to be a propagandist organisation, which would win party support because it had leading peers and cabinet ministers as Vice-Presidents, and would hold public meetings addressed by

[1] Salisbury to Northcote, 11 March 1883. Iddesleigh Papers 1014/4.
[2] Gorst to Northcote, 13 March 1883. Iddesleigh Papers 1043/4.
[3] See p. 106 above. Also H. St J. Raikes, *Henry Cecil Raikes*, *passim*, and R. T. McKenzie, *British Political Parties*, Ch. IV.

leading speakers in various parts of the country. They had also intended it to provide books and pamphlets for party workers, and to supply 'resolution forms' to be used at party meetings in the constituencies. To encourage local party leaders to participate it had also been decided to hold an annual meeting of delegates from the constituencies. But the idea, although a good one, had been only partially carried out until 1870, when Gorst took over the work of the National Union as well as that of the Central Office. The conjunction of the National Union with the Central Office was a sensible one (which has persisted ever since, although in varying forms), and from 1870 to 1876 the National Union was administered as part of-the Central Office. Gorst as party agent helped a constituency with its organisational problems and with the search for candidates, and either he, Keith-Falconer or Colonel Neville, as joint-secretary of the National Union, also supplied it with speakers for public meetings, with suitable posters to erect on hoardings, and with leaflets to push through letter-boxes. Gorst disturbed this comfortable arrangement after his resignation from the agency in 1876 by advocating greater independence for the National Union (whose secretary he remained for a time), but Raikes was able to defeat the proposal at the Annual General Meeting, and nothing came of it.

The National Union in the early eighties was, none the less, a much more important body than it had been in the seventies. This was not because there had been a change in its constitution but because the local associations had come to take a new interest in it. For them the defeat of 1880 seemed more than a betrayal by the party organisers, although they complained bitterly about the Central Office: it seemed to mark the emergence of the caucus in British politics, and many of the local leaders began to see themselves as the organisers of a Conservative caucus, headed perhaps by Lord Randolph Churchill. Ironically enough, it was Gorst who put down the first revolt after 1880, but he was able to do so only after Lord Percy had been allowed to join the Central Committee as the National Union's representative. Indeed, if Liverpool, Manchester and Birmingham had thrown their united energies into the fight, he might not, even then, have been completely successful.

The control of the National Union was vested in its Council, but the Council until 1883 was little more than a creature of the Central Office. It was composed of men who had held office,

or were holding office, like Raikes and Lord Percy, influential
back benchers like Henry Chaplin (who rarely attended), the
party officials at the Central Office, a Whip or two, a few M.P.s
and candidates like Sir William Charley, J. M. Maclean and
Ellis Ashmead-Bartlett, who were used by the Central Office for
the writing of pamphlets or the delivery of lectures, and a few
representatives of the local associations. Such a heterogeneous
gathering was naturally dominated by anyone with a policy
(hitherto the party managers), and it was towards this Council
that Gorst and Lord Randolph Churchill turned their attentions
in 1883. They resolved to 'capture' it at the 1883 Annual Meeting,
to install Lord Randolph as chairman in place of Lord Percy,
to obtain a large grant from the party funds to free the Union
from dependence upon the Whips and the Central Committee, and
then to 'weld the Council into a powerful political organisation
strong enough to set the "front-bench men" at defiance'.[1] And when
it came to propaganda Lord Randolph had an excellent case:

> I should like to see the control of the party organization taken out
> of the hands of a self-elected body, and placed in the hands of an
> elected body. I should like to see the management of party funds
> taken out of the hands of an irresponsible body. The Central Com-
> mittee is a self-elected and irresponsible body, while the Council is
> a responsible and elected body.[2]

Gorst and Churchill at first rather over-played their hands by
making too thorough preparations for the 1883 conference. Their
list of 'approved candidates' leaked out, and was even sent to
Sir Stafford Northcote by Ellis Ashmead-Bartlett some days in
advance of the meeting. And some moderates were annoyed that
the list was so carefully engineered that the names of all Churchill's
most popular opponents (who were sure of election) appeared on
the Gorst-Churchill list. Ashmead-Bartlett, accordingly, constituted himself an unofficial leader of the opposition along with
Edward Clarke, and they, with some assistance, were able to
prevent Churchill winning an overwhelming victory.[3] As it was,

[1] J. M. Maclean, *Recollections of Westminster and India*, Manchester [1901], p. 59.
[2] Lord Randolph Churchill at the 1883 conference, quoted in McKenzie, *British Political Parties*, p. 170.
[3] Gorst wrote to Wolff after the election: 'The election, however, went off badly.
Clarke, Chaplin, Claud Hamilton, and a lot of other undesirable men got elected,
and it will require the greatest care and skill in the selection and election of the
twelve co-opted members to secure us the necessary working majority. I don't quite
understand [Ashmead-Bartlett's] game, but he evidently thinks it his interest now
to do openly everything he can against us?' Gorst, *The Fourth Party*, p. 258.

the bare majority was enough, since it enabled Churchill to become Chairman and to obtain an 'Organisation Committee' composed mainly of his supporters to attend to the fulfilment of his programme.

The Organisation Committee immediately came into conflict with its avowed enemy the Central Committee. It had the advantage of strong leadership, while the Central Committee was more or less dependent on the vacillations of Sir Stafford Northcote. It had, moreover, the at least tacit support of Bartley, the Central Committee's own executive officer. There was a long period of negotiation, of which Sir Winston Churchill's biography of his father gives details, and then in April 1884, an abrupt ending of negotiations. Then a pause before the National Union conference in July 1884, when Lord Randolph won a carefully prepared victory. Finally a compromise (not approved by Gorst) by which Lord Randolph (1) recognised Lord Salisbury as his leader, and (2) gave over the chairmanship of the National Union Council to Sir Michael Hicks Beach who had lately become *de facto* party leader in the Commons. In return Churchill was taken into the party fold as one of its acknowledged leaders and his enemy, the Central Committee, was disbanded.

Without Churchill the National Union was powerless, and easily slipped back into its old dependence on the central office. Moreover, it had already a rival which was beginning to outshine it. Primroses had first been worn in memory of Disraeli on Primrose Day (19 April) 1883, and the Primrose League had been formed soon afterwards on the suggestion of Drummond Wolff of the Fourth Party.[1] By 1885 it had spread all over the country, and was particularly important in rural areas, and by 1886 it was the most important political organisation in the constituencies.

The end of the Fourth Party also marked the beginning of a new harmony at the Central Office. The Central Committee was wound up and the management of the party again entrusted to the Chief Whip and the Principal Agent. But this time there was no difficulty about personalities. During the next ten years Akers-Douglas, as Chief Whip, and Middleton, as Principal Agent, formed a team of unrivalled efficiency, and by co-operation the Central Office at last achieved the independence and prestige which Gorst had always sought for it.

[1] There is a history: Janet H. Robb, *The Primrose League 1883-1906*, New York 1942.

Chapter Seventeen

PARTY FINANCE

I

THE party fund had a peculiar importance for party organisation because it afforded almost the only means by which the party managers could affect the conduct of elections directly, and because the amount of money available prescribed the limits of central organisation. Indeed, the effectiveness of the central organisation depended in the last resort on the amount of money it had at its disposal, for in many constituencies only this outside financial help could ensure that the registration was properly conducted, that good candidates could fight efficiently, and even that some seats should be contested at all. On the other hand, all this was in a sense on the periphery of the main political battle because the overwhelming majority of candidates paid their own way, and because the party election fund occasionally shrank to as little as £15,000: the fund was no more than a reserve which enabled the parties to cope with the unusual constituency, or to subsidise the limited number of candidates with slender resources. Only the Parnellites after 1885 possessed sufficient funds to give the party leaders the whip hand in the selection of candidates and to enable them to pay a salary to the most impecunious M.P.s.

The two major parties recruited their fund in almost identical fashion. Until the Secret Service money for political purposes was abolished in 1886, whichever party was in office received £10,000 a year for the use of the Chief Whip in the Commons (in his capacity of Patronage Secretary of the Treasury) with which he was expected to provide for the business of the House by seeing that the government's supporters were in regular attendance. This sum did not go very far, however, and the bulk of the party income on both sides was obtained by means of an appeal for funds launched shortly before a general election when there was a strong incentive to give freely. In addition, subsidiary appeals were made to office-holders or former office-holders from time to time to help with the expenses of the party offices, and to a wider public in the hope of obtaining subscriptions to the registration associations. On the Conservative side the party clubs also made regular contributions.

The Secret Service money was of considerable value to the party in office, because it enabled it to provide for ordinary recurrent expenses without appealing to its supporters and also to accumulate a small surplus. The whole sum of £10,000 was paid over without question, and without any provision for audit, or for the return of unexpended monies, and was spent at the entire discretion of the Chief Whip.[1] About £1,200 was spent on the routine expenses of the Parliamentary Secretary's office at 52, King Street, most of it on the wages and expenses of the messengers who enabled the Whips to keep in touch with ministers, peers, and M.P.s. These expenses were ultimately transferred to the ordinary Treasury estimates.[2] Another £500 or thereabouts appears to have been spent on the secretarial and travelling expenses incurred by the Chief Whip and his personal (i.e. unofficial) private secretary or in payment of the latter. No accounts have survived of these arrangements, but most Whips travelled a great deal and had both an official and one or two unofficial private secretaries. The remaining £7,500 was available for ordinary political purposes. About £2,000 of this would have been absorbed by the ordinary requirements of the party offices in London and, at least after 1875, another £1,000 by the Scottish and Irish offices. The £4,500, more or less, which was left over could be invested in Consols and saved up for a period in opposition or could be spent on by-elections. The

---

[1] H.C. 267, p. 56 (1884-5). VII, 112.

[2] The details of this transfer are to be found in the Treasury Papers at the Public Record Office, T1/8287B and T1/8373B. The staff of the office paid out of the Secret Service money consisted of an assistant superintendent at £200 a year, seven messengers at £1. 15. 0. a week during the session and £1. 10. 0. or 15s. when Parliament was not sitting (they received numerous 'extras' in addition to their wages) and a charwoman. The estimate for office expenses in 1887 was

Allowance for messengers, etc.	£880
Private Secretaries	£200
Office expenses and incidentals	£50
Travelling expenses	£20
Telegrams, etc.	£30
	£1,180

This sum was later increased to a little over £1,200.

Liberals appear to have saved considerable sums between 1868 and 1874; the Conservatives probably saved less because they were more lavish in spending money.[1] But there is probably no significance in the fact that the Secret Service fund was abolished by a Conservative Chancellor of the Exchequer (Lord Randolph Churchill) in 1886, after its administration had been severely criticised by the Comptroller and Auditor-General and the Public Accounts Committee.[2]

The general election appeal for funds was specifically designed to raise money for poor candidates, but the appeal also had the additional objective of building up a reserve to use between elections. The peers, although they did not always do so, were expected to contribute most of the money, because they had no election expenses to find. The Chief Whip in the Lords became in this way the most important money-raiser; on the Conservative side he acted as one of the trustees of the party funds and sat in at meetings where organisational questions were discussed. The Chief Whip in the Commons was by tradition called upon to raise large sums only when the Lords were reluctant, as the Liberal peers were in 1868 and 1874, but the Liberals were increasingly forced to break with tradition, and after 1885 they could obtain very little money from the Lords.[3]

The amount brought in by the election appeal varied considerably. Disraeli asked for £100,000 for his 1868 election fund, and extracted £10,000 from an unwilling cabinet as their contribution towards it,[4] but there is no evidence that he obtained

[1] The Secret Service fund may have supplied the sums invested in Consols which W. P. Adam inherited from his predecessors in 1874, and which I found mysterious in writing of the subject in 'British Party Finance, 1868-1880', *Bulletin of the Institute of Historial Research*, XXVII, 85-6 (1954). This article contains a list of contributors to the Liberal funds in 1868, 1874 and 1880.

[2] The official statement of the change is contained in *3 Hansard* CCCVIII, 667-8.

[3] The Liberal contributors listed in my article cited above belong to the following categories:

			1868	*1874*	*1880*
Peers .	.	.	8	22	19
M.P.s	.	.	37	13	11
ex-M.P.s	.	.	1	1	3
Candidates .	.		—	—	4
Others.	.	.	2	3	5
			48	39	42

The sum raised in the Lords was on each occasion about £6,000 to £8,000 or about a third or a quarter of the total sum raised.

[4] Buckle, *Disraeli*, V, 56-7.

more than half his target, and the Whips on both sides were always less ambitious. The Conservatives usually hoped for about £50,000, and expected to spend about £30,000 on the election itself; the Liberals usually aimed at from £20,000 to £30,000. The sum required grew considerably after 1885, however, as it became customary to fight more hopeless seats and to put up candidates with less money. Thus Middleton estimated the expenses of the 1892 election as £80,000:

> We have available rather over £20,000—To fight all the English & Irish seats we want £60,000 more which makes £80,000 & with the chance of being out [of office] for a time we ought to aim at a surplus to carry on with—say £20,000—What we want therefore is £80,000 to add to what we have got and with a little management this can easily be done.[1]

On this latter occasion Lord Limerick, the Lords' Whip, collected no less than £45,000 from the peers alone, 'quite an exceptional collection for the House of Lords Whip'.[2] Contrast these very large sums with the £15,000 the Liberals were able to raise in 1868, the £10,000 in 1874, and the £33,000 in 1880 from Lords, Commons and outsiders together.

The success of a particular election appeal depended to a considerable extent on the way in which the Lords Whip went about his business. If he were old or out of sympathy with his fellow-peers he would do badly: if shrewd, disinterested and popular he would do well. Much, too, depended on his backing: the Conservatives always managed to get more through the influence of Lord Abergavenny than they would otherwise have done. The way in which an appeal was launched is made clear by the correspondence between Lord Limerick and Lord Salisbury after Limerick had become Lords Whip in 1889. Limerick was obliged to consult many of his predecessors as to how the appeals for the 1892 election should be made because his immediate predecessor, Lord Kintore, had become governor of South Australia, and was out of the country. Not that Limerick was lacking in shrewdness: he had already given Salisbury very good advice in 1890 on how

---

[1] R. W. E. Middleton to S. K. McDonnell, 15 November 1891. Salisbury Papers. These figures should be compared with those for 1910 given in Blake, *The Unknown Prime Minister*, p. 100.

[2] Limerick to Salisbury, 8 December 1894. Salisbury Papers. In 1895 Limerick obtained only £37,750 from the peers because five peers who had contributed in 1892 gave nothing. Limerick to Salisbury, 18 July 1895.

he should fill the vacant office of Captain of the Gentlemen at Arms with an eye to the next elections.

> I trust you will not mind my expressing a hope that Rosslyn's post may be given to some peer of great local influence and property who can be of use to the party.
>
> When the general election comes it will be necessary to urgently appeal for pecuniary and general support to the principal peers, and we ought to be able to look to those who have received posts or honours from the Government, if they are in a position to give substantial aid. I understand that Abergavenny has recommended Yarborough to you. I think it would be a good appointment, as he is able to assist materially, is regular in the House, and I believe does work locally.[1]

Limerick began his enquiries at the end of November 1891 when he asked for permission to start his appeal.

> After consulting with Douglas and Middleton, I think it would be well, if you approve, to commence taking steps for the collection of the special General Election Fund. I of course direct my particular attention to the peers, and it requires a good deal of personal private correspondence as well as interviews, not being a matter that can be managed by circulars, so that I should like to commence on it before the regular work of the Session begins.[2]

Salisbury demurred at first, and asked for further information, and Limerick had to explain.

> I did not purpose attacking the peers generally at present, but only making lists of those likely to help, ascertaining through whom different peers can best be influenced, and (through Middleton) what peers give material aid in different localities and therefore cannot be expected to give so much to the general Fund. In fact to get together general information of what peers may be expected to do when the time comes. Only in a few cases, if the opportunity served, mentioning the matter to individual peers.
>
> I wrote to Lathom[3] as you suggested and he answers that the Fund ought to be started in good time, but that it would be better not to make any general appeal at present. That the first thing is to get some big men to put down their names for large sums and use

[1] Limerick to Salisbury, 29 July 1890. Yarborough was duly appointed and gave £1,000 towards the 1892 appeal, but nothing in 1895. He did not hold office again.
[2] Limerick to Salisbury, 1 December 1891. Salisbury Papers.
[3] Edward Bootle-Wilbraham, second Lord Skelmersdale and first Earl of Lathom, Conservative Chief Whip in the House of Lords 1874-85, Lord Chamberlain, etc.

them as decoy ducks, so as (privately) to influence others at the proper time. Also that a good deal of the work must be done through others who can influence individuals.

I know that this is the most difficult, and I may say unpleasant, part of a Whip's work. I will take care not to 'rush' the peers, for I have no doubt that many will require to be well warmed by the actual contest—Lathom says that Colville used to work the Scotch peers principally, and should be asked to do so again.[1]

There is an agreeable irony in Lathom's advice, since among Lord Salisbury's papers is Lathom's appeal to him to contribute to the 1880 election fund.

Forgive me for troubling you. As 'Whip' it is my duty to ask you whether you will contribute to the Carlton Fund for the expenses of the forthcoming Elections. As yet I have not been very successful. The Duke of Portland comes forward well with £6,000. Duke of Northumberland £2,000, Ld Egerton £1,000, Ld Wilton & Ld Penrhyn £500 each. Others have not answered me yet.[2]

In addition to the fund raised at elections there were a number of other less important sources of income. The richer office-holders and former office-holders could usually be prevailed upon to give from £500 to £2,000 between them roughly once in two years. The Carlton and Junior Carlton clubs gave £500 each every year to the Conservative fund, and more at election times: then the Carlton gave about £1,000 and a percentage of its profits, and the Junior Carlton about £1,000, the amount being calculated on the basis of ten shillings a member.[3] Small subscriptions to the registration associations brought in perhaps £500 more. There were also variable amounts raised for local purposes in Scotland and Ireland. The sums available in Ireland were sometimes quite large, but all record of them seems to have been lost. The Scots appear to have given little to the Scottish as distinct from the general fund until the late seventies. After that enough money came in to finance most routine Scottish expenditure, and by 1885 the Conservatives had a regular

---

[1] Limerick to Salisbury, 8 December 1891. Salisbury Papers. The 11th Lord Colville of Culross was Master of the Buckhounds 1866-8, and collected the bulk of the party funds in 1868.

[2] Lord Skelmersdale to Salisbury, 15 March 1880. Salisbury Papers.

[3] The *St Stephen's Review*, 2 February 1884, reported that the Carlton gave £1,400, the Junior Carlton half as much, that the St Stephen's 'does not do much', and that the Beaconsfield hoped to do more. For the Carlton see Petrie, *The Carlton Club*, pp. 90f., and [C. 2856-I] pp. 485-8. H.C. (1881). XLIV, 515-18.

income of about £1,000 a year and an election fund of £5,355.

Until the eighties there was very little bartering of honours for money or services. Peel had frowned on the practice, which had not been uncommon in his younger days, and other statesmen followed his example.[1] This did not prevent the Whips from letting it be known that those who expended a great deal of money on elections, particularly in difficult constituencies, would be entitled to some recognition in after years, but there was nothing more than a vague understanding which could hardly be misinterpreted. By the eighties, however, both parties had been so hard hit by the depression of trade and industry on the one hand and of agriculture on the other, that it was difficult for them to find candidates willing to spend £4,000 or more on a doubtful election unless they could offer something in return. Sir Stafford Northcote, while leader of the Opposition, therefore fell into the habit of giving assurances to rich and influential men that if they did fight a difficult and expensive contest, their so doing would be felt 'a great addition to the claims' they already had upon 'the gratitude of the Conservative party'. Usually this assurance was conveyed in such a way that there was no doubt that it amounted to a promise of a knighthood, baronetcy, or peerage, and as a consequence Lord Salisbury was later called upon to redeem it. But there was no attempt by the Conservatives to sell honours. The sale of honours was begun by the Liberals when in 1891 the Liberal Chief Whip prevailed upon Mr Gladstone to exchange a promise of peerages to two insignificant but wealthy men for substantial contributions to the Liberal party funds. As a consequence James Williamson and the Viscount de Stern became (on Lord Rosebery's nomination) Lord Ashton and Lord Wandsworth in 1895. But their story does not belong to this book.[2]

II

The Conservatives placed the party fund in the hands of trustees, and authorised the Chief Whip in the Commons or his deputy to draw on their account. The Liberals left it entirely

[1] Professor Gash, in a letter to the author, writes, 'I have never come across any evidence of *previous* encouragement and promises to candidates fighting difficult seats; though subsequently such services were frequently adduced by the candidates themselves or their backers as constituting a claim on the gratitude of the party. It was not a claim readily recognised by party leaders, however.'

[2] I hope to tell the story in more detail elsewhere.

in the hands of the Chief Whip, who kept it in a special account opened in his own name, and regarded it as an important source of influence. 'I should be sorry', wrote Edward Marjoribanks in 1889, 'to see the dispensation of funds for election purposes in the hands of others than the official Whips. The influence we have is none too great and the power of the purse forms an important factor in what we have.'[1]

There was very little difference in the purposes to which the two parties put their funds. These were outlined in a letter of explanation which George Glyn, the Chief Liberal Whip in 1868, sent to Gladstone after he had expressed some anxiety that the fund should be used only for legitimate purposes.

> With respect to the 'Fund' I can assure you that it is spent entirely upon legitimate election expenses—at least it is given by me with that proviso. The claims upon a 'Fund' are as follows. 1st Registration. We have an office in London with a Secretary etc in communication with all the local agents, giving them advice, supplying them with all forms of claims etc etc also doing most important work *at an election* in looking up the out voters. This is supposed to be kept alive by annual subscriptions, but I find £300 a year is all I get towards an expense of near £1500. I have kept this up this year as it would have been most foolish to lose all this perfect machinery (the only basis of organization which we have) upon the eve of a General Election. Hayter says it costs more than it is worth but Brand has been a strong advocate for it, & I certainly *now* find it *most necessary*.[2] I am sure we have saved thousands of votes by the information & instructions sent to local agents from our head quarters.
>
> The 2d expense is the Office here which it is needful to have for some months before an election, & if anyone sees the daily work here now, the visits of candidates and agents & the correspondence & telegraphs upon matters connected with candidatures the necessity for such a 'house of call' cd not be doubted.
>
> The fund is wanted 3rdly for aid in *some* cases towards local registration & in some degree for expenses of meetings etc to rouse popular feeling which can only be done by sending men down to aid candidates etc etc.
>
> 4thly for direct assistance to *candidates*, & of course here, when the money is given, I cannot tell exactly how it goes but it is given *to the candidate* & upon the understanding that it is in aid of legitimate expenditure. There are many places where special men are necessary

[1] Add. MS. 44,332, f.208. [2] Sir William Hayter and Brand were former Chief Whips.

& sometimes such men may have a little less money to spend than the place will fairly cost . . . I don't think it possible to manage properly without say £10000 to £15000—& *of course* such a sum wd not be near enough if we copied the tactics of our opponents, who start their men with all they want & ask no questions as to the mode of expenditure. I think in nearly all the places I have promised to subscribe to the seats depended upon it and the grant was to make up either for what the candidate or those *locally* concerned *could not do.* In former times if the 'Whip's fund' ran low a few cheques from Brookes soon set matters right but you will gather from Ld B[ess-borough]'s letter that it is not so now & I find it hard to hit the right financial vein, without either going to those who have other claims upon them or putting myself too much in the hands of those to whom I do not think I shd be under an obligation. I have only really troubled you with all this as you wished to hear more of the 'mysterious fund'. I have no doubt it has been & might be used for objectionable objects but I hoped to guard agst this if I had the funds to dispose of as far as I cd by making the grants for legitimate objects only.[1]

The party organisers on both sides felt some anxiety about the way in which the fund was spent because they realised that they had almost no control over the money once it left their hands. They had simply to hand it over to the candidate with admonitions to use it virtuously, and hope for the best. When Sir William Hart Dyke was asked in 1880 whether any measures were taken to see that the money was spent legally he was bound to reply, as any other Whip would have done, 'Well, I confess I have never taken any steps to produce that result.'[2] The Whips always hoped that they would not be driven into paying money towards a corrupt contest, but when they found that a seat might be won by doing so they found it difficult to refuse. They had then to balance the possibility of winning or holding a seat against the possibility that the borough might become a constant drain on their resources and a source of scandal, or that a pure fight might mean the reform of the borough and cheaper elections.

For most Whips this was not, however, the most pressing question. What they had to decide was the extent to which hopeless contests or near-hopeless contests were justified if they had to be fought with party money rather than at the expense of the candidates.

[1] Glyn to Gladstone, 12 September 1868. Add. MS. 44,347, ff.160-4, quoted also by A. F. Thompson, *English Historical Review,* LXIII, 194-5, (1948).
[2] [C. 2856-I] p. 527. H.C. (1881). XLIV, 557.

Both parties were divided on the issue. Glyn on the Liberal side strongly opposed hopeless contests, but his successor, Adam, was inclined to think that few constituencies were really hopeless. Gorst, Middleton, and Salisbury on the Conservative side supported Glyn—'Hopeless seats should never be fought' was one of Salisbury's favourite dicta—Spofforth, on the other hand, took the opposite view. He held that it was absolutely necessary to contest seats 'where your man is either certain to be beaten, or at any rate it is highly improbable he will succeed', and devoted part of a long memorandum on party management to the subject.

> You must make up your mind to one thing; that the enemy will attack you everywhere with a view of expending your resources; for this reason you should naturally do the same and have candidates ready for every place. It doesn't much matter what sort of men they may be so that they are ready speakers. They should be provided merely with funds necessary to pay the strictly legal expenses at the lowest possible rate, such as their share of the Sheriff's expenses in erecting Polling Booths, & also to pay for one or two rooms as may be necessary for committee work and for printing addresses. The attack thus made on a seat although certain not to be won by your man will involve a much larger expenditure by the successful candidate & if he is a poor man and requires assistance will encroach considerably on the funds of his party collected for the purpose of the General Election. So, consequently, you will do more injury to your opponents by causing an unnecessary expenditure of their resources than the mere expenditure of a small sum on your own part to your own cause.[1]

The balance between the two points of view was decided partly by the need to encourage the party at general elections by contesting as many seats as possible, and by local pressure in particular constituencies, and partly by the amount of money in the party coffers. Thus it was possible for the Liberals to fight many constituencies in 1880 which could not be fought in 1868 or 1874 simply because there was considerably more money available and because it was necessary to take advantage of the enthusiasm among party workers created by the Midlothian campaign.

There was a strong tradition, already well-established in the forties and reflected in many of the begging letters received by the Whips, that a deserving candidate was entitled to £500 from

---

[1] This memorandum is in the Disraeli Papers, where it is wrongly attributed to Lord Norton. The punctuation has been altered to clarify certain passages.

the party fund.[1] But in fact the figure was just as often £300. W. P. Adam, Liberal Chief Whip in 1880, left notes about thirty-nine subsidies he granted in that year: seventeen were of £500, ten were of £300, eight were of more than £500, three were of less than £300, and one was of £450. By 1885 the reduction in the area of constituencies and the limitation of election expenses had made the lower figure of £250 or £300 the usual one. Captain Middleton's one surviving letter book (mainly for 1885-6)[2] records fifty-three grants to individual candidates: three were of £150, nine of £200, seventeen of £250, ten of £300, one of £350, seven of £400, and six of £500. At the time, and for many years afterwards, it was a rule of the Central Office that no constituency should be given more than one-third of the expenses allowed under the 1883 Act, unless the circumstances were quite exceptional.[3]

This subsidy was usually given only to poor candidates and to problem constituencies which gave the Whips trouble for many successive elections. Those on W. P. Adam's list for 1880 are an interesting cross-section of them. Eleven of them were English boroughs and eleven were English counties. Blackburn, the first name on the list, was something of a Conservative stronghold, but a strong local Liberal candidate had managed to win one seat in 1874, and required assistance to keep it. This took two forms, a second candidate to reduce the number of split votes, and £300 towards his election expenses. Canterbury was another Conservative stronghold, and a very corrupt one; it obtained £500 to make a contest possible and to take advantage of divisions in the Conservative ranks caused by an independent Conservative candidate, and a further £500 towards the cost of bringing the petition which eventually unseated both the newly elected Conservatives and led to the disfranchisement of the borough until 1885. Dorchester, another Conservative stronghold, was fought by an Irishman, A. W. F. Greville, Irish Whip in the Commons from 1868 to 1874, in the vain hope of winning him an English seat. He was no longer a possible candidate for an Irish constituency because he opposed Home Rule, and the £450 he received was in the nature of a reward for past services and a consolation for losing his seat at Westmeath to a Home Ruler in 1874. He had already contested Perthshire in 1878 and, as it

[1] Professor Gash speaks of it as a 'routine subsidy': *Politics in the Age of Peel*, p. 436.
[2] This letter book is now in the Chilston Papers.
[3] Akers-Douglas to McDonnell, 19 April 1898. Salisbury Papers.

happened, never got back into the House, because his father died in 1883 and he became the second Lord Greville. The Dudley election was more complicated and absorbed no less than £1,000. The seat had once been in the gift of Lord Dudley, but his political career had been an odd one, and since 1857, when he had driven out his nominee, Sir Stafford Northcote, the borough had been represented by a Liberal, Henry Brinsley Sheridan. In 1880 Sheridan was hotly opposed by a strong Conservative and since he lived on director's fees, did not possess the resources to defend the seat unaided. Because he was the only candidate who could hold the seat he was very generously treated. Horsham was fairly evenly divided between the two parties, but because the election was fought very largely on local issues the Liberal sitting member, James Clifton Brown, who was given £250, was eventually defeated. By contrast, the Liberal candidate for the Monmouth district was conducting a campaign almost entirely in national terms, and was carried into parliament on the crest of the wave emanating from Midlothian. This candidate, E. H. Carbutt, was a mechanical engineer and former mayor of Leeds, and the £500 the party spent on him proved a sound investment. Portsmouth, which secured £300, was a marginal constituency, leaning towards the Conservatives, and too important to be neglected. Sheffield received £1,000. One of the Liberal candidates was a local man, S. D. Waddy, who had given up his seat for Barnstaple in 1879 specially to contest Sheffield at a by-election. This had cost about £2,000 and had used up all his resources, so that for his second contest within a year at the behest of the party leaders he required a subsidy. In the event he lost the seat to a Conservative, but the party still kept a fatherly eye on him and he was given a seat at Edinburgh in 1882. At Stoke one of the Liberal candidates was Henry Broadhurst, a working man, and the £500 paid over to the constituency was doubtless a condition of his candidature. The last two boroughs mentioned, Westminster, a Conservative stronghold, and York, a marginal constituency, which each received £300 for poor candidates (John Morley and Ralph Creyke), were the only straightforward boroughs on the list, with no serious problems apart from their lack of money.[1]

[1] The final result in these eleven boroughs was a Liberal gain of four seats (Monmouth, two at Stoke and one at York) and a loss of two seats (Horsham and one at Sheffield) and the unseating of two Conservatives at Canterbury. This amounts to a net gain of four seats.

The thirteen English counties were less interesting. Two obtained assistance, but the candidate did not go to the poll (South Hampshire and North Norfolk), three were quite hopeless constituencies for Liberals (East Devon, Middlesex, and North Northumberland), and the remainder were marginal seats which cost a small fortune to contest (East Cumberland, East Essex, West Gloucestershire, Huntingdonshire, West Norfolk, South Northumberland, East Suffolk, North Wiltshire, and East Worcestershire). Two of them attracted attention because Gladstone's sons were candidates—Herbert in Middlesex, and William Henry in East Worcestershire—but their intrinsic interest was not great.[1]

These orthodox subsidies were supplemented in special cases by much larger grants. These were usually given in cases where there was not enough money to start a contest in a key constituency. Thus W. P. Adam in 1880 gave a loan of £3,000 to the county of Inverness to help start a contest, and George Glyn in 1868 obtained gifts of £1,500 from Lord Yarborough for Cricklade and £2,000 from Sir John Ramsden for the county of Monmouth, which met most of the election costs. The Conservatives were usually more lavish in such exceptional cases, and also at important by-elections, such as those caused by ministers vacating their seats in 1880, when Oxford alone received £3,000.[2] Most special cases involved an approach to friendly magnates and sometimes a collection in one of the clubs as well as a grant from the party fund, which lacked the resources to provide for them without further help. South Shropshire in 1868 is a fairly typical case of this sort.[3] Each party had won a seat in 1865, after a somewhat inconclusive contest, but the new electors were strongly Conservative, and there was no reason why the

---

[1] East Worcestershire received £500 and Middlesex £200 from the party. W. H. Gladstone won the Worcestershire seat, but Herbert Gladstone was defeated in Middlesex and succeeded his father as M.P. for Leeds.

[2] It was the exception rather than the rule to oppose ministers seeking re-election. During Gladstone's 1868 ministry only six ministers were opposed, none of them in 1868 itself, and all kept their seats, although Gladstone himself would probably have lost his seat on becoming Chancellor of the Exchequer had he not dissolved in 1874. During Disraeli's 1874 ministry only three ministers were opposed, and again all kept their seats. During Gladstone's 1880 ministry the opposition was more successful: Sir William Harcourt, the Home Secretary, was defeated at Oxford in 1880, as was John McLaren, the Lord Advocate, at Wigtown, and in 1882 W. H. Grenfell, the Parliamentary Groom in Waiting, was defeated at Salisbury. Two other ministerial seats were unsuccessfully attacked. A. B. Beaven, 'List of Opposed Elections on Taking Office', *English Historical Review*, XXVI, 139-48 (1911). The case of Sir Henry Storks discussed in Chapter XI was an exceptional one.

[3] There is a bundle of correspondence on this election in the Disraeli Papers.

Conservatives should not have both seats, if they could find the necessary money and a second candidate. The Conservative sitting member, Percy Egerton Herbert, Lord Powis's brother, was not well off and could do little to help, while Lord Powis himself and the other Conservative magnates were not very anxious for a fight. However, the local squires, farmers, and clergy were much more zealous, and they had a good candidate, Edward Corbett of Longnor Hall, whose father had been M.P. for Shrewsbury. But Corbett, in the words of a local squire, could not 'afford one farthing', so that nothing was done to promote a contest until three weeks before the election. Then a meeting of local Tories decided to appeal to Disraeli for help through Montagu Corry, himself a Shropshire landowner. They assured him that Corbett could win easily enough, but added that a contest would cost £5,000, of which they could raise only one-fifth, and that Lord Boyne 'ought to give largely because the proper candidate was his son—and then he would have had to have paid all', suggesting £2,000 as a proper sum for that unfortunate nobleman to give.[1] Corry and Taylor, the Whip, discussed the matter, and began immediately to collect promises of financial support. When sufficient money was promised to make a start possible, Taylor agreed to guarantee the remainder (he apparently paid out £1,300), and Corbett came out as candidate. Meanwhile the Liberals, whose slender chances of success depended on their establishing an expensive organisation, had also found that they were desperately short of money. Their only candidate, R. J. More, M.P., of Linley Hall, was himself a poor man, and the Liberal magnates headed by the Duke of Sutherland were as indifferent to the result of the election as their Conservative counterparts. The result was therefore hardly in doubt, and Glyn told Gladstone a few days before the election: 'I am afraid we may lose S. Shropshire. More has no money, Lord Granville & I are trying to help him but the Duke of Sutherland refused to give a farthing, the county & the Carlton find £9,000 for his opponent.'[2] On polling day More did surprisingly well, but he was none the less beaten by 353 votes and did not get back into parliament until 1885.

[1] Lord Boyne owned 8,424 acres in the county but was really a Durham magnate and had chosen to bring his only son forward for the Southern Division of that county, where he was defeated.
[2] Glyn to Gladstone, 12 November 1868. Add. MS. 44,347, f.242.

There was as yet no question of a party salary or subsidy except for Home Rulers, although the trade union members were necessarily assisted by their union. Sometimes a particularly penurious individual (usually an Irishman) would be given a dole by the Whips if he were faced with starvation, or would be pensioned off to some remote colony to drink himself to death, but this was unusual.[1] Bankrupts were usually helped by means of a whip round the clubs and the richer members of the party, and sometimes as much as £10,000 was raised in this way and invested in an annuity, but in such cases the Whips rarely started an appeal themselves, although they might make a contribution to a fund started by others. The necessity for special contributions of this sort was not great before 1885 because it was almost impossible to get into parliament, except in Ireland, without paying one's way, and there was no real shortage of rich or at least well-off men to contest seats. I have been able to find no case of a regular salary being paid to a member before 1886, when Colonel Henry Eyre entered parliament as Conservative member for the Gainsborough division of Lincolnshire after a sharp contest and on condition that the constituency should pay him £300 a year. This it did until 1889 when Eyre's salary was stopped. To avoid a by-election the Central Office then agreed to take over the payments, and maintained them until 1898, although Eyre lost the seat in 1892 and became simply a paid party lecturer.[2] The only other cases of party subsidies were those in which sums of up to £100 were paid to members as contributions towards the cost of keeping up the register in their constituency.

III

The Home Rulers were inevitably financed in a different way from the Liberals or Conservatives.[3] Indeed, for a time they managed without a fund altogether. Isaac Butt, while leader of the Home Rule movement, refused to allow the Home Rule League to have an election fund, and such office space and stationery as was necessary was paid for out of the two guineas

[1] The curious case of The O'Donoghue, who lived very largely by borrowing from his fellow members, is mentioned by Sir Alfred E. Pease, *Elections and Recollections*, p. 101.
[2] There is a long correspondence about Colonel Eyre in the Salisbury Papers.
[3] Cruise O'Brien, *Parnell and His Party*, pp. 133-40, 265-72.

subscribed by each Home Rule M.P. Since neither of the other parties had an adequate Irish fund this is not as surprising as it might seem at first sight, but it was undoubtedly a short-sighted move which restricted the Home Rule movement both in its organisation and in the class of members it recruited: only quite rich men could pay their own way. Parnell would probably have remedied this situation for his own followers by 1880 had he not been chairman of the Land League, which was committed to not spending its very substantial income (£60,000 to £100,000 a year at this time) on elections. As it was, he could only obtain an advance of £2,000 from the League and £300 from other sources for the election, which was of very little practical help, even though the Parnellites usually spent substantially less than their opponents.[1] Fortunately for the party many of the Parnellites who were elected for the first time in 1880 were Irishmen already living in England, so that there was no real question of having to support them between elections.

The end of the Land League in 1881 freed the Parnellites from their dependence on an organisation which was, at least theoretically, hostile to parliamentarianism, and incidentally led to the transfer of over £30,000 held by the Land League in Paris to Parnell and his two senior colleagues.[2] It became possible to build up special party funds both in the hands of the newly formed National League and in those of the party leaders. The National League raised sufficient money for the ordinary routine party expenses in Ireland and for by-elections—in 1883 it spent £1,267 on them alone—while the main party fund was accumulated for fighting general elections and for paying the expenses of members. In 1885 not less than £17,950 was raised for this latter fund, and possibly a great deal more, and by the end of 1886 the fund had grown to £100,000.[3] Out of this very large sum it became possible to pay the travelling expenses of members. But this was all after 1885. Before 1885, when Parnell had not had a chance to sift his followers at a general election, there was still something rather amateurish about the party organisation, and the windfalls of 1881-2 had yet to make their influence felt.

---

[1] The returns are not clear on this point but suggest that the Parnellites spent about £300 on the average. *Ibid.*, p. 137n.
[2] *Ibid.*, pp. 135-6. [3] *Ibid.*, p. 266.

APPENDICES

Appendix I

A NOTE ON MUNICIPAL ELECTIONS

IN most of the larger towns, and many of the smaller ones, municipal and other local elections had long played a vital part in local politics. They were the recognised nursery of electoral organisation, since the municipal ward was universally accepted as the basic unit of election-eering, as well as a constant reminder of the parliamentary struggle to come and a meter which indicated the ebb and flow of party strengths. The pettiness of local politics, the parsimoniousness of local councillors, except when they themselves were interested in a contract, and the blatant corruption at so many municipal elections often kept the better class of manufacturers, merchants, and professional men out of the town council. A Nottingham witness told the Hartington Committee in 1869 that 'the parties nominated are generally of opposing politics, but they are not persons of influence or position in the town, and the contests of late years have subsided into a struggle between persons in the lower rank of life who have accumulated a little property, and who wish to obtain a position in the town . . .'[1] And similar evidence was given by a Bradford witness.[2] But the example of Alderman Cobden was not entirely forgotten. Towns like Bolton and Sunder-land almost invariably returned wealthy and able local aldermen or councillors to parliament. And there were always sufficient local councillors from other big and medium-sized towns to bring the total number of members or ex-members of local councils in the House of Commons up to about fifty or sixty,[3] in addition to the usual six or seven London aldermen and common-councillors.[4] After 1870 there were also a good many members of school boards. Indeed, the great interest in education shown by electors and local magnates alike,

[1] H.C. 352, p. 16 (1868–9). VIII, 16.

[2] *Ibid.*, p. 111.

[3] The standard books of reference do not always mention local government service, but the following figures are approximately correct for the members elected in 1868 and 1880.

Service as	1868	1880
Councillor before election	20	10
Mayor & Councillor before election	35	38
Mayor after election	7	11
	62	59

[4] Full details are given in A. B. Beaven, *The Aldermen of the City of London*, London 1908, pp. 261-328.

tended to attract into local political life, as members of school boards, men who were not interested in municipal politics, such as Herbert Birley in Manchester and Mark Firth and Sir John Brown in Sheffield.[1]

The revival of political enthusiasm which accompanied the passage of the 1867 Reform Act encouraged local politicians to take a new interest in municipal elections. Since 1835 these had always reflected to some degree the shift in national political opinion, although the degree to which particular boroughs were affected depended on local circumstances. There were fewer fluctuations in party strengths in boroughs like Bristol (with a firmly established Conservative majority), or Leeds (with an equally safe Liberal majority), than in those where the result of an election in one or two wards might change the political complexion of the council. The national pattern took the form of a Radical phase in the mid-thirties, followed by a Conservative revival which quickened tempo after 1840 and lasted until a short time after the break-up of the Conservative party in 1845-6.

There was then a long period of neglect of municipal affairs, during which a quiescent aldermanic Liberalism held sway,[2] followed after 1867 by a revival of Radicalism in Birmingham and of Conservatism elsewhere, which culminated in a series of striking victories by the Conservatives in the municipal elections of 1873, and with the election of Joseph Chamberlain as Mayor of Birmingham in the same year. During the middle seventies there was a period of consolidation, which in some places lasted until 1886, and in others was succeeded after 1878 by a long period of Radical gains. After 1886 there was a period of confusion, from which the Conservatives generally profited, then more Liberal gains in the early nineties, followed by another Conservative revival.

The importance of municipal elections was fully recognised by the pioneers of party reorganisation in the seventies, John Gorst and Joseph Chamberlain, and their influence on these elections may conveniently be noted here. Gorst's tenure of the office of principal agent to the Conservative party corresponded with a great burst of municipal electioneering in Lancashire which resulted in severe Liberal defeats. Gorst carefully collated the results of these elections, as Bonham had

---

[1] School board elections were avowedly fought in most places solely on a denominational basis, but in practice politics and denominationalism were inseparable, and the organisers of the two parties became the organisers of the school board elections. The quality of the members of the Sheffield School Board in its first years was quite remarkable: there is an interesting account of it in J. H. Bingham, *The Sheffield School Board 1870-1903*, Sheffield 1949.

[2] There is a good account of a typical council of this period in C. Gill, *History of Birmingham, Vol I, Manor and Borough to 1865*, Oxford 1952, Ch. XVIII. During this period nearly all newspapers ceased to report municipal election results except from their own locality.

been wont to do in Peel's day,[1] and regarded them as one of the most important indications of the trend of popular opinion. As long as he remained at the Central Office he urged on the party leaders the need to take a greater interest in municipal elections and to treat them as a barometer which reflected the changes in public opinion. After the Conservatives had taken office in 1874 these warnings assumed a new importance. Thus in December 1874 he wrote to Disraeli,

> You will remember that our victory in the English Boroughs, at the late General Election was fore-shadowed by successes at the Municipal Elections of 1872 & 1873. I ought therefore to call your attention to the fact that this year we seem, notwithstanding our prestige as the party in office, to be losing the ground which we then gained.
>
> I send you returns obtained from half the Municipal Boroughs: and you may assume this to be the more favourable half, because experience shows that our friends are more ready to report success than failure. These returns show that whereas in the contests of 1873 we won 112 seats & lost 83, in the contests of 1874 we have won 93 and lost 100.[2]
>
> I have always felt some apprehension lest the political reaction in the English Boroughs which brought us into power should prove to be a mere temporary movement of repulsion induced by the unpopularity of the late government; and lest the electors, after once giving vent to their feelings by rejecting the supporters of the late government, might return to their normal allegiance to the so-called Liberal Party. We have seen some indication of this in Parliamentary Elections at Stroud, Bath, Hull & elsewhere; and the Municipal Elections of this year appear to furnish additional evidence of the precarious tenure of our position in the Boroughs. It is worth notice that we seem to have lost ground in places like Bath, Ashton, Colchester, Leeds, & Wakefield, which in the late General Election expressed their condemnation of the late government; and to have gained ground in places like Bolton, Bradford, Hastings and Rochdale, where the movement of repulsion had not spent itself in a Parliamentary victory.

[1] For Bonham see N. Gash, 'F. R. Bonham: Conservative "Political Secretary", 1832-47', *English Historical Review*, LXIII, 502-22 (1948).

[2] In a later letter (22 November 1875) Gorst gave the returns for 1875. The Conservatives gained seats in 24 boroughs, the Liberals in 31, there was no change in 52 and in 30 there was no political contest; nineteen others failed to send in a return. The Conservatives gained 41 seats and lost 91 in the 137 boroughs which sent in a return. In the 52 boroughs for which there were comparable returns for 1874 and 1875 the results were: 1874 Conservatives gained 21 seats and lost 44, a net Liberal gain of 23: 1875 Conservatives gained 19 seats and lost 46, a net Liberal gain of 27. In 1879 the Conservatives lost a very much larger number of seats and suffered a very real setback.

I do not dissent from your view that the mass of the people is, or may be made, Tory. But masses cannot move without leaders; and in English Boroughs we are grievously deficient in Tory leaders. Those of the higher classes in Boroughs who take part in politics have everything to lose & nothing to gain by attaching themselves to the Tory party; and we therefore find wealth, influence, ability, and all local political forces arrayed against us.

I was in hopes that the power and patronage which the possession of office has given us might have been to some extent at least so used as to create in the Boroughs a permanent Tory faction. The Radicals during their long tenure of power sedulously pursued such a policy, and have (I think as a consequence) a staff of Borough leaders immeasurably stronger than ours. But I think your colleagues (who are none of them Borough Members themselves) either fail to see the necessity for such a policy or despair of maintaining permanently our position in the Boroughs. At any rate little has been done to strengthen & consolidate our friends in the Boroughs and much to alienate and discourage them. I think you will find Mr. Dyke of the same opinion.[1]

Unfortunately for Gorst, the Conservative leaders and the party managers refused to take any notice of his warnings. For instance, Hart Dyke, the Chief Whip, shrugged off Gorst's warnings when they were referred to him, although he agreed that the Conservatives were losing ground:

We have been fighting for some years in many of these Boroughs & vast sums of money have been spent on Municipal Elections in view of the struggle supposed to be imminent. In many cases I fear after winning the Parliamentary battle, our friends have rested on their oars & allowed themselves to be beaten in the Municipal Election.

An instance: Mr. Saul Isaac called on me at [the] Treasury a few days ago.[2] I said to him—You have not done so well I fear this time in Municipal Elections. He laughed & said, Ah—but we spent nothing this time. They did all that [on] the other side. I have won my seat. This is I venture to think an instance which by no means stands alone, & that by inquiry it may be shewn that many of our friends have held their hands this time who were working hard in 1873. This is an evil but we must take human nature as we find it, & stir up our friends another year.

1 Gorst to Disraeli, 2 December 1874. Disraeli Papers.
2 Saul Isaac was M.P. for Nottingham 1874-80.

The Birmingham Liberals headed by Joseph Chamberlain believed both in fighting municipal elections on political lines and in the necessity for a systematic campaign to bring all local institutions into party hands.[1] For them political organisation was conceived in comprehensive terms and the 'Birmingham model' or 'Birmingham caucus' was a highly developed machine for securing success in elections for the School Board, the Board of Guardians and the town council as well as in parliamentary elections. There was no difference of principle between the Liberals and Conservatives in Birmingham as to the necessity of contesting local elections on political lines: where the two parties differed was in the type of organisation adopted. The Conservatives had no municipal policy and contested elections haphazardly; the Liberals had a municipal policy and contested local government elections regularly and systematically in order to be able to carry it out.

The Birmingham policy was also adopted by other Liberal associations which had close connections with Birmingham. The Leeds Liberal Association, for instance, had among its objects 'To superintend the registration of Parliamentary, Municipal, and Poor Law Electors. To promote in the Borough the Return of Liberal Representatives to Parliament, the Town Council, the School Board, the Board of Guardians, and the Board of Overseers.' More time was spent on the municipal and other local contests than on any other party work, and something of the atmosphere of the association is reflected in the following paragraph from the report of the Leeds Liberal Association for 1880 referring to the Board of Guardians.

> It scarcely comes within the objects of the Association to criticise the votes of the members of the Board, but as the labours of the Association are, to a large extent, directed towards the consolidation of the Liberal party, and as the political complexion of the Board was changed from a Tory to a Liberal one chiefly by the action taken by this Association, the fact can scarcely be passed by unnoticed that there were Liberals who voted for the election of a Tory Chairman. To say the least, if the same principle were acted upon in other representative bodies in the town, the efforts and aims of this Association would be impaired.

Neither Conservative exhortations nor Birmingham's example persuaded all local politicians of the need to contest municipal elections on exclusively party lines, and there remained a considerable minority of towns where municipal elections were 'non-political'. In some of them there was a genuine conviction that there was no connection between party and municipal affairs, and to Chamberlain's embarrassment the

[1] There is an admirable account of the attitude of the Birmingham Liberals in A. Briggs, *History of Birmingham: Vol. II, Borough and City, 1865-1938*, Oxford 1952, Ch. VI.

chairman of the Portsmouth Liberals expressed this view very forcibly at the inaugural conference of the National Liberal Federation.[1] More commonly there was a feeling that a policy of 'thorough' was not possible, however desirable in theory. A correspondent, writing to the *Manchester Guardian* in 1880, remarked that 'The few gentlemen in each ward who take an active interest in corporation affairs, be they Conservative or Liberal, will bear me out when I say that they often find great difficulty in procuring candidates to fill the office of councillor',[2] and in most boroughs few wards were actually contested except before a general election. Even in Birmingham nine wards were uncontested and only three contested in 1870 and 1871, and sixteen were uncontested and only two contested in 1880 and 1881.[3] In Bristol six wards were uncontested and four contested in 1870 and 1871, while after a redistribution of ward boundaries six wards were uncontested and seven contested in 1880, and seven wards were uncontested and six contested in 1881.[4]

In towns where there was no question of adopting the Birmingham policy of 'thorough', the absence of effective opposition meant that candidates for the council, although known to be partisans of one party or the other, rarely wore party labels.[5] Not that they were classified as Independents except in exceptional circumstances: they simply put themselves forward as individual citizens with an interest in the welfare of their native place, and left the press to classify them as it wished. This explains why it was usual for the press to report the election results in party terms, even when such terms were almost meaningless. As when *The Times* in 1885 reported the elections at Falmouth and

[1] *Proceedings Attending the Formation of the National Federation of Liberal Associations*, p. 25. A conference of Conservative Local Chairmen in 1875 took the same view of municipal elections. Gorst reported to Dyke on 21 December 1875 (Disraeli Papers): 'They think that in those places where Municipal Elections are not conducted on political grounds it is for the interest of the Conservative party to leave things as they are and not to attempt to introduce a political element into Municipal affairs; but in those places where contests are conducted on political grounds the organization of the party should be used to the utmost to promote the return of Conservative candidates for all local offices.'

[2] Reprinted in *To the Ratepayers of Manchester: Corporation Proceedings and Municipal Returns*, Manchester 1880, p. 5.

[3] E. S. Griffith, *Modern Development of City Government*, Oxford 1927, II, 697. Comparable figures for 1920-2 were: 1920 contested 27, uncontested 3; 1921 24 contested, 6 uncontested; 1922 22 contested, 8 uncontested.

[4] A. B. Beaven, *Bristol Lists*, Bristol 1899, *passim*.

[5] The returns sent by John Gorst to Disraeli in 1873-4 listed the following towns as having no party contests: Barnstaple, Berwick, Bodmin, Brighton, Canterbury, Dewsbury, Dudley, Flint, Gloucester, Hull, Hythe, Lincoln, London, Newcastle-under-Lyme, Newcastle-on-Tyne, Pembroke, Portsmouth, East Retford, Ripon, Stafford, Sunderland, Walsall, Wolverhampton and Wycombe. *The Times*, 3 November 1885 reported that there were no party contests in a number of parliamentary boroughs: Andover, Berwick, Brighton, Bodmin, Calne, Dewsbury, Falmouth, Halifax, Kendal, Pembroke, Swansea, Walsall, Wolverhampton and Wycombe.

Blackpool in apparently contradictory terms: 'FALMOUTH—Four Liberals were returned. The contest was non-political. The council is now composed of 11 Liberals and five Conservatives.' 'BLACKPOOL— Contests, which were decided on non-political grounds, took place in four out of the six wards. The council, formerly almost solely Conservative, is now equally divided, the Liberals having gained three seats by the present elections'.

In some of the largest towns, and notably in Manchester, essentially local questions were rarely made an issue between the parties. But in most of them party feeling was whipped up over such issues as the provision of a new gas or water works, the extension of the borough boundaries, and the numerous other schemes which affected the pockets of the ratepayers, or (in Liverpool) their religious convictions, as well as over national issues. Even quite absurd local issues aroused great controversy, although there was perhaps nothing so odd as events in Eastbourne in 1892, of which *The Times* reported: 'In Eastbourne no candidate could hope for success who did not declare himself against Salvation Army bands in the open air.'[1] A typical case was that of Stockport.[2] During the first ten years after the reform of 1835, there was much bitterness at the dispossession of the old corporation and the appointment of a partisan town clerk by the new Liberal council. But it required popular opposition to a Liberal Manorial Tolls Bill in 1846 (when only one ward was uncontested) and 1847 (when all the wards were contested) to bring the Conservatives within sight of victory. Several Liberal councillors changed sides and the Conservatives won a sweeping victory which was capped in 1848 by the dismissal of the obnoxious Liberal Town Clerk. By 1851 it was the Conservatives' turn for local unpopularity, and the elections were decided by hostility to a Conservative proposal to construct a new market hall. In 1864 the Liberals again suffered a setback, this time because they proposed to construct a new bridge across the Mersey. On the other hand, between 1867 and 1874 when the Conservatives steadily gained ground at hotly contested municipal elections, the issues were as much national as local.

In many towns which were only haphazardly contested on political lines, there was considerable pressure in the late seventies and early eighties for a more positive approach to local elections by both Conservative and Liberal Associations. In Manchester and Salford, for instance, although there was a Liberal majority on both councils, the Liberal Associations did not concern themselves directly with local elections, except that in Salford, the School Board elections were regularly compromised between the 'Church' and 'Unsectarian' parties

[1] *The Times*, 2 November 1892.
[2] A 'History of the Municipality of Stockport' was published at intervals during 1873 and 1874 in the *Stockport Advertiser*. It appears never to have been reprinted.

in order to avoid expensive contests.[1] In both towns there was a gradual change of attitude, although neither party adopted the Birmingham policy of 'thorough'.

In Manchester the ward branches of the Liberal Association had long been nominally responsible for sponsoring municipal candidates, but before 1879 they had rarely been given any central encouragement. After 1879, however, there was something like a continuous agitation for help for the wards, which bore fruit in a pious resolution stressing the political value of contesting municipal elections,[2] and in a number of grants to individual wards.[3] But the Liberal leaders, or at least the older men among them, were reluctant to deplete their funds, and managed to avoid adopting any general municipal policy, not only in 1879 when the approaching general election gave the local elections a special significance, but also in succeeding years. The younger members of the Executive Committee, several of them councillors, continued to agitate for a more positive policy, and in 1884 even risked a full-scale row with the officers of the association by demanding that the councillors be allotted a special place within it, and that their elections be fought for them by the association. But after much consultation and several special meetings this policy was decisively rejected in favour of a reaffirmation of the value of the old order, it being formally resolved that the association should, at the discretion of the General Purposes Committee, merely 'if required' give its advice, or pecuniary help, to the Liberal organisation of any ward in the City.[4] The officers became less reluctant to help the wards after this, but the Birmingham policy was never in fact adopted by the Liberals during their remaining years of dominance on the council.[5]

In Salford there was a more decisive change, although only one of degree, which is summed up in the following extract from the annual report of the Liberal Association for 1882.

The question of municipal elections has received the special consideration of the Executive Committee during the past year. Hitherto,

---

[1] The *Manchester Examiner and Times*, 16 November 1882, reports a typical compromise. The cost of an election to the borough ratepayers was estimated at £800.

[2] A resolution was passed by the Executive Committee on 6 November 1879: 'That this Executive recognizes in the recent Municipal Elections in many Boroughs throughout the Country a series of Victories which will give support to the Liberal party and encourage it to new and increased efforts: and the Executive would at the same time record its thanks to the committee of St. Michael's and All Saints' Wards in this city for their valuable and successful services.'

[3] In 1879 £100 was given to St Michael's Ward, in 1880 £50, in 1881 £155, and in 1882 £50. Other wards received £30 and £50. MS. Minutes of the Manchester Liberal Association.

[4] Minutes of a Special Meeting of the Executive Committee, 16 September 1884.

[5] Shena D. Simon, *A Century of City Government*, London 1938, p. 397.

although the rules of the association provide for it, no direct effort has been made by the Council [of the Liberal Association] to secure Liberal candidates at municipal elections, or to employ the resources of the association in securing their return. Many members of our party have decided objections to contesting these elections on political grounds, and they have hoped that our opponents would see the wisdom of relaxing their efforts [to disturb the long-established Liberal majority, which had resulted in the defeat of several prominent Liberals]. Your Council having duly considered this avowed determination on the part of our political opponents, have resolved to counteract this obnoxious proceeding by promoting the candidature of Liberals who will make the efficient management of municipal affairs their first consideration, irrespective of party allegiance.[1]

For local politicians themselves, the almost universal practice of appointing mayor and aldermen from among the active politicians of the majority party and the borough justices from among the political friends of the government of the day provided a convenient system of rewards for party services. There were always those who maintained that aldermen should be chosen either for their personal merit or in proportion to the party strengths on the council, but they were only heeded where one party had a secure majority. Elsewhere, the bad habits of the first reformed councils were impossible to eradicate. In the thirties it had been usual for the victorious reformers to monopolise the aldermanic bench, and when they began to suffer electoral defeats to prolong their majority by their control of it. In many cases the result was that the Conservative minority was forced to use its temporary majority when the aldermen came up for re-election to secure all the vacant aldermanic places to itself, and with them a majority on the council. When the pendulum swung the other way the process was repeated. In any case the occurrence of aldermanic vacancies was often made the occasion for a more vigorous campaign than usual in the November elections.[2]

Not infrequently a strong minority party also felt very bitter about the politics of the local magistrates, particularly in Lancashire where nominations were in the hands of the Chancellor of the Duchy who was in the habit of making straightforward party appointments. Because of the long years of Liberal rule the majority of benches had a distinctly Liberal complexion before 1874, and in places the Liberals deliberately took a party line on the bench. At Ashton, for instance, the mayor in 1869

---

[1] *Manchester Examiner and Times*, 9 March 1882.
[2] As for instance at Nottingham: H.C. 352, p. 15 (1868-9). VIII, 15.

made no secret of the fact that his party acted together on the bench,[1] and this fact undoubtedly contributed towards the dissatisfaction felt in the town at the behaviour of the magistrates at the time of the Murphy riots. In Bolton the Liberals probably lost the 1868 parliamentary election because of popular resentment against sentences inflicted by a Liberal bench dominated by temperance advocates, who were also conducting a systematic campaign for the closing of beershops.[2] The Hartington Committee were also told a curious story of the Scottish burgh of Dumfries, where, at the instigation of the Provost, who was also Liberal agent, many publicans were refused renewal of their licences in April 1868 and granted it in October when their political loyalty could be tested at the general election.[3]

Fortunately for the subsequent history of local government the appointment of active politicians to paid offices in local authorities became increasingly uncommon after the fifties. Political considerations were still important in deciding between candidates for an important post. Indeed Redlich writing at the turn of the century took them quite for granted. 'An important appointment, such as that of Town Clerk, often leads to a party conflict, and the majority commonly insists on appointing a man of its own colour. But Town Clerks are seldom men who have taken an active part in politics.'[4] But there was very little attempt to make such appointments as had been made to town clerkships in the thirties, when active politicians were chosen because of their political usefulness. The first town clerk of Bolton, an active incorporator and Liberal, when dismissed by the first Conservative council in 1844, showed something of his temper when he remarked that 'It was far from his feeling to desire to serve the Conservative Party'.[5] In a few cases appointments to lesser offices under the corporation tended to go to political partisans irrespective of their qualifications. Thus at Crewe in 1892, two Liberals, one a councillor, who had been dismissed from the railway workshops were compensated with the posts of assistant sanitary inspector and assistant rate collector.[6] On the other hand, in Birmingham partisan appointments were rarely made, and Schnadhorst, the Secretary of the Liberal Association, maintained in a letter to *The Times* in 1878 that most of the successful applicants for senior posts were Conservatives.[7]

---

[1] H.C. 352, p. 145 (1868-9). VIII, 145.
[2] Reform League Report: Bolton. cp. p. 312 above.
[3] H.C. 352, pp. 324f. (1868-9). VIII, 324f.
[4] J. Redlich and F. W. Hirst, *Local Government in England*, London 1903, I, 276n. Of course, such appointments are by no means unusual today, but dismissals on political grounds are now almost impossible.
[5] *Bolton Journal*, 9 January 1914.
[6] Chaloner, *The Social and Economic Development of Crewe*, p. 166.
[7] *The Times*, 20 August 1878.

THE CONSTITUENCIES 1868-85

A. *The Redistribution of Seats in 1867 and 1868*

ENGLAND & WALES

Number of Seats

Boroughs totally disfranchised

For corruption: Lancaster, Totnes, Yarmouth (two members) and Reigate (one member)   7

Because of their size: Honiton, Thetford, Wells (two members), Arundel, Ashburton, Dartmouth, and Lyme Regis (one member)   10

Boroughs partly disfranchised

Andover, Bodmin, Bridgnorth, Bridport, Buckingham, Chichester, Chippenham, Cirencester, Cockermouth, Devizes, Dorchester, Evesham, Guildford, Harwich, Hertford, Huntingdon, Knaresborough, Leominster, Lewes, Lichfield, Ludlow, Lymington, Maldon, Malton, Marlborough, Great Marlow, Newport (Isle of Wight), Poole, Richmond, Ripon, Stamford, Tavistock, Tewkesbury, Windsor, and High Wycombe   35

Total reduction . .   52

New county divisions

Two additional members for Cheshire, Derbyshire, Devonshire, Essex, Kent, Lincolnshire, Norfolk, Somerset, Stafford, Surrey, and the West Riding; three additional members for Lancashire   25

New boroughs

Chelsea, Hackney (two members), Burnley, Darlington, Dewsbury, Gravesend, the Hartlepools, Middlesbrough, Stalybridge, Stockton, and Wednesbury (one member) .   13

New university constituency

London (one member)   1

New seats for existing boroughs

A third seat for Birmingham, Leeds, Liverpool, and Manchester; a second seat for Merthyr Tydvil and Salford .   6

Total increase[1] . .   45

[1] The seven remaining seats were allocated to Scotland. The 1867 Act provided only for the abolition of the four corrupt boroughs and left the total number of English seats unchanged, but the Scottish members were able to secure the abolition of the seven small boroughs listed above and their allocation to Scotland in the Scottish Act of 1868.

Counties amalgamated
   Peebles and Selkirk (one member) I
                              Total reduction . . ‾I‾

New county divisions
   One additional member for Aberdeenshire, Ayrshire, and
   Lanarkshire (divided into two single-member constituencies)   3
New burgh
   Hawick district or Border Burghs (one member) . . I
New university constituencies
   Edinburgh and St Andrew's, Glasgow and Aberdeen (one
   member) 2
New seats for existing burghs
   A third seat for Glasgow and a second for Dundee . . 2
                              Total increase   ‾8‾

IRELAND

No change

B. *The Minority Clause 1867-85*

The so-called minority clause of the 1867 Reform Act provided that no voter in a three-member constituency might cast more than two votes when all three seats were being contested, and that no voter in the four-member City of London might cast more than three votes. The three-member constituencies affected were the counties of Berkshire, Buckinghamshire, Cambridgeshire, Dorset, Herefordshire, Hertfordshire, and Oxfordshire, and the boroughs of Birmingham, Glasgow, Leeds, Liverpool, and Manchester. The effects of the clause (which was inoperative at most by-elections) varied considerably. In Birmingham and Glasgow the Liberals were strong enough to carry all three seats when they were united, and a Conservative who won a seat at Glasgow in 1874 had an independent Liberal to thank for his success. In Liverpool and five of the seven counties there was a Conservative majority, but not a large one, so that the clause in effect deprived the Conservatives of six members. In the remaining five constituencies (City of London, Leeds, Manchester, Herefordshire, Hertfordshire), neither party had a safe majority, so that the clause assured each party of one seat and limited the contest between them to a struggle for the remaining seat or seats. The approximate effect of the clause on a division in the House of Commons was to give the Liberals an extra three votes in 1868, an extra eight in 1874, and an extra four in 1880.

C. A Note on Registration in England

In outline the registration machinery established in 1832 was simple enough.[1] First, the Overseers in each township or parish prepared and published a preliminary register: then aggrieved or interested parties served notices of claims and objections in order to secure the inclusion of names which had accidentally been omitted, to correct errors, and to exclude the unqualified: finally the claims and objections were considered by a special tribunal, the Court of the Revising Barrister. But this simplicity was all on the surface, and even after endless tinkering the English system of registration, unlike the Scotch, could never be induced to work without friction, and only the willingness of the parties to employ registration agents saved it from breaking down altogether.

The difficulties began with the Overseers. They had been chosen to take charge of the registers, not because they were competent officials, but because they kept the rate-books which contained the only comprehensive record of valuations. Most of them were ordinary citizens of the shopkeeper or farmer class who were chosen annually by the local justices and entrusted with the general supervision of the rate-collectors. They were totally unqualified, and had become by 1870 a by-word for inefficiency, ignorance, and illiteracy.[2] It is true that the Overseers did their best, and in the countryside their local knowledge often stood them in good stead, but they had no incentives and quite inadequate assistance. As a consequence, they left the almost illiterate rate-collectors to put the register together and made little or no effort to correct the minor clerical errors which abounded and which were sufficient to disqualify an elector. There were exceptions, of course. In London the Overseers were usually party nominees who took great interest in the registers; in a few counties, notably Durham and the West Riding, the town Overseers had adequate clerical help; and in others the party agents were able to give their help in preparing the preliminary registers. Moreover, after 1868 the standard of performance began to improve as a result of the pressure of public opinion, and in the towns it became increasingly common to provide the Overseer with an efficient deputy. But even after this improvement it cannot be pretended that the Overseers did their job well.

[1] The easiest approach to this very complicated subject is by way of a contemporary election manual such as those of Cox and Grady, Glen, Leader, or Rogers. For more recent accounts see Seymour, *Electoral Reform in England and Wales* and J. Alun Thomas. 'The System of Registration and the Development of Party Organisation, 1832-1870', *History*, XXXV, 81-98 (1950).

[2] A leading Conservative agent spoke in 1870 of the Overseers' 'bad education', 'inaccuracy', and 'not understanding what ought to be done', and said that unless there was the very greatest care taken by political organisations, the register would become full of unqualified persons. H.C. 360, p. 1 (1870). VI, 209.

Nor was the only objection to the Overseers a personal one. They suffered from the additional disadvantage that their records of rating and valuations were often thoroughly inadequate. The Union Assessment Committee Act of 1862, which provided for the appointment of a local committee in every Poor Law Union, and charged it with the supervision of the valuation of property, also specifically imposed upon the Overseers the duty of keeping proper records. But they did not do so. The Poor Law Board (and its successor, the Local Government Board), protested about their negligence, but in the face of local opposition to central interference it felt powerless to effect any but the most gradual improvement, and contented itself with a rating system which allowed the rate-books (on which the electoral registers were based) to become hopelessly inaccurate. Entries dealing with landownership and tenancies were often out of date or based on wrong information, and valuations were often entered on the basis of a conventional assessment which gave only a rough indication of the true value of the property.[1] In the long run it was possible for a persistent person, or a party agent acting on his behalf, to overcome these difficulties by application to the revision court, but most electors were not persistent so that many of those whose property was not accurately entered in the rate-book failed to obtain the vote.

Special provision had to be made for those persons who were entitled to vote but whose names were not entered in the rate-book or in the register of pre-1832 ancient-right voters kept by the town clerk. Lodgers and owners of property who were not ratepayers (because in England occupiers were responsible for the payment of rates) were required to make a special claim to the Overseers as soon as they were qualified, and their claims caused very little difficulty except in parts of London.[2] The most serious difficulties and complications were caused by the compound householders. Until 1869 the practice of 'compounding'

---

[1] It took the Local Government Board two years to extract from the local rating authorities the returns which were required for the 'New Domesday', after a preliminary check had revealed over 250,000 errors in those first submitted [C. 1097-Pt. I] pp. 5-6. H.C. (1874). LXXII, 5-6. Even after this check there remained large numbers of conventional assessments based on traditional values not rental, in addition to the vast numbers of erroneous entries which escaped the attention of the Local Government Board. In the Irish counties the position was even worse than in England since the difference between the actual value and the assessment for rating was more marked, amounting in many cases to as much as 30 to 40 per cent. And there was another discrepancy. Whereas in England a rebate of 15 to 25 per cent was usual as a reward for prompt payment of rates and did not affect the value of the property in the rate books, in Ireland this was not so, and the rebate could have the effect of lowering the rateable value *for electoral purposes only*, thus disqualifying the tenant. cp. C. Dawson, *Remarks on the County, Borough, and Municipal Franchises in England and Ireland*, 4th edn, Dublin 1884, p. 7.

[2] Owners once registered remained on the register until their claim was objected to: lodgers were required to make an annual application for registration, and were, therefore, often disqualified because they had not the time to make application.

for the payment of rates, by which the owner of a property collected the rates and paid them (less a 15% to 25% rebate) to the rate collectors, kept the names of most tenants who compounded out of the rate-books altogether. As a consequence, the only way in which such a tenant could be registered was by cancelling the existing agreement with his landlord and paying the rates himself. An Act of 1851 (Clay's Act) enabled him to do this comparatively easily and to claim any rebate available to the landlord, but few compounders actually bothered to register themselves before 1867, and most of those who were on the registers got there because of the zeal of individual Overseers who made it their business to add the names of compounders to their preliminary registers.

The middle classes were not generally compounders, except in London and a few resorts like Bath and Brighton, so that there was no urgent need to deal with the problem of the compounders before 1867. But the adoption of household suffrage in 1867 created a completely new situation since about two-thirds of the occupiers of houses rated at less than £10 were compounders.[1] Disraeli sought to overcome the difficulties which this situation created by abolishing compounding altogether. Accordingly Section Seven of the Reform Act somewhat incongruously directed that in future all tenants whatsoever should pay their rates direct to the rating authority. But the change was intolerable, inconveniencing landlord, tenant and rating authority alike, and all did their best to evade it. The result was wide discrepancies in the effect of the Act upon different districts and, in some cases, a great deal of confusion, with landlords refusing to lower rents although they had stopped paying rates, with tenants refusing to pay rates and being summonsed, and with meetings specially called to denounce the change.[2] In short, it was clearly demonstrated that Parliament could not enforce personal payment of rates, and in 1869 compounding was restored. The Poor-Rate Assessment and Collection Act directed borough Overseers to enter both in the rate-books and in the electoral registers the names of the occupiers of all rateable premises, irrespective of whether they paid rates or not.

The 1869 Act was successful in its immediate purpose of putting an end to the existing confusion, but it by no means solved all the difficulties created by compounding. With the staffs available to them, Overseers found it almost impossible to keep an accurate account of transferred

[1] In 1866 the figures were as follows:

Rent	Compounders	Other tenants
Over £10 p.a.	94,111	550,411
Under £10 p.a.	476,593	245,910

Source: H.C. 136, p. 13 (1867). LVI, 461.

[2] cp. B. Keith-Lucas, *English Local Government Franchise: A Short History*, Oxford 1952, p. 73.

tenancies. The consequence was an increased dependence on the party agents: where they were efficient they supplied the Overseers with a list of changes of tenancy; where they were not, the registers became corrupt. The lawyers also discovered that the position of the tenants of 'tied cottages', for which they paid only a nominal rent or none at all, was extremely obscure. Thus, although the Morpeth miners whose cottages were owned by the collieries they worked for were enfranchised,[1] many other occupants of tied cottages were not. These latter included what Gladstone called 'men of high class' such as senior government officials, as well as the servants and labourers of the gentry and the farmers, all of whom were excluded from the franchise until 1885.[2]

The second and third stages of the registration procedure were intended to safeguard the public against the inefficiency of the Overseers. Consequently, the initiative for correcting mistakes was vested not in an official but in the ordinary elector. Any person whose name was excluded from the preliminary register might send in a claim to be registered, and if no one objected to its inclusion he would be duly registered. On the other hand, any elector might object to the inclusion of any name for any of four reasons: that the entry was inaccurate, that the person referred to lacked the necessary qualifications, that he had moved from the address in the register, or that he had died. These claims and objections were investigated by the Court of the Revising Barrister, where the party registration agents acted for the individual electors. Although nominally a court, this was in fact no more than a minor administrative tribunal with an unqualified or barely-qualified adjudicator and with very limited powers: until 1878 the Revising Barrister was without even the power to amend minor clerical errors in the register or to strike out duplicate entries unless they were formally objected to. A few Revising Barristers were specialists in election law, but the great majority were barristers without practice appointed by the circuit judges because they were relatives or the sons of friends, or because they were promising young men who needed help to establish themselves in their profession.[3]

The Revision Courts, far from being the court of appeal which was originally envisaged, soon became, with the co-operation of the party agents, the keystone of the registration system, and by the eighties had

[1] A. Watson, *A Great Labour Leader*, London 1908, pp. 124-9.

[2] *3 Hansard*, CCLXXXV, 112.

[3] Dudley Baxter denounced the system of appointments in 1870: 'I am sorry to say', he told a Select Committee on Registration, 'that the appointments of revising barristers often go by favour. It is very frequently, indeed, the son or near relative of the dignitary who appoints without regard to fitness as a barrister.' H.C. 360, p. 23 (1870). VI, 231.

virtually supplanted the overseers in the big towns, although not usually elsewhere. In a big town like Leeds or Manchester, at last 3,000 claims and 3,000 objections were usually heard annually, apart from those settled privately between the Overseers and the party agents. Even as late as 1896 the scandal persisted and the Manchester Liberals were able to publish figures from the 1895 revision which were an indictment of the whole system, and which showed clearly that the Overseers were content to let others do their work.[1]

Divisions	Total No. of electors on Overseers' lists	Claims made by both parties		Objections made by both parties	
North-West .	16,314	1,586	(10%)	2,158	(13%)
North . .	14,371	1,067	(7·5%)	2,464	(17%)
North-East .	13,015	1,359	(10·5%)	1,998	(15·5%)
East . .	15,579	1,007	(6·4%)	1,733	(11%)
South . .	14,243	563	(4%)	455	(3%)
South-West .	12,203	523	(4%)	345	(2·8%)

It was, of course, impossible for individuals to make claims on this scale, and the whole work of revision fell into the hands of the parties, who were compelled to employ men specially to do the work for them.

D. The Size of the Constituencies of the United Kingdom (England, Wales, Scotland, and Ireland) in 1881

COUNTIES

Constituencies	Limits of population	Gross population, 1881	Number of electors, 1881	Number of Members	Ratio of population to Members	Ratio of electors to Members
19	Under 50,000	609,235	39,116	21	29,011	1,863
28	50,000 to 74,999	1,762,134	110,121	43	40,980	2,561
22	75,000 to 99,999	1,947,490	140,902	41	47,499	3,436
23	100,000 to 124,999	2,631,433	167,287	47	55,988	3,559
27	125,000 to 149,999	3,554,281	202,706	54	65,820	3,755
15	150,000 to 174,999	2,427,399	136,835	29	83,703	4,718
25	200,000 and over	7,105,149	400,680	48	148,024	8,347
159		20,037,121	1,197,647	283	—	—

[1] Annual Report of the Manchester Liberal Union, 1896. MS. Minutes.

BOROUGHS

Constituencies	Limits of population	Gross population, 1881	Number of electors, 1881	Number of Members	Ratio of population to Members	Ratio of electors to Members
42	Under 7,000	248,990	30,913	42	5,928	736
30	7,000 to 9,999	250,317	33,662	30	8,344	1,122
48	10,000 to 19,999	713,137	91,826	72	9,904	1,275
22	20,000 to 29,999	569,953	74,265	32	17,811	2,320
38	30,000 to 49,999	1,543,466	207,721	55	28,063	3,776
34	50,000 to 99,999	2,309,614	334,961	53	43,577	6,320
18	100,000 to 199,999	2,430,047	340,340	33	73,637	10,313
19	200,000 and over	6,745,594	736,789	43	156,874	17,134
251		14,811,118	1,850,477	360	—	—

Appendix III

SEATS CONTROLLED BY PATRONS 1868-85

THE list which follows covers only the period from 1868 to 1885, but most of the interests listed originated long before. The 1816 edition of Oldfield's *Representative History* assigned thirty English county seats to a patron, and fourteen of these (marked here with an asterisk) were still in the hands of a patron in 1868. In addition, five other seats were virtually in the hands of their old patron's descendants.[1] Only eleven seats had escaped from control, and many of these were occasionally held by members of the former patron's family. After 1885 a number of predominant interests could still be maintained, but the hold of patrons was precarious, and by 1900 very few of them looked upon any seat as if it were absolutely in their gift. The following is a brief list of patrons between 1885 and 1900.

Buckinghamshire, Aylesbury Division	Lord Rothschild
Cheshire, Knutsford Division	Lord Egerton
Derbyshire, West Division	Duke of Devonshire
Durham, Jarrow Division	C. M. Palmer
Hertfordshire, St Albans Division	?Earl of Verulam
Huntingdonshire, Ramsey Division	Lord de Ramsey
Leicestershire, Melton Division	Duke of Rutland
Northamptonshire, North Division	Marquess of Exeter
— Mid Division	Earl Spencer
Nottinghamshire, Newark Division	Earl Manvers
Oxfordshire, Henley Division	??Earl of Macclesfield
Sussex, Chichester Division	Duke of Richmond.

[1] One seat each for South Durham (where the Duke of Cleveland gave his support to the Pease family), North Lancashire (Earl of Derby), North Lincolnshire (Earl of Yarborough), South Nottinghamshire (Earl Manvers), and West Worcestershire (Earl Beauchamp).

A. COUNTY SEATS 1868-85

1. *England*

Constituency	Patron	Members of patron's family who represented the county 1868-85
Bedfordshire	*Duke of Bedford (L)	F. C. Hastings Russell 1846-72 Marquess of Tavistock 1875-85
Cambridgeshire	*Duke of Rutland (C) [to 1874] *Earl of Hardwicke (C) [to 1878]	Lord George J. Manners 1847-57, 1863-74 Visct Royston 1865-73 Hon. Eliot C. Yorke 1873-8
East Cumberland	Earl of Carlisle (L)	Hon. C. W. G. Howard 1840-79 George J. Howard 1879-80, 1881-5
West Cumberland	*Earl of Lonsdale (C)	Henry Lowther 1847-72
North Derbyshire	*Duke of Devonshire (L)	Lord George W. Cavendish 1834-80 Lord Edward Cavendish 1880-5
Huntingdonshire	*Duke of Manchester (C) [to 1880] Edward Fellowes (C) [cr. Lord De Ramsey 1887]	Lord Robert Montagu 1859-74 Visct Mandeville 1877-80 Edward Fellowes 1837-80 W. H. Fellowes 1880-5
North Leicestershire	*Duke of Rutland (C)	Lord John Manners 1857-85
North Northumberland	*Duke of Northumberland (C)	Earl Percy 1868-85
Rutland	*Earl of Gainsborough (C)	Hon. Gerard Noel 1847-83 J. W. Lowther 1883-5[1]
West Sussex	*Duke of Richmond (C) [by agreement with Lord Leconfield]	Earl of March 1869-85

[1] Lowther was nephew (by marriage) of the late member, as well as the son of a local landowner.

Constituency	Patron	Members of patron's family who represented the county 1868-85
Westmorland	*Earl of Lonsdale (C)	Hon. William Lowther 1868-85
	Marquess of Headfort (C)	Earl of Bective (3rd Marquess) 1854-70
		Earl of Bective 1871-85
Yorkshire West Riding (South)	*Earl Fitzwilliam (L) [seat lost 1872-80]	Visct Milton 1865-72 Hon. W. H. W. Fitzwilliam 1880-5
North Riding	Earl of Feversham (C)	Hon. Octavius Duncombe 1841-59, 1867-74
		Visct Helmsley 1874-81

2. Wales[1]

Carmarthenshire	Earl Cawdor (C) [a declining interest]	Visct Emlyn 1874-85
Denbighshire	Sir Watkin Williams-Wynn (C)	Sir W. W.-Wynn 1841-85 Sir H. W. W.-Wynn 1885
Monmouthshire	*Duke of Beaufort (C)	P. G. H. Somerset 1859-71 Lord Henry C. Somerset 1871-80
	*Lord Tredegar (C)	C. O. S. Morgan 1841-74 Hon. F. C. Morgan 1874-85
Montgomeryshire	Sir W. W.-Wynn (C) [to 1880]	C. W. W.-Wynn 1862-80
Radnorshire	?Lord Ormathwaite (C) [to 1880]	Hon. Arthur Walsh 1868-80

3. Scotland

Argyllshire	Duke of Argyll (L)	Marquess of Lorne 1868-78
		Lord Colin Campbell 1878-85
Buteshire	?Marquess of Bute (C)	—
Orkney and Shetland	Earl of Zetland (L) [to 1873?]	Frederick Dundas 1837-47, 1852-72

---

[1] Other predominant influences were (1) that of Lords Hanmer and Mostyn and the Duke of Westminster in Flintshire (Lord Richard Grosvenor was member from 1861 to 1886) and (2) the personal interest of C. R. M. Talbot in Glamorgan, which he represented from 1830 to 1885. (He afterwards sat for Mid-Glamorgan 1885-90). If Talbot had accepted the peerage that Gladstone offered him in 1869 he would probably have become a patron of the more orthodox variety. Ion Trant Hamilton (cr. Lord Holm Patrick 1897) exercised a similar influence in county Dublin but had too little land to make it permanent.

Constituency	Patron	Members of patron's family who represented the county *1868-85*
Sutherlandshire	Duke of Sutherland (L)	Lord Ronald Leveson-Gower 1867-74
		Marquess of Stafford 1874-86

4. Ireland

Constituency	Patron	Members of patron's family who represented the county *1868-85*
Antrim	Lord O'Neill (C)	Hon. Edward O'Neill 1863-80
	4th Marquess of Hertford (C) [to 1870][1]	Admiral G. H. Seymour 1865-9
		Earl of Yarmouth 1869-74
Carlow	Henry Bruen (C) [to 1880?]	Henry Bruen 1857-80
Donegal	Duke of Abercorn (C) [to 1880]	Marquess of Hamilton 1860-80
Down	Marquesses of Down-shire and London-derry (C) [one or two seats]	Lord A. E. Hill-Trevor 1845-80
		Lord Arthur Hill 1880-5
		Visct Castlereagh 1878-84
Fermanagh	M. E. Archdale (C)	Capt. M. E. Archdale 1835-74
		W. H. Archdale 1874-85
	Earl of Enniskillen (C)	Hon. Henry Cole 1854-80
		Visct Crichton 1880-5[2]
Kerry	Earl of Kenmare (L) [to 1872]	Visct Castlerosse 1852-71
Kildare	Duke of Leinster (L) [to 1874]	Lord Otho FitzGerald 1865-74
Tyrone	Earl of Belmore (C) [to 1880]	Rt. Hon. H. T. L. Corry 1826-73
		Hon. H. W. L. Corry 1873-80
	Duke of Abercorn (C) [to 1874]	Lord Claud Hamilton 1835-7, 1839-74

[1] In 1870 the Antrim estates were bequeathed to Sir Richard Wallace, later M.P. for Lisburn, not to the new Marquess. As a consequence Lord Yarmouth, the eldest son of the new Marquess, gave up his seat for Antrim in 1874 and was elected for South Warwickshire, where his father's estates lay.

[2] Viscount Crichton (eldest son of the Earl of Erne) had married a daughter of the Earl of Enniskillen. As a result of a family arrangement in 1880 Crichton gave up his seat for the Crichton family borough of Enniskillen which he had represented since 1868 to Viscount Cole, Lord Enniskillen's eldest son, and in return obtained Lord Enniskillen's support for the county.

Constituency	Patron	Members of patron's family who represented the borough or county 1868-85
Wicklow	Earl Fitzwilliam and the Earl of Carysfort (L)	Hon. W. H. W. Fitz- william 1868-74

B. BOROUGH SEATS[1] 1868-85

1. England

Aylesbury	Sir N. M. de Rothschild (L) [cr. Lord Rothschild, 1885]	Sir N. M. de Rothschild 1865-85 Baron F. J. de Rothschild 1885
Bodmin	Lord Robartes (L)	—
Bridgnorth	? T. C. Whitmore (C) [to 1867] W. O. Foster [1870-85]	Henry Whitmore 1852-65, 1866-70 W. H. Foster 1870-85 (L→C)
Bury St Edmunds	Marquess of Bristol (C) [to 1880]	Lord Francis Hervey 1874-80, 1885-92
Calne	Marquess of Lansdowne (L)	Lord Edmond Fitz- maurice 1868-85
Chester [temporarily disfranchised 1880]	Marquess (later Duke) of Westminster (L)	Earl Grosvenor 1847-69 Hon. N. de l'A. Gros- venor 1869-74 Hon. Beilby Lawley[2] 1880
Chichester	Duke of Richmond (C)	Lord Henry Lennox 1846-85
Chippenham	Sir Gabriel Goldney Bt. (C) Sir John Neeld Bt. (C)	Sir Gabriel Goldney 1865-85
Cirencester	Earl Bathurst (C) T. W. Chester Master[3] (C)	A. A. Bathurst 1857-78 T. W. Chester Master Jnr. 1878-85

[1] There were no two-member boroughs in which both seats were controlled by patrons. To the list below some historians would probably add Leominster, where the dominant interest was that of the Arkwrights and Droitwich, for which see pp. 48-9.

[2] Lawley (who became Lord Wenlock seven months after his election) was eldest son of the Duke of Westminster's sister.

[3] T. W. Chester Master of The Abbey, Cirencester, M.P. for Cirencester, 1837-44, had come practically to control the borough by 1880.

Constituency	Patron	Members of patron's family who represented the borough 1868-85
Dorchester	H. G. Sturt (C) [cr. Lord Alington, 1876]	C. N. Sturt 1856-74
Eye	Sir Edward Kerrison Bt. (C)	—
Hertford	Marquess of Salisbury (C)	A. J. Balfour 1874-85
Huntingdon	Earl of Sandwich (C)	Visct Hinchingbrooke 1876-84
Launceston	Various, see pp. 47-8 (C)	above
Lichfield	Col. Richard Dyott (C)	Col. Dyott 1865-80
Ludlow	Earl of Powis (C)	Col. G. H. W. W. Clive 1860-85
Lymington	?the Burrard family (C)	
Macclesfield [disfranchised 1880]	John Brocklehurst (L)	W. C. Brocklehurst 1868-80
Malmesbury	Walter Powell (C) [1868-81] Col. C. W. Miles (C)	Walter Powell 1868-81 Col. C. W. Miles 1882-5
Malton	Earl Fitzwilliam (L)	Hon. C. W. W. Fitzwilliam 1852-85
Marlborough	Marquess of Ailesbury (L)	Lord Ernest Bruce 1832-78 Lord Charles Bruce 1878-85
Marlow	T. P. Williams (C) T. O. Wethered (C)	T. O. Wethered 1868-80 General O. L. C. Williams 1880-5
Midhurst	Earl of Egmont (C)	C. G. Perceval 1874
Peterborough	Earl Fitzwilliam (L)	Hon. W. J. W. Fitzwilliam 1878-85
Richmond	Earl of Zetland (L)	Lawrence Dundas 1872-3 Hon. J. C. Dundas 1873-85
Ripon	Earl de Grey [cr. Marquess of Ripon 1871] (L)	Earl de Grey 1874-80

Constituency	Patron	Members of patron's family who represented the borough 1868-85
Scarborough	Sir John Johnstone Bt. (L) [to 1869]	Sir J. V. B. Johnstone 1832-7, 1841-69
	? Sir Harcourt Johnstone Bt. [1869-85] [cr. Lord Derwent (L) 1881]	Sir H. Johnstone 1869-80
Shaftesbury [to 1880]	Marquess of Westminster (L) [to 1869]	—
	Dowager Marchioness of Westminster (C) [1869-80]	—
Stamford	Marquess of Exeter (C) [to 1880]	—
Tamworth	Sir Robert Peel Bt. (L→C→L) [to 1880]	Sir Robert Peel 1850-80
Tavistock	Duke of Bedford (L)	Lord Arthur Russell 1857-85
Tewkesbury	?? John Martin (L)	R. B. Martin 1880-5
Tiverton	Sir John Heathcoat-Amory Bt. (L)	Sir J. H. Amory 1868-85
Warwick	? Earl of Warwick (C)	—
Wenlock	Lord Forester (C)	Hon. G. C. W. Forester 1828-74 C. T. W. Forester 1874-85
Whitehaven	Earl of Lonsdale (C)	G. A. F. Bentinck[1] 1865-85
Wilton	Earl of Pembroke[2] (C)	Hon. Sidney Herbert 1877-85
Woodstock	Duke of Marlborough (C)	Lord Randolph Churchill 1874-85
Wycombe	Lord Carrington (L)	Hon. W. H. P. Carington 1868-83 Col. Gerard Smith 1883-5

[1] Bentinck's mother was Lord Lonsdale's sister.
[2] While the 13th Earl was a minor Lady Herbert returned Sir Edmund Antrobus, a Liberal-Conservative, who sat from 1855 to 1877. Her son was, however, a decided Conservative.

Constituency	Patron	Members of patron's family who represented the borough 1868-85
2. Wales		
Montgomery dist.	? Lord Sudeley (L)	Hon. C. D. R. Hanbury-Tracy 1863-77 Hon. F. S. A. Hanbury-Tracy 1877-85, 1886-92
3. Scotland		
Wick dist.	? Duke of Sutherland (L)	—
4. Ireland		
Clonmell	? John Bagwell (L) [to 1874]	John Bagwell 1857-74
Dungannon	Earl of Ranfurly (C) [to 1874]	Hon. W. S. Knox 1851-74
Enniskillen	Earl of Enniskillen (C)	Visct Crichton 1868-80 Visct Cole 1880-5
Lisburn	Marquess of Hertford (C) [to 1870] Sir Richard Wallace [1870-85]	Sir R. Wallace 1873-85
Portarlington	Earl of Portarlington (C)	Hon. L. S. W. Dawson-Damer 1857-65, 1868-80

Party Totals, 1868

	Liberal	Conservative
Counties		
England	4	12
Wales	—	6 (1)
Scotland	3 (1)	1 (1)
Ireland	3	9
Boroughs		
England	18 (1)	21 (3)
Wales	1 (1)	—
Scotland	1 (1)	—
Ireland	1 (1)	4
Total	31 (5)	53 (5)

Doubtful attributions are included in the totals but are also noted in brackets. Wilton is counted as a Liberal borough, under the influence of Lady Herbert.

Appendix IV

PARTY ASSOCIATIONS AND PRESSURE GROUPS, THEIR INCOME AND EXPENDITURE

THE balance sheets which are summarised below show the great difference between the resources of the great noncomformist pressure groups on the one hand and of the two federations of party associations on the other. A balance sheet for the very efficient Leeds Liberal Association is added to set the other figures in perspective. The income of the various bodies may be stated in round figures as

Liberation Society 1881-2	£9,075
United Kingdom Alliance 1881-2[1] . .	£13,458
National Education League (at its peak, 1871-2)	£6,486
National Liberal Federation 1881-2 . .	£1,944
National Union 1881-2	£926
Leeds Liberal Association 1881 . . .	£430

The ordinary expenditure of the party headquarters described in Chapter Seventeen was about £10,000 to £15,000 a year.

[1] This figure excludes the income of the *Alliance News*.

(1) *The Liberation Society*
Income and Expenditure 1881-2[1]

Receipts	£	s.	d.	Payments	£	s.	d.
Balance from previous year	684	9	–	Lectures and meetings . . .	874	11	8
Subscriptions and Donations	5,705	7	10	Travelling . .	820	13	9
Sale of Publications	35	11	10	Salaries of Officers .	1,400	–	–
Drafts on Legacy Account (leaving balance of £7,334. 15. 6)	3,000	–	–	Agents and Lecturers . .	2,078	16	5
				Clerks, messengers, etc. . . .	292	13	3
Interest and Dividends . .	334	11	3	Advertising . .	18	8	–
				Stationery . .	42	3	4
				Publications and printing . .	785	3	5
				Authorship and editorship . .	530	6	4
				Local Committee expenses . .	267	4	–
				Tract distribution and bill-posting .	154	12	5
				Books and Papers .	71	5	2
				Rent, Taxes, and office expenses .	251	8	2
				Postage, parcels and telegrams .	651	7	8
				Parliamentary expenses . .	18	16	2
				Scottish Council Expenses (incl. secretary) . .	736	14	–
				Balance in hand .	765	16	2
	£9,759	19	11		£9,759	19	11

[1] *Liberator*, 1 June 1882.

(2) *The United Kingdom Alliance*
Income and Expenditure 1881-2[1]

Receipts	£	s.	d.	Payments	£	s.	d.
Balance from previous year	1,702	12	6	Salaries to agents and lecturers	5,744	18	5
Subscriptions and Donations	12,600	5	8	Expenses of Agents	1,421	18	9
Admission to Meetings	220	13	8	Meetings and travelling expenses	727	12	–
Bazaar	5	11	6	Parliamentary and electoral agencies	238	19	11
Legacies	120	–	–	Publication of *Alliance News*	3,680	14	7
Sales of *Alliance News*	3,448	7	–	Editorial expenses of do.	311	8	9
Advertisements for do.	426	–	–	Cost of *Alliance News* to subscribers, etc.	2,182	14	3
Sale of books, etc.	236	13	2	Office Salaries	1,005	2	3
Rent of Offices let	267	10	–	Tracts, etc.	488	3	9
Interest	7	5	8	Postages, etc.	219	2	1
				Miscellaneous expenses	171	16	8
				Rent and Taxes (Manchester and London offices) –	806	16	4
				Printing of circulars, etc.	193	2	7
				Stationery	121	1	2
				General advertising	102	6	8
				Newspapers and parliamentary papers	46	7	3
				Bank Charges	15	17	8
				Balance in hand	1,556	16	1
	£19,034	19	2		£19,034	19	2

[1] *Thirtieth Report of the Executive Committee of the United Kingdom Alliance,* Manchester 1882, p. 63.

(3) *The National Education League*

Income and Expenditure 1871-2[1]

Receipts	£	s.	d.	Payments	£	s.	d.
Balance from previous year	997	2	4	Travelling . .	1,489	4	–
Contributions (less amounts retained by branches) .	6,471	18	4	Salaries and wages.	2,046	2	7
				Advertising, printing and stationery	2,383	3	3
Interest and sundries . .	14	6	4	Postage . .	585	–	–
				Office furniture, rent, rates, etc. .	261	9	5
				Book keeping .	122	11	2
				Carriage of books, etc. . . .	85	12	1
				Public meetings and incidentals .	307	5	6
				Balance in hand .	202	19	–
	£7,483	7	–		£7,483	7	–

[1] *National Education League Monthly Paper*, December 1872, p. 7.

(4) *The National Liberal Federation*
Income and Expenditure 1881-2[1]

Receipts	£	s.	d.	Payments	£	s.	d.
Balance from previous year	37	4	9	Salaries and wages	479	2	4
Subscriptions	901	8	–	Printing, stationery and advertising	773	18	–
Sale of publications	142	18	5	Travelling and organisation	80	16	–
Special fund	900	–	–	Conference and deputations	211	16	6
				Lectures	123	10	8
				Rent, rates, coal, gas	78	3	6
				Stamps and telegrams	107	3	6
				Office expenses	88	12	7
				Balance	38	8	1
	£1,981	11	2		£1,981	11	2

[1] *National Liberal Federation. Fifth Annual Report* . . . , Birmingham 1883, p. 20.

(5) *The National Union*
Income and Expenditure 1881-2[1]

Receipts	£	s.	d.	Payments	£	s.	d.
Balance from previous year .	172	16	9	Printing, advertising and stationery	444	10	2
Subscriptions and donations . .	926	10	6	Conference expenses (at Bristol) .	17	8	–
				Lecturers' fees .	125	–	–
				Postage, telegrams, messages, parcels	140	7	4
				Housekeeper, furniture . . .	42	1	8
				Rent and office expenses . .	218	15	–
				Literary fees .	7	7	–
				Travelling expenses	18	2	8
				Sundries . .	4	5	2
				Balance in hand .	81	10	3
	£1,099	7	3		£1,099	7	3

[1] McKenzie, *British Political Parties*, p. 162.

(6) *The Leeds Liberal Association*

Income and Expenditure 1881[1]

Receipts	£	s.	d.	Payments	£	s.	d.
Balance from previous year .	84	15	8	Uncashed cheques from previous year . .	3	15	0
Late subscription to 1880 election fund . .	25	0	0	Secretary's salary .	140	0	0
Sale of publications	3	19	8	Rent, rates, gas, coal and office cleaning . .	61	19	11
Rent from Nonconformist Union & Liberal Cabinet .	3	15	0	Printing, binding, advertising and Stationery .	54	18	6
Subscriptions[2] .	395	7	6	Postages, telegrams etc. . . .	18	2	2½
Interest from bank .	2	11	0	Publications . .	4	18	9
				Rooms for meetings	9	12	6
				Miscellaneous .	5	0	2½
				Overseers' lists .	8	12	6
				Registration agents and office assistance . .	71	8	6
				Legal expenses .	10	10	0
				Subscriptions to Nat. Liberal Federation and National Reform Union . .	12	2	0
				Secretary's expenses to Birmingham and Manchester . .	2	0	6
				Balance at end of year . .	112	8	3
	£515	8	10		£515	8	10

[1] From the annual report of the Association published in Leeds, 1882.
[2] For comments on this item see p. 132 above. The individual subscriptions were: £25 (1), £10 (1), £5 5s. (2), £5 (6), £4 (1), £3 3s. (3), £2 2s. (22), £2 (2), £1 1s. (119), £1 (14), 11s. 6d. (1), 11s. (1), 10s. 6d. (69), 10s. (42), 6s. (1), 5s. (145), 4s. (2), 3s. 6d. (2), 3s. (3), 2s. 6d. (109), 2s. (31), 1s. 6d. (3), 1s. (101).

BIBLIOGRAPHY

THIS bibliography is not intended to be comprehensive, but it includes all the MS. collections and printed material found useful in the preparation of this book, with the exception of works on economic history and Ireland. The majority of the items listed are referred to directly at some point in the text.

The material is arranged under the following heads:

A. Manuscript Collections.
B. Official Papers.
C. Newspapers, Periodicals and Reports.
D. Works of Reference.
E. Biographies.
F. Other Works.

A. MANUSCRIPT COLLECTIONS

1. *In Libraries, Museums, and Record Offices*

Bishopsgate Institute: The George Howell Collection including the papers of the Reform League.

Bodleian Library: The Clarendon Papers.

British Museum: The Campbell-Bannerman Papers (Add. MSS. 41,206-41,252).

—— The Dilke Papers (Add. MSS. 48,874-43,967).

—— The Gladstone Papers (Add. MSS. 44,086-44,835).

—— The Ripon Papers (Add. MSS. 43,510-43,644).

British Transport Commission Record Office: Records of the Great Eastern and the London and North-Western Railways.

House of Lords Record Office: Evidence given at the trial of election petitions.

Liverpool Record Office: The Melly Papers.

Manchester Central Library: The J. B. Smith Papers.

Northamptonshire Record Office: The Fitzwilliam (Milton) Papers.

—— The Ward Hunt Papers.

—— The Knightley Papers.

Public Record Office: The Cardwell Papers.

—— The Granville Papers.

—— The Home Office Papers.

—— The Treasury Papers.

Royal Courts of Justice, Election Petitions Office: Register of Election Petitions.

Sheffield Central Library: Wentworth Woodhouse Muniments.
—— Bagshawe Papers.
—— Spencer-Stanhope Papers.
—— H. J. Wilson Papers.
2. *Private Collections.*
Adam Papers: Papers of W. P. Adam, by courtesy of Captain C. K. Adam, D.S.O., R.N. (Retd.)
Bath Papers: Papers of the 4th Marquess of Bath, by courtesy of the Most Hon. the Marquess of Bath.
Chilston Papers: Papers of the 1st Viscount Chilston, by courtesy of the Right Hon. the Viscount Chilston.
Cranbrook Papers: Papers of the 1st Earl of Cranbrook, by courtesy of the Right Hon. the Earl of Cranbrook.
Devonshire Papers: Papers of the 8th Duke of Devonshire, by courtesy of His Grace the Duke of Devonshire, M.C., and the Trustees of the Chatsworth Settlement.
Disraeli Papers: Papers of the Earl of Beaconsfield, by courtesy of the National Trust.
Hambleden Papers: Papers of W. H. Smith, by courtesy of the Hon. David Smith.
Hampden Papers: Papers of the 1st Viscount Hampden by courtesy of the Right Hon. the Viscount Hampden, C.M.G.
Hylton Papers: Papers of the 1st Lord Hylton, by courtesy of the Right Hon. the Lord Hylton.
Iddesleigh Papers: Papers of the 1st Earl of Iddesleigh, by courtesy of the Right Hon. the Earl of Iddesleigh.
Manchester Liberal Federation Papers: Papers of the Manchester Liberal Association and its successors, by courtesy of the officers of the Manchester Liberal Federation.
National Union of Conservative and Unionist Associations, Records of the: MS. Minutes of the early conferences by courtesy of the Secretary.
North of England Conservative Agents' Association, Records of the: MS. Minutes and other records by courtesy of the officers.
Salisbury Papers: Papers of the 3rd Marquess of Salisbury, by courtesy of the Most Hon. the Marquess of Salisbury, K.G.
Winmarleigh Papers: Papers of Lord Winmarleigh, by courtesy of the Rt. Hon. the Earl of Scarbrough, K.G.

B. OFFICIAL PAPERS

This list does not include any of the several hundred items listed under the heading 'Elections and Representations of the People' in the *General Alphabetical Index to the Bills, Reports, Estimates, Accounts, and Papers, printed by order of the House of Commons, and to the Papers Presented by Command, 1852-1899,* H.M.S.O. 1909, nor the individual papers on particular elections listed in Appendix I of P. and G. Ford, *Select List of British Parliamentary Papers 1833-1899*, Oxford 1953.

Hansard's Parliamentary Debates, Third Series.
Report from Her Majesty's Commissioners on Agriculture.
    [C. 2778] H.C. (1881). XV, 1. and [C. 3309] H.C. (1882). XIV, I.
Report from the Select Committee on County Financial Arrangements. H.C. 421
    (1867-8). IX, 1.
Reports and *Evidence* of the Royal Commission on Land in Wales and
    Monmouthshire: See Index [C. 8222] H.C. (1896). XXXV, 730.
Report from the Select Committee on Malt Tax. H.C. 420 (1867-8). IX,
    235.
Report from the Select Committee on Members Holding Contracts (Sir Sydney
    Waterlow). H.C. 78 (1868-9). VII, 253.
Report of the Commissioners appointed to inquire into Municipal Corporations
    not subject to the Municipal Corporations Act (other than the City of
    London). [C. 2490] H.C. (1880). XXXI, 1.
Report from the Select Committee on Poor Law Guardians, &c. H.C. 297
    (1878). XVII, 263.
Second Report from the Committee of Public Accounts. H.C. 267 (1884-5).
    VII, 37.
Eleventh and Final Report of the Commissioners appointed to inquire into the
    Organisation and Rules of Trade Unions and other Associations. [4123]
    H.C. (1868-9). XXXI, 235.
Civil Servants under the control of the Treasury, who are Candidates for Seats in
    the House of Commons. Treasury Minute. [C. 4229] H.C. (1884-5).
    XLV, 171.
Census of Great Britain 1851. Religious Worship. England and Wales.
    Reports and Tables. [1690] H.C. (1852-3). LXXXIX, 1.
Members of Parliament: Return of the Names of every Member returned to
    serve in each Parliament . . . from so Remote a Period as it can be
    obtained . . . H.C. 69 (1878). LXII, 1.
Return of the Names of every Member returned to serve in each Parliament to
    the end of 1885 . . . H.C. 21 (1887). LXVI, 255.
Return of Owners of Land, 1873. England and Wales (exclusive of the
    Metropolis). [C. 1097] H.C. (1874). LXXII, Pts. I and II.
Scotland. Owners of Lands and Heritages 1872-73. Return. [C. 899] H.C.
    (1874). LXXII, Pt. III.
Land Owners in Ireland. Return of Owners of Land of One Acre and Upwards . . .
    [C. 1492] H.C. (1876). LXXX, 61.

C. NEWSPAPERS, PERIODICALS AND REPORTS

1. *Newspapers* (short titles only)

Auckland Times and Herald.
Bolton Journal.
Cambridge Chronicle.
Cambridge Independent Press.
Chelmsford Chronicle.
Cheshire County News.
Colchester Mercury.
Commercial, Shipping and General Advertiser for West Cornwall.
Daily News.
Dewsbury Reporter.
Dudley Herald.
Irish Times.
Leeds Mercury.
Lincoln Gazette.
Liverpool Mercury.
Liverpool Weekly Courier.
Manchester City News.

Manchester Courier.
Manchester Examiner and Times.
Manchester Guardian.
Morning Advertiser.
Morning Star.
Pall Mall Gazette.
Preston Guardian.
Reynolds's Weekly Newspaper.
St James's Gazette.
The Scotsman.
South Durham Herald.
Stamford Mercury.
Standard.
Stockport Advertiser.
Sunderland Herald.
Sunderland Times.
The Times.
Western Weekly Advertiser.

2. *Periodicals*

Agricultural Gazette.
Beehive.
Blackwood's Magazine.
British Quarterly Review.
Congregationalist.
Contemporary Review.
County Council Magazine.
Economist.
Englishwoman's Review.
Fortnightly Review.
Guardian.
Herepath's Railway Journal.
Inquirer.
Law Times.
Macmillan's Magazine.
Methodist Recorder.
Monthly Review.

The Nation (New York).
National Reformer.
National Review.
Nineteenth Century.
Nonconformist.
Notes and Queries.
Primitive Methodist.
Punch.
Quarterly Review.
Railway Times.
St Stephen's Review.
Saturday Review.
Spectator.
Tablet.
Vanity Fair.
Westminster Review.

3. *Journals of Particular Organisations*
Alliance News.
Financial Reformer.
Journal of the Statistical Society.
Liberator.
Licensed Victuallers' Guardian.
Monthly Record of the Protestant Evangelical Mission and Electoral Union.
National Education League Monthly Paper.
Transactions of the Manchester Statistical Society.
Transactions of the National Association for the Promotion of Social Science.

4. *Annual Reports of the following Organisations*
Leeds and County Conservative Club.
Leeds Liberal Association.
Leeds Liberal Club.
National Liberal Federation.
National Union of Conservative and Constitutional Associations.
United Kingdom Alliance.

5. *Miscellaneous Reports*
Liberal Secretaries' and Agents' Association. Report of its Formation, Rules and Conferences held at Derby 1882, London May 1882, and Manchester June 1883, Liverpool 1883.
Great National Conference of Licensed Victuallers' Delegates in the Exchange Assembly Room Birmingham, January 8th and 9th, 1873. Full Report . . . , Birmingham 1873.
The Land. The Report of the Land Enquiry Committee, 2 vols, 1913-14.
Proceedings Attending the Formation of the National Federation of Liberal Associations, Birmingham 1877.
Report of the Special Conference of the National Reform Union . . . December 15, 1875. Manchester 1876.
Political Economy Club . . . Minutes of Proceedings, 1821-1882, London 1882.
Proceedings of the Bolton Town Council, 1916-17, Bolton 1917.
Representative Reform: Report of the Committee appointed by the Conference of Members of the Reform League and others, on Mr. Hare's Scheme of Representation, London 1868.
To the Ratepayers of Manchester: Corporation Proceedings and Municipal Returns, Manchester 1880

D. WORKS OF REFERENCE
1. *Directories and Lists* (place of publication London unless otherwise indicated)

Annual Register.

Bateman, John. *Great Landowners of Great Britain and Ireland*, 4 edn, 1883.

Beaven, A. B. *Aldermen of the City of London*, 2 vols, 1908-13.

—— *Bristol Lists*, Bristol 1899.

Bevan, G. P. *Statistical Atlas of England, Scotland and Ireland*, Edinburgh 1882.

Boase, Frederic. *Modern English Biography*, 6 vols, Truro 1892-1921.

Bradshaw's Railway Manual, Shareholders' Guide & Official Directory (Manchester).

Burke's Landed Gentry.

Burke's Peerage, Baronetage and Knightage.

Burtchaell, G. D. and Sadleir, T. U. *Alumni Dublinenses*, new edn, Dublin 1935.

Cokayne, G. E. *The Complete Baronetage*, 6 vols, Exeter 1900-9.

Cokayne, G. E. *The Complete Peerage*, ed. Vicary Gibbs, 1910—

Conservative Central Office. *Conservative Agents and Associations in the Counties and Boroughs of England and Wales*, 1874.

Constitutional Year Book.

Debrett's Baronetage.

Debrett's Peerage.

De Burgh, U. H. Hussey. *The Landowners of Ireland*, Dublin 1878.

Dictionary of National Biography, 1885—

Directory of Directors.

Dod's Peerage, Baronetage, and Knightage.

Eton School Lists from 1791 to 1877, ed. H. E. Chetwynd-Stapylton, 1877.

Financial Reform Almanack and Year Book, Liverpool 1851-1912.

Foster, Joseph. *Alumni Oxonienses*, 8 vols, 1887-92.

—— *Men-at-the-Bar. A Biographical Handlist*, 1885.

Harrow School Register 1571-1800, ed. W. T. J. Gun, 1934.

—— *1800-1911*, ed. M. G. Dauglish and P. K. Stephenson, 3 edn, 1911.

Ivey, G. J. *The Club Directory*, 1879.

Law List.

Liberal Year Book, ed. E. A. Judges, 1887-9.

Liberal Year Book, Leeds 1909.

Liberal and Radical Year Book, 1887.

Men of the Time, ed. Thompson Cooper, 9 edn, 1875.

Morrison's Leeds Blue Book, Leeds 1933.

Newspaper Press Directory and Advertisers' Guide.

Post Office Directory of Lincolnshire, ed. E. R. Kelly, 1876. Also the *Post Office Directory* of Cambridge, Norfolk and Suffolk, of Lancashire, of London, and of Yorkshire.

Price, F. G. Hilton. *A Handbook of London Bankers*, 2 edn, 1890-1.

Record of Old Westminsters, ed. G. F. Russell Barker and A. H. Stenning, 2 vols, 1928.
Reformers' Year Book and Political Annual, 1867.
Roberts, T. N. *Parliamentary Buff Book*, [annually] 1873-81.
Rugby School Register, ed. A. T. Michell, 3 vols, Rugby 1901-4.
Shrewsbury School Register, 1734-1908, ed. J. E. Auden, Oswestry 1909.
The Upper Ten Thousand for 1877.
Venn, J. and J. A. *Alumni Cantabrigienses*, 10 vols, Cambridge 1922-54.
Vine, J. R. S. *English Municipal Institutions; Their Growth and Development from 1835 to 1879, Statistically Illustrated*, 1879.
Weller, Edward. *Philips' Atlas of the Counties of England*, revised edn, 1876.
Whitaker's Almanack.
Who Was Who, 1920—
Winchester College, 1836-1906. A Register, ed. J. B. Wainewright, Winchester 1907.

2. Works on Election Law

Anstey, T. C. *Notes upon the Representation of the People Act, 1867*, London 1867.
Cox, E. W. and Grady, S. G. *The New Law and Practice of Registration and Elections*, 10 edn, London 1868.
Gorst, J. E. *An Election Manual, containing the Parliamentary Elections Corrupt and Illegal Practices Act, 1883*, London 1883.
Hazeldine, G. A. *How to Win an Election. A Manual*, Leicester n.d.
Law Times Reports.
Leader, William. *The Franchise, A Manual of Registration and Election Law and Practice*, London 1879.
Leigh, Chandos and Le Marchant, H. D. *A Guide to Election Law*, London 1870-4.
O'Malley, E. L. and Hardcastle, H. *Reports of the Decisions of the Judges for the Trial of Election Petitions in England and Ireland*, London 1870—
Raikes, H. C. 'The New Law of Elections', *National Review*, II, 189-204 (1883-4).
Rogers, F. N. *Rogers on Elections*, 3 vols, numerous editions.

3. Works concerned with the Election of Members of Parliament

Acland, James. *Imperial Poll Book . . . 1832-67*, London 1867.
Albery, William. *Parliamentary History of the Ancient Borough of Horsham, 1295-1885*, London 1927.
Bean, W. W. *Parliamentary Representation of the Six Northern Counties of England*, Hull 1890.

Beaven, A. B. 'List of Opposed Elections on Taking Office', *English Historical Review*, XXVI, 139-148 (1911).

Bennett, Richard. *A Record of Elections . . . for Liverpool . . . 1832-1878*, Liverpool 1878.

Burtchaell, G. D. *Genealogical Memoirs of the Members of Parliament for the County and City of Kilkenny*, Dublin 1888.

Crossley, James. *Statistics of the Manchester Election 1868*, Manchester 1868.

Debrett's House of Commons and the Judicial Bench.

Dobson, W. *History of the Parliamentary Representation of Preston*, 2 edn, Preston 1868.

Dod, C. R. *Electoral Facts from 1832 to 1852, Impartially Stated*, London 1852.

Dod's Parliamentary Companion.

Ferguson, R. S. *Cumberland and Westmorland M.P.'s from the Restoration to the Reform Bill of 1867 (1660-1867)*, Carlisle 1871.

Foster, Joseph. *Members of Parliament, Scotland*, London 1882.

Hill, G. *Electoral History of the Borough of Lambeth since its Enfranchisement in 1832*, London 1879.

Judd, G. P. *Members of Parliament, 1734-1832*, New Haven 1955.

Lawrance, W. T. *Parliamentary Representation of Cornwall*, Truro [1925].

MacCalmont, F. H. *Parliamentary Poll Book of all Elections*, Nottingham 1910.

Memorials of Brooks's MDCCLXIV to MCM, London 1907.

Oldfield, T. H. B. *An Entire and Complete History, Political and Personal, of the Boroughs of Great Britain*, 3 vols, London 1792.

—— *Representative History of Great Britain and Ireland*, 6 vols, London 1816.

Parliamentary Directory of the Professional, Commercial and Mercantile Members of the House of Commons, London 1874.

Pink, W. D. and Beaven, A. B. *Parliamentary Representation of Lancashire, 1258-1885*, London 1889.

The Times. New Parliament, at each election.

Whitley, T. W. *Parliamentary Representation of the City of Coventry*, Coventry 1892.

Wilkie, T. *Representation of Scotland*, Paisley 1895.

Wilks, G. *Barons of the Cinque Ports, and the Parliamentary Representation of Hythe*, Folkestone 1892.

Williams, W. R. *Parliamentary History of the Principality of Wales, 1541-1895*, Brecknock 1895.

—— *Parliamentary History* of the following counties: *Gloucester* (Hereford 1898), *Hereford* (Brecknock 1896), *Oxford* (Brecknock 1899) and *Worcester* (Hereford 1897).

Poll books for the following elections are also referred to in the text: Cambridge 1865 and 1868, Cambridgeshire 1868, North Durham 1868, Lincolnshire 1868. Those for South and West Norfolk and for West Suffolk for the period 1835-71 were used in preparing Chapter IV. Collections of election posters, leaflets, and cartoons which have been found useful are those in the British Museum, the Gloucester Public Library, the Manchester Central Library, the Library of the Bishopsgate Institute, and the Essex Record Office.

E. BIOGRAPHICAL WORKS (arranged in order of subjects: place of publication London unless otherwise indicated.)[1]

Aberdare, 1st Lord. *Letters of the Rt. Hon. Henry Austin Bruce, G.C.B., Lord Aberdare of Duffryn*, 2 vols, privately printed, Oxford 1902.

Acland, Sir Thomas Dyke Bt. *Memoirs and Letters of the Right Honourable Sir Thomas Dyke Acland*, ed. A. H. D. Acland, privately printed, 1902.

Adderley, Charles Bowyer: see Norton, Lord.

Allon, The Rev. Henry. *Henry Allon . . . The Story of his Ministry*, ed. W. H. Harwood, 1894.

—— *Letters to a Victorian Editor*, ed. A. Peel, 1929.

Amberley, Viscount. *Amberley Papers. The Letters and Diaries of Lord and Lady Amberley*, ed. Bertrand and Patricia Russell, 2 vols, 1937.

Argyll, 8th Duke of. *George Douglas, 8th Duke of Argyll (1823-1900): Autobiography and Memoirs*, ed. the Dowager Duchess, 2 vols, 1906.

Astley, Sir John Dugdale Bt. *Fifty Years of My Life in the World of Sport at Home and Abroad*, by Sir J. D. Astley, 6 edn [1895].

Austin, Alfred. *Autobiography of Alfred Austin, Poet Laureate, 1835-1910*, 2 vols, 1911.

Avebury, 1st Lord. *Life of Sir John Lubbock, Lord Avebury*, by H. G. Hutchinson, 2 vols, 1914.

Balfour, 1st Earl of. *Arthur James Balfour, First Earl of Balfour*, by Blanche E. C. Dugdale, 2 vols, 1939.

—— *Chapters of Autobiography*, by A. J. Balfour, 1930.

Ballantine, Serjeant William. *Some Experiences of a Barrister's Life*, by W. Ballantine, new edn, 1898.

Campbell-Bannerman, Sir Henry. *Life of the Right Hon. Sir Henry Campbell-Bannerman*, by J. A. Spender, 2 vols, 1923.

Baxter, Robert Dudley. *In Memoriam. R. Dudley Baxter, M.A.*, by Mary D. Baxter, 1878.

Beach, Sir Michael Hicks Bt., see St Aldwyn, Earl.

Beaconsfield, Earl of. *Life of Benjamin Disraeli, Earl of Beaconsfield*, by W. F. Monypenny and G. E. Buckle, 6 vols, 1910-24.

---

[1] Individual speeches are not included unless referred to in the text.

Beaconsfield, Earl of. *Earl of Beaconsfield*, by H. E. Gorst, 1900.

—— *Letters of Disraeli to Lady Bradford and Lady Chesterfield*, ed. Marquess of Zetland, 2 vols, 1929.

—— *Selected Speeches of the late Earl of Beaconsfield*, ed. T. E. Kebbel, 2 vols, 1882.

—— *Disraeli and his Day*, by Sir Wm. Fraser, 1891.

Beales, Edmond. *Speech of Edmond Beales, Esq., M.A., President of the Reform League, at the Meeting at St. Martin's Hall in Support of the League, May 13, 1865.* 1865.

Bonham, Francis Robert. 'F. R. Bonham: Conservative "Political Secretary", 1832-47', by Norman Gash, *English Historical Review*, LXIII, 502-22 (1948).

Bradlaugh, Charles. *Charles Bradlaugh, A Record of his Life and Work*, by H. B. Bonner, 2 vols, 1895.

Brampton, Lord. *Reminiscences of Sir Henry Hawkins, Baron Brampton*, ed. Richard Harris, 2 vols, 1904.

Bramwell, Lord. *Some Account of George William Wilshere, Baron Bramwell of Hever and his Opinions*, by C. Fairfield, 1898.

Brentford, 1st Viscount. *Jix, Viscount Brentford*, by H. A. Taylor, 1933.

Bridges, John Affleck. *Reminiscences of a Country Politician*, by J. A. Bridges, 1906.

Bright, Sir Charles Tilston. *Life Story of Sir Charles Tilston Bright, Civil Engineer*, by Charles Bright, revised edition, 1908.

Bright, John. *Life of John Bright*, by G. M. Trevelyan, 1913.

—— *Diaries of John Bright*, 1930.

—— *Public Addresses of John Bright, M.P.*, ed. J. E. Thorold Rogers, 1879.

—— *Public Letters of the Right Hon. John Bright, M.P.*, ed. H. J. Leech, 1885.

Broadhurst, Henry. *Henry Broadhurst, M.P. The Story of his Life . . . told by Himself*, 1901.

Brodrick, George Charles. *Memories and Impressions, 1831-1900*, by G. C. Brodrick, 1900.

Brodrick, William St John: see Midleton, Earl of.

Brookfield, Arthur Montagu. *Annals of a Chequered Life*, by A. M. Brookfield 1930.

Bruce, Henry Austin: see Aberdare, Lord.

Burnaby, Frederick Gustavus. *Life of Colonel Fred Burnaby*, by Thos. Wright, 1909.

Burt, Thomas. *A Great Labour Leader, being a Life of The Right Hon. Thomas Burt, M.P.*, by Aaron Watson, 1908.

—— *Thomas Burt . . . An Autobiography*, ed. Aaron Watson, 1924.

Butler, Josephine Elizabeth. *Personal Reminiscences of a Great Crusade*, by Josephine Butler, new edn, 1898.
—— *Portrait of Josephine Butler*, by A. S. G. Butler, 1954.
Caine, William Sproston. *W. S. Caine, M.P. A Biography*, by John Newton, 1907.
Carnarvon, 4th Earl of. *Life of Henry Edward Molyneux Herbert, Fourth Earl of Carnarvon, 1831-1890*, by Sir Arthur Hardinge, 3 vols, Oxford 1925.
Cavendish, Lady Frederick. *Diary of Lady Frederick Cavendish*, ed. John Bailey, 2 vols, 1927.
Chadwick, Sir Edwin. *Life and Times of Sir Edwin Chadwick*, by S. E. Finer, 1952.
Chamberlain, Joseph. *Life of Joseph Chamberlain*, vols 1-3 by J. L. Garvin, vol. 4 by Julian Amery, 1932-51.
—— *A Political Memoir, 1880-92*, by Joseph Chamberlain, ed. C. H. D. Howard, 1953.
—— *Mr. Chamberlain's Speeches*, ed. C. W. Boyd, 2 vols, 1914.
—— 'Joseph Chamberlain and the "Unauthorized Programme"', by C. H. D. Howard, *English Historical Review*, CCLIV, 477-91 (1950).
Channing, Lord. *Memories of Midland Politics, 1885-1910*, by F. A. Channing, 1918.
Chaplin, 1st Viscount. *Henry Chaplin: A Memoir*, by the Marchioness of Londonderry, 1926.
Childers, Hugh Culling Eardley. *Life and Correspondence of the Right Hon. Hugh C. E. Childers, 1827-1896*, by Spencer Childers, 2 vols, 1901.
Churchill, Lord Randolph. *Lord Randolph Churchill*, by W. L. S. Churchill, new edn, 1951.
—— *Lord Randolph Churchill*, by Lord Rosebery, 1906.
—— *Speeches of the Right Honourable Lord Randolph Churchill, M.P., 1880-1888*, ed. Louis J. Jennings, 2 vols, 1889.
—— 'Lord Randolph Churchill and the Popular Organization of the Conservative Party', by F. H. Herrick, *Pacific Historical Review*, XV, 178-91 (1946).
Clarendon, 4th Earl of. *Life and Letters of George William Frederick, Fourth Earl of Clarendon*, by Sir Herbert Maxwell, 2 vols, 1913.
Clarke, Sir Edward George. *Life of Sir Edward Clarke*, by D. Walker-Smith and Edw. Clarke, 1939.
—— *Story of My Life*, by Sir Edw. Clarke, 1918.
Clifford, The Rev. John. *Dr. John Clifford, His Life, Letters and Reminiscences*, by Sir James Marchant, 1924.
Cobden, Richard. *Life of Richard Cobden*, by John Morley, 2 vols, 1881.
Coburn, Charles. *'The Man Who Broke the Bank.' Memories of the Stage and Music Hall*, by Charles Coburn, n.d.

Coleridge, 1st Lord. *Life and Correspondence of John Duke, Lord Coleridge, Lord Chief Justice of England*, by E. H. Coleridge, 2 vols, 1904.

Collings, Jesse. *Life of the Right Hon. Jesse Collings*, by Jesse Collings and J. L. Green, 1920.

Courtney, Lord. *Life of Lord Courtney*, by G. P. Gooch, 1920.

Cowen, Joseph. *Life and Speeches of Joseph Cowen M.P.*, by E. R. Jones, [1886].

Cranbrook, 1st Earl of. *Gathorne Hardy, First Earl of Cranbrook: A Memoir*, by A. E. Gathorne-Hardy, 2 vols, 1910.

Cremer, Sir William Randal. *Sir Randal Cremer, His Life and Work*, by Howard Evans, 1909.

Crosskey, The Rev. Henry William. *Henry William Crosskey. His Life and Work*, by H. W. Armstrong, Birmingham 1895.

Dale, The Rev. Robert William. *Life of R. W. Dale of Birmingham*, by A. W. W. Dale, 2 edn, 1899.

Davitt, Michael. *Michael Davitt, Revolutionary Agitator and Labour Leader*, by F. Sheehy-Skeffington, 1908.

Delane, John Thadeus. *John Thadeus Delane, Editor of 'The Times'*, by A. I. Dasent, 2 vols, 1908.

Denison, John Evelyn: see Ossington, Viscount.

Derby, 14th Earl of. *Lord Derby and Victorian Conservatism*, by W. D. Jones, Oxford 1956.

Devonshire, 8th Duke of. *Life of Spencer Compton, Eighth Duke of Devonshire*, by Bernard Holland, 2 vols, 1911.

Dilke, Sir Charles Wentworth Bt. *Life of the Rt. Hon. Sir Charles W. Dilke Bart., M.P.*, by Stephen Gwynn and G. M. Tuckwell, 2 vols, 1917.

Disraeli, Benjamin; see Beaconsfield, Earl of.

Dufferin and Ava, 1st Marquess of. *Marquess of Dufferin and Ava*, by C. E. Black, 2 vols, 1903.

Edwards, Sir George. *From Crow-Scaring to Westminster: An Autobiography*, by George Edwards, 1922.

Edwards, John Passmore. *A Few Footprints*, by J. Passmore Edwards, privately printed, 2 edn, 1906.

Ellis, John Edward. *The Life of the Rt. Hon. John Edward Ellis, M.P.*, by A. Tilney Bassett, 1914.

Ellis, Thomas Edward. *Thomas Edward Ellis*, by T. I. Ellis, 2 vols, Liverpool 1944-8.

—— *Speeches and Addresses*, by T. E. Ellis, Wrexham 1912.

Escott, Thomas Hay Sweet. *Platform, Press, Politics & Play*, by T. H. S. Escott, Bristol [1895].

Esher, 2nd Viscount. *Journals and Letters of Reginald, Viscount Esher*, ed. M. V. Brett, 4 vols, 1934-8.

Farquharson, Robert. *House of Commons from Within and other Memories*, by R. Farquharson, 1912.

—— *In and Out of Parliament: Reminiscences of a Varied Life*, by R. Farquharson, 1911.

Fawcett, Henry. *Life of Henry Fawcett*, by Leslie Stephen, 3 edn, 1886.

—— *A Beacon for the Blind*, by W. Holt, 1915.

Fawcett, Millicent Garrett. *Millicent Garrett Fawcett*, by R. Strachey, 1931.

FitzRoy, Sir Almeric William. *Memoirs*, by Sir Almeric FitzRoy, 2 vols, 1925.

Forster, William Edward. *Life of the Right Honourable William Edward Forster*, by T. Wemyss Reid, one volume edn, 1895.

Forward, Sir William Bower. *Recollections of a Busy Life, being the reminiscences of a Liverpool merchant, 1840-1910*, by Sir William Forward, Liverpool 1910.

Fowler, Henry Hartley: see Wolverhampton, Viscount.

Fraser, Bishop James. *James Fraser, Second Bishop of Manchester. A Memoir 1818-1885*, by Thomas Hughes, 1889.

—— *Lancashire Life of Bishop Fraser*, by J. W. Diggle, 6 edn, 1890.

Lloyd George, Earl. *Lloyd George, 1863-1914*, by W. Watkin Davies, 1939.

—— *Tempestuous Journey: Lloyd George, his Life and Times*, by Frank Owen, 1954.

Gladstone, Viscount. *Herbert Gladstone: A Memoir*, by Sir Charles Mallet, 1932.

—— *After Thirty Years*, by Viscount Gladstone, 1928.

Gladstone, William Ewart. *Gladstone: A Biography*, by Sir Philip Magnus, 1954.

—— *Life of William Ewart Gladstone*, by John Morley, 3 vols, 1903.

—— *A Chapter of Autobiography*, by W. E. Gladstone, 1868.

—— *Gladstone to his Wife*, ed. A. Tilney Bassett, 1936.

—— *Political Correspondence of Mr. Gladstone and Lord Granville 1868-1876*, ed. Agatha Ramm, 2 vols (Camden 3 Series LXXXI-LXXXII), 1952.

—— *Political Speeches in Scotland, November and December 1879*, Edinburgh 1879.

—— *Political Speeches in Scotland, March and April 1880*, Edinburgh 1880.

—— *The Queen and Mr. Gladstone*, ed. Philip Guedalla, 2 vols, 1933.

—— *Speeches in South-West Lancashire, October 1868*, Liverpool 1868.

—— *Gladstone and Ireland, 1850-94*, by Lord Eversley, 1912.

—— *Gladstone and the Irish Nation*, by J. L. Hammond, 1928.

—— *Rise of Gladstone to the Leadership of the Liberal Party 1859 to 1868*, by W. E. Williams, Cambridge 1934.

—— *Talks with Mr. Gladstone*, by Lionel A. Tollemache, 1898.

Glenesk, Lord. *Lord Glenesk and the 'Morning Post'*, by R. J. Lucas, 1910.

Godley, John Arthur: see Kilbracken, Lord.

Goschen, 1st Viscount. *Life of George Joachim Goschen, First Viscount Goschen, 1831-1907*, by A. R. D. Elliot, 2 vols, 1911.

Gower, Hon. Edward Frederick Leveson-. *Bygone Years*, by Frederick Leveson-Gower, 1905.

Gower, Lord Ronald. *My Reminiscences*, by Lord Ronald Gower, new edn, 1895.

—— *Records and Reminiscences*, by Lord Ronald Gower, 1903

Granville, 2nd Earl. *Life of Granville George Leveson-Gower, Second Earl Granville, K.G.*, by Lord [Edmond] Fitzmaurice, 2 vols, 1905.

Gray, Frank. *Confessions of a Candidate*, by Frank Gray, 1925.

Gregory, Maundy. *Honours for Sale. The Strange Story of Maundy Gregory*, by Gerald Macmillan, 1954.

Gregson, William. *Life of William Gregson, Temperance Advocate*, by J. G. Shaw, Blackburn 1891.

Grey, Sir George, Bt. *Memoir of Sir George Grey, Bart, G.C.B.*, by Mandell Creighton, privately printed, Newcastle 1884.

Grimston, Robert. *Life of the Hon. Robert Grimston*, by F. Gale, 1885.

Halsbury, 1st Earl of. *The Earl of Halsbury, Lord High Chancellor (1823-1921)*, by A. Wilson-Fox, 1929.

Hamilton, Lord George. *Parliamentary Reminiscences and Reflections*, by Lord George Hamilton, 2 vols, 1916-22.

Harcourt, Sir William George Granville Venables Vernon-. *Life of Sir William Harcourt*, by A. G. Gardiner, 2 vols, 1923.

Hardy, Gathorne: see Cranbrook, Earl of.

Harrison, Frederic. *Autobiographic Memoirs*, by Frederic Harrison, 1911.

Hartington, Marquess of: see Devonshire, Duke of.

Hawkins, Sir Henry: see Brampton, Lord.

Healy, Timothy Michael. *Letters and Leaders of My Day*, by T. M. Healy, 2 vols [1928].

Herbert, Auberon Edward William Molyneux-. *Auberon Herbert: Crusader for Liberty*, by S. H. Harris, 1943.

Holden, Sir Isaac, Bt., and Illingworth, Alfred. *The Holden-Illingworth Letters*, privately printed, Bradford 1927.

Holyoake, George Jacob. *Sixty Years of an Agitator's Life*, by G. J. Holyoake, 3 edn, 2 vols, 1893.

—— *Life and Letters of George Jacob Holyoake*, by Joseph McCabe, 2 vols, 1908.

Hooley, Ernest Terah. *Hooley's Confessions*, by E. T. Hooley, 1927.

Hope, George. *George Hope of Fenton Barns*, by his daughter, Edinburgh 1881.

Howes, Joseph. *Twenty-Five Years' Fight with the Tories*, by J. Howes, privately printed, Leeds 1907.

Hudson, Sir Robert Arundell. *Sir Robert Hudson. A Memoir*, by J. A. Spender, 1930.

Hughes, Thomas. *Thomas Hughes: The Life of the Author of 'Tom Brown's Schooldays'*, by E. C. Mack and W. H. G. Armytage, 1952.

Iddesleigh, 1st Earl of. *Life, Letters and Diaries of Sir Stafford Northcote, First Earl of Iddesleigh*, by Andrew Lang, one volume edn, Edinburgh 1891.

James of Hereford, Lord. *Lord James of Hereford*, by Lord Askwith, 1930.

Jones, Ernest Charles. *Ernest Jones, Chartist*, by John Saville, 1952.

Kenealy, Edward Vaughan. *Memoirs of Edward Vaughan Kenealy*, ed. A. Kenealy, 1908.

Kilbracken, 1st Lord. *Reminiscences*, by Lord Kilbracken, 1931.

Kimberley, 1st Earl of. *A Journal of Events during the Gladstone Ministry, 1868-1874*, by John, First Earl of Kimberley, ed. Ethel Drus (Camden 3 Series XC), 1958.

Labouchere, Henry Du Pré. *Life of Henry Labouchere*, by A. L. Thorold, 1913.

Lansdowne, 5th Marquess of: *Lord Lansdowne: A Biography*, by Lord Newton, 1929.

Latimer, Thomas. *The Cobbett of the West*, by R. S. Lambert, 1939.

Law, Andrew Bonar. *The Unknown Prime Minister. The Life and Times of Andrew Bonar Law 1858-1923*, by Robert Blake, 1955.

Lawson, Sir Wilfrid, Bt. *Sir Wilfrid Lawson: A Memoir*, ed. G. W. E. Russell, 1909.

Layard, Sir Austen Henry. *Sir A. Henry Layard G.C.B., D.C.L. Autobiography and Letters*, ed. W. N. Bruce, 2 vols, 1903.

Lockwood, Sir Frank. *Sir Frank Lockwood, A Biographical Sketch*, by Augustine Birrell, Nelson edn, n.d.

Long, 1st Viscount. *Walter Long and his Times*, by Sir Charles Petrie, 1936.

Lowe, Robert: see Sherbrooke, Viscount.

Lowther, James William: see Ullswater, Viscount.

Lubbock, Sir John: see Avebury, Lord.

Lucy, Sir Henry William. *Sixty Years in the Wilderness*, by H. W. Lucy, 1909.

Lyttleton, Alfred. *Alfred Lyttleton. An Account of his Life*, by his widow, 1917.

McClintock, Sir Francis Leopold. *Life of Admiral Sir Leopold McClintock*, by Sir Clements Markham, 1909.

MacColl, Malcolm. *Malcolm MacColl, Memoirs and Correspondence*, ed. G. W. E. Russell, 1914.

McLaren, Duncan. *Life and Work of Duncan McLaren*, by J. B. Mackie, 2 vols, Edinburgh 1888.

Maclean, James Mackenzie. *Recollections of Westminster and India*, Manchester [1901].

Macmillan, Lord. *A Man of Law's Tale*, by Lord Macmillan, 1953.

MacNeill, John Gordon Swift. *What I have Seen and Heard*, 1925.

Magee, Archbishop William Connor. *Life and Correspondence of William Connor Magee, Archbishop of York, Bishop of Peterborough*, by J. C. MacDonnell, 2 vols, 1896.

Malmesbury, 3rd Earl of. *Memoirs of an Ex-Minister*, by the Earl of Malmesbury, one volume edn, 1885.

Manners, Lord John: see Rutland, Duke of.

Manning, Henry Edward, Cardinal. *Life of Cardinal Manning, Archbishop of Westminster*, by E. S. Purcell, 2 edn, 2 vols, 1896.

Maxwell, Sir Herbert Eustace, Bt. *Evening Memories*, by Sir Herbert Maxwell, 1932.

Melly, George. *Recollections of Sixty Years (1833-1893)*, by George Melly, privately printed, Coventry 1893.

Miall, Edward. *Life of Edward Miall*, by Arthur Miall, 1884.

Midleton, 1st Earl of. *Records & Reactions 1856-1939*, by the Earl of Midleton, 1939.

Mill, John Stuart. *Autobiography*, by J. S. Mill, World's Classics edn, Oxford 1923.

Moore, George Henry. *An Irish Gentleman, George Henry Moore: His Travels, His Racing, His Politics*, by M. G. Moore, 1913.

Morley, 1st Viscount. *Recollections*, by Lord Morley, 2 vols, 1917.

—— *Early Life and Letters of John Morley*, by F. W. Hirst, 2 vols, 1927.

Morley, Samuel. *Life of Samuel Morley*, by Edwin Hodder, 2 edn, 1887.

Mowbray, Sir John Robert. *Seventy Years at Westminster*, by Sir John Mowbray, Edinburgh 1900.

Mundella, Anthony John. *A. J. Mundella, 1825-1897. The Liberal Background to the Labour Movement*, by W. H. G. Armytage, London 1951.

—— 'A. J. Mundella and the Sheffield Election of 1868', by Margaret Higginbotham, *Transactions of the Hunter Archaeological Society*, V, 285-93 (1943).

Nevill, Lady Dorothy. *Reminiscences of Lady Dorothy Nevill*, ed. Ralph Nevill, 1906.

Northbrook, 1st Earl of. *Thomas George, Earl of Northbrook, G.C.S.I. A Memoir*, by Sir Bernard Mallet, 1908.

Northcote, Sir Stafford: see Iddesleigh, Earl of.

Norton, 1st Lord. *Life of Lord Norton, 1814-1905: Statesman and Philanthropist*, by W. S. Childe-Pemberton, 1909.

Oastler, Richard. *Tory Radical: The Life of Richard Oastler*, New York 1946.

O'Brien, Lord. *Reminiscences of the Right Hon. Lord O'Brien, Lord Chief Justice of Ireland*, ed. Georgina O'Brien, 1916.

O'Brien, William. *Recollections*, by Wm. O'Brien, 1905.

O'Connor, Thomas Power. *Memoirs of an Old Parliamentarian*, by T. P. O'Connor, 2 vols, 1929.

O'Hagan, H. Osborne. *Leaves from my Life*, by H. O. O'Hagan, 2 vols, 1929.

Osborne, Ralph Bernal, *Life of Ralph Bernal Osborne, M.P.*, by P. H. Bagenal, privately printed, 1884.

Ossington, Viscount. *Notes from my Journal when Speaker of the House of Commons*, by Lord Ossington, privately printed, 1899.

Palmer, Roundell: see Selborne, Earl of.

Palmerston, 3rd Viscount. *Life of Henry John Temple, Viscount Palmerston: 1846-1865*, by E. Ashley, 2 vols, 1876.

Parkes, Joseph. *Joseph Parkes of Birmingham*, by Jessie K. Buckley, 1926.

Parnell, Charles Stewart. *Charles Stewart Parnell: His Love Story and Political Life*, by Katherine Parnell, 2 vols, 1914.

—— *Life of Charles Stewart Parnell 1846-1891*, by R. Barry O'Brien, 2 vols, New York 1898.

—— *Parnell and his Party 1880-90*, by C. Cruise O'Brien, Oxford 1957.

Pease, Sir Alfred Edward, Bt. *Elections and Recollections*, by Sir A. E. Pease, 1932.

Peel, Sir Robert, Bt. 'Peel and the Party System', by Norman Gash, *Transactions of the Royal Historical Society*, 5 Series I, 47-70 (1951).

Pell, Albert. *Reminiscences of Albert Pell sometime M.P. for South Leicestershire*, ed. Thomas Mackay, 1908.

Playfair, 1st Lord. *Memoirs and Correspondence of Lyon Playfair, First Lord Playfair of St. Andrews*, by Sir T. Wemyss Reid, 1899.

Plimsoll, Samuel. *The Plimsoll Mark*, by David Masters, 1955.

Ponsonby, Sir Henry Frederick. *Henry Ponsonby, Queen Victoria's Private Secretary*, by Lord Ponsonby, 1942.

Potter, Edmund. *Edmund Potter and Dinting Vale*, by J. G. Hurst, Manchester 1948.

Powell, Sir Francis Sharp, Bt. *Sir Francis Sharp Powell Baronet and Member of Parliament*, by H. L. P. Hulbert, Leeds 1914.

Raikes, Henry Cecil. *Life and Letters of Henry Cecil Raikes late Her Majesty's Postmaster-General*, by H. St J. Raikes, 1898.

Raper, James Hayes. *A Brief Memoir of James Hayes Raper, Temperance Reformer, 1820-1897*, by J. D. Hilton, 1898.

Rathbone, William. *William Rathbone: A Memoir*, by Eleanor F. Rathbone, 1905.

Reading, 1st Marquess of. *Rufus Isaacs, First Marquess of Reading*, by the 2nd Marquess, 2 vols, 1942-5.

Reid, Sir Thomas Wemyss. *Memoirs of Sir Wemyss Reid 1842-1885*, ed. Stuart J. Reid, 1905.

Rendel, Lord. *Personal Papers of Lord Rendel*, ed. F. E. Hamer, 1931.

Richard, Henry. *Henry Richard, M.P.*, by C. S. Miall, 1889.

Ripon, 1st Marquess of. *Life of the First Marquess of Ripon*, by L. Wolf, 2 vols, 1921.

Roebuck, John Arthur. *Life and Letters of John Arthur Roebuck*, by R. E. Leader, 1897.

Rogers, James Guinness. *An Autobiography*, by J. G. Rogers, 1903.

Rosebery, 5th Earl of. *Lord Rosebery*, by the Marquess of Crewe, 2 vols, 1931.

Russell, 1st Earl. *Life of Lord John Russell*, by Sir Spencer Walpole, 2 vols, 1889.

—— *Later Correspondence of Lord John Russell*, ed. G. P. Gooch, 2 vols, 1925.

—— *Recollections and Suggestions 1813-1873*, by Lord Russell, 1875.

Russell of Killowen, Lord. *Life of Lord Russell of Killowen*, by R. Barry O'Brien, Nelson edn, n.d.

Russell of Liverpool, 1st Lord. *That Reminds Me—*, by E. R. Russell, 1899.

Russell, George William Erskine. *Collections and Recollections*, 2 vols, Nelson edn, 1903-9.

Rutland, 7th Duke of. *Lord John Manners and his Friends*, by Chas. Whibley, 2 vols, Edinburgh 1925.

Rylands, Peter. *Correspondence and Speeches of Mr. Peter Rylands, M.P.*, by L. G. Rylands, 2 vols, Manchester 1890.

St Aldwyn, 1st Earl. *Sir Michael Hicks Beach, Earl St. Aldwyn*, by Lady Victoria Hicks Beach, 2 vols, 1932.

Salisbury, 3rd Marquess of. *Life of Robert, Marquis of Salisbury*, by Lady Gwendolen Cecil, 4 vols, 1921-32.

Salisbury, Mary, Marchioness of. *A Great Lady's Friendships. Letters to Mary, Marchioness of Salisbury, Countess of Derby, 1862-1890*, by Lady Burghlere, 1933.

Salvidge, Sir Archibald. *Salvidge of Liverpool*, by Stanley Salvidge, 1934.

Sandwith, Humphry. *Humphry Sandwith: A Memoir*, by T. H. Ward, 1884.

Saunderson, Edward James. *Colonel Saunderson, M.P. A Memoir*, by R. Lucas, 1908.

Schreiber, Lady Charlotte. *Lady Charlotte Schreiber: Extracts from her Journal 1853-1901*, ed. Earl of Bessborough, 1952.

Selborne, 1st Earl of. *Memorials*, by the Earl of Selborne, 4 vols, 1896-8.

Shaftesbury, 7th Earl of. *Life and Work of the Seventh Earl of Shaftesbury, K.G.*, by E. Hodder, one volume edn, 1893.

Sherbrooke, Viscount. *Life and Letters of the Right Honourable Robert Lowe, Viscount Sherbrooke*, by A. P. Martin, 2 vols, 1893.

—— *Robert Lowe, Viscount Sherbrooke*, by J. F. Hogan, 1893.

Shuttleworth, Sir James Kay-. *The Life and Work af Sir James Kay-Shuttleworth*, by Frank Smith, 1923.

Smith, Goldwin. *Reminiscences by Goldwin Smith*, ed. A. Haultain, New York, 1911.

—— *Goldwin Smith, Victorian Liberal*, by Elisabeth Wallace, Toronto 1957.

Smith, Samuel. *My Life Work*, by S. Smith, 1902.

Smith, William Henry. *Life and Times of the Rt. Hon. William Henry Smith, M.P.*, by Sir Herbert Maxwell, 2 vols, Edinburgh 1893.

Soutter, Francis William. *Recollections of a Labour Pioneer*, by F. W. Soutter, 1923.

Stansfeld, James. *James Stansfeld, A Victorian Champion of Sex Equality*, by J. L. and Barbara Hammond, 1932.

Stephen, Leslie, *Leslie Stephen, His Thought and Character in Relation to His Time*, by Noel Annan, 1951.

Stephens, Joseph Rayner. *Life of Joseph Rayner Stephens*, by G. J. Holyoake [1881].

Sysonby, 1st Lord. *Recollections of Three Reigns*, by Lord Sysonby, 1951.

Tait, Archbishop Archibald Campbell. *Life of Archibald Campbell Tait, Archbishop of Canterbury*, by R. T. Davidson and W. Benham, 3 edn, 2 vols, 1891.

Torrens, William Torrens McCullagh. *Twenty Years in Parliament*, by W. M. Torrens, 1893.

Trevelyan, Sir George Otto. *Sir George Otto Trevelyan. A Memoir*, by G. M. Trevelyan, 1932.

Trollope, Anthony. *An Autobiography*, by A. Trollope, Crown edn, Oxford 1950.

—— 'Trollope and the Beverley Election', by L. O. Tingay, *Nineteenth Century Fiction*, vol. 5, No. 1. June 1950.

Tuckwell, William. *Reminiscences of a Radical Parson*, by W. Tuckwell, 1905.

Ullswater, 1st Viscount. *A Speaker's Commentaries*, by J. W. Lowther, Viscount Ullswater, 2 vols, 1925.

Vaughan, Herbert, Cardinal. *Life of Cardinal Vaughan*, by J. G. Snead-Cox, 2 vols, 1910.

Victoria, Queen. *Letters of Queen Victoria*, second series, ed. G. E. Buckle, 3 vols, 1926-8.

—— *Political Influence of Queen Victoria 1861-1901*, by F. Hardie, Oxford 1935.

Vincent, Sir Howard. *Life of Sir Howard Vincent*, by S. H. Jeyes and F. D. How, 1912.

Waldegrave, Frances, Countess. *Strawberry Fair: A Biography of Frances, Countess Waldegrave 1821-1879*, by O. W. Hewett, 1956.

Wantage, Lord. *Lord Wantage V.C., K.C.B. A Memoir*, by Lady Wantage, 1907.

Waterlow, Sir Sydney Hedley, Bt. *Life of Sir Sydney H. Waterlow Bart, London apprentice, Lord Mayor . . .*, by George Smalley, 2 vols, 1909.

Watson, Robert Spence. *Life of Robert Spence Watson*, by Percy Corder, 1914.

Webb, Beatrice. *My Apprenticeship*, by Beatrice Webb, 1926.

West, Sir Algernon. *Recollections, 1832 to 1886*, by Sir Algernon West, 2 edn, 2 vols, 1899.

Wilberforce, Bishop Samuel. *Life of the Right Reverend Samuel Wilberforce*, by A. R. Ashwell and R. G. Wilberforce, 3 vols, 1880.

Williams, Montagu. *Leaves of a Life*, by Montagu Williams, 2 edn, 1890.

Willoughby de Broke, 19th Lord. *The Passing Years*, by Lord Willoughby de Broke, 1924.

Wilson, Henry Joseph. *Henry Joseph Wilson: Fighter for Freedom, 1833-1914*, by Mosa Anderson, 1953.

Winder, Thomas H. *A Life's Adventure*, by T. H. Winder, privately printed, 1921.

Wolff, Sir Henry Drummond. *Rambling Recollections*, by Sir H. D. Wolff, 2 vols, 1908.

Wolverhampton, 1st Viscount. *Life of Henry Hartley Fowler, First Viscount Wolverhampton*, by Edith H. Fowler, 1912.

Wyndham, George. *Life and Letters of George Wyndham*, by J. W. Mackail and Guy Wyndham, 2 vols, n.d.

F. OTHER WORKS (place of publication London unless otherwise indicated.)

Adam, Sir Charles E. (ed.). *View of the Political State of Scotland in the Last Century*, Edinburgh 1887.

Adams, Francis. *History of the Elementary School Contest in England*, 1882.

Arnold, R. Arthur, *Free Land*, 1880.

—— *History of the Cotton Famine*, 1864.

Ashton, T. S. *Economic and Social Investigations in Manchester, 1833-1933: A Centenary History of the Manchester Statistical Society*, 1934.

Axon, W. E. A. *Annals of Manchester*, Manchester 1886.

Bagehot, Walter. *English Constitution*, 2 edn, 1872.

—— *Lombard Street*, 1915 edn.

'The Banker M.P.' *Three Banks' Review*, December 1956, pp. 33-42.

Barclay, J. W. 'The Grievances of the Farmers', *Nineteenth Century*, XI, 275-87 (1882).

Barker, T. C. and Harris, J. R. *A Merseyside Town in the Industrial Revolution: St. Helens, 1750-1900*, Liverpool 1954.

Bartley, G. C. T. 'Conservative Organisation', *Fortnightly Review*, n.s. XXXVII, 611-19 (1885).

Baxter, R. Dudley. *Local Government and Taxation, and Mr. Goschen's Report*, 1874.

—— *National Income: The United Kingdom*, 1868.

—— *New Reform Bill: The Franchise Returns Critically Examined*, 2 edn, 1866.

—— *Re-distribution of Seats and the Counties*, 2 edn, 1866.

—— *Results of the General Election*, 2 edn, 1869.

—— *Taxation of the United Kingdom*, 1869.

Bedford, 11th Duke of. *A Great Agricultural Estate, Being the Story of the Origin and Administration of Woburn and Thorney*, 1897.

Biggs, W. W. *Some Reasons for the Conservatism of Liverpool, by Vindex*, privately printed, Liverpool [1880].

Bignold, Sir Robert. *Five Generations of the Bignold Family, 1761-1947*, 1948.

Bingham, J. H. *Sheffield School Board, 1870-1903*, Sheffield 1949.

Blackburn, Helen. *Woman's Suffrage: A Record of the Movement in the British Isles*, 1902.

Blackie, J. S. *Scottish Highlanders and the Land Laws*, 1885.

Bowley, A. L. *Wages and Income in the United Kingdom since 1860*, Cambridge 1937.

Brand, C. F. 'The Conversion of the British Trade Unions to Political Action', *American Historical Review*, XXX, 251-70 (1925).

Briggs, Asa. 'The Background of the Parliamentary Reform Movement in Three English Cities (1830-2)', *Cambridge Historical Journal*, X, 293-317 (1952).

—— *History of Birmingham: Vol. II, Borough and City, 1865-1938,* Oxford 1952.

—— *Victorian People: Some Reassessments of People, Institutions, Ideas and Events, 1851-1867*, 1954.

Brodrick, G. C. *English Land and English Landlords*, 1881.

Brodrick, W. St J. (Earl of Midleton). 'The Functions of Conservative Opposition', *Nineteenth Century*, XIII, 155-65 (1883).

Brown, Benjamin H. *Tariff Reform Movement in Great Britain 1881-1895*, New York 1943.

Buckley, K. D. *Trade Unionism in Aberdeen, 1878 to 1900*, Aberdeen 1955.

Burke, Thomas. *Catholic History of Liverpool*, Liverpool 1910.

Burns, Dawson. *Temperance History*, 2 vols [1890].

Butler, D. E. *Electoral System in Britain, 1918-1951*, Oxford 1953.

Buxton, Charles. *Ideas of the Day on Policy*, 3 edn, 1868.

Buxton, Sydney. *Finance and Politics, An Historical Study, 1783-1885*, 2 vols, 1888.

—— *Handbook to Political Questions of the Day*, 5 edn, 1885.

Callender, W. R. Junr. *Trades Unions Defended*, Manchester 1870.

—— *Suggestions on Reform*, Manchester 1866.

Campbell, Peter and Birch, A. H. 'Politics in the North-West', *Manchester School of Economic and Social Studies*, XVIII, 217-43 (1950).

Carlyle, Thomas. 'Shooting Niagara: and After?' *Macmillan's Magazine* XVI, 319-36 (1867).

Carter, Henry. *English Temperance Movement: A Study in Objectives: Volume I, The Formative Period, 1830-1899*, 1933.

Chaloner, W. H. *Social and Economic Development of Crewe, 1780-1923*, Manchester 1950.

Chamberlain, Joseph. 'A New Political Organization', *Fortnightly Review*, n.s. XXII, 126-34 (1877).

Charley, W. T. *Conservative Legislation for the Working Classes, No. 1. Mines and Factories*, revised edn, 1868.

Christie, I. R. 'Economical Reform and "The Influence of the Crown", 1780', *Cambridge Historical Journal*, XII, 144-54 (1956).

Christie, O. F. *The Transition from Aristocracy, 1832-1867*, 1927.

—— *The Transition to Democracy, 1867-1914*, 1934.

Clapham, J. H. *An Economic History of Modern Britain: Free Trade and Steel, 1850-1886*, Cambridge 1932.

Clark, Colin. *National Income and Outlay*, 1937.

Clarke, Thomas. *Failures of the Gladstone Administration*, Manchester 1871.

Clegg, James. *Annals of Bolton*, Bolton 1888.

Cohen, Emmeline W. *Growth of the British Civil Service, 1780-1939*, 1941.

Cole, G. D. H. *British Working-Class Politics, 1832-1914*, 1941.

—— *Short History of the British Working-Class Movement, 1789-1947*, 1948.

—— and Filson, A. W. *British Working-Class Movements: Select Documents 1789-1875*, 1951.

Congregational Union. *Duty of Protestant Nonconformists in Relation to the Irish Church*, 1868.

Coupland, Sir Reginald. *Welsh and Scottish Nationalism: A Study*, 1954.

Cox, Homersham. *History of the Reform Bills of 1866 and 1867*, 1868.

Crapster, Basil L. 'Scotland and the Conservative Party in 1876', *Journal of Modern History*, XXIX, 355-60 (1957).

Crawford, 25th Earl of. *Conservatism: its Principles, Policy, and Practice*, 1868.

Crosskey, H. W. 'The Liberal Association—The "600"—of Birmingham', *Macmillan's Magazine*, XXXV, 299-307 (1876-7).

Crowley, D. W. 'The "Crofters' Party", 1885-1892', *Scottish Historical Review*, XXXV, 110-26 (1956).

Crozier, Mary. *An Old Silk Family, 1745-1945*, Aberdeen 1947.

Davis, W. J. *British Trades Union Congress. History and Recollections*, 1910.

Davitt, Michael. *Fall of Feudalism in Ireland or the Story of the Land League Revolution*, New York 1904.

Dawson, Charles. *Remarks on the County, Borough, and Municipal Franchises in England and Ireland*, 4 edn, Dublin 1884.

Denvir, John. *Irish in Britain from the Earliest Times to the Fall and Death of Parnell*, 1892.

Droop, H. R. 'On Methods of Electing Representatives', *Journal of the Statistical Society*, XLIV, 141-202 (1881).

Eaton, D. B. *Civil Service in Great Britain*, New York 1880.

Ellis, A. 'The Parliamentary Representation of the Metropolitan, Agricultural, and Manufacturing Divisions of the United Kingdom, with Suggestions for its Redistribution', *Journal of the Statistical Society*, XLVI, 59-100 (1883).

Emanuel, Lewis. *Corrupt Practices at Parliamentary Elections*, 2 edn, 1881.

Ensor, R. C. K. *England 1870-1914*, Oxford 1936.

—— 'Some Political and Economic Interactions in Later Victorian England', *Transactions of the Royal Historical Society*, 4 series XXXI, 17-28 (1949).

Escott, T. H. S. *Club Makers and Club Members*, 1914.

—— *Masters of English Journalism*, 1911.

Essays on Reform, 1867.

Evans, Thomas. *Background of Modern Welsh Politics, 1789-1846*, Cardiff 1936.

Eversley, Lord. *Commons, Forests and Footpaths*, revised edn, 1910.

Fagan, Louis. *Reform Club, 1836-1886*, 1887.

Farrer, 2nd Lord. *Some Farrer Memorials*, privately printed, 1923.

Felkin, William. *History of Machine-Wrought Hosiery and Lace Manufactures*, Cambridge 1867.

Finlen, James. *Mr. J. Finlen's Defence of Himself*, 1868.

Fisher, W. J. 'Liberal Clubs and the Liberal Party', *Monthly Review*, December 1904, pp. 127-36.

Forward, A. B. 'Democratic Toryism', *Contemporary Review*, XLIII, 294-304 (1883).

Franklin, T. Bedford. *History of Scottish Farming*, Edinburgh 1952.

Frisby, Alfred. 'Voters *not* Votes: The Relative Strength of Political Parties as shown by the last two General Elections', *Contemporary Review*, XXXVIII, 635-46 (1880).

Fulford, Roger. *Glyn's 1753-1953: Six Generations in Lombard Street*, 1953.

Gash, Norman. *Politics in the Age of Peel*, 1953.

George, Henry. *Progress and Poverty*, 1881.

Gill, Conrad. *History of Birmingham: Vol. I, Manor and Borough to 1865*, Oxford 1952.

Gillespie, F. E. *Labor and Politics in England, 1850-1867*, Durham, N.C. 1927.

Gladstone, W. E. 'Electoral Facts', *Nineteenth Century*, IV, 955-68 (1878).

—— *The Bulgarian Horrors and the Question of the East*, 1876.

Gorst, H. E. *The Fourth Party*, 1906.

Gregory, T. E. *Westminster Bank through a Century*, 2 vols, Oxford, 1936.

Griffith, E. S. *Modern Development of City Government*, 2 vols, Oxford 1927.

Groves, Reg. *Sharpen the Sickle! The History of the Farm Workers' Union*, 1949.

Hall, T. H. 'The Rural Boroughs', *National Review*, III, 373-85 (1884).

Halliley, E. 'A Short History of the National Society of Conservative and Unionist Agents', supplement to the *Conservative Agents' Journal*, December 1947.

Hanham, H. J. 'British Party Finance, 1868-1880', *Bulletin of the Institute of Historical Research*, XXVII, 69-90 (1954).

Hare, Thomas. *Treatise on the Election of Representatives*, 1859.

Harris, William. *History of the Radical Party in Parliament*, 1885.

Hayler, M. H. C. *Vision of a Century, 1853-1953: The United Kingdom Alliance in Historical Retrospect*, privately printed, 1953.

Henderson, G. B. *Crimean War Diplomacy*, Glasgow 1947.

Henderson, W. O. *Lancashire Cotton Famine, 1861-1865*, Manchester 1934.

Herrick, F. H. 'The Origins of the National Liberal Federation,' *Journal of Modern History*, XVII, 116-29 (1945).

—— 'The Reform Bill of 1867 and the British Party System', *Pacific Historical Review*, III, 216-33 (1934).

—— 'The Second Reform Movement in Britain 1850-65', *Journal of the History of Ideas*, IX, 174-192 (1948).

Hewitson, Anthony. *History of Preston*, Preston 1883.

Higenbottam, S. *Our Society's History*, Manchester 1939.

Hill, R. L. *Toryism and the People, 1832-1846*, 1929.

Hodgson, W. E. 'Why Conservatism Fails in Scotland', *National Review*, II, 235-43 (1883-4).

Holyoake, G. J. *Working-class Representation, Its Conditions and Consequences*, Birmingham 1868.

Howard, C. H. D. 'The Parnell Manifesto of 21 November, 1885, and the Schools Question', *English History Review*, LXII, 42-51 (1947).

Howard, James. 'The Farmers and the Tory Party', *Nineteenth Century*, XIII, 1016-35 (1883).

—— 'Landowning as a Business: A Reply', *Nineteenth Century*, XI, 555-66 (1882).

Howell, George. *Conflicts of Capital and Labour Historically and Economically Considered*, 2 edn, 1890.

—— *Labour Legislation, Labour Movements, and Labour Leaders*, 2 edn, 1905.

—— 'The Caucus System and the Liberal Party', *New Quarterly Magazine*, X, 579-90 (1878).

—— 'The History of the International Association', *Nineteenth Century*, IV, 19-39 (1878).

Hughes, Edward. 'Postscript to the Civil Service Reforms of 1855', *Public Administration*, XXXIII, 299-306 (1955).

Humphrey, A. W. *History of Labour Representation*, 1912.

Hurst, G. B. *The Manchester Politician 1750-1912*, 1912.

Hylton, 2nd Lord. *The Jolliffes of Staffordshire*, privately printed, 1892.

Jacobs, Julius. *London Trades Council, 1860-1950: A History*, privately printed, 1950.

Jefferys, J. B. *Story of the Engineers, 1800-1945*, privately printed, 1945.

Jenkins, R. T. 'The Development of Nationalism in Wales', *Sociological Review*, XXVII, 163-82 (1935).

Jennings, G. H. *Anecdotal History of the British Parliament*, 1880.

Jephson, H. *The Platform, Its Rise and Progress*. 2 vols, 1892.

Jerrold, B. 'On the Manufacture of Public Opinion', *Nineteenth Century*, XIII, 1080-92 (1883).

Jevons, W. S. *Methods of Social Reform and other Papers*, 1883.

Johnston, Thomas. *History of the Working Classes in Scotland*, 3 edn, Glasgow [1939].

Jones, J. B. *Annals of Dover*, Dover 1916.

Kebbel, T. E. 'Conservative Instincts in the English People: The Middle Classes', *National Review*, I, 687-701 (1883).

—— *History of Toryism*, 1886.

Kemp, P. K. *The Bentall Story*, 1955.

Kent, C. B. R. *English Radicals*, 1899.

Kitson Clark, G. S. R. 'The Electorate and the Repeal of the Corn Laws', *Transactions of the Royal Historical Society*, 5 Series I, 109-126, 1951.

—— *The English Inheritance*, 1950.

Lamb, W. K. 'British Labour and Parliament 1865-1893', Typescript Ph.D. Thesis, London School of Economics, 1933.

Laski, H. J. *British Cabinet: A Study in its Personnel, 1801-1924*, Fabian Tract 223, 1928.

—— *Parliamentary Government in England*, 1938.

Law, H. W. and Irene. *Book of the Beresford Hopes*, 1925.

Layton, W. T. (Lord) and Crowther, Geoffrey. *Introduction to the Study of Prices*, 3 edn, 1938.

Lee, J. M. 'Stamford and the Cecils 1700-1885', Typescript B.Litt. Thesis, Oxford, 1957.

Levi, Leone. *Wages and Earnings of the Working Classes*, 1867 and 1885.

Leys, Colin. 'Petitioning in the Nineteenth and Twentieth Centuries', *Political Studies*, III, 45-64 (1955).

The 'Liberation Society' and its Triennial Conferences, 1880.

Lipman, V. D. *Local Government Areas, 1834-1945*, Oxford 1949.

Lloyd, Sir J. E. *A History of Carmarthenshire*, vol. 2, Cardiff 1939.

Lloyd, S. *The Lloyds of Birmingham*, 3 edn, Birmingham 1909.

Lowell, A. L. *Government of England*, 2 vols, New York 1908.

Keith-Lucas, B. *English Local Government Franchise: A Short History*, Oxford 1952.

Lucy, H. W. *A Diary of Two Parliaments: The Disraeli Parliament 1874-1880*, 1885; *The Gladstone Parliament, 1880-1885*, 1886.

McCaffrey, Lawrence J. 'Home Rule and the General Election of 1874 in Ireland', *Irish Historical Studies*, IX, 190-212 (1954).

Maccoby, Simon. *English Radicalism 1853-86*, 1938.

McCord, Norman. *The Anti-Corn Law League, 1838-1846*, 1958.

McCready, H. W. 'The British Election of 1874: Frederic Harrison and the Liberal-Labour Dilemma', *Canadian Journal of Economics and Political Science*, XX, 166-75 (1954).

—— 'British Labour and the Royal Commission on Trade Unions, 1867-9', *University of Toronto Quarterly*, XXIV, 390-409 (1954-5).

—— 'British Labour's Lobby, 1867-75', *Canadian Journal of Economics and Political Science*, XXII, 141-60 (1956).

McKenzie, R. T. *British Political Parties*, 1955.

Maltby, S. E. *Manchester and the Movement for National Elementary Education, 1800-1870*, Manchester 1918.

Manchester United Liberal Party. *Representation of Manchester, General Election, 1868: Report of the Office Committee*.

Manning, B. L. *Protestant Dissenting Deputies*, Cambridge 1952.

Marriott, W. T. 'The Birmingham Caucus', *Nineteenth Century*, XI, 949-65 (1882).

Marshall, J. D. 'Corrupt Practices at the Lancaster Election of 1865', *Transactions of the Lancashire and Cheshire Antiquarian Society*, LXIII, 117-30 (1952-3).

Martin, J. B. 'The Elections of 1868 and 1874', *Journal of the Statistical Society*, XXXVII, 193-229 (1874).

—— 'Electoral Statistics: a Review of the Working of our Representative System from 1832 to 1881', *Journal of the Statistical Society*, XLVII, 75-124 (1884).

Martin, J. B. 'The Electoral "Swing of the Pendulum"', *Journal of the Royal Statistical Society*, LXIX, 655-707 (1906).

Marx, Karl and Engels, Friedrich. *Karl Marx and Frederick Engels on Britain*, Moscow 1953.

Mason, J. F. A. *The Borough of Bridgnorth, 1157-1957*, Bridgnorth 1957.

Matthews, A. H. H. *Fifty Years of Agricultural Politics*, 1915.

Matthews, P. W. and Tuke, A. W. *History of Barclay's Bank Limited*, 1926.

Miall, C. S. *Disestablishment Question in Relation to the Liberal Party and Electoral Action*, 1877.

Miller, G. C. *Blackburn: The Evolution of a Cotton Town*, Blackburn 1951.

Mills, W. H. ed. *Manchester Reform Club, 1871-1921*, privately printed, Manchester 1922.

Moses, Robert. *Civil Service of Great Britain*, Columbia University Studies in History, Economics and Public Law, vol. LVII, No. 1, New York 1914.

Musson, A. E. *The Congress of 1868: The Origins and Establishment of the Trades Union Congress*, 1955.

—— *Typographical Association: Origins and History up to 1949*, Oxford 1954.

Namier, Sir Lewis. *England in the Age of the American Revolution*, 1930.

—— *Personalities and Powers*, 1955.

—— *Structure of Politics at the Accession of George III*, 2 edn, 1957.

Noble, John. *Parliamentary Reformer's Manual*, Manchester 1883.

Nonconformist Minister. *Nonconformity and Politics*, 1909.

O'Brien, R. Barry. *Fifty Years of Concessions to Ireland, 1831-1881*, 2 vols, 1883-5.

—— *Parliamentary History of the Irish Land Question, from 1829 to 1869 . . .*, 1880.

O'Connor, T. P. *The Parnell Movement, with a Sketch of Irish Parties from 1843*, 1886.

O'Donnell, F. H. *History of the Irish Parliamentary Party*, 2 vols, 1910.

O'Grady, S. *Toryism and the Tory Democracy*, 1886.

Ostrogorski, Moisei. *Democracy and the Organization of Political Parties*, trans. F. Clarke, 2 vols, 1902.

Palmer, N. D. *Irish Land League Crisis*, New Haven 1940.

Panton, G. *House of Lords, 1882*, Manchester 1882.

Pares, Richard and Taylor, A. J. P. eds. *Essays Presented to Sir Lewis Namier*, 1956.

Paul, Alexander. *History of Reform*, 3 edn, 1884.

Paul, Herbert. *History of Modern England*, 5 vols, 1904-6.

Paul, W. *History of the Origin and Progress of Operative Conservative Societies*, 2 edn, Leeds 1838.

Peel, A. *These Hundred Years. A History of the Congregational Union of England and Wales, 1831-1931,* 1931.

Pelling, Henry. *America and the British Left: From Bright to Bevan,* 1956.

—— *Origins of the Labour Party,* 1954.

Petrie, Sir Charles. *Carlton Club,* 1955.

Phillips, Maberly. *History of Banks, Bankers and Banking, in Northumberland, Durham, and North Yorkshire,* 1894.

Picton, J. A. *Memorials of Liverpool,* 2 vols, Liverpool 1903.

Plumb, J. H. ed. *Studies in Social History: A Tribute to G. M. Trevelyan,* 1955.

Pollock, Sir Frederick. *Land Laws,* 2 edn, 1887.

Porritt, E. and A. G. *Unreformed House of Commons,* 2 vols, Cambridge 1903.

Postgate, R. W. *Builders' History,* 1923.

Questions for a Reformed Parliament, 1867.

Radical Programme, 1885.

Rae, W. F. 'Political Clubs and Party Organization', *Nineteenth Century,* III, 908-32 (1878).

Raikes, H. C. 'The Functions of an Opposition', *Nineteenth Century,* XIII, 140-54 (1883).

Redford, Arthur. *Manchester Merchants and Foreign Trade,* 2 vols, Manchester 1934-56.

Redlich, Josef. *Procedure of the House of Commons. A Study of its History and Present Form,* 3 vols, 1908.

—— and Hirst, F. W. *Local Government in England,* 2 vols, 1903.

Reid, Andrew ed. *Why I am a Liberal* [1885].

Richard, Henry. *Letters on the Social and Political Condition of the Principality of Wales,* 1866. Also published as *Letters and Essays on Wales,* 1884.

—— and Williams, J. C. *Disestablishment,* 1885.

Rigg, T. G. *Political Parties, Their Present Position and Prospects,* 1881.

Robb, Janet H. *Primrose League, 1883-1906,* New York 1942.

Roberts, B. C. *The Trades Union Congress, 1868-1921,* 1958.

Rodgers, Brian. 'The Social Science Association, 1857-1886', *Manchester School of Economic and Social Studies,* XX, 283-310 (1952).

Rogers, J. Guinness. 'Political Dissent', *Fortnightly Review,* n.s. XXII 811-26 (1877).

—— 'Town and Country Politics', *Nineteenth Century,* XI, 826-40 (1882).

Rosenbaum, S. 'The General Election of January, 1910, and the Bearing of the Results on Some Problems of Representation', *Journal of the Royal Statistical Society,* LXXIII, 473-511 (1910).

Ross, J. F. S. *Parliamentary Representation,* revised edn, 1948.

Rostow, W. W. *British Economy of the Nineteenth Century,* Oxford 1948.

Royal Statistical Society. *Annals of the Royal Statistical Society, 1834-1934*, 1934.

Salisbury, 3rd Marquess of. 'The Value of Redistribution: A Note on Electoral Statistics', *National Review*, IV, 145-62 (1884-5).

Salter, F. R. 'Political Nonconformity in the Eighteen-Thirties', *Transactions of the Royal Historical Society*, 5 Series III, 125-43 (1953).

Saunders, William. *New Parliament, 1880*, 1880.

Saville, John ed. *Democracy and the Labour Movement*, 1954.

Scott, Benjamin. *Statistical Vindication of the City of London; or, Fallacies Exploded and Figures Explained*, 1867.

Selley, Ernest. *Village Trade Unions in Two Centuries*, 1919.

Seymour, Charles. *Electoral Reform in England and Wales*, New Haven 1915.

Simon, Shena D. *A Century of City Government: Manchester 1838-1938*, 1938.

Slugg, J. T. *Reminiscences of Manchester Fifty Years Ago*, Manchester 1881.

Springall, L. Marion. *Labouring Life in Norfolk Villages, 1834-1914*, 1936.

Stancliffe, F. S. *John Shaw's, 1738-1938*, Manchester 1938.

Steven, Robert. *National Liberal Club: Politics and Persons* [1924].

Stevens, E. C. Cleveland-. *English Railways, their Development and Relation to the State*, 1915.

Stokes, W. *Representation of Manchester. Who shall be its Third Member?* 2 edn, Manchester 1868.

Sykes, Joseph. *Amalgamation Movement in English Banking, 1825-1924*, 1926.

Taylor, Edward. *An Account of Orangeism. A Key to the late Religious Riots*, Rochdale 1868.

Taylor, E. R. *Methodism and Politics, 1791-1851*, Cambridge 1935.

Taylor, H. A. 'Politics in Famine-Stricken Preston', *Transactions of the Historic Society of Lancashire and Cheshire*, CVII, 121-39 (1955).

Thomas, J. Alun. *House of Commons, 1832-1901. A Study of its Economic and Functional Character*, Cardiff 1939.

—— 'The System of Registration and the Development of Party Organisation, 1832-1870', *History*, XXXV, 81-98 (1950).

Thompson, A. F. 'Gladstone's Whips and the General Election of 1868', *English Historical Review*, LXIII, 189-200 (1948).

Thompson, G. C. *Public Opinion and Lord Beaconsfield, 1875-1880*, 2 vols, 1886.

The Times: History of the Times—The Tradition Established 1841-1884, 1939.

Trevelyan, G. O. *Speeches on the County Franchise*, Manchester 1877.

Victoria County History: the volumes dealing with *Huntingdon, Leicester*, and *Wiltshire* contain important sections on political history.

Waddy, H. T. *Devonshire Club & Crockfords*, 1919.

Wadsworth, A. P. *Newspaper Circulations, 1800-1854,* reprinted from the *Transactions of the Manchester Statistical Society* for 1954-5.

Wake, Joan. *The Brudenells of Deene,* 1953.

Walpole, Sir Spencer. *History of Twenty-Five Years,* 4 vols, 1904-8.

Watson, J. A. Scott. *History of the Royal Agricultural Society of England, 1839-1939,* 1940.

Watson, R. S. *National Liberal Federation,* 1907.

Wearmouth, R. F. *Methodism and the Struggle of the Working Classes, 1850-1900,* Leicester 1954.

Webb, Beatrice. *Co-operative Movement in Great Britain,* 1891.

—— and Sidney. *English Local Government: The Story of the King's Highway,* 1913.

—— *History of Trade Unionism,* new edn, 1920.

—— *Industrial Democracy,* new edn, 1902.

West, Algernon. *Contemporary Portraits. Men of My Day in Public Life,* 1920.

—— *One City and Many Men,* 1908.

White, B. D. *History of the Corporation of Liverpool, 1835-1914,* Liverpool 1951.

White, J. *Borough of Macclesfield: Corrupt Practices (Disfranchisement) Bill, 1882: Speech of Mr. Alderman White, J.P.,* Macclesfield 1882.

Whyte, J. H. *The Independent Irish Party, 1850-9,* Oxford 1958.

Williams, David. *A History of Modern Wales,* 1950.

—— *Rebecca Riots,* Cardiff 1955.

Williams, J. E. 'Paternalism in Local Government in the Nineteenth Century', *Public Administration,* XXXIII, 439-46 (1955).

Williams, P. M. 'Public Opinion and the Railway Rates Question in 1886', *English Historical Review,* LXVII, 37-73 (1952).

Wilson, E. D. J. 'The Caucus and its Consequences', *Nineteenth Century,* IV, 695-712 (1878).

Wollaston, E. P. M. 'The Irish Nationalist Movement in Great Britain 1886-1908', Typescript M.A. Thesis, London, 1958.

INDEX